PSL COMPLETE GUIDE TO MODEL RAILWAYS

PSL COMPLETE GUIDE TO MODEL RAILWAYS

MICHAEL ANDRESS

Patrick Stephens

Originally published between 1979 and 1982 in eight volumes as the *PSL Model Railway Guide* series.
This combined edition first published in hardback August 1985.
First published in paperback September 1986.

British Library Cataloguing in Publication Data

Andress, Michael
PSL complete guide to model railways.
1. Railroads — Models
I. Title
625.1'9 TF197

ISBN 0-85059-849-4

Patrick Stephens Limited is part of the Thorsons Publishing Group, Wellingborough, Northamptonshire, NN8 2RQ, England

Printed in Great Britain by
Biddles Limited, Guildford, Surrey

10 9 8 7 6 5 4 3 2

Baseboards, Track and Electrification

Michael Andress

Contents

Introduction

For many the first introduction to railway modelling is a train set. This is an excellent way to begin the hobby. Nowadays such sets are of very good quality in appearance, accuracy of scale and reliability of operation. Even though the simple train set can provide a great deal of enjoyment in setting up and running, particularly if extra track and points are added, it has many limitations. In time the enthusiast will probably want to progress to a more permanent model railway layout with its greater realism. This transitional phase is a very important stage in the hobby. A successful first layout may well encourage the modeller to go on in a pastime which can give him, or her, much pleasure and satisfaction over the years. Failure at this stage may lead to giving up the hobby altogether.

When building a layout it is tempting to rush ahead in an effort to get something running and to provide the structures and scenery which make a model railway interesting and attractive to look at. Though some more experienced modellers become especially interested in such aspects of the hobby as track construction, electrification and so on, for the beginner baseboard construction, track laying and wiring often seem rather dull and difficult jobs. They may be thought of as tasks to be done as quickly as possible so that one can get on to more exciting projects. Because of this and a lack of knowledge of the basic principles involved these jobs may be inadequately carried out. This is unfortunate as sound baseboard construction, accurate track laying and correct electrification and wiring are basic essentials in the building of a good model railway. By good, I mean one which will look and run well and which will give the enthusiast continuing pleasure and satisfaction.

If this work is not completed properly there can be recurrent problems and much time, effort and additional expense may be involved in attempting to correct faults later. These difficulties may also spoil the enjoyment and cause dissatisfaction and disillusionment with the hobby.

My aim in this book is to provide the beginner with a straightforward guide to these important subjects. I make no claim to originality for the ideas presented here; they are based on the experience and ideas of many modellers and are, for the most part, standard practice. Indeed, this is not the place for experimental schemes or new, relatively untried innovations. The beginner will do much better to stick to well-tested methods.

Although, as I have suggested above, the principles described in this book are based on the work of many modellers, too many to credit individually, there are two whose ideas on baseboard construction are worthy of special mention. They are Cyril Freezer, now editor of *Model Railways*, who has done much to develop and popularise the basic grid form most often used in Britain, and Linn Westcott, formerly editor of the American magazine *Model Railroader*, who devised the excellent and ingenious 'L-Girder' system. Both these experts have also written extensively and with great clarity on model railway electrification.

I would like to thank all those modellers who have allowed me to use photographs of their models or layouts in this book. In particular I am indebted to Graham Bailey, Geoff Barlow, K.J. Churms, Howard Coulson, Paul Drombolis, Jim Gadd, Keith Gowen, P.D. Hancock, Brian Harrap, Terry Jenkins, Betty Kay, John Medd, Ron Prattley, Mike Sharman and Vernon Sparrow.

I am also grateful to those manufacturers who have helped me with information and photographs.

Baseboards

The baseboard is the foundation of a layout. Even though it is largely hidden on the completed model railway its importance should not be overlooked. Remember that if the baseboard proves to be defective you may have to scrap the whole layout and begin all over again!

Why do we need a baseboard?

It is perhaps a logical beginning to decide first of all why we need a baseboard at all. At one time train sets were usually 0 gauge, or even larger in size, and most often they were set out on the floor for use. This was fine as the large and robust track pieces were fairly resistant to accidental damage and much of the fun of laying out the line was to take it under and around the furniture, which in the imagination became tunnels, mountains, cuttings and so on. A few train sets are still made in the larger scales. The Triang Big Big Trains have been discontinued but the Lima, Timpo and LGB models are still available. These run very well on the floor and even out of doors in the garden. However, most train sets are now in 00 or smaller scales. The small size of the track sections in these scales means that care is needed when assembling the track, both to achieve proper alignment and to avoid damage and it is not really satisfactory to try to do this on the floor. There is also the danger that the track may be trodden on causing it to become bent, distorted or broken. The dust, dirt and fluff that collect on the floor will get into the motors and bearings of the locomotives and rolling stock, impairing their running. So in the smaller scales it is essential to work on a table or other surface. The usual choice is to set the railway up on a table—often the dining table. However, there are disadvantages. Often the table is needed for other purposes so that it may not always be available at the time when the operator wishes to set up the railway; or activities may have to be cut short so that the table can be used for a family meal. Another problem is that the table may not be large enough. In 00 scale a reasonable sized table is needed to accommodate just the basic oval, and it is not often possible to add much further track unless the table is unusually large. Also there is always the risk of scratching or otherwise marking the table if, for example, a locomotive derails and damage of this sort will not make the enthusiast popular with the rest of the family if the table is an expensive piece of furniture.

Thus, the ideal arrangement even for a train set is to have a running surface provided specifically for it. Though you will probably want to progress eventually from your train set to a model railway layout there is no need to rush this. There is a good deal to be said for taking the time to try out various track arrangements with the train set track and with additional track sections and points purchased separately. Playing around with the train set in this way is enjoyable in itself and it is also very helpful in deciding what sort of track plan you would like for your first proper layout. To do this you will need a suitable surface on which to set up the track designs and even though you are not yet ready to start on a definitive layout there is no reason why you should not make up a baseboard for this purpose. If a suitable design is chosen it can be retained as the baseboard for the proper layout. It could be a rectangular board of appropriate size or the more flexible scheme of, say, four smaller baseboard sections which can be fitted together in various ways to form differently shaped baseboards. Whichever type is chosen it should be a solid top baseboard so that the track sections can be shuffled about as desired during the experimental stage.

For a train set it is convenient, as I have explained, to have a baseboard; for a model railway layout it is essential. The layout must be built up in a permanent form if it is to be properly developed, both operationally and scenically. Smooth running depends on the alignment of the track and the electrical

A train set can easily be developed into an interesting small layout when it is fitted on to a permanent baseboard. The layout shown here has track from a train set together with three points and some extra track purchased separately. The addition of a few structures and simple scenery completes the model railway.

A view of the underside of the baseboard for the layout in the previous picture, shown during construction. Because the baseboard top is chipboard, stronger and more rigid than wood fibre insulation board, less support is required and a simpler framing can be employed, as seen here, if you wish. However, if the layout is to be moved about frequently it is advisable to use the standard grid framing even with a chipboard top.

contacts; on a train set which is frequently set up and then dismantled fittings can become loosened or distorted which impairs operation. On a model railway layout the track is carefully and accurately aligned initially and then fixed in place so that it cannot move or become distorted. Good electrical connections can be made and maintained. With a temporary set-up the wiring must be kept simple but on a more permanent layout more complicated electrification is possible, permitting more interesting and realistic control and operation. Last, but certainly not least, a permanent set-up is required before realistic scenic work can be carried out and this is essential for a complete model railway layout. Such a layout must have its own baseboard on which everything can be fixed. I have used the word permanent to distinguish a model railway layout from one which is set up afresh for each operating session and not to suggest or imply that a layout, once built, should never be changed. It is almost certain that you will want to alter or extend your railway from time to time. Eventually, with improving standards of modelling, changes in your interests or merely a desire to try something new you will most likely want to scrap your first layout and build another. If the original baseboard was of sound construction there is no reason why it should not be salvaged and reused for your new layout; if necessary being altered or extended for the purpose. Thus the work which you put into making a good baseboard to begin with will not be wasted.

Having decided that a baseboard is essential we can now consider our requirements. Obviously it must be flat and true when constructed. It should also be strong enough not to distort with time, changes in temperature and humidity, or with handling in the case of a portable layout. The baseboard must be rigid enough not to sag or bend from its own weight and sufficiently strong to take the weight of the operator leaning on or against it. Do not be misled into thinking that because you are modelling in N scale a flimsy base will be adequate. For the commonly used scales the weight of the models is insignificant and for the same size of board the construction must be as strong for an N-scale layout as for an 00-scale railway. However, it may be that because of the smaller size of the N-scale models and layout a smaller baseboard can be used and in that case lighter material may be adequate for the framing.

The choice of materials employed may also be influenced by the cost, availability and ease of construction. If the track is to be fixed down with pins, the top surface may be chosen so that these can be pushed into it easily.

The noise produced by the trains running is another factor to be considered and this is influenced to some extent by the materials used in the baseboard construction.

Commercial baseboards

Until recently anyone wanting a model railway baseboard had to build it himself or arrange to have one specially made. Now there are several ready-made boards available commercially. There are two very different types.

One is the base moulded in thick plastic or fibreglass. This type provides not only a base on which to fit the track but also a contoured terrain complete with hills, tunnels, rivers, roads and so on. This does, of course, restrict the design of the layout to one of the arrangements offered but it is a way of completing a scenic model railway layout with an absolute minimum of time and effort.

A variety of baseboards with different track and scenic features are made in 00/HO, N and Z scales by Kibri, Noch, Hornby and DAS, and some of these offer possibilities for extension or combination to produce larger layouts. Most of the bases are pre-coloured and some of the Kibri and Noch boards even have grassy areas represented by flocking. To give greater strength wooden framing is fitted into the Kibri and Noch bases. For the most part the preformed bases are intended for use on a table or other support but the Kibri baseboards have provision for fitting legs which are available as separate items. The moulded bases have the advantage of making it very quick and easy to provide a scenic setting for the train set but they are rather expensive and there is little scope for the modeller to create his own individual layout.

The other form of baseboard available commercially is of the standard type frequently constructed by enthusiasts for their own layouts but provided ready-made or in kit form. This is very convenient but will naturally be more expensive than building your own from scratch. Baseboards of this type are offered by Raitab, Alan Borwell and Puffers. The boards are modular baseboards and can be fitted together as required to give the size and shape wanted for your layout. The bases from Puffers are 4 ft × 2 ft; the other manufacturers offer them in a selection of sizes up to 4 ft × 2 ft. The Raitab baseboards, for example, have wooden framing and legs with metal fittings; the kits are available with or without tops of chipboard or Sundeala as desired.

Faller have recently introduced kits for baseboards and legs of wooden construction with a top surface of re-inforced corrugated board.

Materials

For the modeller who wishes to construct his own baseboard we should now look at the various materials which can be used. Methods of construction will be considered in detail later but a baseboard is essentially a frame or grid with or without a covering top and these two parts are conveniently discussed separately.

Many different materials have been tried for the framing but wood is by far the most commonly employed and is the only one we need consider here. Most modellers will need to use softwood; hardwood has the advantage of greater strength but is more

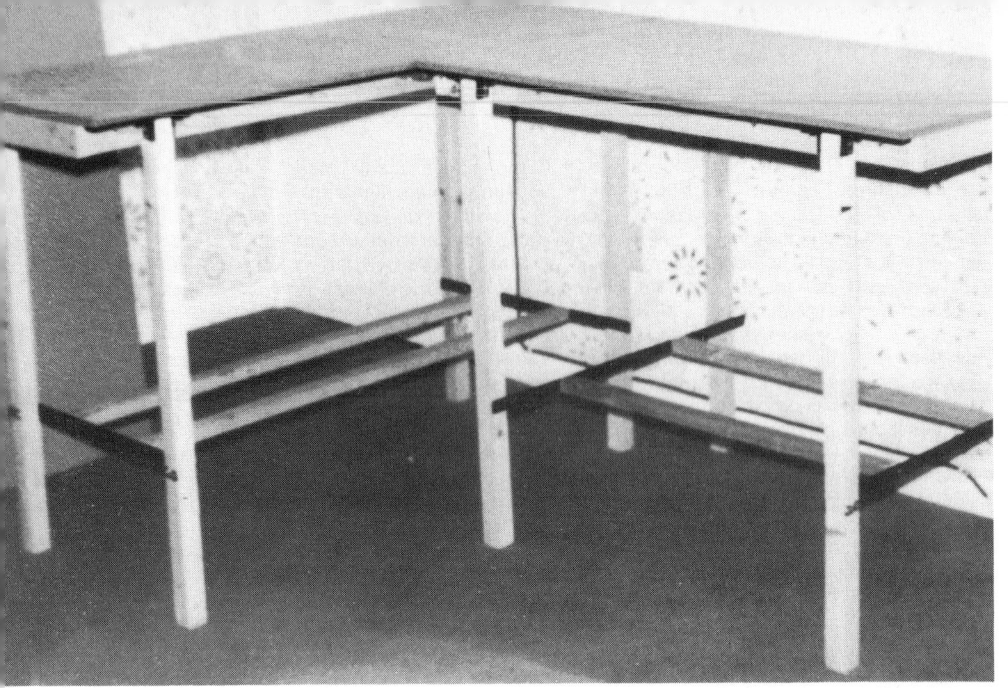

difficult to work and these days tends to be expensive. Sometimes it is possible to obtain old timber cheaply from demolition sites and other sources and provided the wood is free from wood-worm or rot there is the advantage that it will be well seasoned. Usually, however, the enthusiast will have to buy softwood from a local timber yard or DIY shop and this will be perfectly satisfactory. As far as possible choose pieces which are straight, without bends or twists and are free from cracks or large knots. Nowadays the wood will not have been properly seasoned and if there is time it is a good idea to let the timber stand in the house for a few weeks before use, especially if you have central heating. This will allow the wood to shrink before it is made up into a baseboard rather than afterwards when this might cause warping.

The most frequently used size of timber is a nominal 2 in × 1 in, with an actual finished size of 1⅞ in × ⅞ in, but other sizes may also be needed depending on the type and dimensions of the baseboard. Fixing is with wood screws, 1½ or 2 in No 8 flathead are the most useful sizes and white glue such as Gloy.

For the top surface, if one is required, there is a wider choice of materials. These vary in strength and rigidity, weight and cost and the individual modeller should choose the one which best suits his own requirements.

Wood fibre insulation board ½ in thick is very popular. It is cheap, easy to cut with a saw or knife and takes pins and track spikes without difficulty. This material must be

An L-shaped baseboard made up from Raitab baseboard table kits showing the neat construction of these units. The kits are available in a range of sizes from 3 ft × 1 ft to 4 ft × 2 ft and can be combined to form any required size and shape of baseboard. (Photo courtesy of Raitab.)

supported at intervals not greater than a foot to prevent sagging. It is relatively light and has good, sound deadening properties. A useful alternative is Sundeala which is harder and stronger but also more expensive.

Chipboard is another frequently used material. It is stronger and more rigid than the insulation board and requires less bracing, making it useful for portable layouts. The cost and weight are greater and it is also noisier than the wood fibre board. Because it is much harder it is more difficult to work and will not take fine pins or track spikes as they tend to bend instead of pushing in easily.

Plywood was popular and is still often used in the United States, where I suspect it may be less expensive than here. Some saving can be made by using ply with a good finish on one side only and fitting it with the poorer surface underneath on to the framing while the better side forms the top face of the baseboard. Plywood is also more difficult to work than the insulation board and it is quite noisy.

Blockboard is another alternative material. It is rigid but expensive and heavy. It might be worthwhile employing it in areas where rigidity is important and it is not convenient to add extra bracing. For example it could be

Sturdy baseboard construction on a large exhibition layout. Chipboard has been used as the baseboard top and also as the track base for the tracks above baseboard level.

used as the base for a goods yard on a higher level with limited clearance beneath for low level tracks making it impossible to fit bracing.

Hardboard is mentioned only to be dismissed as quite unsuitable. It tends to warp, buckle and distort even when well braced, causing problems with any track laid on it. It is also noisy and the surface is too hard for pins and track spikes to be pushed in without drilling holes first.

Tools

Fortunately only a simple tool kit is needed for baseboard construction and anyone with an interest in carpentry or DIY work will almost certainly have a more than adequate selection of tools already.

For cutting the frame pieces to size and possibly for cutting the baseboard top a saw will be required. A handsaw is perfectly adequate and a tenon saw is a good choice as this will be ideal for making neat joints. A mitre block is helpful in keeping the cuts square and accurate so that the pieces will fit properly together. I have a Copydex 'Joint-master' which is very useful as it enables one to make all types of joints easily and accurately. It is by no means essential but is well worth while considering as an extra item of equipment, particularly if you are planning a large layout or if you do other woodwork as well.

A power saw is also something of a luxury item and is certainly not necessary, though again might be worth purchasing if you plan a large baseboard or if it will be useful to you for other projects as well. The circular saw type is good for the construction of baseboard framing, particularly of the 'L-Girder' type whereas a sabre saw can save a great deal of time if you wish to use the so-called 'cookie cutter' method of baseboard fabrication or for cutting track bases.

Baseboard framing can be made up very satisfactorily using only butt joints but you may prefer to make halved joints and if so you will need a chisel for cutting away the waste wood between the saw cuts. Assembly of the frame will be with screws, so suitable holes must be drilled to take them. For a small layout a hand drill is all that is required but for a larger layout where many holes will be needed you might think it worth buying a power drill. Drill bits to suit the sizes of screws you will use, together with a countersink, are also necessary. It may be most convenient to buy a set of drill bits so that it is easy to drill holes of any size when needed. To fix and tighten the screws a screwdriver will be required; make sure you get one of the appropriate size as too small a blade will damage the slots in the screwheads and the screws will be difficult to tighten or to remove. If you have a power drill you can buy a screwdriver bit to fit into it and this will speed up fixing the screws very considerably. This is not of much consequence on a small layout but can save a lot of time on a large one. A steel rule and a square should also form part of the tool set for marking out before cutting and for checking during assembly.

If insulation board is used as the top surface of the baseboard some people prefer to cut it with a knife rather than a saw as this is less messy, producing much less dust. An ordinary modelling knife is not suitable; a stronger larger knife is needed. The Stanley knife is ideal and this useful tool will also come in handy for many other hobby jobs where the usual modelling knife is not heavy or strong enough. When insulation board is employed for the baseboard surface it is most conveniently fixed onto the frame with nails so a hammer should be included in the tool kit.

For cleaning up the cut edges of the frame and top I use a Surform followed by a file and sandpaper.

Another piece of equipment which is not essential but which I have found extremely useful is a Black & Decker 'Workmate'. This is in effect a combined workbench and large vice or clamp and it folds up for easy storage and carrying. The 'Workmate' makes it easy to hold long pieces of wood for sawing, drilling, filing and other work without needing anyone else to help. It is invaluable for many jobs around the home as well as in layout construction.

In modern houses and flats particularly it is often difficult to find somewhere to carry out the work involved in building a layout baseboard. To achieve good results most easily a clean, well lit area is desirable. In good weather the work can be done out of doors if necessary but railway modelling is most often undertaken in the winter when bad weather and the dark evenings may make this impracticable. The garage, if you have one, is an alternative but it may be cramped when the car is in it and often the lighting is inadequate. A workshop or workroom is the ideal but few of us are fortunate enough to have a room which can be devoted to this purpose. Though it may seem an unlikely choice of site I find the best place to work on a project of this type is the kitchen. The lighting is good and the floor is tiled so there is no difficulty in sweeping up the sawdust and wood shavings. Provided care is taken to do no damage and the room is properly cleaned up afterwards a small layout baseboard can be constructed here without difficulty or undue disruption. But do not

The framing for a 4 ft × 1 ft 9 in baseboard section showing typical grid construction using butt and halved joints. The modeller has fitted the end joists to the ends of the side girders; a stronger frame would have resulted if these joists had been placed between the girders.

forget to check that the kitchen is not needed for cooking or other domestic activities at the time you want to use it!

Baseboard size

There are many factors which may influence the size and type of baseboard chosen. The size and shape of the layout, where it will be located, whether it is to be a permanent fixture, semi-permanent or portable, plans for future modifications and extensions and personal preferences must all be taken into account. I recommend most strongly that a beginner's first layout should be kept small and simple, even if it is designed to permit later extension. There are several good reasons for this. First of all, there are various construction techniques and methods to be mastered and it is much easier, quicker and cheaper to learn these on a small layout where the amount of work required is relatively limited. In a small area progress seems more rapid, encouraging the modeller to carry on. A model railway does not need to be large and complex to be enjoyable to construct and operate. Indeed, the beginner who tackles too ambitious a layout will find construction and, if he ever completes the model, maintenance so time consuming that he may have little time left to enjoy running it.

Even with a small layout it is worth considering whether to make the baseboard in one piece or as two or more sections which are then joined together, either on a more or less permanent basis or temporarily for operating sessions if the layout is to be portable. There is a natural tendency when going on from a train set to a model railway to think in terms of an oval track plan on a baseboard about 6 ft × 4 ft in size, the board then being built as a single unit. Though the plan may not look very big on paper as a small scale plan, a baseboard of this size is surprisingly large, heavy and difficult to carry, particularly as on the finished layout one side of it is covered with fragile scenery and structures. However, for convenience in construction, layouts up to about this size which are not likely to be moved about frequently can be satisfactorily built on a single baseboard. A layout with a length no greater than 6 ft can be carried end up through a doorway and this makes it much more movable than if it is any longer.

For larger layouts, even if the need to move them is not anticipated, it is worth while arranging construction so that the baseboard can be taken apart into smaller units without damaging the layout unduly. If the modeller has to move house or wishes to show the layout at an exhibition it is then possible to transport it. There is also the bonus that smaller units may be more convenient to construct in the beginning, especially if one has to resort to working on the kitchen table!

A portable layout must obviously be small enough, or break down into units which are sufficiently small, for easy handling and transportation. An ideal size for these sections is 4 ft × 2 ft. This is small enough for easy handling by one person, yet large enough that the number of separate units required to make up the layout is not excessive. The individual modeller may, however, decide to make his units a different size, perhaps because of the size or shape of his layout or so that the sections will fit into his car for transportation, or into a large cupboard for storage. The sections need not be the same in size or shape but the use of a standard module can be advantageous both in construction and in storage.

We will look at the construction of these layout sections and methods of fitting them together later in the book.

Baseboard height

There is no 'correct' height for a model railway layout; everyone has his own ideas on the best level for the baseboard. The height chosen may depend on whether the model is to be operated by an adult, a child or both. Because model railways appear more realistic if viewed at about eye level, rather than from above, a position above the normal table level is usually preferred for the baseboard. Conversely it is easier to operate the layout if you have an overall view from above the layout; this is most important on a complicated layout. One compromise solution is to choose the height so that the layout is at about eye level for spectators sitting in low chairs, while the operator has a high stool so that he can see the whole layout easily.

The width of the layout is also relevant in deciding how high it should stand. The greatest easy reach across a layout is when it is at about waist height so this is the level to choose if the layout is wider than 18-24 in.

The baseboard may need to be high up to clear furniture or other items in the room. If it must be high a narrow scenic layout is the most suitable type.

Most layouts are between about 36 and 48 in from the floor with an average of perhaps 42 in. There are some exceptions to the general rules on baseboard height. Coffee table layouts, for example, will of course be quite low, typically about 18 in high. Portable layouts should not be much more than 3 ft high because they would be unstable.

Baseboard construction

Having considered some general points regarding baseboards we can now look at the methods of building them. There are several different types of baseboard construction.

Basic frame or grid

This is the standard form of baseboard construction. The frame is usually made up from 2 in × 1 in timber (these are nominal sizes and the actual dimensions of the finished wood is 1⅞ in × ⅞ in). The main side girders are cut to run the length of the board and they will be braced by joists fitted across between them at intervals not greater than 12 in. Note that the end joists must also be fitted between the main girders and not on to their ends as this gives greater strength. To join the girders and joists simple butt joints with two screws and glue are perfectly adequate though halved joints may be used if you prefer.

For baseboards up to a foot wide no central girder is required but above this width one is needed for each extra foot width. Halved joints are usually employed where these girders cross the joists but these can be avoided if you wish by staggering the joists so that butt joints can be used.

The method of construction is the same whether you are building, for example, a 6 ft × 4 ft baseboard as a single unit, or as three 4 ft × 2 ft boards which will be fitted together to form a 6 ft × 4 ft base, but there will be some duplication of the girders in the latter arrangement and therefore more material will be needed. Sometimes a baseboard which is not rectangular or square may be needed, perhaps an L-shape or a rectangle with arms extending from it. The simplest method is to build it as two or more rectangular bases which are then fixed together to produce the desired form. Take care in assembling the basic frame as it must have a perfectly flat upper surface to take the baseboard top.

If the baseboard is to be made up of two or more smaller units provision must be made for these to be fixed together firmly and accurately. For a permanent layout a convenient method is to bolt the two sections together with coach bolts. To ensure an accurate fit, clamp the two baseboard units firmly together making sure the two pieces are perfectly aligned and then drill through both at once. When clamping them pay special attention to the top surfaces as there must be no step where they

Basic grid for 4 ft × 2 ft layout section made up from 2 in × 1 in timber. Construction employs halved joints for central girder and butt joints elsewhere; if preferred butt joints could be used throughout by staggering the joists at either side of the central girder.

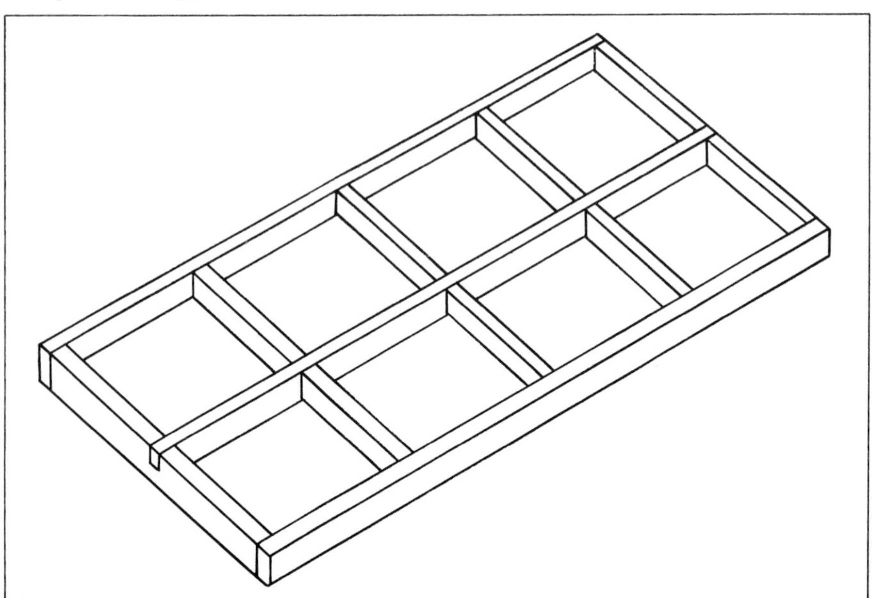

An L-shaped baseboard shown from the underside so the 2 in × 1 in wood framing is visible. Note how the L-shaped board has been made up from two rectangular units, one 4 ft × 1 ft and the other 2 ft × 1 ft. The two have been screwed together and a metal angle has been used for strengthening. The baseboard top is ½ in thick wood fibre insulation board.

join and no twisting of one in relation to the other.

Though the track bases and scenery supports can be fitted on to the frame directly (the open top or open frame baseboard system) the beginner is best advised to fit a top surface on to the basic frame (the solid top form of baseboard).

Solid top baseboards

The material employed for the top surface can be any of those listed in the section on materials earlier in the book. One of the most frequently used is ½ in thick wood fibre insulation board. As previously mentioned this is relatively soft and easy to work, inexpensive and takes pins and spikes easily but must be supported at intervals no greater than 12 ins to avoid sagging. After cutting to size, a top of insulation board should be nailed and glued on to the frame. Another popular choice for the top surface is chipboard. This is stronger and more rigid than the insulation board but is heavier, more expensive and harder to work. A top of this material is fixed down by screwing and gluing. The greater strength and rigidity of chipboard means that it needs less support then the insulation board and on small layouts lighter framing can be used if desired.

The solid top type of baseboard uses more material than the open top method but has the advantage of simplicity. The presence of a complete top surface also means that the modeller can use the baseboard to lay out the track in various arrangements before he decides on a final plan. Then, wherever he wishes to lay the tracks there will be support. It also makes it easy to alter the position of tracks if you change your mind during construction about the layout plan you want.

A disadvantage is that it is more awkward to build a layout with tracks at various levels, particularly if tracks below the level of the baseboard surface are required. Elevated tracks can be carried on a track base cut from chipboard or ply supported by wood blocks fixed on to the baseboard top. If you wish, the track base can be surfaced with insulation board to allow easy insertion of track pins and to reduce noise. Cyril Freezer has described a neat way of giving a smooth start to a rising track where it leaves the main baseboard level. He suggests cutting a tongue of the insulation board top surface and packing it up to the required grade. This tongue then leads smoothly on to the track base which is supported as described above.

If there must be tracks below the level of the baseboard top then this and possibly part of the baseboard framing must be cut away in this area. Alternatively if the baseboard is made up of separate sections joined together these may be planned so that low level tracks can be carried down between two of these sections. Either way such complications are best avoided, particularly by the beginner. If you want to construct a layout with tracks on multiple levels the most suitable type of baseboard is the open top form, either a basic grid frame or an L-girder frame. This should be designed so that the lowest level tracks run on track bases fitted directly on to the surface of the frame and the other tracks and scenery are then built upwards from the base.

If a deep valley or ravine is wanted, part of the baseboard can be dropped down to accommodate it—the area being strengthened with wood bracing or by metal brackets. A convenient arrangement is to

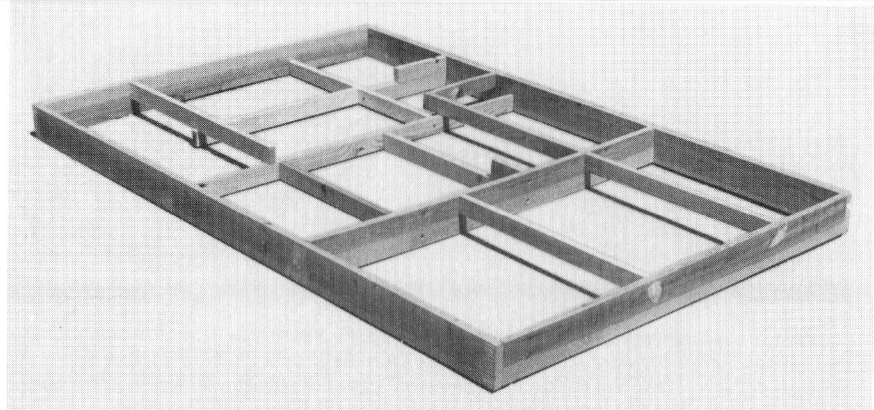

Baseboard for a 6 ft × 4 ft layout during construction. 4 in × 1 in timber was used for part of the framing and 2 in × 1 in for the rest. This has produced an area 2 in below the general ground level for a lake and river to be modelled. An additional joist at the right-hand end of the layout should have been provided to give better support for the top.

Later, during the construction, part of the wood fibre insulation board top has been fitted after cutting it to shape for one side of the lake and river. Further pieces of insulation board will be fixed in place to form the ground at this side and, between and at a lower level, to form a basis for the lake and river.

have the dropped section between two baseboard units.

Open-top baseboards

With this system a top surface is applied over the open frame only where it is needed for tracks or for features such as an industrial or urban area. This method uses less material and gives more flexibility in planning tracks and scenery at varying levels; it is particularly suitable for hilly or mountainous scenery. The track bases are cut from chipboard or ply and faced with insulation board as for the elevated tracks in the solid top method. However, these track bases are supported directly on the framing of the baseboard. For higher level tracks the track bases are carried on risers, wood strips fixed on to the framing and extending up to the required height.

The lack of a flat surface on which to lay

A baseboard section of the open-frame type. Note the track base supported by risers. The gap in the centre is where a large bridge spanning a gorge will be fitted. Note also the scenery supports built up from wood and hardboard.

out the track while planning and building the layout makes things more difficult especially for the beginner. One solution is to fit a top surface temporarily and to plan the track arrangement out full size on this. Once the track plan has been finalised the top is removed and the track locations are transferred to the frame for positioning the track bases and risers.

Model Railroader magazine staff devised a rather ingenious method, descriptively named the 'cookie cutter' technique, which combines the simplicity of the solid top with some of the flexibility of the open top system when it comes to adding high level trackage.

The 'cookie cutter'

The framing, of conventional type, is covered with a flat top of plywood which is screwed but not glued down. The surface is used to lay out the track in various ways until the final arrangement is decided on. If desired the tracks can be fixed down at this stage provided care is taken not to cover any of the screws which are holding the top down. The beginner can thus complete a simple one level layout which he can enjoy operating. This can be accomplished quickly and easily as in the solid top system. Later the modeller may wish to make the layout more interesting by introducing different levels for the tracks. If a track, either a new one to be added or one of the tracks already present, is to be elevated, saw cuts are made through the plywood top at either side of the track, taking care not to cut through any of the joists. Any screws holding this strip are removed and the strip and track are raised to the required height. Wood risers are fitted to support it. Though the technique is said to work well even with tracks already laid being raised up, there would seem to be a risk of such tracks being distorted unless this is done very carefully. However, the method does offer the benefits of easy planning and being able to get the trains running without delay, together with the potential for further development later. As the scenic side progresses part of the baseboard top can be cut away to enable the modelling of rivers, lakes and valleys.

L-Girder Framework

Some years ago Linn Westcott, who was editor of the American *Model Railroader* magazine at the time, devised an excellent new form of open frame baseboard with many important advantages. This is the 'layer' method and the essential feature is that the joists rest on top of the girders instead of lying between them. The main longitudinal girders are usually made L-shaped for greater strength and for convenience in the fixing of joists, risers and other parts to them. Therefore this type of framework is usually known as the 'L-Girder Frame'. The system was originally designed for large permanent layouts and each girder was built up by screwing and gluing a strip of 2 in × 1 in wood along the edge of a 4 in × 2 in plank to form a girder which was L-shaped in cross section. For smaller layouts or modular baseboards the girders can be lighter; 2 in × ½ in and 2 in × 1 in wood is suitable. If a circular saw bench is available L-girders can be cut very quickly and easily. Just two cuts with the saw into a wood strip will leave an L-girder and the piece removed from inside the L can be used as joists. The L-girders are very strong and convenient but are not essential and on a small layout simple girders can be used satisfactorily if preferred.

The important feature of the system is the position of the joists on top of the girders and this gives several advantages. The joists do not have to be cut accurately, as they must be in the basic grid to fit between the girders, so construction is simpler. Because all the screws are fitted from below they remain accessible and are easy to remove, making alterations and extensions to the layout much simpler than with the more conventional framework. Joists can be moved easily either to get them out of the way or to provide support when changes are made to tracks or scenery and the whole system is very flexible. The L-girder framework gives the maximum strength and therefore needs less material than other framing, making it lighter and cheaper to build. It is usually employed as an open-top baseboard and its versatility makes it ideal for layouts with tracks at multiple levels and correspondingly uneven scenic terrain. However, it is also perfectly satisfactory for a small beginner's layout with a solid top fitted on to a simple L-girder frame.

With this system the legs are not placed at the ends of the layout or layout section. The strongest position for the legs is where the long girders are crossed by joists and the best location is about 1/5 of the way in from the front, rear and ends. Legs placed here are also less likely to be accidentally knocked than ones in the conventional positions. 2 in × 1 in or 2 in square timber is used for the legs and these must be braced. This bracing should be at about 45° and reach to within 6 in of the floor at the lower end for maximum steadiness.

Baseboard support

On a permanent free-standing layout legs cut from 2 in square timber can be fixed into the corners of the baseboard frame with screws and braced either with wood struts or with metal angle brackets. To make sure the baseboard top will be level clamp the legs in place with 'C' clamps and set the whole thing up on a flat floor. Put a shallow dish filled with water on top of the baseboard and adjust the legs until the top is perfectly level as shown by the water. Tighten up the clamps and keep them on until you have drilled the holes for the screws fixing the legs. On longer baseboards, legs will be needed at 4 ft intervals. If the layout is semi-permanent only and must be taken down from time to time, bolts rather than screws should be used to fix the legs in place. Fitting wing nuts on to the bolts instead of the ordinary nuts will make them easier to remove.

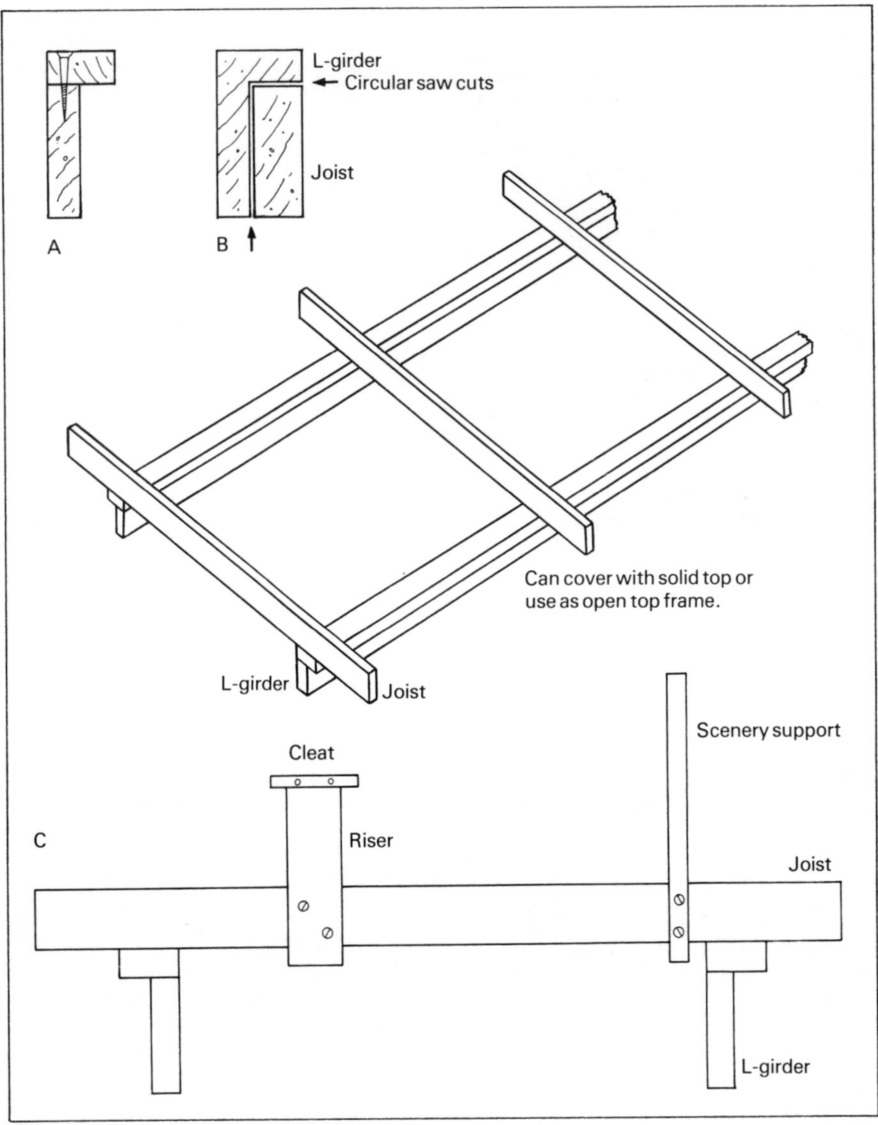

L-girder framing. **A** *Built up L-girder screwed and glued.* **B** *Sawn L-girder.* **C** *Track base for elevated track fixed to cleat (left) and for non-elevated track supported directly on joists (right).*

A beginner's layout is most often made as a free standing unit even if it will be placed against the wall. However, if there is no objection to plugging the wall, the rear of the baseboard can be supported by a batten or brackets of wood or metal fixed on to the wall. If the layout is a narrow one designed to be fitted along the wall or walls of the room it may be possible to support it entirely by fixing it, shelf-like, to the wall. However, most layouts are too wide for this and will also require legs to support the front edge.

It may be convenient to use furniture (a table, chest of drawers, low cupboard or bookcase) to support the layout rather than fitting it with legs of its own. You may have suitable pieces of furniture already; felt pads may be needed between the layout and the

A sturdy, but simply made, trestle used for layout support.

Jim Gadd's attractive 4 mm scale 9 mm gauge model railway layout has been constructed as a number of separate easily transported sections making it completely portable. It has been shown at numerous exhibitions. The photograph shows a passenger train arriving at Moulsett station.

top surface of the furniture to prevent scratching. Alternatively you can often buy secondhand furniture cheaply and you may find some useful items this way. If you make any repairs necessary and repaint the pieces of furniture they can be made very presentable and there may be drawers or shelves which will be useful for storing rolling stock and other models. Another source of furniture which can be used to support a layout is the whitewood range of ready-made and kit items; several matching units can be selected and used for a layout along one wall.

Another way of supporting a layout is to use trestles. These can be fixed or folding trestles and can be of quite simple construction.

Portable layouts

A portable layout must break down easily into units or modules small enough to be transported and stored without difficulty. It is best to design it so that it can be assembled, dismantled and moved by one person working alone. This means that the owner need not rely on anyone else for assistance. As it may well be necessary to set up and take down the layout for every operating session this should be arranged to take as little time as possible. When not in use the layout must be stored away, preferably neatly and safe from dust and accidental damage.

The sections or modules for a portable layout can be fabricated following the usual methods of construction. A grid frame of 2 in × 1 in wood with a top surface of insulation board or chipboard is suitable. The size of each module should certainly not be greater than 4 ft × 2 ft and units 3 ft long and 12-18 in wide may well be better. For these smaller sections 1 in square timber is adequate particularly if chipboard is used for the top of the baseboard. The small units are more convenient to transport in a car and are small enough to be stored in a large cupboard. The sections of a layout need not be identical in size and shape, but there are some advantages in having a standard module. Construction may be faster and easier because they can be mass produced and storage is likely to be simpler if all the modules are uniform. A neat method of storage is to construct a cupboard of the appropriate size to take the modules sliding on to supporting ledges fitted inside each end of the cupboard, very much as if they were drawers in a chest.

To fix the units together coach bolts can be used as with a permanent layout, preferably fitting the bolts with wing nuts to make

Part of a large N-scale layout built by Graham Bailey. The first section, to the right of the picture, is supported on two trestles. Further sections, one of which is shown here, are bolted on and each has one pair of legs at one end, the other end being supported by the trestle or legs of the adjacent section. These additional sections are fitted at both ends of the first unit.

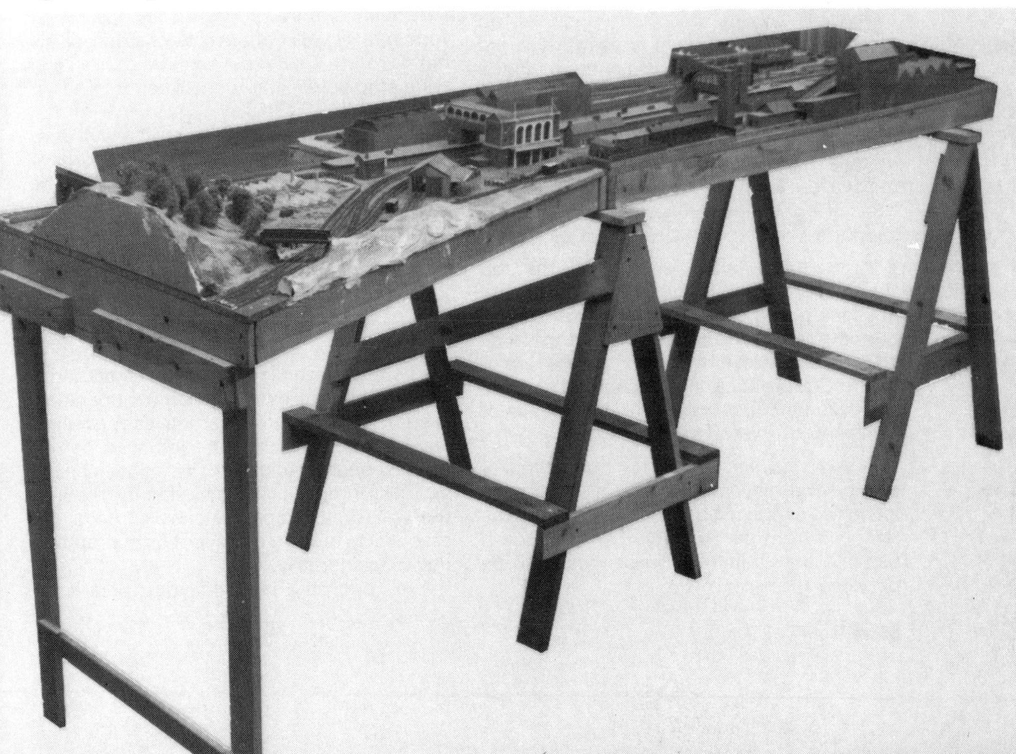

assembly quicker and easier. Unfortunately with setting up and dismantling the layout repeatedly the holes become worn larger so that the bolts are a loose fit and alignment of the sections may not be exact. One solution to this problem is to fit pieces of metal pipe, or tube of appropriate inside diameter, into the holes so that the bolts bear on the metal and do not enlarge the holes. However, an even better method has been suggested by Cyril Freezer. He uses cast brass flapback hinges with the pins removed and replaced with round nails of suitable size with the upper part bent to form handles. The adjacent baseboard sections are clamped together so that they are accurately aligned and the hinges are fixed on with one flap on each side of the join. When the pin is removed the two sections can be taken apart. The two hinge halves make it easy to line up the sections for fitting together again and when the pins are fitted into the hinges at each end of the join the two boards will be held firmly together.

You may find it convenient to make a portable layout so that adjacent units form identical pairs. Each pair can then be hinged together to form a double unit which folds up on itself; this provides protection during transportation and storage. The hinges must be mounted on blocks well above track level to provide clearance for structures and scenery, which should be arranged to interlock so that they do not clash when the module is folded up.

Portable layouts are often supported on furniture or trestles when in use. If legs are needed it is convenient to have them hinged on to the underside of the baseboards and to fit metal braces to lock them in position when the layout is erected. Usually only one module, the largest if they vary in size, needs to have four legs; the others will be fitted with a pair of legs at one end while the other end is supported by the next baseboard section.

If insulation board is used as the top surface for a portable layout it is desirable to fit a facing strip of ½ in square stripwood to protect the soft insulation board at the ends of the baseboard. Firm fixation for the rails of the tracks crossing the baseboard joins is achieved by soldering them to the heads of screws in this wood strip.

When arranging storage for the sections of a portable layout remember that the locomotives and rolling stock may have to be removed from the railway when it is not in use and that suitable storage must also be provided for them.

Lifting sections

If a layout fitted along a wall crosses the door of the room some means of access must be provided. If the layout is fairly high it may be possible to duck under it but a more satisfactory arrangement is to have a lifting section of the baseboard at this point. This is, in effect, merely a small baseboard section constructed in the usual manner. You may prefer to use chipboard rather than insulation board for the top surface to give greater rigidity to the lifting piece. The section is hinged at one end using ordinary flapback hinges mounted on wooden blocks at least an inch thick. A 2 in × 1 in strip of wood is fixed along the lower edge of the adjacent baseboard at the other side of the gap to support the end of the lifting section when it is in the down position.

Foldaway baseboards

Few modellers are lucky enough to have a room which can be devoted entirely to their hobby; usually the model railway layout must be fitted into one of the ordinary rooms in the house and should interfere as little as possible with the other uses of the room. One way in which this may be accomplished is to make a baseboard which is hinged or pivoted at one edge so that it folds up against the wall when not in use. Many successful layouts of this type have been built ranging from small N-scale railways which fold up into a bookcase or cupboard to a complete 8 ft × 10 ft HO scale layout, constructed by an American enthusiast, which swings up to form a false wall right across one end of his dining room. This layout takes up only a 26 in wide strip across the room when it is not in use!

The best arangement is to build a wall unit, complete with shelves and/or cupboards if desired, and to fix this firmly to the wall. The baseboard is then supported from this. A small layout can be hinged on to it but a large layout is better pivoted on lengths of steel rod in metal bearing tubes. On large layouts, counterweights to balance the layout make it easier and safer to raise or lower the baseboard.

There are several points to be remembered with a foldaway layout. When the operating session is over, all the locomotives and rolling stock must, of course, be removed before the baseboard is folded up; it is convenient to include storage accommodation for them in the wall unit. Proper catches or bolts are essential to prevent the layout from dropping down accidentally.

Note that on a hinged layout there is no

access from the rear edge. Therefore on any baseboard wider than 3 ft it is preferable to have a central operating and access well. The layout can be arranged so that the front edge is supported by furniture such as a chest of drawers or a table when the baseboard is down, or it can be fitted with folding or detachable legs. Since raising and lowering the baseboard imposes additional strain on it, rather thicker material than usual may be preferred for the framing.

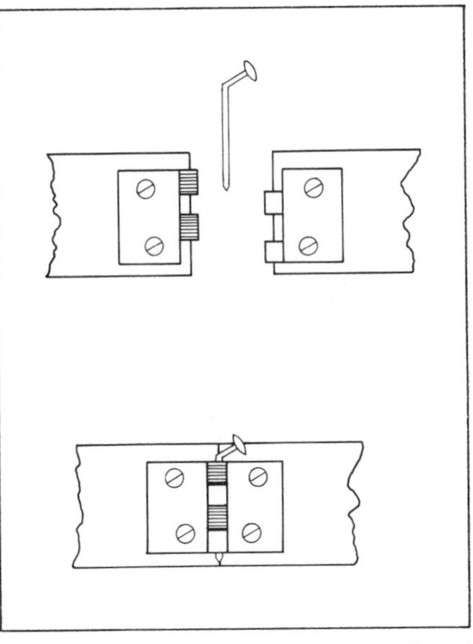

The hinge method of joining baseboard sections. Pin of hinge is removed and hinge halves fitted to baseboard sections. To join the two units, hinge halves are aligned and a round nail of appropriate size is used to hold them together.

Coffee table layouts

The introduction of the very small scales, 009, N and Z, has enabled the construction of an interesting operating model railway layout in a very small space. Some modellers have taken advantage of this to build small layouts into coffee tables. These are very convenient to operate and, of course, there is no problem of storage; when nicely finished these layouts form attractive pieces of furniture and they certainly stimulate interest and conversation amongst visitors.

Typically a layout will be about 3 ft × 2 ft or 18 in in size with a continuous track plan, either an oval or a figure of eight design. The base and sides are often of ½ in thick plywood, with or without a frame of 2 in × 1 in timber beneath the base. The top is made

Baseboard construction for the coffee table layout built by K.J. Churms. A box-like unit was made up from ½-in ply fixed with 1½-in No 8 screws and nails. Angle brackets inside the front corners provide greater rigidity. (Diagram by K.J. Churms.)

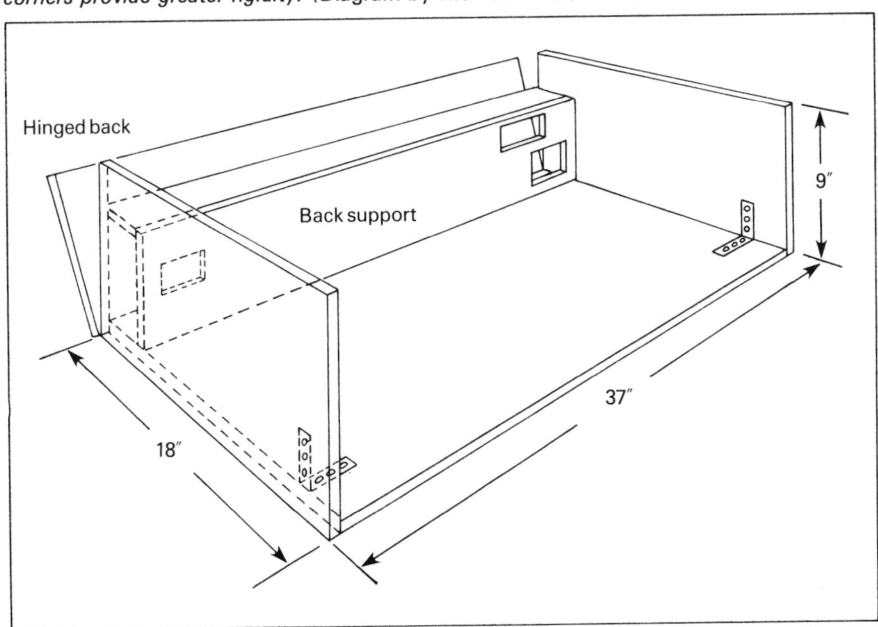

An attractive coffee table layout built by K.J. Churms. The 009 layout measures 3 ft × 18 in and has a twisted figure of eight track plan giving a good length of run. (Photo courtesy K.J. Churms).

from plate glass so that the layout can be viewed while also being used as a coffee table. Sometimes the sides are also made of plate glass. Ready-made legs in a variety of styles and materials are available from DIY shops and only require screwing into place on the underside of the baseboard. In keeping with their use as coffee tables the layouts are quite low, with the top perhaps 18 in above the floor. This also helps to make them more stable and steady.

An alternative method of construction was used by the MAP staff some years ago when they built a layout of this type which was featured in *Model Railway News* magazine. They used ¾ in square steel Dexion Speedframe tubes and joiners to make the frame with a baseboard of ½ in thick blockboard and a top of plate glass. Wooden dowels fitted across the frame below the baseboard formed a convenient rack for magazines. The finished model was a very neat piece of furniture.

Bookcase layouts

The lounge is a pleasant place in which to operate a model railway. The room is usually warm and comfortable and one can be sociable with the rest of the family while enjoying the hobby. The coffee table layout is one way in which a layout can be fitted into the lounge in an acceptable form but the scope of such a model is limited even in the very small scales and the idea is not really feasible for 00 scale.

An alternative is to incorporate a layout into some other piece of furniture. The modern style of wall units show considerable potential for a scheme of this sort, particularly if the modeller can design and build the units himself to suit his railway modelling requirements. If the finished piece of furniture is to be acceptable for the lounge the general workmanship and finish must be good and some ability at woodwork is needed for successful construction. There

A closer view of part of the coffee table layout constructed by K.J. Churms. Attractive scenery makes the layout appear larger than it is. (Photo courtesy K.J. Churms.)

are quite a number of kits and ready-made units which can be fitted together in various combinations now available and the modeller may be able to utilise some of these if he does not feel capable of building the whole thing from scratch.

Ideally the layout should be covered when not in use both to protect it from dust and damage and to keep it out of sight when the lounge is used for other activities. However it should be possible to get it ready for operation with a minimum of effort. The modeller can also take the opportunity to include shelves and cupboards for general use or to accommodate books, magazines and other model railway items.

Ron Prattley has built a fine unit of this type, an attractive bookcase in which the layout is completely hidden when not in use. For operation the layout is revealed by removing the bookcase top; this itself forms a further section of the layout when it is reversed and fitted on to the end of the bookcase. The layout is completed by the addition of the fiddle yard which is stored in the bookcase at other times. Ron built the bookcase from pine and he used self-adhesive plastic over this to give an excellent finished appearance as can be seen in the accompanying pictures.

Vernon Sparrow is another modeller who has been able to fit his layout into the lounge. He has constructed a shelf along one wall above the furniture to carry his model railway; a neat appearance has been achieved by making the shelf match the furniture.

There are a number of shelving systems designed for home assembly, available from DIY shops and the modeller could arrange one of these to provide neatly finished shelves, one for a narrow layout and others for books, magazines and models.

Above *Ron Prattley built this superb bookcase to house his 00-scale layout in his lounge. When not in use the model railway is completely covered keeping it safe from damage and dust.* **Below** *For operation the top of the bookcase is removed, reversed and added onto the end of the bookcase to extend the layout. The fiddle yard (above large shelf in bookcase) has yet to be put in place at the end of the layout.* (Photos by Ron Prattley.)

Above *Vernon Sparrow built this neatly finished shelf matching the other units of furniture which he also constructed, to support his 00-scale layout along one wall of his lounge. The layout is seen here from the usual viewpoint. Although the shelf is only 16½ in wide an interesting track layout has been featured* (*see track plan*). **Below** *This view shows the layout as seen from an armchair.* (Photos courtesy Vernon Sparrow.)

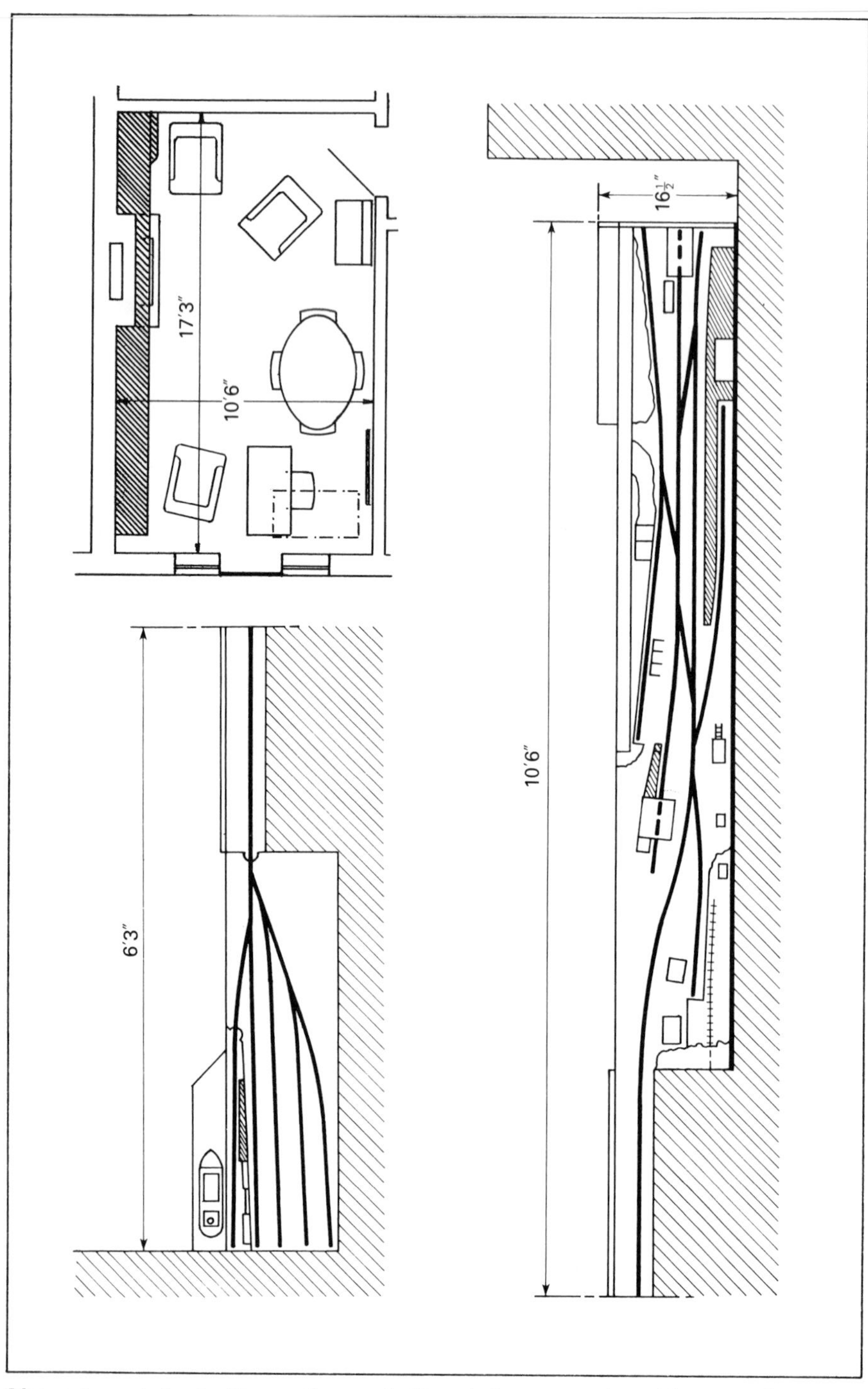

Above *Layout plan for Vernon Sparrow's 00-scale layout together with a plan of his lounge showing how the layout has been fitted into the room.* (Plans courtesy of Vernon Sparrow.)

Track

Much of the appeal of railway modelling is that a layout is not merely a static collection of models built or purchased by the enthusiast but is a miniature working replica of the real railways. To enjoy a layout to the full it is essential that it should work well and realistically. The track is fundamental to this and every effort should be made to lay it accurately. If an item of rolling stock runs badly it can be put aside, or left on a siding, until it can be adjusted and the working of the layout as a whole will not be impaired. However, if a section of track is faulty and causes derailments it may spoil the operation of the railway entirely. It will save time and trouble in the long run if you make sure the track is properly laid at the beginning; it is always more difficult to correct faults later.

The modeller can either buy his track ready-made or he can build it himself from the component parts.

Ready-made track

The made up track now available commercially is of very good quality both in its reliability of operation and in appearance. I would recommend that the beginner should always use this type of track for his first layout. It is convenient and easy to lay and the modeller can quickly complete the basic trackwork so that it is possible to run a train. With reasonable care even a novice can lay smooth and accurate trackwork over which trains will run reliably and without derailments.

Most of the ready-made track has rail of Code 100 section in 00/HO and of Code 80 in N which represents the heaviest rail used on prototype main lines and is therefore overscale for lighter track. However, it has the great advantage of accepting virtually all proprietary wheels, whereas finer section rail will only take fine scale wheels. Provided the track is ballasted and painted (as described later) the appearance of the heavier rail is quite acceptable.

Sectional track

This is the type with which the beginner will be familiar from its inclusion in train sets. The pieces of track have the rails attached to a rigid sleeper base and are thus of fixed shape, straight or curved in a range of radii. The sections are also made in a selection of shorter lengths permitting greater scope in track arrangement. A rail joiner is fitted on one rail at each end ready for fixing the sections together.

Sectional track is the simplest and quickest to lay and can, of course, be set out temporarily and taken up again as soon as the particular track layout is finished with. If it is to be more permanent, pins can be used to hold it in place. Alternatively it can be fixed with double-sided adhesive tape. This will hold it firmly and it is still easy to lift the track again later.

The best way of joining pieces of sectional track is to lay them on a flat surface and gently slide them together so that the rails fit correctly into the joiners. This may sound obvious but it is surprisingly easy, especially with N and Z scales, to let the rail overlap the joiner instead, causing a vertical misalignment at the rail join which can lead to derailments. Similarly when taking the sections apart again slide them on a flat surface. Never twist or strain the track as this may permanently distort it. With a train set or temporary layout which is dismantled after use, the track must be stored away carefully to avoid damage. Do not just pile all the track together in a box or drawer but stack it neatly. A good idea is to wrap each section of track in tissue paper or even newspaper. The points can be kept in their original boxes if these have been retained. Be especially careful that the rail joiners do not get bent as this may interfere with smooth running and also with electrical contact. When joining the sections make sure that they are properly aligned. With the curved sections in particular it is quite easy to have a slight

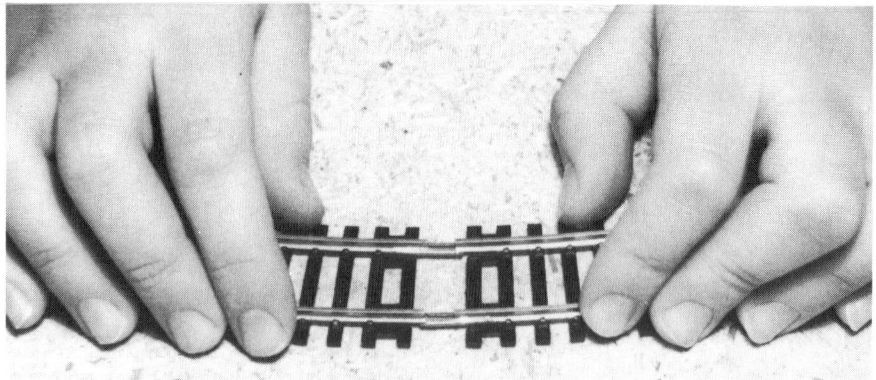

When joining pieces of sectional track place them on a flat surface and slide them together making sure the rail ends fit properly into the rail joiners. Take care not to bend or twist the track.

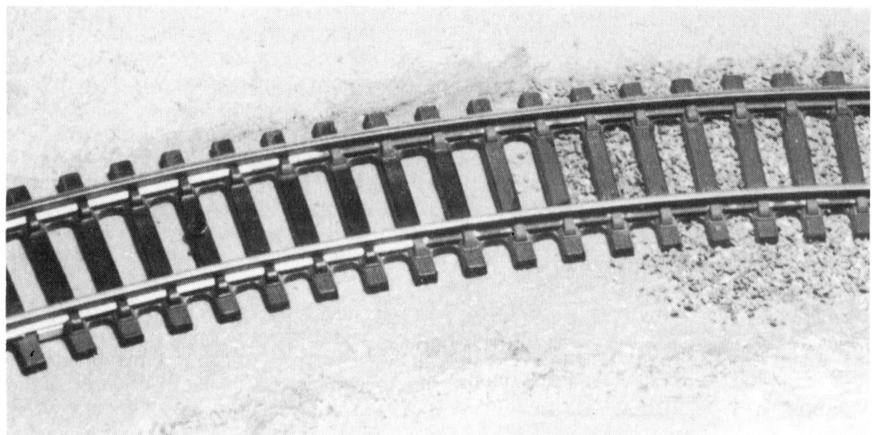

Hornby sectional track on a permanent layout. Note the great improvement in appearance of the track after ballasting and painting the rails and sleepers at the right side of the picture.

angulation at the join. One way of checking is to place another section of the same radius over the join as a guide; another is to use a Tracksetta template of the appropriate curve.

A wide range of sectional track pieces is available from various manufacturers, especially in the most popular 00/HO and N gauges. In many cases the parts from different makers are compatible which provides even greater choice. When setting up a track layout you may find that you need some small lengths of straight or curved track to complete it. Half and quarter sections, both straight and curved, are available and these may be suitable; alternatively a piece can be cut to fit exactly, as described in the section on flexible track. Some of the manufacturers also make extendable or telescoping pieces, the lengths of which are adjustable, within limits, to fit the gap present. The points and special trackwork are suitable for use with either sectional or flexible track and are considered later.

Most sectional track consists of rails fixed to a rigid sleeper base without ballast; if this is required it must be added as with flexible track. However, the Fleischmann N-gauge 'Piccolo' track is complete with a ballast base. In 00/HO the Conrad track system, also manufactured in Germany, is a comprehensive system with a preballasted base

A selection of track pieces from the Conrad range of 00/HO sectional track. Note the textured and coloured ballast base moulded in plastic.

of rigid plastic. The texture and colour of the ballast is realistic and the system is designed for the enthusiast who wants to build a scale layout but wishes to have the convenience of sectional track.

Sectional track is the easiest to work with and is ideal for the beginner. It can be assembled without any cutting or other constructional work and provides a smooth running line. It can also be taken apart and rearranged as often as desired giving the modeller the chance to experiment with a variety of layout schemes. Because most modellers progress to using flexible track they often overlook the uses of the sectional variety on a permanent scale layout. It can be a very quick and convenient way of laying hidden sidings, concealed track, fiddle yards and so on; this will give reliable operation and is very desirable for any track which is hidden or inaccessible. As it is often possible to buy secondhand sectional track which is in good condition, but much cheaper than new equipment, this can be an economical way of laying such lines. There is no reason why the modeller who is going on from a train set to a permanent layout should not incorporate the sectional track he has into the new layout together with the flexible variety, and he may prefer to do this rather than scrap the former or sell it cheaply to a dealer. The sectional track is laid in the same way as flexible.

The main disadvantage of sectional track is that it is restricting. The curves are of fixed radii and this tends to result in a track plan which is rather symmetrical and toy-like. The configurations must be designed to fit the track sections available rather than the situation on the layout. However, there are many interesting and realistic plans which can be made up with this type of track.

Flexible track

On prototype railways the track is designed to fit the location and to give as smooth a ride as possible for the locomotives and rolling stock which pass over it. The track is usually laid out with smooth flowing curves and with gentle transitions from straight to curved track and this is not possible in model form using sectional track. For this reason most modellers use flexible track for their layouts.

Flexible track is similar to the usual ballastless sectional track but the plastic sleeper base, instead of being complete and rigid, has gaps arranged so that it can be curved to any desired radius. It is usually made in pieces about a yard long. To make up a layout this type of track must be curved and cut to length to fit. It must also be fixed down to keep it in position and to retain its curves.

The introduction of the modern plastic sleepered flexible track was a great advance. Prior to this the modeller either had to use sectional track with its limitations or had to make up his own trackwork, which could be very time consuming on a layout with a lot of track. The flexible track is quick and easy to lay and gives good running with a realistic appearance.

The first step is to draw out the track plan full size on the baseboard surface. It can be helpful to use points and pieces of sectional

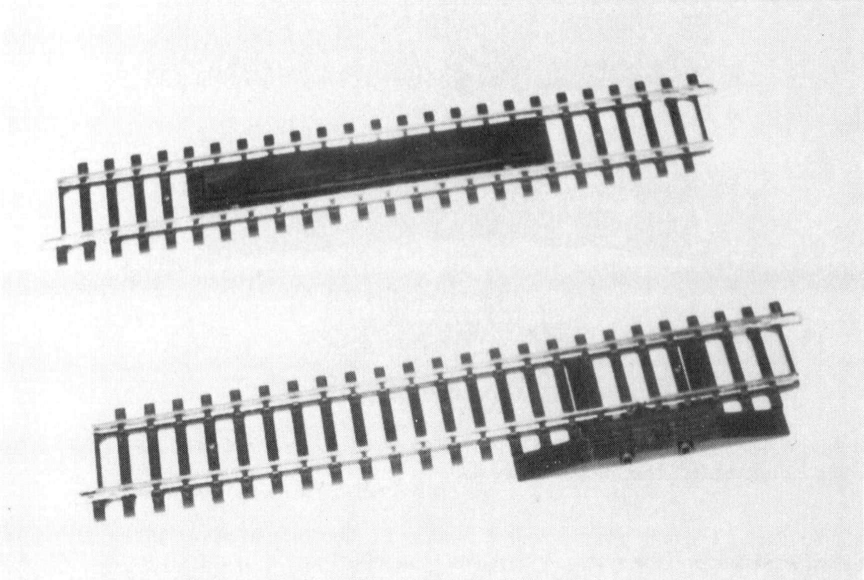

Two items of special track from the Hornby range of sectional track. Above is an uncoupling ramp fitted to a standard straight track piece; below is the isolating track section.

This 6 ft × 4 ft 00-scale layout under construction utilises track from a train set together with additional pieces of sectional track, points and flexible track. The baseboard for this layout is shown during construction in two pictures earlier in the book.

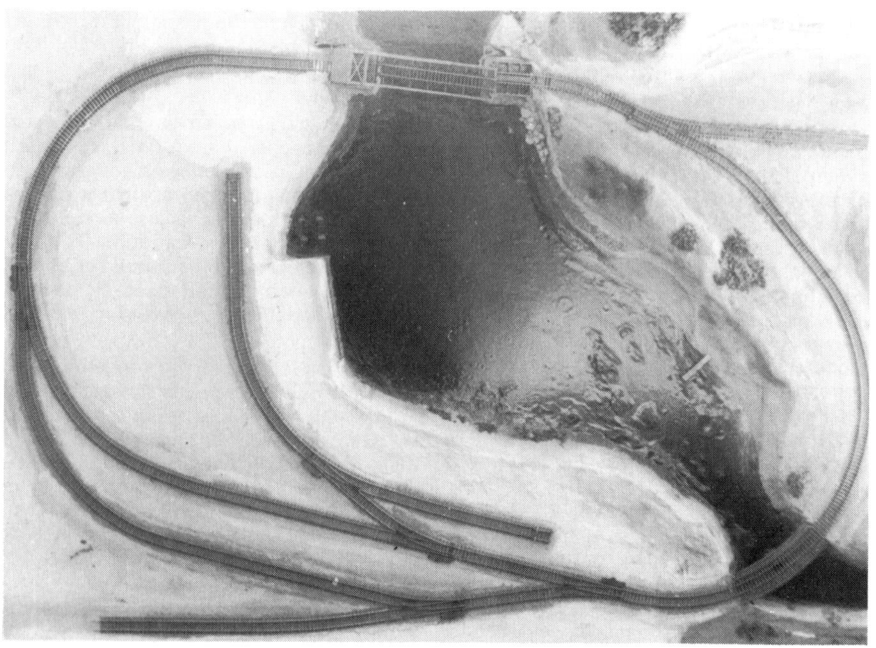

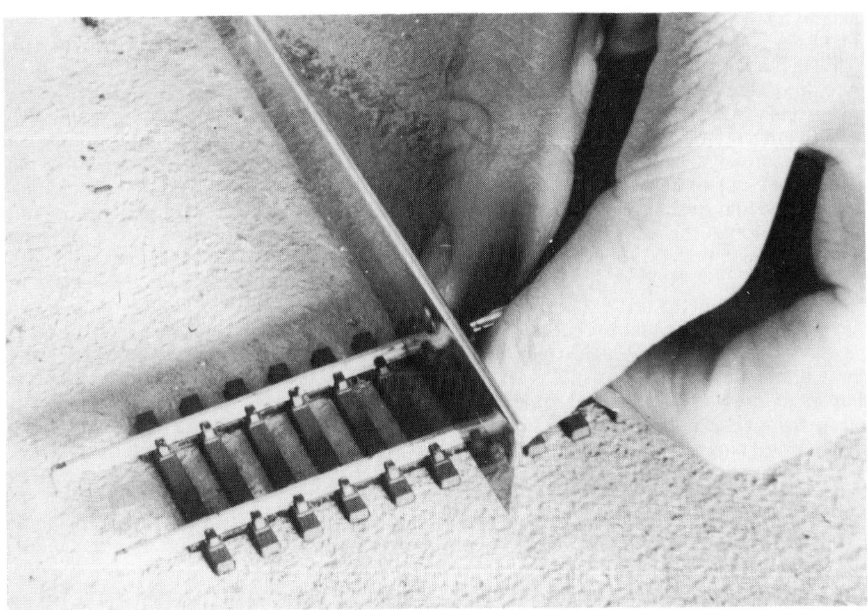

To cut sectional or flexible track to fit, use a razor saw and hold the rails firmly while cutting to avoid damage to the tags which hold the rails on to the sleepers. The best method is to use a track gauge or a block of wood with two slots to fit the rails to hold the rails.

track as guides; you may also find it useful to make templates of the curves needed from hardboard, thin plywood or thick cardboard. As you set the plan out full size you may well find that you wish to make minor alterations and improvements to the layout design. Once you are satisfied with the plan, you can prepare for track laying. You will need track, points, fishplates (both insulating and non-insulating), track pins and white glue. To check each section of trackwork as it is laid you will also need a power unit, a locomotive and some rolling stock; a bogie coach and a 4-wheel wagon will suffice. This will enable you to find any faults at once so that they can be corrected before work progresses any further.

When flexible track is bent into a curve the inner rail will be too long and must be shortened to match up with the outer rail. Also the track must often be cut to fit the other track and points. This cutting is easily accomplished with a razor saw, but the rails must be held firmly while you are cutting so that you do not bend the rails or break the small tags which hold the rails to the sleepers. A small block of wood with two grooves cut in it to fit the rails forms a useful tool for holding the rails while cutting them; alternatively you can put a track gauge on to the rails close to where you cut them. After sawing through the rails use a fine file to smooth the ends, particularly the top and inner sides where the train wheels will run. To allow the rail joiners to slide fully by giving the proper sleeper spacing, you will need to cut along horizontally under each rail end to detach it from the first sleeper; this is easily done either with the razor saw or with a modelling knife. The filing of the rail ends mentioned above not only removes any irregularities which will interfere with smooth running but also makes it easier to slide the rail joiners on, particularly if the edges of the sides and base are slightly bevelled. If necessary the rail joiners (of the metal non-insulating type) can also be eased slightly open with the end of a screwdriver, though take care not to make them loose. Make sure that the rail joiners do not get kinked when fitting them on as this may cause misalignment at the rail joins. The joiners can be tightened after fitting using a pair of fine pliers to ensure good electrical contact. A slight gap between the rail ends will allow for any expansion and contraction with temperature changes. Where rail gaps are required for electrical isolation or sectionalisation use insulating rail joiners instead of the usual metal ones.

Laying ready-made track is not difficult but it should not be rushed. Take your time and make a really good job of the trackwork; it is easier to get it right to begin with than to have to try to correct it later! There are several popular methods of ballasting the track and these will be fully described a little later but I should mention at this stage that in some of these the ballast must be applied at the same time as the track is laid.

If you wish to pin the track down, and this is usually advisable at least for curved track, use the commercially available track pins. Many brands of track have holes in the sleepers at intervals for pinning. If the track you are using does not already have holes, or if you require pins in different positions, you can drill them out with a drill bit slightly larger in diameter than the pins. The pins should not be a tight fit in the holes because this may lead to the sleepers bending when the pins are pushed in. If your layout has insulation board for the baseboard top or for the track bases you can use the fine Peco track pins and with these you do not need to drill holes in the sleepers as they can be easily pushed in through the sleepers and into the insulation board. If your track is laid on a harder surface such as chipboard, plywood or blockboard stouter pins will be required and holes should be drilled both through the sleepers and into the base. The track pins are pushed in using fine long-nose pliers or a fairly strong pair of tweezers. Insert the pins with the pliers while holding the track firmly with your other hand. Push them in far enough just to touch the sleepers but do not force them in any further as this will bend the sleepers and distort the track. It is also easier to remove the pins should you wish to lift the track later to make alterations to your track plan if the pins are not too far in. On a portable layout the pinning should be fairly close to keep the track secure; on other layouts relatively few pins are required and the spacing can be wider.

The track can be glued down using white (PVA) glue. The adhesive is spread over the track area, the track is positioned and either weighted down to hold it in place or lightly pinned to prevent it moving until the glue sets. Ballast is usually applied over the glue immediately after the track is positioned. An alternative method of fixing the track down is to use double-sided adhesive tape. Pieces are cut to the lengths required and carefully fixed down in the line of the track. The protective paper covering is then peeled off and the track is laid on top. No pins are needed. Ballast is sprinkled on and pressed down with the fingers to make it adhere to the tape around the sleepers.

If a foam ballast underlay is used this should be fitted on to the sleepers before the track is laid. Adhesive can be applied to the sleepers before combining the track and underlay if you wish though this is not essential as the glue used to fix the underlay down will soak through the foam and also hold the track firm. A few pins are inserted to hold the combined track and underlay in place while the glue sets. This pinning must be done with particular care not to push the pins in too far as it is easy to compress the underlay where it is pinned producing a switchback effect with the track. The laying of points calls for especial care and details are given in the section on points and special trackwork.

It is generally best to start track laying at the most complex part of the trackwork, usually the station area. Here there may be several points and a runaround track, where the track must match up exactly. Once you have got this correct you can work along the line. In this way with an oval track plan you will be able to work round in both directions from the station and when the tracks meet you will be able to adjust the simple straight tracks to match up smoothly. If, however, you left the station area until last it might be difficult, or impossible, to get the tracks to match up accurately.

Each piece of track should be properly aligned with the preceding section. If you bring your eye down close to track level and sight along the rails you can easily see any bends or kinks and they can be corrected before the track is fixed down. When laying curves it is easy to overlook a slight kink at the join which will jolt and perhaps derail rolling stock passing over it. It is useful to cut a template from thick card, hardboard or thin plywood to the appropriate curve to fit alongside the inner side of the inner rail and the track is then curved to fit this before it is fixed down. Alternatively you can buy Tracksetta templates for the radii you will be using. These metal templates are made in a range of radii, and also straight, for 00 and N gauges and are designed to fit between the rails of the flexible track holding it to shape until it is fixed in position. With either type of template, the Tracksettas or the homemade shapes, joins can also be accurately aligned. If the curve on the layout is to be longer than the template, fix the first part of the curve down, then move the template along so half

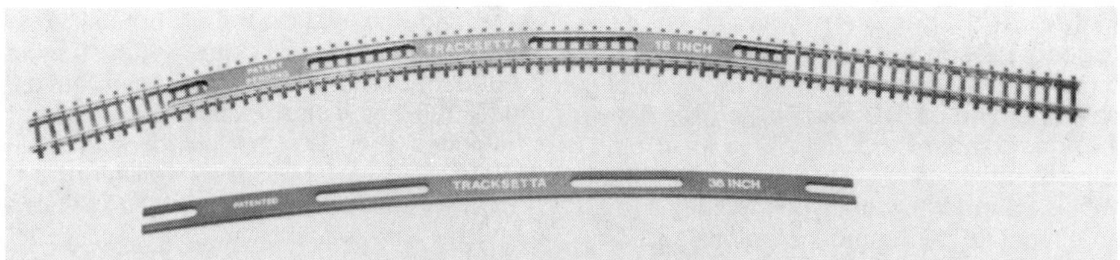

The Melcam 'Tracksetta' metal templates simplify the laying of flexible track in smooth curves and the joining of curved segments of sectional track accurately. Two N-gauge templates are shown in this picture, one of 18 in radius fitted into a length of Peco flexible track above and one of 36 in radius below. Straight templates are also produced.

is still in the fixed section of the curve while the rest curves the next part of the track into place. Continue working along the curve in stages until the whole curve is fixed down. When minimum radius curves are necessary take particular care to make them as smooth and accurate as you can so that you get good running.

It is worth while buying a track gauge even if you plan to lay only ready-made track and using it to check when track laying. Suitable gauges are made by Peco, Millholme Models and Hamblings. The most likely place for the track to get out of gauge is where two sections are joined, particularly if the joint occurs on a curve. If possible avoid having a rail joint too near to the point where a curve starts or ends. If you must have a joint here it may help to pre-bend the rails into the curve required rather than letting it take up the curve itself as you lay it. Another useful dodge when joining flexible track is to cut the track so that two or three sleepers are left beyond the ends of the rails. The rails from the next section are brought into the tags on these sleepers. This will reduce the tendency for kinking at the join.

On model railways the change from straight track to curved is usually abrupt with the track passing immediately into a curve which has the same radius throughout. This tends to cause lurching as rolling stock passes from the straight to the curve and also makes the small radius curves we have to use, due to lack of space, even more noticeable. On prototype railways this change is gradual, the track passing from straight into a curve, the radius of which steadily decreases until it reaches the radius of the curve proper. This linking curve is known as a transition or spiral curve or easement. The plotting of mathematically correct easements is complex and beyond most of us; I believe an American modeller has used a computer to calculate them for his layout! However a very reasonable compromise can be reached by using a curve with twice the radius of the curve proper and about 8-10 in long to link the straight track with the true curve. Using this as a guide you will find that the flexible track will assume a smooth curve which is close to a true easement. To do this will, of course, need a little more space or alternatively means employing a smaller radius for the curve proper so that the curve will fit into the same space. However you will find that the running will be smoother and the appearance better with an easement even though it does mean using a sharper curve for the curve proper.

Sometimes it is necessary to fit a section of track in between two other pieces which are already fixed down, for example when completing a run-around loop or when fitting the last piece in an oval. To do this place a length of track over the gap and mark it off to the correct length. Then cut to the exact size to fit the gap. If the track piece is reasonably long, it can be sprung into place without difficulty after fitting rail joiners on to the rail ends. If the segment of track is too short for this it can still be fitted quite easily. Cut the rail joiners down to about two-thirds of their normal length and cut along under each rail end so that the shortened rail joiners can be pushed far enough back that they do not extend beyond the rail ends at all. The piece of track is then dropped into place, the rail ends lined up with those of the adjacent sections of track, and the rail joiners pushed along to fit across the joins.

On a portable layout the rails must be firmly fixed at the baseboard edge where the track crosses from one section of the baseboard to the next. The rail ends are best secured by soldering them to the heads of small screws fixed into a ½ in square edging strip of wood, if insulation board is used as the top surface, or into the chipboard if this is employed as the top.

Points and special trackwork

A good selection of ready-made points and other special items of track is available, particularly in 00/HO and N gauges. These include standard points of various radii, curved points and crossings of different angles. Symmetric or Y-points save space compared to the standard points and this may be very useful in cramped situations. Two Y-points together form an arrangement similar to a double slip-point. Another space saver is the 3-way point and the rather similar lap-point; these are typically seen giving access to industrial sidings. In model form these points not only look interesting and authentic but also allow extra tracks to be fitted in. Double slip-points are expensive but well worth considering both for their impressive appearance and for the operational flexibility they introduce in a station approach, goods yard or industrial area.

I have not provided a listing of the types of points available from different manufacturers as these change with the introduction of new items and the withdrawal of others. Also from time to time a new firm begins production. When planning or constructing a model railway layout consult the current catalogues and also check with your local dealer for advice on what is available.

In many cases the points are made as both manually and electrically operated types. Some manufacturers make manually operated points to which point motors, sold as separate items, can be fitted very simply.

The points offered by some manufacturers, particularly in N scale, are designed for function rather than for authentic scale appearance. The choice is up to the individual but I would advise looking at as many different makes as possible before buying any of the points needed for your layout. The Peco 'Streamline' points and track are particularly realistic in appearance and provide smooth running as well.

Catch-points are designed to derail any stock which comes on to them when they are set against that track. They are located

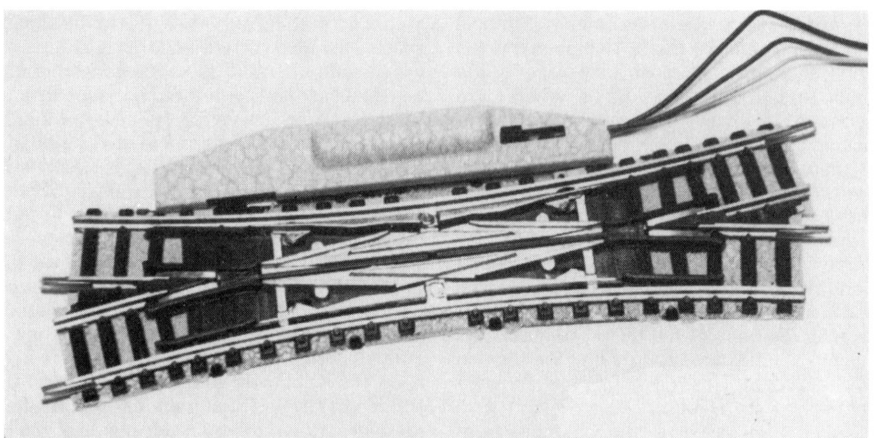

An electrically operated N-gauge, left-hand, double slip-point by Fleischmann.

A Peco 00-scale, double slip-point. This impressive point will add interest to the trackwork while providing flexibility and saving space.

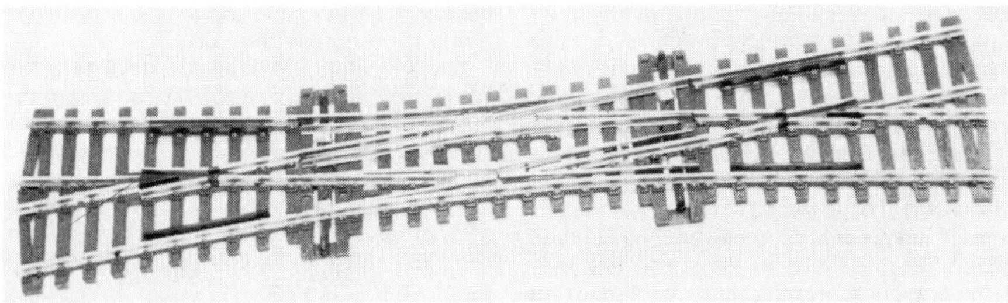

on sidings before they join main lines to make sure that stock cannot run on to the main line accidentally. They are also used on inclines to derail any wagon becoming detached from a train going up the incline. Right- and left-hand catch-points are made in N, 00 and 0 gauges by Peco.

Other special track pieces include power input sections, isolating rail sections and uncouplers. I have already mentioned the extending rail pieces made by various firms; these sections of straight track can be lengthened or shortened, within limits, to suit the gap left between two sections of track and are intended for use with sectional track. Another special item is the Fleischmann contact treadle (00/HO and N) which can be fitted on to the track and when the contact button on the underside of a Fleischmann locomotive contacts it as the engine passes over, an electrical impulse is produced which can be used to operate points, signals, and so on. A similar device is available in N scale from Arnold which is activated by the metal wheels of a passing locomotive.

Fleischmann make models of rack and pinion locomotives in HO and N scales and special track for these is produced, though no points are made. For HO scale, flexible rack rail in 8 in lengths, designed to be fitted on to ordinary straight or curved track, is available. In N-scale, flexible track is manufactured complete with a centre rack rail.

The Conrad system of sectional track, complete with moulded ballast base, was mentioned earlier. The pointwork is very interesting being based on a modular system of switches and crossings from which different types of points and crossings can be assembled. Point motors are concealed within the ballast base. There is also an uncoupling rail section.

When laying points they should be pinned down taking great care not to twist, bend or otherwise distort them; when fixed in place check that the point blades move freely. Glue

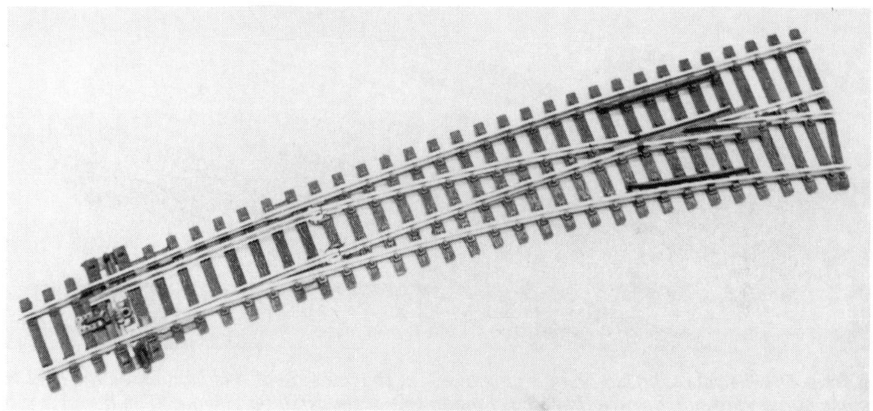

An attractive curved right-hand point in 00 scale by Peco; this is a dead frog point but the Peco 00-scale 'Streamline' points are also available with live frogs, except for crossings and double slip-points.

A Peco 0-scale, left-hand point. The 0-scale 'Streamline' points are live frog (Electrofrog) points with the frog energised through a switch built in to the toe-end of the point.

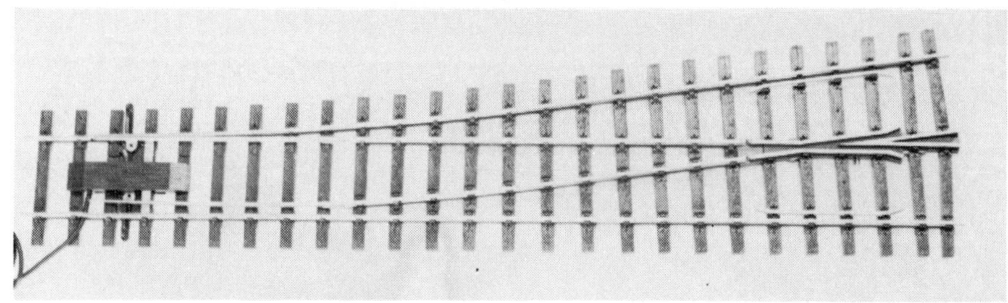

Realistic track at 'Stonepark Lane', an 00-scale branchline terminus. The track is Peco 'Streamline' with foam ballast underlay and a little additional loose ballast. Both the track and ballast have been painted to enhance the effect.

Above *The Fleischmann lap-point is employed, at the left side of this picture, as the lead to these hump yard sidings on a fine Fleischmann HO-scale exhibition layout. The hump is just out of view to the left.* **Below** *The hump section. The whole layout including the hump yard is worked automatically using standard parts from the Fleischmann range.*

may be used in addition if necessary for the ballasting though Peco recommend that glue should not be used with their points as the adhesive may adversely affect the plastic of the base. When laying standard right- or left-hand points hold a straight edge alongside the straight stock rail to make sure that the point is fixed down with this rail perfectly straight.

If foam ballast underlay is used take care not to push the pins in too far causing distortion; the heads of the pins should be just clear of the tops of the sleepers. If loose ballast glued in place is used it is essential that the ballast be kept clear of the moving parts of the point as otherwise the point may be jammed or at least have its movement impaired. Also make sure the ballast does not get between the running and check rails. When the ballast and glue have set, remove any loose ballast and check the point movement again. If necessary use a small screwdriver to scrape away any ballast which is fouling the point. Make sure that the sharp ends of the point blades rest tightly against the stock rails so that the wheel flanges will not run between; it may be necessary to file the ends of the blades very slightly to ensure this.

Point control

For points which are within easy reach of the operator simple inexpensive point levers are perfectly adequate. On a small layout, all the points may be readily accessible and these levers may be all that is needed. However, on many layouts some, at least, of the points are likely to be out of reach and some form of remote control is required. This may be electrical or mechanical.

Electrical control is generally more expensive but is very convenient, is easier to install than mechanical control and can be used to work points at any distance. It is also suitable for portable layouts as the wires can be connected at the baseboard joins to link different sections; mechanical methods could only be used to control points on the same baseboard as the control position. Many of the manufacturers offer their points as either manually or electrically operated or they make electric point motors which can simply be clipped on to the manual points to convert them. These are usually fitted on top of the baseboard surface but the Arnold (N scale) and Fleischmann (HO/00 and N scales) point motors are designed to allow mounting either on top of the baseboard or set into it, so that they can be covered and concealed. It should be noted that for the Arnold and Fleischmann motors a right-hand point motor is used inverted and set into the baseboard for a left-hand point and vice versa. The Peco point motors are designed for fitting beneath the baseboard but can be used, with an adaptor, above the baseboard. Though fixing point motors beneath or set into the baseboard gives a very good effect visually it does make access more difficult and for this reason some modellers prefer to have the motors on top of the baseboard but concealed by removable features such as a small lineside hut or a dummy, hollow stack of sleepers. The electrical details are discussed later.

A variety of mechanical methods for point control have been devised. I think the neatest and probably the easiest to install successfully is the wire-in-tube system. The points are changed by a fine wire moving within copper or plastic tubing; at one end the wire is connected to the switch blade tie bar or point lever and at the other to a lever worked by hand. A standard lever frame forms a neat arrangement for grouping together the controls for a number of points; if desired the frame can be fitted within a dummy building which is open at the rear for access to the frame.

Generally the tubing should be kept in a straight line as far as possible but curves with a radius down to 2 in can be made in it. The plastic tubing is very flexible and easy to use but must be fixed down with care so that the tubing is not constricted causing the wire to stick. When bending the more rigid copper tubing a former should be used to get a smooth curve. The tubing is relatively unobtrusive, especially if painted, and can be mounted on the baseboard surface. If the point to be controlled is beyond another track the tubing must be set into a groove to pass under the track. In fact some modellers prefer to set all the tubing into grooves so that it is concealed; the grooves are most conveniently made before the tracks are laid over them. The grooves are easy to cut if insulation board is used; they should be a good fit for the tubing to help hold it in place. Special fittings are provided to hold the plastic tubing; the copper tube can be held by, or soldered to, pins pushed into the baseboard.

Where the wire joins the point-switch blade and the lever frame, the tubing should be in a straight line with the movement of the tie bar and the lever. Bring the tube up from the groove in a gradual slope rather than at an angle. If the point control wire must turn through a right angle, an angle crank can be

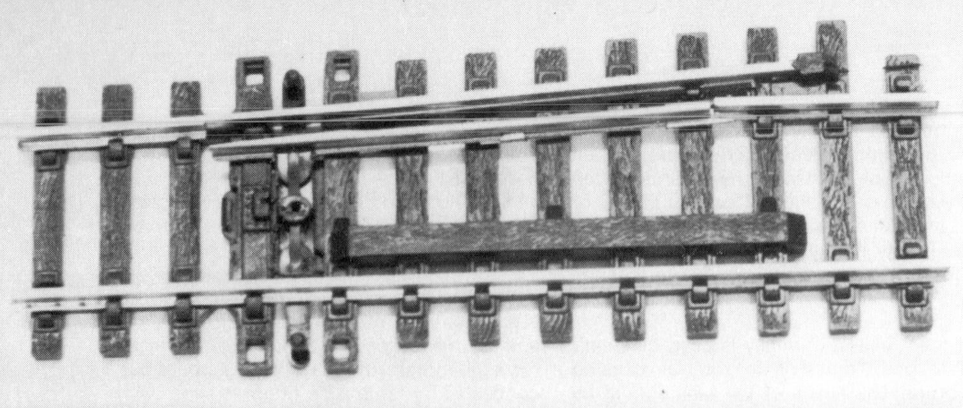

A Peco 00-scale left-hand catch-point. Catch-points are used on sidings and on inclines to derail rolling stock which might otherwise obstruct the main line and in model form they make an interesting and authentic detail. Peco make catch-points in N, 00, and 0 scales.

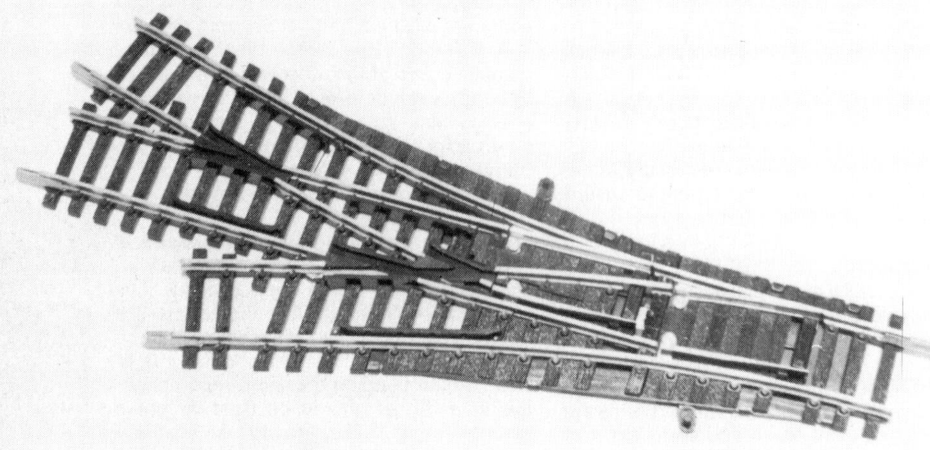

The lap-point is similar to a 3-way point but is not symmetric. It is a useful space saver in a goods yard or industrial area. The HO-scale lap-point shown here is from the Fleischmann range of points.

A diamond crossing in N gauge, by Roco. Note the insulated frogs.

used rather than bending the tubing. The point itself must be firmly fixed down so that the wire moves the tie bar and not the whole point.

The wire-in-tube method is not suitable for control over long distances. The maximum is probably about 10 ft but I prefer to limit the length to 6 ft if possible.

Constructing track

Though the introduction of flexible track has made it possible to lay very realistic track using ready-made products there are still limitations. For complete freedom in track laying giving flowing curves and pointwork to suit the particular situation, hand-built track is still the ideal if the modeller has the necessary skill and is prepared to put in the time and effort required. It also means that finer section rail than that normally used for ready-made track can be employed giving a more realistic appearance; though this will also entail the adoption of finer wheel standards for the locomotives and rolling stock.

In 0 scale Peco make sleepers, chairs which are fixed on to the sleepers with fine pins, bullhead rail and point parts enabling easy construction of well detailed track and points which match up with the ready-made items they produce.

In 00 and TT scales flat-bottom rail can be spiked down and Peco make the necessary components including 'Readiflex' sleeper bases which ensure accuracy of gauge and sleeper spacing. Alternatively flat-bottom rail can be fixed in place by gluing; this is particularly convenient in N and Z scales.

Most modellers who construct their own track in the smaller scales, 00/HO, TT and N, use soldered assembly. The rails can be soldered to pins or staples inserted into card or thin plywood sleepers, but recently the use of copper-clad sleepering has become popular for this type of construction. This material is available cut to size and ready for use with a shallow cut already made across the centre of each sleeper to insulate the two sides from one another.

Provided the modeller has some experience with soldering, construction of the track is straightforward, particularly if a jig is used. A simple jig can be made by fixing small wood strips on to a wooden base arranged so that sleepers placed between the strips will be at the correct spacing. One rail is laid alongside the ends of the strips and is soldered to the sleepers in the jig. The sleepers and single rail are moved along and the rail is soldered to more sleepers put into the jig until the single rail has sleepers fixed along its whole length. The unit of one rail and sleepers is then laid, either straight or curved as required, and if desired ballasted. The second rail is then soldered in place using a track gauge to ensure proper positioning.

There are various methods of constructing points and the subject is rather beyond the scope of the present book. Typically the construction sequence would begin with laying the straight and curved stock rails; these are grooved to take the ends of the point blades. The frog is fitted next having carefully filed the ends of the two rail pieces which form it so that they fit accurately together. A track gauge is used to ensure correct positioning of the frog in relation to the stock rails. The point blades are shaped

A Roco N-gauge, left-hand point fitted with a point motor for electrical remote control.

An example of the wire-in-copper-tube method of control here used for an N-gauge point. The tubing will be much less conspicuous when scenic work is carried out. Alternatively the tubing can be fitted into grooves in the baseboard top surface.

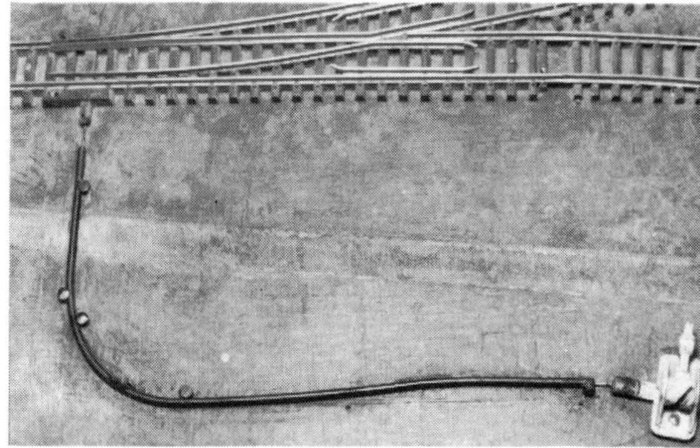

Track on the 4 mm scale Swanage Branch layout constructed by the Isle of Purbeck MRC was hand-built with rail soldered to brass pins in thin-ply sleepers. Excellent overall finishing of the track and lineside area has created a very realistic appearance. Note the telegraph poles and wires, often neglected on model railways.

Points on the Swanage Branch layout were also hand-built and this picture provides a closer look at the track and points.

Two scenes on P.D. Hancock's superb 'Craig & Mertonford Railway' layout. The model is 4 mm scale 9 mm gauge and all track was hand-built. Note the unusual point at Dundreich Halt. (Both photos by P.D. Hancock.)

Superbly modelled broad-gauge track on Mike Sharman's 4 mm scale period layout. Flat-bottom Peco rail was soldered on to brass pins in sleepers of balsa. Note the authentic point levers, pointman's hut and disc signal.

A very neat TT-scale point constructed by soldering Code 65 nickel silver rail on to copper-clad sleepers. The point is on the Great Wessex Railway layout built by John Medd.

and fitted and are fixed to the tie bar. The final pieces are the check rails.

Obviously the modeller should gain experience in the making of standard points before tackling more complex pointwork.

Narrow-gauge track

Ready-made flexible track is produced by Peco for the most popular narrow-gauges, 009 (4 mm scale 9 mm gauge) and 016.5 (7 mm scale 16.5 mm gauge) and this firm also makes points, standard right- and left-hand, for 009. It is also possible to use the ordinary track and points made for the gauge in question even though they are intended for standard gauge in a smaller scale. The sleeper size and spacing will not be correct but if the track is well ballasted and the sleepers are largely hidden this is not obvious and the appearance can be perfectly satisfactory. This method does give the convenience of a much wider range of track and points.

Of course the modeller can scratchbuild his own track and points using the components available for standard-gauge track and employing the same methods.

Dual-gauge track

Modelling narrow-gauge prototypes introduces the possibility of including some dual-, or even triple-gauge track on a layout. Such trackwork can be complex and a great many

A scene on Howard Coulson's very attractive 4 mm scale 9 mm gauge layout based on East African narrow-gauge prototypes. Howard used standard N-scale track to represent 00-scale narrow gauge and the effect is very good even though strictly the sleeper sizes and spacing are not correct, as the track is well ballasted.

Two 009 narrow-gauge points of soldered construction built by Terry Jenkins for a quarry line. The method is similar to that for standard-gauge pointwork.

varied arrangements for points are possible. Though a few ready-made dual-gauge track items have been commercially produced such special trackwork will generally have to be built by hand. Methods are essentially similar to those used for ordinary track but there are more parts to be fitted. The modeller would be well advised to gain some experience of building single-gauge track and points before tackling dual-gauge. It is also best to study the prototype arrangements and to choose one of the simpler examples for a first attempt.

Ballasting

Unless you are using track already complete with a ballast base, such as the Conrad range, the track you lay, whether it is ready-made or hand-built, must be ballasted to give a realistic appearance.

There are various methods of ballasting most of which must be carried out at the time the track is laid. An easy and convenient method is to use foam plastic underlay. The foam has a cushioning effect which helps to produce quiet, smooth running. The only disadvantages are the greater cost and the fact that it has a slightly less realistic appearance than loose ballast. However, with painting and a sprinkling of loose ballast applied over glue the appearance of the foam underlay can be very good indeed. (The method of laying track with foam underlay was described earlier.) Do not use an

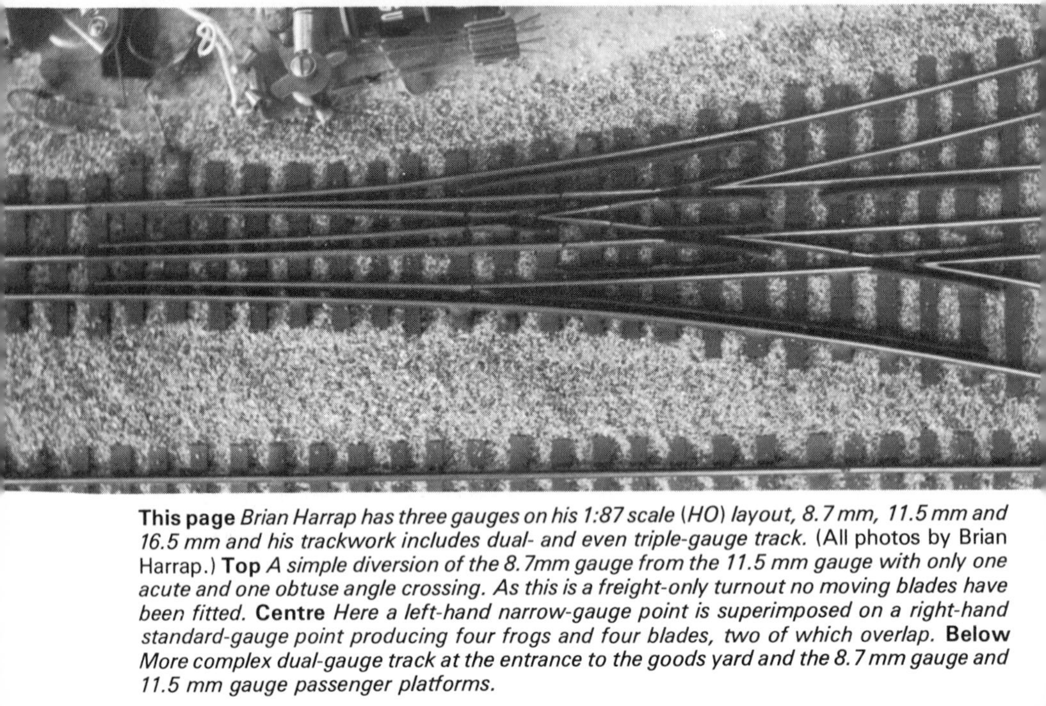

This page *Brian Harrap has three gauges on his 1:87 scale* (*HO*) *layout, 8.7 mm, 11.5 mm and 16.5 mm and his trackwork includes dual- and even triple-gauge track.* (All photos by Brian Harrap.) **Top** *A simple diversion of the 8.7mm gauge from the 11.5 mm gauge with only one acute and one obtuse angle crossing. As this is a freight-only turnout no moving blades have been fitted.* **Centre** *Here a left-hand narrow-gauge point is superimposed on a right-hand standard-gauge point producing four frogs and four blades, two of which overlap.* **Below** *More complex dual-gauge track at the entrance to the goods yard and the 8.7 mm gauge and 11.5 mm gauge passenger platforms.*

excessive amount of adhesive as this will soak through the foam and when it hardens will make the underlay stiff, thus reducing its cushioning effect.

If you wish to use loose ballast, usually cork granules appropriately coloured, or fine granite chippings, it is best applied when the track is laid as it is almost impossible to paint glue neatly around the sleepers for later ballasting without getting it on to the sleepers or rails. The track area is marked out and a covering of latex adhesive is applied. The track is then laid in position and pinned down. Ballast is sprinkled on covering the whole area and is pressed down into the glue. The whole thing is then left to set until completely dry after which excess ballast can be brushed off for re-use elsewhere. Any bare patches are touched up with a little glue and extra ballast. As I mentioned earlier it is essential to make sure that no adhesive is applied to the base where the moving parts of points will be and that no glue gets on to these parts. Failure to take sufficient care here may spoil the smooth working of the points; particularly important if the points are to be controlled electrically as the motors may be unable to overcome any increased resistance to movement. Peco points should not be glued down and with these the glue must be applied around the sleepers after laying for ballasting, again taking care not to get any glue on the moving parts.

An excellent method of ballasting devised in the United States is the so-called 'bonded ballast' technique. Loose ballast is applied dry to the track after laying and is spread out around and between the sleepers using a small brush. The ballast is kept clear of the moving parts of points. Once you are satisfied with the appearance of the ballast it can be sprayed with water containing a few drops of detergent such as washing up liquid, using a perfume spray, atomiser or airbrush. This spraying must be gentle so that the ballast is not displaced; the idea is to apply a mist of water, just enough to dampen the ballast. Then drops of a solution of 1 part of acrylic matte medium (available from art shops) to 6 parts of water are applied using an eyedropper. The drops spread easily through the ballast due to the previous damping with the detergent solution. When the process is completed leave to dry overnight. Then gently brush off any loose ballast and do any touching up needed. Remove any adhesive or ballast which has stuck to the running surfaces of the rails.

As an alternative to the acrylic matte medium, diluted white glue can be used. However the glue dries hard whereas the matte medium remains more flexible and resilient giving a cushioning effect.

Track detailing

For the most realistic appearance the track requires further detailing. Before starting on this I would suggest that you go and have a good look at the real thing. Usually we spend our time watching the trains or looking at the buildings rather than the track but just a few minutes study will make you much more aware of the colours of the rails, sleepers and ballast, and of the many small details always present on and near the tracks.

The most important single aspect is the colouring. Real rails are either dark brown or rust colour on all surfaces except those on which the train wheels run. Painting the rails of the track on your layout with rust colour (Humbrol include 'Rust' in their range of paints) and wiping off the top surfaces before the paint dries will give a great improvement in appearances. It will also do much to conceal the fact that the rail used in ready-made track is overscale. You may also like to paint the sleepers with dark brown paint (Humbrol 'Track Colour' is suitable) to give them a more weathered appearance. The colour of the ballast can be toned down with a light overspray of brown in an airbrush if you want to make it look less clean and new. An easy method of representing old track and ballast is to spray the whole thing with track colour, wiping the tops of the rails clean and touching up the sides of the rails with rust colour. In areas where coal dust and oil drop onto the track the ballast will be discoloured and this can be simulated with black paint.

Buffer stops are available ready-made and in kit form for both sleeper and rail built types; these should also be carefully painted and weathered. Dummy point levers are made by Peco and by Dart Castings and are a nice detail touch even if the points are actually operated electrically by concealed motors. Colin Waite has introduced a kit of parts for accurate modelling of the point rodding used on prototype railways to control many points. Assembly is rather time consuming and requires care but the results are very realistic and greatly enhance the appearance of the track.

There are many other small items which can easily be added; ATC (Automatic Train Control) ramps between the rails, spare rails and track parts beside the track, speed restriction signs and warning notices, mileposts, gradient posts and so on.

In dock and industrial areas tracks are often inset and this can be effectively represented in model form. The 00-scale track shown here was modelled by fixing extra rails on to Peco track leaving a sufficient gap for the wheels. Polyfilla was then used to fill the space between these inner rails and was also brought up the outer sides of the running rails. After the filler had set, a scriber was used to mark out the setts. The final step was painting.

The scratch-built point levers add the finishing touch to the track on Jim Gadd's 009 layout. Note also the pile of sleepers, a typical lineside feature.

An attractive scene on a 4 mm scale diorama by John Piper (Accessories) Limited showing the use of many of their scenic modelling products. Note the realistically ballasted track and the neat lineside fencing of various types.

Trackside details on Keith Gowen's TT-scale layout include token exchange apparatus (just in front of the goods shed). Note also the railwaymen's track crossing simply modelled from scraps of wood.

Two views of the late Eric Kay's Sherrington Branch. Note how good ballasting has given a very realistic appearance to the proprietary track. The effect has also been enhanced by the painting of the rails with rust-coloured matt enamel.

Track cleaning

Any dirt on the track will interfere with the electrical pick-up by the locomotives. For smooth running on a layout it is essential that the track is kept clean. One method of cleaning is to rub over the running surfaces of the rails with an abrasive cleaner such as the type made by Peco. This is like a hard rubber eraser. Never use sandpaper to clean the track as this will scratch the rails; dirt then collects quickly in the scratches causing further problems.

Alternatively one of the solvent cleaners can be applied to the track, either with a small piece of rag held in the hand or with one of the special track cleaning wagons produced by various manufacturers. Several cleaners marketed specifically for track cleaning are available or you can use one of the electrical cleaning fluids. If you use an abrasive cleaner this produces loose dirt and it is advisable to wipe the rails afterwards with one of the electrical cleaners.

A completely different approach to the problem is the use of a high frequency generator unit as described later.

Electrification

Much of the fascination of model railways lies in the fact that they can duplicate in miniature virtually all aspects of prototype railway operation. The use of electricity to power the models has made such realistic control possible. Almost all model railways nowadays are run on 12 volts DC and utilise 2-rail electrification and I propose to discuss only this system in this book.

In their efforts to create even greater realism many expert modellers have devised complex and sophisticated control schemes. Such projects often benefit us all directly or indirectly because they lead to improvements and advances in the equipment produced commercially and hence to better control for our layouts. However, they may lead the beginner to believe that model railway electrification must always be complicated and difficult. This is not so; the electrification of a simple layout of the type a beginner is likely to be constructing is quite straightforward if a few simple rules are followed.

The basic circuit

The basic 2-rail model railway circuit consists of a power source, leads to one rail and from the other, the two rails themselves and the locomotive linking the rails. So that the current flowing through the circuit cannot be short-circuited, bypassing the motor of the locomotive, the two rails must be insulated from each other and similarly the wheels on the two sides of the engine must be insulated. The current passes from one rail to the wheels on that side of the locomotive where one or more pick-ups make contact and carry the current to the motor. The circuit is completed by the pick-ups and wheels on the other side of the engine. The current causes the motor to turn and the locomotive to move. Reversing the current direction results in the motor turning the opposite way and the locomotive moving in the opposite direction.

Though the motors used in model locomotives are rated at 12 volts DC they usually operate at less, working at between 4 and 12 volts depending on the speed; the greater the voltage applied, the faster the engine will run. The current drawn will vary for different locomotives but for any one depends on the load (number of coaches or wagons hauled, steepness of a gradient, etc).

To control the speed and direction of travel of a locomotive a variable source of power is required and this is an opportune time to consider the types of power units available.

Power units

Train sets generally include only a battery controller; this is adequate at first but control is limited and the regular replacement of the batteries becomes expensive. As you develop your train set into a more elaborate system or into a permanent layout you will want to change to a unit working from the mains supply.

Mains power units usually have a transformer, to reduce the mains voltage of 240 to 12, a rectifier, to convert the AC (Alternating Current) to DC (Direct Current) and a controller for speed and direction, mounted together inside a single unit. It is important to remember that although the output from such a unit is perfectly safe the input is the potentially dangerous mains voltage and under no circumstances should the unit be opened up; if there is a fault take the power unit to a dealer or return it to the makers.

While I do not want to confuse the issue with unnecessary details, there are a few general points which will help you to decide which of the three main types of unit to choose. Each type has a transformer and a rectifier but the method of control employed differs.

In the simplest type, the variable resistance controller, a variable resistance is placed in series in the 12 volt DC output from the transformer and rectifier. This resistance takes part of the voltage, wasting it in the form of heat, leaving the remainder for the locomotive motor. If most of the resistance is included in the circuit relatively little voltage is available for the motor and the locomotive moves slowly. As the control is moved to leave less and less of the resistance in the circuit the engine moves faster. This system is cheap and works adequately but there are disadvantages. A basic defect is that it does not directly control the voltage to the locomotive. The track voltage depends not only on the resistance of the controller but also on the ratio between the resistances of the motor and the controller. Thus different motors need varied settings on the controller for the same voltage and ideally the resistance of the controller should be matched to the locomotive motor. The voltage wasted in the variable resistance also depends on the load and unfortunately it increases with an increase in load. Thus on a layout with gradients, instead of maintaining a uniform speed the train will slow down going uphill and speed up going down. For various reasons, including pole locking and mechanical friction, slightly more voltage is required to start the motor turning than to keep it turning slowly once it has started. This means that as the voltage increases the locomotive suddenly moves off at speed; not at all a realistic representation of the gradual start of a real train! With a variable resistance controller this is aggravated because as the locomotive starts to move the load drops and causes a rise in voltage making the engine move even faster.

The addition of a pulse power facility will help to give slower, smoother, more realistic starts. Normally full wave rectification is used so that both phases of the AC cycle are utilised; by changing to half wave using only one phase of each cycle a series of pulses are delivered to the motor with 60 pulses each second. These pulses nudge the motor into rotating without supplying enough steady voltage to send the train racing off. This results in smooth starts, good slow running and pulling power but does cause motors to become hotter than on full wave rectified DC. A power unit with pulse power is usually arranged so that half or full wave can be selected merely by moving a switch. Thus half wave can be used to start the train, with a change to full wave for running it if desired.

The variable transformer type of controller overcomes the basic failing of the variable resistance type. Here the voltage is directly controlled and the voltage selected determines the speed of the motor. Variations in load do not affect the speed as the extra load is automatically provided by the transformer. The voltage required is produced by the primary unit and this is supplied to the track; there is no need for voltage to be wasted as heat, and so less heat is produced. Pulse power can be provided on units of this type as with the variable resistance controllers.

The most recently developed type is the transistor controller. These are very efficient and produce an almost constant output regardless of varying load, and hence current. In units of this type very sophisticated control can be provided by electronic means. These include representation of the inertia and weight of the prototype with slow starting and stopping, coasting and braking. Transistor controllers can give very realistic operation even with simple proprietary locomotive models.

On power units of all types the control of speed and direction may be by a knob or lever. In some cases there is a centre 'off' position with forward one side and reverse the other. In others there is a separate reversing switch and the whole range of

This Airfix unit is typical of the battery controllers supplied with train sets.

The H & M (Hammant & Morgan) 'Safety Minor' is a variable transformer power unit with pulse power and is an ideal unit for a beginner. In addition to the controlled DC output there are uncontrolled 16 volt AC and 12 volt DC auxiliary outputs.

The Digitol 'Gemini T', by Southern Electronic Consultants, is an electronic controller with excellent control, including automatic load compensation, inertia and weight simulation and smooth stopping and starting.

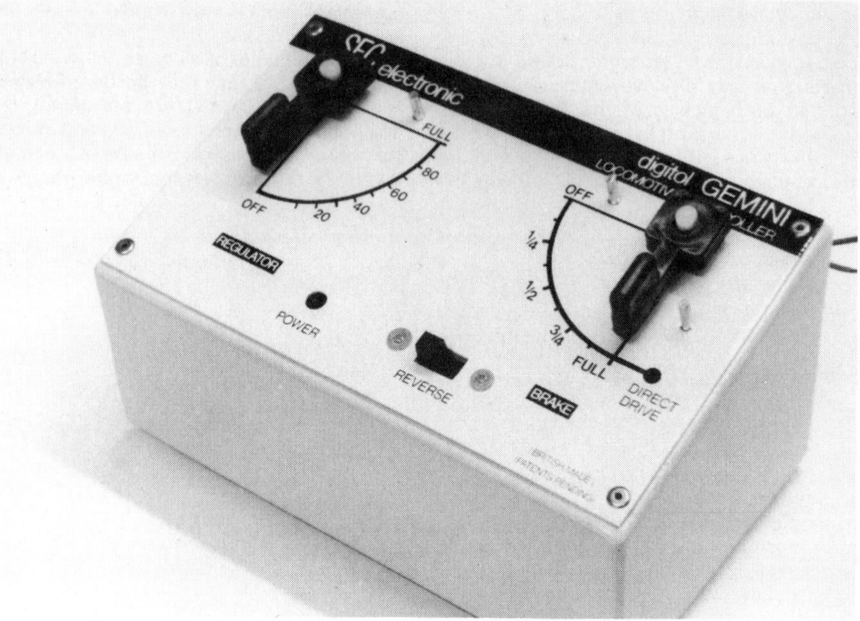

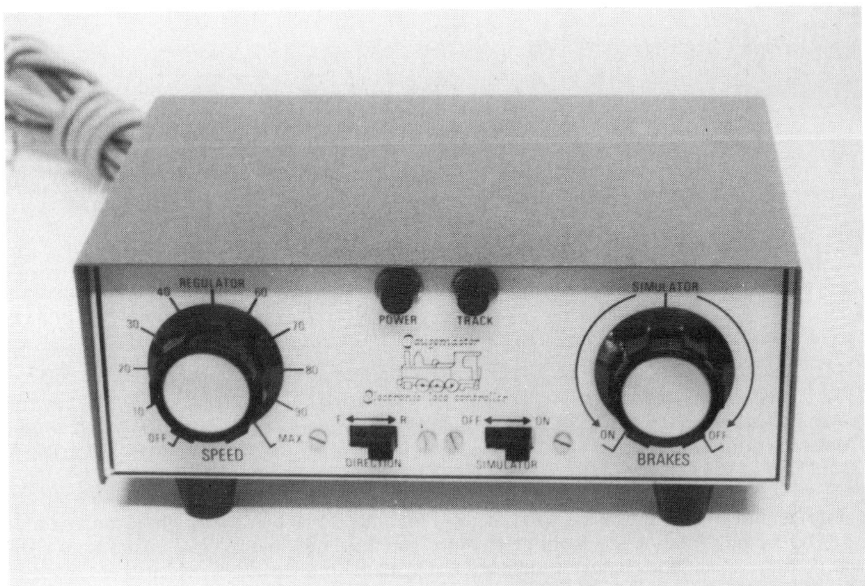

The 'Gaugemaster' is another electronic controller giving realistic operation.

movement of the knob or lever is used to control speed.

Many power units have, in addition to the controlled 12 volt DC output to the track, an auxiliary 16 volt AC uncontrolled outlet for working point motors and other accessories.

Basic wiring

To run a locomotive on a section of track all we need do is connect wires from the controlled DC output terminals of the power unit to the rails. There are terminal rail sections and clips of various types designed for fixing these wires to the rails for sectional track. These can be used on a permanent scale layout but the best method is to solder the wires to the sides of the rails. Suitable wire is available from model railway dealers and electrical shops.

This is all that is required for a length of track, a basic oval, or even for a simple layout, provided dead frog points are employed and we wish to run only one locomotive.

In considering the wiring of a layout we must distinguish carefully between the different types of points available, and here I am referring to the electrical differences not to those in the geometric pattern. The essential feature is whether the frog is electrically live or not as this affects the wiring required.

Dead frog points

In these the frog is made from plastic and is electrically dead. This type of point is very simple to wire but has the disadvantage that locomotives may stall or falter as they pass over the non-electrified frog. Dead frog points can themselves be divided into two types, non-isolating and self-isolating. In the former type the rails beyond the frog are wired so that all the rails are live whichever way the point is set. This makes wiring a layout extremely simple; the current can be fed in at any point and the whole layout will be live at all times. This is, however, at the expense of the convenience of using points for isolation.

In the self-isolating type the point blade is wired to the rail, beyond the frog, on to which it leads, but not to the stock rail. The point blades have a contact so that the one which touches the stock rail is live while the other is isolated. This means that a siding from a self-isolating point is live when the point is set for it but dead when the point is set against it. Unlike a layout with non-isolating points the whole layout is not live and the feed point must be suitably positioned.

The rule for wiring dead frog points is that the current must be fed to the toe-end of a point. This does not mean that a separate feed is needed for each point as a series of

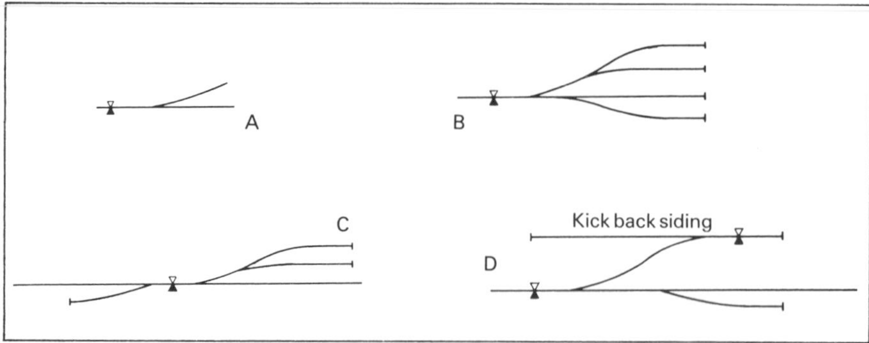

Wiring dead frog isolating points. **A** *Feed must always be at the toe-end of a point.* **B** *Only one feed is needed for a series of points all facing the same way.* **C** *One feed will supply points at either side provided the feed is at the toe-ends of the points.* **D** *For a kickback siding another feed at the toe-end of the point leading to it is required. Dead frog points require gaps only for isolating purposes.*

points facing the same way can all be supplied by one feed at the toe-end of the first point. If a kick-back siding is included a further feed will be needed at the toe-end of this point as shown in the diagram.

The wiring of a small layout with dead frog points of either type is very simple and I would recommend that the beginner use points of the dead frog variety. Any pick-up problems causing locomotive stalling on the dead frogs can usually be overcome by making sure that the wheel treads and current collectors are kept clean. It is also important that there is pick-up from at least two pairs of wheels and preferably more; on tender engines collectors can also be fitted to pick up from the tender wheels with advantage.

Live frog points

In this type of point the frog is metal and is electrically live ensuring good pick-up as a locomotive crosses over it. The frog is wired to the point blades to that both blades and the frog have the same polarity as the stock rail with which the blade is in contact. In this way the track for which the point is set has rails of opposite polarity. The rails of the track against which the point is set have the same polarity and therefore no current will flow; this is because they are electrically linked at this setting.

There are two rules for the electrification of live frog points. As with the dead frog isolating type, current must be fed in at the toe-end of the point. Because there would be a short-circuit if current were fed directly to the frog in this type of point there is also another requirement. Where a feed does lead directly to a point frog there must be an electrical gap in both rails of the track. This applies to an oval, in which there must be gaps in both rails between the feed and the frog of a point leading to a siding, and whenever two points are arranged so that the frogs face each other, as in a crossover or passing loop. Diamond crossings and slip-points are complicated to wire for live frogs and I would advise the use of dead frog crossings and slip-points even if live frog standard points are employed on a layout.

Sectionalisation

So far we have been concerned with using only one locomotive on a layout. Once we add further engines we must arrange the electrification of the layout so that we can control each locomotive. To do this we divide the system up into sections, each of which can be switched on or off as we wish. Provided we only intend to move one locomotive at any one time the single controller is all that is required; it is connected to all the sections but only those in use are switched on. Any locomotive on a section which is switched off will not move.

A simple form of section is the isolated section on a dead-end track, for example an engine shed siding. One rail is gapped by cutting through it with a razor saw and inserting an insulating rail joiner. The rails at either side of the gap are linked by a wire with an on/off switch. If you do not want to make this arrangement up you can use one of the isolating track units designed for use with sectional track instead. In this case the track section would be included during construction or, if you decide to fit it later, a section of

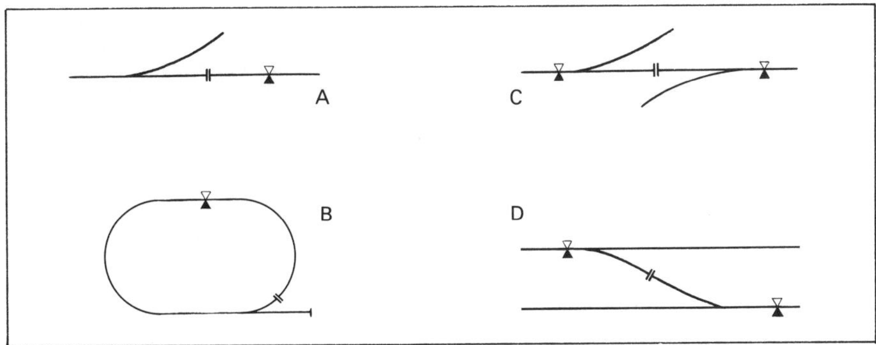

Above *Wiring live frog points.* **A** *Feed must be at the toe-end of the point; wherever a feed leads directly to a point, the frog must have insulating gaps in both rails.* **B** *In an oval with a siding there must be gaps in both rails between the feed and the frog.* **C** *Wherever the frogs of two points face each other there must be gaps in both rails.* **D** *Similarly on a crossover the point frogs face each other and both rails must have gaps.*

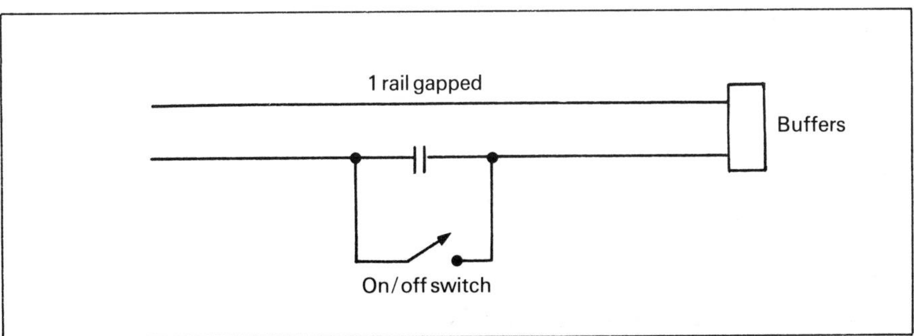

Above *Isolating Section. One rail only is gapped and this is bridged by a wire with an on/off switch. When the section is switched on it receives power from the adjacent live section.* **Below** *Sectionalisation. Full sections are, unlike the simple isolating section, completely independent with both rails gapped and with their own feeds. Return can be grouped into a common return. Each section has its own on/off switch; in the diagram, sections 2 & 3 are 'on', section 1 is 'off'.*

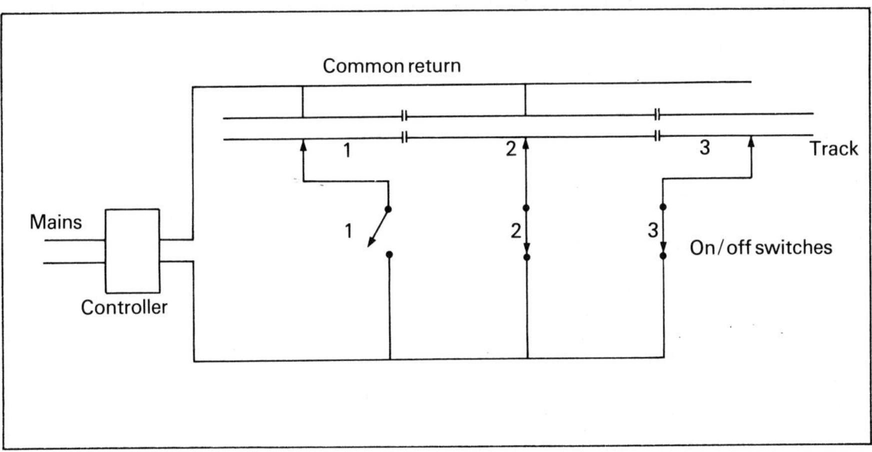

track would be removed to allow the unit to be fitted. When switched on the isolated section receives current from the live section next to it; when switched off the section is dead and a locomotive stored here will not move when another engine is run elsewhere on the layout.

With dead frog isolating points there is a similar effect but with the switching carried out by the points instead of by on/off switches. A siding is isolated if the point is set against it and a passing loop will be isolated if the points at the ends are both set against it.

On a small layout sectionalisation of this type may be perfectly adequate and has the advantage of being very simple to arrange. However, greater flexibility of operation will be achieved by more extensive sectionalisation using independent sections each of which is completely isolated from the others and has separate current feed and return with an on/off switch.

The arrangement of the sections depends not only on the particular layout plan but also on the way in which you will operate the system so no precise instructions can be given. There are, however, some general principles which can be applied. The rules given for wiring live frog points also form a useful basis for sectionalisation whether you are using live or dead frog points. Working from your layout plan look for places where tracks lead off in one or both directions and site feeds here at the toe-ends of the points. For a series of points all facing the same way a feed at the toe-end of the first point will serve them all. Gaps in both rails are required wherever the frogs of two points face each other or the frog of a point is directly connected to a feed.

In meeting these requirements the gaps can often be placed anywhere along the length of track. To decide on the best positions think about train movements on the railway and place the gaps where they will be most convenient for the planned operational pattern.

In addition wherever trains are run on the layout there must be at least one pair of gaps between any two trains. After locating the gaps and feeds as above it may well be that some of the sections are very long. Dividing these into two or more separate smaller sections may provide more flexibility in operation. I have already mentioned isolated sections for dead-end tracks and these can be added as desired to the layout.

The system described above permits us to have two or more locomotives on the layout and to control whichever of these we wish, using a single power unit, provided that we are content to run only one engine at any one time. As a layout develops and becomes more extensive and as additional locomotives are acquired the modeller may wish to run two trains simultaneously on the railway.

Running two trains

Apart from the electrical requirements the layout must obviously be sufficiently extensive to accommodate two trains in action at the same time. Two separate power units are needed for control and the layout should be divided up into sections as described above.

The simplest method is to bring the sections together into two groups each controlled by one power unit. Two trains can be operated simultaneously on the layout provided one is in each group of sections. However, if the trains are in different sections in the same group only one can be in action the other being isolated in a switched off section. Thus, there are limitations to this simple system. Another problem arises in the transfer of a train from a section controlled by one power unit into an adjacent section under the control of the other unit. To do this the two controllers are adjusted to approximately the same setting and the train runs across from one section to the other.

An alternative arrangement to this is the provision of a section between the two groups which can be connected to either controller. In operation a train is run from one group of sections into this common section and stopped at a station. Control of this section is then switched to the other controller and the train is restarted and run on into the other group.

However, the system still has limited scope and a much better arangement is the method known as cab control in which all sections are common to both controllers.

Simple cab control

In this system the operator takes over a cab and by switching on the sections on which he wishes to run his train he can take it anywhere on the layout except on to sections already in use for another train. There are various forms of cab control depending on the size of the layout and its complexity, on how many operators and trains there will be, and on whether the system will be worked from one central point or from a number of different positions.

For a small to moderate sized home layout on which two trains will be run by one or two operators from a central control panel, a cab control system can be simply and easily set up. Two separate power units are used, so that common return wiring can be employed, and these are placed one at either side of the control panel. On this central panel are mounted a series of single-pole double-throw centre 'off' position switches, one for each section of the layout. These switches are wired uniformly so that the same end of each is linked to one controller, and the other to the second controller. If the switches are mounted so that the lever movement is from side to side, instead of the more usual up and down, the wiring can be arranged so that the controller towards which a lever points will be the one to which the section is linked at the time. The levers can be mounted in the appropriate positions on a diagrammatic panel, on which the layout plan is drawn out in schematic form, making a very neat panel which is easy to work. Alternatively the switches can be arranged in one or more ranks, labelled to match up with a separate track plan.

Once an operator has finished using a section he should switch it to the centre 'off' position on the panel so that it is available for the other operator to use. With this particular system a section can only be linked to one controller at one time because of the switching method used.

The cab control system is an excellent one and in its simple form, as described here, is certainly not beyond the scope of the beginner once he has become familiar with the basic principles of model railway electrification.

Reversing loops

When the diverging tracks from a point are joined up to form a reversing loop, so called because the direction of travel of a train passing round the loop will have been reversed when it passes back on to the main track, an electrical problem arises. If we follow one of the rails around the loop we find that it meets the other rail at some point resulting in a permanent short-circuit. To prevent this the loop is made in a separate section isolated from the remainder of the layout by gaps in both rails at both ends of the loop.

The loop can be powered in several different ways. A simple method, which also has the advantage of allowing trains to pass round the loop without stopping, is to wire the loop directly to the controller while the leads to the main line go via a DPDT (Double-Pole Double-Throw) switch.

As the train passes on to the loop section the point is changed and the DPDT switch is thrown reversing the current in the main line; this then matches the polarity of the far end of the loop and the train can pass back on to the main line without stopping. As the feed

Simple Cab Control. Each section is linked to both controllers so either operator can use it. Each section has its own single-pole, double-throw (SPDT) switch with centre 'off' position; thus a section can be linked to one or other controller or to the 'off' position. In the diagram, section 1 is linked to controller A, section 3 to controller B and section 2 is switched off.

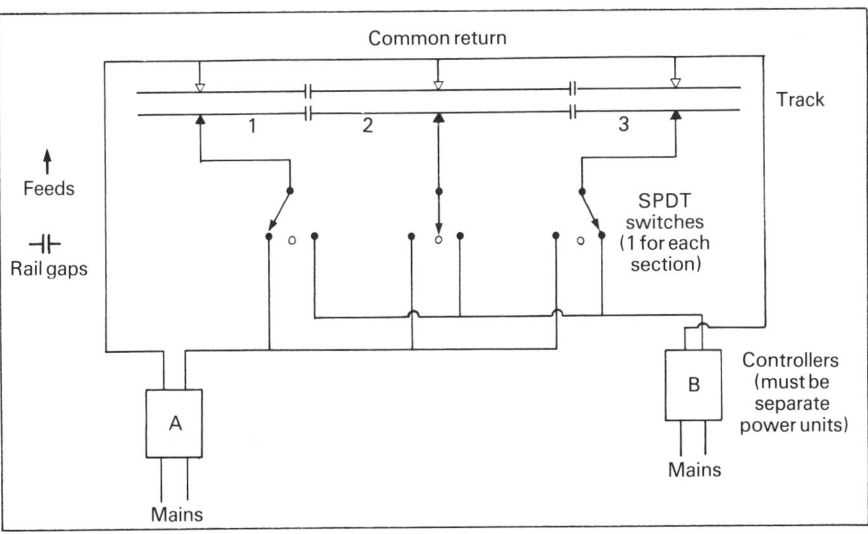

reversal in the main line has been carried out by the reversing switch the direction of travel of the locomotive still matches that selected on the controller.

The reversing loop of this type is easy to identify but in designing layouts, particularly complicated ones, reversing sections can sometimes be incorporated unintentionally and without the modeller realising that they are present. An example is in the so-called dog bone or dumbell type of track plan in which the two sides of a long oval are brought together and resemble true double track. The modeller may then be tempted to introduce a crossover between these tracks. In fact the tracks are not true double track but two single tracks in opposite directions and a train passing over a crossover here will have its direction around the layout reversed. In other words a reversing section has been created. One way of checking for hidden reversing sections on a layout plan is to draw arrows in one direction along the main route. Then follow along in this direction over the

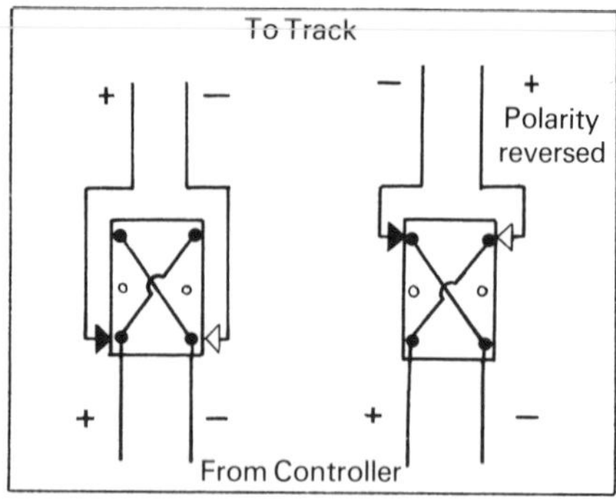

Details of DPDT switch showing how it reverses polarity when its position is changed. Centre position is 'off'.

possible routes and if at any time you find that, without stopping and reversing, you are travelling against the arrows then you have traversed a reversing section. This must either be eliminated or suitably wired. In general I would advise the beginner to avoid

Reversing loop wiring. Wiring arrangement shown permits the train to run round loop and back on to the main line without stopping. Once the train is on the loop section, which is completely isolated by gaps in both rails at both ends of the loop, the DPDT (Double-Pole Double-Throw) switch is changed, reversing polarity on main-line.

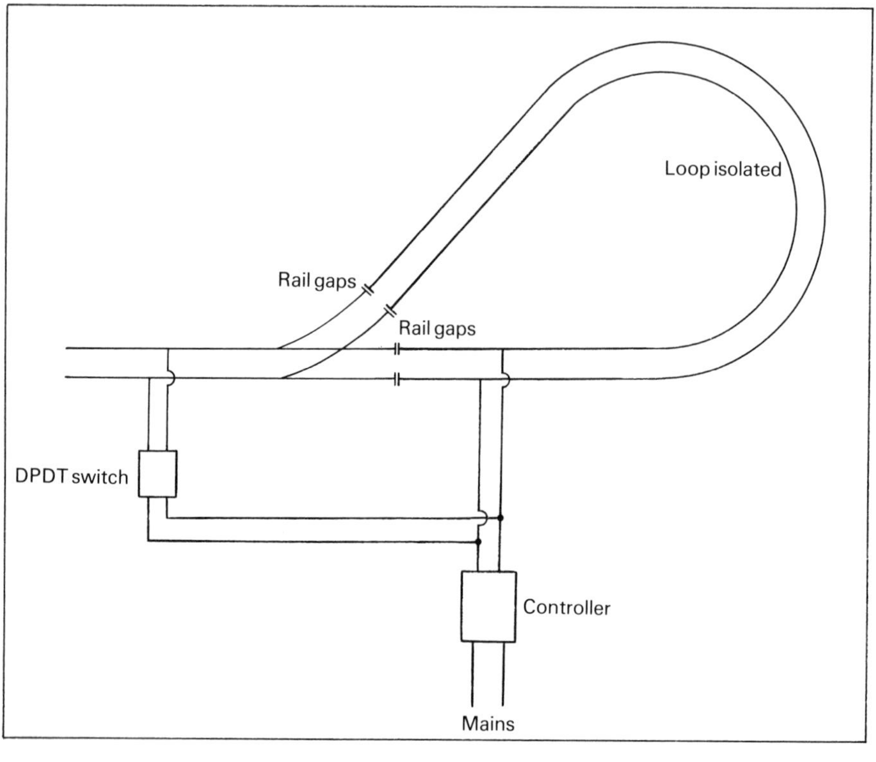

Vollmer N-scale catenary on a German prototype layout. The locomotive is a Fleischmann track cleaning engine.

Highly detailed working catenary system constructed from Sommerfeldt parts on a Fleischmann HO-scale exhibition layout.

including any reversing sections on his layout.

Catenary

A good selection of electric outline locomotive models is available in HO and N scales, mainly of American and Continental prototypes and many of these have working pantographs which can be used as the electrical pick-ups for power and control of the models. The provision of a working catenary not only adds to the realism but also provides the opportunity to control two locomotives independently and simultaneously on the same stretch of track, one being powered from the track and the other from the overhead. The simplest and cheapest working catenary was manufactured by Triang but this is no longer produced and is difficult to obtain secondhand. Two Continental firms, Vollmer and Sommerfeldt, produce parts for constructing working catenary in HO and N scales. The Sommerfeldt parts, available in Britain from M & R (Model Railways) Ltd., are highly detailed replicas of various European prototype catenary parts and are very realistic; however, it would be expensive to install more than a very limited system. Excellent working catenary systems in 00/HO scale are now also available from Lima and Hadley/J.V. The Arnold N-scale catenary is a dummy non-working system intended for appearance only. Some modellers have constructed successful catenary from scratch but this does involve a good deal of work on any but a very small layout.

Electric point control

Electric point control is very convenient to install and operate and can be used to change points at any distance. Normally twin-solenoid motors are employed in which two opposing coils move an iron core, linked to the point tie bar, changing the points. There must also be a device to lock the point after it has been thrown. The motors take a high current but for only a very short time so any number of points can be operated from a single power unit provided they are changed one at a time and not simultaneously. Many control units provide a suitable auxiliary low voltage AC output for this purpose. Using the train controller to power point motors can sometimes lead to momentary slowing of the train as points are changed so you may prefer to use a separate transformer for point control.

The impulse must be only momentary or the coil may burn out so special passing contact, or flash, switches are employed. As with the cab control section switches mentioned earlier these can be fitted at the appropriate positions on a diagrammatic control panel. Alternatively they can be mounted in a bank or banks and numbered or otherwise coded for identification. Various firms produce suitable switches; H & M produce a neat unit containing six switches.

Some point motors, for example the H & M SW3, have an automatic cut-off switch incorporated in them so that they can be used with ordinary on/off switches instead of requiring flash switches.

An alternative method of switching points is to use two pushbuttons for each motor. However, this system does not give a visible indication on the control panel of which way the point is switched. Another popular scheme in conjunction with a diagrammatic track layout control panel is the use of an electric pencil probe, such as those made by ECM and Peco, for point changing. Two small roundheaded brass screws are inserted into the panel, one at either side of the point. Where the screws protrude through the rear of the panel, wires are attached and led to the point motor. The wiring is arranged so that the point movements match the screw positions. The electric probe is attached to the AC outlet lead. To change a point the probe is touched on the appropriate screw.

The pushbutton and electric pencil methods have the advantage that they can be kept in contact until the point is thrown whereas flash switches may not always change the point. The addition of a capacitor discharge unit will eliminate the danger of point motors burning out and also doubles the energy for operation overcoming sticking. The ECM unit, for example, is easily inserted into existing systems and can be fed from the normal 16 volt AC auxiliary supply. One unit only is required for the whole layout. The Codar 'Track King' electronic controller includes built in switching for 6-point motors and a capacitor discharge power supply output for use with any number of point motors.

Recent developments

I mentioned at the beginning of the section on electrification that expert modellers with a special interest in electrification and electronics had made many advances in the development of systems and devices giving better and more realistic operation. Fortunately the great popularity of railway modelling makes it worthwhile for manufacturers to produce many of these commercially, to the benefit of us all. I would like to conclude by mentioning three recent developments of interest.

Multiple train control

It has long been the ambition of the keen operator to be able to control several locomotives independently on the same tracks, just as on the prototype. The old Trix Twin system permitted two engines to be operated together under individual control but this required the use of 3-rail track. The centre rail was common and the other two rails each supplied one of the engines. A similar form of control is possible using working catenary with one locomotive controlled from the overhead wire and the other from the track.

However, these are special cases and in addition allow control of only two engines. The ideal is independent running of several locomotives on 2-rail track and without the need for the complication of sectional cab control. Some advanced modellers have devised various ways of achieving this including radio control and complex electronic systems but these have been beyond the ability of the average modeller.

Now multiple train control systems are being developed commercially in this country. Two major manufacturers, Airfix and Hornby, and two firms specialising in electrical equipment for model railways, H & M and ECM, are producing systems which should be on the market during the next year or so. Full technical details are not being released by any of the firms but the four systems are probably similar in principle though it seems likely that none will be compatible with any of the others.

The Airfix system, which will probably be the first to appear in the shops, permits the simultaneous independent control of four locomotives and up to 16 locomotives can be on the same track without the need for any isolating switches. This is achieved with only two wires to the track. The track is powered with 20 volts AC with each train selecting part of the current to operate only when commanded by the console. Each locomotive has a small easily fitted electronic chip inside which is set to respond only to its own signals from the control panel. The constant track power at 20 volts AC allows full coach lighting even when the train is stationary. The system will also be able to control other parts of the layout such as points and signals.

Though it will obviously take time to assess the various systems once they appear it does seem certain that electronic multiple train

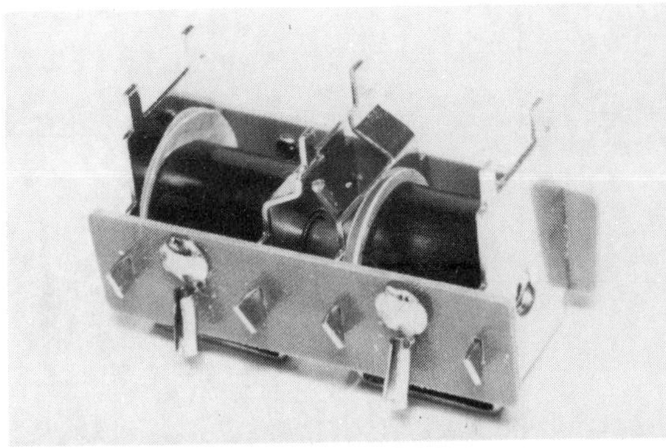

The Peco point motor fits beneath the baseboard or, with an adaptor, on top of the baseboard. The motor does not have a locking device as it is designed for use with Peco points which themselves incorporate a locking spring.

Below *A Hammant & Morgan point motor mounted on top of the baseboard for convenient access.* **Bottom** *The motor is concealed by this small hut made from Superquick kit parts.*

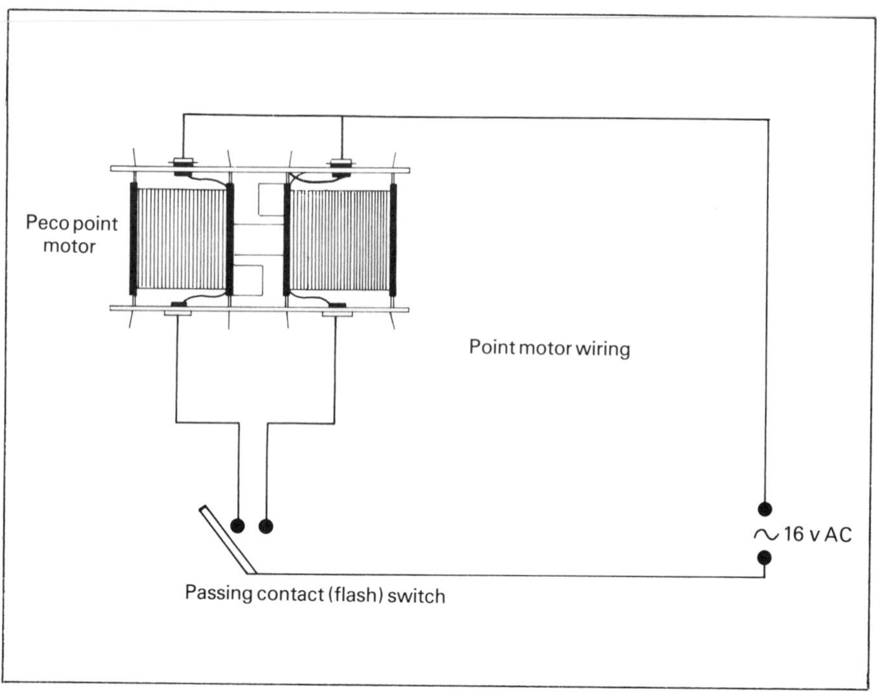

Point Motor Wiring. **Above** *Passing contact or flash switch.* **Below** *Electric pencil probe.*

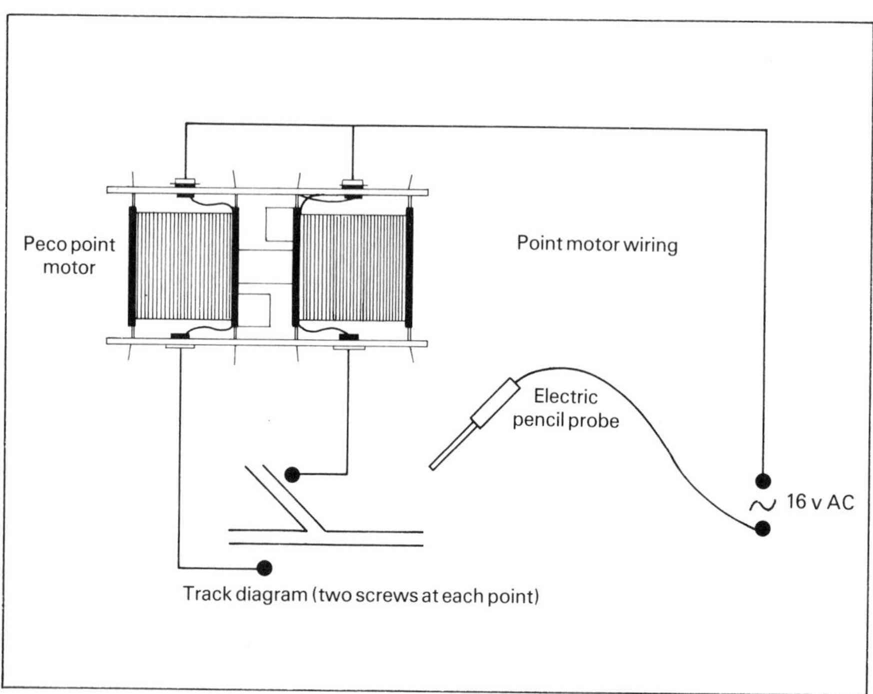

The control panel on Vernon Sparrow's 00-scale layout. Note the electric pencil probe just to the left of the centre of the controls and the roundheaded screws, two per point, fixed into the adjacent track diagram and used to make contact for changing the points. (Photo by Vernon Sparrow.)

The console for the Airfix Multiple Train Control system with the four control units for independent running of four locomotives. (Photo courtesy of Airfix.)

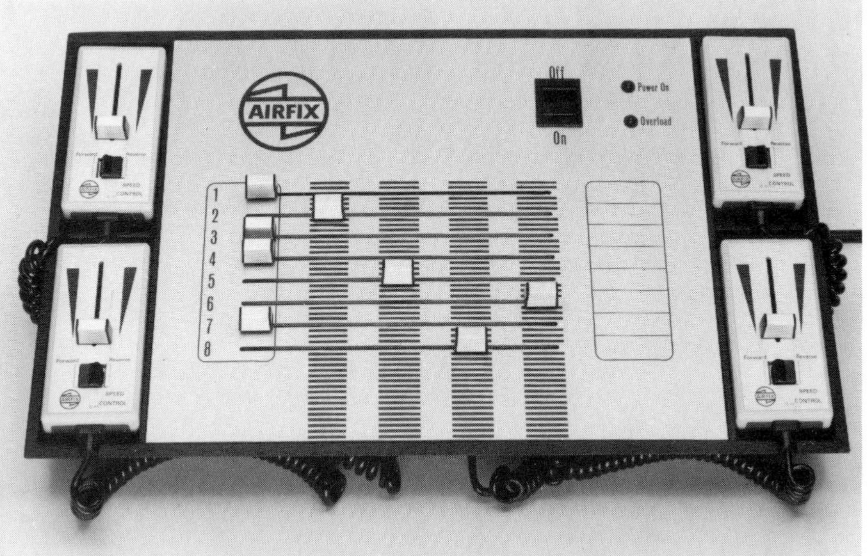

control will revolutionise model railway electrification, perhaps making much of what I have written in this book obsolete and of historic interest only!

Sound

Another electronic development which has become popular, particularly in the United States, is the production of simulated steam and diesel locomotive sounds synchronised with the movements of the model engines. Many enthusiasts find that such a unit adds greatly to the effect and realism of operating their locomotives and gives them much enjoyment. No tapes or recordings are necessary, the sounds being synthesised electronically. The Codar 'Steamsound' unit realistically simulates all the sounds of a real steam locomotive including the exhaust beat (variable in speed and character), steam hiss, safety valve blast, the whistle (variable in pitch for different engines), and other effects!

Electric track cleaning

One of the problems in ensuring good and reliable operation is the need for the track to be kept clean so that electrical conduction is maintained. An alternative to the physical cleaning methods described in the section on track is the use of a high frequency generator. The Relco HF Generator, which had the distinction of being demonstrated on the 'Tomorrow's World' BBC TV programme, uses high frequency superimposed on the normal supply to ionise the gap due to dirt on the track and restore electrical contact. The unit converts the 12 volt DC input into high frequency AC only when the circuit is broken, burning away the dirt and restoring conductivity. The normal DC current then flows again. The generator is easily wired into the layout input and is perfectly safe to use.

The Relco HF Generator for track cleaning.

The Codar 'Steam-sound' electronic synthesiser.

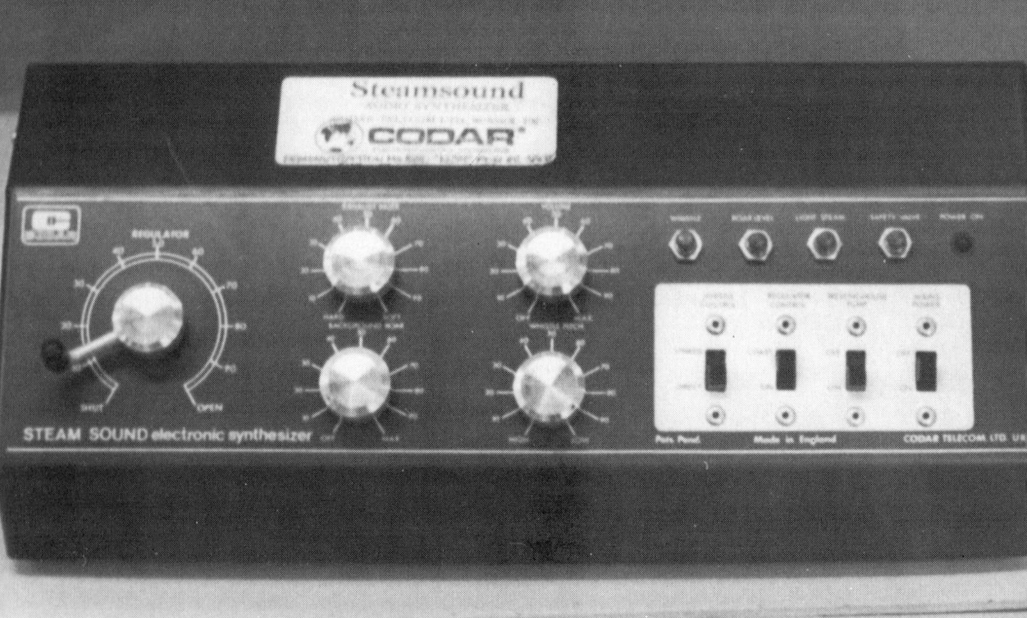

Layout Planning

Michael Andress

Contents

Introduction

Railway modelling is a very popular pastime with more enthusiasts taking up the hobby every year. Many of the newcomers start with a train set and the transition from this to a more permanent model railway layout is an important step for them. The scope of railway modelling is very wide indeed, ranging from the miniature engineering involved in constructing model locomotives, through the applications of electrical and electronic circuitry in model railway control, to the artistic aspects of structure and scenery modelling. The many different interests brought together in the hobby lead to great variety in the types of layouts built. This is one of the attractions of the hobby but the great choice can also be bewildering to the beginner who does not yet know where his special interests and skills may lie.

Railway modelling is also different from most other constructional hobbies in that we do not only model locomotives or trains just to be displayed as static items, or to be operated as individual models. Instead, our model represents a working railway complete with its surrounding landscape. This adds greatly to the interest. It also means that even though a layout may be complete enough for enjoyable running, construction can continue with the addition of extra models and details, and perhaps by extending the layout. The modeller can thus alternate construction and operation as he pleases, maintaining the interest and enthusiasm. In this way some layouts have been built up over many years and are now very large and elaborate. There is a danger that the beginner, when he sees pictures of these, may be tempted to tackle something too ambitious.

For the construction of a model railway layout which will continue to provide pleasure for the owner, some advance planning is necessary. It is also important to have some idea of what sort of layout is wanted. Often the beginner does not have the knowledge or experience to decide. My aim in this book is to give him some idea of the possibilities and to provide advice on the type of layout he can successfully tackle as a first project.

The term layout planning can be used in a rather restricted sense to describe the designing of the actual track arrangement, the number and positions of the platforms and other details. However, there is a great deal more than this for the modeller to consider in his planning and I want to use the term in a much wider context. We must decide on the size, shape, location and type of model railway layout and even the sort of structures and scenery which will be added. These, and other aspects, are all of importance in the creation of a satisfying model railway layout.

The book covers planning for 00-scale and N-scale layouts of types suitable for beginners. These are the most popular scales in this country, particularly 00, and are the ones best suited to the inexperienced modeller.

The ideas and information presented here are based on the experiences of many modellers. Over the years there have been many interesting developments in layout planning, particularly with regard to small layouts suitable for modern houses. Because an idea devised by one modeller is often modified and improved by others it is difficult to know how any particular scheme first originated. I would, however, like to give credit to the work of Cyril Freezer, now editor of *Model Railways* magazine, who has designed many interesting small layouts and who has done much to popularise the concept of branch line modelling.

I would like to thank all those modellers who have kindly allowed me to use photographs of their work to illustrate this book. In particular I am grateful to Graham Bailey, Tony Butler, Leo Campbell, K.J. Churms, Howard Coulson, Brian Dorman, Keith Gowen, David Hammersley, Dave Howsam, Terry Jenkins, Bob Jones, Ron Prattley, Phil Savage, Mike Sharman, Allan Sibley and Adrian Swain.

Some general considerations

Because we are modelling a whole system rather than just a few separate items which could be displayed on shelves or in a cabinet we must find space to accommodate our layout. To complete a model railway there are many models to be constructed or purchased and time and money will be required. Thus when deciding what sort of layout to build we must take into account the amount of space, time and money we can afford and also how long a period we are prepared to let the construction of the layout take. Obviously there is no point in planning a large and complex system if there is space for only a very small layout. What is often less evident to the beginner is the heavy commitment in hours of work and in cost involved in the building of a large model railway. Many

The Isle of Purbeck MRC 4 mm scale Swanage Branch layout was modelled very closely on the prototype line and is very realistic. However most modellers do not have the space or time to construct such a large layout and must compress and compromise much more.

Part of the attractive DJH Models 00-scale demonstration layout which was constructed entirely from commercially available items. Note how the small factory utilises the space in the corner of the layout providing not only scenic interest but also a siding to add to the operating scope of the line.

really big layouts have been built over many years by modellers who have been able and willing to devote a great deal of time and money to the hobby. It is essential not to be too ambitious in the choice of a first layout. Later, if the modeller finds he can spare more space, time and money he can tackle a more extensive project.

The track design is very important in determining the appearance of a model railway and how it can be run so it should be planned with some care. However, do not worry too much about trying to make your plan perfect; it never will be! Your first layout is most unlikely to be your final one and, indeed, will probably be very different from what you eventually decide you want in a layout. As you gain knowledge and experience you will want to modify, improve, alter and extend your layout and later you will probably decide to scrap or sell it and build a new and better one, incorporating those features you have come to realise you want to include. So, while it is wise to give some thought to planning your model railway before starting construction, do not spend too long 'armchair modelling'—planning, designing and dreaming without actually building anything! There is no substitute for practical experience.

Though track planning will be discussed later in this book I would suggest that the beginner may well do best to choose a published plan, the basic design of which appeals to him, and to modify it as necessary to suit his own tastes, rather than try to make up his own plan. Small changes will give individuality to the published plan without affecting the essential features. In this way problems of design, some of which may only become apparent too late in construction for easy correction, will be avoided. Do not feel that you are showing a lack of originality by copying a plan in this way. There is only a limited number of workable schemes suitable for small layouts and most, if not all, of these must already have been utilised. Many track plans have been published in the model railway magazines, particularly in *Railway Modeller*, and Cyril Freezer has collected many of his layout plans into three books of which *60 Plans for Small Railways* is especially useful to the beginner.

When we plan a model railway we should always remember that the function of the prototype, with the exception now, perhaps, of the preserved lines, is to provide transportation. On some railways this is very specialised, for example, commuter lines carrying only passengers, mining railways transporting only ore; on others the traffic is mixed, with passengers, both long distance and local, and a wide variety of freight. If a model railway is to be realistic and interesting it should seem to be a replica of the real thing not only in appearance but also in operation. We can add variety to the running of the layout and to the rolling stock required by the provision of lineside industries, each with a siding or sidings to be shunted. There is an almost unlimited choice of possible industries, some of which require special types of rolling stock to serve them, and this is another way in which individuality can be introduced into your model railway.

The restrictions of space, time and money obviously limit what can be included on a layout. We have the choice of representing much of the prototype in outline only or of concentrating on a particular part and modelling it in much greater detail. Interesting layouts of both types have been built but model railways which specialise in an aspect in which the constructor is especially interested are usually more successful than those in which an attempt has been made to include almost everything. However, do remember that railway modelling is a hobby for your pleasure and enjoyment. Plan and build your layout the way you would like to have it and not how others tell you it ought to be. There are so many different aims, interests and ideas among railway modellers that the type of layout other enthusiasts like may not suit you at all. Your model railway is your own private little kingdom where you can express your own ideas and creativity, and where you can make your own rules. Some enthusiasts will say that you must do this or that on your model because it is prototype practice to do so, but this is not necessarily a valid argument because we can never copy the real thing exactly anyway. Selection and compression are always needed and it is up to the individual to select the parts that he likes and which to him represent the best aspects of the prototype. Provided your layout gives you enjoyment and satisfaction it is a success!

The train set

The train set is the traditional introduction to railway modelling and it remains an excellent way of starting the hobby. The basic set usually consists of a locomotive, coaches or goods stock, and an oval of sectional track about 3½ ft × 2½ ft. Many different sets are produced with various combinations of steam, diesel or electric outline locomotive and coaches or goods vehicles. Some sets include additional track and one or more turnouts for sidings or a passing loop. Nowadays the models are generally of very good quality, they are accurate and well detailed and make an excellent basis from which to develop your layout. If the set is a gift the choice will already have been made for you, but if you are buying the train set yourself try to select a set which will not only meet your present needs but which will also

This simple first permanent layout was developed easily and quickly from a train set.

be appropriate for your future layout. Your interests may change or become more specialised but it is obviously helpful if you have some idea of how you might want your railway to develop; if it is to follow British, American or European prototype, if it will be period steam or modern image diesel and so on. This may help to avoid the need for the replacement of locomotives and rolling stock at a later date.

Although it may be tempting to select a large and impressive express locomotive with main line coaches, a better choice is a small steam or diesel engine with a train of goods stock. A large locomotive will look out of place on a small layout with sharp curves, whereas a small engine will be equally at home on the train set oval or on the larger and more complex layout which you may build up from it eventually. I suggest goods vehicles as the initial items of rolling stock because they provide more opportunities for shunting when you add a few sidings. When you later acquire passenger stock, select short branch line coaches rather than full length main line stock. They will look better on sharp curves and will allow you to use shorter platforms with a consequent saving in space.

Although the simple oval is convenient it has very limited operational scope. You can run a train clockwise or anti-clockwise around the track and that is all! While the oval is a useful basis for a small layout, providing as it does a continuous run in a small area, it needs additional features to make it more interesting. Even a single siding will permit us to drop off and pick up wagons. A run-around loop will give greater scope for shunting because the siding can then be worked by a train running in either direction. Further sidings provide additional permutations for shunting and extra interest. For example, we can represent a small industrial line with, perhaps, three sidings, each serving a factory or warehouse, and this will give considerable operating potential. As the track is sectional you can try out various

Eastern Models feature a timber works on their HO-scale demonstration layout. This industry is served by two sidings giving extra scope for shunting.

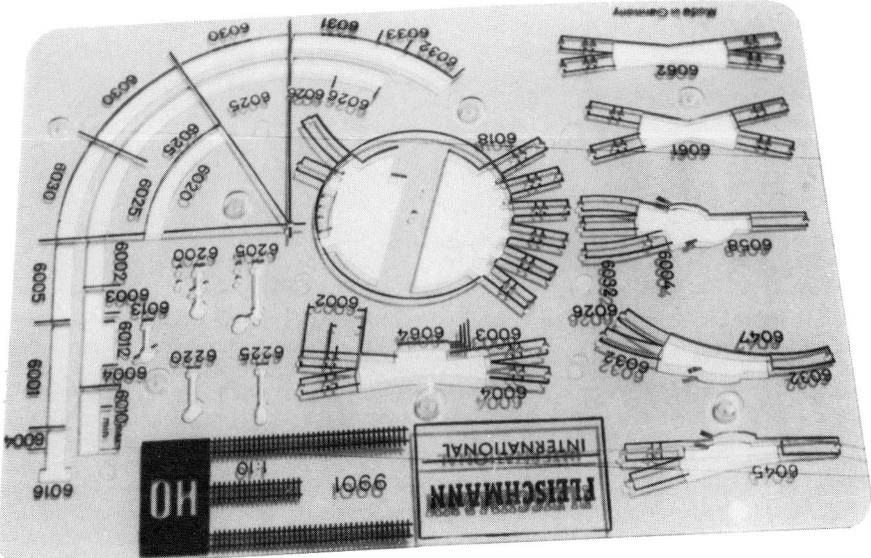

The Fleischmann HO-track stencil allows accurate planning to 1:10 scale of layouts with Fleischmann track pieces, points, crossings, etc.

arrangements as you buy extra track and points. This can be a very valuable period of experimentation. There are many different ways of setting out the track and these will produce a variety of operating patterns. Running trains over these different track layouts may give you some idea of the sort of permanent layout you would like to build. You may, perhaps, enjoy watching the trains run steadily on a continuous line or you may prefer the challenge of shunting on a small, but complicated, industrial layout.

It is best to add gradually to the train set rather than to buy a lot of additional parts all at once. In this way you can experiment to the full with the track you have as you go along and you will have more idea of which extra pieces you would find most useful. Similarly with additional locomotives and rolling stock it is preferable to build up gradually from the basic set, so that you can, if you wish, change your mind about the type of railway you want without having to dispose of a lot of equipment, previously acquired but now unsuitable.

For a permanent model railway layout using flexible track a track plan is required as a guide, but it is more difficult to draw out a small scale plan for a layout using sectional track because it must be very accurate or the fixed pieces of sectional track may not fit when you come to lay the track. The easiest method is to lay it out full size using actual track pieces to make sure of the positioning. However, you may want to try out various designs on paper without having to buy the track sections until you decide on one particular plan, so that you can then buy just the pieces needed. Some manufacturers produce track stencils to enable the drawing up of accurate small scale plans of layouts which can be built using the sectional track which they make. They include Hornby (00 scale), Arnold (N scale) and Fleischmann (HO and N scales).

The train set has much to recommend it as a starting point for railway modellers. The sets are relatively inexpensive and you can build up from them gradually as your finances permit. The track is easy to assemble and provides good running; being sectional it allows the modeller to try out many different track layouts. The models are realistic and the train set can give a great deal of enjoyment as well as providing useful experience. It can be incorporated into a permanent layout later if you wish.

Scale and Gauge

Some of the basic terms in railway modelling are often used rather loosely and the beginner may become confused by them. In view of this I feel that it is worthwhile first of all to explain the difference between scale and gauge and the relationship between 00 and HO scales and between Continental and British N scales.

Scale refers to the proportion between the prototype and the model. *Gauge* is the track width, measured between the inner surfaces of the running rails. The British prototype standard gauge is 4 ft 8 ½ in.

For 00 the scale is 4 mm to the foot; that is each foot on the prototype is represented by 4 mm on the model. Alternatively this can be expressed as a ratio of 1:76. The track gauge for 00 is 16.5 mm. HO scale is 3.5 mm to the foot or a ratio of 1:87, also with a track gauge of 16.5 mm. As we have two different scales with the same track gauge, representing in each case the standard 4 ft 8 ½ in gauge prototype, the track gauge must be incorrect for one of the scales. In fact it is in 00 scale that the track width is wrong, being narrower than it should be. This discrepancy arose soon after the commercial introduction of 00 gauge. At first it was intended that the scale should be half 0 scale, making it 3.5 mm to the foot with the virtually correct track gauge of 16.5 mm. However, manufacturers soon found that the small size of the British prototype loading gauge (the maximum permissible height and width for locomotives and rolling stock), compared to those in Europe and the United States, created two problems. The first was the difficulty of fitting the electric motors commercially produced at that time into the British prototype locomotives. The second concerned parts such as axle guards, bogie sides and locomotive valve gear. These parts had to be made thicker than scale to give them enough strength for commercially produced models. It was also necessary to increase clearance in proportion to the prototype to allow models to run on the sharp curves needed on model railway layouts. The small British loading gauge allowed insufficient width for these increases and so the manufacturers adopted the slightly larger scale of 4 mm to the foot while retaining the 16.5 mm track gauge, the combination being named 00. With the development of smaller scales it is clear that the compromise is no longer necessary but manufacturers and modellers are now so heavily committed to 00 scale that a change to HO scale for British modelling is most unlikely. European and American manufacturers, with the benefits of the larger prototype loading gauges retained 3.5 mm scale and 16.5 mm gauge as HO scale.

00 in Britain and HO in Europe and America have become the most popular of all scales and this is reflected in the vast ranges of ready-to-run equipment, kits of all types, and parts which are produced. These scales are a good compromise in size, being small enough for an interesting layout to be built in a reasonable space, but large enough for good detailing and for relatively easy kit construction and scratch-building. The models are also easy to handle. The convenience of having such a wide variety of products on the market should not be underestimated. It means that a layout can be fairly quickly brought to the stage where it can be operated, whereas progress would be much slower if many of the items had to be hand-built, and the delay might then cause the modeller to lose interest and enthusiasm, particularly if he is a beginner. The proprietary models used to complete the layout initially can be replaced later by more detailed kits or scratch-built items if desired. Another advantage of the availability of good quality commercial products is that the modeller has more time to concentrate on those aspects of the hobby which interest him most. In addition the large potential market for products in 00 and HO scales encourages manufacturers to offer models of less popular prototypes and of more specialised items which in other scales could

not be profitably produced. Thus the modeller has a wider choice. The greater opportunities for mass production also means that the models may be less expensive.

Most modellers of British prototypes are prepared to accept the incorrect scale/gauge ratio of 00 for the convenience and advantages of the large range of commercial items on the market, and so that their models will be compatible with those of their friends. If you find the slightly narrow gauge appearance of 4 mm scale on 16.5 mm gauge unacceptable you can model to EM scale (4 mm scale on 18 mm gauge) or to the exact Protofour standards (4 mm scale on 18.83 mm gauge) but either will involve you in more conversion and construction work than is necessary in 00 scale.

N scale was introduced commercially in the early 1960s by the German firm Arnold, with models to a ratio of 1:160, representing a scale of approximately 1.9 mm to the foot, running on track of 9 mm gauge. Unfortunately, for exactly the same reason that British prototypes were modelled to 00 scale instead of HO, it was considered necessary for the slightly larger scale of 2 1/16 mm to the foot, a ratio of 1:148, to be used for commercially produced models of British locomotives and rolling stock, and this has become the standard for British N scale. The track gauge is the same as for Continental and American N scale—9 mm.

N scale is well established and is now second only to 00 and HO scales in popularity. It offers a significant space advantage over the larger scales. A wide variety of models is available and the range of ready-to-run equipment, kits and parts is steadily increasing all the time. N scale has the advantage that standards for track, wheels and couplings were established early on so that all the models produced are compatible in these respects. Thus the modeller does not have the expense or trouble of having to change wheels or couplings to match his own equipment. The present N-scale standards for wheels and track are rather coarse in comparison to those in the larger scales. This makes for reliable running but does detract from the appearance. There have been moves to introduce finer scale standards in N scale and it may be that the manufacturers will adopt these eventually.

I have discussed 00 and N scales in some detail because these are the scales the beginner is most likely to choose; I would certainly recommend that one of these be selected. Of course the choice may already have been made by the gift or purchase of a train set, by the gift of some equipment from a railway modelling friend, or because someone you know has a layout and you want to work to the same scale.

If you have not yet decided I suggest you look at the models in the shops, at exhibitions, or on a friend's layout to see which scale appeals most to you. You might even like to buy one or two kits and make them up to see how you find working in the different scales before you commit yourself too far to want to change. 00 scale has the advantage of being less fiddly to handle and kit construction and scratch-building tend to be easier because of the larger size. Though, conversely, some workers in N scale claim that as less detail is required they find it easier to build models in the smaller scale than in 00. Really it all comes down to your own preferences and to getting used to modelling in any particular scale. The small size of N scale may make it possible for you to fit a more interesting layout into the space you have available. The choice is up to you depending on the circumstances and on your personal feelings about the appearance and feel of the models. Do not make the mistake of thinking that it will be cheaper to model in the smaller N scale! The locomotive and rolling stock models tend to be fairly similar in price in 00 and N scales for comparable quality because the expense of manufacture is much the same. In fact an N-scale layout may well cost you more because you can fit so much more into the same space than on an 00-scale model railway.

Definitions

As I have already indicated I feel that the beginner should start with 00 or N scale. The following brief listing of scales and gauges is provided for general interest and information and so that you will be familiar with them when you see them mentioned in model railway magazines, rather than because I am suggesting other alternative scales for the beginner. Later, after experience in 00 or N scale, the modeller may wish to try out another scale and by then he will be in a better position to assess what this will involve.

Z scale (1.4 mm to the foot or 1:220; 6.5 mm gauge; prototype gauge equivalent 4 ft 8¼ in).

This is the most recently introduced commercial scale. The models, by Märklin, are remarkably well detailed but are expensive and only Continental prototypes are produced. A few plastic structure kits are made for this scale by Kibri.

N Scale—US and Continental (1.9 mm to the foot or 1:160; 9 mm gauge; prototype gauge equivalent 4 ft 8½ in).

Now well established and second only to HO scale in popularity in America and Europe. There is a wide range of ready-to-run models of high quality with the advantage that wheel and rail standards are generally uniform and that there is a universal coupling, so that stock from different manufacturers can be run together. Many kits and parts are also marketed.

N Scale—British (2 1/16 mm to the foot or 1:148; 9 mm gauge; prototype gauge equivalent 4 ft 4½ in).

This is also now very popular being second only to 00 scale in Britain. There is a reasonable selection of ready-to-run locomotives and rolling stock and a steadily increasing range of kits, including a variety of cast metal locomotive body kits to fit onto commercial chassis. Many structures and accessories are now on the market, either ready-made or in kit form. The large range of excellent Continental structure kits can also be utilised, sometimes with minor modifications to make them appear more British. These European kits are strictly speaking slightly underscale for British N-scale layouts but this is not really noticeable in practice and can even be an advantage, particularly in the case of large buildings, as the structures will occupy a little less space than if they were to exact scale.

000 Scale (2 mm to the foot or 1:152; 9.5 mm gauge; prototype gauge equivalent 4 ft 8½ in).

This is a scale for the enthusiast who is prepared to hand-build most of his models himself and it is not suitable for inexperienced workers. There is an active 2 mm Scale Association which provides considerable assistance for modellers working in this scale.

TT Scale—Continental (2.5 mm to the foot or 1:120; 12 mm gauge; prototype gauge equivalent 4 ft 8½ in).

There has been a revival of interest in this scale in Germany recently with the re-introduction of the old East German Zeuke products in revised and improved form as Berliner Bahnen. This firm offers a good range of locomotives and rolling stock and also figures and road vehicles.

TT Scale—British (TT3) (3 mm to the foot or 1:100; 12 mm gauge; prototype gauge equivalent 4 ft).

Though the scale received a setback with the introduction of N scale and no ready-to-run models are at present made, there is still a range of kits and parts available and modellers are supported by an active association, the 3 mm Society, which produces its own magazine *Mixed Traffic* for its members. The scale offers a compromise between 00 and N scales but the lack of ready-to-run equipment makes it unsuitable for the beginner.

HO Scale (3.5 mm to the foot or 1:87; 16.5 mm gauge; prototype gauge equivalent 4 ft 8½ in).

The most popular scale by far in the United States and on the Continent with a very extensive range of ready-to-run equipment, kits, parts and accessories.

00 Scale (4 mm to the foot or 1:76; 16.5 mm gauge; prototype gauge equivalent 4 ft 1½ in).

The most popular scale in Britain with many advantages for the beginner despite the inaccurate scale/gauge ratio.

EM gauge (18 mm gauge with 4 mm to the foot scale; prototype gauge equivalent 4 ft 6 in) gives a much better appearance and track is now available from Ratio, though locomotives and rolling stock must be modified by the modeller. The EM Gauge Society provides assistance for workers in this gauge.

Protofour—P4 (18.83 mm gauge with 4 mm to the foot scale; prototype gauge equivalent 4 ft 8½ in). This is a system with an exact scale/track gauge ratio and also a set of fine scale standards for track, wheels and other details. The Protofour Society provides advice and information and a number of items are now commercially available for the system. The results are excellent but the beginner should acquire experience with 00 scale first.

S Scale (3/16 in to the foot or 1:64; 7/8 in gauge; prototype gauge equivalent 4 ft 8 in).

There are some commercial items available for this scale in the United States but not in Britain. It is a useful compromise between 00 and 0 scales but is not suitable for the beginner because models must be hand-built.

0 Scale—British (7 mm to the foot or 1:43; 32 mm gauge; prototype gauge equivalent 4 ft 7 in).

An attractive scale because of the size and weight of the models and the detail which can be included, but generally not suitable for the beginner because of the expense involved and the space needed. There are a number of inexpensive locomotives and rolling stock models of Continental manufacture available, some of British prototype, but the range is very limited.

1 Scale (10 mm to the foot or 1:30.5; 45 mm gauge; prototype gauge equivalent 4 ft 6 in).

Even more expensive in space and cost than 0 scale. There is a range of ready-to-run locomotives and rolling stock of Continental prototype from Märklin.

Narrow gauge

Narrow-gauge modelling has become very popular in recent years, partly because of the numerous preserved lines now in operation but mainly due to the introduction of commercial ready-to-run models, kits and parts in some scales. A railway is narrow gauge if its track width is less than the standard 4 ft 8½ in, but most modellers tend to choose prototypes of metre gauge or less. Apart from the undoubted charm of these railways there are advantages for the modeller because the sharp curves, steep gradients, small locomotives, short trains and simple stations typical of narrow-gauge lines enable a model to be built in a smaller space than a standard-gauge model railway would need.

If we set out to model a narrow-gauge prototype we can use one of the commercially produced gauges and choose the appropriate scale to go with it or we can decide on the scale we will model to and make the gauge to suit. Generally it is best to employ a recognised gauge so that commercial wheels, mechanisms and, if desired, track can be used. If the scale and gauge are chosen so that the scale is also one which is catered for by the trade we have the ideal arrangement. We can use items such as structures, figures, road vehicles, and other accessories from the scale chosen while employing wheels, mechanisms, bogies and so on from the smaller scale which has the gauge we are using.

The following are the most usual scale/gauge combinations:

Nn3 (N scale on Z gauge representing 3 ft gauge prototype). I have not heard of any modellers in Britain using this combination so far but a few American enthusiasts have built narrow-gauge layouts in N scale using locomotives and rolling stock converted from Märklin Z-scale models. Unfortunately the high cost of the Z-scale models is likely to deter many modellers but the combination has considerable potential for the modeller who would like an extensive narrow-gauge system in a limited space.

00n2 and HOn2½ (These are respectively 4 mm scale (usually known as 009) and 3.5 mm scale (usually known as HO9 or HOe) on 9 mm gauge track). Strictly speaking the former is equivalent to 2 ft 3 in gauge prototype and the latter approximately 2 ft 6 in but both are used to model prototypes of from 2 ft to 2 ft 6 in gauge. Some ready-to-run models of Continental prototype are available and a variety of British kits are produced including cast metal locomotive body kits to fit onto N-gauge commercial chassis. The modeller can also utilise N-scale locomotive mechanisms, wagon underframes and wheels, coach bogies and so on for his own models. 009 track and points are made by Peco, or N-scale track can be used if the sleepers, which are wrongly spaced, are largely hidden by the ballast. The latter choice enables the modeller to benefit from the more extensive range of points, crossings and other special track available in N scale. Lilliput make a useful dual-gauge (16.5 mm and 9 mm) crossing for 00- or HO-scale layouts which have both standard- and narrow-gauge track.

HOn3 (This is 3.5 mm scale on 10.5 mm gauge track for 3 ft gauge prototypes). It is popular in the United States where brass ready-to-run locomotives and rolling stock, numerous parts and a variety of rolling stock kits are on sale. Ready-made track is also produced. Some of these items are available in Britain from specialist model railway shops.

00n3 (4 mm scale on 12 mm gauge representing 3 ft gauge prototype). Gem in Britain market a number of metal kits for the Isle of Man Railway equipment and TT3 mechanisms and other parts can be used also.

HOm (3.5 mm scale on 12 mm gauge track for metre gauge prototypes). This scale/gauge combination was formerly catered for by Zeuke of East Germany but ready-to-run locomotives and rolling stock together with sectional and flexible track and points are now produced by Bemo.

0n2¼ (7 mm scale on 16.5 mm gauge track; equivalent to approximately 2 ft 4 in gauge prototype but used to represent gauges of 2 ft 3 in and 2 ft 6 in also). This is an attractive combination as the models are large enough to allow considerable detailing but a layout can be built in the same space as a comparable one in 00 scale. The vast range of mechanisms, wheels, underframes and track parts intended for 00 and HO can be used for convenience and economy and there is a good selection of accessories such as figures and road vehicles for 0 scale. The

Peco locomotive and rolling stock cast metal kits for this scale/gauge combination should help to make it popular.

On2½ (¼ in to the foot scale on 16.5 mm gauge track). This is the American equivalent of the above and has similar advantages.

10 mm, 14 mm and 16 mm scales on 32 mm gauge track (Representing respectively 3 ft, 2 ft 3 in and 2 ft gauge prototypes). The large size of these models means that they can be very well detailed. Some modellers have used the inexpensive Triang Big Big Train (0 gauge) locomotives and rolling stock as a basis for models to these scales. The Triang models are no longer produced but they can sometimes be obtained second hand. Some accessories are available in 10 mm scale and others can be adapted from military modelling kits.

G-gauge (14 mm scale on 45 mm gauge track). The LGB range of ready-to-run locomotives and rolling stock is quite extensive and is being steadily enlarged. The manufacturer also makes sectional track and points to complete the system. The models are mainly of European prototypes but a few American models are also made. The scale/gauge combination is equivalent to metre gauge.

Broad gauge

The broad-gauge prototypes have not become popular for modelling in the way that the narrow-gauge railways have, though a few layouts have been built featuring models of the Irish 5 ft 3 in gauge railways. Mike Sharman has modelled the old Brunel 7 ft gauge very effectively on his superb Victorian period 4 mm scale layout which also includes standard- and narrow-gauge tracks together with some complex mixed gauge trackwork. Mike Sharman also offers a number of cast metal kits commercially for broad-gauge modelling in 4 mm scale.

A layout built by Terry Jenkins. This 00-scale model railway is typical of the sort of layout a beginner can tackle successfully. The structures are mainly modified kits and the scenic work is straightforward but effective.

Layout size

I have already cautioned the beginner not to be tempted, by seeing large and elaborate model railways, into tackling something too ambitious for his first layout. It is also very easy when studying layout plans drawn to a small scale to underestimate the size that these layouts will be when built. When considering a plan it is a good idea to measure out on the floor the dimensions of the layout so that you can visualise more easily how much space it would occupy. Even a 6 ft × 4 ft layout, usually classified as small, will take up quite a lot of a small or medium sized room, and if you need to carry it at all, you will find it surprisingly massive.

The beginner sometimes has the belief that if a small layout will be good then a large one must be even better! This is quite wrong. A model railway does not have to be large and elaborate to be successful. Indeed, the greatest entertainment comes from a layout when it is fully used and as most modellers usually operate single-handed the layout should not be too big.

There are many advantages in building a small layout as your first model railway. As I indicated earlier the three basic limiting factors when constructing a layout are the time, money and space which we are able and willing to afford. For a small layout the initial financial outlay will be low, particularly if the modeller is progressing from a train set and already has much of the equipment he needs. The further costs incurred during construction will also be small and there will be no danger of progress being held up through lack of money.

Because only a limited number of models can be accommodated on a small layout the modeller can afford to make sure they are of a high standard, either by purchasing more expensive models or by taking the time to build well detailed ones himself. In the relatively small area, progress on scenic work will be encouragingly good for only a few evenings of modelling, and there is again time to attend to all the small details which make a layout more interesting.

A model railway is a working model and if it is to provide the maximum enjoyment for its owner it must work well. Good track and wiring are essential and it is much easier both to construct and to maintain smooth, accurate track and good electrical contact on a small layout than on a large one, simply because there is so much less of it.

Often lack of space limits the size of layout which can be built and the modeller has no alternative but to settle for a small model railway. However, even if a large area is available it is still advisable to start out modestly. If the plan is chosen with some forethought a small simple layout, which can be completed fairly quickly and easily, can later be extended or incorporated into a larger system. If possible select the site for your layout with this in mind. Many excellent layouts have been developed in this way. John Allen's HO scale 'Gorre & Daphetid', one of the finest model railroads ever constructed, started out as a small layout approximately 6½ ft × 3½ ft in size and this original section was retained, with only minor alterations, as part of the eventually very large and complex system.

Alternatively, when the layout has been completed and has provided all the operating entertainment it can, you may decide to scrap it rather than use it as part of a larger layout. It may be that your ideas have changed and that it will be easier to build a completely new layout as you want it rather than to try to alter the old one. The standard of your modelling work may also have improved so that the original section is no longer up to the standard you want. Though the beginner tends to think of his first layout, while he is planning and building it, as his final one, most modellers do construct more than one layout, in many cases several. This is another advantage of starting with a small layout as you will be more likely to scrap it and start again than if you are heavily committed in time and money to a large layout. Scrapping a small layout is not the extravagance it may seem. The original cost of the layout will have been amply repaid in the pleasure and experience you have gained in building and operating it and many of the parts, perhaps even the baseboard, can be saved and re-used. A fresh start may also stimulate your interest and enthusiasm.

For the beginner I would suggest a layout no larger than about 6 ft × 4 ft for a rectangular layout accommodating a continuous run track plan of some type. If possible it is best to have a central operating well in layouts of this sort. Access to all parts of the layout is then much easier, particularly as it will probably be necessary to have one side of the layout against a wall. The model railway also appears much more realistic to operate as the trains look as if they are really going somewhere rather than just round and round. This seems to be because you have to turn to watch the train as it passes behind you instead of being able to see it all the time from one position as you can when you view the layout from one side.

For a long narrow layout for a point-to-point design, perhaps as an L-shape fitting into the corner of a room, a baseboard with arms of up to about 6 or 8 ft long and 1-2 ft wide is the maximum size I would advise for a first layout.

The track plan for whatever type of layout is selected should be fairly simple with relatively few points. This is important because the number of points included on a layout influences considerably the time taken to build and later to maintain the model railway.

Even if you anticipate that the layout will be a permanent fitting in the room there is much to be said for constructing it as a number of units, each preferably no larger than about 4 ft × 2ft, which can be fixed together rigidly but which can be taken apart if necessary for storage or transportation. Obviously for a portable layout some arrangement of this sort will be essential.

I believe it was Cyril Freezer who once wrote that it is easier to build a good small layout than a good large layout. This is a very true statement and one which all beginners would do well to keep in mind!

Layout location

When planning a layout the beginner may well look around the house trying to find a large space for his model railway. I can remember planning a grandiose scheme and then looking for the largest possible site to accommodate it, but fortunately as a beginner I never got as far as actually trying to build my dream layout! These larger spaces include sites such as the loft, the garage or a garden shed and all of these have been utilised very satisfactorily by many modellers. As an example, Mike Sharman's large mixed gauge period layout is now being built into the owner's loft. However, Mike is an expert modeller with great experience, capable not only of constructing a large layout on which almost everything is hand-built but also of fitting out his loft to house the railway. It is worth mentioning though that his layout began as a much smaller portable section which has since been incorporated into the present system.

Personally, I would not recommend any of the above sites for the beginner. Generally I do not feel it is the right approach at this stage because in an effort to obtain the use of a space which is probably much larger than is required the modeller is accepting some serious disadvantages. For example, it can be very dusty in a garage, making operation troublesome and causing problems in maintenance. Fitting out a loft or erecting a garden shed may involve so much work and cost that the modeller may never actually get round to building the layout which was the real object of the exercise! All these sites are likely to be cold in winter, so you will either end up not using the layout then or providing heating which will add to the expense. On wet nights the idea of going out to a garden shed to run your railway is not very inviting! There is also the danger that, having created a large space exclusively for a model railway, the modeller may be tempted to start on too large a layout. I also feel that it is a pity to isolate yourself from the rest of the family while working on or running your railway.

Now I know there are exceptions to the comments I have made above. A friend of mine who lived in a bungalow had a fully fitted-out loft with easy access already, so he erected his portable layout in the centre of the loft and used the rest to store his kits, tools, books and so on. In this case the loft was really the equivalent of a spare room and my objections about work needed for fitting out and lack of comfort do not apply. However, most of us are not so fortunate and in general I think it is best to try to find a site within the main part of the house. There are many places in most houses where a small layout of the sort a beginner should be tackling can be accommodated. Indeed successful layouts have been built in small flats, bedsitters and even a caravan!

If you are lucky enough to have a spare

room which can be devoted exclusively to your hobby then there is no problem. More frequently, however, the layout must be accommodated in a room which will be used for other purposes also and it must not interfere unduly with these other activities. Often a youngster will want to develop his train set into a permanent continuous-run layout on a baseboard in his bedroom. A rectangular baseboard of this type does occupy a considerable part of the free area of a room even if its size is kept to a minimum. As it will almost certainly need to be pushed back against a wall, a baseboard with a central operating well is the best arrangement so that access to the whole layout is easy. Unfortunately there is a tendency for a layout like this in a bedroom to become untidy. The models themselves get dusty and things may be left on and under the baseboard making cleaning up difficult. A neat solution to the problem is to arrange the baseboard so that it folds up against one wall when the layout is not in use, leaving the room clear. The layout should be hinged along one edge onto a strong frame fixed firmly to the wall. Shelves or cupboards can be built into the lower part of the frame below the layout to store the locomotives and rolling stock between operating sessions. Hinging the layout in this way does involve additional construction work but it may mean that a layout can be built in a room where it would not otherwise be acceptable. It also ensures that the layout is kept tidy, because loose models, tools and so on, must be removed before the baseboard is folded up. There will also be more protection from dust and accidental damage for the layout.

An alternative way of installing a permanent layout in a room is to fit a long, narrow baseboard along one or more walls. The most suitable arrangement for the beginner is a layout limited to only one or two of the walls. In this way the door of the room can be left clear avoiding the need for any form of lifting section to be included. This type of layout can conveniently be supported on storage units; many suitable pieces of furniture are available at very reasonable prices from discount stores, either as ready-made units or in kit form for home assembly. If preferred, the baseboard can be fixed to the wall as a shelf. A neat and convenient method is to use one of the slotted shelving systems obtainable from DIY shops. A layout of this type can be fitted into a bedroom with very little effect on the usual purposes of the room. Similarly, if an along-the-wall layout is very neatly finished it may be acceptable in the lounge. If you are really stuck for space do not overlook the possibility of installing a narrow layout along the wall in the hall. In many houses the hall is too small for this but in others there would be ample, otherwise wasted, space.

If you fit a layout into the lounge you may like to have a cover so the layout will be concealed when not in use. This will also protect the model from dust and damage.

A close view of part of a neat 00-scale bookcase layout built by Dave Howsam and Ron Prattley showing the goods yard. Layout is realistic and interesting even though actual width available is only 10½ in. (Photo by Ron Prattley.)

An interesting 009 narrow-gauge layout built in a coffee table. Design is essentially a dog bone with the loops overlapped. (Model, photo and plan by K.J. Churms.)

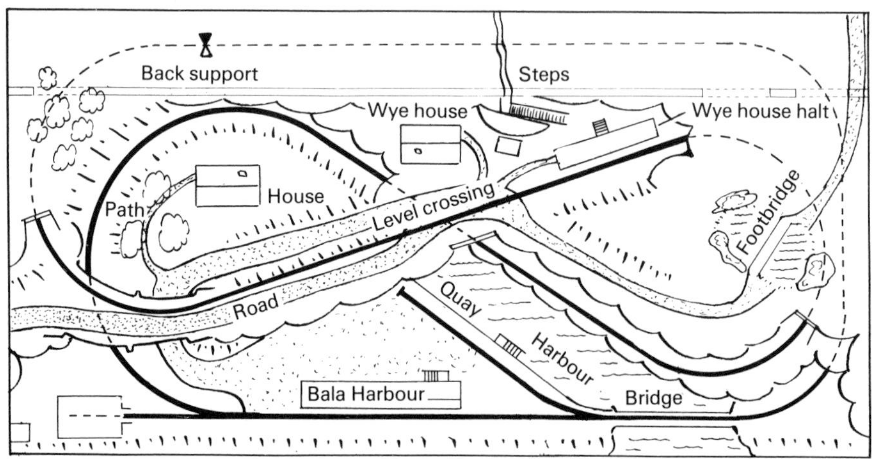

Dave Howsam and Ron Prattley have constructed a very neat bookcase to house a terminus to fiddle yard design model railway. When not in use the model is hidden and the unit looks like a typical bookcase. To set up for operating, the top is removed to reveal the terminus on the fixed part of the bookcase. The top is reversed and fitted onto one end of the unit where it forms the remainder of the layout, including the fiddle yard. The complete layout measures 16 ft in length. The bookcase also provides useful bookshelves and cupboards. An advantage of a unit of this type is that it is free standing and does not require any fixing to the wall as would be needed with a shelf layout. If a more extensive layout is wanted further units can be constructed to carry the railway along a second wall as well. Dave and Ron built their bookcase up from wood and chipboard, but you may well be able to find suitable units, either ready-made or in kit form, which could be adapted for this purpose.

If you do not want to tackle the

An L-shaped portable N-scale layout following German prototype. The model which includes a double-track mainline and a single-track branchline is not yet complete, requiring two further sections at the right-hand end. When not in use the layout breaks down into four sections which can be easily carried and stored.

One of the sections of the German N-scale layout. Three of the units, including this one, measure 40 in × 20 in, the other section is 60 in × 20 in. The modules are bolted together to assemble the layout.

construction of a unit as large as a bookcase, but would like a railway layout that can be kept in the lounge, you might consider building a coffee table layout. These very small layouts in 009, N or Z scale usually measure about 3 ft × 1½ or 2 ft, and have a continuous run track plan, either an oval or a figure of eight design. The model is built into a coffee table the top, and sometimes also the sides, of which are plate glass. Obviously the scope of such a layout is limited, but nevertheless the construction can provide good experience in everything from track laying to scenic detailing. As can be seen from the layout shown, constructed by K.J. Churms, the finished result can be a very attractive piece of furniture and it will certainly promote interest in railway modelling!

For the modeller with limited space, particularly if his accommodation may not be permanent, a portable layout can be the answer. The layout is made up of a number of sections, each of which should be a maximum of 4 ft × 2 ft, which are set up for operating sessions and stored away afterwards. It is important that they are stored neatly both to keep them out of the way and to avoid damage. Keith Gowen's TT-scale branch line layout is a portable model railway and is stored in a large cupboard when not in use; this is a very convenient scheme and if you have a suitable cupboard it would be worth making your layout sections the correct size to fit into it. An advantage of a portable layout is that construction work can be carried out very conveniently as each section is small and, not being fixed down, can be carried to the workbench or a table. In this way you can work on the model in comfort and under ideal conditions.

The idea of constructing the layout as a series of sections has been taken rather further by some modellers, particularly in the United States. These enthusiasts often build a number of separate units or modules completing each one fully, even to the smallest details, before going on. In some cases the modules offer little or no possibility for operation at the time and are intended more as a convenient way for a modeller without much space to enjoy construction. Eventually if space for a layout becomes available the modeller will have several modules which can be fitted together as the basis of a layout. The module method of building also has some advantages for the beginner in that he can practise construction techniques and enjoy a variety of work on a small unit. Obviously this method does not provide much scope for those interested in operation, though if you can run trains on a club layout or one belonging to a friend you might like to consider it as a way of enjoying construction at home. The modules can be made to a standard size for convenience in building and storage, but need not be the same.

A further step has been taken in the United States with N scale with a system called N-Track. A number of modellers are building standard size modules on which the tracks are arranged so that they are in set positions at the ends of each module. This enables any module to be joined to any other. Standards such as the minimum radius for curves are also set. The system allows units to be linked to form large layouts for exhibitions or for operating sessions when several modellers get together.

Market Redwing station on Keith Gowen's TT-scale portable layout. Neat modelling has resulted in a very realistic appearance. Note the token exchange apparatus in the lower left corner of the picture.

Track schemes

There are only a few basic track designs and all layouts employ one or more of these. The best known, from its train set origin is the oval. It is a very useful arrangement but its appearance must be disguised if it is to be realistic. Concealing part of the oval with scenery is desirable. Part of the toy-like look of the train set oval is due to its symmetry and distorting the oval will help to disguise its nature. Positioning the tracks so that they are not parallel with the edge of the baseboard will also improve the appearance. Often straight track can be replaced by a gently curving line, again showing greater realism. The layout will also look much more realistic if viewed from within the oval by providing a central operating well. The oval gives a continuous run on which the train can travel as long as you wish without the need to stop, turn or reverse and this can be very convenient, especially if you just enjoy watching your models run.

The figure of eight layout provides a greater length of run per lap in the same area as an oval. However it either involves a track crossing at the same level, a feature more typical of US prototypes than on British lines, or at different levels. For a realistic figure of eight layout the scenery must be planned to justify the track arrangements and gradients. This is best done with hills, rivers and other natural obstacles.

The oval—the simplest continuous run design, derived from the train set.

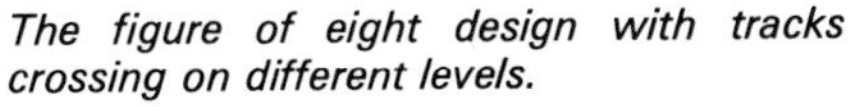

The figure of eight design with tracks crossing on different levels.

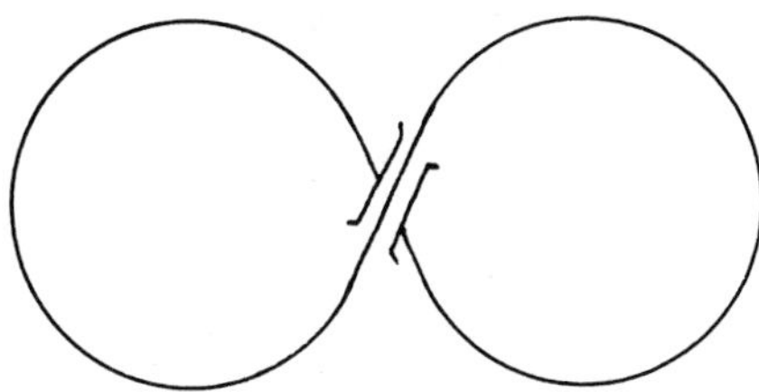

The one level figure of eight design with track crossing provides more length of run per lap than the oval.

The twice around track plan which provides almost double the length of run of the oval in the same area.

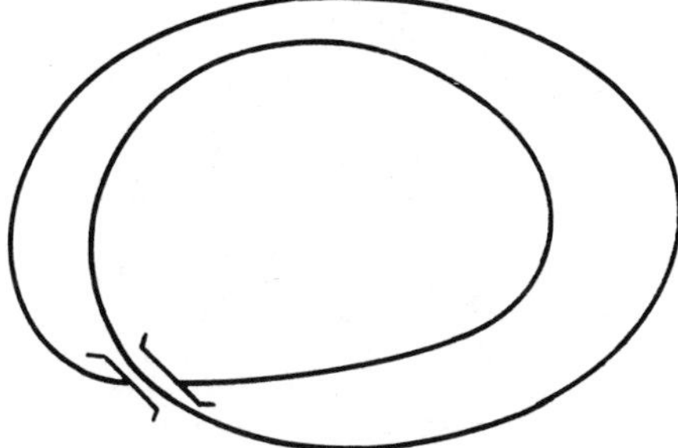

If the design is twisted further a twice around, continuous run plan results. This is a very useful arrangement as it gives about twice the length of run per lap of a simple oval, but again the scenery must be designed to make the track design appear plausible. With a plan of this type it is best to avoid having too much exactly parallel track as this will make the layout less realistic.

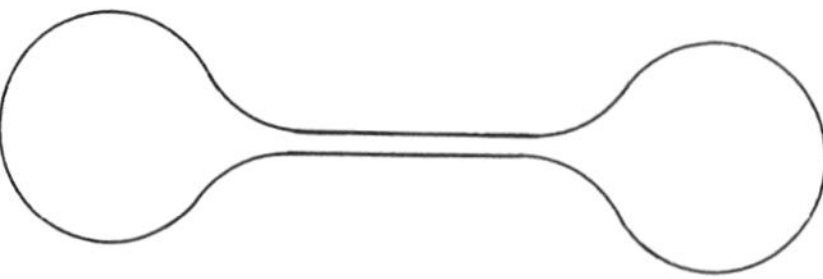

The dog bone is a variant of the oval.

Another form of continuous run scheme is the dog bone, essentially an oval with the sides brought closer together. It can be extended and twisted on itself to give a much longer run. As the two sides of the dog bone can be brought together to resemble double track this design can be used for a main line layout. The loops are the least realistic parts and are best concealed; it may be possible to place one above the other and hide them both together thus saving space on the layout.

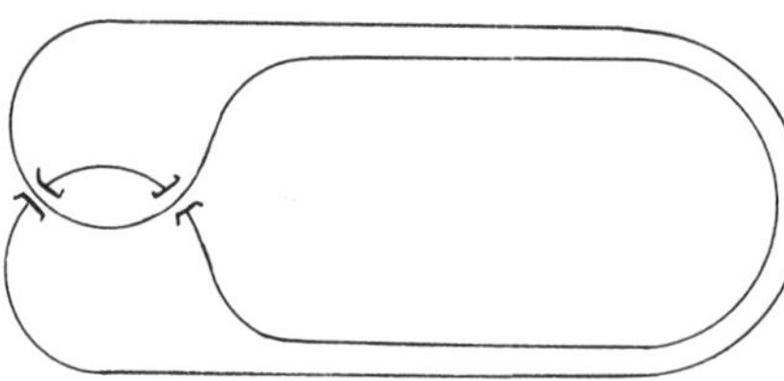

The folded dog bone provides greater length of run. Positioning one loop above the other, either partly as here or completely, saves space.

An entirely different arrangement is the point-to-point track plan. Whereas the oval is derived from the train set, this scheme is based on the prototype resulting in realism and authenticity. The only major disadvantage of the point-to-point layout is that the length of run for the train is limited. The usual design for this kind of layout is a long, narrow one, often running along one or more walls of a room. However, a point-to-point layout design can be twisted on itself into a spiral to

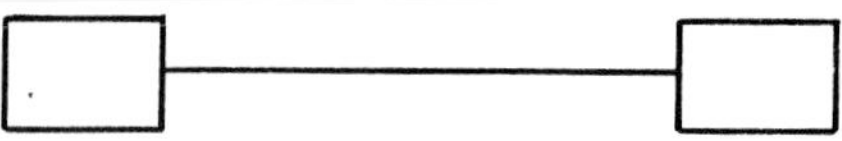

The point-to-point scheme, here as a straight design is often bent into an L-shape to fit into the corner of a room extending along two walls, and can also be bent further into a U-shape to fit onto a rectangular baseboard.

fit onto an ordinary rectangular baseboard. One terminus on a point-to-point layout may take the form of a fiddle yard.

A variant is the out and back scheme in which one terminus (or the fiddle yard in a terminus to fiddle yard design) is replaced by a loop so that the train is brought back to the terminus from which it started. This is a useful arrangement, particularly if the loop is combined with an oval so that the train can

A variant on the point-to-point scheme is the out and back design where the fiddle yard, or one terminus, is replaced by a reversing loop. This design can also be twisted to fit onto a rectangular baseboard.

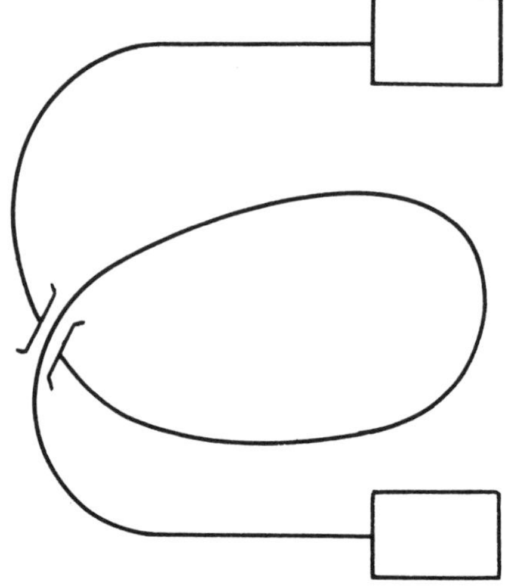

Further twisting results in a spiral point-to-point design giving greater length of run.

make as many laps around the oval as desired before coming back to the terminus. It does, however, require a special wiring arrangement for the reversing loop part of the system. An out and back design can be built on a long, narrow board—though a wider part will be needed to accommodate the loop. Alternatively, the track plan can be twisted into a spiral or figure of eight shape to fit on a shorter, wider rectangular baseboard. A more elaborate reversing loop with extra tracks acting as hidden sidings will make for more interesting operation by allowing the order in which the trains return to the terminus to be varied from that in which they left it.

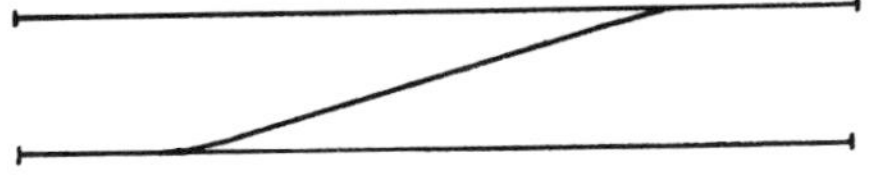

The Z-shape, zig-zag, or switch-back track arrangement.

An entirely different concept in track planning is the Z-shaped or switchback arrangement. Here a greater length of run for the trains is achieved by having three tracks form a Z-shape, each track being nearly the full length of the baseboard. In fact even more than three tracks can be included if desired. On such a layout the train travels three times the length of the layout (if three tracks are used) and the interest of operation is further increased by the reversing that is needed. Obviously, for the sake of reality we must introduce a good reason for the presence of three parallel tracks. On a small industrial layout the excuse may be that the track arrangement is needed to provide access to all the various factories, warehouses and other industries. Another way in which the scheme can be justified is to provide vertical separation between the tracks. For example on a mining layout a switchback track arrangement can be employed to bring the railway down the hillside in a situation where we can claim that it would have been too difficult or expensive for the prototype to have built curves to bring the line down in one continuous run. The scenery on such a layout must be rugged enough to support this argument. Though the beginner is perhaps best advised to build a single level layout for his first attempt, the switchback design on different levels has some interesting features and is worthy of consideration if lack of space forces you to build a narrow layout. This scheme does not appear to have been used much in Britain but is more popular in America.

It is of course possible to combine more than one of the basic track arrangements in one layout. For example, a continuous oval plan with a branch leading to a terminus combines the oval and point-to-point types.

Your choice of basic scheme will be influenced by your interests. If you enjoy watching your trains run in a realistic landscape, pick a simple continuous design—do not put in too much track and hide some of the track you have in tunnels and behind hills. If you are more interested in shunting then a point-to-point, or a Z-shaped design with lineside industries to shunt, will probably appeal more.

Basic concepts—Fiddle yards

The idea of the fiddle yard is one which has largely developed with the concept of the branch line point-to-point model railway layout. In the restricted space often available for this type of railway, rather than have two limited terminal stations unrealistically close together it was felt better to concentrate on constructing one rather more interesting terminus. The other end of the line was then led to some hidden sidings which represented the rest of the railway system. At first these sidings were provided with a run around arrangement and were operated much as a normal station would be. Sometimes a turntable was included to allow the engine to be reversed. However, as the sidings were hidden from view anyway, modellers soon found it quicker and more convenient to ignore prototype practice and to provide merely a bank of storage sidings on which the locomotives and rolling stock were rearranged by hand. Hence the name 'fiddle yard'. This is a most useful device as it allows reversal and rearrangement of the trains easily and quickly while using a minimum of space. In fact the yard can often be made detachable so that it is fitted onto the layout during operating sessions only. In this way it increases the rolling stock capacity of the railway and makes operation more interesting. An alternative arrangement to a bank of sidings fed by points is the provision of a traverser table with a single track lead. The table is moved to give access to its sidings. Such a traverser need not be elaborate, but merely a simple sliding board moved by hand, with spring brass contacts for electrical supply to the tracks.

Finding that the rearrangement of trains in the fiddle yard was a rather uninteresting chore for one operator on his well known

Fiddle yards. Typical fiddle yard (a). A traverser fiddle yard (b). Fiddle yard on concealed part of oval (c).

'Buckingham Branch' layout, Peter Denny devised an ingenious detachable 5 track fiddle yard. When all the trains have entered the fiddle yard it is detached, turned end for end reversing all the trains at once, and replaced. Small end doors are slid in to prevent any stock falling from the yard during turning. Operation can then immediately continue. This method has the additional bonus that stock can be stored in the fiddle yard when the layout is not in use. Not only is the stock kept safe from damage but the trains are ready for running as soon as the yard is fixed onto the layout. The Rev Denny has since further developed his fiddle yard by arranging for reversal without detaching. With a mechanism based on Meccano parts the yard is designed to move away a short distance to give clearance, and the whole fiddle yard then rotates as a train turntable to reverse it. The yard is then moved in again to meet the layout.

An alternative to a fiddle yard for turning trains is to use a series of reversing loop tracks but this requires much more space.

A most ingenious form of fiddle yard has been devised by an American modeller, in the form of a train ferry. The model ferry is mounted on a wheeled cart, very much like an old wooden tea trolley, which he has constructed to match the height of his layout. The trains are run onto the ferry which then 'sails' by being wheeled away on its cart. The ferry could be double ended so that it could be wheeled back into place with the trains reversed. Again, a ferry fiddle yard can be used for storage, and there will also be space for storage on the trolley underneath it. Plans for a 4 mm scale train ferry are included in the range of Skinley Blueprints and would enable a modeller to construct a realistic model of a British ferry.

Though fiddle yards and hidden sidings are particularly associated with point-to-point branchline layouts they can also be usefully employed to add operating potential to layouts based on other track patterns. For example, the rear of an oval can be concealed and sidings can be provided here for train holding or for use as a fiddle yard. Similarly on an out and back scheme hidden sidings can be led from the reversing loop.

Extendable layouts

A model railway layout, even a small one, will take some time to build. Indeed, as much of the pleasure of railway modelling is in the construction work we would not want to complete the layout too soon. However, it is nice to be able to alternate building and operating as the mood takes us. Ideally we need a layout which begins small, so that we can get something running on it as soon as possible, but which can be extended in stages thus maintaining its interest. In this way there will be a period of track laying and wiring to reach the next stage, followed by a

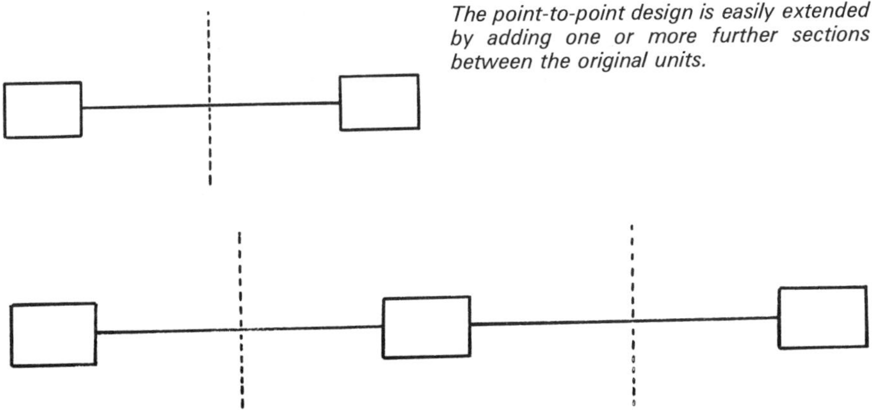

The point-to-point design is easily extended by adding one or more further sections between the original units.

pause to build structures and scenery and perhaps more rolling stock. You can also enjoy operating the extended layout. The layout should be arranged so that it is fully usable at each stage. Thus there will be no need to go on to the next stage until you feel you want to.

The point-to-point type of layout, for example a branch line of the terminus to fiddle yard design, is very easily extended particularly if the terminus and fiddle yard are on separate baseboard sections. All that is needed is to add extra sections between the two original units. At every stage the layout will be fully operational and further sections can be completed at your leisure. Such a system can be very versatile. You can, for example, remove a section you no longer want and replace it with another more interesting one, or you can take one unit out for rebuilding and still run the layout in the meantime. If you want you can even arrange the sections so that they will fit together in more than one order to give extra variety to the operation of the layout. While the additional sections for a point-to-point line will probably be narrow units carrying a single line there is no reason why an oval or spiral should not be included if it suits the space available and you want it.

Many enthusiasts start with an oval track plan, often developed from the train set. The simple oval needs a passing track and a few sidings to make it sufficiently interesting to operate. For the next stage of the layout one of the sidings on the outside of the oval can be extended to form a branch line. This can be carried away from the main oval on an extension of the baseboard or it can be kept on the original base but raised up to a higher level. Alternatively the main oval can be elevated so that the branch can lead down to a reversing loop beneath it.

Another development of the oval is to raise part of it so that it crosses over the level section to result in a spiral point-to-point scheme. There are many possible ways in which the simple oval can be added to and modified particularly if the so called 'cookie cutter' method of baseboard construction is employed. In this system a simple grid frame is used to support a baseboard top of plywood which is fixed on to the frame with screws only. The tracks are then laid and the railway is used until the modeller wants to develop it further. To raise the level of a track saw cuts are made with a keyhole or sabre saw along each side of the track, taking care not to cut the frame beneath the plywood. Any screws holding this strip down are removed and, the strip and the track it supports, are elevated to the required height. Wooden riser blocks are fitted to hold it in its new position.

It is helpful when planning to extend a layout in this way if you have some idea at the beginning how you will want to do this later. You can then put sidings on the original layout at points where branch lines or other tracks will leave the oval later. Thus the points needed will already be in place avoiding the job of taking up part of the track and fitting points in later.

One of the benefits in building up your layout in stages is that you do not need to decide on the details of these later stages until you actually start work on them. Thus the experience you gain from the first part of the layout will influence the form which the extensions will take, and the finished layout will be more likely to meet your eventual requirements.

The oval can be developed by adding branches inside or outside.

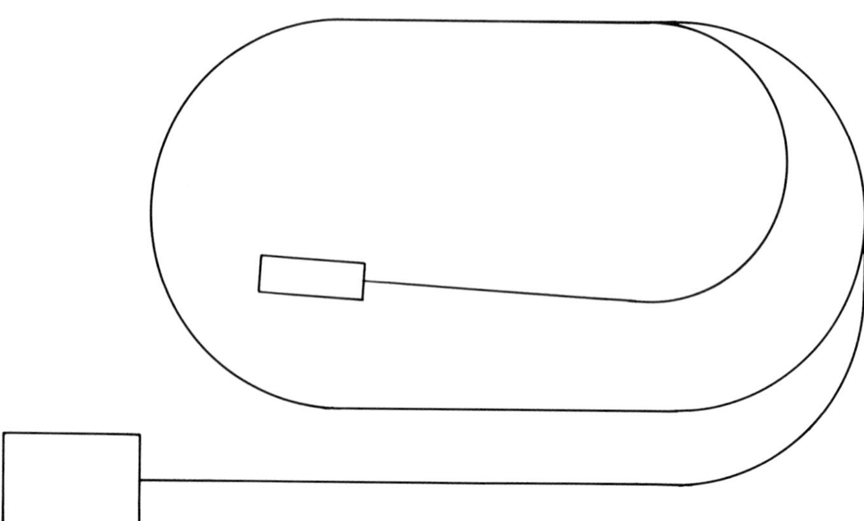

Here two branches have been added but the design is not a good one as a train proceeding from one terminus must reverse, at some stage after reaching the oval, to get onto the other branch.

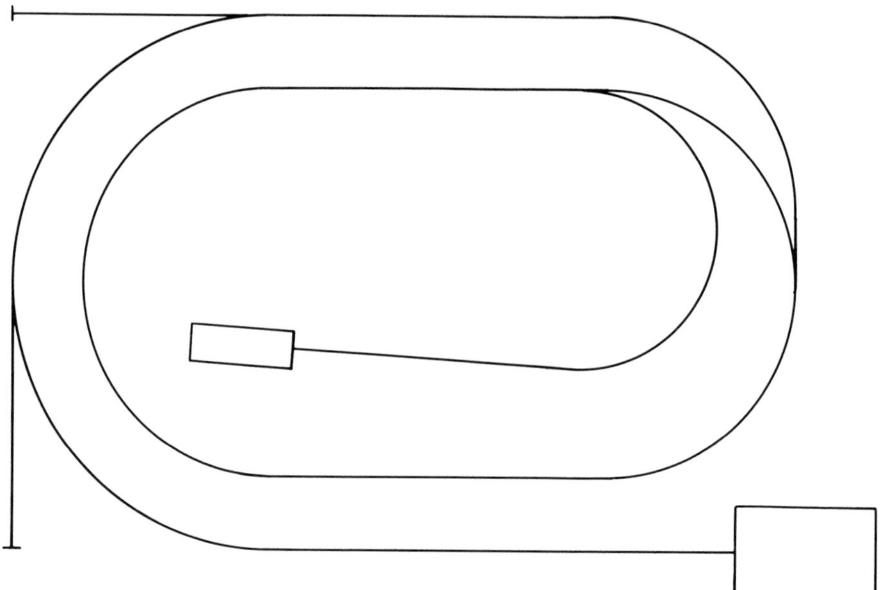

This is the better design and allows interesting operation combining, as it does, a continuous run on the oval with point-to-point operation on the branches.

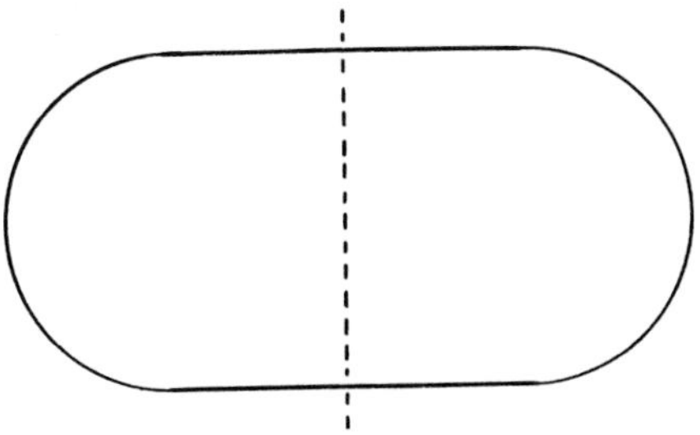

Another method of developing the oval is to divide it as shown (preferably building it in two sections to make this easy), drawing these apart and fitting additional tracks between.

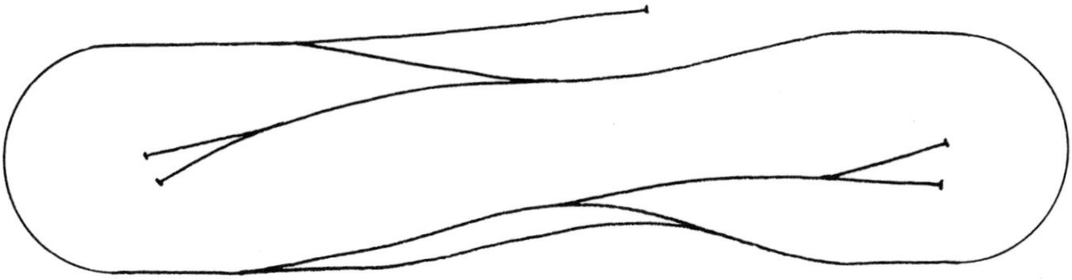

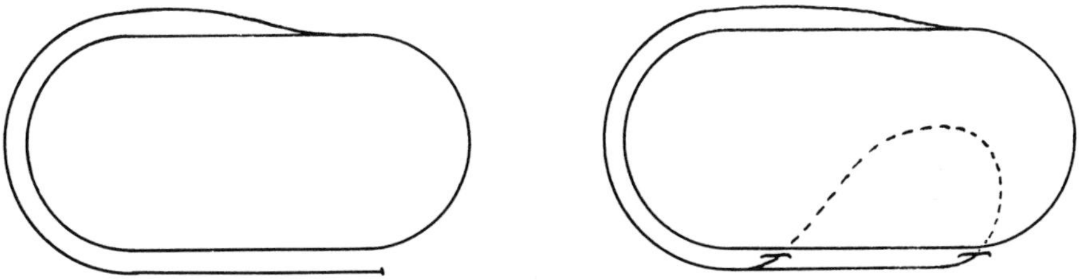

Here the original oval has been elevated so that the branch can go to a reversing loop situated beneath the oval.

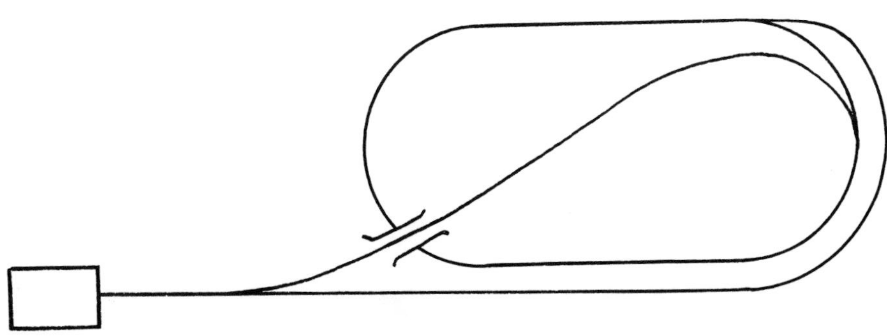

This oval with a single branch has a reversing loop incorporated so that trains can run out and back from the terminus and do as many laps as desired round the oval.

Railway types

On a model railway layout it is quite impossible to include everything and compromise and selection are essential. Obviously it is best to concentrate on the parts of the prototype which interest you most. If your interests are rather varied there is nothing to stop you mixing prototypes and periods on one layout, if you wish, but your model railway is more likely to be satisfying to view and operate if it is more realistic and authentic. The highly accurate and detailed models now available commercially will also look at their best in a proper setting.

Your modelling will benefit from knowledge of the real thing, either from direct observation of the prototype or from the study of photographs, drawings, railway and model railway magazines and books. Though basing your model on the prototype will help realism it is not generally possible, or even desirable, to try to copy part of a real railway exactly. Instead, select the features which you find the most characteristic and appealing, and leave out those you feel are unnecessary or undesirable, so creating your own ideal representation of the prototype.

There are various types of railways depending on the location, circumstances and type of traffic. We can model our layout on any of these and the following listing gives some idea of the possibilities. There is often some overlap between the different categories; it may also be possible to include more than one type of railway on a layout.

Main line

The main lines with their fast long trains are a very interesting and exciting part of the real railways and there is an excellent selection of suitable model locomotives and rolling stock now available, making a main line a tempting choice. However, to do the prototype justice a large layout with a good length of run, large radius curves, double track and platforms able to accommodate long trains is really desirable. A main line 00-scale layout can be built in a small space but this involves considerable compromise. Train lengths of only 4 or 5 coaches and curves of 18 or even 15 in radius may be required. However, some imagination must be used with any model railway layout, and you may be prepared to stretch it further if you are really set on the idea of a main line layout. A convenient arrangement is a continuous run scheme, either a simple oval or a twice around or figure of eight design so that length of run can be achieved by letting the train make a number of laps of the circuit.

Though I am hesitant to recommend it to the beginner for a first effort, because of its greater extent and the need for a lifting section at the door, a layout around the walls of a room is an ideal arrangement if you are sure you want a main line model. If you have a suitable site and you wish to tackle a layout of this type, start very simply with just a single track circuit. Planning in advance where points will be needed later is helpful as they can then be included in the correct positions in the basic circuit as you lay it. In this way you will avoid the need to remove sections of track later to fit the points in. In due course you can install a second circuit to make the line double track. Station tracks, goods yards, an engine depot, sidings and so on can all be added in stages as time and money are available.

An alternative to the continuous run layout is an L-shaped terminus to fiddle yard scheme of the type developed for branch line models, but with the station adapted for main line practice, though again with restricted train lengths. If the layout is fitted into the corner of a room, it could later be extended, if circumstances permit, by introducing new sections between the station and the fiddle yard. Eventually it could be carried right round the room to form a complete circuit, with the station converted from a terminus into a through type.

In N scale a 180° turn can be made on a 2 ft wide board and this makes it possible to model a main line through station on a

The main station on Graham Bailey's modern period British Rail N-scale layout uses parts from three Pola kits for the glass roof while the remainder of the station was scratch-built.

narrow board along one wall, or curved to fit onto an L-shaped baseboard along two walls, with the baseboard widening to 2 ft at each end to accommodate loops to provide continuous running. The loops can be hidden by scenery to conceal their sharp radii and also the fact that the trains go round and round on the layout. If it is important to keep the layout as narrow as possible throughout, 9 in radius Peco Setrack sectional track can be used for the loops and the turn can be made on a baseboard only 20 in wide.

If the modeller merely enjoys seeing his trains run in a realistic setting, but is not concerned about operation, a very simple diorama type of layout can be constructed in N scale which can be fitted along one wall as a shelf. A dog bone track design will produce what appears to be double track main line while the loops at each end, allowing continuous running, can be concealed. The scenic work should be carried out carefully to give a realistic effect. The landscape can rise at the rear of the layout to cover hidden sidings holding other trains.

Branch line

If we want to achieve a model railway as realistic as possible within the restrictions imposed by a small layout we must look for a suitable prototype and the country branch line in the days of steam is an ideal choice. Trains often consisted of only two or three coaches pulled by a small tank engine and the station track layouts were usually fairly simple. An attractive branch line type of layout can easily be developed from the train set oval and can be an ideal first permanent layout with considerable scope for attractive scenery and structures.

During the 1950s the branch line model railway layout concept was developed considerably. The idea was not so much to provide a suitable subject for beginners as to enable more experienced modellers to create a model railway which would look and operate realistically in a small space. The short prototype trains allowed the modeller to run authentic length trains despite the small size of his layout. Also because the station track layouts are simple on branch lines they can be compressed to fit onto a model railway while still retaining their essential features, so that the model can be operated according to prototype practice and following a proper timetable. Rather than copy any particular station exactly, the modeller will usually do better to select desirable features from various prototypes to produce an interesting and attractive station.

A branch line terminus modelled in 00 scale. The layout is operated as a point-to-point line with a fiddle yard at the other end.

Because the aim was realistic operation, the point-to-point track arrangement was preferred to the continuous run schemes and the now classic branch line terminus to fiddle yard (hidden sidings representing the rest of the system) design was developed. Such a track plan can be fitted onto baseboards of various shapes but a popular arrangement is on two narrow baseboards in an L-shape, often fitted into the corner of a room. This design has the advantage of providing the greatest running possibilities in a minimum area and often a layout of this shape can be fitted into a room whereas a conventional rectangular baseboard would not be accept-

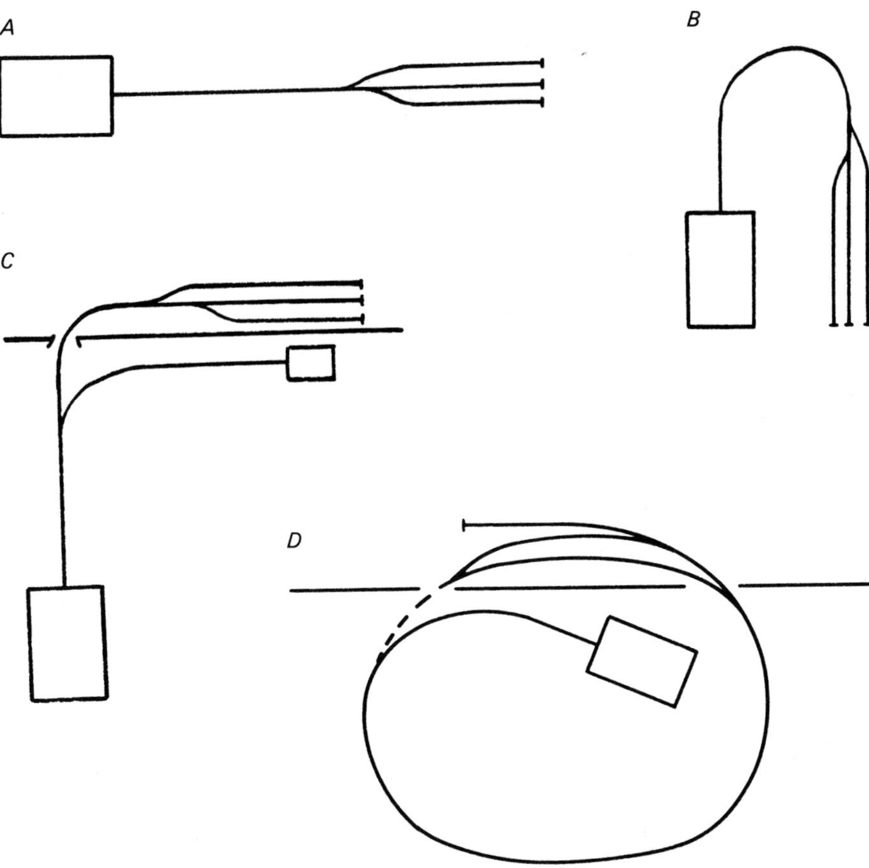

Branch Lines. The basic branch line terminus to fiddle yard design (a). This can be bent to a U-shape if desired (b). An L-shaped terminus to fiddle yard scheme with an additional station, dock, factory or other feature in front of the fiddle yard and separated from it by a backscene (c). The Maurice Deane terminus to fiddle yard design with a backscene separating the two (d). Note the optional link track (dotted) providing a continuous run if required.

able as it would block the centre of the room too much.

A branch line layout of this type is also very suitable for the beginner as it can fairly quickly be brought to a stage where it is interesting to view and operate. However, the scope is limited and in time the modeller will wish to extend the layout. This is another reason for not basing the model accurately on a specific prototype because if you do, once you have completed the model no further development is possible. If, however, your layout is merely based in general terms on the practice of the prototype you have chosen, you are free to alter or add to your model indefinitely.

An interesting alternative to the usual scheme, first employed, I believe, by Maurice Deane, is to fit the branch line on a rectangular baseboard with the fiddle yard behind the terminus but concealed by a low backscene. This has two advantages. The modeller can easily reach both the terminus and the fiddle yard from his operating position in the central well. It also makes it easy to include a link to allow continuous running for locomotives to be run in or when the modeller would like to just sit back and watch the trains in action. The link can be concealed so that the realism of the point-to-point scheme is not impaired.

The branch line provides the opportunity for realistic operation and also has great scenic possibilities. GWR branches are

The Market Redwing GWR branch layout is a portable one which has been exhibited on several occasions. At shows the railway is operated on an hourly programme and the card system illustrated here indicates to the spectators what the next train movement will be. As each operation is completed the next card is turned down.

particularly popular and are very well catered for with commercial models, but other prototypes can also be followed very satisfactorily if preferred.

Modern image

There is considerable interest in modelling present day British Rail, particularly among younger enthusiasts. The locomotive and rolling stock requirements are generally well catered for by the trade with even the High Speed Train available, as a ready-to-run model in 00 and as a kit in N scale. There is a reasonable range of diesels and a few electrics with further models planned in the ready-to-run category and there is also a selection of diesels and multiple units in kit form, particularly from MTK and Q kits which helps to complete the motive power scene. There is also a good variety of rolling stock suitable for a modern layout.

As the mainline will probably be chosen to model, some compromise will be needed on a small layout but there are some advantages to modern image modelling compared to a mainline layout in steam days. In many cases the trains are now shorter and many tracks have been lifted simplifying track layouts and goods yards. Engine servicing facilities are also much simpler with diesel fuel tanks replacing coal and water and with no need for turntables. The modeller can introduce some modern architecture in addition to the older buildings still in use giving an interesting variety. Overhead catenary is also very effective in model form and a working catenary can be assembled from parts made by Vollmer or Sommerfeldt. In this case two trains can be controlled independently on the same stretch of track, one from the track as usual and one from the overhead.

One of the great advantages of modelling modern railways is that one can still study the real thing easily to gain information on anything from locomotives down to small details such as signs and noticeboards. On the goods side a Freightliner depot would make an interesting working model. As modern trains are often run as block units

The attractive Hornby 00-scale model of the British Rail High Speed Train seen on the exhibition layout of the Bournemouth & Isle of Purbeck MRC. Note the non-operating model of a miniature railway on the promenade below the station and the beach at lower right.

Mike Sharman has constructed a fine Victorian period 4 mm scale layout which features standard-, narrow- and broad-gauge track together with some complex multiple gauge trackwork. Careful research and accurate modelling, mostly from scratch, has recreated the atmosphere of the railways of that period very effectively. Locomotive No 10 is a model of Timothy Hackworth's 0-6-0 built in 1838 for the Stockton & Darlington Railway and is the oldest prototype represented on the layout. The working beam engine behind No 10 was also scratch-built.

there is rather less opportunity for train marshalling and shunting on a modern layout, but we can still install some industrial sidings for local shunting.

Period

Though strictly the term refers to any era, including the present, I use it here to mean historical, for any time prior to the contemporary scene. Construction of an historical layout requires research and also care to avoid introducing anachronisms. Depending on the period chosen the modeller may also have to build more or less all his locomotives and rolling stock himself.

The most popular period seems to be the pre-nationalisation era, particularly of the 1930s, and of the four main railway companies, the LMS, the LNER, the SR and the GWR, the greatest following is for the GWR, with especial interest in its branch-lines. There is now a good selection of ready-to-run models and kits enabling the modeller to construct a successful model of this type.

A period which has many advantages but which is not yet particularly popular is the post-nationalisation era of the 1950s. A layout based on this period can mix an interesting variety of steam, diesel and electric locomotives and of rolling stock. The modeller is well served with commercial models and there is no problem in obtaining information and photographs.

At the other end of the time scale are the early Victorian railways. The modeller who chooses these as his prototype will need to carry out considerable research and there is little available commercially to help him in construction. However, if well executed such a layout can be most interesting and attractive. Mike Sharman has built a superb 4 mm scale layout of this period; careful research and skilled scratch-building has created an authentic atmosphere as can be seen in the above photograph.

Going back to even earlier times, 1825-30, the American MRC of Darlington chose the Stockton & Darlington Railway as their prototype and built a fascinating model of great historical interest for the Rail 150 exhibition in 1975. The scale was also 4 mm.

A view of W. T. Butler's Dalcross layout, a 4 mm scale model of a 19th century ironworks. The accurate modelling of an unusual prototype and the inclusion of many small, but authentic details, has resulted in a fascinating model. The locomotives, rolling stock, structures and steam lorries were all hand-built.

Industrial

The industrial railway layout has considerable potential in a small space as it can be essentially a shunting layout and need not have an oval or other form of continuous run, though one can be included if desired and if there is sufficient space. In its simplest form the track plan need only have a run-around loop and a number of sidings though the addition of hidden sidings or a fiddle yard, concealed by structures, low relief buildings or a backscene, will add to the operating potential. For a long, narrow layout the switchback type of track plan is useful for an industrial line, while if a rectangular baseboard can be used an oval with sidings can be a convenient track arrangement.

As the locomotives will be small steam or diesel engines and the rolling stock mainly goods vehicles, the layout can have sharp

There are many prototype industries which can be adapted to make interesting features for model railway layouts. This small scrap yard in 4 mm scale was based on a yard in Newcastle but was considerably compressed to suit the space available on a layout.

curves. If the modeller wishes he can include some interesting trackwork as the prototype is often cramped and needs slips, 3-way or lap points, curved points and crossings. The track is often set into roads or wharves so that road vehicles can cross the tracks easily and this should also be represented on the model.

There is a good selection of suitable small locomotives in ready-to-run and kit form. Centre Models have specialised in industrial steam locomotives, offering cast metal kits for four different types in 00 scale, and some of the smaller engines made by other cast metal kit manufacturers are also ideal for a layout of this type. A wide range of suitable rolling stock both ready-to-run and in kit form is on the market.

The layout can be based on one major industry such as a mine and processing plant, a large factory or a shipyard, or can represent an industrial area or estate with a variety of different types of industries giving scope for a wide range of rolling stock. A dock or canal is often very attractive in model form.

The small size of N scale makes it possible to represent the larger industries more realistically than is usually possible in 00 scale. Graham Bailey modelled this shipbuilding yard for his N-scale British Rail layout using a modified Novo Shell Welder kit as the ship under construction.

An industrial layout also offers excellent opportunities for structure modelling and detailing. Because the prototype is often cramped, with tracks winding between numerous buildings we can fit a great deal into a small area on a layout without loss of realism. There are a number of fine kits for industrial structures on the market, mainly plastic kits manufactured on the Continent. These can be modified and combined to produce even greater variety or the modeller can scratch-build his structures, perhaps following actual prototypes. Several working models are also available as kits including a dock crane, a gantry crane, an aerial ropeway, gravel loaders and a conveyor belt, and these will add extra activity and interest to the layout. The possibilities for detailing an industrial model railway layout are almost limitless and the modeller might like to illuminate the buildings, perhaps employing fibre optics.

If the opportunity arises to build a larger layout eventually the industrial layout can be incorporated into it forming a factory area which can generate much interesting traffic and shunting activity.

Narrow gauge

Not only are the narrow-gauge prototypes very attractive and appealing but they also have many other features which make them ideal subjects for modelling. The short trains, small locomotives and rolling stock, sharp curves, steep gradients and simple station track plans are all useful to the enthusiast trying to fit a model railway into a small space.

The modeller may choose to base his layout on one of the preserved lines, either as it is today or as it was in its earlier days. There are a number of locomotive and rolling stock kits now available, mainly in 009, for British prototypes which will assist the modeller in a project of this sort but he will also need to do some converting and scratch-building to complete the roster. Obviously if the modeller chooses to represent the line as it is today there will be no problem in gaining accurate information about the railway and its stock. There is also a good deal of data available about the better known railways in their earlier days so it should not be too difficult to make an authentic model.

Alternatively, the enthusiast may prefer to model an imaginery line thus giving him more scope for introducing features he finds interesting or attractive. He may base his model in a general way on one prototype or perhaps on aspects of several.

The Vale of Tallynog is a model of a small Welsh narrow-gauge railway constructed by Phil Savage, a member of the Wessex 009 Society. The fiddle yard can be seen behind the retaining wall. The excellent detailing of the railway terminus and dock gives the layout a very realistic appearance.

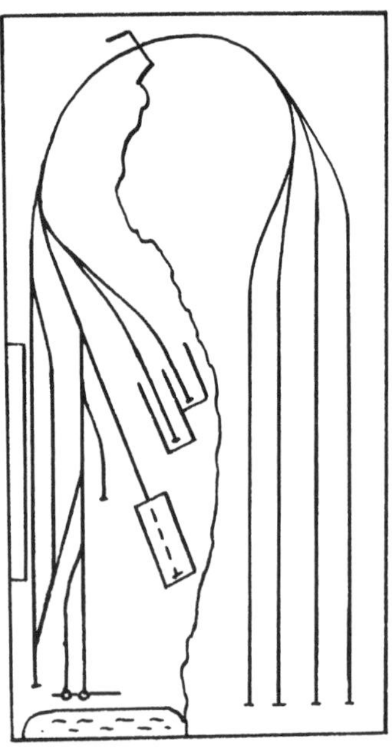

Track plan for Phil Savage's 009 Vale of Tallynog layout, a U-shaped terminus to fiddle yard design. (Plan not to scale.)

Many of the overseas narrow-gauge lines are also very appealing and with the selection of ready-to-run models, particularly Swiss and Austrian prototypes, in HO9 a layout can be built without difficulty. For realism, the modeller should try to create the atmosphere of the original by studying book or magazine pictures and perhaps by visiting the real thing on holiday. The track arrangements differ from those typical of British practice and the model should be based on actual track plans if possible. While the availability of ready-to-run equipment and the greater familiarity of European prototypes tempts modellers to choose these there are many attractive narrow-gauge railways in other parts of the world which could also make excellent layouts. An example is Howard Coulson's 'Eitomo' layout in 009 based on East African prototypes. Study of the real thing from books and magazines together with good scenic work has enabled Howard to capture the atmosphere of these lines very effectively. Most of his locomotives and rolling stock are conversions of commercially available 009 or N-scale models and are closely based on East African prototypes.

Many American narrow-gauge modellers work in HOn3, HO-scale models of 3 ft gauge

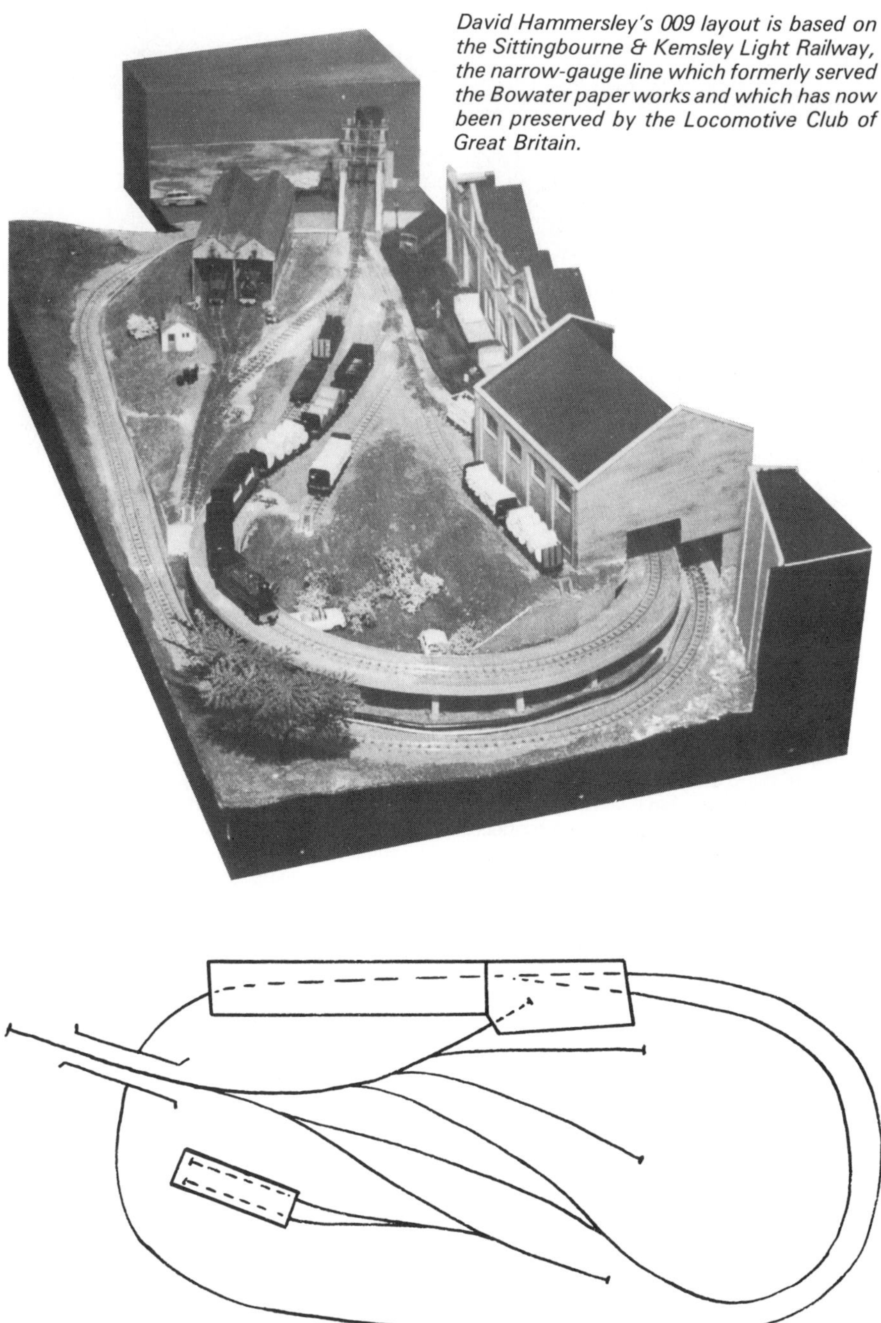

David Hammersley's 009 layout is based on the Sittingbourne & Kemsley Light Railway, the narrow-gauge line which formerly served the Bowater paper works and which has now been preserved by the Locomotive Club of Great Britain.

Track plan of the 009 layout built by David Hammersley and based on the Bowater Railway. The track design is an oval, partly concealed by structures, with a branch rising from it to the higher central part of the layout. (Plan is not to scale.)

Howard Coulson has based his 009 narrow-gauge 'Eitomo' layout on East African prototype lines. With careful research and imaginative modelling he has given his layout the atmosphere of the real thing. The locomotives (including the Climax shown here) and rolling stock are mostly conversions of commercial 009- and N-scale products.

prototypes, but some are using 9 mm gauge to model lines such as the Maine 2 ft gauge railways in HO scale, and this would be a more convenient choice for modellers in Britain as there are more commercial items available for conversion.

The introduction of ready-to-run models in 009 led to the development of the so-called 'rabbit' layouts. Modellers took advantage of the sharp curves and steep gradients possible in this scale to pack a great deal of track at various levels onto a very small baseboard, with mountainous scenery and with trains popping in and out of tunnels like rabbits in and out of burrows. Realism is of course compromised but the layouts are very entertaining to build and operate. With good scenery they are very attractive and make an ideal coffee table or display layout for the lounge.

An alternative to an entire layout in narrow gauge is the addition of a narrow-gauge feeder to a standard-gauge layout. This is an ideal arrangement as it gives you a chance to see how you like narrow-gauge modelling without committing yourself to more than a short length of track to start with. If you like it you can then extend the narrow-gauge section. I should perhaps warn you that there is a tendency for it to take over at the expense of the standard gauge! A narrow-gauge line will add interest and extra activity to the layout using only space which would not be of much use for standard-gauge tracks.

Combining standard and narrow gauge on the layout gives the opportunity for including interesting dual-gauge trackwork. However, with the exception of a dual 16.5 mm/9 mm gauge crossing made by Liliput, you will have to build any dual-gauge track yourself, a task for the more experienced modeller.

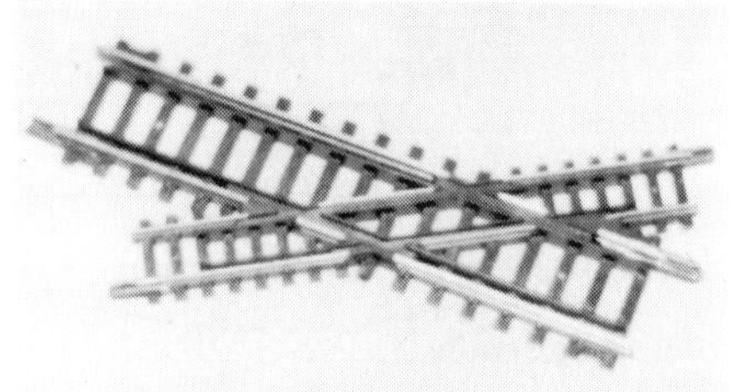

Liliput make this crossing for 00 gauge (16.5 mm) and 009 (9 mm) which may be useful when combining a standard- and narrow-gauge line on a layout.

Foreign

I have made some mention of modelling foreign railways in the section on narrow gauge and similar principles apply to standard gauge with regard to familiarising yourself with everything about the prototype and its setting if you hope to create a realistic

This 009 narrow-gauge layout owned by the Poole & District Model Railway Society measures only 36 in × 27 in but includes a track run of over 12 ft, two sidings, two stations and many interesting scenic features! It is an example of the so-called rabbit layout.

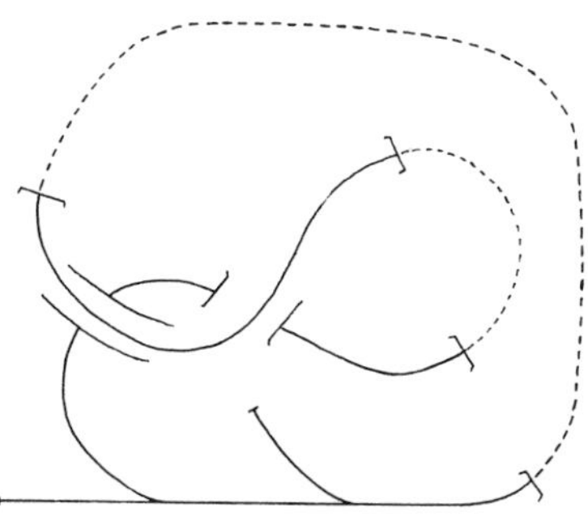

The Poole & District MRS 009 layout is a simple 'rabbit' type with a dog bone design where one loop partly overlaps the other. Two sidings add extra interest. (Plan not to scale.)

model. Operating practice and track layout is often rather different from the British system and this should be taken into account when designing a layout.

For US modelling the range of ready-to-run models, kits and parts in HO and N scales is excellent and the enthusiast can obtain a great deal of information about modelling American railroads from reading one or more of the excellent model railroad magazines produced in the States.

The range of European models in HO and N scales is also very good though the emphasis is almost entirely on ready-to-run equipment; this is generally of excellent quality. Some countries, particularly Germany, France and Switzerland, are very well catered for by the manufacturers but for others there is much less available. There is a good deal of prototype information, in England, for the modeller and several countries have model railway magazines, though here there may be language problems of course. Ideally one should visit the country concerned and take as many photographs as possible to guide you in modelling the setting, the trackside details and so on.

For other countries of the world much converting or scratch-building will be required to complete a layout and such a project is only suitable for the more experienced modeller with a particular interest in and knowledge of the railway system concerned.

Preserved line

I briefly mentioned the possibility of modelling a preserved line in the narrow-gauge section. For the modeller who likes, and has perhaps already collected, a wide variety of locomotives which would not normally be seen together because of their origins, period or type, a very attractive solution can be a preserved standard-gauge line. One could even include some foreign

A scene on a typical US branchline modelled in HO scale. The beautifully detailed corrugated iron warehouse was built from a Campbell's kit. (Photograph by courtesy of Leo Campbell.)

Jouef offer a wide selection of French prototype models in HO scale including this interesting train of double-decker commuter coaches seen here on the Hestair Models' exhibition layout.

engines if desired as there are several prototype precedents for this!

The modeller might like to base his layout on an actual preserved line. This has the advantage that he can visit the railway to see and photograph everything and there is often plenty of published data about the locomotives, rolling stock and so on. The model could be a representation of the line as it is, or as the preservation society hope to make it. Such a model could be very satisfying and could also have considerable publicity value for the railway. Providing locomotives and stock for most lines should not be a problem using the standard commercial products.

Another approach would be to model a branch line you like and which has been closed, as though it had been preserved. This will give you more freedom in the design of the layout and in the choice of locomotives and rolling stock than if you were modelling an actual preserved line. A third alternative is to model an entirely imaginary preserved line of your own design.

There are many interesting details which could be added to a layout of this type. There may be locomotives and stock awaiting or undergoing repair, some scrapped items kept to provide spare parts for other stock, many parts lying around, and numerous visitors, some with cameras taking pictures. There could also be a small museum of other items such as traction engines, vintage cars or buses, and so on.

If you model a station on the preserved line as one combined with British Rail then you have the perfect excuse for including everything from vintage steam engines on the preserved line to the High Speed Train on the BR tracks! All on the one layout!

The working traverser on Mike Sharman's period layout with its nicely detailed vertical boilered donkey engine. The locomotive is 'Pegasus' a 2-4-0 built in 1870 by Joseph Beattie for the London & South Western Railway. Locomotive and traverser were both hand-built.

More specialised railway types

Engine depot

One approach to modelling on a small layout is to choose a prototype line which can be compressed without losing its essential features, the branch line being a good example. Another method can be to select a small part of a larger prototype system and model only that section. As many modellers buy or build more and larger locomotives than can reasonably be accommodated on the usual small layout, an apt choice can be to model a motive power depot. Such a model need occupy only a small area but will be ideal as a setting for displaying and operating locomotive models. If hidden sidings are included the layout could even be

Part of the garden railway layout built by Dave Howsam and Ron Prattley. Figures, plants and garden fittings are Britains' models. (Photo by Ron Prattley.)

operated to a timetable, with locomotives leaving the shed, taking on coal and water and proceeding to their duties. Later they will return from the hidden sidings to be prepared for the next day's work.

Though such a layout is unusual it could be interesting to build, with plenty of opportunities for super-detailing interesting structures and, if desired, a turntable. A crane and a snowplough are among the items of unusual rolling stock which can be stored on sidings on the layout. Extra details could include a hoist and perhaps an engine undergoing repairs, or one which has been scrapped. The scope of the model can be increased by providing facilities for diesels as well.

A layout of this type could be ideal for the modeller who is a club member and can enjoy more conventional operating on the club layout but wants somewhere to display his locomotives. It is also a useful unit for the modeller who has no space for a layout at present but is building up a collection of locomotive models for the time when he will be able to construct a layout. The engine depot will allow him to enjoy some construction work, provide a setting for his engines and can be incorporated into a layout later.

Military railways

From the American Civil War right through to the Second World War, railways have played an important military role. With the great popularity of both railway and military modelling I am sure that many enthusiasts are interested in both and I am surprised that so few military railway layouts have been built. The ideal prototype would perhaps be the extensive narrow-gauge railway system which operated in France during the First World War. *Light Railways of the First World War* by W.J.K. Davies (David & Charles) covers this subject in detail, even including dimensioned drawings of the locomotives and rolling stock. In 009 the equipment could be represented well with commercially available items, modified in some cases. Such a layout could be built in a small space and the scenic work could be very effective, with ruined buildings, First World War tanks, soldiers and horse drawn equipment, trenches, look-out posts and so on. The Airfix 00-scale military models would be especially useful in this detailing.

Some of the most interesting and impressive pieces of military railway equipment are the railway guns, and the enthusiast may well like to include several of these models on his layout. One approach might be to construct an industrial railway layout based on a factory producing these guns. Such a model would permit shunting and also act as an effective setting for displaying the model rail guns.

A different type of military railway layout would be one based on one of the military railways operated in Britain. The Longmoor Military Railway used for training army personnel in railway operating has been well documented and could make an interesting model. The Royal Aircraft Establishment railway at Farnborough would make an unusual variant on the industrial railway theme. The major traffic here is coal brought in by rail to the power station, but wood and steel sections are also transported.

Rack railways

Mountain railways may be fitted with a rack in the centre of the track with which a driven gear on the locomotives meshes thus ensuring good traction and no slipping. The only British prototype is the Snowdon Mountain Railway.

In model form Fleischmann provide locomotives and track, but no points, for both HO and N scales. The lack of points mean that only a simple single track line can be constructed unless the modeller is prepared to make points himself. However, a rack railway can be an attractive addition to a conventional layout, providing extra activity and an excuse for some mountainous scenery.

Underground railways

Underground railways have been rather neglected by modellers though there does seem to have been more interest recently with the appearance of a few layouts including models of London Transport tube trains, one built by an enthusiast in Holland! An LT layout would make an interesting model. Much of the track should be modelled on parts of the system above ground with only part of it in tunnels. Alternatively, an underground model could be added to an ordinary urban or suburban area layout, in which case it might be best to keep it entirely beneath ground level so that it does not take up space which could be used for the rest of the layout.

Garden railway

Dave Howsam and Ron Prattley produced a most unusual but attractive model some years ago of a garden in 10 mm to the foot scale using Britains' figures and garden fittings with N-scale model locomotives,

ESSO

The relatively small size of N-scale models has enabled Graham Bailey to provide comprehensive steam and diesel locomotive servicing facilities on his moderate sized British Rail layout. These include a steam locomotive roundhouse (above left), coaling stage (above), diesel engine house (left), diesel fuelling depot (below left) and a train washing unit (below).

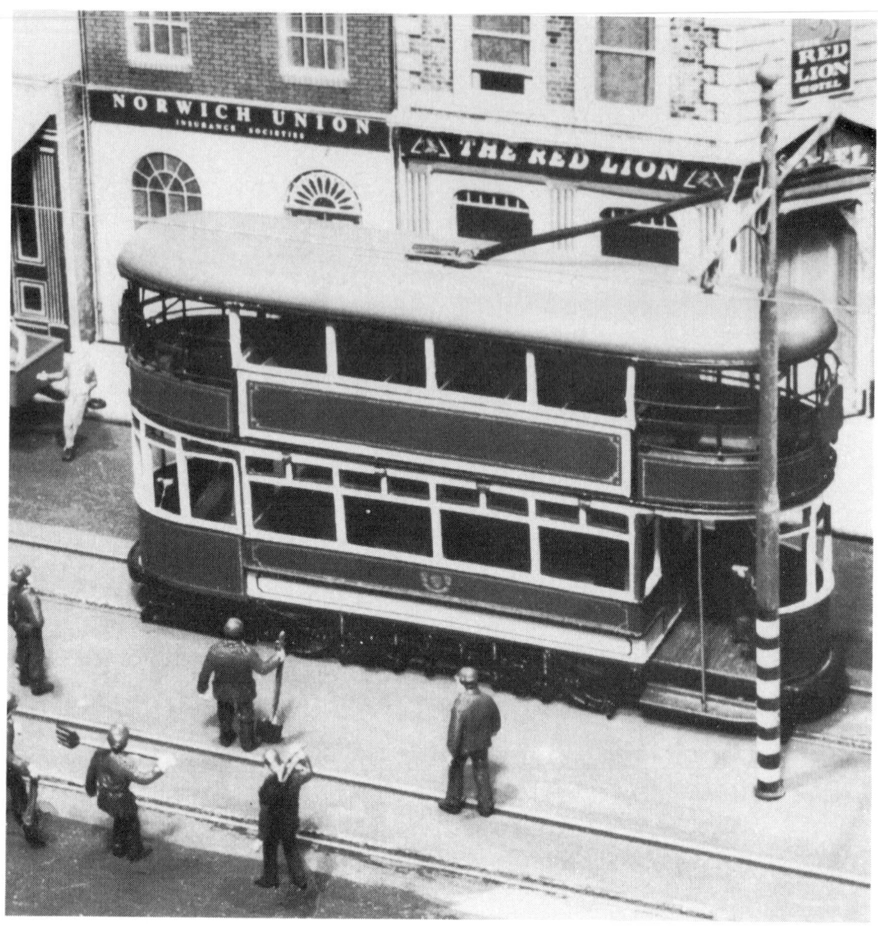

A model tramway system can be an interesting addition to a model railway layout. The two views above and right are of Adrian Swain's 00-scale tramway. British tram models are available in 00 and N scales as cast metal kits; Continental prototype models are manufactured as ready-to-run items in HO and N scales.

rolling stock and track representing a 10¼ in gauge garden railway. The track layout on this model was very simple so operating scope was limited but the layout was intended especially for display and was very successful. There is no reason why a more extensive system could not be modelled in this way. A miniature railway, though not of course in the garden, which would make a very interesting prototype for a project of this sort is the well known Ravenglass & Eskdale Railway.

Monorails

These make intriguing models but do call for scratch-building by the modeller. Though model monorails are rather rare, the Listowel & Ballybunion (an early Irish monorail) seems to be an appealing prototype, perhaps because it is so unusual. I know of models of this line in various scales by no fewer than five modellers; the largest of these models are the superb 16 mm scale locomotives made by Don Boreham and Adrian Garner.

Trams

Trams are not strictly railway models in the usual sense, though a tramway layout can be very appealing. The sharp curves and short 'trains' (for British prototypes usually a single

tramcar, though European trams often pull trailers) enable an interesting layout to be built in a small area. As the setting will probably be an urban one the possibilities for structure modelling and detailing are considerable. A tram system can also be added to a model railway layout and will increase the action on the layout, even with a very simple tram system.

Ready-to-run European tram models are available in HO and N scales while British cast metal kits are made in 00 and N scales. A few HO-scale German prototype cast metal tram kits are also produced.

Most modellers will want to build a conventional type of layout, the branch line and industrial railway being particularly suitable for the beginner. However, I feel it is worth while to indicate, as I have above, that the possible scope in the hobby is much wider than that; it is always worth while considering something a little different for your modelling, provided it is a subject which appeals to you and in which you are sufficiently interested to do any research which is necessary.

Track planning

00 scale

Having looked at the basic track schemes and considered the various types of railways that can be modelled we have reached the stage of planning the track arrangement for a layout. The usual method is to draw to scale the outline of the layout baseboard and then to plot in the tracks on this plan. A convenient scale is 1 in to the foot or, for small layouts, even 2 in to the foot. Unfortunately many plans are not drawn properly, either through lack of care or due to a desire to squeeze that little bit more into the layout. The errors particularly relate to points, for which inadequate allowance is made for lengths and radii, and to clearances which are insufficient. It is very important to draw everything accurately to scale as errors here will cause problems later when you try to construct the layout. Though a neatly drawn out plan (complete with attractive scenic details sketched in) looks very nice it is by no means necessary for this planning work. A roughly drawn plan is perfectly adequate provided the modeller keeps accurately to scale measurements.

Tracks should be arranged so that the centre lines are not less than 1½ in from the baseboard edge and a greater clearance is better if it is possible. The track centres for 2 tracks running parallel should be 2 in apart. The curve radius chosen as the minimum will depend on the type of equipment that will be run on the layout, on the space available and on the type of railway modelled. The usual minimum for proprietary models is 15 in radius, but 18 or 24 in curves are desirable, and curves of larger radius still will look better if they can be accommodated. When plotting the track positions we must start a curve at a point a distance at least equal to the radius of the curve plus the clearance needed, from the end of the layout. If the curve can be started further back we can either use a larger radius curve or allow more clearance. As the curve is often one of 180° at the end of the layout we must also check on the width, which will be twice the sum of the radius and the clearance, in relation to the baseboard width. The appearance of small radius curves can be improved considerably by fitting a curve of twice the radius between the straight and the true curve as a transitional section. This will require more space than the simple minimum radius curve, of course, and suitable allowance must be made if you wish to do this.

Points are more difficult to draw to scale and care should be taken to allow sufficient space for them. You should measure the points you intend to use and use this length as a guide, preferably allowing a little extra to give you some leeway in case of any slight errors during track laying. For example, I allow 7 in for Hornby, 8 in for Peco 2 ft radius, and 9 in for Peco 3 ft radius points, and 8 in for a Peco crossing. I want to stress that you should stick closely to the measurements for points and crossings and resist any temptation to cut things finer. These parts cannot be altered so if you have not allowed the right amount of space your layout will not be correct—other parts being distorted with detrimental effects.

A fairly commonly employed track arrangement is a reversing loop. This requires a distance of three times the radius of the curves for the loop itself, together with another radius on the end to join with the other tracks. The width of the loop is twice the radius. Clearances must be added to these figures.

If one track is to pass over another a clearance of at least 2½ in and preferably 3 in is required. As the maximum gradient that should be used is 1 in 30 a distance of 90 in, 7 ft 6 in, is needed to clear the low level track if only one track is on a gradient. If one track rises and the other falls, both at 1 in 30, the distance is halved to 45 in, 3 ft 9 in respectively. These figures assume the more desirable minimum of 3 in clearance is adopted. If the track is curved we need to

Diagram A

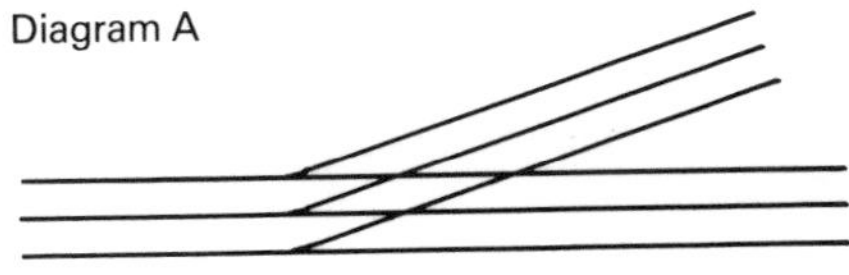

Diagram B

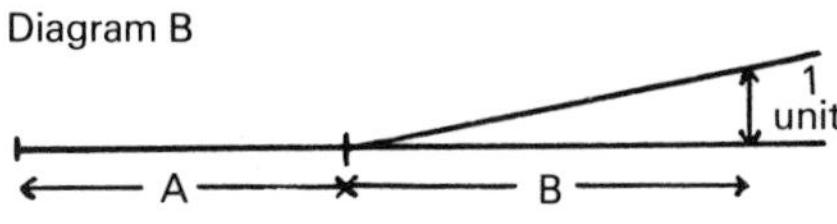

Track planning in 00 scale *Many modellers when drawing out a scale plan make the points too short and give them too wide an angle; this causes problems when you try to construct the layout as the points will not fit into the space allowed.*

If we draw in the centre lines for the straight and diverging tracks on a pair of points as in Diagram A we can see there is a point at which these lines meet and that they meet at an angle. To draw points accurately on our track plans we need to locate the point at which the lines meet correctly and to draw the true angle from it.

We can do this as in Diagram B, using the dimensions given in the table for 'A' and 'B', and we can then be confident that the plan will be accurate with respect to the points.

Point radius	'A'	'B'
18 inch	*2½ inch*	*3½ units*
24 inch	*3 inch*	*4 units*
36 inch	*3½ inch*	*5 units*

These dimensions are easily obtained by measuring directly the points you intend to use and you can make your own listing to suit your choice of points.

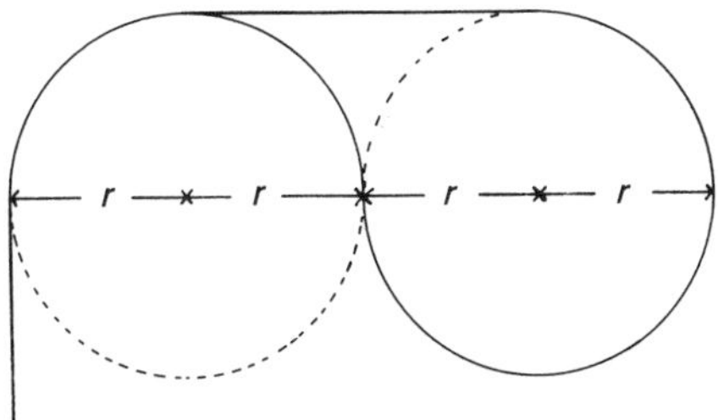

The reversing loop together with a lead out is equivalent in space to two circles side by side and the length required is therefore at least four times the minimum radius.

know its length for working out the gradient. As the circumference of a circle is given by $2\pi r$ we will be close enough if we call π 3 and reckon the circumference as 6 times the radius. That is in every ¼ circle the track distance is 1½ times the radius. For 18 in radius curves therefore, the distance for a quarter circle is 27 in.

Station platforms will be 4½-5 in wide and the platform edge should be an inch from the track centre line. Platform lengths depend on the train lengths and a convenient estimate is to allow 1 ft per coach. If platforms must be short, model a small station and keep train lengths down also. Stations are usually modelled with straight platforms but the introduction of a slight curve can be attractive.

A terminus station will need a run-around loop so that the engine can be moved to the other end of the train for the return journey. The loop can either go alongside the platform or can be on the line beyond the platform so it may also be used for goods trains. The loop must, of course, be long enough to hold the trains and there must also be sufficient room on the track beyond it for the locomotive, say 8 in for a tank engine and as much as 12 in for a tender locomotive.

Goods facilities can be very simple, merely a siding or two entered by trailing points, or there may be a larger yard with a headshunt, so that shunting can take place without blocking the main line. A run-around loop may be provided but often the passenger loop can be shared. When planning sidings and passing loops try to avoid reverse or 'S' curves.

Kick-back sidings are sometimes included on a model railway layout. Access to one of these is only possible if the siding from which it leads is empty already or is cleared at the time. Because of this the modeller may find that he does not use the kick-back siding as he does not want to be bothered with carrying out the extra moves required. Conversely, however, we can take the view that anything which involves more shunting movements adds to the operating activity and makes the layout more interesting. It is a matter of personal choice whether you want to keep operation simple and easy or to make it as complex as you can. Modellers who particularly enjoy operation and shunting may choose to model an industrial line on which numerous complications such as kick-back sidings, several industries being served by one siding making access more difficult, and so on, can be introduced.

Engine servicing facilities may also be very

Some examples of station plans—not to scale.

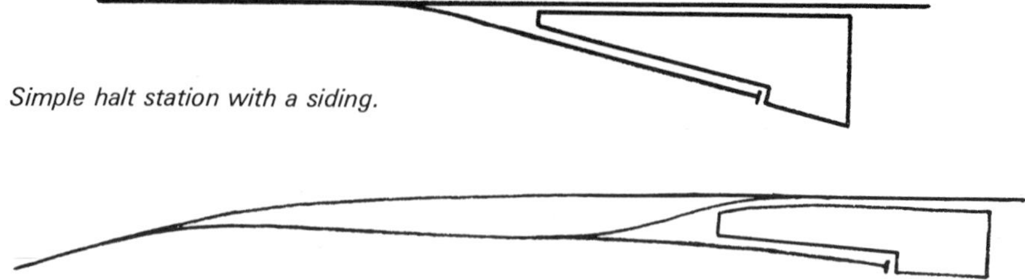

Simple halt station with a siding.

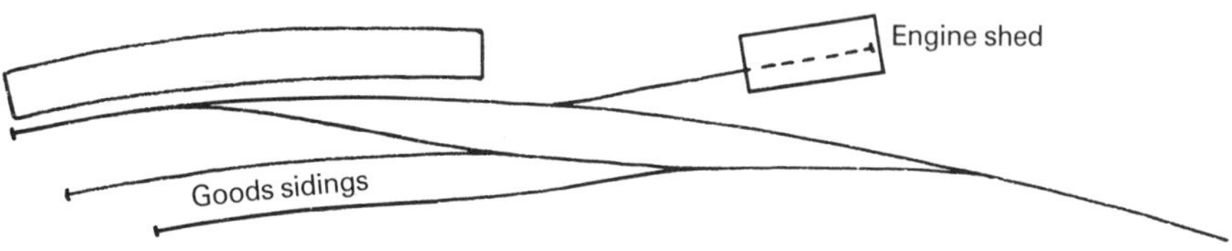

Simple through station with run around loop so trains from either direction can shunt the siding and so trains can be reversed. The loop can also double up as a siding.

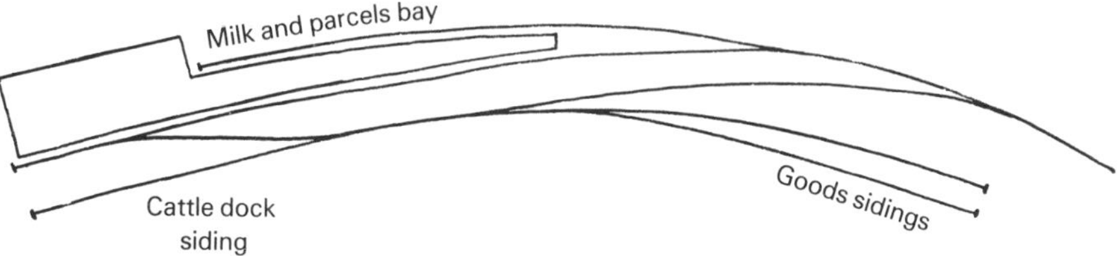

Small terminus station with run-around loop, goods sidings and engine shed.

Slightly larger terminus station with parcels, milk and cattle dock sidings but no engine shed.

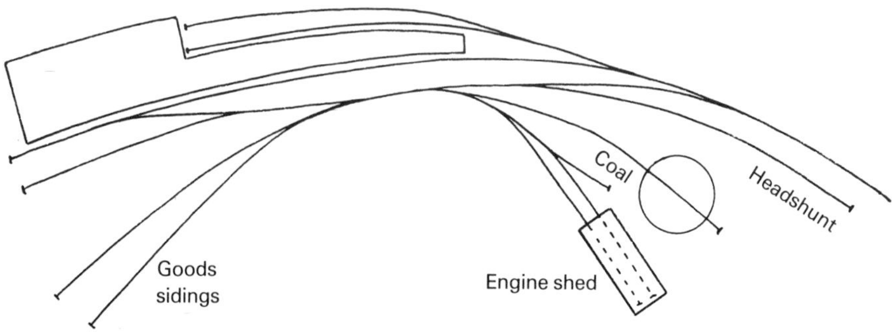

Larger terminus station with more comprehensive engine servicing facilities including a turntable so tender locomotives can be turned. A headshunt has been provided so shunting can be carried out without blocking the main line.

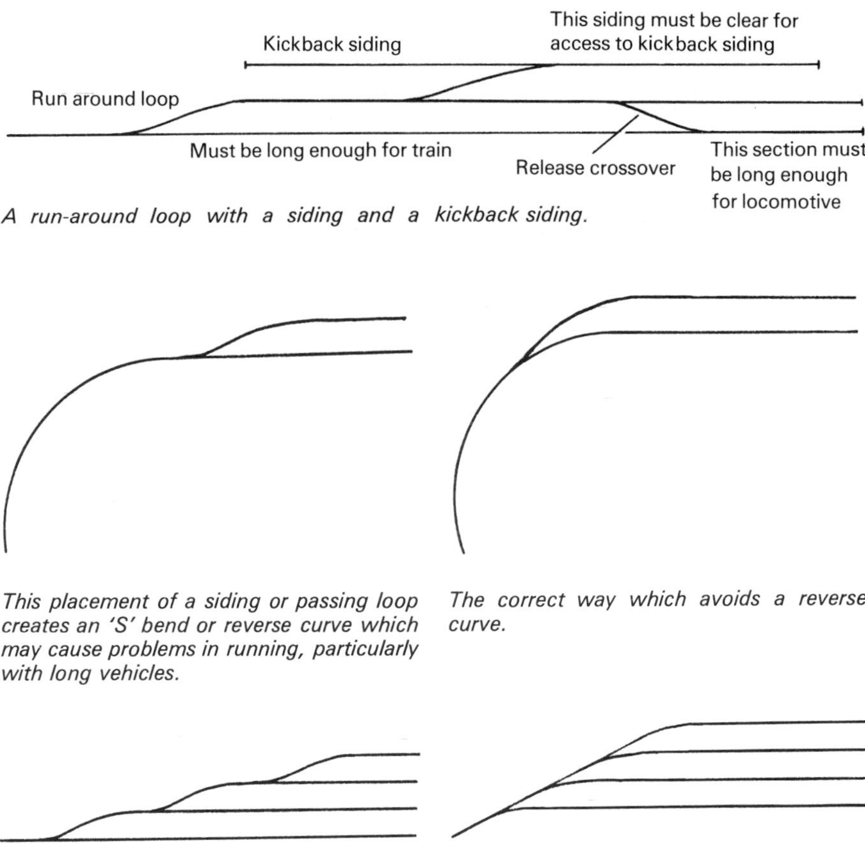

A run-around loop with a siding and a kickback siding.

This placement of a siding or passing loop creates an 'S' bend or reverse curve which may cause problems in running, particularly with long vehicles.

The correct way which avoids a reverse curve.

This arrangement of sidings creates a whole series of reverse curves and also wastes space.

The correct design for a series of sidings.

simple, merely a single track engine shed with coaling stage, water tower and ash pit for one engine at a branch line terminus, or a larger depot may be modelled with a 2 or 3 track shed and perhaps a turntable for tender locomotives. If a point-to-point system has a turntable at one terminus there should also be one at the other terminus (except, of course, if it is a fiddle yard) so that engines can always run facing the correct way. A turntable is quite a large feature so you should consider carefully before including one if you are short of space. A 9 in diameter table will accommodate small engines but larger locomotives will need an 11 in table.

It is essential to provide proper access to track, points and rolling stock; check your own easy reach at the height you intend to have your layout and use this as a guide when planning the layout. If you want to have a central operating well do not make this too small; 4 ft × 2ft is a reasonable minimum. Make sure that access to tunnels will also be easy.

For the actual drawing out only fairly simple drawing instruments are needed; a sharp pencil, a pair of compasses, a set square, a ruler and an eraser are the essentials. Templates, for the curves you will be using in the scale of your drawing, can be cut from card or, even better, transparent plastic, and will be very useful. Many modellers work on white card rather than on paper when drawing up layout plans as frequent alterations can be made without crumpling the material or spoiling the surface.

While it is very convenient to draw out plans to 1 or 2 in to the foot scale in the early stages, there is much to be said for drawing

Small motive power depots.

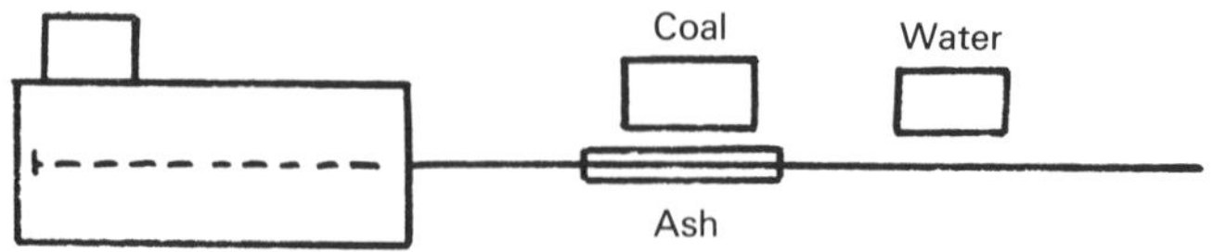

Very simple engine facilities for a small station.

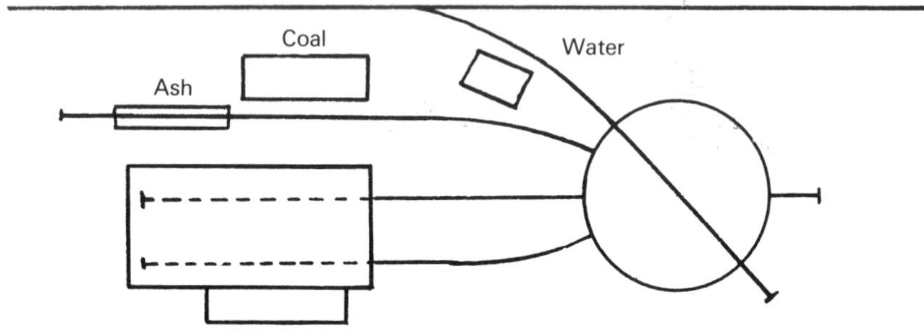

Larger dead-end type of shed with turntable.

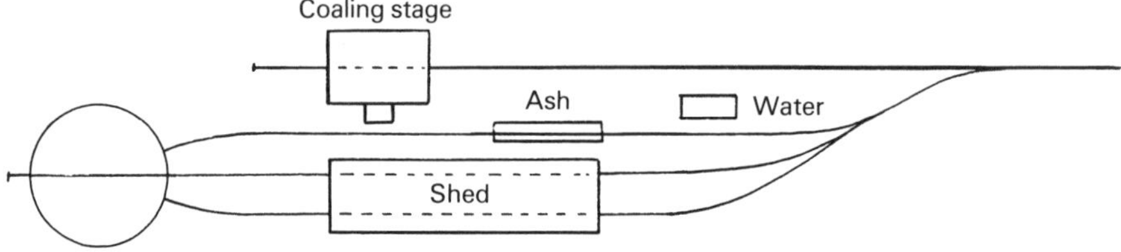

Through type of engine shed with turntable.

out your plan full size when you have reached what you think may be your final design. Lining paper used for wall-papering is cheap and convenient for this purpose. You will need a long ruler, a pencil, an eraser, and some templates for the radii you will be using—cut from card, hardboard or ply. It is usually most convenient to work on the floor. If you are planning to use Peco points you will find a set of the Peco point plans valuable. By working full size you can avoid errors that can easily arise in small scale plans.

N scale

In general the principles of planning in N scale are similar to those for 00 scale with an appropriate reduction in dimensions, but there are a few special points to bear in mind. As the majority of published track plans are designed for 00 or HO scale it may well be that the modeller will wish to adapt such a plan for N scale. As a rough guide we can halve the linear dimensions reducing the area to a quarter. However, a direct conversion in this way may be neither possible nor desirable. The size of the operator is, of course, the same no matter what the scale of the layout, thus if there is a central operating well or some access openings it will probably be impossible to reduce the size of these. However, as the overall dimensions will be greatly reduced, while the operator's reach remains the same, the whole of the layout may now be accessible from any of the edges allowing the modeller to operate from one side instead of from the central well, which can then be covered with scenery. If a central wall is retained the layout size cannot be reduced as much but if you have enough space it is worth while keeping the well. The layout will appear more realistic if viewed and operated from the centre as only part will be visible at any one time making the round and round nature of the line, if a continuous run design, much less apparent.

It is often undesirable to reduce an 00-scale plan to quarter size for N scale; the resulting appearance is likely to be very disappointing with a much more toy-like effect than if it had been built in the larger scale. This is because the actual size of the layout is so much smaller and the eye sees so much more of it at a single glance. This is aggravated by the fact that the viewing position remains the same height above the layout, and is now twice as high in proportion. If you measure out a 6 ft × 4 ft rectangle and a 3 ft × 2 ft rectangle and compare them you will get some idea of this effect. If there is an oval, its continuous design is more obvious than in the original size. Things can be improved a little by building the layout higher from the ground so that you do not look down on it as much, but if possible it is better to reduce the linear dimensions only to about three-quarters of the 00 size rather than to half. This will allow the use of larger radius curves and give a generally less cramped appearance.

Another point which must be considered is the clearance for raised tracks crossing over low level tracks beneath. As the track base thickness will probably be the same as for 00 scale and as the same or greater clearance in actual terms will be required, the clearances cannot be reduced proportionally with the other dimensions. This will mean that an increase in the gradient will be needed for the N-scale layout. This is another reason for reducing the layout size by less than the full half.

If you have a larger space available but are thinking of N scale rather than 00 to allow you to build a more extensive and interesting model railway it is essential not to be too ambitious. We have become used to thinking of an 00-scale layout of say 8 ft × 4 ft as being within the capabilities of a beginner and it may be tempting to think of an N-scale layout in the same area. If the track plan is kept simple with not too many points, and emphasis is more on sweeping curves, gentle gradients and realistic landscape, this may be very successful. However, it is likely to be disastrous if an attempt is made to use the space for an N-scale version of a complex 16 ft × 8 ft 00-scale layout designed for a group of advanced modellers! This may be an exaggeration but it is very easy to get carried away with enthusiasm in the circumstances and some restraint is needed.

The fact that a 180° turn can be made in N scale (in as little as 20 in of baseboard width) creates some possibilities not open to the modeller working in 00 scale. For example, on a branch line terminus to fiddle yard scheme it is possible in N scale to include a reversing loop with some hidden sidings arising from it in place of the usual fiddle yard, making operation more convenient. Similarly, loops can be fitted at each end of a long, narrow layout to make it a continuous run design without making the layout too wide to be fitted along a wall or two walls of a room.

Eight Oaks station on a British N (1:48) scale layout built by Bob Jones. In N scale, platforms long enough to look realistic can be provided without needing a large space.

Structures

The structures on a model railway layout are a very important part of the landscape. Not only do they add scenic interest but in some cases they also provide extra operational possibilities for the line by creating traffic. For the best effect, both for individual buildings and for the overall appearance of the layout some planning in the selection and positioning is essential. Any temptation to just rush out to the local model shop once the track is down and to buy whatever takes the eye, or happens to be in stock at the time, is to be resisted!

In some cases a structure model needs to be planned accurately at an early stage. For example, the beautifully modelled machine shop on Mike Sharman's period layout is an integral part of the layout design so its size and position, and the position of the tracks, standard, narrow and broad gauge, entering it all had to be decided before the track laying was carried out. In other situations it may be important to plan ahead to ensure that there will be sufficient space for a particular model building, and that the sidings will be suitably positioned in relation to it. This will give a more realistic result than merely making the structures fit in later with the tracks already in place. The dimensions of model buildings constructed from the kits of some manufacturers are listed in their catalogues and this can be useful in advance planning.

We can divide model railway structures into three main groups, the railway buildings, such as stations, goods sheds, engine sheds and so on; buildings associated with the railway and providing traffic for it, factories, mines, warehouses, etc and incidental buildings in the landscape, houses, farms, hotels, garages, shops, and so on.

There is a good range of model buildings, mostly in kit form, available commercially in 00/HO and N scales, and these can often be easily modified or converted to suit your requirements more closely and to give you some individuality for your layout. Another popular technique is the combination of parts from two or more kits, known as cross-kitting, to make larger or different structures.

The greatest choice and scope, of course, comes with scratch-building structures for your layout. A good selection of materials is stocked by model shops including brick, stone and tile papers, balsa, plastic and corrugated copper.

Whether you use kits or construct your own buildings from scratch you should choose prototypes appropriate to the locality in which your railway is supposed to be set and to the type of railway you are modelling. The architectural style and details and the construction material used—wood, brick or stone—are often characteristic and the right selection can do much to make your layout appear authentic.

Most of us have space for only a small layout and beginners should start modestly even if there is plenty of room available, hence there is space for only relatively few buildings so we should be quite selective. Each should be worth its place on the layout and must add to the interest and overall appearance. We need buildings with character which will fit in with each other and generally they should be fairly small as large structures may tend to dwarf the rest of the layout. Buildings with interesting or irregular lines, with varying textures due to the use of several different materials such as brick, stone, wood, corrugated iron, and with additions, alterations and repairs over the years, together with the effects of weathering, often make good modelling subjects. Generally I find the older buildings more attractive in model form than the new modern structures. Remember that on a layout the view point is almost always from above and roofs are particularly noticeable. Thus buildings with varied rooflines due to gables and dormers, and with interesting chimneys and other roof details are especially suitable for modelling purposes.

Just as important as the selection of which structures will make good individual models

These low relief warehouses at the rear of the industrial layout built by Allan Sibley and Brian Dorman complete the scene and also conceal a fiddle yard.

This superbly detailed railway workshop on Mike Sharman's period layout is an important feature of the railway. Note the three different track gauges inside the building with, from the front, broad-, narrow- and standard-gauge tracks.

is the choice and arrangement to form a visually effective grouping. This takes a bit of practice and experience but can make all the difference in the final appearance. Develop a sense of arrangement by studying groupings which you find visually appealing—both in pictures of prototype structures and of layouts built by the expert scenic modellers and shown in the model press—and try to decide why they look good. Experiment with separate models, putting them in various positions in relation to one another until you find the best arrangement. You will soon learn how to achieve a good effect on your layout. In general avoid very regular patterns with straight streets and buildings in orderly

The arrangement of the structures in this attractive 00-scale display layout featuring Builder Plus kits has been planned to create a realistic model town and the railway blends naturally into the scene.

rows. More irregular arrangements are not only more typical of the prototype but will also make your layout appear larger.

A very effective technique where space is limited at the rear of a layout is the use of low relief structures. These are buildings with only the front wall and the front parts of the side walls and roof modelled while the rest is omitted. Although the models have a depth of only an inch or so they look correct from any viewing angle provided that other buildings, trees or other features are placed to conceal the lack of depth. The appearance is much more realistic than merely using a painted backscene. Some special kits are available for structures of this type, for example, the card kits made by Superquick and Hamblings, or alternatively you can use ordinary kits and employ the front and back separately as low relief models. If you prefer to scratch-build these models they are, of course, much quicker and easier to construct than conventional structures as only the front is fully modelled.

Structure models can also be utilised as scenic barriers to visually break up a length of track to make it appear longer, or to conceal part of an oval of track or a fiddle yard. Low relief structures near the back of the layout are especially useful in covering hidden tracks, storage sidings or a fiddle yard. A row of buildings along the centre of the baseboard, with or without a double-sided backdrop, can divide the layout into two separate towns making the railway seem longer and the stations further away from each other.

There are a number of kits available now for structures which are motorised. These include windmills with moving sails, water-mills fitted with small pumps so that real water can be circulated to turn the wheels, factories with moving conveyor belts and so on. Though some modellers may feel that these are rather gimmicky they are well worth considering, particularly on a small layout where any extra movement which can be introduced, in addition to the trains, will add to the interest of the scene. There are also some excellent working crane models for dock and goods yard use.

You may like to include on your layout two linked industries, between which there is rail traffic—for example, a mine from which ore is taken to a processing plant. For the most realistic effect the wagons in trains from the mine should be loaded with ore, while trains of empty wagons run back from the processing plant to the mine. To avoid the task of loading and unloading by hand many modellers ignore the inaccuracy and run full and empty wagons indiscriminately. However, a neat scheme to allow correct running

Many excellent industrial structures are available in kit form so it is easy to provide an interesting variety for a layout. Although the Continental kits are in HO or Continental N scale they can be used satisfactorily for 00- and British N-scale layouts respectively. This well detailed model is the Kibri HO-scale Large Gravel Silo.

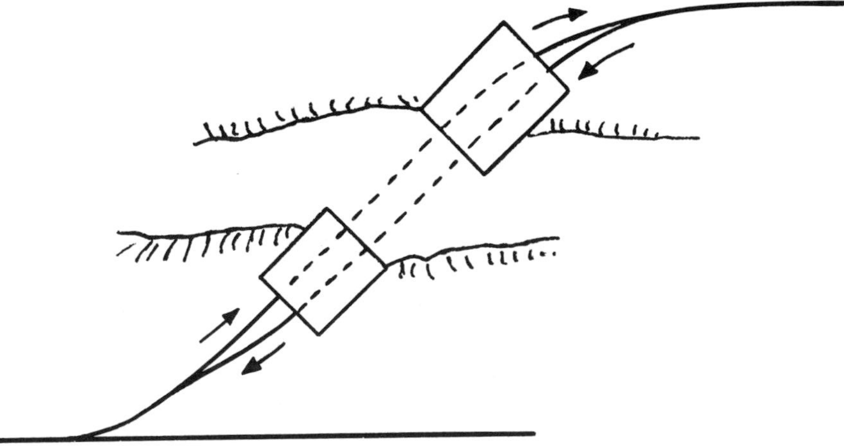

This arrangement allows empty wagons to enter the mine and full ones to leave it, while at the processing plant the reverse occurs, without the need for any loading or unloading of wagons.

has been devised by some modellers. The two industries are positioned either side of a ridge of hills, a row of industrial buildings or a double sided backdrop and hidden tracks connect them as shown in the diagram. Thus full wagons pushed into the processing plant are removed from the mine (and conversely empty wagons pushed into the mine are pulled out) at the other end of the hidden track from the processing plant.

Scenery

There is often a tendency for the modeller to concentrate on the designing of a track plan which will provide interesting operation, on the laying of smooth track for good running and on the correct wiring of the track. Once satisfied with these aspects he then adds scenery very much as an afterthought. Unfortunately such scenic work often appears unnatural and contrived. This is a pity because scenery can do a great deal to make a layout more realistic and interesting. Good scenic work not only makes the layout more attractive but also makes it look larger than it actually is. The scenery can also help to disguise such operationally necessary features as sharp curves, hidden tracks and fiddle yards. It can also be used to emphasise features we wish to show up.

It is important to plan the scenery in a general way with the track plan. Do not worry about the smaller details at this stage, as there will almost certainly be minor changes you wish to make during construction. In the prototype the landscape is, obviously, there before the railway which is planned to run through it. In the model the scenery is added last, but we should try to make it look as if it were there first. We must consider the type of terrain we want to model (hilly or flat, rural or urban) and the placing of a river, lake or canal. If your model is to be set in a particular location it is worth while visiting the area to see what the landscape is like. Make sketches or take photographs to guide you later when you are working on your layout.

By building up the scenery in the central part of this small 00-scale layout Terry Jenkins has created a dividing barrier between the two sides of the layout helping to conceal the oval track plan and making the layout more realistic.

Wherever there are tracks hidden by scenery, adequate access must be provided for track maintenance and in case of stalling or derailment. This is particularly important if there are concealed points or crossings. On the Isle of Purbeck MRC the problem has been solved by making part of the scenery lift out to give access to the track and points inside a tunnel. The removable section includes the farm.

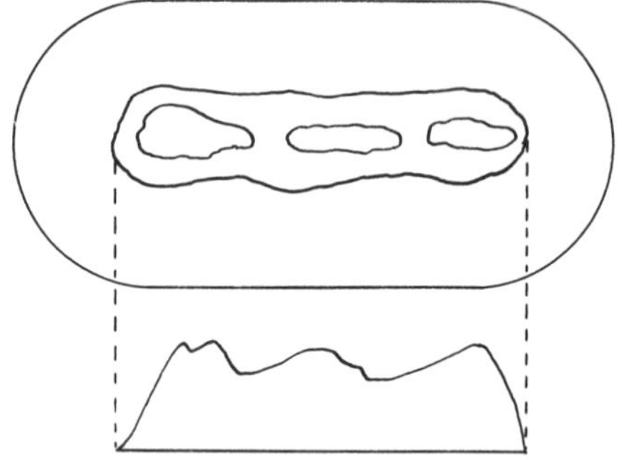

Scenery can be used to separate visually the two sides of an oval to make the layout appear larger and more interesting. A ridge of hills can be modelled to form a scenic barrier.

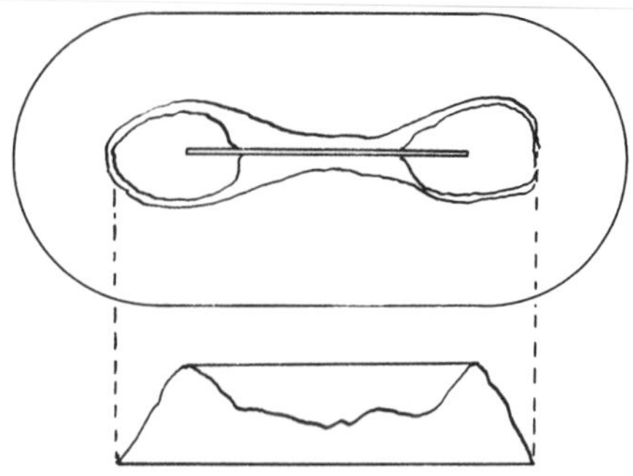

Extra height can be given by modelling a peak at each end of the ridge and fitting a double-sided backdrop between.

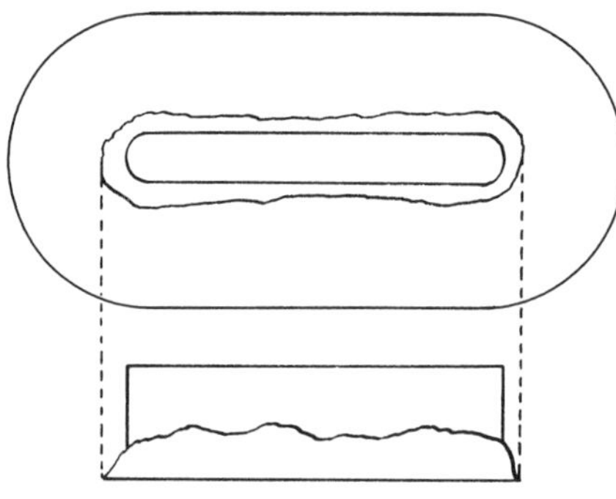

If the modelled scenery cannot be made high enough, an oval backscene can be erected within the track oval. This continuous backdrop will be more realistic than a simple, flat, double-sided backscene in which the ends would be visible.

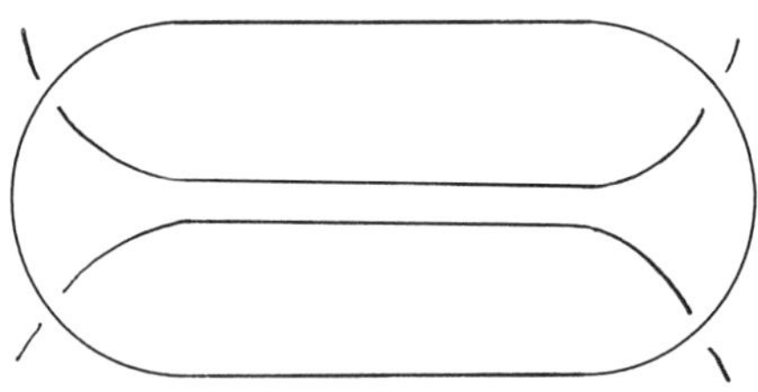

Taking the idea of a scenic barrier even further, the two sides of the track oval can be completely separated visually with backscenes as shown and the scenery can be quite different on each side. If a station is provided at each side this set-up is a good one for two operators, one at each side of the layout.

In scenic modelling considerable compression is needed and we must choose small examples of natural features, hills, rivers, trees and so on for modelling because otherwise they will be too big for the layout. It is better to select a narrow, winding river rather than a wide, straight one because the former will appear longer making the layout look larger. Another useful technique is to model a number of separate scenes, each one forming a centre of interest to attract the attention of the viewer, within the layout as a whole. Breaking the layout up into a number of parts like this makes it seem bigger. In the same way visually breaking lengths of tracks up into sections by bridges, cuttings, tunnels and buildings will also make them appear longer.

Tunnels are very useful on a model railway for hiding tracks, for example, to conceal part of the continuous run of an oval track plan and as a scenic break. However, real tunnels are very expensive for railways to bore so they are only constructed where they are really needed. Thus for a convincing appearance on a model railway the hill through which the tunnel passes must look high and large enough so that it would not have been possible to carry the track around the hill or through a cutting. If the model is set in a generally flat landscape it may be preferable to use some other scenic feature such as a group of trees, a road bridge or a structure to act as a scenic barrier, rather than to introduce an unlikely hill and tunnel. If you have one or more tunnels on your layout make sure that the clearances inside the tunnels are adequate for your widest models and that access is provided for maintenance of track, and points (if any) and for retrieving trains which have stalled or derailed within the tunnels.

On an oval plan layout a useful scenic arrangement is a high central ridge of hills. This device divides the layout into two areas viewed separately and makes the layout appear larger and the length of run seem longer. It also means that as there is a barrier the two areas can be made quite different scenically, adding variety to the model. If the ridge cannot be high enough to give visual separation without being unrealistically steep, some trees can be added along the top. If the scenery in the centre cannot be built up high enough, an alternative is to use a double-sided backdrop, either between a peak at each end or as an oval (see diagrams).

Scenic backgrounds fitted to the rear of a layout can do a great deal to improve the appearance by blocking from view irrelevant and distracting features such as wall-paper, curtains and so on, behind the layout and by making the layout appear larger by giving the impression that it extends into the distance as far as the eye can see. A scenic background can also be useful in concealing tracks or a fiddle yard.

For the most realistic effect it is important to match the modelled scenery and the background so that they appear to merge imperceptibly. This requires some advance planning particularly if a commercially produced backscene is employed as the modelled scenery must then be designed to blend into this.

Well modelled suburban scenery adds interest to this scene on a Fleischmann exhibition layout in HO scale. Study of such model railways can provide many ideas for scenic work on small home layouts.

A model of the layout

It is often difficult, particularly for the beginner, to visualise from a small scale layout plan just what the completed model railway will look like. This is especially so when the layout will have track at various levels. One way of deciding if you want to build from a particular plan is to make a small model of the layout at perhaps 1 in to the foot scale. A layout 6 ft × 4 ft would thus be modelled as a 6 in × 4 in miniature. Construction is easy in card and balsa, starting with the lowest level and adding any elevated tracks with card. The terrain can be modelled with plaster, or a modelling clay such as Das and, if desired, structures and even trains can be added using small pieces of balsa. You can keep such a model very simple using it only to give a rough guide to the appearance of the projected layout or you can add detail and colour to produce a more accurate model. Modifications to the plan can be made easily if desired and you can check that there will be no problems in making such changes. This can save you a lot of time and work later when you come to construct the full size layout.

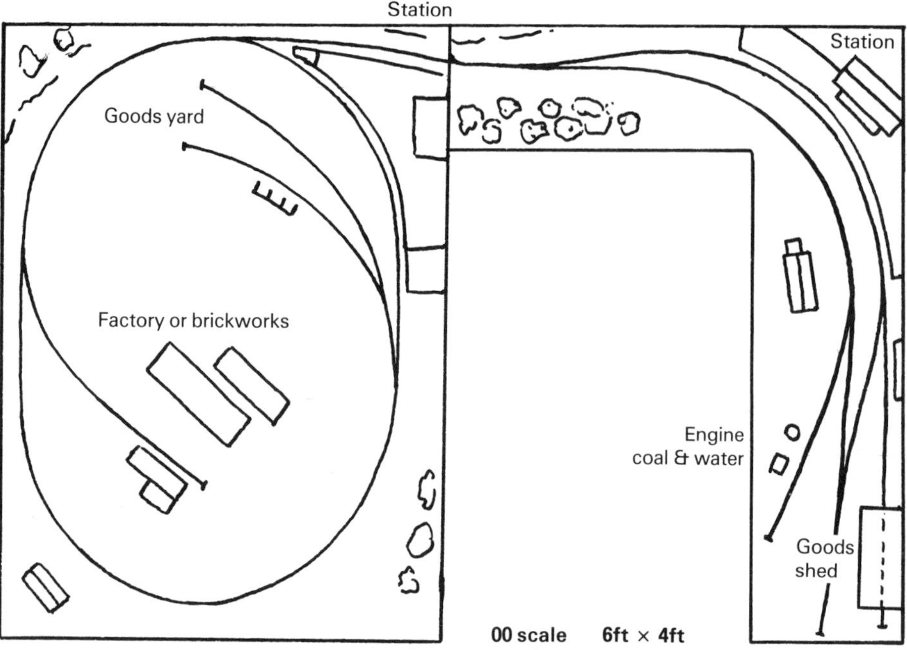

Layout plans *This layout can be developed very simply from a train set. First the oval is laid on a 4 ft × 3 ft baseboard and sidings are added as desired. Finally the extension can be constructed. The design is based on train set track using Hornby or Airfix points. Operation is limited but the layout should be interesting for the beginner to build and run. The layout also provides a good introduction to structure and scenery modelling.*

Model Railway Guide 2

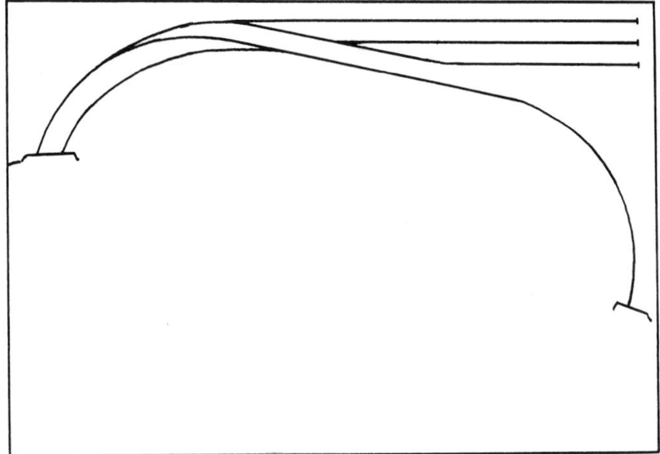

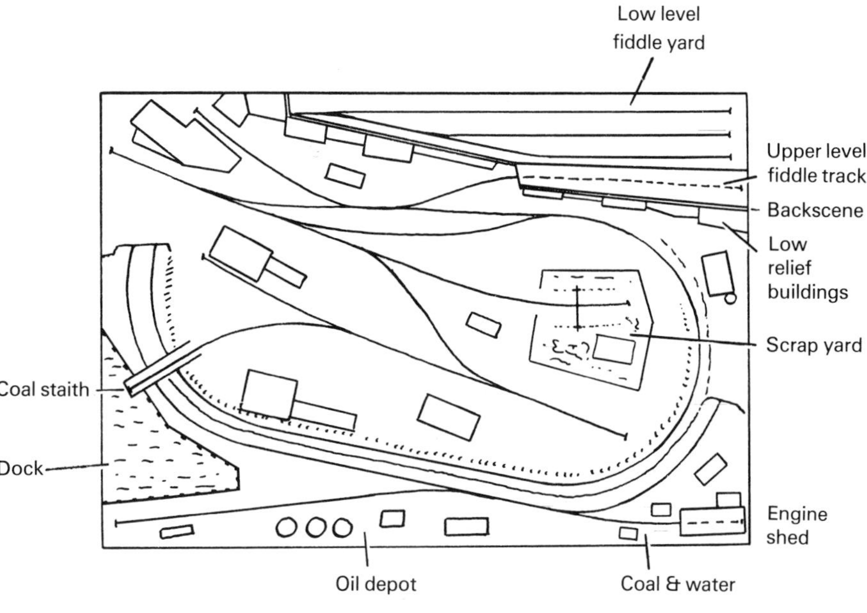

00 scale 6ft × 4ft

This industrial layout is also a development of the basic oval and again uses Hornby or Airfix points (one Hornby curved point is employed). The low level tracks are laid first and the layout can be operated at this stage. Later the modeller can construct the upper level and the track leading up to it. There is great scope for structure modelling and for scenic detailing and the operating potential is also good if you enjoy shunting. Trains of wagons are brought from the hidden sidings at the rear of the oval and up to the high level where the wagons are distributed to various industries including a scrap yard and a coal staith which passes above the low level tracks to load barges at the dock. Use of one of the card order schemes for deciding which wagon must go to which siding will add to the operating interest. The traffic will be mainly goods but you can also run an occasional workmen's train.

A model of the layout

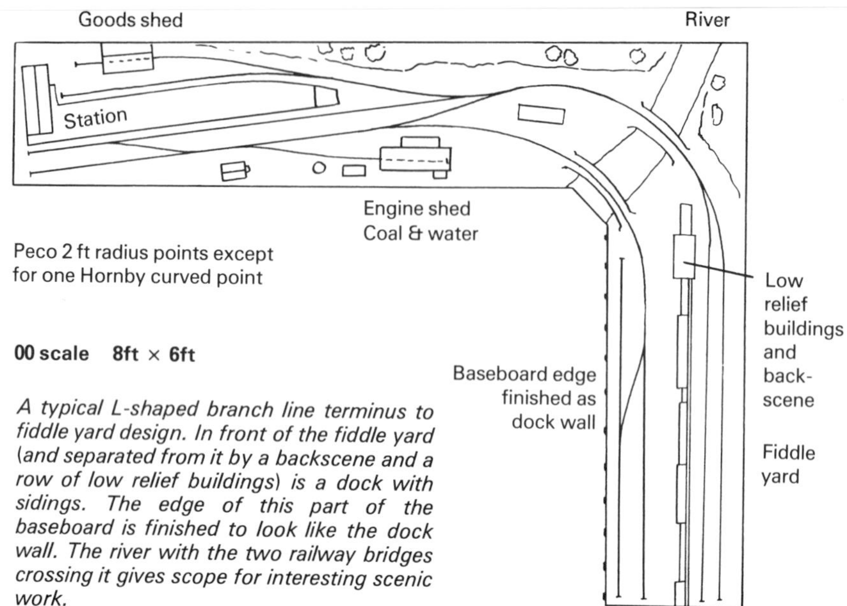

Peco 2 ft radius points except for one Hornby curved point

00 scale 8ft × 6ft

A typical L-shaped branch line terminus to fiddle yard design. In front of the fiddle yard (and separated from it by a backscene and a row of low relief buildings) is a dock with sidings. The edge of this part of the baseboard is finished to look like the dock wall. The river with the two railway bridges crossing it gives scope for interesting scenic work.

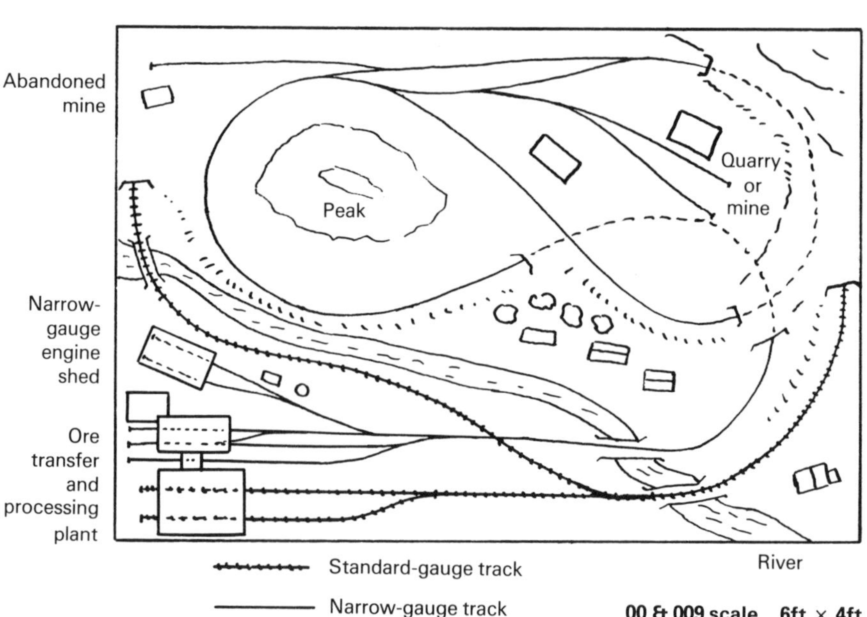

00 & 009 scale 6ft × 4ft

A simple dual-gauge 00/009 layout. The standard-gauge oval with sidings can be laid first and the layout can be operated in this form until the modeller wishes to add the narrow gauge. The hidden standard-gauge tracks have been omitted from the plan for clarity, they merely complete the oval though hidden sidings can also be included if desired. The narrow gauge is an out and back design and the reversing loop requires special wiring. The dual-gauge crossing is a Liliput product. The standard-gauge points are Hornby or Airfix.

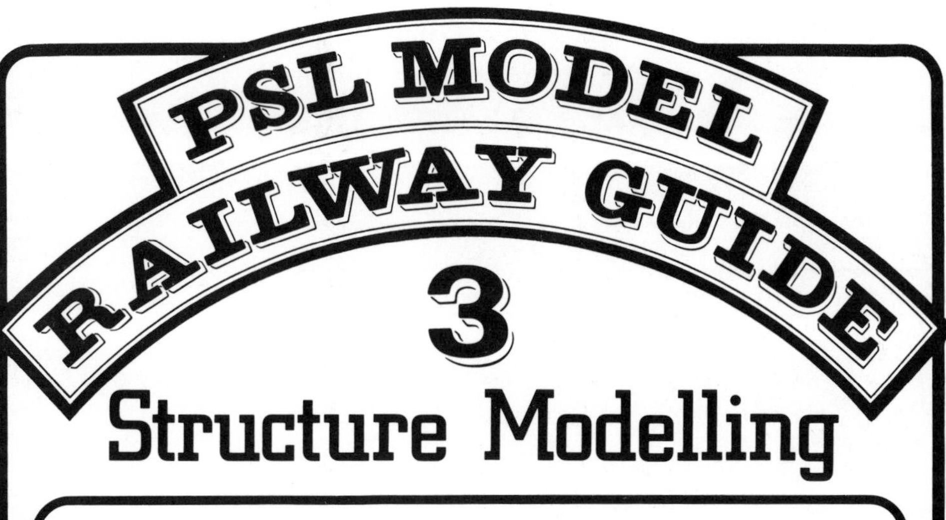

Structure Modelling

Michael Andress

Contents

Introduction

The construction of model buildings can be a very enjoyable pastime. While architectural modelling is an important part of the professional modelmaker's work, most amateurs only become involved indirectly, usually through railway modelling. At one time the only buildings to be found on a model railway layout were essential railway structures such as stations, goods sheds, signal boxes and bridges, and these were often unrealistic, toy-like items. Now, however, the landscape which provides the setting for a model railway has become much more important and there has been a marked improvement in the scope and standard of both scenic and structure modelling in an effort to achieve greater realism.

The steadily increasing interest in this aspect of the hobby has led to the commercial production of kits of various types and there is now a range available which is excellent in both extent and quality, particularly in 00, HO and N scales. There have also been a number of new materials and techniques applied to scratch-building which have brought about an increase in realism. The standards are now high with the best structure models being remarkably accurate, realistic and well detailed.

My aim in this book is to indicate to the beginner what is available and to give him or her some ideas on how to utilise effectively the many kits, parts and different materials in building structures for a model railway layout. I include both sexes in the last sentence quite deliberately as this is a facet of railway modelling which the ladies often especially enjoy and which they tackle very successfully! Though the examples will be mainly relevant to railway modelling, many of the kits, materials and construction techniques are equally suitable for military modelling and wargaming, fields in which there is now considerable interest in building structure models for inclusion in settings for military figures, tanks, guns and vehicles. Bus modellers may also want to construct buildings as these vehicles are often displayed on large or small layouts or dioramas, a bus depot being a favourite choice of subject. I have also seen interesting ship model displays where the vessels are shown in a harbour, dock or shipyard setting with appropriate structures completing the scene. Aircraft models are sometimes displayed on dioramas which include buildings—a small airfield being a good example. Tramway layouts usually need numerous structures as such models are typically set in town or city surroundings. Last, but not least, there are those modellers whose primary interest is in architectural work. Thus, the scope for structure modelling is considerable.

This book concentrates mainly on the most popular railway modelling scales, 00, HO and N, though some examples from other scales are also included. However, some of the information relating to kits and all the scratch-building data can be applied to most scales used in modelling structures.

I would like to thank all those modellers who have helped me with photographs and information for this book. In particular I am grateful to Graham Bailey, Tony Butler, Olive Clark, Howard Coulson, Steven Dewhirst, Allan Downes, Roy England, Len Fidkin, Keith Gowen, P.D. Hancock, Trevor Hughes, Terry Jenkins, Bob Jones, Betty Kay, The Middlesbrough Model Railway and Tramway Club, Dave Rowe, George Sellios, Doris Stokes and Colin Woolridge. I am also grateful to those manufacturers who have assisted me with information and pictures of their products.

Some basic points

As there are relatively few ready-made structure models available, though Grafar and Bachmann offer N-scale ranges, most beginners start their model making with a few structure kits, often to add to a train set or a small and simple first scale layout. Such kit models are an excellent introduction because they are generally easy and quick to build and they provide useful experience in constructional work. As they are usually static items they need only look attractive and accuracy in assembly is less important than for models such as locomotives and rolling stock which must run well to be successful. Mistakes or poor finishing in the original construction can often be improved by a little extra work later when the modeller has gained in experience and skill. Alternatively if the first attempts are completely unsuccessful they can be discarded or put into the scrap box as a source of parts for other buildings without much loss as the kits are, on the whole, not very expensive. The knowledge and practice gained with structure modelling will be of benefit for other aspects of the hobby and the successful completion of a few small and simple building kits can do much to boost the confidence and interest in the tackling of more difficult projects.

As I have already implied, the beginner is most likely to find enjoyment and success in structure modelling by starting with something simple. Choose a fairly small and easy-to-build card or plastic kit first, then progress to larger and more complex kits, trying all the time to make each model better than the one before both in neatness of construction and in the finishing. Ideas for extra detailing and then for alterations and conversions from the basic kits will soon come once you get started. Once some skill in kit assembly and conversion has been achieved there is no reason why the modeller should not build from scratch if he or she wishes. For a first attempt at scratch-building there is much to be said for following one of the many articles which appear in the modelling magazines describing the construction of various types of buildings. Such an article will provide all the prototype information needed as well as detailed instructions on how the model can be made. You will find it of value to read as many of these articles as you can,

Below and over page *Two views of the remarkable city model, based on London, constructed in 1 mm scale by Norman Clark. The trains and road vehicles move on endless belts and the model is also lit for viewing as a night scene. The buildings have been constructed largely from card.*

even though you do not plan to build the actual models described, as you will learn much about the methods of construction which can be used. The knowledge you acquire in this way can then be applied to the modelling of buildings which do interest you. Quite often you will find that the authors of these articles have made improvements to conventional construction methods or have devised new techniques and these may help you in your own modelling by making construction easier or the results more realistic.

Unless you are an architectural modeller, and perhaps not even then, you will not be making single models of buildings to be displayed individually, but a number of structures to be placed together on a model railway layout or a diorama of some type. Thus the choice of models, whether kits or scratch-built, must be judged not only by their suitability as regards your skill and experience and their individual appeal but also in relation to the overall effect required. This selection is essential if you are to achieve a realistic appearance for your layout as a whole, and it does require care and thought. You will also need to be able to resist the temptation to acquire models you like but which are unsuitable for the scene you are planning!

Ideally your layout, even if not a model of a particular prototype line, should be based in a more or less specific geographical location and the buildings chosen should be appropriate in architectural style and in the materials, such as brick, stone or wood, used in construction. If your layout is to be a period model, care must be taken to avoid introducing anachronisms. The different structures should also blend in well together though this is more difficult to assess in advance, particularly for the beginner, unless a group of structures from a prototype setting are reproduced together. The railway buildings of a particular region or railway company often have a characteristic style and it is important to model this correctly if the right effect is to be produced. In real towns and villages there is often considerable variation in style and period between the buildings, with new concrete and glass office blocks next to timbered houses and so on. However, in model form we must be a little cautious in what we copy, selecting, as an artist may in painting a picture, the best features and omitting those which would spoil the scene. This is important because of the compression we must carry out in modelling a town or village on a small layout and because we get an overall view of the model rather than just seeing part at a time as we do when walking along a real street. Thus we must try to create a somewhat idealised or representational scene with the character and atmosphere of the prototype rather than an exact copy. Some of our most successful scenic and structure modellers, John Ahern, P.R. Wickham, and P.D. Hancock, for example, have created detailed historical and geographical backgrounds for the imaginary

Opposite page *Three views of an 009 narrow-gauge layout constructed by the Middlesbrough Model Railway and Tramway Club. The railway buildings and mine have been scratch-built with similar architectural styles and construction materials giving a harmonious appearance which adds much to the realism and atmosphere of the layout. Note the unusual, but prototypical, water tank by the engine shed.*

TIME TABLE
WOLF'S RAKE

This footbridge at Market Redwing station on Keith Gowen's TT-scale layout is a Triang model which has been modified to give it a more characteristic GWR appearance.

prototypes on which their layouts were modelled. While these modellers obviously gained enjoyment from this I realise that many others would not be interested in such a digression from their practical modelling. Even so the results are likely to be much better if the modeller is prepared to give a little consideration at the beginning to the background for his layout. He can then choose appropriate structures and will have some idea of what he is trying to achieve as far as the overall appearance is concerned.

The arrangement of the model structures is also important in the creation of a realistic and visually effective grouping on the layout or diorama. You may be uncertain at first how to obtain this but you will find that a little experimentation and practice will help. It is also valuable to think about groupings, either of real buildings or of models on layouts built by the experts, and to decide why they are effective. There is much to be said for planning all the structures for your layout at an early stage, rather than adding them piecemeal, as this will give you more chance of creating a well-composed scene. A useful technique is to make from scrap card rough mock-up models of the structures you plan to have. These shapes can be tried in various positions and groupings until the most satisfactory is determined. You may find that some modification to one or more of the buildings will be advantageous or that one of the structures cannot be fitted in successfully. It is, of course,

Beautifully modelled farm buildings in 4 mm scale by Allan Downes. The structures have been grouped to make an interesting and attractive scene. (Photograph by John Priest.)

Natural grouping adds to the realism and effectiveness of these superb 4 mm scale models scratch-built by Allan Downes. Note the accurately modelled stone walling and the creeper on the wall of the cottages. (Photograph by John Priest.)

much better to find this out before you actually build the models! Some of the kit catalogues provide the dimensions for each of the models in the range and this will also be helpful for the modeller in advance planning before purchasing the kits. The structures should obviously be planned in conjunction with the scenery to provide the most effective setting for a model railway.

Incidentally, the architectural models built by the professionals are worthy of study because great care is taken to present these in the most visually effective way possible. After all the appearance may make the difference between winning or missing out on an important contract! Study these models carefully and you will often pick up useful ideas for your own layout.

As there is space on most model railway layouts for only a limited number of buildings we should be selective and choose only interesting and attractive structures, each of which will add to the overall appearance. If they are not to dwarf the rest of the layout and if we are to have enough buildings to provide interesting variety, our structures should be small. By this I do not mean that they should be underscale, though this can be useful for background models as we shall see later, but that we should select small prototypes. Generally these structures will also be more appropriate to the scope of the railway facilities, the number and length of sidings and so on, which we will have space for on a layout. However, you may find an interesting subject you would like to model but which would be too large for your layout if copied exactly. It is often possible by applying what has been called 'selective compression' to such a building to retain the original character while significantly reducing the size of the model. Industrial buildings such as factories and warehouses are often made up of a number of repeated similar or identical units or sections and some of these can be omitted to make the model smaller. A three-storey structure can be cut down to two, the number of doors and windows can be reduced, windows can be made smaller and closer together, and chimneys and skylights can similarly be reduced in size. However, the height of doors and of loading platforms should not be altered and the clearances for any openings through which railway rolling stock passes must, of couse, be maintained. Using these techniques it should be possible to reduce the size of a structure to about two thirds of the linear dimensions and this will cut down the ground area to approximately a third, an appreciable saving.

For buildings in the background and away from the tracks so that they will not be compared directly to the size of the locomotives and rolling stock, a reduction can be made simply by modelling to a smaller scale. In

Above *Typical of the superb architectural models produced professionally is this one of a Middle Eastern army barracks built by Thorp Modelmakers Ltd of London. The amateur will benefit from studying work of this type.* (Photograph by courtesy of Thorp Modelmakers.)

Below *The choice of prototype is important in an effective model. The rock bunker on which this HO-scale Fine Scale Miniatures kit was based is an excellent subject with its interesting lines and many surface details such as the wood framing, the stairway and the conveyor belts. Note the shelter over the railroad track with the fully detailed corrugated iron roof. This superb craftsman wood kit includes many cast metal detailing items and is complete except for the figures shown in this picture.* (Photograph by courtesy of Fine Scale Miniatures.)

The small size of N-scale models may allow relatively large industries to be featured on a model railway layout. Graham Bailey constructed this realistic ship-building and repair yard, complete with a ship being built, for his modern British prototype layout. The ship is a modified Novo 'Shell Welder' kit and the gantry crane in the background is a cut down Pola HO-scale kit model. The rest of the structures were scratch-built.

most cases the modeller uses a scale only slightly smaller, for example $\frac{1}{8}$ in to the foot on an 00 or HO-scale layout. However, this can be taken much further to give the impression of great depth to a scene, even though there are only a few inches of actual distance available in front of the backscene, by forcing the perspective. This is similar to the way an artist uses perspective drawing to make his two-dimensional picture appear to have depth as well. It is a technique which is extensively, and expertly, employed in museum dioramas and you can see examples in many museums, for example, the Science Museum in London. It has not been much used by railway modellers, partly because the viewpoint must be rather strictly limited for the most successful results and this cannot usually be achieved on an ordinary model railway layout. However, the late Jack Nelson applied perspective modelling most effectively in a number of superb dioramas of the LNWR, and I believe there are plans for these models to be put on public show. The subject is rather beyond the scope of this book and I would refer readers to an article by Mr Nelson in the November 1971 issue of *Model Railways* magazine for more information. I can, however, give an example of how forced perspective can be applied simply but effectively on a layout. At a branch line terminus there may be a street running along behind the station, parallel to and a few inches in front of the backdrop. The houses or shops along this street are modelled to full scale for 00. Running back from this street towards the backdrop, but curving round, is another road. The buildings on this are constructed as if drawn in perspective, with the end nearest the viewer higher than the end away from the onlooker. This can be quite marked with the scale going from 00 at the front to N scale at the rear in only a couple of buildings. Positioning figures of appropriate scale in relation to the front and rear structures enhances the effect. Any features in these distorted walls must also be modelled in the same way, for example, doors, windows and so on. Making the road curve round so that it goes out of sight behind the other buildings avoids the need to continue the perspective on the drawn backscene, a task which may prove difficult unless the modeller has some artistic skill. Because the road runs back the viewpoint is relatively limited to more or less in front, thus helping to overcome one of the problems with perspective modelling. It is important, however, to view the scene from close to model ground level for the best effect. Looking down from above will distort the appearance. The buildings on the rear of the curve can be modelled as low relief structures (see later), as well as in perspective, to save space.

Sources of ideas and information

The beginner can learn a great deal by reading the model railway magazines and books and by looking at photographs appearing there of layouts built by experienced modellers. Often the techniques employed in construction are described and study of the pictures also helps in understanding how these workers have achieved realistic arrangements and groupings and the all-important 'atmosphere'. Many kit conversions have been described in the model press and following one of these can be a good introduction to this type of work. These conversions will also give you ideas for other, original modifications of your own. Visits to model railway exhibitions will prove very helpful as well as most enjoyable. Provided you choose a moment when they are not too busy operating to talk to members of the public you will find that most exhibitors are very willing to answer questions about how they built the models on their layouts and to explain any construction techniques which they use. Membership of a club can also be very beneficial as you can learn a great deal from the more experienced members. Not only will they advise you on how to build your models and give you practical assistance too if necessary, but they can also help you to avoid the mistakes they have made in the past!

Museum models and dioramas are worthy of study as they will give you ideas on the most effective methods of presentation, particularly regarding aspects such as perspective modelling and lighting. A visit to the Pendon Museum is especially recommended. Not only can you see what must be some of the finest structure modelling ever carried out in 4 mm scale in the Pendon Parva village (some pictures of which are included in this book) and other displays, but also John Ahern's famous 'Madder Valley' layout which is on permanent loan to the museum.

For scratch-building, many photographs and plans of railway and other suitable structures appear in the model railway magazines and there are also articles detailing the construction of various models. As I mentioned earlier a good approach for the beginner is to build at least one model based on an article of this type before going on to choose his own prototypes

A scene at Madderport on John Ahern's famous 00-scale 'Madder Valley' model railway layout, now on display at the Pendon Museum. The buildings were constructed from card and were based on real structures; the building at the left of the photograph, for example, is a model of the harbour office at Poole, Dorset. Note the low relief structures at the rear of the layout. (Photograph by courtesy of Pendon Museum.)

Some of the buildings from the 4 mm scale Pendon Parva village model at Pendon Museum. The structures, which are all accurate replicas of real buildings, are built to the highest museum standards and the degree of detailing is almost unbelievable. Construction is mainly from card while the windows are glazed with either real glass, microscope cover slips, or mica. Thatching was carried out with human hair but tow is now used. The interiors are fully modelled. (Photographs by courtesy of Pendon Museum.)

to model. A few plans are available commercially. The Skinley range includes some structures, while MAP have a selection of plans in 4 mm scale for buildings designed by John Ahern. Many pictures of prototypes are to be found in books and magazines, on picture postcards and so on, and these can all be useful. It is a good idea to build up a file of pictures of structures and details of buildings which interest you so that you can use them for reference purposes in your modelling.

Best of all is to go out and look for buildings you would like to model. You will be surprised how interesting and enjoyable a stroll around an industrial, railway, dock or other area can be when you have such a purpose. If possible take a pencil and notebook, a camera, and perhaps a tape-measure with you and make notes and sketches, take numerous pictures and keep a record of a few basic dimensions for any buildings which you like. It is also useful to collect information on small details which you can model, even if the structure as a whole is not suitable. Modelling such features accurately will add authenticity and realism to your model buildings. Industrial structures in particular often have a great deal in the way of pipes, tanks, valves, ventilators, ducts, extractor fans and so on visible on the exterior and adding appropriate features to your models will make them more interesting. There is no need to model any building exactly as it is unless you wish to, and you will often find that you would like to make alterations to suit your own ideas and to meet the requirements of your layout more closely. Sometimes combining features from several different prototypes may result in the most suitable building for your scene.

If you are one of those lucky people who can sketch well this will be very useful in collecting information on prototypes. Even if your drawing is not good you can still make rough sketches which can be adequate as a record, especially if you keep them fairly simple and if you note down enough dimensions from which to model accurately. Personally I find photography the most convenient method and I take my camera with me whenever I think I may be somewhere that there may be buildings of interest. I document any structure of interest photographically, when I have the opportunity, even if the information does not seem to be of immediate use. I may want to refer to it in the future and I also find that a look through my file often gives me ideas for modelling projects. As black and white film is cheap it is worth while taking plenty of pictures. Straight on views of the front, sides and back are useful for modelling purposes and, if you can show a person of known height in the pictures, this will help you in estimating the dimensions and will usually enable you to draw up a sufficiently accurate plan from which to build a model. Though the film is more expensive it is also a good idea to take some colour pictures if possible as this will be helpful when you come to paint the model. Even if you do not follow the original colour scheme the pictures will be a good guide to weathering.

If you do take a considerable number of pictures it is desirable to have some form of filing which will permit convenient storage and retrieval of any particular negative. I take mainly 35 mm films and I store the negatives in Paterson and Photo Science negative files which are loose-leaf folders holding separate sheets each of which will take a 36 exposure 35 mm film cut into strips of six pictures. Before filing the negatives I contact print each film on to a sheet of 10 in × 8 in enlarging paper in a Paterson contact printer. The contact sheet for each film is then filed with the loose leaf holding that film. This makes it easier to locate the negative for a particular picture but ideally the negatives should also be cross indexed according to subject. A simple method is to give each sheet a number and also each negative, for example 10/18 would be the 18th negative on sheet 10. File cards are made up for different subjects, for example, signal boxes, and filed alphabetically. The relevant negative numbers are then listed on the cards together with further brief identifying notes.

Industrial structures are often interesting in model form. This attractive processing plant is a source of extra traffic on P.D. Hancock's well-known 4 mm scale narrow-gauge 'Craig & Mertonford Railway' layout. The model was scratch-built from card, stripwood and corrugated copper sheet. (Photograph by P.D. Hancock.)

Tools

Relatively few tools are needed for structure modelling and the beginner can easily and inexpensively assemble a suitable selection. My tool kit contains the following items.

Modelling knife I use Swann Morton knives but the X-Acto ones are equally suitable. Both are of the type with replaceable blades and both manufacturers offer a range of different blade shapes for varying purposes. I find it convenient to have two handles and to fit a new blade in one. As this blade becomes less sharp I transfer it to the other handle and fit another new one to the first. The handles are marked appropriately and I can use the sharper blade for fine work and the other for rougher jobs. Always fit a new blade when embarking on any delicate or difficult work as you will find it much easier to get good results with a really sharp knife. For heavier work I use a Stanley knife. This again has replaceable blades but both the knife and the blades are of sturdier construction then the Swann Morton ones, making it useful for cutting thicker material.

Razor saw This is very useful for cutting thicker plastic sheet and thick kit parts as well as wood strip and sheet. I use an X-Acto saw handle with replaceable blades, but other makes are also available. The X-Acto Mitre Box designed for use with the saw is very convenient for cutting right angles and 45-degree angles.

Steel rule and steel square These are required for accurate measuring and marking out and I always use a steel rule as a guide for cutting with a modelling knife. It is handy to have a 6 in rule for small parts and a 12 or 18 in one for longer cuts.

Scriber This can be used for marking out and is also good for scribing planking on plastic, card or wood. An alternative is to use a needle held in a pin vice.

Pin vice This, with a selection of fine drills, enables me to make small holes for fixing small details on to structure models.

Hand drill This is used with drills too large for the pin vice when larger holes are required.

Fine files I have a set of needle files of different shapes, round, square, flat, oval, half round and triangular and these are very useful for a variety of tasks including smoothing, shaping, enlarging openings and so on.

Fine sandpaper This is also essential for smoothing and finishing.

Tweezers These are needed for handling small parts and I have two pairs, one coarse and one fine with pointed tips.

Scissors These are useful for cutting out parts especially along curved or irregular lines which may be more difficult with a knife. I have several pairs including one very fine pair suitable for very delicate work.

Small clothes pegs These are extremely useful for all sorts of holding jobs in model making. Bulldog clips and rubber bands are also good for this purpose. Uses for these items include keeping parts together and correctly aligned while glue is setting, holding parts while you cut, file or sand them and holding small items while they are painted and until the paint dries.

Small vice This is also used to hold parts and materials while they are cut or shaped.

Fine pliers These are employed for various jobs particularly for bending wire and metal when modelling piping and other details.

Wood burning tool This tool is intended for burning decorative designs on wood but it can also be used to model stone, brick and various types of wood planking by burning appropriately placed grooves into sheet balsa. The model I have can also be used as a soldering iron. The Pyrogravure, popular with military modellers, who use it to achieve a variety of effects in plastic, is a similar but rather more sophisticated and controllable piece of equipment.

Soldering iron This is not often needed for structure modelling but is sometimes useful in making details such as handrails, piping and so on.

Painting equipment will be discussed in a later section.

Board A surface on which to work and cut is

essential. I often use chipboard or hardboard as they have no grain to catch the knife blade and direct it away from the line of the cut. The hardboard needs replacing fairly frequently as the surface quickly becomes marked, but it is inexpensive. If you do use hardboard always work on the smooth face. Some modellers recommend glass as a working surface but this has the disadvantage of being breakable and it also tends to blunt the knife blades quickly.

The tools I have listed above are ones which I have found useful but they are by no means essential for all structure modelling. If you build only from pre-cut card kits for example it is possible to get by with almost no tools at all. Conversely you may find items which I have not listed are useful to you in your modelling. Always be on the lookout for tools which can be employed to help in your construction work as you can come across some surprisingly useful items quite unexpectedly, particularly now so many tools are available for do-it-yourself work.

It is, of course, important to take care of your tools and to store them when not in use so that they do not become broken or blunted. It is also much easier to find the particular item you need if your tools are kept neat and tidy.

Last, but not least, it is essential to learn to hold and use your tools correctly. Not only will your work be better, with less likelihood of damaging the tools, but even more important you will not run the risk of injury as you may if you use them incorrectly. Make sure whenever you are cutting, sawing, drilling or filing that if the tool should slip it will not reach your hands. If possible hold parts in a vice if they are small or difficult to hold by hand while you are working on them.

You will find that your modelling is better and more enjoyable if you have good working conditions. I find it most comfortable to work at a table or desk sitting on a chair of appropriate height. As one may spend a whole evening at work on a model a good position will make neck or backache less likely. Perhaps most often overlooked is the importance of good lighting, arranged so that you are not working in your own shadow. When marking out and cutting you must be able to see well if you are to do accurate work. Poor lighting also leads to eyestrain, headaches and tiredness, none of which is conducive to enjoyable or successful modelling! I find an Anglepoise type of lamp ideal as this can be adjusted to exactly the right position for whatever I am doing. When using some model cements and solvents you should ensure that there is good ventilation and that you are not inhaling excessive amounts of vapour. It is not advisable to smoke when using these chemicals.

Materials

The materials you use will be influenced by the type of modelling you are doing and perhaps the construction materials employed for the prototype you are following, but also by your own personal preferences. Modellers, being inventive and imaginative people, have tried many different raw materials for scratch-building and for detailing and conversion work on kit models. The following list includes most of those commonly used and the beginner will find it advantageous to try out a variety of these before deciding which he will utilise for his models.

Card This is the traditional material for model building construction and is still the choice of several of the experts despite the introduction of plastic card. It is generally best to buy good quality card as the extra cost will not be very great for the relatively small quantities required. Smooth-surfaced card in different thicknesses and in a variety of colours can be purchased at art shops. For interior floors and bracing, cheaper quality card can be used if desired but this should be fairly thick and strong.

Balsa wood This light, soft wood is available in model and toy shops as blocks, sheets and strips of varying sizes. It is easy to cut and shape and is useful for floors, internal bracing and for walls which are to be faced with some other material. It is also useful for models of buildings of timber construction and for trestle bridges, though the surface texture and grain are rather too coarse.

Hard wood Some British model shops stock obechi stripwood in various sizes and this is useful for timber buildings. The larger sizes of stripwood can also often be obtained from DIY shops and can be employed for interior bracing. In the United States a wide range of sizes of bass is available including very small sizes and also a variety of sections such as T, L, H and I girders. Sheetwood machined to represent planking, capped siding, lapboard siding and so on, is also produced. These materials are marketed in Britain by some of the specialist shops such as Victors of Islington.

Drawing paper This is available in a variety of thicknesses and surface finishes from art shops and has many uses including modelling slates, tiles, individually applied bricks and stones.

Plastic card This is sheet polystyrene in a range of thicknesses and in various colours

Superb scratch-building in 2 mm scale by Len Fidkin. This oil derrick model was constructed following an article by American modeller George Allen in Model Railroader *magazine in September 1952. The model was made almost entirely from wood.*

This prize-winning 2 mm scale American trestle bridge was scratch-built by Len Fidkin using fine stripwood.

including white and black. It is very easy to cut, using a modelling knife for the thinner sheets and a razor saw for the thicker material. Shaping is also easy with files and sandpaper and the finish is very good with no grain visible. Plastic card models can be assembled using solvent adhesives which are very convenient to use. These qualities have made this material very popular with modellers and it is widely used in scratch-building structure models. It can also be used very satisfactorily in carrying out conversions of plastic kits. Plastic card is also sold as fine strips of various sizes, and this is very handy when quantities of fine strip are needed for a model as it saves a great deal of cutting. Clear plastic sheet is produced for glazing windows. Plastic card is also made in embossed sheets for representing brick, stone course and random stone, cobblestones and so on, in various scales. When appropriately painted the effect is very good as the embossing provides a realistic relief to the surface.

Plastic shapes Plastruct offer a wide range of girders, rods, tubes, beams and many other shapes for various scales made in ABS plastic. These parts were originally marketed for professional workers constructing models of industrial installations but are now available also for amateur modellers. Fine plastic rod is made by various manufacturers.

Plastic filler Used to fill gaps and holes in plastic before finishing and painting and also useful for making alterations in plastic kits. Suitable fillers are made by several manufacturers including Humbrol. Milliput make a useful two part epoxy filler.

Expanded polystyrene This light foam plastic is easy to work and is quite strong. It can be used for constructing model building walls, stone walling and so on. This material is sold at DIY shops either as sheets of varying thicknesses or as ceiling tiles but large quantities are used as packing and you may be able to obtain this material as scrap without cost. Expanded polystyrene can be dangerous if inhaled so care should be taken when working with it, particularly if you are sawing or filing it.

Brick, stone, slate and tile paper These papers, printed in colour, are produced in the main small scales by various manufacturers including Builder Plus and Superquick. Faller make a range of thicker printed materials which have the pattern embossed for greater realism.

Corrugated metal This represents corrugated iron sheeting on model buildings. Slaters make corrugated copper sheet for this

Above *The late Eric Kay built this impressive viaduct for his N-scale 'Sherrington Branch' using polystyrene foam sawn and carved to shape.*

Below *Eitomo station building on Howard Coulson's 'N & M R' an 009 layout closely based on East African narrow-gauge railways. The model was scratch-built after study of photographs of prototype stations. Corrugated iron walls and roof were represented by corrugated copper sheet.*

purpose. In the United States Campbell Scale Models market thin corrugated aluminium sheet which is exact scale for HO and very realistic in appearance. You may be able to obtain this from specialist shops in Britain.

Plaster A material which has been used very effectively in structure modelling particularly for stone-walled prototypes. Either ordinary hardwall plaster or dental plaster can be employed. Plaster fillers such as Polyfilla and Tapwata are also useful in modelling buildings.

Das This is a type of modelling clay which has been used successfully in modelling stonework.

Kos (Pyruma) A fire cement which can be used in structure modelling.

Peco texture modelling compound A modelling material with a variety of applications in model building construction.

Perspex Buildings with large and numerous windows can be conveniently built from perspex with overlays of thin card or plastic card cut out to reveal the perspex beneath where the windows are to be.

Glass Some modellers like to use real glass, usually microscope cover slips, for windows in model buildings.

Miscellaneous There are innumerable odds and ends which can be employed in modelling, especially for detailing purposes on industrial buildings. Many are things which are being discarded and so will not cost you anything! As you become more experienced in detailing, converting and scratch-building you will find that you develop the knack of seeing the modelling potential in many apparently unlikely objects, though you must be careful not to get too good at it or you will be reluctant ever to throw anything away, an attitude which is not generally popular with other members of the household!

Wire of varying thicknesses can be used as ducts, piping, handrails, bracing wires, cables and so on, while staples are convenient for modelling grab-irons. Old toothpaste tubes opened out provide a supply of thin, easy-to-work metal from which pieces of corrugated iron, metal covers and other details can be fabricated. Old, broken toys and domestic utensils often provide useful bits and pieces as do old plastic kit models.

As with your tools, the materials and parts you have in stock should be stored neatly to avoid damage and also to enable you to find what you are looking for quickly and easily. For the storage of small items I bought several inexpensive sets of plastic parts storage drawers from a local DIY shop. These are very convenient as they can be stacked up on top of each other against a wall and so do not require much space. As the drawers are transparent it is possible to get some idea of where things are even without opening them, but I have also added labels for extra convenience.

Kits and kit construction

There is now a very wide range of kits of various types and materials, particularly in the most popular railway modelling scales.

Card kits These offer the largest selection of British prototype structures. The standard material for scratch-building is card, usually covered with brick- or stone-paper. By using good-quality card, printed in full colour, the manufacturers offer the modeller convenience in construction with an excellent finished appearance.

The Hamblings Bilteezi range was first introduced in 1948 and was later expanded. There is a good range of railway and other buildings in 00 scale and a smaller selection in TT. There was also an N-scale series but only two of these are still available, one being the row of low relief suburban shops shown in one of the accompanying pictures. The windows on the Bilteezi sheets are printed not glazed, but the colour reproduction is good and the models have a realistic appearance when completed. The card used is relatively thin and bracing is desirable.

The Superquick card kits are another popular series, again with a good selection of railway and other structures. These kits are made only in 00 scale. They are printed in full colour on thick card and the parts are pre-cut for ease of cutting out and folding. Clear plastic glazing material, silk screen printed with window frames is included. Construction is straightforward and results in sturdy realistic models.

The Builder Plus kits have been more recently introduced and the range, which includes 00- and N-scale models, is being steadily expanded. The models are again printed in full colour, are pre-cut and pre-creased, and include transparent silk screen printed glazing material.

At the time of writing a new range, Gilmour kits, have just come on to the market, and these appear to be of similar type.

Prototype Models make a selection of card kits, printed in colour, complete with clear glazing material with printed window frames, in 2 mm, 4 mm and 7 mm scales. All the models are accurate scale replicas of actual prototype structures, mainly railway buildings. The range includes a number of models which are ideal for a branch line layout.

In addition to the British models, a variety of card kits for US and Continental prototype structures have appeared, mainly in HO scale. There are also a number of kits in varying scales, some suitable for use on model

This bottle kiln and workshops model in 00 scale constructed from a Novus (W & T) card kit is a small industrial unit which can be accommodated on even a very small layout, adding both scenic interest and extra goods traffic.

Low relief shops built from a Hambling's Bilteezi sheet provide a neat finishing touch to Colin Woolridge's attractive N-scale layout. The houses were also built from Bilteezi kits. Note the details in the gardens.

railways, of castles and other historic buildings.

Card kits are easy to build and make a good introduction to structure modelling for the beginner. As with any kit it is important to study the parts together with any written or diagrammatic instructions before starting work. The parts should be cut out carefully, using a sharp modelling knife. The pre-cut models may still have small tabs which need cutting, rather than tearing, to avoid leaving rough edges and the risk of bending or creasing the parts. Often the number or other identifying mark is printed beside rather than on the part. To avoid any possible confusion later, mark the number lightly in pencil on the rear of each part immediately after cutting it out so that it can be definitely identified later. While this may not be important with simple models, mistakes can occur if there are more numerous parts, so this is a good habit to get into from the beginning.

Though the parts have the front surface fully coloured, the cut edges, of course, are not. When the pieces have been cut out these edges should be coloured to match the printed front surfaces using either paint or a felt-tip pen of appropriate colour. If the kit is not pre-creased the card should be scored with the knife before bending. Use a steel rule as a guide when bending to make sure the fold is straight and clean. Even with the pre-creased

Two church models in 00 scale constructed from card kits. **Below left** *A Superquick kit.* **Below right** *A Builder Plus kit.*

This realistic 4 mm scale model of Stamford Engine Shed, LNER ex-GN, was built from a Prototype Models card kit. The kits from this manufacturer are all accurate replicas of actual buildings and the range includes models in 2 mm, 4 mm and 7 mm scales. (Photograph by courtesy of Prototype Models.)

kits take care when making the bends, particularly with the smaller parts, as these can easily become distorted.

For assembly I use a quick-drying tube adhesive such as Uhu or Clear Bostik. Make sure that the parts all match up accurately before applying any glue, then use it sparingly taking care not to let any smears or blobs get on to the outer surface of the card. Some models will need extra bracing of card or stripwood inside to add strength and rigidity. If the card is not very thick it may be advisable to mount the printed walls on to thicker card before assembly. This will avoid warping, bending and buckling later and will make the models less liable to damage from handling or accidental knocks. You may want to paint the interior black or another dark colour; if so, this should be done before the roof is fitted unless access will still be possible from the bottom of the model.

If you want to fit interior details this should also be done before access becomes difficult or impossible. Even if you do not want to go to the lengths of modelling full interior detailing you may wish to add floors and dividing walls so that the viewer cannot see right through from one side of the building to the other, and so the model does not appear to be just an empty shell. These, together with just a suggestion of interior fittings, can do much to make a model look more realistic.

I have already mentioned that the Bilteezi sheets have printed and not glazed windows. While the effect is still good, particularly when the models are in the background, a more realistic appearance can undoubtedly be achieved by cutting out the windows and fitting transparent glazing material behind. On these sheets projecting brickwork is also represented by the printing and not in actual relief. An improvement is to cut this brickwork out on a second kit, mount it on thick card, touching up the edges with appropriate colour, and then glue on to the first kit as an overlay. This does require the purchase of a second kit but this is well worthwhile, especially if the model will be in the foreground on the layout. Window sills, doorsteps, and so on can be similarly treated.

There are some details which can be added to any of the kits. Doorknobs made from pinheads, guttering and downpipes from plastic strip and rod, ventilation ducts on industrial buildings from scraps of card, wood or plastic, and so on. Modelling some windows and doors in a partly open position is another realistic touch. Strips of tiles or slates, or individually applied ones, can be added, as described in the section on scratch-building, on top of the printed kit roofs giving additional relief.

Some of the printed sheets already have a weathered appearance; others will benefit from a little dirt and dust painted on, as will be discussed later. As with all model buildings, the setting is important and many details can be added to the ground around the structures.

Plastic kits The largest choice of structure models is in the form of plastic kits. As many of the manufacturers are Continental the majority of the kits are for European prototypes, though recently there has been a significant increase in the number of British prototypes available. The scales range from Z scale, for which Kibri and Märklin make a few model building kits, through to G, in which kits by HMB are designed for use with the large-scale LGB

Above *This town scene on a Fleischmann exhibition layout gives some idea of the wide range of plastic kits available in HO scale for models of European prototype structures both old and modern. Note also the realistic arrangement of the buildings on this layout.*

Below *This attractive model of a modern motor hotel, complete with rooftop café above the restaurant, is on a large Fleischmann HO-scale exhibition layout. The model was constructed from a Kibri kit.*

model railways. However, the great majority are for 00, HO and N scales.

Considering the models of British prototypes first of all, there is now a good selection available. The Airfix range in 00 scale includes a variety of railway structures. These kits are easy to assemble and form an excellent basis for further detailing and for conversions. There was also, at one time, a selection of non-railway buildings, including a windmill and a thatched cottage. These are not at present available but they may well be re-issued at a future date.

Hornby have recently brought out a range of 00-scale railway structure kits with clip-together plastic parts which are printed in full colour. These models are designed for easy construction by beginners and make up into realistic and attractive buildings especially suitable for use with the Hornby train sets.

The Danish manufacturer Heljan, in addition to Continental and American prototypes in HO and N scales, now makes a series of British railway and other building models in 00 scale which are realistic and well detailed.

In N scale Peco offer a range of railway structures, some of which are illustrated here, as well as several houses, while S & B Mouldings make kits for a selection of railway buildings.

Merit, well known for their small accessories, make a plastic kit for a typical modern signal cabin in 00 scale, and in the same scale Malvern Models have just introduced an attractive GWR halt station.

The greatest variety is in the Continental prototypes from the European manufacturers. These are mainly West German firms such as Faller, Herpa, Kibri, Pola and Vollmer, but others include Jouef (France), Heljan

This attractive signalbox in 00 scale was constructed from one of the range of pre-coloured plastic clip-together kits for model railway buildings produced by Hornby. The model includes some interior details. The trees are from Woodland Scenic kits marketed by Hammant & Morgan. (Photograph by courtesy of McLeish Associates Ltd.)

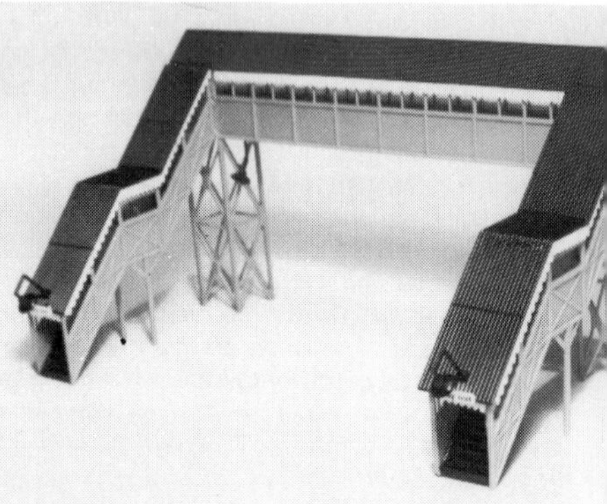

Top left and right and above left *An engine shed, goods shed and signal cabin constructed from Peco N-scale plastic kits.* (Photographs by courtesy of Peco.)

Above right *Heljan have recently introduced a range of 00-scale plastic kits for British prototype railway structures including this realistic footbridge.*

(Denmark), Lima (Italy) and Vero (East Germany). The kits are mainly in HO and N scales but include other railway scales. Though many of the models are unsuitable for use on layouts using British prototypes some, particularly the industrial structures and modern railway buildings, can be employed, if necessary with a few minor alterations. Many of the kits are remarkably well detailed and make up into excellent models. Though strictly the HO and Continental N scale models are slightly underscale for 00 and British N scale respectively the discrepancy is generally not very noticeable and the structure can be utilised.

A good selection of kits of American prototypes are also available from some of the Continental manufacturers and from American firms such as AHM, Atlas, Bachmann, Lifelike, Model Power, Revell and Tyco.

Plastic kits are generally easy to construct but, as always in modelling, care and thought will lead to the best finished model. Before starting work study the instructions and identify the parts. Remove the pieces from the sprues carefully, cutting them off with a knife or razor saw. Do not just break them off as this can cause damage at the point of attachment. Any flash or blemishes should be removed with a modelling knife, fine file and fine sandpaper. If there are any small defects these can be filled. If there are larger defects or if parts are badly formed, damaged or missing, go back to the shop where you bought the kit or write to the manufacturer direct. Many kits include complaint slips for this purpose.

This modern signal cabin was built from an 00-scale plastic kit manufactured by Merit.

This attractive 4 mm scale model GWR halt station was constructed from a plastic kit recently introduced by Malvern Models. (Photograph by courtesy of Malvern Models.)

With a simple kit where the pieces are easy to identify you can remove them all from the sprues and clean them up before assembly. With the larger, more complicated kits it is easy to confuse some of the parts. Many of them may be numbered on the pieces themselves, but others may have a number adjacent to them on the sprue and these pieces should be left in place until needed, as this will make identification easier. You may also find it easier to paint small pieces if they are left attached to the sprues, so that they can be handled and held without difficulty during painting and while they are drying. You will need to touch them up slightly when you do remove them but this is easily done. Many of the plastic kits are moulded in suitably coloured plastic so that painting is not essential. However, good painting will produce a more realistic finish. It is often easier and neater to paint some or all of the parts before assembly especially if there are small parts of one colour to be attached to a larger piece of another colour. Some parts may be inaccessible in the finished model so must be painted before or during assembly. Thus the painting sequence depends partly on the model and partly on the preferences of the builder.

The parts should be checked for a good fit by trying initially to assemble them without glue. If they do not fit together well, file or cut them to the proper shape for an accurate join. For assembly, plastic tube cement can be used but one of the liquid solvent cements such as Mek Pak is the most convenient, especially for the smaller parts. The liquid is simply painted on to the surfaces to be joined and these are then held together until firmly fixed. As the liquid is drawn by capillary action into joins, parts can be cemented conveniently by holding them together in the correct position and then drawing a brush loaded with the solvent along the join. It is important not to get either the tube cement or the solvent on to plastic surfaces which will show on the finished model as this will mark them. If this happens accidentally then wait until the cement is properly dry and hard, then file or sand off the marks, but the surface detail will also be lost. Take care not to touch the surfaces of the model if you have glue on your fingers, as this will also mark the plastic. Any cracks or gaps between parts should be filled using one of the plastic fillers available. This is another reason why it is better to paint these models even if the plastic is an appropriate colour; if you do not then you must get a perfect fit without

Graham Bailey built this market garden from his N-scale layout creating an unusual but attractive scenic feature. The greenhouses are from Faller plastic kits.

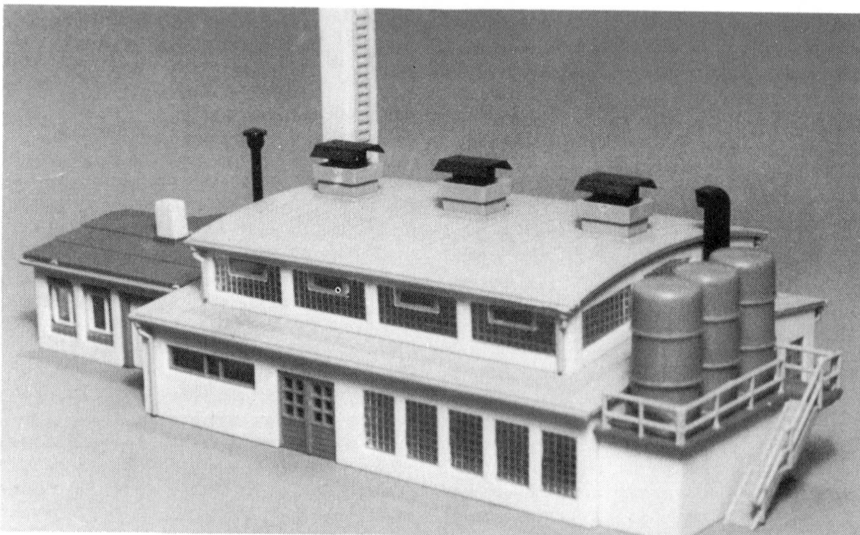

using filler, and this is not always possible. After filling, allow time for the filler to set hard then file and sand it to a smooth finish at the join.

Some of the plastic kits are very highly detailed and complete but others are more basic and will benefit from the addition of extra details as mentioned in the section on card kits.

In addition to their series of HO- and N-scale plastic kits Faller make a range of Combi kits which include embossed card parts, printed in colour, for the walls together with plastic parts and details. These kits combine the advantages of both card and plastic kits with attractive results. Lima have recently introduced a selection of British prototype building kits in 00 scale with plastic bases and roofs and pre-printed card walls. The parts slot together for easy assembly.

Scenerama produced a very neat kit for a pair of semi-detached town houses in 4 mm scale with plastic parts forming the basic structure over which brick and tilepaper were applied. Window frames, doors and other details were moulded in plastic. The completed model is very realistic but unfortunately the kit has apparently been discontinued though at the time of writing W & H Models, and perhaps other shops also, had some still in stock.

A number of structure model kits have also been made in the form of vacuum-moulded plastic. WMH Models offered a series of attractive models in 00 scale including farm buildings and ruined stone cottages. The models were ideal for both railway and military purposes but I have not seen them in the shops for some time now and I suspect they are no longer available. Houses and cottages are produced in 00 scale as vacuum-formed mouldings by Midland Model Railway Supplies and these are designed for use as low relief background models.

Wood kits In Britain manufacturers have tended to concentrate on card structure kits and there have been very few wood kits produced. Builder Plus, who make an extensive range of card kits, have recently extended the scope of their models to include two wood kits in 00 scale, a goods depot and a sawmill. These kits, which make attractive structures, include die-cut planking, stripwood of appropriate dimensions, clear glazing material and black paper to represent bitumen roofing. The goods depot is more typical of a US prototype but the sawmill is suitable for a British layout.

Marlow Models make two 4 mm scale kits of windmills. These are replicas of actual structures, Lacey Green Smock Mill and the National Trust Postmill at Pitstone Green. These are wood kits with details such as windows, millstones, etc, supplied as white metal castings. The kits can be motorised if desired.

It is in the United States, where there are many prototype structures of wooden construction, that the wood kits have been most developed. They are nearly all for HO scale though a few N-scale models are available. The structures are often of older prototypes and in many cases are exact models of particular buildings. The kits include wooden sidings, marked out or cut to size, stripwood, paper shingles, metal castings for windows, doors and other parts, and where the prototype has walls of brick or stone these are represented by brick or stonepaper, by embossed card or, in some kits, castings in dental plaster or urethane are provided. The better kits are remarkably complete even to posters and signs for the walls, and the instructions are often very detailed, even including advice on weathering and providing a proper scenic setting. In some kits there are dozens, even hundreds, of white metal castings for detailing purposes and full interior detailing may be provided, as in the Fine Scale Miniatures Rail Car Shed kit illustrated.

As some experience in modelling is desirable these American kits are not really intended for the beginner but with time, care and some skill, models of exhibition standard can be built from them. Not surprisingly, these kits tend to cost more than the mass-produced card or plastic kits and the larger and more complex ones are quite expensive. However, they do provide many enjoyable hours of construction and a fine model afterwards. These 'craftsman' wood kits are available in limited numbers in Britain at specialist shops such as Victors of Islington.

While the British wood kits are less complicated than many of the US models, construction is more difficult than for card and plastic kits, and a little previous modelling experience will be helpful. It is important to read the instructions or study the diagrams carefully before starting work and to identify

Top left *A realistic girder bridge constructed from a Vollmer plastic kit carries an electrified branch over the main line on this N-scale German layout, based on a prototype. Note how the bridge supporting walls are set into the scenery without any unsightly gaps or cracks.*

Centre left and left *There are many interesting industrial structures available as plastic kits from Continental manufacturers. These pictures show two examples in N scale. A modern chemical factory from the Vollmer range and a timber plant from Pola.*

Above left and right *Marlow Models have recently introduced two kits for 4 mm scale windmills which are models of actual prototype structures—Lacey Green Smock Mill and Pitstone Postmill. The kits are wood with cast metal parts such as windows and millstones.* (Photographs by Angy Jackman.)

Below *Wood craftsman kits are popular in the United States. This superb HO-scale coal dock was constructed by C. Emmerson from a Fine Scale Miniatures kit.* (Photograph by courtesy of Fine Scale Miniatures.)

Above far right *The roof has been removed from this HO-scale rail car shed built from a Fine Scale Miniatures kit to show the incredibly detailed interior. Everything shown, with the exception of the human figures, is included in this remarkably complete kit.* (Photograph by courtesy of Fine Scale Miniatures.)

correctly the materials to be used for each part. It is easy to use the wrong stripwood, for example, so that later you find you have not sufficient of a particular size. In the Builder Plus kits many identical parts must be cut and assembled and care is required to do this accurately. This is important because errors here will spoil the appearance of the completed building. Tube adhesive such as Uhu or Bostik, or balsa cement can be used for assembly. Allow sufficient time for the cement to harden before trying to proceed with construction as many of the separate items are rather fragile until fitted together and if the glue has not set firmly these units may distort while you are fixing them in place. The models can be painted or alternatively stained to represent weathered, unpainted wood. The modeller with a little experience, particularly if he has done some aero-modelling in which the construction work is rather similar, will find that he can build successfully from these kits and that the resulting models are realistic wooden structures. The kits are also a good introduction to this type of work for those who would like to go on to scratch-building models of wooden prototypes.

Metal kits In Britain these are restricted to cast metal kits and the cost and weight of this material limits the choice to small structures such as lineside huts. Mike's Models offer cast metal kits in 4 mm scale for a GWR pagoda halt station building, a Victorian cast iron 'gents' and a GWR corrugated iron lamp hut. Roxey Mouldings make 4 mm scale kits for a Southern Railway platelayers' hut and a tool hut and the Dart Castings range, also 00-scale, includes a GWR lineside hut. W & H Models make a 4 mm scale 'gents' white metal kit. In N scale Fleetline Models make lineside huts and girder and plate girder railway bridges.

Assembly of these small cast metal kits is straightforward. The castings should be cleaned up with a fine file to remove any flash and to ensure a good fit of the parts. The pieces can then be assembled using a tube cement such as Bostik, an epoxy adhesive or a cyanoacrylate adhesive. After washing the model with warm water and a little detergent to remove any dirt and grease it can be painted. For priming I find Duplicolor Grey Primer, supplied in aerosol cans for car touching-up work, convenient, followed by Humbrol or other model paint for the final coats.

In the United States another type of metal kit is available from Suydam. These HO-scale models, mainly of mines and other industrial structures, are made from metal with a corrugated surface covering representing corrugated iron. Assembly requires soldering.

Plaster kits A very effective method of reproducing brick and stone walls is to model a handmade original, make a mould from it and then cast the parts in plaster. These walls are then glued together to form the building and are painted as required. Ossett Mouldings produced a very useful range of castings of this type, including the roof tiling used on the factory model shown on page 33, using plaster with a reinforcing backing of cloth. This firm also made a series of structure kits including lineside huts and a half-timbered pub in this material. Unfortunately I think they must have been discontinued as I have not been able to

With the Linka system the modeller uses the moulds provided to cast parts which can then be used to make up a wide variety of 00-scale model buildings. Two examples, a farm and a castle, are shown in these pictures. (Photographs by courtesy of Thomas Salter Ltd.)

The main roof is made from roofing tiles mouldings from the Ossett range of plastic castings. The ventilator duct was assembled from stripwood with thin strips of plastic card around it (see also page 39).

find any in the shops recently. Some of the US manufacturers, as I have already mentioned, include castings in dental plaster in their 'craftsman' type wooden kits, where stonework is needed.

Thomas Salter have taken a different approach in their new and justifiably popular Linka system. In these sets the modeller is provided with a wide range of moulds for brick and stonework, logs and lapboard, including window openings, doorways and so on, together with Linkalite casting compound. Windows of various types printed on clear glazing material are available and guttering, drainpipes and sheets of signs are also provided for detailing purposes. The parts are supplied as kits of various selections, for example, brickwork or stonework, but are also available separately. Plans, giving full details of the parts needed and how they must be assembled, are produced for a range of 00-scale structures of interest to the railway and military modeller but, of course, the scope for constructing models of the builder's own choice or design is almost limitless.

The system is easy to use. The mould required is first prepared by rinsing it with a little washing-up liquid in warm water. The Linkalite Moulding Compound is gently mixed with water using the measures provided and is then poured into the mould cavities, taking care to push it well into all the corners. The mould is tapped to remove any air bubbles and, as the mixture begins to set, a straight edge is drawn across the surface of the mould to scrape off any excess mixture. After about half an hour the casting is removed by flexing the mould and easing the rubber away. It is then left to dry for 24 hours at room temperature or for four to eight hours in an airing cupboard.

The castings interlock for assembly and they are fixed together with a little of the adhesive provided. Windows, cut from the printed glazing material supplied, are glued in place behind the window openings. Basic paints are provided in the sets but poster paints, ordinary household emulsions or Humbrol enamels can also be employed for colouring.

There is a special thatch-making kit with brushes and a special slow setting Linkalite compound so that the surface can be textured to represent this type of roofing.

Because the moulds can be re-used as often as the modeller wishes and additional moulding compound, adhesive and other items can be purchased separately, the system has great scope and flexibility for the scratch-builder as well as the kit modeller.

Kit conversion

I have already mentioned the possibility of adding extra details to make kit structures more interesting and realistic. From this the modeller may well progress to kit conversion in which the kit is modified so that the finished model has a different appearance. There are several possible advantages in this. It can provide variety and individuality in your structures, and can make kit buildings more suitable for the type of scene you are modelling or for the location in which your layout is supposed to be set. It also enables you to construct more easily, more quickly and perhaps, more successfully than by scratch-building, models of buildings for which no kits are produced. It will, generally however, be more expensive than building entirely from scratch.

Obviously your own interests and the amount of time you can devote to modelling will influence how you choose to model structures. If you are keenest on operation you may be happy to use only basic kit-built structures, perhaps the quickly assembled clip-together Hornby kits for 00 scale, or even, if you are working in N scale, the ready built models made by Grafar. If your interests are more general and include construction as well as operation you may want to convert kits so that you can enjoy more interesting structure modelling and also give your layout some individuality. Alternatively you might particularly like building construction and find that this becomes a main interest in the hobby. In this case you may want to spend most of your time making highly detailed structure models from scratch while keeping other aspects of your layout relatively simple. Indeed, one of the nice things about railway modelling is the wide choice it offers. While I do enjoy scratch-building, my free time is limited and this is one reason why I convert kits. However, I also like the challenge which this type of modelling presents.

The scope of kit conversion is very wide,

Above left *The Airfix 00-scale signalbox plastic kit is also useful as a starting point for conversion work. This picture shows the basic kit assembled according to the manufacturer's instructions.*

Left *A view of a 4 mm scale gantry signal cabin. The cabin itself was constructed from parts of an Airfix signalbox kit while the supporting gantry was made up from Plastruct girdering. The stairs from two kits were used and the additional handrails required for the stairs and around the cabin were cut from thin plastic card.*

Right *This small signalbox for a 4 mm scale narrow-gauge line was largely scratch-built from plastic card but parts from the Airfix signalbox kit were used for convenience. Kit parts used included cut down sides and stairs.*

Below right *Terry Jenkins built this 00-scale factory using Hambling's Bilteezi dairy/small factory card kits. The crane is from an Airfix military vehicle plastic kit.*

Bottom *Keith Gowen constructed the station buildings for the terminus on his TT-scale branch line from Hambling's Bilteezi Stone Forge card kits. The platform canopy is a scratch-built addition.*

ranging from minor alterations in appearance, for example, in modifying a Continental structure to make it look more typical of a British building, to using a few kit parts in a model where so much is fabricated from other materials that the structure could more accurately be considered as scratch-built. This latter situation is not as extravagant as it may at first seem. Many plastic kits are relatively inexpensive but contain well detailed parts which cannot be obtained as separate items. To make up these parts from scratch may be difficult and time consuming and, for the inexperienced modeller, the final result will probably not be as good as the kit parts. Thus it may be worth the cost of the kit to obtain the parts you want; the rest of the kit can be kept and may well provide parts for further conversions in the future. The two signalbox models illustrated here utilise the more-difficult-to-fabricate parts such as sides, with windows, and the steps, from Airfix Signal Cabin kits resulting in a considerable saving in time and work compared to scratch-building. Do take care when converting or using kit parts that the kit or components are suitable for the model you are attempting to make and that the alterations will not involve more work than building from scratch. It can be rather easy to get so carried away with the idea of converting

Two views of an interesting conversion from an 00-scale Super-quick low relief card kit. The modeller has used parts from a second kit to alter the low relief models to full-depth structures. Note the painters on the centre roof and the bird on the higher roofs.

that it can become an end of its own rather than a means to an end. Remember that the idea is to enable you to build a model more easily and quickly, and perhaps with a better result, than if you were to try to build it from scratch.

The card kits are easy to convert and some examples are shown in this book. Many others have been described in the model railway magazines over the years. R.G. Vacy-Ash, the designer of the Hambling's Bilteezi sheets, has built several attractive models converted from these kits and, in fact, some of the kits have been designed to permit construction in different forms. Another well-known modeller, the Rev Edward Beal, has also made a number of interesting models by converting these kits.

However, the plastic kits offer the greatest possibilities for the kit converter and the scope is almost unlimited. I made a point of collecting all the catalogues issued by the structure kit manufacturers so that I can check on just what is available. Just browsing through these will often give me an idea for a conversion. Familiarity with the kits on the market also means that when I see a prototype structure I like I may recall a kit which would be a suitable basis for conversion into a model of this building or which might provide suitable parts for an otherwise scratch-built model.

Whenever you carry out any kit construction or conversion always save any left-over parts. In time you will build up a very useful selection which you can utilise for further projects. As these parts accumulate it is worth separating them into different items such as doors, windows, stairway parts, chimneys, piping, handrails, sections of brick, stone or wood planking, and so on. Store the different lots in labelled boxes or small drawers so that you can quickly check through to see just what you have and so that you can find any particular item without delay. I also keep the instruction sheet from any kit I assemble in a file so that I can refer to it again. Checking through these can also be helpful in finding suitable parts for conversions as most of these sheets include diagrams showing all the kit parts.

A common form of conversion is the combination of two or more identical kits to form a larger structure. This is usually fairly straightforward and, indeed, some kits are designed to permit this as an alternative to the single kit form. Several of the engine shed kits, both card and plastic, come into this category. However, others particularly for factories, warehouses, goods sheds and mine buildings can often be assembled without difficulty with two or more kits combined.

For the more complex conversions quite drastic alterations may be required with extensive cutting and fitting of the parts. These models must be carefully planned and the parts accurately marked and cut if we are to avoid mistakes which may be difficult to rectify. If pieces are wrongly cut it may even be necessary to buy an extra kit to replace the parts and this can be annoying and expensive! Walls, roofs and bases are usually of fairly thick

A medium-sized engine shed constructed in N scale by combining four Peco engine shed kits. The kit is designed to allow any number of units to be fitted together to form a suitable-sized shed. (Photograph by courtesy of Peco.)

plastic and this is most easily cut with a razor saw. Use a file and sandpaper for cleaning up the cut edges and to achieve a perfect fit. If the rear wall of a structure will not be visible when the model is placed on the layout the part or parts making up this wall can be replaced by thick card if desired and the kit wall used elsewhere in the conversion. In this way I was able to construct the small factory (shown in some of the photographs) from a single Airfix engine shed kit even though the factory is twice as long as the kit structure.

When carrying out a conversion you may need to fill in some window or door openings. There may be left over parts from the kit, or from previous conversions, which can be used to fill these gaps or you may need to employ plastic card, either plain material scribed to match, or embossed brick or stone sheet. Any gaps or cracks should be filled, then filed and sanded smooth in the usual way. Joins between parts, for example, in the middle of a wall, can often be concealed by appropriately placed drainpipes, notices, posters, ventilation ducts, piping, lean-to buildings, even planks of wood leaning against the wall.

If in a conversion the cut edge of a section of stone course or brick wall is visible at a corner of the building, a fine file or model knife should be used to carry the grooves representing the mortar between the brick or stone courses around the corner to give a more realistic

A neat N-scale overbridge using Peco moulded plastic girder bridge sides. The stonework is embossed plastic card. Longer bridges can be constructed by employing more than one pair of sides. (Photograph by courtesy of Peco.)

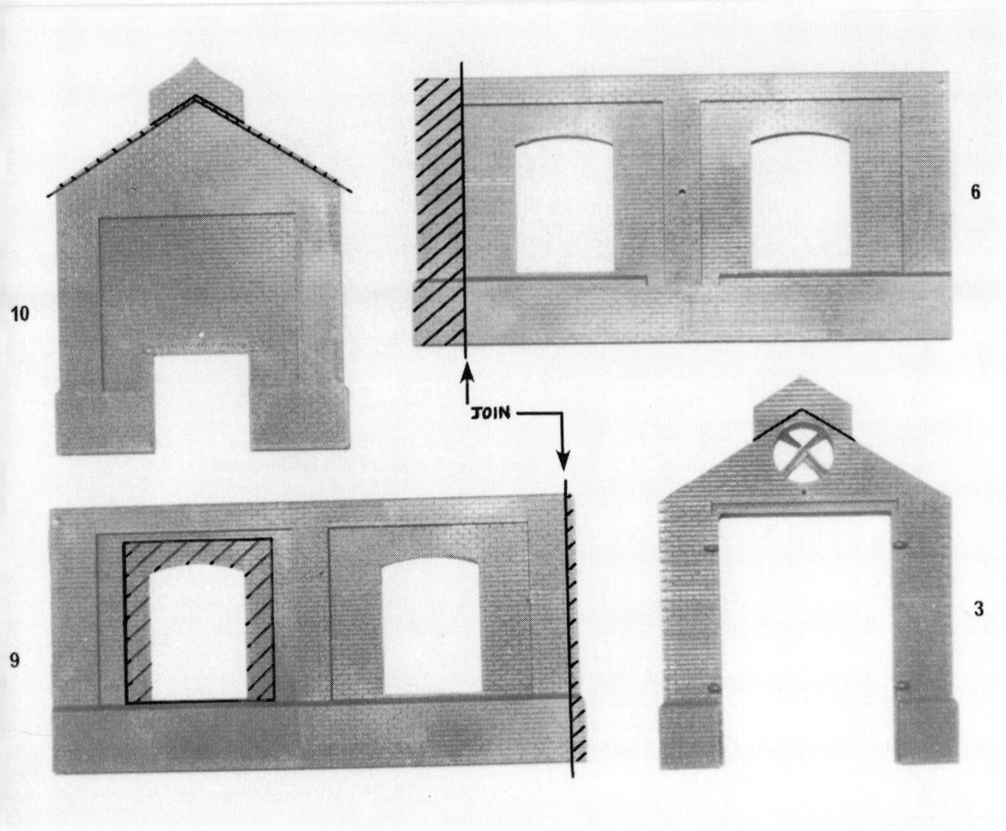

10

6

JOIN

9

3

The Airfix 00-scale engine shed plastic kit is an excellent basis for conversion work and these pictures illustrate the construction of a small lineside factory using parts from this kit. **Left** *Parts from the kit showing how they are modified. Cuts were made with a razor saw. Numbers refer to the kit part numbers. Parts 6 and 9 are joined to form the front wall of the factory.* **Below left** *Front, rear and ends assembled and windows fitted. As the rear of the model will not be visible on the layout, plain card was used for this wall. Alternatively parts from a second kit could be employed to model this wall more fully.* **Above** *A loading platform cut from wood together with doors and a canopy made from balsa wood have been added. The lean-to at the right-hand end was constructed from thick card covered with corrugated copper sheet. The additional roof supports are thick card.* **Below** *The completed model with roof added. See also photograph on page 33.*

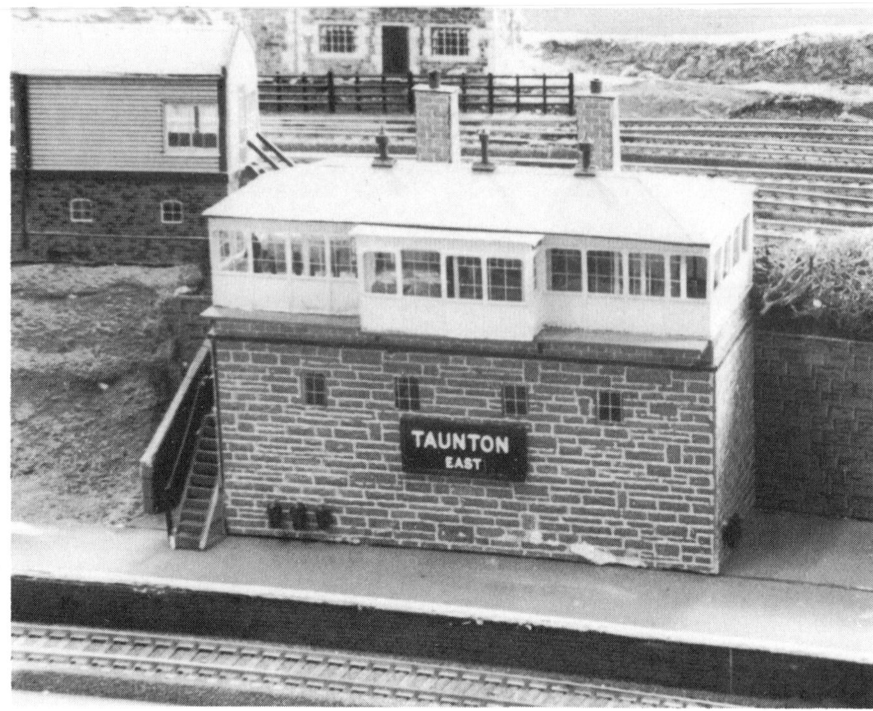

Above *Terry Jenkins used parts from Airfix signal box kits together with a scratch-built base for this large signalbox on the Bournemouth & Isle of Purbeck MRC 4 mm scale layout.*

Below *Graham Bailey used Pola station roof kits with additional parts scratch-built from card for the large station on his N-scale modern layout. The fire station in the foreground was constructed from a Hambling's Bilteezi card kit.*

appearance. Additional parts needed for a conversion, if not to be found in the scrap parts box, can be modelled from plastic card, wood, card or other materials as in scratch-building.

When carrying out conversion work there is no need for the modeller to restrict himself to a single kit or to two or more identical kits. Different kits can be combined with advantage giving great scope for variety, a form of modelling sometimes known as 'cross kitting'. Some models may utilise parts from quite a number of different kits. It all depends on what parts appear most suitable and on the contents of your spare parts box. It is also possible, with a little care, successfully to combine kits of different materials, for example, card and plastic, making the scope even greater. In such cases the plastic parts should be painted, and overall weathering is useful to tone down any differences in surface texture and in colour between the painted plastic and printed card parts. Balsa or hardwood is useful for constructing wooden additions such as lean-to sheds and outbuildings.

One of the advantages of kit conversion is that by building a variety of structures all based on one or two kits we can create a similarity of style and construction material which will give unity and harmony to the scene, enhancing the realism and atmosphere. Railway buildings in a particular area, for example, often show this sort of similarity due to standardisation of architectural style, construction materials and the design of small fittings and details by the railway company concerned.

As the projects become more complex and advanced the work tends to merge into scratch-building and when the modeller comes across a structure which cannot be conveniently converted from any available kit he should find no difficulty in tackling its construction from scratch.

Kit conversion has now outgrown the somewhat derogatory 'kit bashing' title it was once given and is a valuable form of structure modelling. It provides interest and variety without the commitment in time and work required for scratch-building and, best of all, it can be great fun!

Working models

Some modellers dislike structure models which have moving parts, regarding them as gimmicky. Perhaps this follows from the manufacture of toy train gadgetry such as exploding boxcars, head-bobbing giraffes and so on, leading the scale modeller to feel that all working structures and accessories are out of place on a scale layout. However, the kits available are generally well detailed and realistic models which are entirely suitable for use on a scale model railway. The extra movement and interest which these working models can add to the scene are of benefit, particularly on a small layout where the train-operating potential may be rather limited. One of the most popular subjects is the windmill and a variety of types are available in both HO and N scales from Faller and Pola, and in HO scale from Vero. One of the HO-scale Faller kits is for a windmill complete with a waterwheel as well. These models are all of Continental prototypes and will require modifications to make them more typical of British mills. However, the Marlow Models 4 mm scale wooden windmill kits can be motorised by the modeller if desired and these are replicas of actual British windmills. Another attractive choice is a watermill with kits in HO and N scale by Faller and Pola. The Faller HO model is remarkable in that the wheel is driven round by real water which is circulated by means of a small pump. This pump can also be employed to provide moving water for model fountains and waterfalls. Brawa also make a pump of this type. The Faller range also includes sawmills in HO and N scales with waterwheels. As with the windmill kits the prototypes are typically European and modification is needed for a British layout.

The windmills and watermills are appropriate for a rural setting but there are also kits for working models suitable for industrial areas. Vollmer make a working conveyor-belt in HO scale which can be used in conjunction with a loading platform and a warehouse and this will add extra activity to a goods depot or industrial scene. Faller also offer a working conveyor-belt in this scale which can be combined with a dumping tip and storage hopper as part of an interesting gravel works complex. A very effective item from Brawa is an HO-scale working model of an aerial ropeway of the type used to carry ore, rock, coal and so on from a mine or quarry to a processing plant. This firm also uses a similar mechanism for models of a cable railway in HO and N scales and a ski-lift in HO scale. These latter two are more suited to layouts based on Continental prototypes but the mineral ropeway is ideal for British or European model railways.

Container terminals are now part of the

This HO-scale Pola windmill is fitted with a small electric motor to make the sails rotate. The model adds movement as well as scenic interest on this small 009 layout owned by the Poole & District MRS. Note the many small details which make the scene appear larger than it really is.

Above left *An interesting 4 mm scale model of the beam pump at Wheal Busy built by Steve Dewhirst. The building was constructed from card which was painted with shellac and then coated with a thin layer of Polyfilla. When dry this was smoothed over and the stonework was scribed into it. Painting was with poster colours. The chimney is made from plastic card with computer punchings glued on to simulate bricks. The working parts for the beam engine were fabricated from plastic card.*

Above right *Another interesting working model is this cable car system manufactured by Eheim and seen here on a Continental layout built by Terry Jenkins. Models are available in both HO and N scales.*

British railway scene and Faller produce a working model in HO scale which is suitable for a large or moderate-sized goods depot on a modern image layout. If your model railway serves a dock you might like to include one of the impressive Wiad HO scale dockside cranes. Powered by four motors the crane can move along on rails on the dockside, or along on its own bridge track, can rotate and can lift a load, all by remote control.

Lifting bridges are not uncommon on full-size railways and they make interesting models. Working versions of a rolling lift bridge were available in N and HO scales from Pola; the HO-scale model was later marketed by Hornby. However, I am not certain about the present availability of these two models.

There is, of course, no reason why the modeller should not convert the working model kits in the same way as ordinary structure kits. Alternatively the motors and other mechanism parts can be utilised for scratch-built models, or the modeller can buy suitable motors as separate items and make up the remainder of the parts needed from metal or plastic. An example of an interesting and authentic 00-scale working model of a Cornish tin mine beam pump and winding engine scratch-built by Steve Dewhirst is illustrated here. Steve used plastic card to make the working parts and the pump is driven by a slow-speed mains synchronous motor. The mine is the central feature of a small 009 model railway layout and below baseboard level Steve has included part of the network of passages and caverns which would make up the underground workings, creating a most unusual and intriguing model.

Whether or not to include working model structures on a model railway layout is obviously a matter of personal choice but I feel that these models do warrant serious consideration particularly on a small layout where any extra movement and activity which can be provided will add to the interest. They are also popular with visitors to model railway shows and therefore can be fitted on to exhibition layouts to advantage.

Scratch-building

The construction of a model from basic materials is often known as scratch-building and it offers the greatest choice of subject and materials, though does, of course, involve more work, both in actual construction and in the preparation needed beforehand. This preliminary work involves choosing the subject and acquiring the necessary data, obtaining or drawing up plans, selecting and assembling the various materials. Once all this is done you can plan out your order of construction and begin the actual modelling. If you are working from a fully detailed plan you may find it convenient to trace from it a simplified version showing only the basic dimensions of the walls and the sizes and positions of the window, door and other openings. You can then work from this when constructing the basic shell without being confused by all the additional details which are not important at this stage. This will make the job easier and quicker with less chance of making errors.

Various materials can be employed for the basic structure. The surface finish may be modelled by working on the outer surface of this basic shell or may be in the form of an overlay applied to it. Most modellers use card, wood (balsa, hardwood or ply), or plastic card but other materials such as plaster or expanded polystyrene can be employed just as successfully. If card is used we have a choice of two methods. The whole building can be drawn in opened-out form on the card, with or without the roof, as in simple cut-out card models. After cutting out the walls in one piece, the door and window openings are also cut out. The corners are then scored or cut part way through with a knife and are bent using a metal straight-edge held behind to act as a guide so that the corners are folded sharply and accurately. The basic form is then bent to shape with the two ends brought together to form the fourth corner. Gummed paper tape can be applied to hold the ends at this corner and pieces of stripwood added inside each corner will give the structure strength and

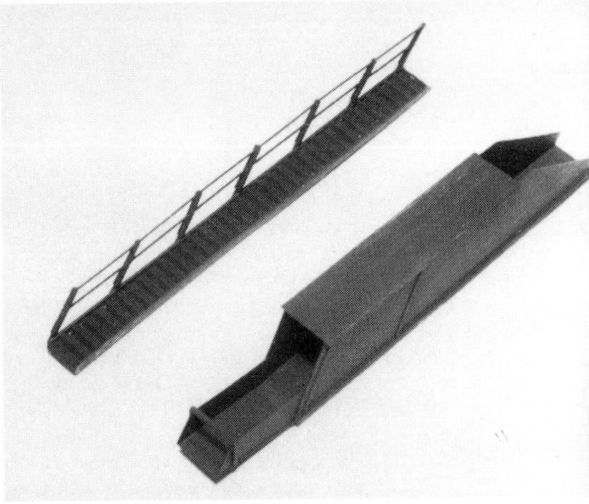

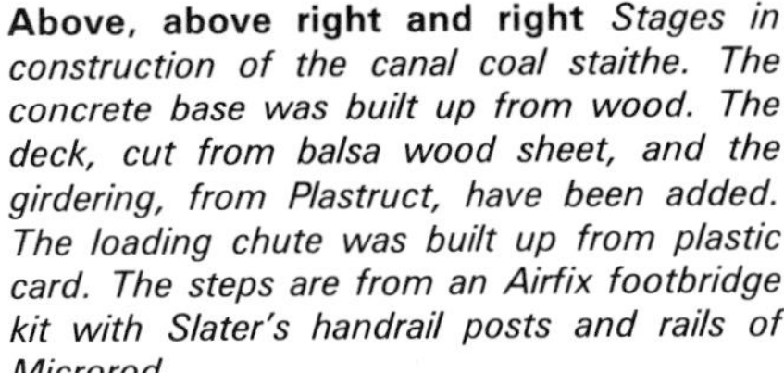

Above, above right and right *Stages in construction of the canal coal staithe. The concrete base was built up from wood. The deck, cut from balsa wood sheet, and the girdering, from Plastruct, have been added. The loading chute was built up from plastic card. The steps are from an Airfix footbridge kit with Slater's handrail posts and rails of Microrod.*

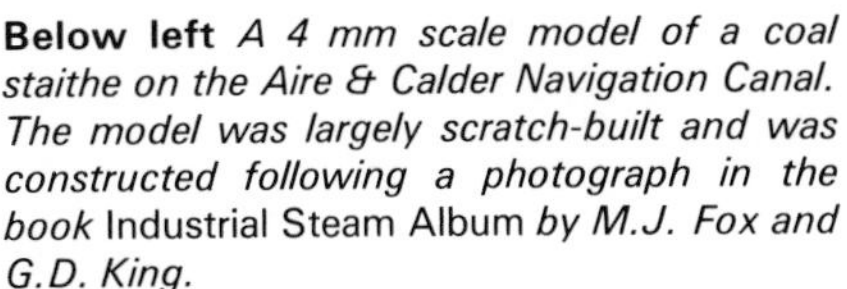

Below left *A 4 mm scale model of a coal staithe on the Aire & Calder Navigation Canal. The model was largely scratch-built and was constructed following a photograph in the book* Industrial Steam Album *by M.J. Fox and G.D. King.*

rigidity. A further inner wall, also of card, can be fitted inside each wall. In these inner walls the window and door openings are also cut out but slightly smaller than the openings in the outer walls to form the window and door frames. With these inner walls glued in place the structure will be quite sturdy. If you plan to use brick or stonepaper on the walls this should be applied before the inner walls are fitted.

Alternatively the walls can be cut out separately from card, wood or plastic card. Either the corners must be bevelled to fit, or you must allow for two of the walls to fit inside the others, for example, the ends between the front and back, and subtract the thickness of the front and back from the width of the end walls. With this method they can either be assembled immediately after cutting out to form a basic structure similar to the folded card type, or each wall can be fully modelled before being assembled with the others. This latter method can be very convenient, especially if there are additional facings and fittings or signs and lettering to be applied, as such work can then be carried out with the walls laid flat on the workbench. If card is used, stripwood bracing will again be desirable in the corners but with wood it may not be required. When working with plastic card I usually fit triangular pieces of scrap plastic into the corners to hold them square and to strengthen the structure generally. Interior walls and floors are best added after the windows have been fitted. The choice of material for the basic shell is not important but it is essential that the structure is accurate in dimensions and squareness (unless deliberate distortion is to be introduced to model an old prototype), and sturdy so that it will not become warped or twisted later.

An example of an unconventional material which has been employed recently is expanded polystyrene. This packing material is light and strong and is convenient for modelling the basic structure of buildings. It is especially

L N E R

popular for ruined buildings on military dioramas. The plastic is easily cut with a knife, saw or, best of all, a hot wire cutter. The construction of such a device has been described by Dave Rowe in an article in the August 1979 issue of *Model Railways* magazine. The surface of the expanded polystyrene can be scribed to represent stonework but the finish is rather coarse and a better effect is achieved by covering the plastic with Polyfilla, Das or Artex. To assemble a structure most universal adhesives are satisfactory but ordinary polystyrene cements must not be used as they will dissolve the expanded plastic.

There are various surface finishes we can choose and these can be modelled in a number of different ways. The choice is up to the individual modeller for the most part and I would recommend that the reader try out different materials and techniques before deciding on which are selected. In the following sections I will endeavour to cover the main ones in use. All give good results if used with care.

The traditional method for modelling brickwork is to use brickpaper and this is still a very satisfactory system. Suitable papers, printed in full colour, are available from various manufacturers. The colouring is generally good and in some cases the brickwork is represented with a realistic weathered appearance. The paper is glued on to the basic structure. When applying the paper to card I often use photomount spray but other adhesives are equally suitable. If plastic card is employed for the basic form, the paper can be applied easily by placing it on the plastic and then painting solvent adhesive liberally on to it. The solvent soaks through the paper and bonds it to the plastic. I apply the paper to each wall separately allowing for an overlap of about $\frac{1}{4}$ in around the corners for the front and back walls. The paper is then fixed on to the end walls and covers this overlap. This method strengthens the corners and avoids the risk of the paper peeling away from the corners as it might if the paper on all the walls goes up to but not around the corners. Use a modelling knife and cut diagonally across the window openings; fold the four flaps thus formed back and glue them to the inside of the walls. In this way the edge of the openings are covered with the brickpaper giving a neat and realistic appearance. Treat the door openings in a similar way.

Stonepapers are employed in exactly the same way as are the brickpapers and also give

Top left *Most of this large N-scale factory complex was scratch-built from 1 mm thick card by Graham Bailey. Brickwork is represented by a covering of Builder Plus brickpaper. The structures at the right-hand end were built from Hambling's Bilteezi sheets.*

Left *An unusual but realistic and interesting model is this derelict factory modelled in N scale by Graham Bailey. The walls are 1 mm thick card covered with Builder Plus brickpaper; beams and rafters are balsa stripwood.*

Below left *Bridges on the 'Eight Oaks' N-scale layout built by Bob Jones. The bridge in the foreground was constructed from stripwood while the stone structure behind is of wooden construction with a covering of stonepaper.*

Below *Terry Jenkins scratch-built this small goods shed in 00 scale using Faller embossed card of stone wall pattern for the walls.*

an attractive finish when applied carefully. Faller make a selection of brick and stone facings which are printed in full colour on card and are embossed to give a more realistic surface texture. These are designed for HO scale but are also suitable for 00. The sheets are applied in a similar manner to brick and stonepapers except that their greater thickness makes it advisable to cut out the window and door openings and not to fold flaps back.

Another popular method now is the use of embossed plastic card for brick and stonework. This material is thin so must be applied as a facing, usually on to a shell made up from thicker plastic card. It can be fixed on the plain walls either before or after they are assembled. Care must be taken to make a square cut along the bottom edge before fitting the facing on so that the brick or stone courses will be parallel to the lower edge of the walls. This cut should be along one of the mortar lines so that the courses on each wall will align properly at the corners. Ideally the corners should be bevelled so that the courses appear to go round the corners. Alternatively, a fine file or modelling knife can be used to make grooves in the edge of the facing piece when a butt joint is used, to match up with the grooves on the adjacent piece. The window and door openings are cut out neatly and if necessary filed true. A fine file or knife is also used here to extend the courses on to the cut edge of the apertures giving the impression of a solid brick or stone wall. The embossed plastic must be painted an appropriate colour depending on the type of brick or stone you wish to represent. A good effect of pointing can then be achieved by applying a thin cream of Polyfilla or Artex over the wall and rubbing most of it gently off. After it has dried further a second rub over will remove any filler which is not in the grooves. The material remaining in the courses gives a realistic representation of the mortar.

A very effective but more time consuming method is to scribe the brick or stonework in the card of the basic structure. This is the technique employed for some of the superb Pendon models. The walls are International Pasteboard and are scribed with a blunt point following the prototype brick or stonework as exactly as possible. An overall coat of paint of mortar colour is applied and then the bricks or stones are touched in individually, varying the colours slightly, giving a very realistic texture and colour.

An alternative, and even more time consuming, method is the application of individual bricks or stones. These are cut from paper, thin card or thin plastic card. A very useful source of rectangles of card of approximately the right size for 00-scale bricks is the punchings from computer cards and if you can obtain some of these you can save yourself a great deal of time and effort by not having to cut out your bricks. The bricks or stones are then positioned one by one on adhesive which has been coated over the basic wall surfaces. The easiest way to do this is to pick the bricks and stones up with the point of a needle. Later the whole is painted as described above for the scribed walls.

A different technique is to use household

Terry Jenkins again used Kos fire cement for the coaling stage and the base of the water tower in this model of the engine servicing facilities at Swanage on the Bournemouth & Isle of Purbeck MRC layout.

Coursed stonework of two different types modelled with Peco Texture Modelling Compound. Variation in the colour of the stones in painting adds to the effect. (Photograph by courtesy of Peco.)

filler such as Polyfilla or Tapwata applied as a coating over a shell of thick card or balsa wood. The brick or stone courses are then scribed into the filler either while it is still soft or after it has dried and hardened. I have used this method effectively for stonework and see no reason why it should not also be satisfactory for brick walls, though the latter will be more work to produce.

The modelling clay Das and fire cements such as Kos can be used in a similar way over wood or card shells. An application of PVA adhesive before the Das or Kos is spread on will make sure that the coating of clay or cement will not come away from the shell as it dries. These materials are scribed before they set. This should be done with a sharp modelling knife taking care to leave only a groove and not to raise a ridge at either side of the groove. Such ridges are unsightly and unrealistic and make it obvious that the material has been scribed, thus spoiling the illusion we are trying to create of a wall made up of separate bricks or stones. When dry the model is painted appropriately using model paints.

Peco Texture Modelling Compound is very useful for modelling brick and stonework. The material is spread over a wood or card shell which has been built up in the usual way and while still moist is scribed to represent the brick or stone walling. The compound remains workable indefinitely provided it is kept moist, and by laying a damp cloth over partially completed work the modeller can leave it and return to it when convenient. The material dries to a natural stone colour but can be painted to give other colours. An inexpensive method is to use household emulsion with powder poster colours mixed in as necessary to give the required shades. Alternatively ordinary model paints can be employed.

I have already described the Linka system in the section on kits and kit construction but, of course the sections of brick and stonework which can be made with the Linka moulds can be used just as successfully for scratch-built models. Modellers can also take the process

A Welsh farmhouse beautifully modelled in 4 mm scale by Dave Rowe using Peco Texture Modelling Compound. This model can be seen at the Peco Modelrama exhibition in Beer, Devon. (Photograph by courtesy of Peco.)

further and make their own moulds. This involves the construction of a master and the making of a mould from it. This is then used to cast as many copies as required. Various materials can be used for the master and for the mould. The master, for example, can be wood or dental plaster carved to represent stonework, or can be made from Das scribed to produce a similar result. The mould itself can be latex, white silicone rubber, or Meltamould remeltable rubber made by Turner Research Ltd of Leeds. This last is available from many toyshops. The final castings can be made from Linkalite or one of the other commercially produced casting powders or from dental plaster, available from Boots chemists.

Trevor Hughes, in addition to casting stonework from his own moulds using techniques similar to those mentioned above, has devised an ingenious and very effective method for modelling stone-built cottages and other structures. He casts a simple slab of plaster about ⅜ in thick. This is then cut up into individual blocks of stone and these are used to build up the structure block by block giving a very realistic appearance. The process was described fully in the May 1979 issue of *Airfix Magazine.*

Another method of modelling brick and stone walls for model building is by detailing balsa wood with a wood-burning pen or Pyrogravure. The tool is used to make the grooves between the stones or bricks by burning them into the surface of the wood. A metal rule is used to guide the burning pen. I have used this method very satisfactorily for stonework. Brickwork can also be modelled successfully but the tip of my woodburning tool is not really quite fine enough for this. This instrument is also ideal for modelling wood planking. The narrow-gauge engine and carriage shed illustrated here has a wooden extension which was made by this method. The walls are balsa with the grain running vertically. The wood-burning pen was used to make the grooves between the planks and also to create the appearance of splits, cracks and knots in the planking. This was easily and quickly carried out. The pen does darken the wood where the burning takes place so painting is necessary.

In the United States an excellent selection of stripwood is available enabling modellers to build up models of wooden prototype structures almost as board by board replicas of the originals. This method is very time consuming but the results can be superb.

Plaster and other textured finishes for walls of buildings can be modelled by coating the basic walls with PVA adhesive and sprinkling on fine sand or other material. When dry the walls can be painted. Many industrial buildings are of corrugated iron construction and this can be modelled with corrugated copper (Slater) or aluminium (Campbell Scale Models) sheet in 00 and HO scales. For the best appearance cut the model corrugated iron into scale-size sheets and apply these individually to the basic shell. Weathering and streaks of rust will give the finishing touches after painting.

When the walls have been modelled the windows can be added. The window frames are usually cut from card or plastic card and can be painted before fixing in place. Clear plastic glazing material represents the glass conveniently. The glazing bars can be painted or scribed on the clear plastic. If scribed, the bars can be coloured by smearing on a little paint and then rubbing it off; the little which remains in the scribed grooves will colour them. A convenient alternative is the use of 'Downesglaze' a clear plastic with silk screen printed frames and glazing bars. This was designed by expert structure modeller, Allan Downes, and gives a realistic appearance with a minimum of effort for the modeller.

If desired, the glazing bars can be incorporated when cutting out the window frames. This is tricky and time consuming and must be done neatly, but can be very effective. Another popular method is to use the neat and ingenious Slater grid system. This manufacturer produces fine plastic card strip, notched at intervals. Lengths of this strip can be fitted together by the notches to produce a grid of the size required for the window. A variety of notch spacings allows the modeller to select the strip needed for the pane sizes he wants. The grid system is easy to use and results in very neat windows.

An alternative to plastic glazing which is preferred by some of the experts is thin glass such as microscope cover slips which are used to cover specimens on slides before they are placed under the microscope. This thin glass is easily snapped to size after scoring and is ideal for modelling windows. One advantage is that it does not become warped, as can occur with plastic.

Bay windows are best modelled as separate units which are then added to the basic structure after they are complete. Construction can be from card or plastic card with clear plastic glazing following the usual methods of construction employed for the main structure.

Doors are modelled in a similar way to windows with the frame and then the door itself fitted behind. A realistic touch is to model some of the windows and perhaps one of the doors of a building in the open position. This

Above *For this 1:64 scale model of the bridge below Tan-Y-Bwlch station on the Ffestiniog Railway, Trevor Hughes cast the abutments in situ from plaster and then scribed them with a sharp needle to represent the stonework. The main bridge girders were cast in epoxy resin in a rubber mould and the handrails are expanded metal.*

Below *Beautifully modelled stone cottage and outbuildings from a prototype at Blaenau Ffestiniog. The model was constructed by Trevor Hughes for a 1:64 scale narrow-gauge model railway layout and the walls were built up from separate blocks cut from cast plaster to represent the stone blocks of the real structure.*

Two views of a scratch-built engine and carriage shed for a 4 mm scale narrow-gauge railway layout. The stone buildings were modelled with walls of plastic card faced with embossed stone plastic card. The slate roofs were covered with overlapping strips of thin card cut to represent individual slates. The wooden extension at the front of the building has walls of balsa scribed with a burning-pen to simulate planking. This section was roofed with corrugated copper. The windows are from Airfix kits.

will involve cutting round the window or door in question and bending it outwards or inwards.

With the basic walls complete and after adding any interior walls, floors and details which you want, the roof can be fitted. The basis of the roof is cut from card, wood or plastic card as for the walls. On this is applied detailing to represent the roofing materials. Slates and tiles are most simply modelled by applying an appropriate commercially-produced slate or tilepaper. This is glued on as with brick and stonepaper, but usually without the complication of openings unless there are skylights or dormer windows. Faller include slate roofing, and small and large tile roofing in their range of coloured embossed card sheets and these give a more realistic texture then the ordinary slate and tilepapers.

An even better effect is achieved by applying

Realistically modelled thatched cottages at the rear complete this scene on the 4 mm scale 'Pipers Mead' layout constructed by Allan Downes. Note also the damaged roof of the engine shed and the workman about to climb up the ladder to repair the hole. Small details like this add greatly to the realism and interest. (Photograph by John Priest.)

individually modelled tiles or slates cut from thin card or plastic card. However, this process is rather laborious and a good compromise which gives a very similar appearance with much less work is to use strips of tiles or slates. Each strip is cut a little longer than the roof length and twice the visible tile or slate height in width. Cuts are made half-way across each strip from the lower edge at intervals equal to the width of the tiles or slates. These sections between the cuts represent the individual tiles or slates. Broken or missing tiles can be simulated by cutting part of the card away. To tile a roof start at the lower edge and glue a strip of half the width of the tile strips along the roof. Then fix one of the tile strips on with its lower (cut into) edge along the lower edge of the roof. Then work upwards gluing strips on with each strip overlapping the upper half of the one below until you reach the ridge at the top of the roof. Do the same on the other half of the roof. Then fit a capping strip, also of card and folded along its centre, to complete the roof. Painting and weathering is then carried out.

A little time can be saved if we take a short cut by using a commercial slate paper and glue it down on to thin card for use in cutting up into strips for roofing. The printed lines on the paper are then a guide and we do not need to measure the strip widths and slate spacings.

Corrugated iron roofs are simply modelled by cutting commercially available copper or aluminium into scale-sized sheets and gluing them on to the roof. For tar-paper roofing I use paper tissues glued down, with a few wrinkles, and then painted black or very dark grey.

Thatch is more difficult to model. Pendon Museum at one time used human hair but this was very expensive and had to be specially mothproofed, so they now use plumbers' hemp, available cheaply from ironmongers, instead. This is glued down with PVA in bundles, arranged much as in real thatching, and is then painted. Allan Downes uses thick knitting wool glued on to a shaped roof. The wool is then brushed with 'Resin W' and flocked with an earth mix texture. As the glue dries it contracts and draws the flock into the strands giving a realistic thatch appearance. Examples of thatched cottages built by Allan Downes can be seen in one of the accompanying pictures. Another alternative method is to use modelling clay textured with a modelling knife to give the surface appearance of thatch and then painted.

Chimneys show a wide variation in style and type and it is a good idea to observe these and to make notes, sketches and photographs as a record to which you can refer when modelling. Chimneys are conveniently made from wood cut to size and shape. Brick or stone chimneys can be modelled with the same surface finish as used for the rest of the building as described earlier. Used ball-point refills provide tubing suitable for the chimney pots.

As you gain experience in scratch-building you will come across new methods and materials and new applications of ones already used for other purposes. Such experimentation is an enjoyable and rewarding part of this type of modelling.

Interior modelling

Whether or not to provide interior details for structure models is largely a matter of personal preference, partly influenced perhaps by the size of your layout and the number of model buildings there are on it. Many modellers feel it is a waste of time and effort to fit them as so little, if any, of the interior is visible, particularly in the smaller scales, once a building is placed on the layout. Others like to make the interior as fully detailed as the exterior and may arrange for the roof or one wall of the structure to be removable so that the inside of the building can be seen properly. Several American modellers have carried out very fine work of this type with structures which are exquisitely detailed both inside and out and certainly for success in the major competitions in the United States full interior details do seem to be necessary! In this country some of the best examples of interior modelling in 4 mm scale must be the model buildings in the Pendon Museum. One of the interiors is complete right down to a stuffed owl in a case, a wireless set with headphones and even pairs of socks drying in front of the fire!

Interior fittings are not for the most part included in kits though some of the craftsman type wood structure kits produced in the United States do include full details permitting the construction of a model of exhibition class, as can be seen in the Fine Scale Miniatures rail car shed kit. I am not aware of any parts made in Britain for interior detailing in the usual railway modelling scales though, of course, a selection of excellent items are available for military modelling in 54 mm scale. In the United States a remarkably complete range of furniture and other interior detailing models in the form of white metal castings are produced in HO scale by Scale Structures Ltd. This manufacturer offers furniture of all types, staircases including a fine spiral stairway, office equipment, a carpenter's bench and tools, bathroom fittings, even a barber's chair and pool tables, as well as smaller parts such as books, bottles, jars and musical instruments! Also in the range are wallpapers, curtains, paintings, rugs and carpets all printed in full colour. There is also a beautifully detailed selection of workshop machinery including a lathe, power saws of various types, a planer, a milling machine, a wheel grinder and a jointer, all accurate models of real equipment and ideal for a factory or machine shop model. With the excellent models made by this firm full interior detailing can easily be added to any structure of American prototype. These parts may be available in Britain from one of the specialist suppliers but they are quite expensive.

Furniture, machinery and other items for modelling interiors can also be made from scratch using scraps of wood, card and plastic together with odds and ends from the scrap

A fascinating historical model by Thorp Modelmakers Ltd of a cathedral interior showing how construction work was carried out. (Photograph by courtesy of Thorp Modelmakers Ltd.)

Because of their large windows and often prominent positions on model railway layouts it is worth while fitting interior detailing in signalboxes even if this is not done for other buildings. This 4 mm scale cabin is largely scratch-built but the windows and stairs are parts from an Airfix kit. Interior details include the levers, table, chair, sink and a clock and track diagram on the wall, all easily made from scrap materials.

box. Unless you plan to make the interior accessible for viewing and want full interior details these models can be relatively simple. If seen only through the windows the fittings inside need be little more than simple shapes suggesting the furniture or machinery within.

Generally a compromise between an absence of any interior fittings and full detailing will probably suit most modellers. It is desirable to include at least some interior walls and floors of card, wood or plastic card, in model buildings to avoid the appearance of an empty shell. If the structure has large windows and is near the front of the layout it is worth adding at least simple interior details. Signal boxes which face the onlooker need interior fittings as the large and numerous windows make the inside clearly visible. It is also essential to dress up the windows of shops with suitable goods. If you find that you enjoy this aspect of modelling you may want to go further and add as much detailing as you can. Knowing that a model building is fully detailed inside as well as outside can be very satisfying to the modeller. If you have only a small layout with space for very few structure models, detailing the interior will prolong the enjoyment of construction and will also improve the standard of your models. If you do model the interior fully it is best to arrange access, usually by having a removable wall or roof, so the details can be displayed to full advantage.

If there is interior lighting some interior fittings will often be needed and conversely if you have modelled details inside the structure you may well want to include lighting to make these more visible. Such lighting can be provided with 'grain of wheat' bulbs and these may be necessary if the bulbs themselves will be visible, as may be the case if the interior is fully modelled. However, it is more economical to use larger bulbs, either torch bulbs or, even better, the low-consumption 14-volt bulbs. If these are run at a lower voltage they will last very much longer. The light output will be reduced but this is of no consequence and may even be more realistic. These larger bulbs should be installed so that they illuminate the interior without being visible themselves. One method is to fit the bulb underneath the building and to make shafts from card so that the light only reaches the places in the building where it is required.

A most interesting recent development is the application of fibre optics to modelling. In this system light is transmitted along the fine glass or plastic filaments making up the fibre, which can be bent around curves if necessary. In a model, light can be transmitted along these fibres from a bulb or bulbs beneath the structure or under the baseboard to situations where there is insufficient space for even the smallest 'grain of wheat' bulb. The transmitted light is emitted at the end of the fibre as a pin point; if the tip is slightly melted to make it more bulbous a good representation of a very tiny light bulb is obtained. Fibre optics can be used to light rooms in a model building; even table lamps and standard lamps can be modelled if desired. It is also possible to light small signs; by positioning a rotating disc with holes in it between the light source and the fibres these signs can be made to flash on and off. With appropriately arranged holes and several fibres, lights can be made to go on and off in a pre-set order. The potential of fibre optics for lighting model structures is almost unlimited and the modeller may find some experimentation rewarding. One source of fibre optic materials and parts for modellers is Makemass Ltd of Crayford in Kent.

Low relief models

The modelling of structures at the rear of a model railway layout or military diorama in low relief is an ingenious solution to two problems which confront the modeller. One is the lack of space available to most of us for our layouts; low relief models occupy much less area than corresponding conventionally modelled buildings, a considerable advantage. The other problem is the difficulty of making a two-dimensional backscene look realistic when it can be viewed from a wide range of positions; scenes drawn in perspective to give an impression of depth are only correct for a very limited viewpoint and, when viewed from other positions, there will be distortion which spoils the effect. If low relief structures are employed the flat backscene need only be a simple sky blue background or one of the commercially-produced sky and cloud sheets.

Low relief buildings have the fronts fully modelled but are only an inch or so deep so that only the front parts of the sides and roof are constructed. This full modelling of the fronts means that they can have proper detailing giving a depth and texture which cannot be achieved with a two dimensional backscene. The fact that the buildings are not complete can be disguised by adjacent structures or by trees or other features.

Several manufacturers have realised how useful these models are to the military and railway modeller and have included examples in their ranges of kits. There are several models in the 00-scale Superquick series and in 00, TT and N scales in the Hamblings Bilteezi range. Builder Plus also now offer some kits of this type. These kits are all printed card models but Midland Model Railway Supplies make a range of vacuum-formed plastic mouldings including low relief scenic backgrounds and low relief buildings in 00 and N scales.

It is also possible to modify ordinary kits for

These three 00-scale structures were built from one of the Superquick low relief kits. The models have a realistic appearance but the depth is only about 1¼ in.

A very effective low relief factory on an 00-scale layout built by members of the Poole & District MRS. The model is a conversion from Builder Plus factory kits.

use as low relief models. This has the advantage that the front and back can be used separately so that each kit will provide two models instead of only the one. You may need to add some extra parts or details to complete the models. Alternatively you can, of course, scratch-build low relief structures giving you complete freedom of choice of prototype. Thus you can select buildings which are appropriate to the locale. The usual methods and materials are employed in construction but the models will be much quicker to build as only the front and part of the sides and roof need be modelled. Whether the models are kit- or scratch-built remember that if there are any windows or open doors the interior of the model should be painted black so that the viewer cannot see that the model has very little depth. If desired, interior lighting can be fitted. Interior fittings can also be included if the modeller wishes. If the low relief models are shops the windows should be detailed with appropriate goods on sale.

It often gives a good effect if a row of low relief buildings are modelled so that some extend a little further forward than others. This variation will give a more natural and realistic appearance and it also enhances the illusion of depth. When modelling a row of low relief buildings it is generally best if they are all approximately the same height. If not then the lack of depth of the structures which are higher is more apparent and tends to spoil the effect.

Low relief models are not only very useful from the purely scenic point of view but are also valuable for concealing hidden sidings or tracks, or a fiddle yard. In these circumstances it may be desirable to arrange for the buildings, preferably as a unit, to lift off the layout to provide easy access to the hidden tracks when necessary.

Painting, weathering and lettering

These finishing touches for a model building, or indeed any type of model, are very important in achieving a realistic appearance. No matter how skilfully you construct a model a poor paint job can spoil all your previous efforts. Conversely a very ordinary model can be made to look very good by expert finishing. Thus it is well worth while making an effort to become good at this aspect of modelling. Practice is probably the most important factor but I hope that some of the comments which follow may also be helpful.

The card kits are printed in full colour and apart from a little touching up, particularly of the cut edges, painting is not usually required. Wood kits can be painted if desired, using model paints such as Humbrol, but often staining gives a realistic and natural finish. When assembling these kits a little glue almost always gets on to the wood around the joints and even if it is wiped off immediately a trace is likely to remain. As the stain will not take over glue there will be pale marks at these places. It is therefore a good idea to stain the wood sheet and strip before assembly. These are various wood stains available from DIY and paint shops which can be employed. Alternatively I have used a thin wash of brown/black model paint effectively on wooden buildings, such as the gold mine shown in one of the photographs, to give a natural weatherbeaten wood appearance.

The metal kits should be primed; I find the Duplicolor automobile grey primer in aerosol cans convenient for this. After the primer has dried the models can be painted with ordinary model paints of appropriate colours.

Many of the plastic kits have their parts moulded in suitably coloured plastic to make painting unnecessary. In many cases the appearance without painting is quite good especially if the models are weathered to tone down the colours a little and to introduce some variation in tone. However, most plastic surfaces have a slight sheen and do look like plastic rather than the construction material they are supposed to represent, and good painting will give a better finished appearance. On the other hand a poor paint job will probably give a result which is inferior to the original unpainted plastic!

Because the gloss paint used on real buildings soon becomes dirtied and loses some of its shine from deposits of dust and grime and from the effects of rain and sunshine, and because the distance at which we view our models is equivalent to looking at real structures from much further away, we need to paint our models with matt and not gloss colours. Another good reason for doing this is that a gloss finish will show up every little

A small gold mine in HO scale scratch-built in balsa sheet and stripwood. The model was constructed following an article by an American modeller, Earl Cochrane, published some years ago. A weathered effect was achieved by painting the wood with a thin wash of black and brown paint.

imperfection whereas a matt paint will obscure these faults. Because there are no reflections a matt finish shows up details better and more clearly than gloss paint does.

Several manufacturers offer suitable ranges of paints. Humbrol is one of the best-known makes and I usually use these paints but there are others which are equally suitable. These paints are also fine for wood and card though for these materials I often use poster colours, such as those made by Winsor & Newton or Rowney. These paints are easy and convenient to use and have the advantage of being water-based. Whatever paint you are using, a dark grey will give a better appearance than a pure black for parts which in the prototype are black. It will also make small details more visible. Humbrol include a Dirty Black in their range but you can also add a little white and perhaps a touch of brown to the ordinary black for a similar result.

I have already mentioned that it is often easiest and neatest to paint some or all of the parts of a model before or during assembly rather than after the structure is complete, particularly if various parts are to be different colours. For buildings with more complicated paint schemes or lettering it is very convenient if construction can be arranged so that the walls can be fully modelled, painted and lettered before they are fitted together to make up the building. In this way the painting and lettering can be carried out with the sides flat on the workbench making the task much simpler. A little touching up may be required after assembly but this is not difficult if most of the work has been done beforehand.

For brush painting you will need a selection of different sizes including a very fine brush for small parts and details. Always buy good quality brushes. Though they are more expensive they will last longer and will not shed their hairs as you use them. They will also give a superior finish. Never apply more paint than is needed; excess will merely obscure detail and fill in corners. Many of the good paints now produced will cover well with only one coat of the darker colours. For the lighter colours a further coat or coats will be needed. If a single thin coat is not covering properly do not try to put the paint on more thickly as this will give a poor finish, very likely with blobs and runs. For the best results flow the paint on smoothly from the brush, covering the whole surface quickly and evenly without going back to apply more paint or to rebrush areas already done. Then leave the model for the paint to dry thoroughly and apply a second coat after that if necessary. Do your painting in a dust-free spot away from where you do your sawing, filing and sanding. Bedrooms are also to be avoided as there is usually a good deal of dust from bed clothes. Always clean your brushes thoroughly after use. A good method is to clean them first in the appropriate thinner or solvent and then follow this with a wash in warm, soapy water. Rinse and dry them before putting them away. The brushes should be stored so that they are not standing on the bristles and so that they will not be damaged.

The best results of all can be achieved with an airbrush. For long a tool only for the professional worker there are now a number of airbrushes on the market intended especially for the amateur modeller. They are still quite expensive but if you do a reasonable amount of model painting the outlay can be worth while for the convenience and for the excellent finish which an airbrush can give.

Lettering is always difficult to do well by hand unless you are a skilful draughtsman, particularly when working in the smaller scales. Dry print lettering from the Letraset, Blick and other ranges can be the answer to this problem. If you do your own photographic work you can produce perfect lettering and signs to any required size or scale by photographing either the original full-size sign or a sign hand drawn or made up with dry print lettering to a larger scale, for ease and neatness, and then printing the resulting negative to produce a sign of exactly the size you want for your model. Once the original has been photographed it is, of course, easy to print as many copies as required so there is no difficulty in providing numerous identical signs for your own buildings and also for your friends.

There are also some excellent commercially-produced signs, notices and posters on the market. Many of these have been photographically reproduced from original signs and advertisements. Dart Castings, for example, offer a selection of railway posters in 2 mm and 4 mm scales which are from posters preserved in the Uplands Railway Museum, Bristol. Builder Plus have a large sheet of advertising signs and posters in full colour and suitable for use for N, 00 and 0 scales. A few of these colourful posters will add greatly to the interest of an otherwise blank wall. If appropriately selected they will also help to set the period of the scene. Notices and signs for use on railway buildings are also available commercially from various manufacturers. Chris Leigh, for example, produces a very neat set of etched brass GWR notices for 4 mm scale.

Some modellers, particularly in the United States, enjoy making up amusing names, often

Two views of a 4 mm scale model railway layout constructed by G. Iliffe Stokes showing some of his superb model buildings. Note particularly the selection and grouping of the structures to give a natural and authentic appearance. Excellent weathering also adds greatly to the realism of the scene. (1st view by J.H. Russell, 2nd view by John Himmens.)

involving a pun, for the shops, factories and firms on their layouts. Again, this is a matter of personal preference and others do not regard the idea with favour. For myself, I must admit I enjoy these little touches with names such as the 'Lee King Pipe Company' and the 'Term Oil Co' (the latter being an industry on the layout built by American modeller, Art Curren). The idea is not new. I can recall that the late John Ahern had 'Quibble & Cuss' estate agents, on his famous 'Madder Valley' layout in pictures taken in the 1940s. A favourite of mine is on a factory model constructed by another American modeller, Earl Smallshaw. The firm is the Miracle Chair Company and the slogan reads 'If It's A Good Chair It's A Miracle'!

Full-size structures do not appear newly painted for long and, if your model is to look like the real thing, a little weathering to simulate dust, grime, mud, rust and spillage must be applied. This weathering not only make the building model more realistic but also enhances its appearance by making details more noticeable and by giving the impression of distance. The further we are away from a real building the more dulled or muted and greyed the colours appear because of the atmospheric haze and fine dust particles in the air. Thus the application of weathering will help to make our model look more like the real building at a distance, than a small model seen close to.

The weathering can be quite light if the structure is supposed to be in good condition and well kept up, or heavy if you want to give the impression of neglect and disrepair. Take care not to overdo it, however, as it is easy to spoil the effect by too much dirt and rust thickly applied. The best guide is the real thing and colour photographs are very useful as a permanent record to which you can refer when actually painting your models. Various colours in the Humbrol range are suitable for dust, dirt and grime, and the selection includes Rust. These colours can be applied as they are, or as a thin wash. A dilute wash of grey or black will give an overall dulling or toning down of the original colour. Powder poster paints are also useful; they can be dusted on and then most of the powder brushed or blown off. Some will remain, more if the brush used is slightly damp, giving the appearance of dust or dirt. Applying more water on the brush will cause streaking, simulating the results of exposure to rain and wind. An airbrush is very useful for weathering as it is easy to apply a light overspray of paint giving a very realistic appearance. Oil spillage on storage tanks can be simulated with a little black gloss paint. Clear gloss varnish can be applied to give the appearance of damp areas due to water leaking from pipes or tanks.

Final details

When your structure model is complete some attention should be paid to its setting on the layout. If the model is just set down on top of the surface of the scenery there will almost certainly be unsightly gaps and cracks between the bottom edges of the walls and the ground, which can completely ruin the effect. After fixing the building down, a little plaster or filler should be used to fill in these gaps. When dry, touch this up with earth colour. If there are to be grass and weeds around the structure, apply a little glue along the ground against the bottom of the walls and sprinkle on green scenic dressing. If the building is to be rather neglected, glue can also be applied to the lower parts of the walls before the scenic dressing is put on, so that the effect will be of grass and weeds growing up the walls. Creepers on the walls can be modelled in a similar way, with the stems drawn in with paint or ink. On the structure models for the Pendon Museum the walls extend at least 3 cm below the ground level and the buildings fit into recesses left in the surface of the scenery. This is an excellent arrangement because the joins are much less noticeable than when a building is set on top of the ground and are also easier to conceal giving a very realistic effect of structures which have proper foundations.

Because the setting for a model building is so important in enhancing its realism we should pay almost as much attention to detailing the immediate surroundings as to the construction of the model itself. Often structure models will be placed in relatively inaccessible positions on model railway baseboards making it very difficult to work on these details. An excellent solution to this problem is to provide structure models with their own small bases, either for single

Terry Jenkins built this 4 mm scale country pub using 1 mm thick card for the basic structure. This was covered with Builder Plus sandstone paper on the walls and chimneys. Individually laid tiles were cut from paper. The model was mounted on its own base for neatness and convenience. It can easily be fitted on to a layout later as a unit.

Another public house modelled by Terry Jenkins again in 00 scale. Terry used embossed stone pattern plastic card for the walls in this model but construction is otherwise similar to that for the model in the previous picture.

buildings or, where convenient, for groups of models. The structure, or structures, can be fixed on to this base and all the necessary modelling and detailing of the immediate surroundings can be carried out with the unit still on the work bench. The small unit can be turned around to allow complete access to all parts and the modeller can benefit from the convenience and comfort which will not only make the job more enjoyable but will also permit him to do his best work. It is usually easy to fix the whole unit on to the baseboard when it is complete and its edges can be concealed by applying a little extra plaster at the join. One of the accompanying photographs shows a 4 mm scale model of a country pub built by Terry Jenkins and fitted on to a small base of its own on which the drive, lawns, walls and other details have been modelled. The whole unit can later be fitted on to a layout.

There are many small details which can be added to complete the scene. Fences and walls are needed, either commercially-produced

The realistic details in front of this building give a more authentic look to the scene. Note also the effectiveness of the numerous accurately modelled roof details on this 4 mm scale factory building constructed from scratch by Tony Butler.

The setting is very important if model buildings are to appear realistic. This superb scene is part of the 4 mm scale Pendon Parva model at Pendon Museum. Note the perfectly modelled fencing, hedge, grass and paths together with the accurate model of a ladies cycle standing against the wall of the house on the left. (Photograph by courtesy of Pendon Museum.)

items or made from scratch. The yards of industrial buildings are often littered with scrap wood, old crates, scrap metal, oil drums, barrels, dustbins, carboys, and rubbish. Many suitable items are available from manufacturers such as Merit. Airfix 00-scale military vehicle kits are a good source of scrap parts including nicely detailed wheels and gears. These are very effective as scrap when painted with rust and weathering colours.

Houses can be provided with detailed gardens which have lawns, bushes, trees, and plants. There are many other items which can be added including a greenhouse or cold frame, children's toys, swings and so on.

Human figures will add life to the scene and there are numerous figures available commercially both painted and unpainted. If interior detailing is added to your models you may want to have people inside as well as outside the buildings.

Scenery

Michael Andress

Contents

Introduction

The construction of scenery is an important and enjoyable aspect of railway modelling. With the development of the small scales, 00 and HO, the idea of modelling a railway as part of a landscape, rather than as a separate entity in isolation, has become popular. The later introduction of the smaller N scale and more recently still the minute Z scale has allowed even wider scope for the creation of the surrounding countryside in model form as a setting for the line. Scenic work has become accepted as an essential part of the hobby and nowadays no model railway layout can be considered complete without scenery. Indeed, the provision of scenery is one of the important differences between the train set temporarily laid out on a table or on the floor and a scale model railway layout with a realistic scenic setting on its own baseboard.

This scenic work is not only attractive and interesting in itself but it also makes the railway models appear more realistic. It also gives the enthusiast the opportunity to introduce individuality and originality to his layout and to make his railway different from every other model. One of the satisfying aspects of the hobby is the scope it gives for the creation of your own little world with everything arranged as you wish. The excellent locomotive and rolling stock models, now commercially available as ready-to-run items, enable everyone to run accurate, well detailed models on their layouts without the time and skill needed to build their own. This is a tremendous advantage, particularly as these high quality products are very reasonably priced, but the models are, of course, identical to those on many other layouts. It is with the modelling of the setting, the structures and scenery, that the modeller can make his layout unique.

Beautifully modelled structures and scenery provide a natural setting for this 4 mm scale railway layout constructed by Allan Downes. The realism and interest of the locomotive and rolling stock are enhanced by the landscape and the train really appears to be going somewhere rather than just running round and round. (Photograph by John Priest.)

Right *Scenic modelling techniques are of interest to military modellers now that dioramas have become a popular method of display for model soldiers and military vehicles. This attractive set piece was built in 1/32 nd scale by Mike Watt. The effect of a well worn country track was obtained by sprinkling real stone chips and powder over Tetrion.*

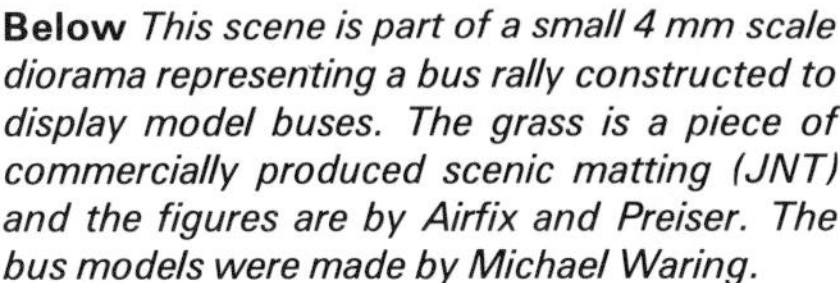

Below *This scene is part of a small 4 mm scale diorama representing a bus rally constructed to display model buses. The grass is a piece of commercially produced scenic matting (JNT) and the figures are by Airfix and Preiser. The bus models were made by Michael Waring.*

Other hobbyists have also realised the benefits of providing a scenic setting in which to display their models. Military modellers have employed the idea to great advantage both for very small settings for single figures and for large dioramas with numerous figures or vehicles. To a lesser, but increasing extent, ship, aircraft, bus, car and other modellers are also constructing scenery for their models. The principles are the same whatever the purpose of the scenic setting and in the past most of the modelling techniques employed have been ones devised by railway modellers. However, now other workers, particularly military modellers, have developed new methods which can be usefully applied to railway modelling and generally the different groups of modellers can all benefit from keeping in touch with the techniques used by all the others.

Structure modelling is discussed in the third book in this series and will not be covered further here.

Many products are now available to help us in our scenic modelling; in fact there are more than ever before and further items are appearing on the market with pleasing frequency so that we are very fortunate to be so well catered for. Not only is there an excellent range of scenic materials and kits for modelling the hills, rocks, grass, trees and other natural features of the landscape but there is also an extensive selection of models and kits for details such as

Above *Part of an interesting and realistic model bus depot layout in 00-scale constructed by John Tincknell. The buses were built from cast metal kits, the JCB excavator is an Airfix model and the lorries are die-cast toys. Note the pipelaying gang with Merit figures, wheelbarrow and pipe sections.*

Below *Tree kits and scenic materials from Hammant & Morgan's Woodland Scenics range have been employed in creating this rural scene in 00 scale.* (Photograph by courtesy of McLeish Associates Ltd.)

Structure models are enhanced by good detailing of their immediate surroundings as with this superb sawmill in HO scale constructed from a Fine Scale Miniatures kit. Note the tree stump, clumps of grass, weeds, scrap wood and old drums. (Photograph by courtesy of Fine Scale Miniatures.)

fences, signposts, telegraph poles, and so on as well as human and animal figures and road vehicles, both motor and horse drawn.

My aim in this book is to provide the beginner with a basic guide to scenery construction and to give some indication of what products are available for scenic modelling. Scenery construction is not difficult and it is a most enjoyable part of railway modelling. It is a facet of the hobby which has given me great pleasure and I hope that this book may encourage you to have a go yourself, and that you may find as much enjoyment as I have in scenic modelling.

I would like to thank all those modellers who have kindly allowed me to use pictures of their scenery to illustrate this book. In particular I am grateful to Graham Bailey, K.J. Churms, Howard Coulson, Allan Downes, Keith Gowen, P.D. Hancock, Trevor Hughes, Terry Jenkins, Bob Jones, Betty Kay, Maurice Kelly, John Norman, the Romsey & District Railway Modellers' Society, Mike Sharman, G. Iliffe Stokes, Glen Tandy, John Tincknell, Michael Waring, Mike Watt, Colin Woolridge, and the 2 mm Scale Association. I am also grateful to those manufacturers who have provided information and pictures of their products.

Some general points

Scenery construction is a very enjoyable and relaxing pastime and it makes a pleasant change from the more demanding types of modelling involved in making a model railway layout. Unlike the construction of locomotive, rolling stock, or structure models where measurements must be exact for a realistic result, scenery modelling is much less precise. After all, hills, rivers, trees and other features vary greatly in size and shape from one to another so it does not matter if you make your model a little larger or smaller or rather different in shape.

Some beginners believe that artistic ability is essential for scenery modelling and feel that as they cannot draw or paint well they will be unsuccessful at scenic work. However, we are working in three dimensions unlike the artist who has to depict a scene with depth on a flat two dimensional surface, and our task is much easier. Modellers sometimes also feel rather lost simply because scenery modelling is less precise than other types of railway modelling. Whereas they are confident when following instructions in assembling, for example, a structure kit, they are unsure how to go about scenic work. The main thing is to have a go; it's easier than you might think! The materials are generally inexpensive and are easy to handle. Your first attempts may not work out very well but it is simple enough to alter or remake a section of scenery until you get the appearance you want.

Just because scenery modelling is not precise do not overlook the importance of observing the real thing. You would not expect

Rugged scenery complete with a mountain railway adds variety to this section of a large HO-scale Fleischmann exhibition layout.

Above *Snow scenes are rarely included on model railways but Terry Jenkins created this realistic ski-slope on a Continental TT-scale layout. The skiers are Merten figures. Polyfilla was used for the snow on the ground while the snow on the trees was applied with a Christmas decoration aerosol.*

Below *This snow scene was set up for photographic purposes using Tapwata filler as the snow. The sledge was scratch-built from plastic card, with driver and horses from Airfix.*

Attractive scenery on the late Eric Kay's 'Sherrington Branch' N-scale layout. Good texturing and attention to small details has helped to create a realistic overall appearance.

to be able to build a realistic model of a signal cabin without having studied a prototype cabin or at least pictures or plans of the real thing. Similarly to model a rock face, a stream or a tree we must observe the real ones. Though individual examples vary greatly in size and shape there are important characteristic features which must be included in our models if we are to achieve the realism we want. The texture and colour are of particular importance and every effort should be made to get them right. Colour can be a problem as it is difficult to remember colours accurately from the time when you see the real thing to when you come to model it. Colour photographs, especially transparencies, can be very valuable for reference. Another difficulty is that many colours look very different when seen under natural and artificial light. Ideally you should try to get the colours on your layout correct for the usual lighting conditions.

Because we have only a small space for a layout it is not possible to model a section of the countryside to true scale. By choosing small examples of various features to model we can save a little space without loss of realism. Hills, trees, rivers and the other natural features of the landscape come in a wide range of sizes and we should select small examples to model. Not only is it more realistic to model a small item accurately than a larger one noticeably underscale, but these features will appear more natural in the small area we have for our layouts. In addition there must be considerable selective compression of the landscape. In fact this necessity can be an advantage because our model will have the more interesting parts of the scenery while omitting the relatively uninteresting areas found between them in the real countryside. We must, however, take care that the scene we model does not look cramped and we must choose features which will blend harmoniously together. Obviously any attempt to include widely varying types of scenery on a small layout is likely to be unsuccessful.

Sources of ideas and information

The modeller will find much useful general information and many pictures, both colour and black and white, of scenery of all types in a wide variety of books and magazines. These cover all areas of Britain and also other parts of the world. There are also many books on more specific topics, useful for reference, which cover aspects such as geology, trees and plants, and so on. There are often diagrams and drawings which are of value in designing and constructing the scenery for your layout.

If you are modelling a particular area you may find it useful to collect picture postcards and other photographs from that part of the

Two views of a superb architectural and scenic model built by John Piper Limited which include a large number of their tree models. Note the small yacht with lowered sails and the seagulls on the shore. (Photographs by courtesy of John Piper Limited.)

country. Obviously it is desirable to visit the area yourself if this is possible and to take notes, make sketches and take numerous photographs, both colour and black and white, for future reference. Study of the real scenery of the area is essential if you are to capture the characteristic appearance in miniature, so important in creating a realistic layout.

The beginner will find many articles appearing in the model railway magazines describing the construction of scenery, sometimes in general terms, others covering specific features. These can be very helpful particularly as they often include photographs of completed model scenery built following the techniques described which show you the sort of appearance you can achieve.

The study of pictures in the magazines showing layouts built by more experienced scenic modellers will also give you ideas and inspiration. Often some indication is given regarding the methods of construction employed, but even without this you will find the pictures helpful. Not only will they show you just what can be achieved in this type of modelling but they will give you ideas for features to include on your layout and show you how these can be arranged to give a realistic effect. The many small details often present on these layouts will also suggest extra touches you can add to your scenes.

I would also recommend visiting model railway exhibitions; the layouts on show are always a source of new ideas for scenic work. Provided you choose a time when they are not too busy most exhibitors are very willing to answer questions about how they built the scenery on their layouts and to give you useful advice. Membership of a model railway club can also be very beneficial for the beginner. The enthusiast can learn a great deal from the more experienced members of the club and he can also gain experience in practical construction by working under supervision on club layouts.

Visits to museums give the modeller the opportunity to see scenic work constructed by experts. The Pendon Museum contains some of the finest 4 mm scale structure and scenery models ever made and a visit is well worth while as I am sure you will come away inspired to improve your own scenic work! Many other museums contain excellent examples of dioramas and other scenic models; the Science Museum in London, for example, and the Imperial War Museum, also in London. Even though these models may not feature railways they are worth studying as they are fine examples of scenic modelling. Particularly noteworthy in these professional models are the standard of finish, the lighting which is often very effective, and the skilled use of perspective modelling to give the scenes great apparent depth.

Planning

Because of the limitations imposed by the necessarily small size of many layouts, considerable thought and ingenuity is often required in fitting in a track plan which will provide interesting operation. The modeller is then fully occupied in laying smooth trackwork and in wiring it up correctly so that the layout will operate well. Once all this is accomplished he sits back with a sigh of relief and a feeling of satisfaction and then thinks about completing the model railway by adding some scenery to fill in the gaps. Unfortunately such scenic work usually appears unrealistic and contrived; in fact it looks just like the afterthought it was.

This is a great pity because scenic work can make a layout much more realistic and interesting if carried out well, but it must be planned along with the track design from the beginning. This planning need only be of a general nature as you will almost certainly want to alter details as you construct the scenery. In the real thing the landscape is obviously there before the railway, which is then planned to run through it. On a model railway the scenery is usually added last but we should try to give the impression that it was there first as in the prototype.

We must decide what type of terrain we wish to model. Will it be flat farming country or hilly and forested, will it be rural or urban, will there be a river, lake or canal, and so on? This may be decided for us if we are basing our layout on a particular prototype line or are setting our railway in a specific geographical locale. Even if not restricted in this way, the type of track plan chosen may influence the scenery modelled. For example, the so called rabbit layouts in 009 need hilly or mountainous scenery to be realistic as this will provide a reason for the tracks at different levels and the

A small timber yard on an 009 layout built by Glyn Tandy. Details include small twigs representing logs and balsa stripwood for the sawn planks. The bushes are lichen.

A village scene on the Bournemouth & Isle of Purbeck MRC 00-scale 'Swanage Branch'. The stone walls were modelled using Kos fire cement. Note the geese in the foreground.

tunnels needed to conceal some of the trackwork. The scenery can be designed to help to conceal or disguise features which are not true to prototype but which are necessary for operational purposes on a model railway layout. These include sharp curves, 180 degree turns, hidden sidings and tracks, and fiddle yards. The scenery can also be used to emphasise good features which we wish to display to full advantage. It tends to make a layout appear larger if the scenery is well modelled and this is another good reason for taking care in the planning and execution of scenic work.

Tunnels are very convenient on a model railway for hiding part of the track, either a section of a continuous run oval track design so that it does not appear to be a simple oval, or on a length of line to break it up visually and make it appear longer. However, real tunnels are very expensive for railway companies to build and they are only bored where they are really needed. Therefore, to be convincing on a model railway, the tunnel must pass through a hill which looks large and high enough to warrant the construction of a tunnel rather than diverting the line around it or making a cutting through it. If the layout has generally flat terrain a single hill with the tunnel through it is likely to appear unrealistic and it may be better to employ some other feature such as a road overbridge, a building or a group of trees to conceal part of the track from view.

On a model railway layout the scenery can be designed to act as a visual barrier between different parts of the layout. A commonly used track plan is the type based on an oval continuous run design, a development of the train set. This is a convenient scheme but has the disadvantage that if the whole of the track is visible it is evident that the train is just going round and round. If the scenery is designed so that there is a high central ridge along the centre of the layout, the layout becomes divided visually into two separate parts with a scenic barrier between. This has several advantages. It makes the layout appear larger than it is and gives the impression that the train is really travelling somewhere rather than just going round an oval. Because only one side of the layout is viewed at a time the two sides can be treated quite differently from the scenic point of view, for example, one side can be rural and the other urban. If the central ridge is not high enough, modelled trees can be added on the top to form a further screen. Another alternative is to fit a double-sided backscene above the ridge of hills.

The scenery must be planned so that the clearances inside cuttings and within tunnels is adequate for the largest locomotives and rolling stock to be used on the line. Take particular care where there are sharp curves as the overhang with long vehicles can then be considerable. It is also essential to arrange that access is provided for maintenance of track and points and for the retrieval of trains which have stalled or derailed within tunnels or on other parts of the layout which are difficult to reach from the usual operating or viewing positions. If there are tracks which you will need to reach, for example, to couple and uncouple wagons during shunting, make sure that they are easily accessible from the edge of the layout and also take care not to place easily damaged scenic items such as trees between the tracks and the layout edge where they are likely to be knocked.

Scenic backgrounds fitted to the rear of a layout can greatly improve the realism by blocking from view irrelevant and distracting features such as wall paper, curtains and furnishings. Such backdrops make the layout appear larger by creating the illusion that the scenery extends into the distance as far as the eye can see. Tracks and fiddle yards are also conveniently concealed by scenic backgrounds.

For the most realistic effect the modelled scenery and the two dimensional background should be matched so that they merge apparently imperceptibly. This is best achieved by advance planning rather than by making or selecting a backscene afterwards and hoping it will look right. Indeed, if a commercially produced backscene is to be employed there is much to be said for choosing this first and then

A scene on the 4 mm scale Swanage Branch layout built by the Bournemouth & Isle of Purbeck MRC. The stone bridge and wall were modelled with Pyruma (Kos) fire cement over card and wood. This material was scribed before it set to represent the individual stone blocks. The fisherman sitting just to the left of the bridge is a Preiser figure. Note the telegraph wires made from thread.

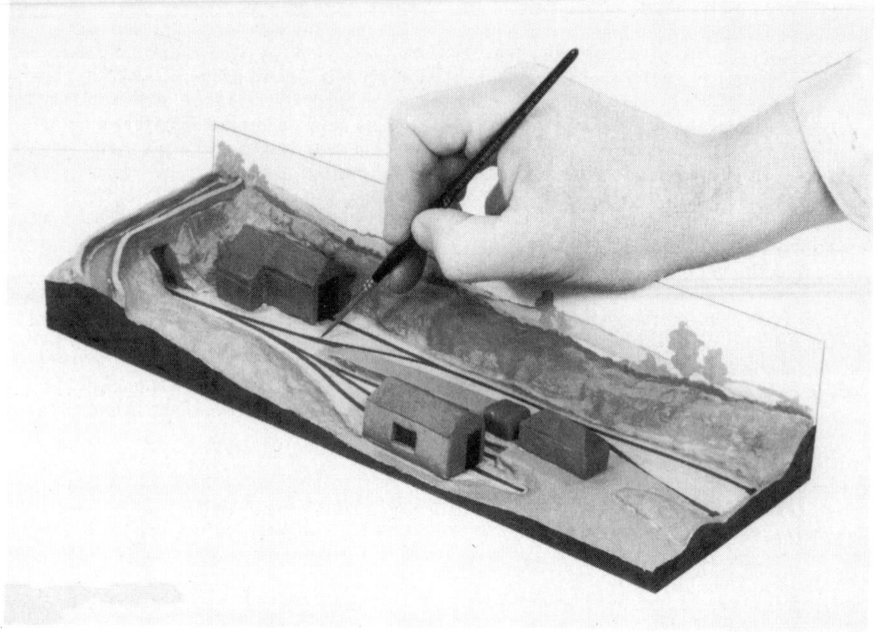

A small scale model of a proposed model railway layout can be very helpful in designing the scenery and other features. This mock-up was made with Peco Texture Modelling Compound. (Photograph by courtesy of Peco.)

planning, constructing and painting the modelled scenery to match up with it.

A model of the layout

It can be difficult, particularly for the beginner, to visualise from his own layout design or a published track plan just what the completed model railway will look like. This is especially true if there are tracks at various levels. The constructions of a small model of the proposed layout can be very helpful indeed in showing how the plan will look when translated into three dimensions. It is also very useful in the planning of suitable scenery.

Such a model can conveniently be constructed to a scale of 1 in to the foot using balsa wood and card. By beginning with a base at the level of the lowest tracks, card can be used to add the elevated tracks at the appropriate heights. Scenery can then be formed using plaster, Plasticine, or other modelling material and, if you wish, you can also represent the structures with balsa or card. The accompanying illustration shows a model of a branch line terminus constructed from Peco Texture Modelling Compound. As can be seen from this picture the model is of great assistance in planning the scenery so that it appears realistic.

You can keep the model very simple, using it only to give a rough guide to the appearance of the projected layout, or you can add many details and colour the model fully to produce an accurate representation. Any alterations or improvements which appear necessary or desirable from the small model can easily be made at this stage before construction of the actual layout begins. This saves time and trouble later and will help to ensure that the finished layout is to your liking.

Baseboards

The baseboard forms the foundation of a model railway layout and hence is of relevance when we consider the modelling of scenery. Indeed, it is only when we fit our track down permanently onto a baseboard that we can carry out true scenic modelling. The train set which is laid out at the beginning of an operating session and taken up again afterwards cannot be provided with realistic scenery or a proper setting. Because the baseboard is hidden on a completed model railway layout it is easy to overlook its importance. However, a well designed and constructed baseboard can make subsequent work much easier and more successful whereas a poor one can lead to many problems later on. The baseboard should be constructed so that it is level and true and it must be sturdy enough not to bend, twist or otherwise distort even if it is lent on or against by the operator. It must also be strong enough to withstand accidental knocks and, in the case of a portable layout, it must be rigid enough to remain true despite frequent erection and dismantling.

Baseboards and their construction are discussed in more detail in the first book in this series, *PSL Model Railway Guide 1 : Baseboards, Track and Electrification,* but the subject is of sufficient importance to warrant a few comments here also. Though most modellers will make their own baseboards there are now a few ready-made bases and kits for baseboards on the market. These are of two main types. The first are moulded bases of plastic or fibreglass such as those manufactured by Hornby, Kibri, Noch and DAS. These incorporate contoured and even, in some cases, coloured scenery and they are intended for use with train sets. The scope for individuality in the scenic modelling with bases of this type is obviously very limited and they do not really come within the scope of this book. The second type are wooden modular boards of the sort which the modeller may construct himself but are in ready-made or kit form for greater convenience. The beginner, or the more experienced modeller who has very limited facilities for wood working, may like to use baseboards of this type. Raitab, Faller, Puffers and Alan Borwell all offer these boards.

However, as I mentioned above, most modellers make their own baseboards up from raw materials. This is cheaper and also permits the construction of exactly the required size and shape of board. For convenience in construction and storage, and for portability, layout baseboards should be made up in units or modules each of which measures no more than 4 ft × 2 ft. Even if a layout is to be set up permanently you may eventually move house and wish to move the layout. This is much easier if the layout can be dismantled into units of small size. As most model railways are developed gradually from a relatively small and simple beginning, the addition of small baseboard units is a convenient way of extending the initial small layout.

Typically baseboard construction is in the form of a wooden frame or grid of 2 in × 1 in timber screwed and glued together with the longitudinal girders running the length of the baseboard and joists across at intervals not greater than 12 in. The joints can be halved or butt joints. For baseboards up to a foot wide no central girder is required but for wider boards one is needed for each additional foot of width. Where the joists cross the central girder or girders, halved joints are usually employed. However, the simpler butt joints can be used by staggering the joists at either side of the central girder.

On this frame a top of wood fibre insulation board or chipboard can be fixed to form a solid top baseboard. This type of base has the advantage of simplicity and is especially convenient for the beginner. Because the whole baseboard has a surface the track can be moved around until a good arrangement is achieved. Wherever the tracks are finally placed there will be support for them and there is no need to decide beforehand where they will be positioned. Similarly the modeller is free to place structures and other features wherever he wishes. Again they can be moved around without restriction until the desired effect results. However, this type of baseboard does impose some limitations on the scenery and there is a tendency for the landscape to be made rather flat and sometimes uninteresting. If a valley, river, lake, or other feature extending below ground level is to be modelled it is necessary to cut away part of the baseboard surface. This can be tricky unless planned in advance so that the board can be cut before fixing it down, and the modeller may therefore omit these interesting scenic features. The solid top baseboard uses more material than the open frame type and is therefore heavier and more expensive.

For an open frame baseboard the wooden framework is constructed as above but is not covered except where tracks, structures, or roads are to be positioned. Track bases can be cut from chipboard and faced with wood fibre insulation board; they are supported directly on the framing of the baseboard. The track bases for high level tracks are carried on risers—wood strips fixed onto the framing and extending up to the required height. This type of baseboard provides more flexibility, particularly for scenic work and for layouts with tracks at different levels, but does require that the layout be planned more accurately at the beginning. As track bases are fitted only where the tracks will be, any change in the positioning of these tracks will involve alterations to the track bases and, in the case of elevated tracks, to the risers also. Thus the open frame baseboard is more suited to the modeller with some experience. This type of board is cheaper and lighter than the solid top type.

There is a special type of open frame baseboard which has many important advantages; this is the 'layer' form designed by an American modeller, Linn Westcott. The key feature is that the joists rest on top of the girders instead of lying between them. Because the main longitudinal girders are usually made L-shaped for greater strength and convenience the system is usually known as the 'L-Girder Frame'. Though designed for large permanent layouts the system is also suitable for small layouts, including portable ones. The L-girder framework gives the maximum strength and therefore needs a minimum of materials so it is light and cheap. It is also a very flexible system and is ideal for layouts with tracks at different levels and for rugged scenery. It also allows modifications to be made fairly easily.

With a solid top baseboard, flat areas of scenery at ground level can be modelled directly on the baseboard surface. The landscape at higher levels is built up above this using supporting formers as necessary. The modelling of any features extending below ground level will involve cutting away a section of the baseboard top and possibly part of the baseboard frame also.

On open frame and L-girder baseboards scenery is supported on the main frame and by supports fixed on to the frame and extending up to the required height. Scenery going below the top of the baseboard can be accommodated between the girders and joists of the frame. With the L-girder frame particularly there is considerable flexibility in the positioning of the joists and they can be placed for the greatest convenience in scenery construction. For a deep valley a section of the baseboard can be lowered to take it. The section is strengthened with wood bracing or metal brackets. On permanent layouts with mountainous scenery a most impressive effect can be achieved by extending the scenery right down to floor level at the front of the layout and by taking the scenery and sky backscene up to ceiling height at the rear of the model railway. Some American modellers have done this with startlingly realistic results.

The basic shape

When we consider the basic landscape for a model railway layout there are three main aspects, the shape or contours, the texture of the surface, and its colour. In this section we will look at the first of these, the modelling of the basic shape or form of the scenery.

In flat areas at the level of the baseboard surface on a solid top type of board only the texturing and colouring will be required. Elsewhere an appropriately contoured basis is needed over which detailing can be applied. As this will be covered and hidden in the final model it does not matter what we use to construct it. However, there are obvious advantages in choosing a material which meets the following requirements. We want it to be easy and convenient to work with and once formed the contours should be retained without sagging or changing shape. The scenery should be sufficiently strong and rigid that it will not be damaged if it is leant on or accidentally knocked. As there may be quite a large area of scenery it is an advantage if the material we use is inexpensive.

Many different materials have been successfully employed and you may find it beneficial to experiment a little with various methods before deciding which will suit you best. The availability of materials may also influence your choice. For example, it may be that rather than buy one material you can use an alternative that you can obtain free of charge as scrap.

A typical form of construction is to cut formers to the appropriate profile from wood fibre insulation board, hardboard, plywood or thick card and to erect these on the baseboard using small blocks of scrap wood to fix them in position. To fill in the gaps strips of card can be

Scenery during construction on an 00-scale model railway layout. Supports are wood and thick card and the base for a road in the foreground is also card. The rocky hillside has been modelled in plaster over Mod Roc plaster bandage material.

Above *The walls of this cutting were modelled with Mod Roc plaster bandage material and Polyfilla.*

Below *An unusual scenic feature on Colin Woolridge's N-scale 'Longbourne' layout is this prehistoric stone circle. Scenery construction was from expanded polystyrene shaped to the contours required and covered with plaster strengthened with old net curtain material. The surface was then painted and covered with dyed sawdust.*

glued, stapled or pinned across between the formers. This card can be cut from old cereal or other packets as it does not have to be of good quality. Alternatively, chicken wire or aviary wire (similar but of smaller mesh) can be pinned or stapled down to cover the formers. Over either of these is applied some material to form a complete surface. One of the plaster bandage materials such as Mod-Roc is easy to obtain and convenient to use. Lengths of the bandage are cut off, dipped briefly into water, gently squeezed to remove excess water, and then moulded into place using the fingers to shape the material into the required contours. It quickly hardens and dries and will then be quite rigid and strong. A cheaper alternative is to use pieces of torn up newspaper or paper towels dipped into plaster made up to a creamy consistency, and then laid out onto the supporting framework. Several layers are applied to give sufficient strength and the surface is smoothed and shaped as with the plaster bandage material.

Jack Kine, an expert scenic modeller who has constructed many of the models used on BBC TV programmes, employs a supporting framework made up from card strips over which he applies pieces of cut up dress stiffener, tarleton or buckram, lightly coated with a creamy mix of Artex modelling powder. This method gives realistic results and is convenient for the modeller because the materials required are available as a scenery kit from Mr Kine's shop in Surbiton.

With any of the above methods the contours can be altered by the addition of extra plaster bandage or other material and by further shaping until the result is as the modeller wishes.

Where there is only a low bank or rocky outcrop we do not need a built up framework of the type described above. All that is required are a few pieces of scrap wood fibre insulation board carved roughly to the shape wanted, glued down onto the base and covered with plaster bandage material, pieces of newspaper dipped in plaster, or other surface covering.

The use of expanded polystyrene for scenery construction is becoming increasingly popular with modellers. This material can be purchased at Do-It-Yourself shops either as blocks or sheets, or as ceiling tiles. However it is extensively used as packing for TV sets, record players, and other delicate equipment. After delivery this packing is discarded and you may well be able to obtain all the expanded polystyrene you need for your layout free of charge. Although the surface is relatively soft and this type of plastic is easy to work, the material is quite strong and will be perfectly suitable as a

Authentic scenic work on a narrow-gauge layout based on the Ffestiniog Railway constructed by Trevor Hughes. The scenery is shaped from expanded polystyrene covered with a thin layer of plaster. Sawdust mixed with Polycell and painted with poster colours gives the realistic grass effect. Note the beautifully modelled stone walls. Those in the foreground were built up from individual pieces of card while the dry stone walls were made from pieces of real stone held together with Polycell.

support for your scenery. It has the advantage of being very light, a particular asset if you are constructing a portable layout.

To glue expanded polystyrene, water-based adhesive or one of the glues sold specifically for fixing ceiling tiles should be used; the ordinary modelling cements and solvents will merely dissolve the plastic with disastrous results! The blocks can be cut with a saw or sharp knife and shaped with a rasp or file but the dust produced can be irritating if inhaled so take care when working with this material. It can also be rather messy as the dust spreads easily so it is worth while having a vacuum cleaner close at hand and clearing up as you work. Even better is to work outside if you can.

The most convenient method of cutting is to use a hot wire cutter. These can be purchased but it is also fairly easy to make an instrument of this type for yourself. The basis of the tool is a length of resistance wire which is heated by passing a current through it. The current is adjusted to give a suitable temperature which will allow the wire to cut through the plastic easily without melting too much of the material. The construction of hot wire cutters has been described in various hobby magazines. Two recent articles which include information on this subject have appeared in model railway magazines. There was an article by Dave Rowe in the August 1979 issue of *Model Railways* and another by Malcolm Clarke and Trevor Hughes in the April 1979 issue of *Railway Modeller.*

Once the expanded polystyrene has been shaped its surface can be covered with plaster or plaster bandage to protect it and to form a basis for detailing the surface.

Scenic modules

The idea of constructing scenic modules or dioramas has become popular recently with modellers, particularly in the United States. I am really referring here to railway (or railroad) modelling but, of course, military modellers are also very interested in this form of presentation for their models. Sometimes a model railway diorama is constructed purely for static display as in the example illustrated here of a period model featuring the 'Rocket' made by Terry Jenkins. However, more often a unit is built with the intention of incorporating it, sooner or later, into a layout.

There are advantages in constructing scenic modules separately, even if the layout is ready to take them immediately. A structure, or group of structures, for example, can be fitted onto a separate base. The scenic work and detailing of the ground surface on the base around the buildings can be carried out more

Below *Terry Jenkins built this small diorama to display the 00-scale Triang 'Rocket' and coach. The period figures are Merten models and the backscene is a Peco product.*

Bottom *This small scrapyard in 4 mm scale was constructed as a unit which can then be fitted into a layout. In this way the work can be carried out in optimum conditions on the workbench rather than on the layout where it may be more difficult.*

Right *Terry Jenkins mounted this scratch-built country pub on its own small base making it easier to conceal the join between the building and the ground. The surrounding details can also be added with the model still on the workbench rather than having to work on the layout.*

Below right *The building on its base has now been fixed on to the layout and the surrounding scenery covers the edges of the base concealing the join. The telephone box is a Merit product.*

easily and more successfully with the unit on the workbench where access is easy and lighting conditions are good, than on the layout where it may be difficult to reach the model. The model scrapyard shown here was built as a unit on its own base and was fully modelled, complete with all details, prior to placing it on a layout. The country pub modelled by Terry Jenkins was fitted onto a base of thick card on which the driveway, lawns and other details were added. The photographs show the model before and after installation on the layout.

On an along the wall layout it can be difficult to reach into the corners for scenery construction. It is often much easier to make the scenery for each corner section as a separate unit on its own base, carrying out all the modelling on the workbench, before fitting it into place on the layout. There is often sufficient space in these corners for fairly extensive scenic work and interesting features, and the full potential is more likely to be realised if the modelling is done in separate units.

The idea of constructing separate units can be taken further with the modeller building a series of dioramas or modules designed so that they can be joined together later to form a complete layout. This can have a number of advantages. The beginner can start on a relatively small unit which will give him the opportunity to try various types of construction work without taking too long to complete. The successful completion of one section will encourage him to go on to construct further, more complicated modules until he builds up a layout.

The more experienced modeller may also find modular construction a convenient method of working, particularly if he has at present insufficient space for a complete layout. He can enjoy some practical modelling in the construction of one or more units and later, if space becomes available, he will already have part of his layout built. In the meantime the scenic modules provide an excellent setting for the display of his locomotive and rolling stock models.

Ground surface texturing

Over the basic contours of the scenery we need to apply a covering which will reproduce the texture and colour of the ground surface. This is conveniently carried out using plaster, a household filler such as Polyfilla or Tapwata, or Artex modelling powder. The material chosen is made up into a mix of thick creamy consistency and is applied over the basic form. By stippling or smoothing the surface with a brush before it sets, the desired surface texture can be achieved. Alternatively, or additionally, material such as sawdust, sand, dust from sawing or filing wood fibre insulation board, and so on, can be mixed in with the surfacing material to create an appropriate texture.

To colour the scenery I use household emulsion paint and poster colours, either the liquid paint or the powder colour. There are advantages to adding powder colour to the plaster or filler mix used for the surface covering to give it a uniform earth colour. This provides a basic colour from which to build up the varied shades needed for realism. It also ensures that if the surface of the scenery becomes chipped it will be earth colour and not unsightly white which shows. Household emulsion paint is cheap, particularly as it is often possible to buy oddments at reduced price, and is convenient to use as the brushes can be cleaned with water. The paint not only colours the scenery but also seals the surface of the plaster or filler. The emulsions can be mixed to produce better shades and the colours can also be modified by mixing in poster colours to give exactly the colour you want. Alternatively you can select a colour

Fishermen's cottages on Mike Sharman's period 4 mm scale layout. The boats are lifeboats from plastic ship kits. Note the muddy track, modelled in plaster, leading over the bridge and the nets spread out to dry. The water surface is plaster painted and then varnished.

A beautifully modelled pond on a 4 mm scale display diorama made by John Piper (Accessories) Limited. The very realistic fencing is etched brass and is among a number of scenic items available from this firm. The ploughed field was modelled with corrugated cardboard with a surface covering of scenic texturing material from the range marketed by this manufacturer.

from one of the ranges in which the colours are mixed to order by retailers; these shops will also endeavour to mix colours to match samples you take in if these are not included in the ranges.

When painting the surface, additional texture can be produced by sprinkling sand, sawdust, plaster, and so on, over the wet paint. Alternatively after the paint has dried, white glue can be brushed on and dyed sawdust, flock powder and scenic dressings can be added as required. For realistic scenery the colours should be kept subdued and should blend into each other. A light overspray with a spray painter or airbrush with a thin grey or black will help to tone down the colour realistically.

In areas of rough ground small stones, gravel or granite chippings can be used to represent rocks and stones. Ploughed fields can be modelled very realistically, as can be seen in the photograph of the John Piper (Accessories) Ltd scenic display module, with corrugated card covered with dark brown scenic dressing. The modelling of grassy areas and other vegetation will be considered later.

For sandy areas such as beaches and deserts the plaster surface is painted and fine sand is sprinkled on, either on the wet paint or later, after the application of diluted white glue. The colour will be yellow for a sandy beach; for a desert scene more grey and brown can be added to the basic colour. Deserts often have dry earth with many small stones and rocks rather than sand and this can be modelled with gravel and stone chippings.

Modelling rock

Rock faces are popular for model railway layouts because they are scenically interesting and also because they require little space to provide vertical separation between tracks or other features. On US and Continental prototype layouts very rugged rocky and mountainous scenery is often featured and this can be very attractive and spectacular. Some imaginative American modellers have extended their scenery down to the floor in front of the layout and up towards the ceiling at the rear giving the mountainous sections of their lines a very realistic and effective appearance. On British prototype layouts the scenery will be less dramatic but cliffs and rock faces can still be included to great advantage. Care must be taken in the planning so that a rock face appears natural and not just added by the modeller for reasons of convenience. Scenery of this type also provides a good excuse for the use of tunnels, but again, these must appear necessary and not contrived.

Various materials and techniques have been employed in the modelling of rocks. The methods described here have all been used successfully and the choice is up to you. Try out different methods and then use the one you find most successful for your layout.

A logical beginning is to consider the use of pieces of real rock. Obviously smoothly

Left *This large cliff forms a most impressive scenic feature on an extensive HO-scale Fleischmann layout. There is a rack railway track running alongside the road at the base of the rock face.*

Below *Terry Jenkins made extensive use of pieces of real rock in modelling this quarry in 00 scale. Note also the derelict building and the abandoned tracks of the narrow-gauge railway.*

rounded rocks and stones are unsuitable; instead we need small rocks with irregular surfaces which look very much like real rock faces in miniature. This method does not seem to be very popular generally with modellers but it can give very good results. One of the accompanying photographs shows a quarry constructed by Terry Jenkins for a large 00-scale layout; in modelling the quarry Terry used numerous pieces of real rock. The pieces should be carefully chosen for size, shape and surface detail to suit the situation on the layout. The rocks are embedded into wet plaster to hold them in place and plaster or filler can be used to fill in the gaps between and around the pieces and to blend them into the scenery. When dry the plaster should be painted to match up with the rocks or to represent earth or grassed areas between the rocky outcrops. The modeller may also wish to apply some paint to the pieces of rock themselves to get just the right effect. On ledges and in cracks in rock faces a few small plants often manage to take root and in the model these can be represented by a little lichen or scenic dressing applied over dabs of white glue.

A disadvantage of using pieces of real rock on a layout is that they are heavy and the weight can be a problem, particularly on a portable layout. However, if only a few smallish rocks are required, using pieces of real rock can be a convenient and realistic solution even on a portable line.

Perhaps the most popular method, in this country, for modelling cliffs and rock faces is to use cork bark. This material is available from model shops and also from florists. The chunks as bought do not look too promising but when cut into suitable pieces and blended into the rest of the scenery the results can be very good. The bark has the advantages of being very light, easy to work with, and readily available. The ridging on the bark gives the effect of

Right *Cork bark was employed to model this rock tunnel mouth on a 4 mm scale narrow-gauge layout owned by the Poole & District MRS.*

Below right *A corner of a small 009 layout owned by the Poole & District MRS. The rock-face at the rear was modelled from cork bark. The bicycle and rack, the wheelbarrow just behind it, and the lamp are all Merit products.*

rock strata and the pieces should be fitted onto the layout so that the ridges run in approximately the same direction in different pieces which are near to each other. These ridges should be horizontal or sloping but not vertical. The bark has a grey/brown colour which is suitable for representing rocks, but an even better effect can be achieved with careful painting. Again vegetation in cracks and on ledges can be modelled using small pieces of lichen or by sprinkling dyed sawdust or scenic dressing onto glue.

Another very light material which is especially useful for portable layouts is expanded polystyrene. I have already mentioned how this plastic can be used as a light but strong support for the scenery generally. It can also be employed for rock faces. The basic size and shape of the rock face is built up from pieces of the plastic and the surface is carved with a knife or shaped with a soldering iron tip to represent the type of rock being modelled. A layer of plaster or Artex modelling powder is applied to cover the surface. This protects the plastic and also enables final detailing to be carried out, both in shaping the wet plaster as it is applied and also in carving the surface when the plaster has set hard.

One of the most realistic methods of modelling cliffs and rock faces is with plaster, roughly shaped during application and then detailed either before or after it sets hard. Over whatever basic scenery foundation is used plaster or Polyfilla is applied where the rock faces are to be. The mix should be fairly stiff and, using a spatula or old table knife, the basic shape of the type of rock formation required is built up. Then with an old blade in a modelling knife and a scriber the details such as cracks, fissures, ledges, crevices and so on are modelled. Final detailing is carried out after the plaster has set, again using a modelling knife and scriber. The rock faces are then painted and vegetation is added to ledges as described earlier. Damp patches where water seeps out and drips down the rocks can be simulated by painting a little clear gloss varnish in the appropriate places.

If the modeller refers to real rock faces, or photographs of them, as a guide for shaping and detailing the plaster, and spends the time and effort needed in modelling all the small details, the results from this method can be very realistic indeed. However, the technique is quite time consuming, particularly if large areas are involved when the work becomes rather tedious.

There is a much easier and quicker method of modelling rocks in plaster which produces surprisingly good results. Plaster or Polyfilla, as a fairly thick mix, is applied to the area over the basic scenery foundation. However, instead of using tools to shape and carve the rock face the modeller takes a piece of metallic cooking foil, crumples it up, then roughly flattens it out again. The foil is then placed over the wet plaster and pressed down onto it. This area is left to set hard before the foil is peeled off. When the foil is removed the plaster will be seen to have an irregular surface reproducing the crumpled foil and giving a very effective rock face appearance. A little touching up and extra detailing can be carried out if desired using a modelling knife and a scriber, and the plaster is then painted. By working in sections, so that the foil can be applied before the plaster

sets, large areas of rock can be modelled very quickly with this technique.

Rocks with a marked strata can be modelled realistically by using wood fibre insulation board. If you have used this material for the baseboard surface on your layout, and perhaps also for the scenery formers, you will probably have scrap offcuts left over. These can be broken up into irregular pieces which are then glued on top of each other to build up the rock face or outcrop. The shaping can be carried further with a knife and rasp until the desired contours are obtained. A final brush over with a wire brush will remove rough edges and fuzziness. Over this a thin layer of plaster, Polyfilla or Artex is applied to seal the surface and to add a little further texture. Though strata are sometimes horizontal they more often slope a little; this can be achieved by using a wedge shaped piece of board at the base of the rock formation.

Whatever method you use for modelling rock, the best results will be obtained by carefully studying the appearance of the real thing and by trying to reproduce it accurately in miniature. There is much to be said, especially if you are a beginner, for choosing an actual example and copying this as exactly as possible.

The colouring is also very important in creating a realistic model of a rock face. Except when using pieces of real rock, I apply a coat of ordinary household emulsion, either white or grey depending on the type of rock being

Above *Part of a small N-scale layout built by John Norman. The narrow-gauge locomotive and trucks are static scenic models made from scraps of plastic card. Cork bark was used to model the rock faces at the back of the scene on the left.*

Left *A quarry on a small narrow-gauge layout. The basic shape was built up with Mod Roc plaster bandage material and the detailing has been applied with Polyfilla. The bulldozer, which is an inexpensive die-cast toy of appropriate size, adds the finishing touch to the scene.*

modelled, to the cliff, rock face or rock outcrop. If desired, sand, plaster or fine sawdust can be mixed into the paint to give more texture to the resulting surface. The emulsion paint not only provides a basic colour over which other shades and tones can be added, but also seals the surface satisfactorily.

The colours depend on the type of rock. For granite I use a coat of grey household emulsion (or white with black powder colour added). Over this basic colour I apply a thin wash of black. This collects in the cracks, fissures and crevices accentuating them and enhancing the three dimensional modelling of the rock face. I then brush on darker greys and a little brown in patches, blending them together to give subtle variations in shade. An alternative and very effective method of adding these other colours is to splatter them on using an old brush or toothbrush, drawing a small piece of card across the bristles so that they flick back causing small drops of the paint to splatter onto the rock. The prominences can be realistically highlighted with a little white paint using an almost dry brush and just touching the surface. For limestone and chalk a little thinned grey or black is applied over a basic coat of white emulsion. Sandstone is a red/brown colour with a little yellow and white blended in. For slate use grey with a little brown. It is very helpful to have colour slides of the type of rock you are modelling to guide you when colouring the scenery. Keep the colours subdued to give the effect of distance and remember to allow for the lighting by which the layout will be viewed. This is usually artificial light rather than daylight.

Water

A well modelled stretch of water can be a very striking scenic feature on a model railway layout, even if it is only a small pond. Lakes, rivers, harbours, canals and other areas of water are not only interesting and attractive in themselves but there are also many associated items such as bridges, jetties, ships and boats, watermills, boathouses, locks and so on, all of which add extra interest to the layout.

There are also other important, though less obvious, benefits in the use of these features as scenic barriers. On a small layout with an oval continuous run track plan, modelling a lake in the centre will visually separate the two sides of the oval. This will help to make the layout more realistic as the trains will appear to be travelling from one side of the lake around to the other, rather than merely going round and round an oval. If part of the oval is concealed by a tunnel the effect will be even better.

Similarly a river or a canal can provide an excellent scenic break between two roughly parallel tracks and will give a good reason for having the two tracks running in more or less the same direction. By breaking up the layout, visually, into separate parts a lake, river or canal will also make it appear larger.

Various materials have been used to model water. The methods I will be describing here are the most popular with railway modellers. All can produce very realistic results if carefully carried out.

The simplest way of representing water is to use paint and varnish. For a dead calm stretch of water, as sometimes found on canals, ponds

A canal and lock on the 2 mm Scale Association layout. Note the small details such as the lifebelts and their holders. Len Folkard constructed the 'Navigation Inn' from scratch.

paints are applied with an airbrush they can be blended very realistically without difficulty. White paint can be used to simulate foam around rocks in a river. Remember that much of the apparent colour of the water in lakes, rivers, canals and harbours is due to reflections from the sky and surrounding trees, hills and so on. Because our models will normally be viewed indoors the sky cannot be reflected in the modelled water and we must make the colours correspondingly lighter by mixing in white, pale grey or light blue. Also make the colours lighter than you want them to be for the finished water as the coats of clear gloss varnish which will be applied to make the surface appear wet will make the colours look darker. Any form of water can be modelled with this plaster, paint and varnish method. Lakes, rivers, ponds, canals, the sea, rapids and even waterfalls can be realistically and

Left *The selection of an unusual feature to model can add interest and individuality to your layout. A good example is this dam on the Hestair Models HO-scale exhibition model railway.*

Below *A scene on Mike Sharman's fine 4 mm scale 19th century period model railway layout. The water in the canal is represented by painting and varnishing the surfaces. The canal boat in the upper lock was scratch-built.*

and small lakes, a piece of hardboard, smooth side up, can be used for the water surface. Unless the hardboard is only a small piece it should be well braced to prevent any warping or sagging. More often there will be ripples or waves and the surface should be modelled with plaster or Polyfilla. This is applied over a wood fibre insulation board or chipboard base. As the plaster is put on, use fingers or a soft brush, dipped frequently into water, to smooth the surface and to create ripples, waves or turbulence. Sand banks or mud banks in a river can be modelled with plaster; rocks protruding from the surface can be represented by small pieces of stone or gravel embedded in the plaster.

When the plaster has set it is painted. As usual I like to apply a basic coat of household emulsion paint to seal the plaster; this can be white or the basic colour of the water. Over this other colours can be applied and blended into each other to give the required appearance of deep or shallow, clear or muddy water. Generally the colours will vary from deep blues and greens in deeper areas to browns, yellows and greys for muddy shallow water. If the inexpensively reproduced in miniature in this way.

Another method is to employ a sheet of transparent material, usually glass though perspex or clear styrene are equally suitable and have the advantage of not being breakable. For modelling dead calm water a flat sheet of glass can be used, but more often some type of ripple glass is chosen to give the appearance of water with small waves or ripples. To achieve a ripple effect with perspex or styrene sheet the material can be heated over a spirit lamp or propane torch. Apply only enough heat to give a gently rippled surface; excess heat may cause unrealistic distortion.

The glass, perspex or clear plastic is then placed over a painted surface representing the lake, river or canal bed, which is painted, as with the plaster, paint and varnish method, to give the impression of varying depths and of clear or muddy water. The transparent material can be placed directly on top of the painted surface of, for example, a sheet of hardboard, but more often the glass or plastic is suspended a little above a bed modelled in plaster giving a very realistic impression of depth to the water. Underwater details such as rocks, waterweed, submerged logs, and even a sunken rowing boat can be included by placing them on the lake or river bed before the water surface is fixed in position.

Because it is easiest to obtain and work with relatively small pieces of glass or plastic this method is more suited to modelling ponds and small lakes rather than a long river or canal. However it may be possible to model these latter features using two or more separate pieces if the joins can be concealed by bridges, weirs or locks. Glass has the disadvantage of being fairly heavy and fragile, both of which qualities are particularly undesirable for portable layouts. Perspex and clear plastic are better in these respects but the surface can be easily scratched when using or cleaning the layouts.

A relatively new technique for modelling water is the use of clear casting plastic. This method is growing in popularity and is now quite widely used by both railway and military modellers. Casting plastic is made by several manufacturers and is widely available from toy and craft shops. I use Plasticraft made by Turner Research Ltd of Leeds, but other materials are equally suitable. There are two components, liquid plastic and hardener, which are mixed just before use.

Terry Jenkins modelled this scene in 4 mm scale. The river bed was shaped with plaster and, after painting, received several coats of clear gloss varnish to give the appearance of water. Note the farmer taking the cows for milking.

Above *Llareggub Harbour on Dave Rowe's well known 4 mm scale narrow-gauge 'Milk Wood' railway layout. Homekraft rough texture modelling clay, carefully shaped to form a breaking wave, was used for the realistic sea. This was then painted and while still wet, the white foam of the wave was added. Several coats of clear gloss varnish completed the sea. The stone buildings and the sea wall were modelled with Peco Texture Modelling Compound.* (Photograph by courtesy of Peco.)

Below *Realistic reflections in a superbly modelled waterfront scene in 4 mm scale, on a layout built by G. Iliffe Stokes. The water surface is represented by thick gauge plastic which is very pliable and ripples sufficiently to give distorted reflections.* (Photograph by T.H. Woollard.)

The bed of the river, lake, canal, etc is modelled with plaster over a base of chipboard or wood fibre insulation board and the banks are built up with Mod-Roc and plaster. The bed need not be very deep as a quite shallow layer of the plastic gives a good impression of depth for the modelled water. The bed is painted in the usual way, blending the colours and using darker blues and greens where the water is to appear deepest, merging into paler colours with browns and yellows where the water is shallow or muddy. Keep the colours on the light side as the plastic makes the finished colours appear darker. The bed must be complete or the casting plastic will leak out. If the water area extends to the edge of the baseboard you must put a strip of card or wood across or seal the gap with Plasticine so that the liquid plastic will be contained. After the model is complete these can be removed. Any detailing of the base with rocks, logs, weed, rubbish and so on can be carried out at this stage. The plastic is then mixed according to the manufacturer's instructions and poured on. Apply several thin layers rather than one thick coating as the latter may crack. Allow each application to set hard before adding the next. Setting can be speeded up by warmth if you wish. If desired extra underwater details, even model fish(!), can be added between the layers. Dyes are available for use with the casting plastic and can be added to one or more of the layers to provide additional colouring. A little white paint can be applied around any rocks giving a realistic impression of foam. If much more hardener than recommended is added to the final layer the setting is speeded up. This fast hardening causes rippling of the surface giving a realistic appearance, with the water apparently having small waves and ripples due to wind and current. Make sure that no dust can get onto the surface of the plastic while it is setting because otherwise it will become adherent to the surface spoiling the effect. If any of the items to be wholly or partly submerged in the modelled water are made of plastic they must be painted beforehand as the liquid plastic will attack and dissolve unpainted plastic.

Of the various methods of modelling water this is probably the most realistic. It is more expensive than the paint and varnish method, though as only a relatively thin casting is required to give a good impression of depth, the cost is not all that great even for quite large lakes or rivers. An alternative which gives similar results but which is, I believe, rather cheaper is fibreglass resin available from motor accessory dealers and firms stocking materials for boat building. Graham Bailey used this material for the realistic harbour, illustrated here, on his modern British prototype N scale layout.

Both the casting plastic and the fibreglass

A busy dock scene on Graham Bailey's N-scale layout. After painting the harbour bed with appropriate colours, fibreglass resin was poured on giving a realistic water effect. The ship model was constructed from the Novo 'Shell Welder' kit originally produced by Frog.

have a strong and unpleasant smell and good ventilation is essential during the modelling and while the material is hardening.

Readers may wonder why, after having recommended the use of pieces of real rock as a good method for modelling miniature rock faces, I have made no mention of using real water for lakes, rivers, ponds or harbours on model railway layouts. In fact it is generally unsuitable. The main disadvantage is that, except when used for very large lakes or harbours, it does not really look right. It also tends to become stagnant and smelly, and there is always the danger of leakage with potentially disastrous results! However, real water can be used very effectively on a small layout with the scenic models such as those offered in kit form by Faller, which are designed to take real water. One model is a water mill, another an ornamental fountain, and in both there is a small pump to circulate the water. In the case of the water mill the water which is pumped round actually rotates the water wheel. With these kits the water is contained within the models and leakage is unlikely.

Vegetation

Vegetation of various types forms a major part of the landscape and thus the representation of grass, bushes, plants and trees is of considerable importance to the scenic modeller. As in other aspects of the scenery, texture and colour are of particular importance. We will consider each of the main types of vegetation in turn.

Grass

It is not sufficient merely to apply a coat of green paint, no matter how accurate the colour may be, to model grass; there must also be some attempt to simulate the texture. The method used will vary according to whether, for example, we are modelling short uniform grass, as in a lawn, or long grass in clumps as might be found in a marshy area. I have already mentioned that the plaster or Polyfilla covering the surface of the scenery can be stippled after it has been applied to give a textured effect. This can be carried further by brushing on a coat of emulsion paint and also stippling this as it dries. Where the grass cover is to be fairly complete the paint can be a yellowy green; if the grass is to be sparse use a light earth colour as the basic coat and later apply patches of green for the grassy areas. Though this provides some texture a better effect will be achieved by adding more with dyed sawdust. This is available commercially or the modeller can colour his own using household dye or

Below *Allan Downes made extensive use of natural plant cuttings in modelling the trees and bushes in this realistic country scene.* (Photograph by John Priest.)

Above right *A scene on the N-scale 'Eight Oaks' layout constructed by Bob Jones. The realistic grassy countryside was shaped with old dress material over crumpled newspaper. The surface was then given two coats of paint with dyed sawdust sprinkled onto the second coat before it dried. The stream in the foreground and the river it leads into were modelled with Polyfilla. This was coloured with poster paints and then several coats of clear gloss varnish were applied to make the surface appear wet.*

Right *A scene on Keith Gowen's TT-scale branch line layout. The grassy banks were modelled with Mod Roc plaster bandage material over chicken wire, painted and sprinkled with flock powder.*

emulsion paint. Choose two or three shades of green, taking care to select natural looking colours; avoid blue greens, which will not appear realistic, and use yellowy greens instead. The colours should be relatively subdued as very bright colours look unnatural on a model railway layout.

After painting the surface of the area with diluted white glue, sprinkle on the dyed sawdust, mixing the different shades in places to give some variation in tone. An alternative to sawdust is flock powder, also on sale in model shops in a range of colours. This material has a finer texture and is thus suited for use at the rear of the layout; here the colours should be more subdued to give the illusion of distance. When the glue has dried fully, gently brush off the surplus sawdust or flock powder for re-use elsewhere. If there are any bare patches, or if you want a thicker covering, the application process can be repeated. A light overspray with grey paint can be very useful for toning down colours which are too bright to make them appear more realistic. It is also effective, for the areas towards the rear of the layout, to make them appear more distant.

Another excellent method for modelling grass is to use medical lint, obtainable from chemist shops. The surface of the scenery is painted with diluted white glue. The amount of glue applied is varied from place to place, more or less being put on according to how thick or

Ground surface texturing

sparse the grass is to be. The lint is then pressed on to the glue with the backing uppermost; the pressure is applied lightly or more heavily according to the thickness of grass wanted. After the glue has dried the backing is torn off leaving the fibres sticking up over the scenery. After painting with a spray painter or an air-brush the effect is very realistic indeed.

Other materials have also been used with success. Old pile carpet stuck down and then trimmed with a modelling knife or scissors to make the surface irregular also gives a good representation of grass when it is painted appropriately. Old felt underlay can also be similarly employed. An old bath towel suitably coloured with dye, paint or felt tip marker pens and cut with scissors to give a more irregular appearance gives a very good representation of long grass and weeds as found in marshy areas.

Sheets of grass matting are available commercially from various manufacturers. Some are very realistic both in colour and texture but others are too uniform in shade and thickness. The latter can be improved by scraping some areas with a modelling knife to thin the matting there, giving a more patchy appearance. Touching up with different shades of paint to provide some variation in colour using a brush or airbrush will also improve the effect. If the colour is too bright, an overall spray with an airbrush can do much to improve the realism by toning down the colour.

Individual clumps of long grass can be modelled using threads from sisal string. Unravel the string, soak in water with a little detergent in it and hang the strands up with a clothes peg at the bottom so that they dry fairly straight. The strands can be dyed or painted green, cut into shorter lengths and glued in place in clumps using white glue. The Landscape Model Co offer ready-made clumps of foliage and rushes which need only to be glued into place on a layout. Bristles from an old toothbrush, brush or broom can also be used to model long grass, reeds or rushes. Another method of making clumps of grass is with ordinary electrical wire. Cut a short piece of wire, strip off most of the insulation leaving only a short segment at one end to hold the strands together and for mounting into a small hole in the base. The fine wire strands are unwound and trimmed to a suitable length. When painted the effect of a small clump of grass is very good.

For larger areas of coarse and long grass, weeds and other ground cover, a good appearance can be achieved easily and quickly by cutting up scraps of lichen unsuitable for modelling bushes or trees, into tiny pieces and sprinkling them fairly thickly onto white glue applied to the area. Diluted white glue is then sprayed over the lichen and a scenic dressing is sprinkled on top giving a thick ground cover of a realistic texture. Flowers can be simulated by tiny spots of paint of a bright colour or by adding a little brightly coloured dyed sawdust or flock powder to the scenic dressing.

Bushes

Bushes and hedges are useful in filling bare areas in a scene and also for helping to divide the landscape up, making the layout appear larger. They can also be useful in separating roads, railway tracks and other features. The easiest way of modelling them is with pieces of lichen. This material is readily available from model shops in a variety of colours. Choose the finer tips for small neat bushes; the coarser pieces can be utilised for larger, straggly growth. A good effect can be achieved with lichen by dipping the pieces into white glue and then sprinkling on sawdust or flock powder of

Left *This close view of a commercially produced grass mat shows the realistic texture of the material. The soldier is to 00 scale.*

Above right *An attractive scene on Keith Gowen's TT-scale layout. The bushes around the tunnel mouth were made from lichen.*

Right *Simple but effective scenic work on an 009 layout built by the Romsey & District Railway Modellers' Society. Lichen has been used for the bushes and trees. Note the abandoned track on the bridge in the left foreground, a realistic and interesting detail.*

Ground surface texturing

Modelling a gorse bush. Fine wire, either fuse wire or wire from electrical flex, is twisted into a bundle and then partly unwound to form the branches arising from the trunk. This is then dipped into matt brown paint. When dry, glue is painted onto the branches and small pieces of green crêpe paper are sprinkled on to represent the foliage. Spots of yellow paint on the foliage give the effect of flowers.

appropriate colour. The glue makes the lichen stiff and the dyed sawdust or flock powder gives a good surface texture. Hedges can be similarly modelled using suitable pieces of lichen and mounting them so as to form a continuous strip of hedge. Rubberised horse-hair is another useful material for modelling bushes and hedges. It is cut into pieces of suitable size and shape, glue is applied and scenic dressing sprinkled on. The whole thing can then be dipped into paint or sprayed with paint. When dry the pieces are mounted on the ground using white glue. There are many other materials, some of which are found around the house, which can be pressed into service in this way. Bob Jones made realistic hedges for his N-scale layout from plastic scouring pads of the type which are used for washing pots and

A selection of materials useful in modelling plants. **A** *pipe cleaner;* **B** *old toothbrush;* **C** *electrical flex;* **D** *JNT fern;* **E** *lichen;* **F** *string.*

pans. He cut the pads to the required shapes and then painted them to produce attractive and inexpensive hedges and bushes.

Bushes can also be built up on a wire skeleton, in the same way that some model trees are constructed, but on a smaller scale. One of the photographs shows a small bush, in this case a gorse bush, during construction using this technique. Several strands of fine wire, from old electric flex were twisted together at one end and splayed apart at the other to form the stem and branches pattern of the bush. The wire was painted brown. When dry, white glue was dabbed on and the whole thing was then dipped into a pile of small punchings from green crêpe paper representing the foliage. Finally small touches of yellow paint gave the effect of flowers on the gorse bush. The bush was easily mounted on the layout by making a small hole in the ground for the stem; a dab of white glue on the base of the stem secured it in place.

Other plants of all types can be modelled using various materials and methods. Ivy and other creepers on walls are easily reproduced using dyed sawdust applied over glue painted onto the parts of the wall to be covered. Stems can be painted on with black or brown using a fine brush. Small pieces of lichen in rows give a good impression of potato and other vegetable plants while longer pieces can be fixed onto a trellis made from scraps of wood to represent climbing plants. Cabbages can be modelled using beads or ball bearings of appropriate size painted green and set out in rows. Small pieces of fern material are available in some ranges of scenic products and these are useful in the modelling of various types of small plants. If you have a small pond on your layout, water lilies can be modelled with small discs punched from green paper, or white paper painted green, for the leaves. The flowers can also be made from paper.

The ultimate in modelling plants and flowers in 4 mm scale can be seen at Pendon where exact scale models of a variety of garden plants and flowers have been created. Many of these have been built up leaf by leaf, flower by flower, from paper tissue coloured appropriately. The results are incredibly realistic and show just what can be achieved with skill and patience!

Finally, something rather different and not very relevant for a British prototype railway, unless you are modelling a botanical garden as a lineside feature, is the cactus plant shown in the photograph on page 41. However, it made an interesting change and was easily modelled using pieces of green pipe cleaner bent to the right shape and glued together. It does serve as a good example of how unlikely items can be pressed into service for scenic modelling; it is always worth while keeping a look out for possible new modelling materials!

The heavy growth of creeper on the goods shed wall was modelled by applying scenic dressing over glue painted onto the building. A scene on the late Eric Kay's N-scale 'Sherrington Branch'.

Above *An interesting but rarely modelled feature is a market garden. This N-scale model was constructed by Graham Bailey. The fruit trees are ready-made commercial products of Continental manufacture while the rows of plants were simply modelled with foam plastic scenic material. The greenhouses were constructed from Faller kits.*

Below *Gardens modelled in 00 scale by Terry Jenkins. The trellis was made from thin strips of wood, and pieces of lichen form the climbing plants. Note the wooden fence built up from strip-wood. The greenhouse is from a Faller kit.*

Above right *A neatly modelled garden on Colin Woolridge's N-scale layout. The hedges and bushes were modelled from lichen.*

Right *The water lilies on this pond have leaves punched from typing paper painted green. The rest of the vegetation is lichen.*

Below right *This cactus plant was modelled from green pipe cleaners cut and bent appropriately and then glued together. The clumps of grass were made from electrical flex.*

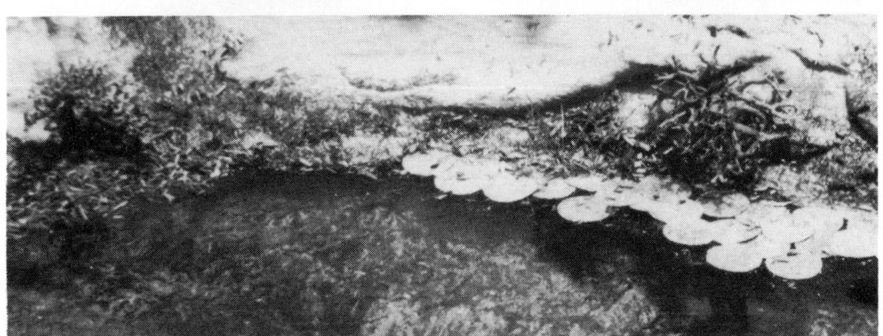

Ground surface texturing

Trees

Trees are, of course, a very important part of the landscape and almost every model railway layout will need at least a few, and more likely a considerable number, if the scenery is not to appear unrealistically bare. This can pose problems for the modeller. While it is possible for the skilful worker to construct very accurate and realistic tree models from scratch the job is time consuming and most modellers would not wish to expend the time and effort required to make more than a few trees in this way.

Fortunately several manufacturers have taken an interest in the production of more authentic tree models, either as ready-made scenic items or in kit form, recently. These firms include John Piper (Accessories) Limited, Woodland Scenics (marketed in Britain by Hammant & Morgan), and Jack Kine Models. These products are much more realistic than most of those previously available and they make it possible for the average modeller to have trees of excellent appearance on his layout with a minimum of effort. The ready-made tress include models of particular species of trees as well as general types which, though realistic and attractive, are not based on any particular tree type. The models are made in various sizes; there is, of course, some overlap between trees as far as scale is concerned as a small tree for 00 scale is just as suitable for use as a large tree in N scale.

The kits make construction easy while still allowing the modeller considerable scope in the size and shape of the tree models he makes. The John Piper kits, for example, have trunk and branch pieces cast in white metal which are glued together to form the tree skeleton. By the choice of which pieces are used, and how many pieces are included, the modeller can vary the size and shape of the tree. The soft metal can be bent easily to give the required branch shape. Rubberised horsehair is used to give bulk to the foliage while the leafy appearance is achieved by covering the horse-hair with scenic dressing. Selections of cast

Left *This realistic tree on the late Eric Kay's N-scale 'Sherrington Branch' is a commercial tree model which has been improved by the addition of scenic dressings giving more texture to the foliage.*

Below left *Though trees on a model railway layout are usually best set out in a natural rather random arrangement there are exceptions to this rule. Poplars are often planted in rows beside roads and along boundaries and Bob Jones has reproduced this realistically on his N-scale 'Eight Oaks' layout.*

Below *A selection of ready-made tree models of general type made by John Piper (Accessories) Limited.* (Photo by courtesy of John Piper Limited.)

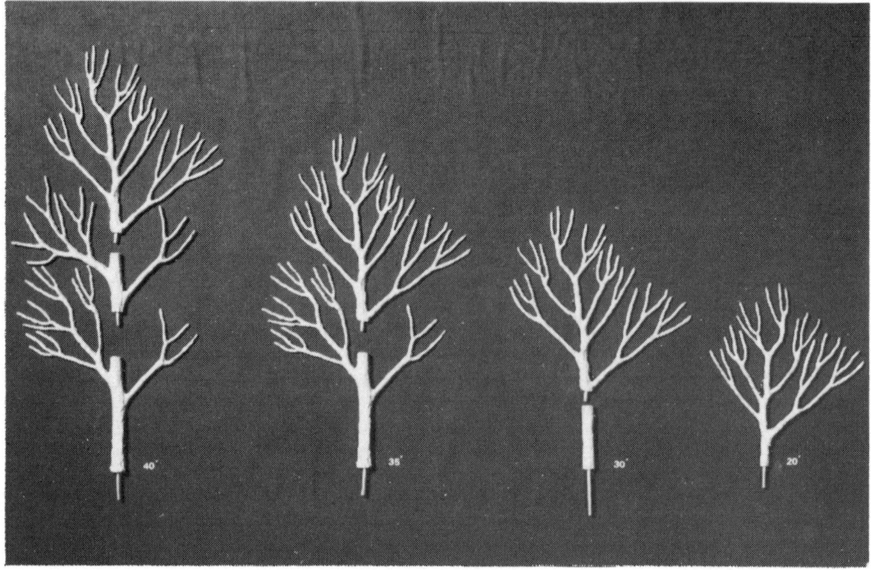

Top *A selection of realistic tree models made up from Woodland Scenics kits from Hammant & Morgan.* (Photo by courtesy of McLeish Associates Ltd.)

Above *Cast metal trunk and branch parts from John Piper tree kits showing how trees of varying heights can be made up by using different combinations. As the castings are soft metal they can be bent to the desired branch arrangements. The foliage is modelled with rubberised horsehair and scenic texture material.* (Photo by courtesy of John Piper Limited.)

metal trunk and branch pieces are also available separately from the kits enabling modellers to add their own foliage or to leave the trees bare to simulate a winter scene. Another very interesting product from this firm is sheets of etched brass leaves, accurate models of specific species. These are really intended for 54 mm scale for military modelling but they can be used effectively, with care, in 00 scale as can be seen in the picture of the old tree on a small exhibition diorama built by the firm.

Understandably, these ready-made tree models and kits, while reasonably priced, are not cheap and if numerous trees are required for a layout the expense could be considerable. In these cases a compromise is probably the best solution. For a few trees in key foreground positions on the layout, highly detailed trees, either purchased ready-made or built up from kits, can be employed. For less important situations nearer the rear of the layout simpler and cheaper commercially produced or hand-made models can be used. When there are numerous trees close together to give the impression of a wooded area some of the simpler models can be very effective as can be seen in the pictures of the N-scale German prototype line shown on page 47.

Though the kits mentioned above are very convenient the modeller may wish to scratch-build some or all of his tree models. This may be because he wants to have a few highly realistic models, more authentic than those available commercially, for the foreground of his layout. Conversely, he may require numerous trees and may wish to make these as simply, quickly and cheaply as possible, his aim being acceptable rather than super-detailed tree models.

Many different materials and methods have been used for scratch-building tree models. Construction can be divided into the modelling of the trunk and branch system, and the representation of the foliage.

The simplest form of trunk construction is to

A beautifully modelled old tree on an exhibition diorama made by John Piper (Accessories) Limited. The tree was made from a skeleton tree kit with etched leaves and with fibre and cork textures giving the ivy effect, all these items being available from this firm.

Above *Two inexpensive, commercial ready-made tree models. The model on the left is of the bottle brush type while the other tree has a plastic base and trunk with foliage modelled from lichen.*

Below *Three more commercially produced tree models. On the left is a poplar made up from a Merit plastic kit. The other two trees are ready-made models of Continental manufacture.*

Two views of an N-scale layout based on German prototype. Extensive use is made of ready-made evergreen tree models of the bottle brush type. Even though these trees are relatively simple models, the effect can be very good, especially when numerous trees are used to give the appearance of a forest.

Bob Jones scratch-built these trees for his N-scale 'Eight Oaks' layout using the bottle brush type of construction. Note also the realistic tarmac road complete with dotted white line along the centre.

use a length of wooden dowel, roughened and painted or a suitably shaped twig which can represent the trunk and two or three of the main branches. Privet and yarrow plants will provide useful twigs for this purpose, but many others are also suitable. If lichen is employed for the foliage simple trees can be easily and quickly made at very little cost. Such trees are sufficiently realistic for background use or where large numbers of trees are required to give the effect of a wood.

Another simple but effective method of making tree models is the so called 'bottle brush' technique. Soft ironwire, such as garden tying wire, is made into a loop a little longer than the required tree height. Sisal string is cut into pieces two or three inches long and these are teased apart and laid between the two sides of the loop. One end of the loop is held firmly by looping it around a nail fixed into the workbench while the other end is twisted. This tightens the wire on the string holding it firmly and produces a bottle brush similar to those used in the kitchen. The string is then fluffed out and trimmed into the shape wanted for the type of tree chosen. This method is particularly suitable for poplars and pines, but other types of trees can be effectively modelled by combining three or four of these basic trees. Simply twist the trunks together and then bend the upper parts of the individual trunks to form main branches. Trim the string to the appropriate shape for the type of tree you are modelling. The whole tree skeleton is now painted matt black or dark grey preferably with an airbrush or aerosol spray. After this has dried dip the tree into clear varnish and sprinkle dyed sawdust over the string to form foliage. This adheres to the varnish and after this has dried the tree is complete except for a coat of grey-brown paint on the trunk.

A more accurate, but more time-consuming, technique for tree modelling is to build up the trunk and branch structure from wire. With this method it is possible not only to accurately model a particular species with the anatomy characteristic of that species but even an actual example of that tree! The trees shown in the accompanying photographs made by P.D. Hancock and by Maurice Kelly all have trunk and branches modelled with wire. It is convenient to use multistrand wire such as electrical cable or picture wire and this should be cut rather longer than the tree height required. Enough pieces of wire or cable are placed together to produce the thickness of trunk needed. The trunk can then be wrapped with gummed paper or masking tape starting at the base. The strands of wire are pulled out to form branches where these are to arise. These are unravelled forming smaller and smaller branches. During this shaping process refer to pictures of the type of tree you are modelling taken in the winter, for deciduous trees, so that the structure is clearly visible and not masked by the foliage. The gummed paper or masking tape is also used to wrap the main branches. The trunk and main branches can then be

Above left *A Scots Pine modelled in 4 mm scale by P.D. Hancock. The trunk and branches were made from wire covered with Pyruma and the foliage is fine loofah.* (Photograph by P.D. Hancock.)

Above right *Pine trees, and on the left a silver birch, modelled in 7 mm scale by Maurice Kelly. Note the dead tree on the ground and the ivy on the trunk of the old tree in the foreground.* (Photograph by Maurice Kelly.)

covered to give a more realistic texture. P.D. Hancock uses plastic wood or Pyruma (Kos) for his models, while Maurice Kelly employed Polyfilla on the trees shown here. The trunk and branches are then painted matt grey or a greenish grey with a brush, spray painter or airbrush.

Various materials can be used for the foliage. Maurice Kelly used dyed lichen for the 7 mm scale pine trees in the photograph whereas P.D. Hancock chose loofah with a covering of dyed sawdust to represent the leaves. Ground up foam and dyed tea leaves (used) have also been used very effectively for leaves on model trees. The modeller can also use the foliage materials available from John Piper (Accessories) Limited, as supplied in their kits and also marketed separately.

It is very important if you want to scratch-build realistic model trees to look at the real thing or pictures of trees in reference books so that you know what sort of appearance you are trying to reproduce. After all you would not attempt to model a locomotive without referring to the prototype! It is also important to record in some way the colour of the foliage for later reference. One method of doing this is to stand some distance away from the tree, preferably a distance comparable to the scale distance from which you will view the model on your layout, and hold up a colour chart with various shades of green. Note the closest match. Remember also to allow for the type of lighting conditions under which you will view the tree model on your layout.

The positioning and arrangement of tree models on the layout is also important. Do not put them in lines or rows unless they have been obviously planted in this way, for example, a row of poplars lining a road. Generally aim for a natural placement with varying sizes of trees. They often grow in groups with larger trees in the middle of the bunch and smaller ones around these. Introduce variety with different types of trees rather than modelling only one species. Make sure that you fix the tree models in place so that they do not droop or lean unrealistically and take care to fill in any gaps around their bases with plaster or scenic dressing.

Extra details such as an occasional dead tree, fallen tree trunks, broken branches on the ground and dead leaves beneath the trees can be added. Ivy and other creepers can be modelled with dyed sawdust sprinkled over dabs of white glue on the trunks and branches.

Ground surface texturing

Scenic backgrounds

The addition of a scenic background will do much to enhance the appearance of the scenic work on a model railway layout. Without one it is all too evident to the viewer that the scenery stops abruptly at the rear edge of the layout. With good scenic modelling we can create the illusion of a landscape in miniature but if full size household items such as furniture and curtains are visible immediately behind the layout they will detract from the effect and make it obvious that the scenery is just a model.

There are two major benefits we can hope to achieve by the provision of a scenic background. One is the blocking out from immediate view of all the distracting extraneous features in the room behind the layout. For this purpose a plain background is effective. This can even be just a plain white background but obviously a sky blue sheet, with or without clouds, will be much more attractive. The second aim is a little more ambitious, to create the impression of much greater depth than the layout actually has with the illusion of the landscape receding far into the distance. To achieve this with a flat two dimensional backscene the usual artist's techniques of perspective and the use of colour are employed to give the effect of depth.

Most modellers use the commercially produced backscenes. These are specially designed for the purpose and are generally very satisfactory. Most are printed in colour from artists' drawings except for the Faller scenes which are reproduced from colour photographs and the Skinley sheets which are line drawings for the modeller to colour himself as he wishes. The scenes are usually designed so that the different sheets of the set made by any one manufacturer will fit together in any order with

One of the range of scenic backgrounds made by Faller. These full colour backscenes have been produced photographically.

Top *An attractive N-scale scene created with Peco kits and scenic products. The backscene is one of a range of full colour printed backgrounds from this firm.* (Photograph by courtesy of Peco.)

Above *This interesting city scene is featured on one of the Peco range of backdrops.* (Photograph by courtesy of Peco.)

the joins matching. If trees, buildings or other features are used to conceal the joins it may be possible to join sheets from different manufacturers successfully, though the variance in styles and colour may cause problems. Some of the ranges include sheets showing only sky and clouds.

Between them, manufacturers in Britain, Germany and the United States offer quite a wide variety of scenes. Obviously the type of landscape, and the structures on town, village or city scenes, must match up with the modelled scenery and buildings on your layout. Usually a suitable backscene is available but this is a limitation of the use of these commercially produced backgrounds. Another disadvantage is that they are employed on many other layouts making them familiar to the viewer and taking away some of the individuality we have tried to give to our models. Having created a miniature landscape which is exactly as he wishes it to be the modeller may be reluctant to complete it with a backscene which someone else has designed and which inevitably will differ from his own concept of how the scene should look. However, in spite of these possible objections, the commercially produced backgrounds have much to commend them. They are generally well designed and produced, they are not unduly expensive, and they enable even a beginner to add a final professional touch to his layout with a minimum of effort.

Though the sheets are intended for specific scales there is some flexibility in this regard. The features shown on the backscene must, of

An HO-scale Airfix Union Pacific 4-4-0 locomotive hauls its freight train past impressive scenery provided by an HO West scenic background. This is one of a series of very realistic full colour backscenes made by this American firm but unfortunately production has been discontinued for the present.

course, be smaller in scale than the modelled items which are in front of the background because they are supposed to be further away. However, the actual size is not too critical as they may be more or less distant. Background sheets which include items of recognisable size, such as buildings, permit the least scope with regard to scale whereas those with features of more variable size such as trees, hedges, mountains and fields allow much more freedom.

The modeller can introduce some variation and make it less obvious that he is using standard backscenes by cutting out parts of the sheets, for example, a low foreground hill, and mounting these onto other sheets. One of the sheets from the Peco series is designed to be cut up in this way. This method can also be used to make cut out profiles which can be mounted an inch or two in front of the background sheet proper to give a greater impression of depth to the scenery. These can be mounted on thick card or on hardboard and the edges of this backing material should be bevelled and painted matt black so that they are not visible to the viewer. If the pieces are larger they should be braced at the rear to prevent warping or curling as this will also spoil the effect.

For modellers who do not wish to be restricted to the commercially available scenic backgrounds there are various possibilities. One method which has been used very successfully is to build up a backscene from a number of pictures taken from old calendars and other sources. Care and thought is essential in the selection of the pictures and in their combination to form a realistic scene, but the results can be very good. The modeller may sometimes find that he needs to draw and paint in parts of the backscene to link the available pictures satisfactorily.

Another method is to use a large photographic enlargement, either a colour print or, less expensive, a tinted black and white print. Photographic backgrounds can be very effective; they are particularly realistic if the model scene is to be photographed when, if correctly arranged, they can be indistinguishable from the real scene. An alternative to using a photographic print as a backscene is the use of colour slides as a guide to drawing and painting a scenic background. Suitable slides can be projected onto white paper and the modeller can trace around the parts he wants to feature on the background. The slides also provide a guide to the colouring when painting the scene.

Finally, the modeller can draw and colour the scenic background working, as it were, from scratch. He may use pictures, photographs or sketches as a guide, particularly if he wishes to represent the scenery of a specific area. The choice of medium is up to the individual. Some modellers prefer oil paints, others water colours or poster paints. One of the accompanying photographs shows a backscene rendered very effectively in pastels by Jo Norman. It is important to keep the background simple. In distant scenes most of the small details are too far away to be visible so to achieve the illusion of distance we require a broad general view rather than a picture cluttered with detail. Another good reason for simplicity is that we do not want the background to compete with the modelled scenery for the viewer's attention. The effect of distance is achieved partly by the size of the features; the smaller they are the further away they seem to be. The representation of atmospheric perspective is also important. The haze in the atmosphere causes the colours of distant objects to be toned down and greyer. Thus to colour the background we should use soft colours to which some grey or white has been added. Sometimes the addition of a little blue or purple as well is effective for the far distance.

For a permanent layout, scenic background sheets can be fixed onto the wall but it is usually better to glue them down onto hardboard; I find wallpaper paste very satisfactory as it is easy to use, inexpensive and gives good results. The hardboard sheets can then be fitted along the back of the layout; it may be necessary to brace the hardboard to prevent bending or warping. On a portable line screws or bolts can be used to fix the backing onto the layout so that it can be detached easily for moving and storage. After the backscenes are

Below *For this photographic set-up the background was merely a piece of card painted dark grey with a yellow disc to represent the full moon.*

Bottom *Jo Norman drew this scenic background using pastels.*

mounted onto the hardboard a light spray with a clear matt varnish will protect the surface. Prior to this the modeller may wish to apply a very thin spray of grey to tone down the colours slightly and enhance the effect of distance by simulating the appearance of atmospheric haze.

If we are to create the illusion of the scenery continuing into the distance the join between the modelled and painted or printed scenery must be concealed as completely as possible. We may be able to mask the junction with trees and bushes, low hills, an embankment or structures, perhaps modelled in low relief. Leaving a gap between the modelled and painted scenery of about half an inch or an inch gives a good effect of depth. At the rear of the layout there can be an embankment or a low ridge of hills and at the back this drops straight down, just in front of the backscene. The join is concealed effectively and easily and the method gives good results. It is important to make sure that no trees or other modelled features can cast any shadows on the backscene as this will spoil the effect.

Another method which requires more careful modelling, but which can also be very realistic, is to bring the modelled scenery right onto the scenic background. This is most suitable for mountainous scenery, the plaster being carried up to and just on to the backscene. The scenery is then painted and the background is coloured at the same time unless a commercial sheet is being used. Trees and bushes can be a mixture of fully modelled, partly modelled ones stuck onto the backscene at the junction, and painted ones. By using smaller and smaller modelled trees as we go further back towards the rear of the layout, the apparent perspective creates more feeling of depth and distance.

I mentioned the use of cut-outs mounted in front of the backscene earlier. These are very useful in making the transition from modelled

Below *Keith Gowen's TT-scale layout showing how the low relief banks are placed just in front of the scenic background. When seen from the usual viewing positions this gives a realistic impression of depth and distance to the scene.*

Opposite page *Howard Coulson's 'NMRR' is an 009 layout based on East African prototypes and imaginative scenic work has created an unusual and interesting model which captures very well the atmosphere of the real thing.* **Top** *A view of the 'Eitomo' station area with a passenger train ready to depart. Scenery is modelled from plaster and cork bark. The hills to the right and at the back of this scene are low relief features.* **Centre** *This view taken from a higher angle and with oblique lighting shows the distant hills modelled in low relief. Note that there are slight gaps between the fully modelled scenery in front, the low relief hills (also formed in plaster) and the backdrop behind. This gives a greater effect of depth but takes very little extra space.* **Bottom** *Another part of the layout in closer view showing some of the many small details. Note the native hut and the realistically modelled muddy track. The horses have broken away from the cart in the foreground.*

Scenic backgrounds

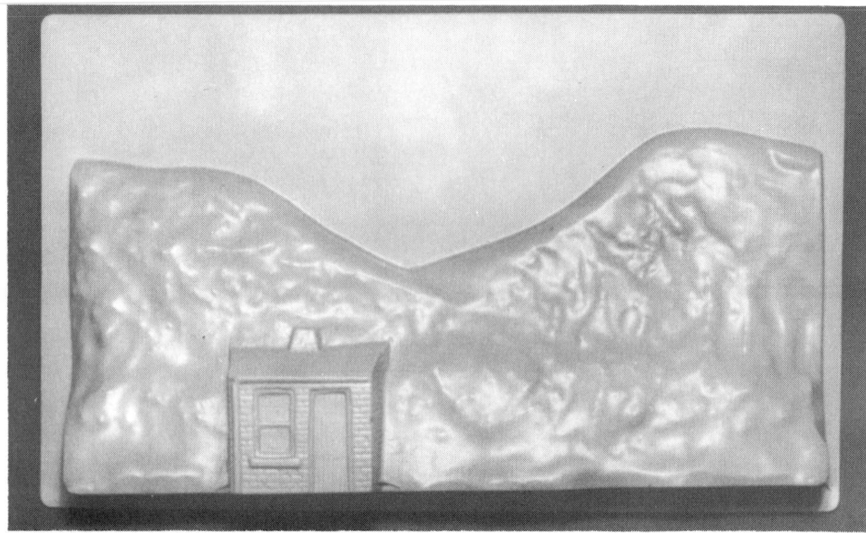

One of a range of 00-scale low relief vacuum formed plastic mouldings made by Midland Model Railway Supplies. These backgrounds give an effective three-dimensional appearance even though they occupy very little depth. This example is shown before painting.

scenery to flat backscene by masking the junction while also creating a greater effect of depth. These cut-outs can be hills, trees, buildings, and so on and they can be cut from commercial backgrounds or from calendars or other pictures, or can be drawn and painted by the modeller. A very good effect can be achieved by modelling low relief hills similar to these cut-outs but giving them surface texture and detail by a thin covering of plaster on the front face. Low relief structures are also useful for masking the junction area in urban or industrial parts of the layout, again without taking up too much space. Midland Model Railway Supplies make a range of low relief scenic backgrounds which are vacuum formed plastic mouldings. The low relief gives these backdrops a realistic appearance of depth even though they measure no more than an inch and a half in depth. The mouldings require painting and the modeller can also add extra detailing with lichen, scenic dressings and so on if he wishes.

Often the scenic background is added as something of an afterthought when the rest of the scenery has been finished. However, it is obviously better to plan this part of the layout at an earlier stage so that the modelled scenery and the backdrop can be designed to match up well. In fact if a commercially produced backscene is employed there are advantages in fixing it in position at an early stage of layout construction before the modelled scenery is built. The terrain shown on the backdrop is then used as a guide so that the modelled scenery can be made to match up with it. The colouring of the backscene will also aid the modeller when he comes to paint the scenery.

The small details

So far in this book we have looked at the various aspects of modelling the landscape but even when the basic scenic work has been completed there are still many small details which can be added to make the layout more attractive and interesting. The possibilities are almost limitless and this detailing can provide enjoyable modelling work for the enthusiast long after the layout is essentially complete.

Among the most important of these miscellaneous small details are human and animal figures. Figures are available for all the popular model railway scales but the largest selection is for 00 and HO. These include cast metal models, such as the neat series of period figures made by John Piper (Accessories) Ltd and the smaller range from Ratio, and painted and unpainted plastic models. The modeller in 00 scale can usually employ HO as well as 00 scale figures and this enables him to select from the excellently detailed and very extensive Preiser and Merten ranges. These are sold as ready painted figures in small sets and are quite expensive, especially as most layouts need large numbers. However, many of the Preiser figures are also available as unpainted selections of 120 or so figures which are very much cheaper and are excellent value. These figures are made of polystyrene and are easily painted with matt model railway paints. However figures made from polythene, for example, the Airfix 00 scale figures, do not take these paints well unless they are given an undercoat first. Unibond PVA adhesive,

Many small details add interest to this HO-scale demonstration layout while the numerous figures give the scene life.

suitably diluted, is very satisfactory for this purpose.

It is easy to alter figures to different poses either to suit them to some particular situation or task on the layout or just to provide variety. A limb can be bent after warming or can be cut off with a sharp modelling knife and reattached in a new position. It is also possible to exchange parts between two or more figures. Tools can be modelled from scraps of wood, card or plastic and fitted to the hands of workmen or placed nearby. The John Piper (Accessories) Ltd range of cast metal parts in 4 mm scale includes a useful selection of well detailed tools and implements and some of the Preiser sets also contain neat model tools of various types.

Some commercial figures are fitted with large unsightly and unrealistic bases. These should be removed or at least concealed when fixing the figures onto the layout. Take care to mount the figures in natural positions and make sure they do not lean over unrealistically. It is also important to arrange the figures in relation to each other so that the grouping appears natural.

There is also a fine range of animals of all types including farm animals, wild life and even pets. The ranges of cast metal accessories made by Dart Castings and by MS Models are particularly useful for the modeller who wants to add small animals such as rabbits, cats, and birds of various species to his layout.

A farm can be an attractive lineside feature and suitable animals are on the market in the ranges of plastic and cast metal models. A good selection of farm equipment is also available especially in the N-scale range of cast metal kits from Langley Miniature Models.

Walls and fences are essential to complete the landscape. Stone walls can be modelled

Below *A selection of N-scale figures from Peco. The detailing is excellent despite the small size.* (Photograph by courtesy of Peco.)

Right *The barrels, sacks, carboys and oil drums on the loading platform at this 00-scale branchline station goods depot are all Merit products. The articulated lorry is a conversion of an Airfix military Matador lorry kit.*

Below right *Terry Jenkins modelled a detailed churchyard as a setting for this 00-scale church model built from a Bilteezi kit. The headstones were included in the kit while the stone bases and the stone walls were made from Kos fire cement. The Morgan three-wheel car in the left foreground was constructed from an Autoreplicas cast metal kit.*

The small details

Opposite *Two views of Henblas Farm superbly modelled in 4 mm scale by Dave Rowe. Peco Texture Modelling Compound has been extensively used in modelling the structures and the very realistic stone walls. The many accurately portrayed small details give the model great atmosphere and authenticity. Note the low relief modelling giving a smooth transition from fully modelled scenery to hand-painted backdrop.* (Photographs by courtesy of Peco.)

Above *The road on this 4 mm scale branch line layout was modelled in plaster. The section around the level crossing was scribed to represent cobblestones. The whole was then painted grey and while the paint was still wet, fine sand was sprinkled over the section at the left. The lorry is a conversion of an Airfix Matador army lorry and the figures are also Airfix products.*

from plaster or Polyfilla over a card or wood former. Peco Texture Modelling Compound is also ideal as can be seen in the pictures of Henblas Farm superbly modelled in 4 mm scale by Dave Rowe. Trevor Hughes has used pieces of real stone held together with Polycell to realistically model dry stone walls; other stone walls on his layout have been built up from individual pieces of card. Fencing can be modelled with wood, card or plastic and there are also commercially available fences of various types. Peco, Airfix, Slater and Ratio offer a range of plastic fencing and John Piper (Accessories) Ltd make 4 mm scale fences, including mesh and barbed wire fencing, as etched brass items which are excellently detailed.

Roads are essential for most model railway layouts. Rough tracks can be modelled in plaster, Polyfilla or Peco Texture Modelling Compound. Tarmac roads can be represented with card, hardboard or plastic painted grey with fine sand sprinkled onto the wet paint to provide a little texture. Cobblestones can be very realistically modelled with Peco Texture Modelling Compound as shown in the accompanying picture. Many accessory items for detailing and roadside are produced, particularly in 00 scale. The Dart Castings range, for example, includes various types of signposts, a horsetrough and drinking fountain, letter boxes and so on. The range of kits for road vehicles, mainly cast metal models, had been steadily increasing in the last few years and is now very good indeed in 00 scale and quickly improving in N scale. The Airfix military vehicle kits in 00 scale are useful for conversion into civilian vehicles and one of

Above *This country track was modelled with plaster over a card base. The motorcycle and side-car is a Langley Miniature Models cast metal kit.*

Below *Roads are an important part of the landscape and can be realistically modelled with Peco Texture Modelling Compound. Cobbled road and pavement; road and pavement complete with drain cover and lamp post; a cart track with characteristic ruts.* (Photographs by courtesy of Peco.)

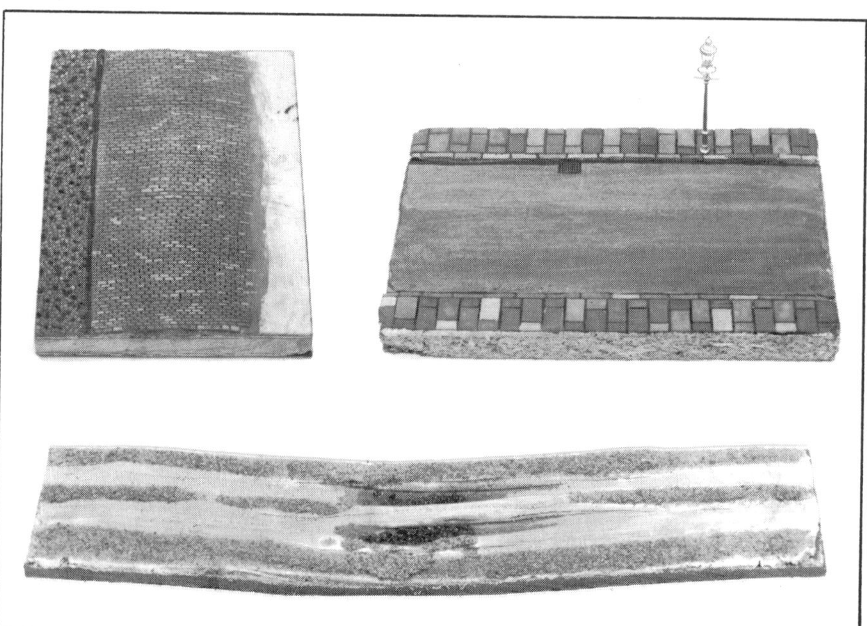

Above *Terry Jenkins modelled this caravan site for the Bournemouth & Isle of Purbeck MRC 00-scale layout. The caravans and cars are die-cast toys. Hedges around the site are lichen.*

Below *This 'Whitbread' brewer's wagon in 4 mm scale was constructed from a Transport Replicas cast metal kit, one of a range of models of motor and horse-drawn vehicles made by this firm.*

Top *Gordon Riggs scratch-built these two 4 mm scale coach models from balsa and card. The figures are from the Airfix range.* (Photograph by Gordon Riggs.)

Above *This realistic 4 mm scale model of a canal narrow boat was constructed from a Novus (W & T) card kit. The model is ideal for a canal scene on a railway layout.*

the kits, the RAF Recovery Set, includes two neatly modelled motor cycles as well as the two lorries. Road vehicles can also be scratch-built from card or plastic card.

Lakes, rivers, canals and harbours offer great possibilities for extra detailing. Ship and boat models can be made from scratch or some of the plastic kits can be employed, with modifications if necessary. A canal scene with a lock is especially interesting and Langley Miniature Models offer kits in both 00 and N scale for canal boats, lock gates and other details and kits for canal boats in 00 scale are available from Novus (W & T) and from Craftline Models.

The details mentioned in this section cover only a small part of the potential scope; the pictures in this book will give further examples and may provide you with other ideas. As always in any form of modelling, observation of the real thing is of great benefit in giving both inspiration and the information required for modelling scenic details. Keep a lookout for interesting items wherever you are and, if possible, make sketches or take photographs. If you build up a file of data in this way you will have all the ideas and facts you will need when the time comes to add details to your layout. Always try to include a few items which are a little out of the ordinary, at least in model form, so that your layout will be more interesting and unusual.

Operating your layout

Michael Andress

Contents

1A86

Introduction

The construction of a model railway layout can give the builder a great deal of enjoyment and satisfaction, but this is by no means all that the hobby has to offer. Operation of the completed layout in a realistic manner, following the principles of real railway practice, can provide continuing interest and entertainment for the enthusiast and his or her friends. Many modellers never realise the full potential of this aspect of the hobby and their running is merely haphazard. My aim in this book is to show the beginner how even a small and simple model railway can be operated in an interesting and realistic manner. There are various methods of running a model railway and we will look at the basic principles of some of these so that you can choose the one most suitable for you and your layout.

If the modeller is to gain the maximum pleasure from operating his layout it is essential that the model railway should run smoothly and reliably. For a layout to operate properly regular maintenance and repairs are required. Many beginners are uncertain just how to go about keeping their layouts and equipment in good order, and also feel that such work is likely to be a tedious chore anyway. However, for the most part, simple care and maintenance that you can easily carry out yourself is all that is needed and I will cover these basic procedures in this book.

Participation in model railway exhibitions and shows can be a very enjoyable and satisfying activity for the enthusiast but also demands careful preparation for the most successful results. In the final section of this book I want to give the beginner some suggestions regarding this preparation and also about attendance and actual operation at the exhibitions themselves.

I would like to thank all those modellers who have kindly allowed me to use pictures of their models and layouts to illustrate this book. In particular I am grateful to Harold Bowcott, members of the Brooklands Railway Society Model Group, Allan Downes, members of the Greenwich & District Narrow Gauge Railway Group, Brian Monaghan, Bob Petch and Dick Wyatt. I am especially indebted to Chris Ellis for permission to include the description of how he compiled a timetable for his N-scale layout and to Geoff Barlow for his advice on maintenance and repairs. I am also grateful to those manufacturers who have provided information and pictures of their products, and particularly to Matt Ascough of M & R (Model Railways) Ltd for his assistance with information on the Fleischmann hump yard.

Left *Modern railway operation is a complex business but is built up from many simple train movements. In the same way model railway operation should be kept simple at first and developed later as experience is gained.*

The train set

The gift or purchase of a train set is the introduction to railway modelling for many enthusiasts and it is probably a good place for us to begin in considering model railway operation. With the basic train set oval the scope for operation is very limited indeed. We can run a train clockwise or anti-clockwise around the oval, we can stop it, start it and reverse it, and that is about all. Even if we place a station or two on the oval and use our imagination to pretend the train is running, say from London to Newcastle, with stops at various stations en route, the layout will not be very interesting to run. No matter how realistic the structures and scenery providing the setting for the railway are, the modeller will soon tire of the layout.

The operational interest and variety will be considerably increased by the addition of even two or three sidings as then we can carry out shunting duties. Trailing sidings are easily worked. The train stops short of the points and it is divided immediately behind the wagon or wagons intended for the siding. The engine and front part of the train then pulls forward over the points, these are changed and the train reverses on to the siding. The wagon or wagons for the siding are uncoupled and left there as the engine moves out of the siding on to the main line. The points are changed again and the engine backs up to reform the train. For a siding served by a facing point it is more difficult. The train stops short of the siding and is split immediately in front of the wagon or wagons for the siding. The engine must then run right round the oval to reach the rear of the train. The siding point is changed and the locomotive then pushes the train on to the siding. The wagon or wagons for the siding are uncoupled and left there while the engine pulls the remainder of the train out of the siding on to the main line again. The point is changed and the locomotive must again run right round the oval, this time to reach the front of the train once more. Normally when a train is made up, wagons destined for the same siding will be placed together but, if for any reason they have not been, then further moves will be required to sort them out at the siding. Similarly, if there are one or more wagons to be collected by the train from the siding this will add to the movements needed as they must be removed

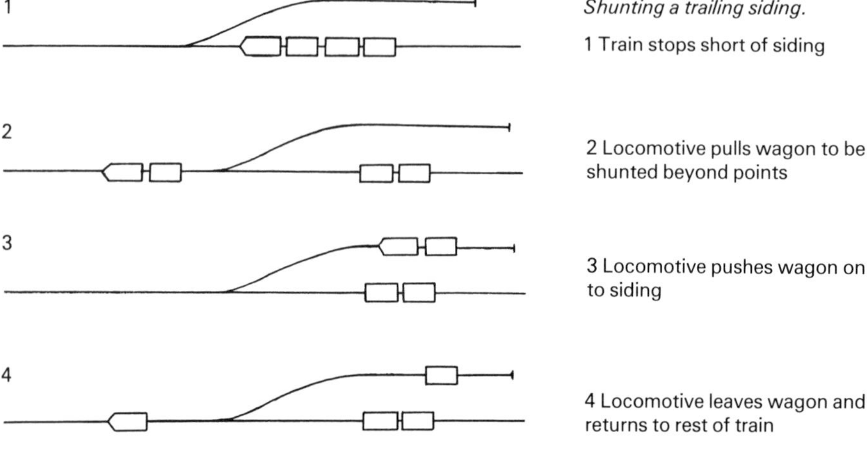

Shunting a trailing siding.

1 Train stops short of siding

2 Locomotive pulls wagon to be shunted beyond points

3 Locomotive pushes wagon on to siding

4 Locomotive leaves wagon and returns to rest of train

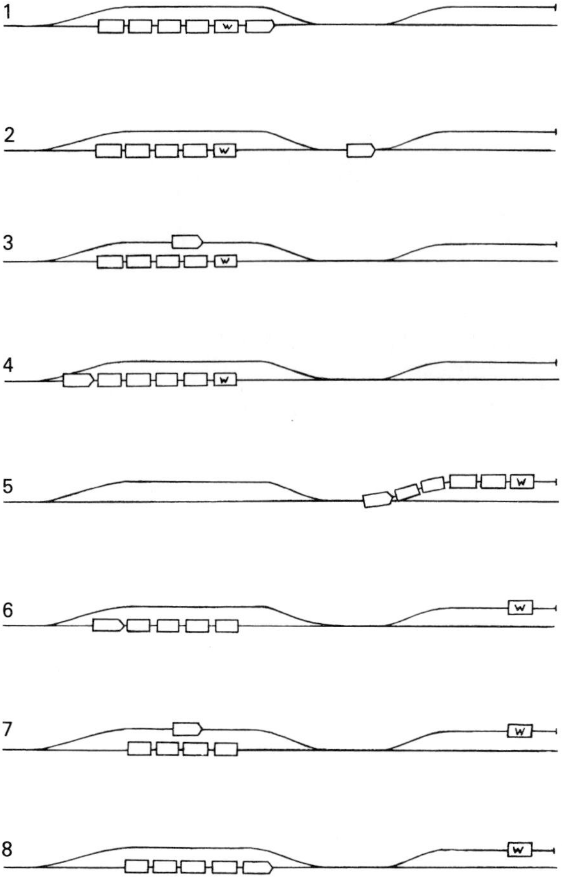

Shunting a facing siding, using a run-around loop. On an oval layout an alternative is for the locomotive to run round oval to reach the rear of the train.

1 Train stops on run-around loop. Wagon 'W' to be dropped
2 Locomotive runs forward to clear points
3 Locomotive runs round train
4 Locomotive at rear of train pushes train forwards
5 Train pushed on to siding
6 Wagon 'W' left on siding. Train pulled back on to run-around loop
7 Locomotive runs round train again
8 Train reformed and ready to move off

Placing two industries on one siding adds to the traffic and to the number of moves required in shunting. To shunt vans to warehouse, wagons at factory must be removed then replaced.

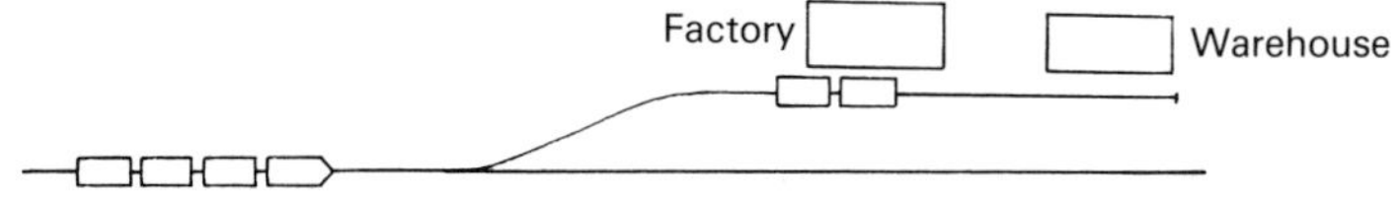

A kick-back siding also increases the shunting moves needed. To shunt wagons on to kick-back siding serving factory warehouse, siding must first be cleared.

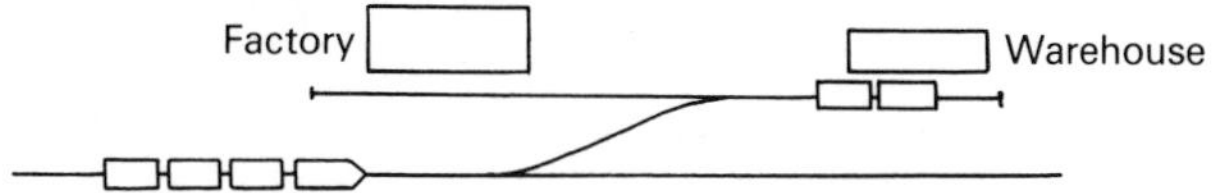

Above *The addition of a run-around loop and a siding to the basic oval makes it possible to run two trains on the layout, though not simultaneously, and to carry out a little shunting, as on this small simple layout built by Terry Jenkins.* **Below** *Here a Mainline 0-6-0 Tank Engine shunts the goods siding on Terry Jenkins' small layout.* **Right** *If a run-around loop is added to the basic train set oval the engine can reach the rear of the train for reversing direction. It also makes the shunting of facing sidings more convenient.*

from the siding before the arriving wagons are shunted on to the track. Further complications arise if one siding serves two different facilities or industries. In this case a wagon at the nearer one may have to be temporarily removed to allow access to a wagon further along the siding, and then replaced in position at the conclusion of the shunting. If there is a fan of sidings, a set of two or more sidings from a single lead from the main line, then there is additional scope for sorting of the arriving wagons. We can provide various facilities, a goods shed, a cattle dock, coal staithes and so on, for these sidings, adding to the interest and the appearance. A kick-back siding is a track leading off, in the reverse direction, from another siding. Because the main siding must be cleared to allow the locomotive to shunt the kick-back siding such an arrangement adds to the number of shunting movements required. Some modellers find this a nuisance and hence do not bother to shunt the kick-back siding. However, if you like shunting, and particularly if your layout is small and thus needs as much operating potential as possible in what space is available, you may benefit from including one or more sidings of this type on it. An advantage of such sidings is that they enable you to place extra tracks in situations where the space could not otherwise be utilised for sidings.

With a simple oval layout with sidings it is possible to accommodate two trains, one on the main line and the other stored on a siding, though they cannot both be run at the same time. The provision of a run-around or passing loop will make shunting more convenient and will add to the operational flexibility. To reverse the train it is stopped on one track of the loop, clear of both points, and the locomotive is uncoupled and run ahead to clear the points. It is then moved back along the other track past the train and over the points behind the train. The engine is then advanced to be coupled to the rear of the train. If it is a goods train with a guards van to be transferred as well as the engine, then additional moves will be required. Similarly, when shunting a siding served by a facing point the locomotive can run round the loop to reach the rear of the train and does not need to travel right round the oval. A passing loop also makes it more convenient to operate two trains on a small oval layout, as one can be held on one track of the loop while the other travels around the main line, using the other track of the passing loop to go by the stationary train. When desired the moving train can be stopped on the loop track and the other train can be run on the main line. Again, only one train can be in action at once.

On a point to point layout the provision of a

The train set

passing loop at an intermediate station will allow trains running in opposite directions to pass at the station, and will also facilitate shunting. At a small terminus a run-around loop is almost always provided so that the locomotive of an arriving train can move round to the other end of the train for the return journey. The presence of the loop also means that both facing and trailing sidings can be shunted. Often the loop is made up by including a release crossover between two tracks and the loop is frequently positioned alongside the platform or platforms saving space on the layout. However, it can alternatively be placed before the platform where it may be more convenient for goods trains, which usually share the same run-around loop at small stations. In this case, the passenger trains will be reversed on to the loop after arrival for the engine to run round and then return to the platform to await departure.

With this arrangement it is easy, if you wish, to provide separate arrival and departure tracks and platforms. Push-pull or auto-trains, railcars and multiple units do not, of course, require a run-around loop as they can operate equally well in either direction. Occasionally at small termini, and often on the platform roads at larger termini, no release crossover is provided. In this situation the arriving train, after the passengers have left, is uncoupled from the locomotive and is then pulled away to the carriage sidings by another engine, often the station pilot. Once the coaches have been removed the original train locomotive moves away to the engine servicing area. Except at small stations a head shunt is usually provided. This is a track parallel to the main line and linked to the sidings so that a locomotive can shunt the goods sidings without the need to use the main line; thus the latter is left clear for trains arriving at and departing from the station.

If we have double track on our oval or point to point line then it becomes easy to run two trains simultaneously, but in many ways operation is more interesting with the difficulties imposed by using single track with passing loops. The need to time train movements correctly so that the trains can pass each other at the loops with the minimum of delay will add to the interest. Thus, even with a simple layout built up from a train set we can carry out most of the basic train movements. Though many of these are straightforward the beginner does need to familiarise himself with the correct methods. He will also find that, with practice, he will become more adept and efficient, both at carrying out the actual movements and also at planning his shunting so that the minimum number of moves will be required. He will also become skilled at running his locomotives smoothly and at a realistic speed while shunting.

These moves, though an essential part of running a model railway, are the 'how' rather than the 'why' of operation. Having considered some of the details of train movements we can now look at the aims of operation.

Aims and advantages of operation

For some modellers the great interest in the hobby comes from the construction. They may enjoy all types of this work or may tend to specialise in one or more aspects, for example, trackwork, scenery or locomotives. For them the enjoyment comes with building the layout and, in many cases, once the work is essentially completed, they lose much of their enthusiasm. They may run a few trains in a rather haphazard manner, but are soon planning extensions, alterations or even a new layout. Now, of course, railway modelling is a hobby and it is up to the individual how he wishes to enjoy it. Indeed, one of the great advantages of this hobby is the very wide range of different activities which it offers. However, I do feel that many beginners who successfully construct layouts with much enjoyment and entertainment in the process are then rather uncertain of what to do with the completed model. They run trains in a random manner, in train set fashion, but are unaware of the great potential for entertainment that model railway operation can offer. Indeed, for some enthusiasts, construction of a layout, though satisfying in itself, is really just a means to an end—the operation of the layout. These modellers have created a fascinating form of game, with the entertainment value of a complex board game, but with the added attraction of seeing authentic models in action in a realistic scenic setting. One of the American pioneers in model railway operation, the late Frank Ellison, likened the operation of a layout to the presentation of a play in a theatre and certainly the running of some of the large and complex model railroads in the United States, by teams of skilled operators, can be a dramatic and exciting performance.

Already we have seen that, even on a small oval layout of the type easily developed from a train set, running a train, especially a goods train, can involve us in a considerable number of train movements. However, interesting though they can be, the movements I have described are really only the mechanics of how we handle the train once we have decided when and where that train will run.

For operation which will remain interesting and entertaining on a model railway layout, we must base it as realistically as possible on the way in which prototype railways are run. The aim of the real railways is to transport people and goods as efficiently and economically as possible, within the limitations imposed by safety regulations and any commitments with regard to services they are obliged to provide, even though they may be unprofitable. Obviously there are limitations, particularly due to lack of space, on our layouts but, as far as possible, our trains should reproduce the operation of the real ones. Thus our trains should appear to have a purpose when they move and not just look as if they are running haphazardly, as the whim of the operator takes them. On the prototype, goods vehicles are moved according to the needs of the customers and we must be sure that we distribute our rolling stock in a realistic manner representing the transport of goods between customers.

Thus what we require is some system or scheme of operating which will give the impression that our trains are travelling around the layout in the same way as prototype trains on the real railways. Generally, the best results will come from using a system based on or adapted from prototype operation. Because of this some familiarity with prototype practice is beneficial and, indeed, finding out more about how the real thing runs can be very interesting in itself as well as helping you to operate your own layout more realistically.

Various methods have been devised by different modellers to suit their own layouts and the type of operation which interests them most. The majority of these schemes are based either on timetable, or sequence, operation, on some system of rolling stock distribution, or on a combination of both. Later in this book we will look at some of the possibilities that you could employ on your model railway.

Now you may be thinking that the idea of prototype-based operation and the use of a timetable is all very well on a large and complex

A small branch line terminus beautifully modelled in 4 mm scale by Allan Downes. All the structures were scratch-built. Such a station provides a good introduction to model railway operation but the scope is somewhat limited as prototype branch lines usually run rather restricted timetables. (Photograph by Brian Monaghan.)

layout with several operators, but that it is not relevant for a small and simple one-man model railway. However, this is not so and, even on a small oval layout, such as might be developed from a train set, it is perfectly feasible to run a timetable or sequence operation scheme. Admittedly, some imagination is required. For example, the journey is often made up of a number of laps of the circuit and we must ignore the fact that the train keeps passing the same features on each lap of the track. However, a model railway can never be an exact replica of the real thing so we must always use some imagination; indeed it is part of the fun to do so. An example of how interesting operation can be provided by a minimum space layout is given by a 3 feet by 2 feet N-gauge layout recently built by Chris Ellis. Despite the small size and simple track plan, a realistic and entertaining schedule has been devised. In a later section in this book Chris Ellis explains how he drew up the timetable and the reasoning behind it.

It was the search for greater realism in railway modelling despite limited space and other resources that encouraged the development of the concept of branch line modelling. Because the branch line model railway forms a good introduction to operation, and in fact to scale railway modelling in general, I would like to consider the subject in more detail.

Branch line operation

If we are to have a realistic model railway in a small space with a necessarily simple track plan we must select a suitable prototype—the country branch line in the days of steam is an ideal choice. Trains often consisted of only two or three coaches or a few wagons pulled by a small tank engine and the station track layouts were usually fairly simple.

During the 1950s the branch line model railway concept was developed considerably. At that time the idea was not so much to provide a suitable subject for beginners as to enable more experienced workers to create a model railway which was realistic in appearance and operation in a small space. The short prototype trains allowed the modeller to run authentic length trains despite the small size of the layout. Also, because the station track layouts were simple on branch lines, they can be compressed to fit on to a model railway while still keeping their essential features. Thus the model can be operated according to prototype practice and following a proper timetable.

The aim was not to make an exact scale model of a particular branch line station; even the simple stations on country branches occupied a considerable ground area and would take too much space on a layout if reproduced accurately to scale. If space for this was available it would be better utilised in modelling a more complex and more interesting station with greater operating potential. In fact, though some enthusiasts have been very successful in basing their branch line stations closely on particular prototypes, many modellers find that it suits them better to combine features from a variety of real stations to produce an interesting and attractive model with all the features they want.

To reiterate then, the key points are having realistic trains operating in an authentic manner. The advantage of branch line stations is that their simple track plans, with few points, permit considerable selective compression without affecting the essential features which influence the way the station can be operated.

Because the aim was realistic operation, the point to point track arrangement was usually preferred to the continuous run schemes, and the now classic branch line terminus to fiddle yard (hidden sidings representing the rest of the system) design was developed. Such a track plan can be fitted on to baseboards of various shapes but a popular arrangement is on two narrow baseboards in an L shape, often fitted into the corner of a room. This design has the advantage of providing the greatest running possibilities in a minimum area and often a layout of this shape can be fitted into a room whereas a conventional rectangular baseboard would not be acceptable as it would block the centre of the room too much.

A branch line layout of this type is also very

A branch line layout can be the ideal introduction to model railway operation for the beginner.

Above *Bob Petch's 00-gauge layout features a GWR branch line through station, Limpley, with a fiddle yard at each end of the line to complete the layout. Here a milk train has been held in the loop at the station to allow a mineral train to pass. Modelling a through station enables the operator to run traffic on the line for which there are no facilities at the station, giving greater scope than with a terminus. This photograph was taken at an exhibition; note the chairs at top right employed to keep the viewers clear of the model.*

Left *One of the two fiddle yards on Bob Petch's layout. Note the sheet of instructions for the fiddle yard operator at bottom right of the picture.*

suitable for the beginner. Now that so many high quality ready-made items such as track, locomotives and rolling stock are available at very reasonable prices such a layout can quickly be brought to a stage where it is interesting to view and operate. The good quality of the commercial items means that, with reasonable care, even the beginner should achieve satisfactory running and be able to enjoy organised operation. It is also easy to add structures and scenery to give an attractive appearance.

The terminus to fiddle yard scheme lends itself very well to authentic operation, based either on a prototype timetable or on one devised by the modeller to suit his own stock and interests. Prototype branch line timetables were usually simple and were often operated on the 'one engine in steam' principle so there is no reason why the beginner with only one locomotive and a limited selection of rolling stock should not be able to run his layout in a realistic manner. The fiddle yard represents the rest of the branch and the junction station. Here trains are made up by hand, without worrying about any pretence of realism and are then despatched to the terminus station where any necessary shunting or other train movements are carried out in an authentic and realistic manner. The train then returns to the fiddle yard. The terminus can operate realistically following the timetable and dealing with all the trains from the imaginary junction.

Such a line is an excellent introduction to operation for the newcomer as it will get him started without difficulty. As he gains experience and additional rolling stock he can extend the basic timetable to make it more fun to operate. The disadvantage is that traffic on a prototype branch line was rather limited in scope and extent and, if the model is to be realistic, operation on it must necessarily also be relatively restricted. Running too intensive a service on a model branch line will destroy the illusion of realism which we are trying to create. Because of these limitations the modeller is likely to find that, in time, he loses interest and will then need to extend the layout or even scrap it and change to a larger system.

Though the classic terminus to fiddle yard scheme described above is the most popular design, there is an interesting alternative arrangement which was, I believe, first employed by Maurice Deane. This is to fit the branch line on a rectangular baseboard with a central operating well and with the line curved round so that the fiddle yard is behind the terminus, concealed by a low backscene. This has the advantage that the modeller working alone can easily reach both the terminus and the fiddle yard beyond it from his operating position in the central well. It also makes it easy to include a link to create an oval so that continuous running is possible if desired. The link can be concealed so that the realism of the point to point scheme is not impaired.

Another idea in which there has been more interest recently, perhaps partly to provide a change from the usual design, is the modelling of a through station on a branch line rather than the terminus. Such an arrangement can be operated as an oval with hidden sidings on the side opposite to the through station, or as a point to point design with a fiddle yard at each end, a reversing loop at each end or with a fiddle yard at one end and a reversing loop at the other, making up an out and back arrangement. The choice of a through station does have certain advantages, particularly in allowing greater scope for traffic on the line.

Traffic on your railway

Before we can plan a timetable or schedule for a layout we must have some idea of the traffic it should carry. The prototype railways, of course, must cope with whatever traffic they are offered. Passengers wish to travel from town to town, commercial and industrial customers want goods and freight transferred to and from their factories, warehouses and depots, and so on. Trains are run to handle these demands and the make up of these trains may be adjusted from day to day and from season to season according to variations in the traffic.

Now if we are modelling a specific station or are basing our layout on a particular line, more or less closely, then the type of traffic will largely be determined for us. From the working timetable of the prototype, if it is available, from details about the line in books and magazine articles, and from a knowledge of the nature of the countryside served by the railway, we can build up an accurate picture of the traffic the line would carry. If we have, on the other hand, created our own station and line we must also develop a background for it. We may choose to base it on a particular area and we can then follow the general traffic trends for lines in the part of the country concerned. Alternatively, we may wish to create our own imaginary countryside for the railway to run through.

Whatever course we choose, it is important to build up a background picture of this sort if we are to have a realistic pattern of traffic for the layout. The branch line again serves as a useful example, partly because it is a good subject for a beginner's first scale layout, and partly because the simple timetable of the prototype makes a good introduction to model railway operation. Let us consider the small branch line terminus first of all. It is likely to be in a country area or serving a small coastal port or seaside town. If we model a terminus station then traffic on our layout from the fiddle yard to the terminus must stop there. All movements on the layout should have a purpose, if our operating is to appear realistic, so wagons will only be moved from the fiddle yard to the terminus and back if there is freight to be carried to or from the station. As the station is a terminus, the type of rolling stock on the line will be limited by the traffic handling facilities at the station. For example, if we have no cattle dock then we cannot run cattle wagons, and so on. If you find this unduly limiting you may prefer to model a through station. This is much less restricting regarding the rolling stock we operate on the line as we can always say that stock for which there are no facilities at the station is merely en route to other destinations further along the line!

Coming back to our small terminus we can first of all consider the passenger traffic. We will need a train early in the morning to take people from the small town to work at the junction town or at other places along the main line from there (all represented by the fiddle yard) and a train to bring them back in the late afternoon or early evening. A train going later in the morning and one back during the afternoon will provide a service for shoppers while a train each way in the evening will cope with passengers wanting to spend an evening at the cinema or at other entertainments in the

Top right *This wooden extension to the platform was provided for milk traffic at Watlington and has been faithfully reproduced on the Mid Hants Model Railway Group model of the station.* **Above right** *The Mid Hants Model Railway Group's accurate model of Watlington station, an Oxfordshire branch line terminus, in EM gauge. This picture shows part of the goods yard which has facilities typical of a small country station. The beautifully detailed goods shed was scratch-built by Barry Fisher. The track on the right is used for coal wagons and storage.* **Right** *Typical traffic at a country branch line station includes livestock and farm equipment as seen here on the EM-gauge model of Watlington station. Note the many small details which add interest and realism to the scene.*

Traffic on your railway

Above *A Hornby 0-6-0 Pannier Tank Engine and an auto-coach made up from a BSL kit form this typical auto-train seen at Stonepark Lane, an 00-gauge country branch line terminus. Because these trains run in either direction the engine does not need to run round the train at the terminus.* **Above right** *Livestock was an important part of the goods traffic on many branch lines and the pens at Corfe Castle station on the 00-gauge model of the Swanage branch, built by the Isle of Purbeck Model Railway Club, contain cattle, sheep and pigs.* **Right** *The provision of industrial sidings will add greatly to the scope and interest of operation. On Harold Bowcott's 00-gauge layout, sidings serve this large factory and the hopper for the transfer of minerals from the narrow-gauge line at the left of the picture.* (Photograph by Brian Monaghan.)

larger town. Some of these services can be by push-pull train or a railcar but these involve less movements as no running round by the engine is required. Therefore it is best to have some of the services provided by ordinary trains so that there will be more shunting. Extra trains will be needed on Saturdays and on market days. If we place our terminus at a seaside or holiday resort then we will need more trains in the summer and may run through coaches or even through trains from London or other cities for the holiday visitors. In rural areas we may need additional trains for seasonal workers depending on the crops grown in the district. Thus variety can be introduced in the passenger traffic for even a fairly small terminus.

When we look at the freight side there is even more scope. Domestic coal was an important item in the days of the steam-operated branch line and our station should have a siding with coal staithes for this traffic. In addition, if we base a locomotive at the terminus with a small engine shed and water tower we will need to provide coal for it and this will make up extra coal traffic on the line.

In a rural area much of the freight traffic will be related to agriculture. This may be crops, grain, vegetables or fruit which will need to be shipped out. Incoming traffic will include fertilisers and occasionally farm equipment such as a plough or tractor. The area may be more concerned with livestock so that we need to provide a cattle dock or sheep pens at our terminus, together with appropriate rolling stock to transport the animals. If horses are to be carried we will need one or more horse boxes on our rolling stock roster. Animal feed shipped in will further add to the traffic. There will also be goods coming in for the shops and the local pub, together with items ordered by people living in the town or village and on nearby farms.

If we have room for a dairy, a small sawmill or a quarry we can introduce suitable extra rolling stock to handle this special traffic; the

additional operational scope will also increase the interest. However, we should not run any stock for which there is clearly no traffic being generated if we are to maintain the realism. If we have chosen a small port as the setting for our terminus we can introduce fish traffic with a special fish train running through to the junction or beyond. There may also be goods brought to the dock for shipment in coastal freighters.

We may have space for a larger station and this will enable us to include more facilities and to introduce more types of traffic, making both the selection of rolling stock and the scope of operation more interesting. The terminus would be serving a larger town and we can probably provide some light industry. This will require incoming raw materials and perhaps coal as fuel, and there will be finished goods to be shipped out.

No hard and fast rules need be laid down regarding the traffic. The important thing is for there to be visible facilities and reasons for the traffic and that it should be appropriate to the area and to the type of community that your station serves. It is useful to decide on this sort of background to your line before planning the traffic and timetable so that you are quite clear just what your aims are. Otherwise you may be tempted to add this and that and to acquire unsuitable rolling stock, resulting in an unrealistic overall effect.

The whole concept can be approached in

Above *Motorail services are now widely available in Britain and Europe. These two pictures show the facility at Narbonne on the SNCF. Special services of this type can be an interesting addition to model railway operation.* **Below** *Such services are often not exclusive to the contemporary scene. Here we see 'Motorail' Victorian style modelled on Mike Sharman's 4 mm scale period layout!*

various ways. One method is to decide on the location and type of line and to build up a picture of the sort of traffic pattern the railway should have. The layout can then be designed to fit in with this. Alternatively you can start with an already completed layout plan, perhaps a published design, and then plan out from this a traffic pattern which would be appropriate for the facilities provided. If you work from a prototype track plan, such as often appear in magazines and books, you can carry out a similar exercise but you will also have additional information available about the line and the area in which it was situated to help create a realistic and authentic operating scheme.

Once we have decided on the sort of traffic our line will carry we will have a good idea of the type of trains we will be running and of the rolling stock required. For the amount of traffic, most modellers use prototype lines of a similar nature as a guide or, if they are copying a particular prototype, they follow the pattern of that line. Often country branch lines had very simple timetables with relatively few trains, and modellers may wish to introduce a little more activity with a few extra trains, though this must not be overdone or the character of the model will be distorted. Even if your station serves an imaginary town you can work out the amount of traffic which would be likely by using real towns of a similar size as a guide. For example, David Jenkinson calculated the daily wagon movements for cattle, coal, minerals, milk and general goods stock on his Marthwaite layout using statistics from Settle and Carlisle stations as a basis. His excellent description appeared in the December 1966 issue of *Railway Modeller* magazine and gives a good example of how the traffic pattern for a model railway layout can be logically built up to give a realistic and authentic operating scheme.

Once we have a clear idea of the traffic our line will carry, we can go on to produce a schedule or timetable setting out the details of how our trains will run. Before devising a timetable for our layout it is perhaps a good time to look briefly at the real thing.

Prototype timetables

The railway timetables with which everyone is familiar are the public timetables which cover only the passenger train schedules listing only their times for the stations at which they stop. Much more useful for the railway modeller interested in operation are the working timetables, issued to employees of the railway. These list all trains on the line concerned, passenger and freight, with their timings and with many other details such as train numbers and classification, speed restrictions, information regarding stops for shunting, for other trains to pass, and so on. These timetables are private and not for publication or general distribution. However, many are available unofficially in railway enthusiast circles and a number, mainly from steam days, have been published. For example, The Oxford Railway Publishing Company Ltd can offer Cambrian Railway (1904), Somerset & Dorset Railway (1920), Southern Railway (West Division) (1932) and Southern Railway (Isle of Wight) (1932) Passenger and Working Timetables, and more timetable reprints are to be published in due course. Many books on particular branch lines include details of their working timetables and these are invaluable to modellers building layouts based on these lines. The excellent books *Great Western Branch Line Termini* Vols 1 & 2 by Paul Karau, published by The Oxford Railway Publishing Company, for example, include working timetables for the branches concerned and also very useful details on how the termini were operated. Even if you are not modelling one of these lines the timetables would be a useful guide if you are operating a branch line layout.

If the modeller has chosen a specific branch, either to model exactly or as a general basis for his layout and he can obtain the working timetable for the period he wishes to model then there will be no difficulty in running an accurate timetable service. As mentioned earlier familiarity with the economy of the area modelled and with the type of traffic the branch carried will enable him to realistically represent operation on the line. If it is not possible to find a copy of the authentic timetable it is still possible to devise a reasonable schedule from the track plan, station facilities and from what is known of the general type and extent of the traffic. Alternatively a timetable from a similar branch could be employed, perhaps with modifications to suit the needs of the modeller.

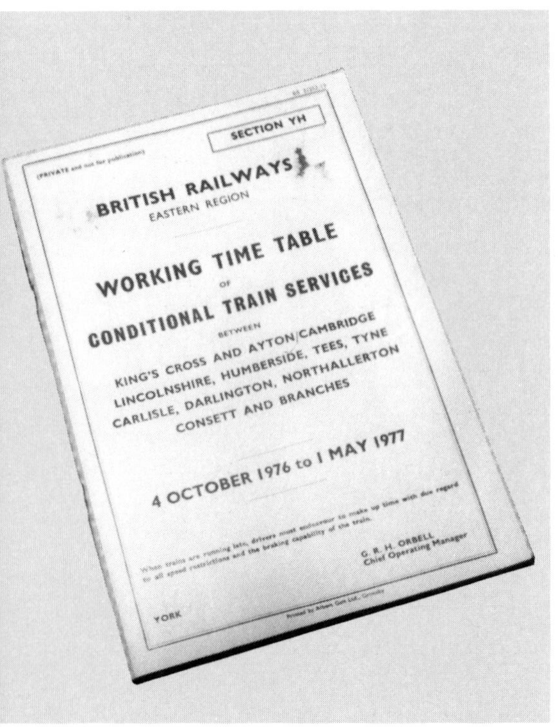

Left *Working timetables are issued to employees and give much more information than the ordinary public timetables, making them especially useful for railway modellers interested in operation.*

Compiling a simple timetable

Having considered the type of traffic we will have on our line, and perhaps with some prototype timetables to guide us, we can tackle the job of producing our first simple timetable. It is important not to try to devise anything too complicated at first as it is easy to become confused by too many details even though the principles may be straightforward. Because of its simplicity a branch line terminus timetable makes a good beginning. Again as branch line timetables were often very simple, frequently such lines operated on the one engine in steam principle, they can be conveniently carried out in model form using the sequence method. This type of running is well suited to the beginner to model railway operation and is also especially suitable for one modeller operating on his own, as is often likely to be the case with a small branch line layout.

Sequence operation is a simple but orderly pattern of operation which overcomes the difficulty that, with a simple timetable (such as would apply to a small branch line terminus or through station) there will be long time intervals between trains. Because of this there are likely to be periods when the operator has nothing to do for some minutes, even when using a speeded-up clock system. With sequence operation a list of train movements is drawn up, as with an ordinary timetable, but these are carried out in simple sequence without regard to the time. Once one move-

A simple timetable.

SX = Except Sunday. **SO** = Sunday only. **Auto** = Auto Train. **Pass** = Passenger.

DOWN TRAINS	PASS	AUTO SO	AUTO SX	MIXED SX	AUTO SO	PASS	AUTO	AUTO
	am	am	am	am	pm	pm	pm	pm
FIDDLE YARD	7.30	9.40	9.55	11.30	1.06	5.10	6.30	8.35
HALT	7.38	9.48	10.03	11.46	1.14	5.18	6.38	8.48
TERMINUS	7.49	9.59	10.14	12.08	1.25	5.29	6.46	8.59

UP TRAINS	PASS	AUTO SO	AUTO SX	GOODS SX	AUTO SO	PASS	AUTO	AUTO
	am	am	am	pm	pm	pm	pm	pm
TERMINUS	8.02	10.20	10.30	1.04	1.35	5.40	7.00	9.05
HALT	8.13	10.31	10.41	1.26	1.46	5.51	7.11	9.16
FIDDLE YARD	8.21	10.41	10.49	1.42	1.54	5.59	7.19	9.24

ment has taken place the operator goes on to the next. Thus it does not matter how quickly or slowly the enthusiast carries out the operations. If he wishes to pause he can do so, merely commencing again with the next train on the list. This is ideal for the beginner as he can get used to running the trains at realistic speeds and to carrying out shunting, also in a smooth and authentic manner, without being under any pressure to keep to time. And conversely there are no periods when he has nothing to do but wait. There is no reason why the modeller should not work through a prototype timetable using this system. Instead of sending out a train at, for example, 2.25 pm either by real or scale time, the train is despatched in its turn, and the time then is regarded as being 2.25 pm. Sequence operation, as I have mentioned previously, is particularly suited to operation of a simple layout, especially a branch line terminus or through station layout with one engine only running at any one time. Here there is not the need, as there may be on a larger more complex layout with two or more operators, for trains to pass or meet other trains or to clear trackage by a certain time. When there are more operators and there are trains which must interlock in their running we need some standard, most conveniently provided by all running to the same clock, whether speeded up or not, so that operation maintains an orderly pattern. Otherwise chaos may result.

As I have already indicated, sequence operation is particularly suitable for the single handed operator though it can still be used with two or more modellers. In this case they can all work from the same sequence card. Alternatively, they can work from cards of their own but provision must be made for keeping the sequence, either by exchanging cards between operators at the appropriate stages, or by including instructions that a particular movement must not be carried out until after the other operator has made some move.

Ideally at the end of the sequence all the stock should be back where it started so that the next sequence can begin. Generally, as with timetables, it is a good idea to begin with a simple limited sequence, then add to it as you gain experience and stock. If a particular sequence becomes boring after a time through repetition, then rearrange it to provide some variety. Extra interest can also be added by running some unscheduled trains such as a track repair train, a special passenger train, perhaps to bring people to an agricultural show, a seasonal goods train for a fruit crop, and so on.

To complete this section I would like to give you an example of how one modeller has created an interesting and realistic operating scheme for a very small layout. Chris Ellis recently built an N-gauge layout only 3 feet by 2 feet in size. He has described the construction of the layout in a series of articles in the magazine, *Model Train,* and I am most grateful for his permission to include here his working timetable and an outline, based on his description, of how he developed this timetable. His layout is based on an American prototype, the Chicago & North Western Railroad, but the basic principles are essentially similar to the making of a timetable for a British line.

The Warren, Beresford and Chicago Railroad was designed to provide interest in operation as well as in construction, and the operating concept of the layout was evolved as

Opposite and following three pages *Operation on the N-gauge American prototype Warren, Beresford and Chicago layout built by Chris Ellis.* (All photographs by Chris Ellis.) **1** *An operator using the timetable alongside the controller. A Scoot is in the fiddle yard, at the rear centre of the picture, ready to run to Warren.* **2** *The Scoot moving along the fiddle yard siding heading up the branch to Warren.* **3** *Switching at North Warren. The Illinois Central reefer (refrigerated car) is being pulled out of the dairy siding. It will be put on the 'main line' and the Lackawanna boxcar will replace it at the dairy loading bank. The tank car will then go on to the Shell siding.* **4** *The Lackawanna boxcar is now being spotted at the dairy.* **5** *The branch freight approaching Warren headed by the Fairbanks-Morse H-12-44 switcher (Minitrix model repainted in Chicago and North Western colours).* **6** *Scoot (Train No 914) heading for Chicago (pushing) while the local freight is switched at North Warren.* **7** *Local mine train (No 910) arrives in the fiddle yard and is removed from the track.* **8** *Switching is suspended while Scoot No 913 arrives at the station at Warren. The local freight locomotive has gone to North Warren to lay over.* **9** *The Scoot has departed and the local freight locomotive arrives back at Warren to resume switching, bringing with it the cars picked up at North Warren.* **10** *Local freight locomotive laying over at North Warren while the Scoot occupies Warren station (see photo 8).* **11** *Switching the mine—Train No 909 changing loaded hoppers for the empties it has just brought in. Note the flagman on the road crossing.* **12** *Train No 912—the local freight returning from Warren/North Warren to Chrystal Lake.*

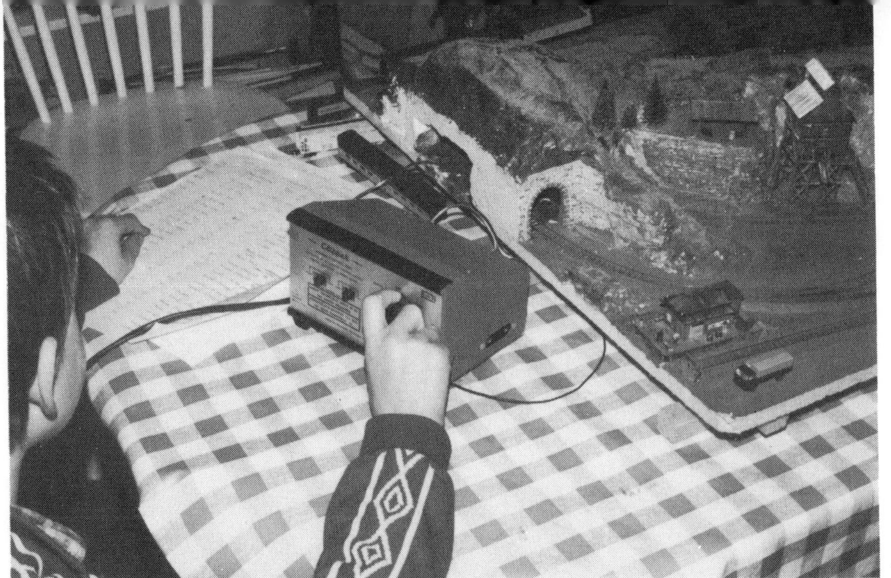
1

2

3

4

5

6

7

8

9

10

11

12

follows. First of all, think in basic terms. What is the aim of the railroad? The answer is to carry people and goods from one point to another. Our layout is the most basic form of railway, a simple single track branch line doing exactly that, carrying goods and people from an 'off-stage' location (the equivalent of the fiddle yard on the classic branch line terminus type of layout) to the stations and depots on the board. From here it is a matter of choosing a location for the line. You can make up a completely mythical line with a 'company' name of its own if desired. Or you can do as we did and find a suitable railway to which your 'branch' can be connected as a fictional addition. The further alternative of modelling an actual location was not really practical for a small oval layout like this because there is insufficient space to represent it properly.

This led us to a 'fictional addition' to a real railway. We wanted a railway which would lend itself to a simple compact branch line, offer a busy service in real life, and enable us to use ready-to-run N-scale items with a minimum of adaptation. One line (but by no means the only one) which fitted these requirements was the Chicago North Western Railroad which operates out of Chicago, west and north-west as its name implies. This may seem somewhat exotic to some readers, but it is colourful in its snappy green/yellow paint scheme, it has a wide selection of motive power, it is a relatively small, tightly managed company, and it has lots of very rural country branch lines, almost as though the old Great Western Railway was still running its 1948 network in this modern diesel age. All the locomotives and stock required to operate a CNW layout are readily available in current N-gauge production, even though a little repainting and adaptation may be necessary. Above all, it operates a commuter service into Chicago which runs further out into the country than any of the other lines in the area with commuter service. Its route to the furthest commuter outpost, the holiday and residential resort of Lake Geneva, Wisconsin, is 73 miles by rail from Chicago on a branch of great charm and beauty.

By American standards the commuter trains offer a very frequent service, and these trains operated by double-decker (or bi-level) cars are short. So a branch line similar to the Lake Geneva branch offered us a modern era setting, with short trains, which could be dove-tailed neatly into the existing network. The sketch map of the CNW routes, over which a commuter service operates, is included here and our branch is added to it, running to Warren (and North Warren—freight only) from Chrystal Lake. This new branch lends itself so

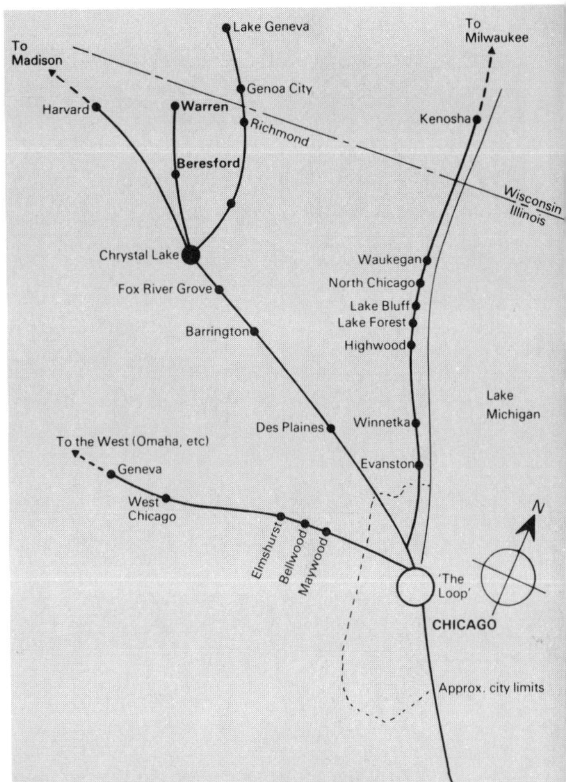

Sketch map showing the actual suburban routes from Chicago of the Chicago and North Western Railway system, with the addition of the fictional Warren branch coming off at Chrystal Lake. Only major stations are shown—there are actually more than 70 in the area of the map. Clybourn, mentioned on the train schedule, is the first junction out of Madison Street station in Chicago. (Courtesy Chris Ellis.)

well to existing CNW operations that we could readily produce a passenger schedule exactly like all other CNW leaflets you can pick up at stations on the line! If you do have access to a home printing set, it adds an amusing extra element to your layout if you have some realistic timetables to display and give to visitors.

A printed schedule, however, is really only the icing on the cake. It will impress your friends and help to bring the layout to life. To operate the layout with a logical schedule of runs you need something more mundane—a working timetable. Real timetables can appear very complicated and on a large model railway

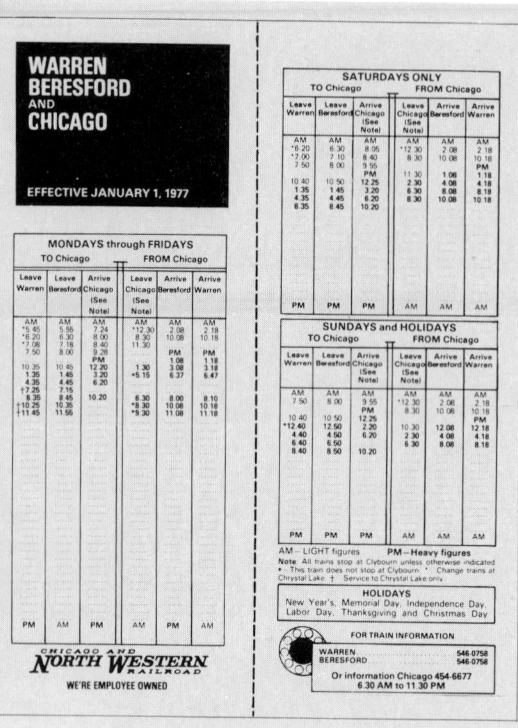
WARREN BERESFORD AND CHICAGO

EFFECTIVE JANUARY 1, 1977

MONDAYS through FRIDAYS

TO Chicago			FROM Chicago		
Leave Warren	Leave Beresford	Arrive Chicago (See Note)	Leave Chicago (See Note)	Arrive Beresford	Arrive Warren
AM	AM	AM	AM	AM	AM
*5.45	5.55	7.24	*12.30	2.08	2.18
*6.20	6.30	8.00	8.30	10.08	10.18
*7.08	7.18	8.40	11.30		
7.50	8.00	9.28		PM	PM
		PM		1.08	1.18
10.35	10.45	12.20	1.30	3.08	3.18
1.35	1.45	3.20	•5.15	6.37	6.47
4.35	4.45	6.20			
†7.25	7.15				
8.35	8.45	10.20	6.30	8.00	8.10
†10.25	10.35		*8.30	10.08	10.18
†11.45	11.55		*9.30	11.08	11.18
PM	AM	PM	AM	PM	AM

CHICAGO AND NORTH WESTERN RAILROAD

WE'RE EMPLOYEE OWNED

SATURDAYS ONLY

TO Chicago			FROM Chicago		
Leave Warren	Leave Beresford	Arrive Chicago (See Note)	Leave Chicago (See Note)	Arrive Beresford	Arrive Warren
AM	AM	AM	AM	AM	AM
*6.20	6.30	8.05	*12.30	2.08	2.18
*7.00	7.10	8.40	8.30	10.08	10.18
7.50	8.00	9.55			PM
		PM	11.30	1.08	1.18
10.40	10.50	12.25	2.30	4.08	4.18
1.35	1.45	3.20	6.30	8.08	8.18
4.35	4.45	6.20	8.30	10.08	10.18
8.35	8.45	10.20			
PM	PM	PM	AM	AM	AM

SUNDAYS and HOLIDAYS

TO Chicago			FROM Chicago		
Leave Warren	Leave Beresford	Arrive Chicago (See Note)	Leave Chicago (See Note)	Arrive Beresford	Arrive Warren
AM	AM	AM	AM	AM	AM
7.50	8.00	9.55	*12.30	2.08	2.18
		PM	8.30	10.08	10.18
10.40	10.50	12.25			PM
*12.40	12.50	2.20	10.30	12.08	12.18
4.40	4.50	6.20	2.30	4.08	4.18
6.40	6.50		6.30	8.08	8.18
8.40	8.50	10.20			
PM	PM	PM	AM	AM	AM

AM – LIGHT figures PM – Heavy figures

Note: All trains stop at Clybourn unless otherwise indicated • – This train does not stop at Clybourn. * Change trains at Chrystal Lake † Service to Chrystal Lake only

HOLIDAYS
New Year's, Memorial Day, Independence Day, Labor Day, Thanksgiving and Christmas Day

FOR TRAIN INFORMATION

WARREN 546-0758
BERESFORD 546-0758

Or information Chicago 454-6677
6.30 AM to 11.30 PM

WORKING TIMETABLE – WARREN

No.	Time (Warren)	From	To	Duty/Remarks
901	2.18 am	C	W	Scoot — lays over at W
902	5.45 am	W	CL	Scoot — shuttle to CL and re
903	6.10 am	CL	W	Scoot — 902 returning to W
904	6.20 am	W	CL	Scoot — shuttle to CL and re
905	6.55 am	CL	W	Scoot — 904 returning to W
906	7.08 am	W	CL	Scoot — shuttle to CL and re
907	7.40 am	CL	W	Scoot 906 returning to W
908	7.50 am	W	C	Scoot — through to Chicago
909	8.15 am	CL	W	Mine train — work mine
910	8.45 am	W	CL	Mine train returning to CL
911	9.45 am	CL	W	Local freight from CL
912	As required	W	CL	Local freight returning to CL
913	10.18 am	C	W	Scoot — 8.30 from C
914	10.35 am	W	C	Scoot through to Chicago
915	As required	CL	W	Local freight from CL
916	As required	W	CL	Local freight to CL
917	1.18 pm	C	W	Scoot — 11.30 from C
918	1.35 pm	W	C	Scoot — through to Chicago
919	2.00 pm	CL	W	Mine train — work mine
920	2.30 pm	W	CL	Mine train — return to CL
921	3.18 pm	C	W	Scoot — 1.30 from C
922	4.35 pm	W	C	Scoot — through to Chicago
923	As required	CL	W	Local freight from CL
924	As required	W	CL	Local freight to CL
925	6.47 pm	C	W	Scoot — 5.15 from Chicago
926	7.05 pm	W	CL	Scoot — to Chrystal Lake
927	8.10 pm	C	W	Scoot — 6.30 from Chicago
928	8.35 pm	W	C	Scoot — through to Chicago
929	9.15 pm	CL	W	Mine train
930	9.45 pm	W	CL	Mine train — return to CL
931	10.18 pm	CL	W	Scoot — shuttle from CL (926 returning)
932	10.25 pm	W	CL	Scoot — shuttle to CL
933	11.18 pm	CL	W	Scoot (932 returning)
934	11.45 pm	W	CL	Scoot — to CL
901	2.18 am	CL	W	Scoot (934 returning) Lays over at W to form 902

Notes:
C = Chicago, Madison Street Station W = Warren CL = Chryst
All times in column 2 are arrival/departure Warren

Left *The train schedule for the Warren, Beresford and Chicago layout was reproduced to the exact size and style of the real CNW passenger timetables.* (Courtesy Chris Ellis.) **Right** *Working timetable for the Warren, Beresford and Chicago layout.* (Courtesy Chris Ellis.)

operation can be complex. However, here we have only the simplest of single line branches on which it is physically impossible to run more than one train at a time. Consequently, our timetable should be a simple one.

For a start, we forgot about time, real or speeded up, since ours is a layout for leisurely home operation and the pace of working is entirely up to you. Yes, there are nominated arrival and departure times for all the trains operating in a sequence throughout the day, but these times are descriptive rather than actual. Looking at the working timetable given here you will see that the first train in the 24 hour weekday schedule is the 2.18 am arrival in Warren from Chrystal Lake—representing the connecting train (at Chrystal Lake) with the last train of the day out of Chicago. So if you choose to start an operating session with this train it is simply the 2.18 am, no matter what time your operating session starts.

Obviously, to work this out we had to know some basic timings and make some assumptions. So to start with we got hold of the train schedules for all the commuter runs on the CNW network. Using the train schedule for the Chicago-Harvard route (on which line is the all-important Chrystal Lake junction) it is easy enough to plot the frequency of passenger trains to and from the CNW station in Chicago. We made an early assumption here which was dictated by the limited trackage at Warren; because there are no spare sidings at Warren we could not have passenger trains 'laying over' waiting for their next turn, except for the last train at night which could lay over to become the first train in the morning. On the real railway, where most commuter runs are crowded into the morning or evening rush hours, the trains lay over in sidings in Chicago, Harvard, Chrystal Lake, etc, until they are next required for service. At Warren any such lay over would impede the running of freight trains, so incoming passenger trains are marked on the working timetable as returning to Chrystal Lake to lay over. A more likely alternative to this would be a siding 'off the board' beyond Beresford, where the train could be held until it returned to Warren for the next scheduled run to Chicago. At present this does not worry us—the train just runs back to siding A and is taken off the track until next required. If and when we extend the layout on to another board, we will worry about the actual destination then.

The other point peculiar to the CNW operation is that all trains are made up of bi-level (double-deck) cars and are push-pull operated using F7 or E8 diesel locomotives. So there is no need for the locomotive to run around the train at Warren. On the actual CNW commuter routes there may be anything from two to six passenger cars, the outer one a driving unit, depending on the density of the route. A single car is not usual, but may be seen on late or holiday workings on some routes. For the compact Warren branch we decided that a single trailer would be used for early and late trains running to Chrystal Lake only and two trailers would be used for trains running 'through' to Chicago. This is actually a happy assumption. As Chrystal Lake is on the Harvard-Chicago route, itself a main line, with a very frequent commuter train service, we reasoned that trains coming off the Warren branch would not be likely to duplicate runs to Chicago on an already busy main line. So we make only the most important trains run 'through' to Chicago and for the rest the passengers boarding at Warren and Beresford change at Chrystal Lake to a train already running on the Harvard-Chicago route.

Having placed all the key passenger train times at what is roughly the correct timing by real CNW standards, we could then pencil in all the freight train timings on the branch. It is most unlikely there would ever be 'through' freight workings on a small branch like this. So we assume that all freight cars for on-line customers or facilities are dropped or picked-up overnight by main line freight trains at the Chrystal Lake interchange sidings, then brought up the branch by a small locomotive assigned to the branch. In practice this is a Minitrix Fairbanks-Morse H-12-44 or an Atlas GP9.

It so happens that the timings we have invented dove-tail quite neatly with the passenger trains, but the assumption must be made from the timings that some of the freight trains must go into passing loops or sidings down the branch to let passenger trains through. We also ignored for the present that somewhere along the 18 miles of track between Warren and Chrystal Lake there may be other on-line industries with traffic to exchange and so make further complications. At present, therefore, all the freight cars which arrive at Warren are for sidings 'on the board', not off it.

Of particular interest is the complication with the 9.45 am local freight. Long before it can finish its work at Warren and North Warren, the 10.18 am passenger train is due. So the freight locomotive has to clear the station tracks and in practice it goes round to North Warren and the train crew take a coffee break until the passenger train has departed again as the 10.35 am.

Following the American style, we have given each train working a number, odd numbers out from Chicago and Chrystal Lake, even numbers inbound. The prefix '9' is supposed to indicate the line or branch—in this case the Warren branch. Actually this reference number is much easier to follow and remember than the time of the train and in practice the number is used rather than the time. Thus the 9.45 am referred to above is called Train No 911 when we are operating. A full weekday schedule has no less than 34 workings—17 in each direction, and it takes a very full evening operating session to get through it all. Sometimes, in fact, we do not complete it, but the beauty of the system is that you can start and stop when and how you please. If you have only a spare half hour, run as many trains as you have time for, mark your progress on the timetable (tick off each working with a pencil when completed) and carry on from where you left off when you next get time for an operating session. In CNW parlance the push-pull commuter trains are known as 'Scoots' (because they scoot along

Track plan of the Warren, Beresford and Chicago N-gauge layout built by Chris Ellis. **1** *Beresford Station;* **2** *Oil depot;* **3** *Dairy;* **4** *Corn and feed elevator;* **5** *Farm machinery and produce merchant;* **6** *Mine;* **7** *Freight depot;* **8** *Warehouse;* **9** *Warren Station;* **10** *North Warren;* **A** *fiddle siding. Each square measures 12 in.* (Courtesy Chris Ellis.)

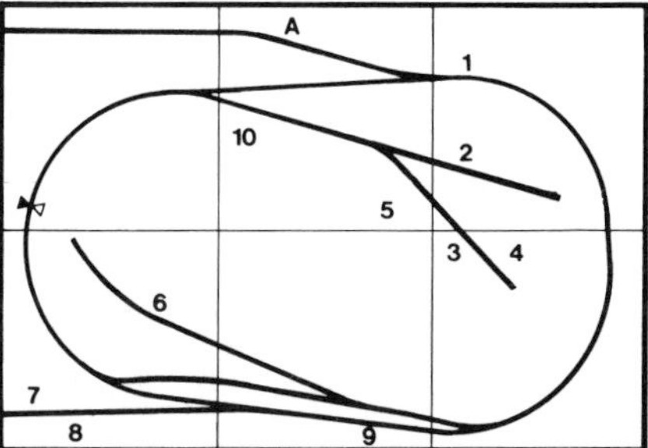

quite fast!), and to save time on the timetable we have marked all passenger trains as 'scoots'. The working timetable reproduced here should be self-explanatory.

Do not be put off in any way by the fact that the trains and timetable on our actual layout are modern Chicago and North Western Railroad. You can run any trains that take your fancy on this type of layout without fundamentally changing the timetable. You can, of course, work out your own running sequence and times to suit yourself, but if you do not want to be bothered with this just photocopy our printed working timetable, change the station names and trains to suit your particular interest and away you go! With appropriate adaptations the line could be set in Wales, Scotland or Germany, the basic principles of the operation remain the same.

The other important point is that the layout and setting can equally well be in the steam or diesel age as you wish. Though our CNW 'scoots' are push-pull, there is no reason why the passenger trains should not be perfectly conventional with the locomotive running around the train for the return journey. We have done this ourselves by switching the diesel era of our layout over to steam on occasions, using the Minitrix Pennsylvania Railroad B6 0-6-0 and an 0-4-0 saddle tank. In this case the passenger train has been made up of a single 'steam age' PRR combine coach.

What we hope our timetable has shown is that even a very simple layout like this, little more than a development from a basic train set oval, still has massive operational potential far removed from merely running model trains round and round in circles. We found that when trying to work a full week-day timetable in an evening session there was not actually much time available for running trains round and round but, if you want to make a few laps to simulate 'mileage' before bringing the train into the station, that is entirely up to you.

The above description by Chris Ellis clearly demonstrates that a simple sequence scheme of operation can create interesting and entertaining running on even a very small and simple layout, extending the enjoyment such a layout can give well beyond the period of construction. Such sequence operation is ideal for the beginner, new to the concept of model railway operation and still gaining skill in actually carrying out the various train movements. Indeed, many modellers find that the system suits them well and they continue to use it on their layouts without going on to anything more complicated. However, others feel that much of the interest, even excitement, in model railway operation comes from meeting the challenge of running to time, just as the real railways strive to do. It can be argued that as we have no real passengers on our model trains, and there is nobody sending out or waiting to receive the goods we pretend to be transporting on our railway, then we have no pressure to provide an efficient service unless we run to time. The protagonists of this argument feel that this is the best way to duplicate the operation of the real railways on a model layout. Certainly such operation can be an absorbing activity.

When introducing an operating system on a layout it is best to begin as a sequence scheme without the pressure of working to the clock. Later, as the operators become familiar with the system and gain experience generally, working to time can be added to the operating method. Basic to any system of operating to the clock is the matter of time and how we apply it to the model railway, and I would like to consider this subject next.

Time and the speeded-up clock

Now it can be argued that time is a constant factor and applies equally to models as to the real railway. And, indeed, if our model train is travelling at 60 scale miles per hour it will proceed a distance of 1 scale mile in 1 actual minute, just as the prototype at 60 miles per hour will travel 1 mile in the same actual time. So we could deduce that this is a logical argument and that we should run our timetable in accordance with an ordinary clock, and there are some modellers who do just that.

However, when we look a little further into the subject we find that there are definite disadvantages to this method. One very significant problem arises because of the short time it takes a train to run from one station to the next. Because it is usually quite impossible to model even a short branch line exactly to scale in the space we have for a layout, considerable compression is unavoidable in the model. This is selective, affecting particularly the length of track between stations. Thus, on most model railways the time taken for a train to travel between stations can be measured in seconds rather than minutes. Timetables both for the prototype and for model railways are made out to minutes, not seconds, so that these times between stations would have to be rounded up or down to the nearest minute and it is not possible to construct a satisfactory timetable on this basis. For example, if we have three stations, A, B and C on an 00-scale layout, with 10 feet of track from A to B and 20 feet from B to C, a train travelling at 20 scale miles per hour will take just under 30 seconds to go from A to B, which we must count as 0 minutes or 1 minute for our timetable. The time B to C will be just under 60 seconds, again counted as either 0 or 1 minute for the schedule. If the train travels at 40 scale miles per hour the times will be halved but must again be taken as either 0 or 1 minute for the timetable. Thus the use of standard time is quite inadequate for our purposes. If, however, we use fast time with a 12:1 ratio (5 minutes actual time becomes 1 hour fast time) the times A to B will become approximately 6 minutes and 3 minutes respectively for 20 and 40 scale miles per hour, and similarly the times B to C will be about 12 minutes and 6 minutes. These enable us to compile a meaningful timetable.

There are many prototype operations that are unnecessarily long and it would be uninteresting on the model to allow the actual time they require. Another advantage of speeded-up time is that these functions will now take much less time. The use of fast time also makes it convenient to make small alterations in the schedules as found necessary by experience in running the layout. Say we have allowed 90 seconds for our train to pass between two points on the layout. If we use actual time this will be represented as either 1 or 2 minutes on the schedule. However, with 12:1 ratio speeded-up time this will be 18 minutes and, if necessary, we can adjust this to say 17 or 19 minutes, whereas with standard time we would still have to list it as 1 or 2 minutes.

Another reason for using speeded-up time is to retain the character of the operation of the real railways. To take an example, we can consider the intervals between trains, one following the other. On the prototype there may be an interval of 5 or 10 minutes and any delay of the first train will immediately affect the running of the second. On a model railway with an interval of 5 or 10 actual minutes the first train would have reached its destination long before the second train started, and the situation is not really representative of the operation on the prototype. With speeded-up time the actual interval on the model will be much less and the situation will be more like that on the real railway.

With many prototype timetables there are gaps in the schedule when there is no activity and these times can be boring interruptions to an operating session for which standard time is used. However, if we employ a speeded-up clock, these gaps will be very much shortened and will not be a significant interruption to the flow of operations.

Another benefit of the fast clock is that a full

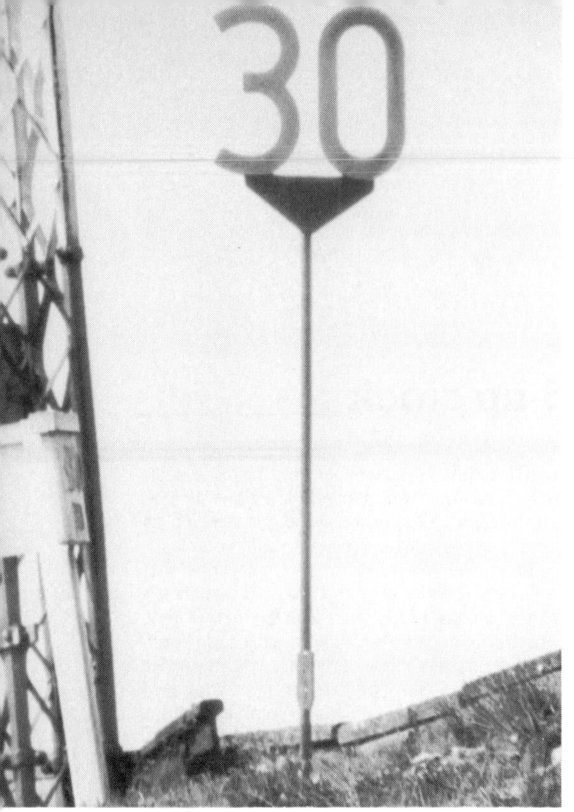

Prototype railways impose speed restrictions which must be obeyed by drivers. This is a standard British Rail speed restriction sign, the numbers indicating the limit, here 30 miles per hour. The front faces of the numbers are yellow, the rest black.

24-hour timetable can be worked through in a single operating session. This means that the whole range of railway activity, day and night, can be enjoyed giving variety and hence extra interest to the session. It also has the advantage that, by working through the complete timetable at each session, the operators become familiar with it and, as they gain experience and skill, the running of the layout will be smoother and more enjoyable.

Having put forward a case for the use of fast time in model railway operation we must now consider just how fast this time should be. Some modellers assume that the ratio of fast to real time should relate to the scale in which they are working in some mathematically calculable way, but this is not so. A fundamental principal of the use of fast time in model railway operation is that there is no 'correct' scale time ratio for a particular scale; the ratio depends only on operating considerations. At first sight this may seem illogical but if we consider the situation in more detail we can see that it is not basically the scaling down that introduces the need for fast time. As I mentioned in an example earlier, a model train will travel a scale mile at, say, 60 scale miles per hour in the same actual time, 1 minute, as a real train will take for a mile at 60 miles per hour. So, purely on the basis of scaling down, there is not necessarily any reason why we should not use standard time. It is the further compression of distances along the track, beyond that called for by scale, needed to fit a layout into a reasonable space that is a fundamental reason for using speeded-up time. We also find that many manoeuvres can be carried out more quickly on a model railway than on the prototype and this is a further reason for employing fast time.

This speeded-up time is often known as 'fast time'. Sometimes the term 'scale time' is used but, as this may be thought to imply some relationship to the scale of the model, it is perhaps not as good a term as 'fast time'. There have been attempts to justify the use of a particular relationship of this fast time to scale using various mathematical principles. For example, it has been suggested that we should apply Froude's equation, which is used to relate findings from the testing of models in wind tunnels and water tanks to the prototypes. Or that we should use the equation employed by movie makers when filming models to determine the appropriate camera speed so that, when screened at normal projection speed, the models in the film will move, and particularly fall, like the real thing. However, the idea of applying these principles to model railway operation is fallacious because, as explained above, the ratio depends not on the scale of the layout but on various operating considerations, though as it happens the results obtained do come within the range used by railway modellers.

Factors which do influence your choice include the distance between stations, train speeds and the efficiency of the operators at shunting and in carrying out other train movements of this type. It is also useful to choose a ratio which is convenient for measurementrs and calculations; the minimum interval of time should be a fast minute as we do not want to be involved with fractions of minutes in our schedule. The length of the 'day' on your railway, which may be 12 or 24 hours or some other period, and the average time you like an operating session to last may also influence your choice as there are advantages in being able to work through a full 'day' at a single session.

The ideal ratio depends to some extent on the type of operation on your railway. If it is

Operating your trains at scale speeds will improve the realism of your layout and you can impose appropriate scale speed limits. Suitable model signs are available from Smiths of Solihull and from R. Alderman of Yeovil. The 4 mm example shown here is from a Smiths set.

mainly running trains out on the line then, because of our greatly compressed distances, considerable speeding up of the time is desirable, especially if our stations are close together. On the other hand, if operation on our layout is largely shunting, perhaps on an industrial railway model, then the ratio should be smaller. One argument put forward against the use of fast time is that the discrepancy between the two types of operation will make it impossible to select a suitable ratio. These modellers claim that as shunting on the model will take much the same time as on the prototype, then using a speeded-up clock to make main line running more realistic will leave insufficient time for shunting to be carried out properly, or that inordinately long times will be needed on the timetable for shunting operations to be completed. In fact, two American modellers carefully timed shunting activities of various types on both prototypes and model railroads and found that, though it varies between different types of shunting, on average such operations were still appreciably faster on the model. They were, incidentally, very careful that all model locomotive movements were carried out at scale speeds and in accordance with prototype practice. It is, therefore, quite feasible to find a compromise ratio which will improve operation on the main line and still permit realistic shunting.

The usual range of ratios of fast to standard time is somewhere between 6:1 and 15:1, with 12:1 perhaps the most popular, though 10:1 also has its advocates. The 12:1 ratio is convenient in that 5 minutes of standard time is equivalent to 1 hour of fast time, and a 24-hour day on the timetable can be worked through in a 2-hour operating session. The choice of ratio is up to the individual modeller and there is no reason why he should not adjust it later if he finds that it is set too high or too low for his layout. It has been suggested that a variable speed clock, or 'rubber' clock, is advantageous with inexperienced operators. If they fall behind schedule or are having difficulties of one sort or another then the clock can be slowed, or even stopped, until they catch up or sort out the problems. This has benefits when learning, both for training the operators and in deciding which will be the best ratio for your layout. However, once the operators have sufficient experience and the appropriate ratio has been selected it is best to try to stick to the proper timing and not to alter the clock. With practice in working at a particular ratio, the operators become used to the fast time and familiar with the time needed for various manoeuvres and this is valuable in running the layout well. If the clock is being continually varied it takes much longer for this skill to be acquired.

Obviously, the most convenient method of working to fast time is to have a clock, or clocks, which have been adapted or altered in some way so that fast time can be read directly from it. Various modellers have modified clocks in different ways, usually by altering the gearing, so that they run faster. The details will vary with the particular clocks and with the degree of speeding-up required, and such alterations are beyond the scope of this book. I understand that digital clocks with integrated circuits can be altered by replacing the original time-base oscillator with one of higher frequency, or even with a variable frequency to produce a variable clock. Two articles have appeared in the American magazine, *Model Railroader,* one on altering an electric kitchen clock in the November 1955 issue, and one on modifying a digital clock in the November 1974 issue, and modellers wanting further information may like to refer to these articles.

A much simpler method is to use a clock without altering the mechanism but removing the hour hand and using the minute hand to read off the hours on a new face made up to suit the ratio selection. If you choose 12:1 you do not even need to make a new face, merely read off the hours as usual but with the minute hand. You can judge the intermediate times fairly well, especially if the spaces are marked out into minutes on the dial. If you are making a new clock face yourself you can divide the spaces between the hour marks into four quarters, each representing 15 minutes of fast time. Obviously reading a clock of this type will not be quite as accurate as one with the mechanism altered to speed it up but the times can still be judged sufficiently accurately for satisfactory operation.

To conclude our consideration of speeded-up time there is one final concept, that of the shortened mile, named the 'smile' by its originator, the late Frank Ellison, a pioneer of realistic model railroad operation. This measure is not related to scale but to the fast time ratio. A model train travelling at 60 scale miles per hour goes 1 scale mile in 1 minute of standard time; it also goes 1 'smile' in 1 fast minute. Thus the length of a 'smile' depends on the fast time ratio employed; for 10:1, for example, 1 'smile' = 0.1 scale mile. Though some modellers do install 'smile' posts at appropriate spacing on their main lines, 'smiles' do not really apply visually or in construction, but relate to timetable operation.

The train graph

Earlier we looked at a very simple timetable for a branch line with only one engine in steam. Here scheduling is very simple as there is only one train to be concerned with at any one time, running from the fiddle yard to the terminus and back. Because of the simplicity of the train movements, a mere list or table of the times is easy to compile and to interpret. On a more complex layout with perhaps two or three trains making journeys at the same time, and the need to arrange for trains to pass at specific places where there are passing loops, then a table of that type is much more difficult to compile and to understand. We need some other method which will enable us to determine more easily and quickly the relative positions and movements of the trains.

The simplest method is to follow the example of the prototype railways and make up a train graph on which the information is built up in an easy to understand visual form. It enables us to see, at a glance, where any train should be at any time and where and when it will pass other trains. These graphs, by convention, are laid out with the distance on the vertical axis. For the modeller this can be in scale miles, in actual feet, or if using fast time, in 'smiles'. It is useful to include a schematic track diagram along this axis also, together with the station names appropriately positioned. This is set out along the horizontal axis of the graph, either actual time or fast time, depending on the system you use on your layout. On such a graph the slope of the train lines is related to their speeds. When a train is stopped the train line will be horizontal, that is, though time passes, the distance does not change. The operators can work from train graphs or timetables can be compiled from the graph for running purposes. If you plan to work from the train graph it is convenient to make photocopies of the original graph for the

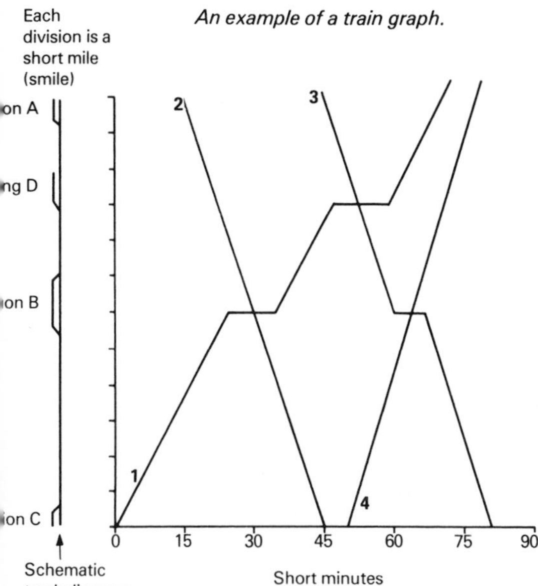

An example of a train graph.

If vertical axis scale miles instead of 'smiles', plot real time along horizontal axis instead of short minutes (fast time). Goods Train **1** leaves Station C at 0 minutes and stops at Station B at 25 minutes to shunt and to allow Train **2**, a non-stopping passenger train, to pass. Train **1** also waits on Siding D to allow Train **3** to pass. Train **2** reaches Station C and is turned to become Train **4** leaving 5 minutes later. Train **3** is a goods train which stops at Station B to shunt and to allow Train **4** to pass.

Average speed of a train is given by the slope.

Train 2 travels 12 smiles from A to C in 30 fast minutes—average speed thus 24 miles per hour.

Above *Once we have established our standard timetable we can increase the operating activity by adding extra unscheduled trains. An interesting example is an enthusiast's special which will give us the opportunity to run a locomotive and stock which might otherwise be inappropriate to the line. This scene was specially set up on the Isle of Purbeck MRC's 00-gauge Swanage branch layout with a Triang 'Lord of the Isles' heading the train.* **Below** *Another instance where a special unscheduled train can add to the interest of timetable operation. This is the snowplough train, rather rarely required in Britain, but regularly needed on many European and American lines in the winter. This train is on a Swiss narrow-gauge line.*

operators to use, and these can be marked to show the features of importance to the particular operator. For example, if one operator is concerned with running an intermediate junction station on the line, a red line can be drawn horizontally across the graph at the level of the station. It is then easy for that operator to see exactly when the various trains reach his station as this will be where the train lines cut the red line. Alternatively, if one operator will be running certain trains then on his copy of the train graph his trains can have their lines marked in red. The train graphs represent a point to point system but can also be applied to an oval layout perfectly satisfactorily. In this case one point on the oval (perhaps one station or yard, or, best of all, if there are hidden sidings at one side of the oval serving as a fiddle yard) is included at both the top and the bottom of the vertical axis of the graph. To avoid confusion it can be named differently for the two positions. Once a train has arrived at this point it can either reverse forming a train returning from this yard or it can go on when it will be a new train starting at the other end of the axis on the train graph.

Ideally, the train graph is constructed, as mentioned above, with distance plotted on the vertical axis, positioning stations and other points accurately on this axis according to their situation on the layout, measuring in scale miles, actual feet or 'smiles'. We can then plot the train lines exactly either working from the times we want the trains to be at particular points, or on the basis of the speed, because the slope of the train lines relates to the speed—the faster the train the more nearly vertical the train line. Thus working from the time the train leaves a station we can determine by drawing in the appropriate slope when it will reach the next station travelling at the speed we have chosen. This may, for example, be 60 scale miles per hour for a passenger train, and only 20 miles per hour for a slow goods train.

However, if we want to keep things simple and do not wish to measure the distances on the layout, or calculate them in terms of scale miles, it is still possible to construct a train graph by working more empirically. To do this we run the various trains we intend to include in the timetable over the layout. Taking care to run them at what appear to the eye to be suitable scale speeds, each journey is carefully timed for each point on the trip and these are noted down. We then construct a train graph as before but, instead of plotting distances on the vertical axis, we merely list the stations on the route in their correct order along this axis. They can either be spaced evenly regardless of their actual distances apart or they can be placed approximately as they are located in relation to each other on the layout. Such a graph will not yield all the information that the more accurately plotted one will; we cannot, for example, calculate the train speed from the slope of the train line. However, the graph can still be a very useful method of constructing a suitable timetable for operating the layout and a helpful visual presentation of that timetable for the operators.

So far both in simple timetable construction and in the train graph we have been concerned only with the scheduled trains which are run regularly on the layout. After a time when the timetable becomes very familiar and perhaps a little repetitious, some enthusiasts like to add a little extra challenge and interest to the proceedings by introducing unscheduled extra trains and other complications. The need to cope with these, while at the same time interfering as little as possible with the regular trains on the timetable will certainly stop the operators getting bored! One method of introducing these complications at random, thus making the session more exciting, is to have a set of cards, sometimes called situation or hazard cards, on each of which is listed a situation which will affect operation. These can include changes in the traffic needs necessitating the running of an extra train or of providing additional coaches for one which is already scheduled, breakdowns or derailments which may entail delays or diversions as well as the making up of a breakdown train and running it to the location, and so on. The list of possibilities is almost limitless and you can easily select some which are appropriate to your layout. The cards are shuffled and the pack is placed face down. Then, at predetermined times during an operating session, a card can be taken from the top of the pack and the instructions carried out. The introduction of unscheduled events at random in this way can do a great deal to add interest and challenge to a session, even if the basic timetable is becoming rather routine.

Bell codes

On the prototype railway bell signals sent from one signal box to the next advise the signalmen of the trains passing into the areas which they control. The messages are passed in a code system with which the signalmen are as familiar as a radio operator is with the morse code. Rather than merely exchanging information by direct conversation, some railway modellers like to use the standard British Rail bell signalling codes for communication between two or more operators running a model railway layout. The system is not only convenient, particularly if the layout is a large one with the operators some distance apart, perhaps even in different rooms, but is also authentic, adding realism to operating procedures.

The prototype codes are designed to cover every possible contingency, and are further complicated by the fact that some codes apply to all British Rail regions, some to all regions except the Southern, and some to the Southern Region only! For the full details I would refer you to the very useful book, *British Railway Signalling* by G.M. Kichenside and Alan Williams, published by Ian Allan, where the BR Standard Signal Box Bell Codes are given in full in an appendix. Most modellers find that a restricted code is adequate for their needs and is much easier to learn, so that operators quickly find they no longer have to keep referring back to the list. As an example, the bell code presented here is the one that Eric Kay used on his Sherrington Branch and which proved perfectly adequate for normal operation, both at home and at exhibitions. When there were two operators on his layout, one would man the terminus station, Sherrington, and the other the fiddle yard and the bell code was employed for communication between them to offer and accept trains.

I would advise the beginner who would like to use the bell code system to start with a simple selection, rather than with too full a list which will be difficult to use. It is easy to add further codes as necessary later. The actual bells can be merely bell gongs, struck by hand, or an electric bell system can be installed, arranged so that each press of a button or switch gives a single ring.

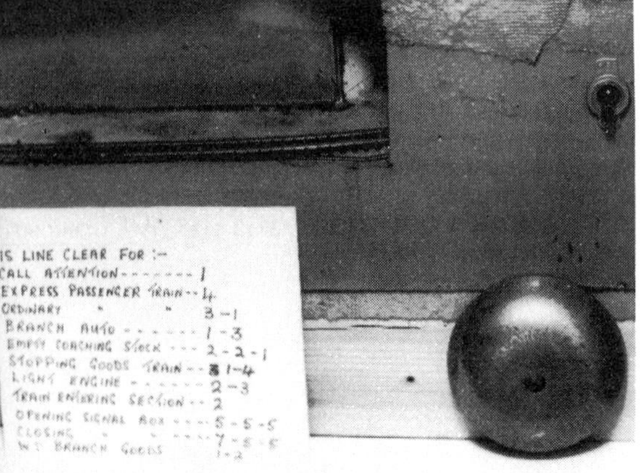

Below *Part of the fiddle yard on Eric Kay's N-gauge Sherrington branch. The fiddle yard operator uses the gong at the right to communicate by bell code with the other operator at the station. Note the check list showing the codes commonly used on the layout.* **Below right** *Simple bell code system as used on the Sherrington Branch.*

Opening signal box	5-5-5
Closing signal box	7-5-5
Call Attention	1
Is line clear for:	
Express passenger train	4
Ordinary passenger train	3-1
Branch auto-train	1-3
Empty coaching stock	2-2-1
Light Engine	2-3
Train entering section	2
Branch goods train	1-2

Card order systems

In looking at operation on a model railway layout, so far we have concentrated on the movement of complete trains, passenger and freight, over the line in accordance with a schedule. We have considered how to compile a timetable based on a realistic pattern of operation to handle the traffic appropriate to the line. As yet we have not taken into account the distribution of individual goods wagons, vans and other stock. On a branch line we have merely sent a goods train made up from what appears to be a reasonable selection of stock from the fiddle yard to the terminus. At this destination we have perhaps exchanged the incoming wagons for ones already at the station and which are assumed to be ready to go back to the junction (fiddle yard).

While recognising that it is desirable for realism that our goods stock should appear to be moving in response to the traffic needs, we have no automatic method of producing an authentic traffic flow and must either improvise as we go or have a set scheme laid down for our sequence operation or timetable. Neither system is ideal. The former tends to lead to any wagons which are not easy to get at, being ignored when shunting is carried out, while the latter is likely to become too well known to the operator in time, making operation too predictable and, therefore, less interesting. On the prototype railways the needs of the customers dictate the traffic and, as these needs fluctuate, so the goods traffic varies, but we have no customers on our model railway.

In an effort to create, artificially, realistic and varying goods traffic in model railway operation, a number of systems of freight car distribution have been devised. I use the American term 'freight car' deliberately because there has been a particular interest in this subject in the United States and most of the schemes have originated there. The systems have been designed to represent American prototype railroad practice, particularly the operations of the 'way freight' train which travels the single track main line stopping to drop and pick up cars at numerous stations and lineside industries. However, the schemes can also be applied with good effect on British layouts with only minor adaptations. Freight car distribution systems are ideal for small shunting layouts such as those based on industrial railways and can create very interesting operation on a small layout. On other lines, for example a country branch, the systems can be used in combination with a timetable, and will provide the basis for the distribution of goods stock to and from the terminus and any intermediate stations or lineside industries by the trains listed in the schedule.

In one of the simplest forms of random distribution selection, modellers have used playing cards, deciding beforehand which card or cards from the pack will represent which destination for the rolling stock. When the train is ready to depart the cards are shuffled and dealt from the top of the pack. The first card shows where the first wagon is to go, the second card the second wagon, and so on. As all destinations will not be appropriate for all wagons it will be necessary on occasions to ignore the card turned up for a particular wagon and to turn up others until a suitable one is found.

A variant which will overcome the problem of unsuitable destinations is to have groups of destinations, each of which can accept any wagon. For example, one group could be made up of several industrial sidings. If a wagon is directed here it can be shunted onto a siding which is appropriate for use. Another group may be a goods yard with various facilities; thus a cattle wagon directed to the goods yard would be put on the siding serving the cattle dock. If we have four groups we can, as suggested by Mr Evens in *Model Railways* magazine (January 1974) use a pack of cards with the court cards removed and use the categories of cards red-even, red-odd, black-even, and black-odd, to give the four groups.

The true card order systems, however, do not rely on playing cards but have cards, one for each wagon on the railway, on which enough information to identify each individual wagon,

OWNER:	HIGHLEY MINING COMPANY.
TYPE:	10 TON OPEN WAGON.
NO.	425.

DESTINATION:

Colliery.
Coal Staithes.
Smiths Factory.
Crowley Manufacturing Company.
Johnson's Foundry.
Fiddle Yard.

A wagon card for a simple card order system. A paper clip is used as a marker to indicate destination on left.

van, tanker, etc, is provided. There are many ways in which distribution of the rolling stock can then be organised. One simple system is to have another set of cards with all possible destinations, again one card for each. The two sets of cards are shuffled separately and the top card from each is turned up providing a wagon and its destination. This process is then repeated as many times as there are to be wagons in the train. Again there may be the problem of inappropriate destinations turning up with the need to go on to another card. A similar system could be employed to determine which wagons the train picks up, or alternatively, one wagon could be collected for each one dropped.

Another scheme is to include on each wagon card a note of the appropriate load and the origin and destination for that load. The cards belonging to the wagons which are at a particular station are kept in a small box at the station. When a train arrives the driver takes a number of cards from the box, collects the wagons concerned, and takes them, and their cards, to the appropriate destinations; if a wagon begins at its destination then it is returned to its origin as an empty. The number of cards taken can be at the driver's discretion, or previously decided, or determined at the time by throwing a dice. This system in its simplest form will mean that any particular wagon will only move between two places, origin to destination and back. A more interesting variant is to have all the possible destinations for a particular wagon listed across the top or along one side of the card and to select one of these, indicating which with a paper clip, before the run.

There are many variants of the card order system but I would like to describe one simple system which can be applied to a small layout and which you may find suitable for your model railway. If you do employ it you should find it a useful basis, though as you gain experience you will probably wish to make modifications to suit the particular features of your line.

Strictly, card order systems should apply to loads and allow for whether or not a wagon, van, etc is empty or loaded, but if we concern ourselves only with rolling stock movements we can simplify the system to advantage. The method can be applied to a fiddle yard to terminus layout, to a through station type of layout with a fiddle yard at each end, or to an oval continuous scheme. Obviously the more stations, sidings and industries that we can include on the layout, the greater will be the scope for stock distribution and the more entertaining the operation.

The initial step is to list all the possible destinations including goods sidings of various types at different stations and any industries at these stations or along the line. A card (a plain postcard is suitable) is made out for each item of goods rolling stock on the railway indicating its type, number and, in the case of Private Owner stock, the name of the owner, to help easy identification during operation. Below this list the possible destinations. If you have a layout with one or more through stations and a yard or fiddle yard at each end, or a continuous layout with part concealed and used as a fiddle yard for trains coming either way round the oval, you can also include TGA and TGB at regular intervals in the listings, standing for 'Through Goods' with the 'A' or 'B' indicating the direction of travel along or around the track. In this case the wagon will be taken through to the yard at the other end of the journey and will wait there until another train is made up. At each station, yard or industrial site there will be a box for cards, divided into an arrivals side and a departures side. If there are several sidings at that point the two sides will each be subdivided into sections for each siding. These boxes can easily be made from stout card with thinner card for the subdividing pieces.

When we start an operating session the stock will normally be spread around the layout on various sidings and the card for each wagon will be in the box at the site at which the wagon is located. We can make up a train in the yard or fiddle yard by taking the required number of cards from the box there and then assembling the wagons concerned in the yard. On each card there will be a paper clip marking one of the destinations and the operator distributes the stock from the train into the indicated sidings as the train makes its journey along the line. On arrival at a siding for which his train has a wagon the driver looks in the box. If there is a card, or cards, in the departures section he removes this and then transfers any card in the arrivals section into the departures side. The card or cards for any wagons to be dropped at the siding he places in the arrivals side. After carrying out the necessary shunting to drop and pick up wagons as required, the driver takes his train on, together with the remaining cards from his original selection, plus the cards for any wagons he has picked up here. On the cards he picks up he moves the paper clips down to the next destination on the list. If it is on his route he can drop these wagons, if not he takes them through to the yard at the end of the journey where they will wait for a train in the other direction.

In fact there are quite a number of variations possible regarding picking up wagons. One frequently used is to only pick up wagons that are to travel in the direction of the train; others are left for the first train in the opposite direction. Some modellers like to pick up the same number of wagons at a siding as are dropped there; this has the advantage of balancing the stock around the layout automatically. Although on this system each wagon runs through the same pattern of distribution repeatedly, the clip being moved back to the top of the list when it reaches the bottom, the number of destinations on the cards will vary from wagon to wagon so there will be almost limitless variation in the way trains are made up, especially if there are a reasonable number of wagons and destinations. Variety can also be added by listing destinations in differing orders on the various cards.

Though this system is a fairly simple one I think you will find that it gives a sense of purpose to the running of goods trains on your layout. No longer are you just picking up a few wagons here and there as the mood takes you, and for no particular reason; instead you are moving wagons following the instructions given providing a fair representation of the real railway, responding to the needs of its customers.

One of the main criticisms of the card order systems is the need for the cards to be carried by the driver from place to place with the train, and the difficulty of marrying up a wagon with its card again if the two become separated. In fact these problems only really apply on large layouts with numerous wagons and with considerable actual distances between different parts of the layout. On a small layout a simple card order system, as described above, should be perfectly satisfactory. On some layouts, in an attempt to overcome the problems just mentioned, systems have been devised where the freight car itself carries either a slip of paper or a drawing pin, the head of which is coloured according to a code, which tells the operator where it is to go.

Cliff Young, a modeller living in Britain but modelling American prototype, uses a card and waybill system for freight operation based on one devised by an American modeller, Doug Smith, but modified to suit his own requirements. The system is more complicated than the simple one I described above but correspondingly is more flexible and realistic. He has given details of his system in an article in the November 1966 issue of *Railway Modeller* magazine and also in the recently published book *The Encyclopaedia of Model Railways* from Octopus Books Ltd, and I would recommend that readers interested in taking the subject further should consult his articles.

Loading and unloading

As we have already seen, for realism in the operation of a model railway layout we must give the impression that it is actually transporting people and goods from place to place, reproducing in miniature the function of the prototype. However, because our miniature railway workers cannot load and unload our wagons and vans for us, we do run into problems with appearances in this respect. So often on model railways we see a train arrive and shunt a wagon loaded with coal on to a siding, only to have the wagon taken away again by the next train still full of coal! With much of our rolling stock there is, of course, no difficulty. Though a few modellers do include passengers inside model coaches, it is not generally very noticeable whether coaches are full or empty so we can consider them as whichever we need according to the requirements of our timetable. And there is obviously nothing we can do to simulate passengers getting on and off the trains! Similarly with goods stock such as vans, tankers, cement wagons, salt wagons, and so on, the loaded and empty stock appears identical. If we wish to preserve the correct procedures we can shunt vans into a goods shed or under a canopy outside the door of a warehouse, tankers can be positioned alongside storage tanks, cement wagons beneath a hopper, and so on, where we can imagine loading or unloading is taking place without distorting realism too much.

The difficulty comes with open wagons, timber bolsters, flat wagons, and suchlike. Some modellers just load and unload openly by hand, ignoring appearances for the short time taken. If you are exhibiting your layout you may prefer to arrange things so this procedure takes place out of sight of the public. One possibility is to run the stock into a goods shed, warehouse or factory building which has no back so that you have access to the interior for loading and unloading without viewers being aware of this. Alternatively you may be able to run the stock on to a hidden siding or to the fiddle yard. Whatever you do, the process of loading and unloading is made much easier with specially made loads. For an open wagon, cut a rectangle of balsa or thick card to fit neatly into the top of the wagon. On top of this glue the coal, rock chippings, sand, barrels, sacks, boxes, or whatever other load you wish to represent. On the underside glue a small block of wood, of the right size to support the load at the correct level inside the wagon, at the centre. This arrangement makes it easy to remove the load; merely pressing on one end will cause it to tilt so that you can pick it up. Replacing the load is also easy and, of course, the loads can be used for different wagons provided the dimensions are the same.

A system which can be very realistic if we are modelling trains transporting bulk loads between two places, for example, ore being taken from a mine to a processing plant, is to have two trains which are identical, except for the fact that one has full wagons and the other empty wagons. With the arrangement of the tracks it appears that loaded trains are emerging from the mine and running into the processing plant, while the reverse is taking place with the empty trains.

There are also a number of working model loaders of various types now available as kits or ready-to-use models and, with these, wagons can actually be loaded and unloaded adding to the realism of operation. An example is the Faller Gravel Works complete with storage silos, working conveyor belts and operating hopper wagons.

Removable wagon load with narrow central support beneath false floor. Pressing at one end tilts load for easy removal.

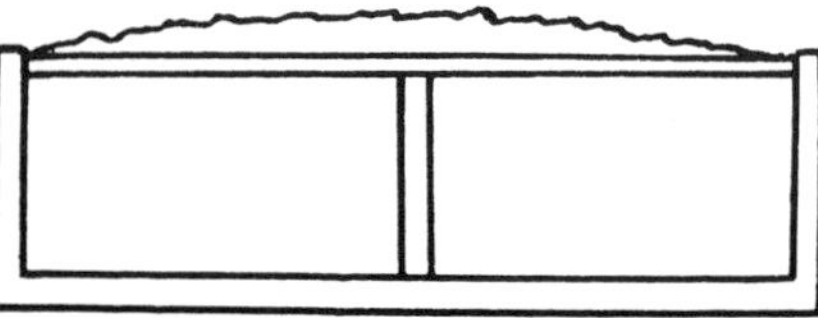

Above *The marshalling sidings of the hump shunting yard at the Tyne Yard. Though, obviously, considerable simplification and compression is necessary, an interesting and realistic hump yard can be included on a large or moderate sized model railway layout.* **Below** *A van passing through a retarder on the Tyne Yard hump yard.*

Two views of an operating model hump yard on a large HO-scale Fleischmann exhibition layout. **Top** *The hump itself is in the centre of this picture.* **Above** *The five marshalling sidings of the hump yard are shown in the right centre of this photograph. On this automatically operated layout, wagons are distributed at random on to these sidings.* **Below** *Part of the track plan of the HO-scale Fleischmann exhibition layout. The small black triangle near the left side indicates the site of the hump, the lap point (three-way) is labelled 227, and the five tracks of the marshalling yard are in the central part of the diagram.* (Courtesy of Fleischmann.)

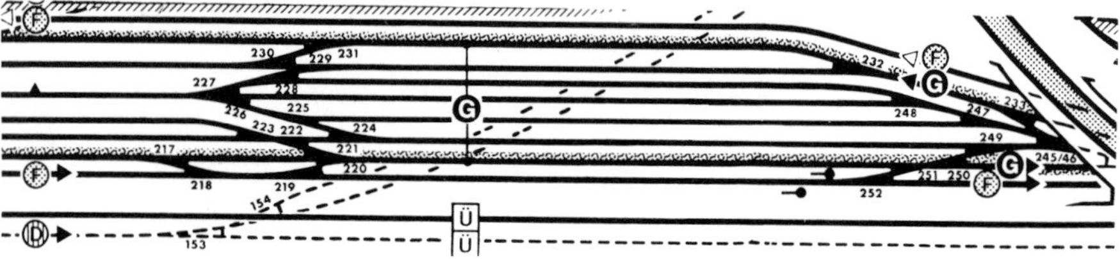

One of the most interesting aspects of the handling of freight traffic on modern prototype railways is the marshalling of wagons and vans in hump yards. Models of these yards are not often seen though the Reverend Edward Beal built one for his well-known West Midland layout nearly 30 years ago! Real hump yards occupy a great deal of space but considerable compression is possible for a model and, while one could not be included on a small layout, it would be possible to fit one in on a moderate sized home or club layout if desired. The accompanying photographs show an HO-scale working hump yard, automatically operated, on a large Fleischmann exhibition layout. An interesting point is that the yard was built entirely with standard Fleischmann parts. The single track passing over the hump has an uncoupler on the slope beyond the hump after which it divides into three by a lap point. The outer two tracks then divide again by ordinary turnouts giving a total of five marshalling sidings on which the trains are assembled. By means of contacts on the tracks, wagons passing along the tracks change the points for the following wagons.

Shunting competitions

With many systems the operating of a model railway layout can be considered as a form of game, with the challenge of keeping the layout running efficiently while overcoming any complications which arise or are deliberately introduced, all the time obeying the rules and trying to maintain realism. Part of the skill developed in operating relates to shunting, so that with practice the enthusiast becomes better both at planning his moves and at actually carrying them out smoothly, realistically and efficiently. Taking this a little further some modellers have produced small shunting modules designed to be used as a form of competitive game. One of the most successful of these was devised by John Allen, who was a very well-known American modeller. Basically the track plan is a run-around loop with a selection of sidings and the aim is to distribute a number of freight cars placed on the module in accordance with a pre-set plan. There are many different ways in which the module can be used and the game has proved very popular.

Often with puzzles of this sort the number of moves taken are counted but John Allen chose instead to arrange for a constant slow locomotive speed and for the competition to be carried out against the clock. Thus it is important to be quick rather than to take the least possible number of moves. Used in its original form the module was very interesting but a further development was to build a mirror image unit and to link the two, so that two people can operate, one on each module, at the same time. Though the two could compete against each other, the game is carried out with them trying to help each other so that their time is taken as the time for both to have completed the required moves.

Shunting games of this type have great potential for entertainment and also for practice in operation. Full details of John Allen's layout were given in the November 1972 issue of *Model Railroader* magazine and anyone contemplating building such a module might like to refer to that article.

Loading and unloading

Maintenance

If the model railway layout is to provide interesting, enjoyable and realistic operation it is essential that the models should work well. Even for very simple operation poor running, frequent derailments, coupling faults and other interruptions will spoil the fun and may well cause the modeller to lose interest. Most of the ready-to-run equipment now available is of very good quality, but, for continued good running, regular maintenance is necessary. Some modellers neglect such attention because they feel it will be an uninteresting and time-consuming chore, others, particularly beginners, because they do not know how to tackle the job. Undeniably on a large and complex layout a great deal of time must be spent on cleaning, checking, adjusting and repairing and this is one of the reasons why the beginner should be careful not to attempt to build too ambitious a model railway layout. If he does manage to complete such a model he may find that he has so much maintenance to do he has little time left to sit back and operate his railway. However, on a smaller, simpler layout even the beginner should be able to carry out these important tasks quickly and easily and there is no doubt that the enjoyment and satisfaction obtained from the consequent smooth, reliable running will more than compensate for the time and effort.

Obviously prevention is always better than cure, in railway modelling as well as in medicine! Much can be done to avoid future troubles by good initial construction and by care in handling, operating and storing locomotives, rolling stock, track, structures and other items. Care of your models is very important and right from the beginning, with the train set, it is worth getting into good habits. After all the standard of many ready-to-

Below *Maintenance vehicles are important on the full size railways. This SR two-car electric set is a rail cleaning and de-icing unit.* **Below right** *A re-railer makes the placing of rolling stock on the rails easier and is especially useful for N-gauge bogie rolling stock. Because it makes it easier to re-rail stock less handling is likely to be necessary and there is therefore less risk of accidental damage. In this picture an Eggerbahn re-railer is being used to place a Peco N-gauge tank wagon on the track.*

run models is now so good that you may well want to retain them for use on a scale layout. Alternatively, if you come to sell or exchange them you will get a better deal if they are in good condition and have clearly been properly looked after. With the train set, track and points can easily be broken, twisted or bent when setting up or dismantling the layout if due care is not taken. Do not hold pieces of track in mid air when fitting them together as this may lead to twisting and distortion of the pieces with consequent derailments. Instead, place the two track sections on a flat surface and slide them together. Never force together any pieces you are having difficulty with. Instead look carefully to see why they will not join up. Damage may also occur during storage between operating sessions, particularly if the models and track are just dumped into a large box, drawer or cupboard. The models can be conveniently and safely stored in their original boxes when not in use. Many manufacturers now include a pre-formed plastic packing piece into which the locomotive or item of rolling stock fits snugly within the box, and this helps to avoid damage. Alternatively, if the boxes are no longer available you can wrap the models in paper, preferably tissue paper, but newspaper will do, and pack them carefully into a box. Take special care not to damage couplings or wheels. Small detail fittings are also especially vulnerable. Pack track sections face to face in pairs in a box with the points on top. Slight, almost unnoticeable damage to or twisting of the track pieces may lead to troubles in running for which there is no apparent cause, so take the time and trouble to protect them during storage by proper packing. While considering the train set it is worth mentioning that, though you may have to lay the set out on the floor you should not put it down on carpet if you can avoid doing so because fluff and dirt from the carpet will quickly get on to the wheels and axles and into the mechanisms.

One of the major problems for the railway modeller is the dust so often present in the atmosphere. Airborne dust and dirt are a nuisance in many ways affecting both the appearance and the performance of a model railway layout. In most rooms a deposit of dust settles over a layout in a surprisingly short time, even if the layout is in fairly regular use. It is especially noticeable on locomotives and rolling stock but soon makes the scenery and structures appear grimy also. The real thing is, of course, exposed to dirt, grime, dust and rain giving a weathered look which we try hard to duplicate to make our models realistic, but unfortunately the dust which settles on the layout does not give this effect but instead merely looks dirty!

Dust also interferes with the smooth running of our models in various ways. Dirt from the air becomes trapped in the oil or grease used to lubricate gearboxes and bearings and causes wear while dust deposits on electrical contacts and on the rails interfere with current flow making operation erratic. We can tackle the problem in two basic ways; preventing dust from reaching the railway and removing any which does. Ideally, the layout should be in an atmosphere as free of dust as possible. However, most railway modellers are only too pleased to find anywhere to put a model railway and cannot afford to be too choosy about the room where they set up their layout. Often a bedroom is the only possibility and, unfortunately, is particularly bad from this point of view as the bedclothes give rise to a lot of dust and fluff, most of which seems to find

its way on to the layout! Even in the lounge there is a good deal of dust from the furnishings as people move about the room, sit in the chairs, draw the curtains, and so on. The ideal is a room set aside solely for the layout, but few of us are this fortunate. If you are lucky enough to have a model railway room, plastic or lino floor tiles or covering, rather than a carpet, will reduce the amount of dust. If you want to cover in the space beneath the layout, hardboard panels are a better choice than old curtain material which is likely to harbour dust and dirt. The room should be kept as clean as possible and any sanding, filing, sawing or other work which produces dust should, if possible, be done elsewhere. Some American modellers, more accustomed to air conditioning than we are in Britain, have experimented with fans and filter-blower units in an attempt to keep dust out of the layout room but such arrangements are more elaborate and expensive than most modellers would wish to consider using.

If we cannot exclude dust from the room we can try to keep it off the layout itself. The difficulty is that most model railways are rather large compared to other types of models. It is much easier for car, ship and military modellers, for example, to put their creations into small cases or into bookcases or cabinets to keep them away from dust and dirt. Cabinets or cases of this type, preferably with glass doors, can be ideal for storing locomotives and rolling stock safely away from dust and from the risk of damage. They are easily and quickly accessible when wanted for operating and, if the doors are fitted with glass, the models can be seen by the modeller and by visitors without the need for handling. A few modellers have built small enclosed layouts, usually in the form of coffee tables with glass tops, occasionally in glass cases. An example of a small layout built into a coffee table is the 009 narrow gauge model railway constructed by Mr K.J. Churms which was illustrated in *PSL Model Railway Guides 1* and *2.* Such an arrangement creates an interesting and attractive piece of furniture and also keeps most of the dust out. However, unless the layout is very carefully sealed up, a little dust will creep in and the model will require occasional cleaning.

Covering larger layouts is less convenient but is certainly desirable unless the room is relatively dust free. The easiest and cheapest method is probably to use a sheet of clear polythene. Some form of support to hold the sheet clear of the structures, scenery and details is desirable as otherwise they are likely to be damaged by the cover as it is fitted or removed. A convenient method is to use hoops bent up from wire and fitted on beneath the polythene. The cover will not be airtight so some dust will get under it, but it will help by keeping out most of the dust. The plastic will become dirty and should be washed from time to time. Covering and uncovering the layout for operating takes only a few minutes and is more than compensated for by the time saved in cleaning.

An even better scheme is some form of hinged lid which covers the layout when not in use but is easily raised for operation. Such an arrangement does require more work to construct and the materials needed will be more expensive. The details will depend on your layout size and shape. The Reverend Peter Denny constructed a very neat hinged cover for his Buckingham Branch layout some years ago using wood, hardboard and strawboard. His cover was counterweighted and was also fitted with lights, giving good illumination of the layout when in operation. A detailed description of the cover and its construction was given in the June 1961 issue of *Railway Modeller* magazine and I would recommend that you refer to this if you are considering making a cover of this type for your layout.

If the only place available for a model railway layout is in a room which is regularly used for other purposes such as the lounge, hall or a bedroom, an excellent arrangement is to build the layout into a piece of furniture such as a bookcase or a chest of drawers. The top can be hinged so that, when not in operation, the railway can be concealed by closing the lid, making the unit look like an ordinary piece of furniture. This system also protects the layout from accidental damage and, to a considerable extent, from dust and dirt. Ron Prattley has built a fine example of a bookcase containing an 00-gauge layout for his lounge. He made the lid removable so that it could be reversed to form an extension to the fixed part of the layout in the bookcase. The fiddle yard is a further detachable piece which fits as a drawer in the bookcase when the railway is not in use, and is illustrated in the *PSL Model Railway Guide 1: Baseboards, Track and Electrification.*

Another method sometimes employed by modellers who are short of space for a layout is to hinge the baseboard on to a wall or into a unit of furniture so that the railway can be folded down for operating and then swung up against the wall, or into the cabinet or cupboard out of the way when the running session is over. This scheme also has advantages from the point of view of keeping the layout clean as less dust will settle on it while it is standing on edge, particularly if it swings up into a unit of furniture so that there

Above *Harold Bowcott's 00-gauge layout is hinged on to the wall so that when not in use it can be stored folded up out of the way. This arrangement also helps to keep the layout clean as much less dust will settle on it in the vertical position. Shelves on the wall, arranged to fit into the operating well when the layout is folded up, provide storage for locomotives and rolling stock.* (Photograph by Brian Monaghan.) **Below** *A British Rail ballast cleaner. All the railway modeller needs is a vacuum cleaner and a soft brush!*

is a covering strip above it. Harold Bowcott has constructed an 00-gauge layout which is hinged on to the wall so that it can be folded up against it, thus taking up a minimum of space when not in use. This position also keeps most of the dust off the layout.

In addition to keeping as much dust and dirt as possible away from the layout it is also important to avoid extremes of temperature, direct sunlight and damp as these can cause damage, warping, fading of the colours, and even melting of plastic structures and other items. For these reasons, sites such as lofts, where temperatures may vary greatly, cellars, garages and garden sheds, all of which may be damp, should be considered carefully before building a layout there to make sure that conditions will be acceptable. All these locations are also inclined to be dirty and dusty unless properly finished inside.

For general cleaning of the layout a vacuum cleaner with a nozzle attachment fitted is ideal. There is no need to touch the layout with the nozzle, it can be held an inch or two above the surface thus avoiding the risk of damage. If you wish you can cover the nozzle end with wire mesh so that if any small details, such as figures, have become detached from the layout surface they will be caught by the mesh and not sucked up into the cleaner bag. A soft brush may be needed for more persistent dust, especially on structures. For locomotives and

Above *Eric Kay made this track cleaning wagon from an Atlas N-scale railroad car by drilling a hole in the floor to take the plastic nozzle and fixing a foam rubber pad beneath the floor. Track cleaning fluid poured into the nozzle soaks the pad and cleans the track as the car moves along the track. Lead weights fixed inside the car apply pressure on the pad.* **Below left** *This neat electric outline locomotive model is the Fleischmann N-scale track cleaning locomotive.* **Below right** *This view of the underside of the Fleischmann N-scale track cleaning locomotive clearly shows the two pads which clean the rails as the model runs on the track.*

rolling stock a small soft brush is useful for cleaning ; a convenient brush to use is one of the type sometimes employed for cleaning camera lenses and interiors in which the brush is combined with a rubber puffer so that dust in crevices can be blown out. This enables easy cleaning without risk of damage to small details. Even with fairly regular cleaning of the scenery the colours tend to become dull and dingy after a while and repainting may be necessary eventually. Lichen used for modelling bushes and trees may become brittle in time and it is then likely to crumble if touched. Its pliability can be restored by spraying it with a mixture of one part glycerine to three parts of water.

Track cleaning is especially important as it affects operation as well as appearance. Regular running of the trains does much to help keep the rails clean on their running surfaces, but most of us cannot run our trains often enough for this alone to be sufficient. In addition we will need to clean the rails with a little solvent fairly regularly to remove oil and dirt. The solvent can be methylated spirits or one of the commercially available track cleaners on the market. It can be applied with a soft piece of cloth or with a track cleaning wagon. Several manufacturers produce model wagons or vans which actually clean the track, either by means of a foam pad or by one or two rotating pads beneath the vehicle. In addition Fleischmann make a track cleaning locomotive in N gauge. Some modellers use WD 40 for

track cleaning and this is effective but, as it is a little oily, it should be kept off the track surroundings. For more vigorous cleaning, perhaps when the layout has not been run for some time, a track cleaning rubber such as that made by Peco can be employed. Do not use abrasives such as sandpaper or emery cloth as these will leave scratches on the rails which predispose to the accumulation of more dirt with a recurrence of the problems. Points should also be carefully cleaned including the backs of the blades and stock rails to ensure good electrical contact. Make sure that there is no dirt or loose ballast preventing full movement of the point blades. Remove any fluff which is caught up on the rails and brush away any dust. Also check the frog for any build up of dirt deposits. When cleaning the track check also for any loose track pins, any loss of alignment at track joins and for loose fishplates, and carry out any repairs needed.

A recently introduced device which maintains good electrical conduction, even if the track is dirty, is the Relco High Frequency Generator. This unit uses high frequency superimposed on the normal supply to ionise the gap due to dirt on the track and restore electrical contact. The device converts the 12-volt DC input into high frequency AC only when the circuit is broken, burning away the dirt and restoring conductivity. The normal DC current then flows again. The generator is easily wired into the layout input and is perfectly safe to use.

It is also worth mentioning that the Multiple Train Control systems now on the market from Airfix and Hornby are less affected by dirty track than the conventional system because of the higher voltage employed and because it is constantly applied. On the ordinary 12-volt DC system the actual voltage applied is often much lower than 12 volts. I understand that the Relco HF Generator must not be used with the Multiple Train Control systems.

The full benefits of track cleaning will not be realised unless you also clean the wheels of your locomotives and rolling stock. Dirt collects on locomotive wheels and interferes with electrical pick-up; it can also spread from

Top right *When the layout has not been operated recently the use of a track cleaning rubber such as that made by Peco is an effective way of cleaning the rails.* **Above right** *A pipe cleaner with the tip dipped into methylated spirits or other track cleaner is useful for cleaning points.* **Right** *A Relco HF Generator for track cleaning.*

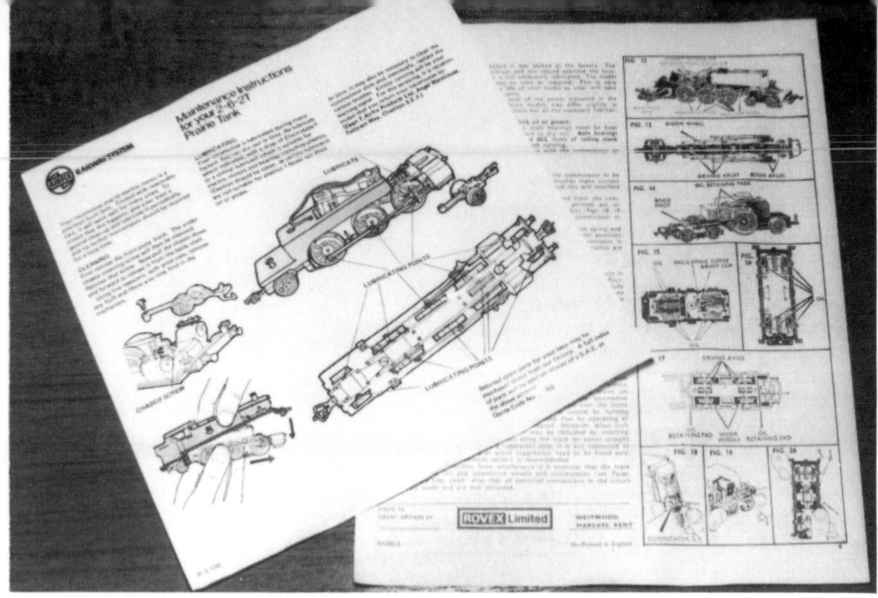

Above *The manufacturers issue instruction sheets for their locomotives and other models detailing how lubrication and maintenance should be carried out and the modeller should study the relevant information carefully. The examples shown here are from Airfix and Hornby.* **Right** *A van derailed at Gävle on the Swedish State Railway system. When any incident of this type occurs on the prototype railways a careful check is made to determine the cause. On a model railway layout we need not be so painstaking but if repeated derailments occur at the same spot or with the same piece of rolling stock then some investigation is called for.*

the wheels on to the track. For cleaning locomotive driving wheels Peco make a wheel cleaning brush and scraper set which is very effective. The wires from the brush and scraper are connected either to the 12-volt power unit terminals or to the track and, when the brush and scraper are applied to the driving wheels, one on each side, the wheels rotate making cleaning easy and effective. Sometimes scraping with a small screwdriver is necessary to remove firmly adherent dirt. On rolling stock wheels the dirt has less direct effect on running but it will spread on to the track so cleaning the rolling stock wheels is also important. Gentle scraping with a small screwdriver is the most effective method. Also look for fluff and hairs wound round axles and in bearings on both locomotives and rolling stock and remove them with a needle point and a pair of fine tweezers.

Generally locomotive mechanisms require relatively little attention and, if running well, they should, for the most part, be left well alone. Most are ready to run when purchased and do not even need oiling. In fact, many more problems arise from over oiling model locomotives than from them having insufficient lubrication. It is particularly important to avoid getting oil onto the commutator or brushes of the motor. The correct type of oil should be used; do not use thick oil or grease. Some oils can damage plastic so it is advisable to use one of the oils especially marketed for railway modelling such as Peco Electrolube. The instruction leaflets provided by the manufacturer will indicate the lubricating points on the locomotive concerned and you should follow the advice given in these instructions. Only apply a tiny drop of oil at each point. These include the axle bearings, the coupling rod pins, valve gear pivots, and the felt oil retaining pads on the armature shaft bearing.

From time to time it may be necessary to clean the slots between the segments of the commutator as carbon from the brushes accumulates here and interferes with smooth running. To do this the brush pressure on the commutator is relieved or the brushes are removed and a wooden toothpick can then be used to remove the deposit. It is important not to scratch the surface of the commutator or the armature windings. Any oil on the commutator should be wiped off with a clean rag. If the brushes are worn they can be replaced at this time.

If you are in any doubt about your ability to carry out any of these jobs do take the model to your local dealer rather than risk causing damage. Always read the instruction leaflets carefully before doing anything to your model locomotives. Never take them apart just for the sake of it if they are running satisfactorily and never remove the magnet from the motor as it will lose its power unless it is kept in contact with a keeper all the time.

If a locomotive will not run, though it has operated satisfactorily previously, this may be due to there being no power to the track or to a fault in the locomotive or its electrical pick-up. A simple means of checking for a fault in the supply to the track is to try another locomotive on the same piece of track. If this will not run either make sure that the power is actually switched on and that there are no loose connections between the power unit and the track. Also check that the fishplates are tight and providing proper electrical contact. Never fiddle with the mains side of the power unit and never open the power unit casing, as accidents with the mains supply can be fatal. If you suspect a fault here take the unit to your local dealer for expert advice.

If the track is not at fault we need to check the locomotive. Remove the body and apply wires from the 12-volt DC output of the power unit direct to the brushes, one to each. The motor will then usually run. If so, then the current is not reaching the motor from the track and this may be due to dirty wheels, a pick-up not in contact with its wheel, or a lead which has come loose. It is usually fairly easy to spot which of these is the cause. If, when the wires are applied to the brushes, the motor moves only slightly, it suggests that the problem is mechanical, either due to binding or breakage, or due to hairs and fluff wound round the axles and bearings. If there is no sign of life in the motor when the wires are applied and the brushes are in good condition, then it would appear to be the motor which is at fault and you will need to take the model to your local dealer for attention.

The best way of maintaining your model railway in good working order, with a minimum of effort, is to carry out the necessary servicing and repairs regularly. If you set aside part of an operating session each week or two for these jobs you will find that only a short time will usually be required, whereas if you let too many jobs accumulate, you will be in for a long session when you eventually get round to attending to them. In the meantime your railway will not be running as well as it should.

Some modellers like to keep a notebook to list any faults which they notice during operating sessions so that they do not forget them when they have a maintenance and repair session. One system which has advantages, especially on a large layout with several operators, is to have some way of marking points on the track at which derailments occur and the locomotives or stock concerned. If several markers accumulate at one point on the track it suggests that there is a fault here and that the derailments were not just unlucky isolated incidents. Similarly, if one engine or wagon collects several markers it would seem that a careful check for the fault is indicated. The necessary repairs or adjustments to the track, locomotives or wagons can then be carried out.

Exhibiting your layout

I am always impressed by the number of model railway exhibitions which are staged, mostly by the many clubs and societies throughout the country, each year. Though some of these shows are disappointing because of poor choice of layouts or bad organisation, most are successful and provide a great deal of pleasure and entertainment, both for model railway enthusiasts and for other members of the general public who visit the shows. It can also be very enjoyable and satisfying for the railway modeller to participate in such exhibitions by showing his or her own layout.

To provide the greatest possible interest the organisers should try to bring together a good variety of different types of layouts, large and small, of differing prototypes, standard and narrow gauge, of different scales, and so on. They should also try to achieve a reasonable balance so that all the visitors will find something of particular interest to them. It is also desirable that the organisers should ensure that all the layouts are of a good standard and that they have not appeared in the same area too often without alterations or additions having been made. When members of the public are paying for entry I do feel that they have a right to expect that the layouts on display will not be inferior and will not be largely the same ones as at the previous show! It is also important for the club in question in the long term, both for recruitment and for success in staging future shows, that the standards be kept up.

In general the layouts shown fall into two categories, personal and club layouts. The former are usually designed and built purely for the owners' enjoyment and the idea of exhibiting only arises much later. However, some individual modellers have constructed personal layouts with shows in mind. In some cases lack of space at home makes it difficult to operate a model railway and they concentrate more on construction there, taking the opportunity to indulge in some interesting operation while at exhibitions. An example of such a model is Keith Gowen's 'Market Redwing' TT-gauge branch line layout which has been regularly and successfully exhibited in recent years. Keith has little space for a layout

Below *A view of Keith Gowen's TT-gauge branch line layout which was built for exhibition use.* **Right** *A scene on the Bridport branch 00-gauge layout built by the Model Group of the Brooklands Railway Society. Note the effective backscene which not only makes the layout appear larger but also serves to conceal the operators. The road overbridge neatly hides the exit of the track through the backscene to reach the fiddle yard.* **Below right** *A neatly lettered name board completes the exhibition presentation of the Brooklands Railway Society Model Group 00-gauge Bridport branch layout.*

at home so he planned his model railway for exhibition use. The layout was designed so that the four sections which make it up are easy to transport and assemble, and so that they can be conveniently stored in a large cupboard at his home when not in use.

Club layouts are often built specifically for exhibition use by the members. Whether or not the layout was designed for show purposes there are some points to be considered. The layout should be an operating model railway and it should work well. There is a place for static models at exhibitions but layouts should be seen in action. It is preferable that the layout should appear to be complete even if further work is, in fact, still to be carried out later. So, if you have been invited to exhibit your layout this is a good reason for completing any areas of scenery that are as yet unfinished, for building any missing structures, and for adding figures and other details to bring your layout to completion. A possible exception is if you have a particular construction method, for example for scenery, and you wish to show how this is carried out, perhaps as a series of step by step stages. However, this would probably be best shown as a separate static display in conjunction with your layout, rather than leaving parts of the layout unfinished.

When a layout is on show the presentation is important. Though the surface of the layout may have been properly coloured, detailed and finished, the edges, the framing of the baseboard, may have been left as bare wood. If so a better appearance will result if these edges, after any necessary filling and sanding, are painted with matt black paint. This gives a neat but unobtrusive finish. If your layout lacks a scenic background consider installing one. It will give an impression of greater depth and realism to your scenery and, if you will be operating from behind the layout, the backscene will partly conceal you from the viewers. A backdrop can also be useful for hiding a fiddle yard from view.

Also part of the presentation is a neat name board for your railway. You may also like to provide some explanatory information about

the layout and perhaps a track plan. If your model is based on a particular prototype line, for example a branch line, you might like to feature a display of photographs of the real thing to show visitors what you have modelled. If you are running the layout to a timetable or are following a sequence of operation during the exhibition you may wish to have a copy of the timetable mounted beside the layout so that members of the public can follow the movements that are taking place at any particular time. Prior to the show you will probably be asked to provide some details of your layout and perhaps a track plan for inclusion in the official printed exhibition guide or handbook. Try to cover the things which you would like to know about the layout if it belonged to someone else when you write these brief notes about the model.

If you are invited to show your layout at an exhibition, check on its transportability well before the date of the show. Can it be carried in sections in a car or estate car or will it be necessary to borrow or hire a small van? If you own a car and are planning to build a layout it may be worth while designing it in sections which will fit into your car. If you do not take your layout down very often, try a few practice runs of taking the sections apart and reassembling them so that the process will be quick and easy when you come to set it up at the show. Constructing the layout so that fragile items such as structures and details can be removed for transportation or storage will help to avoid damage. If you do this keep the removable items in boxes or cartons so that they do not get mislaid when not on the layout. The Mid Hants Model Railway Group's exhibition model of the Watlington Branch in EM gauge is a portable layout on which almost all the structures and details, such as telegraph poles, lamps, figures, road vehicles, and so on, can be removed for moving or storing the layout. Each human figure has a wire fitted beneath one foot which fits into a suitably placed hole in the platform or other surface. It is also important to have some means of carrying your locomotives and rolling stock safely to and from the exhibition. This may simply be a cardboard box within which the individual models are placed after wrapping in tissue paper or after putting into their original boxes. If you anticipate attending a number of shows it is worth taking the time to make a wooden carrying case fitted with partitions in appropriate positions and lined with foam rubber to protect the models.

The Mid Hants Model Railway Group model of the Watlington branch in EM gauge is a portable layout and many of the small details, such as the human figures and the telegraph pole in this view of the station approach, together with the structures, are detachable for storage and transport.

It is a good idea to keep the electrical arrangements for your layout as neat and tidy as possible. This will make it easier to set up and there will be less risk of people getting snagged by the wiring with the danger of disconnecting or damaging it. As you may need assistance from club members in running your layout, particularly when you want to have a break so that you can have a meal or visit the rest of the show, it is helpful if your control arrangements are straightforward and clearly labelled. Thus another operator taking over will be able to run the layout without too much difficulty and without the need for elaborate instructions.

At some exhibitions the lighting is poor. Often the hall is a hired one, not equipped with suitable lighting and there may be little the club can do to provide better illumination. Poor lighting may make it difficult for the visitors to see the detail work on your layout properly and can also give the impression that it is dull and lifeless instead of doing justice to your realistic colouring. It is well worth while fitting effective lights to your layout if you plan to attend a few exhibitions; the lights may also be useful when running the model railway at home. Effective lighting can do a great deal to enhance a model railway but it is an aspect of presentation that

Above *Dick Wyatt has several bright lights which he fixes above the corners of his narrow-gauge layout at shows. These enable the beautifully detailed and coloured scenery and structures to be seen to full advantage. These two pictures were taken at an exhibition and the excellent even illumination is evident.* **Below** *The control panel of the Mid Hants Model Railway Group EM-gauge model of Watlington station is neatly laid out and fully labelled, making it easy for operators, even those who do not regularly run the layout.*

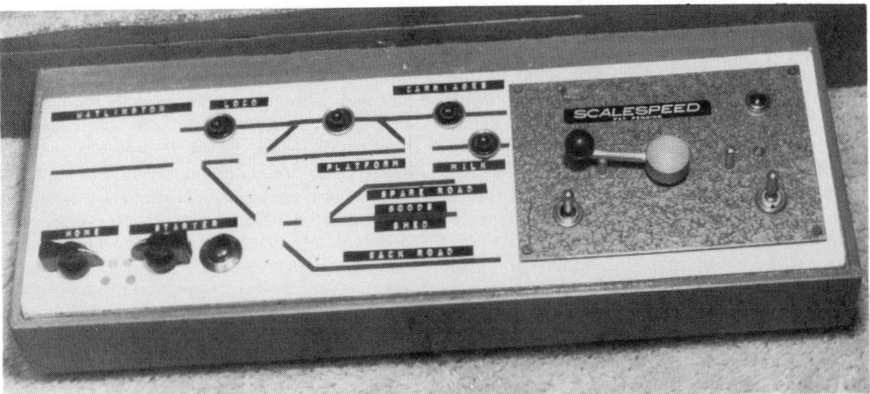

Plate glass or perspex panels provide effective protection for a layout at shows without interfering with viewing, as on this exhibition layout owned by Hestair Models. The top edge of the screen is just visible in this picture as a white line across the lower part.

is often rather neglected. As a temporary exhibition measure even a couple of adjustable reading lamps can be of use on a small layout if positioned to illuminate important parts of the model. An ideal arrangement is to fit fluorescent strip lighting over your layout as this gives even illumination, but this is more suitable for home use than at exhibitions.

At shows there are inevitably visitors usually, though not always, children, who seemingly must touch everything, including your layout, with the risk of damage to small details. Efforts are made at exhibitions to keep the public from getting too close to the layouts, often by putting a row of chairs in front of each layout. This can be reasonably effective but it is difficult to stop children from moving or climbing onto the chairs. If you are planning to attend several shows as an exhibitor you may feel it is worth the effort and cost of fitting perspex panels along the front edge of the layout. These panels of perspex, thick enough to be rigid, should be about 10 or 12 inches high and are very effective in preventing handling of the layout by the public but do not interfere with viewing. They are best fixed in place with screws along the lower edges so that they can be fitted for shows but easily removed when the layout is again set up at home.

Operating models such as cranes, windmills, watermills, and so on seem popular with visitors to model railway shows and you might consider installing one or more on your layout. Some modellers feel that models of this type are inappropriate on a scale model railway layout, regarding them as gimmicky and toy-like. However the kits available are generally well detailed and realistic models and the extra movement and interest which these working models can add to the scene are of benefit, particularly on a small layout where the train operating potential may be rather limited.

I have already mentioned that it is important to check and prepare the locomotives, rolling stock and track on your layout beforehand so that operation will be as smooth and reliable as possible during the exhibition. Conditions at shows are often unfavourable because of dust and dirt, humidity, and so on. If the show lasts more than one day it is a good idea to clean the track before starting operation each day.

Rather than run the trains at random it is much better to have some system of operation for exhibitions. Haphazard running of the trains may give a toy-like impression to the visitors whereas systematic operation will create a much more realistic effect. Rather than have to decide what you are going to do on the spur of the moment, have a simple sequence arranged and practised beforehand. Try to make this series of train movements interesting and authentic so that visitors will find them realistic and will want to see what happens next. Keep the sequence fairly simple and make sure that you are really familiar with it so that with the distractions of the exhibition you can still remember what you are doing and what you

Above *Operating models add interest and are particularly beneficial on a small layout. This interesting working lift bridge was built from a Pola/Hornby kit. The bridge spans the entrance to a small harbour on an 00-gauge layout.* **Below** *A scene on the Bridport branch 00-gauge layout built by the Model Group of the Brooklands Railway Society. The attractive scenery has been realistically blended with the back scene giving a very spacious effect. Note the card system indicating to viewers the train movements which are taking place. As each is completed the card is flipped over to reveal the next.*

should do next! It is helpful to have a card or a series of cards on which the moves are clearly printed to use as an aid to memory and for the benefit of any assistants or relief operators who are not familiar with operating the layout. The interest of your model railway for the viewers will be enhanced if it is made clear to those watching what train movements are taking place. A convenient method is to have a series of cards with the moves on them. These cards are mounted in a suitable place arranged so that, as each move is completed, the card concerned can be flipped up to reveal the next. Keith Gowen uses this scheme with a convenient variation. In addition to the information on the front of each card intended for the viewer, there are details on the rear for the operator. Any sequence should not be too long so that it can be completed reasonably quickly. There can then be a pause before it is repeated. During this natural break spectators will move away making room for others to take their places to see the layout in action. Equally important, it gives an opportunity for visitors to ask questions and to talk to the operators.

Exhibitions have an important role to play in public relations for railway modelling in encouraging people to take up the hobby and

Opposite *Two views of Graham Lindley's attractive 009-gauge 'Lydd Valley' layout. The track plan includes a through station and hidden sidings used as a fiddle yard. The layout is designed to link up with one built by a friend for exhibition purposes.* **This page** *The Greenwich & District NGRS 009-layout provides excellent publicity for the preserved 2 foot 3 inch gauge Talyllyn Railway in Mid Wales.* **Above** *The Wharf Station is an accurate replica of the prototype, complete even to the locomotive and slate wagon on static display outside the museum building.* **Below** *Pendre, where the sheds and workshops are situated, is not an exact model but does capture the atmosphere of the real thing.*

in helping less experienced modellers. You will find this contact very interesting, enjoyable and satisfying and often you can pick up new ideas and information yourself. If there is some particular feature of your layout which is unusual or of special interest you may find that there are numerous comments and questions about it. For example, Graham Lindley has found that so many visitors are interested in the method of modelling grass on his 009 Lydd Valley layout that he now takes a sample of the grass matting he used to show to those visitors who enquire about the construction technique.

An idea which has great potential, but which has been little exploited so far, is the use of a taped commentary to accompany and explain the operation of the layout. Not only does this indicate to the audience what movements are taking place and why, making operation more interesting for them, but the commentary can also be a useful guide for the operator. The idea has much to recommend it, particularly as so many modellers must surely own or have access to cassette recorders now. The only modeller that I know of who has employed this technique is the Reverend Awdry, well known not only for his railway modelling but also for his very popular children's books. If the large crowd gathered around his layout throughout the show is any indication, the commentary was very popular with the visitors!

Models are always very effective in attracting public interest and attention and the railway preservation societies are finding that models of stations on their lines are an excellent form of publicity. Not only can the model show the station or line as it is today but it can also show planned future developments, and in a much more effective way than plans or drawings. In this way the general public can get a very clear idea of what the society is trying to achieve and they are more likely to support the preservation and restoration work with donations or with offers of voluntary work. If you are a member of one of the preservation societies a very interesting and useful project for you to undertake could be the modelling of part of the railway for exhibition purposes.

Railway modelling is a hobby and the important thing is to enjoy your participation. For your own personal modelling you should feel that you can please yourself what you do. It should not become a chore and, if you do not feel like modelling at any particular time, then you should give it a miss. However, when you agree to show your layout you have a commitment to be ready on time and to put on a good show. You should not back out without very good reason as the organisers are depending on you. Be sure when you agree to attend that all the details of where and when the exhibition will be held are clear. Check on whether you will be paid expenses for travelling, if accommodation has been arranged if necessary, and so on.

Modellers often do not realise the value of their layouts and of their locomotives and rolling stock, having built them up gradually, and are particularly prone to underestimate the amount of work which would be involved in replacement. When exhibiting your layout the risks of theft, damage or loss are inevitably increased and it is important to consider the matter of insurance. Sometimes the exhibition organisers arrange insurance cover for all the models involved but you should check on this and, if none is provided, consider obtaining your own.

Branch line railways

Michael Andress

Contents

Introduction

Railway modelling is perhaps the most popular of all constructional hobbies and part of the attraction must surely be the very wide scope which the hobby offers. Though I have dabbled in various other modelling hobbies I have yet to find one which has such diversity of construction and operation. Much of the lasting appeal of modelling railways comes from the fact that, after we have built or bought models which are accurate replicas of the real locomotives and rolling stock, we can run them in a manner which realistically duplicates the operation of prototype railways. Because we do not just have models of individual locomotives, coaches, wagons, structures and so on, but create a whole unified system, the model railway is much more interesting. In addition the layout will be different from that constructed by any other modeller even though many of the individual parts may be the same. Thus one creates one's own unique model railway and this increases the satisfaction and enjoyment of the hobby.

For the many beginners who take up railway modelling each year a very important step is the construction of their first scale model railway layout. Ideally, this should be a layout which will be interesting to build and operate but which will not demand too much in the way of skill, time and money so that there is every chance of it being successfully completed before the initial enthusiasm and interest are lost

An excellent choice is a branch line model. Such a layout will give the novice the opportunity to try out all aspects of construction work—baseboard building, tracklaying, structure modelling, scenery construction,

An attractive branch line scene modelled in 4 mm scale by Terry Jenkins. The typical GWR halt station is a John Day Models plastic kit and the locomotive is the Airfix 1400 Class 0-4-2T.

and, if he or she wishes, locomotive and rolling stock modelling—in a small area and at relatively little cost. When completed the model railway can be operated in a realistic and authentic manner. Thus a branch line layout can provide useful experience in construction together with continued operating enjoyment.

In this book my aim is to introduce the subject of branch line modelling to the beginner and to point out some of the advantages and disadvantages of such a choice. I also want to look at typical arrangements for branch line layouts and to consider the alternatives of accurately following a specific prototype and of merely basing the model more generally on one company or area. A selection of branch line layouts in various popular scales are included to show the reader how different modellers have tackled the subject and to give the beginner ideas for his or her own layout. Finally I have taken three prototype branch lines which are still in operation today to show how each could be used as the basis of a layout. Alternatively features from them could be included in other layouts.

The ideas and information presented here are not for the most part new or original but are based on the work of many modellers, the development of branch line modelling to its present state having taken place over a period of some 30 years. Because an idea devised by one person may be modified, developed and improved by others it is often difficult to know just who first thought up any particular scheme. Modellers such as the late John Ahern (Madder Valley Railway), the Reverend Peter Denny (Buckingham Branch) and Maurice Deane (Culm Valley Branch) have been leaders in branch line modelling and I am grateful to them for the information, enjoyment and inspiration I have received from reading about their models. Much credit is also due to Cyril Freezer, now Editor of *Model Railways* magazine. As the idea of modelling branch lines has developed he has presented the concepts involved with clarity and enthusiasm and his many excellent layout plans based on these principles are ideal for the modeller wanting to build a layout of this type.

I would like to thank all those modellers who have kindly allowed me to use photographs of their work to illustrate this book. In particular I am grateful to Graham Bailey, Harold Bowcott, Alan Copas, Allan Downes, Keith Gowen, Terry Jenkins, Betty Kay, the members of the Mid Hants Model Railway Group, Brian Monaghan and Mike Sharman. I would also like to thank John Brewer, Editor of *Railway Modeller* magazine, for permission to reproduce the photographs of Harold Bowcott's layout.

Prototype branches

We should perhaps, at this early stage, decide just what we mean by a branch line, both in general prototype terms and in the more limited definition usually applied for modelling purposes. Strictly speaking a branch line is any line which diverges from the main line and this category includes even major routes. These latter are double tracked, and in appearance and in operation are virtually identical to the main line. As on the main route the trains will be long and hauled by heavy locomotives.

However, when we speak of modelling branch lines we usually refer to the short, single track, country branch serving a small seaside or country town, perhaps with one or more small intermediate stations or halts. Such lines proliferated in those optimistic days when the railway network was spreading over the whole country and when every small town was anxious to be linked to the railway system for the increased trade and prosperity it was hoped would result. Some of these branches were built by the many small independent companies which were formed and were later taken over by the larger concerns; others were backed from the outset by the main line companies. Many of the branches were successful and profitable, especially when there were local trades and industries to provide traffic and where the new line formed the most convenient link to the main routes enabling passengers and produce to reach their destinations easily. For other lines it was a struggle for survival from the beginning. Often the stations were built to be large enough to cope with the amount of traffic the promoters optimistically assumed would develop, but which in many cases did not. At seaside towns and in holiday areas facilities were provided for the peak traffic of the summer period but the income from this was not sufficient to make up for the lack of passengers during the rest of the year.

Though the branch line closures from the 'Beeching Axe' were the most dramatic and most familiar to the general public they were by no means the first. The best years for these lines were before the First World War and there has been a steady decline since then. The increasing numbers of cars, lorries and buses appearing on the roads provided competition for the railways and the branch lines were particularly affected. For reasons of economy some stations had been built at a distance from the towns and villages they served so that passengers had a long walk at the end of their rail journey. The bus could offer a much more convenient service at a lower fare. Thus even in the 1920s many lines had already had to cut back on their services, and there were many closures in the 1930s. After the Second World War British Railways continued to reduce

Rural branch line atmosphere preserved at Buckfastleigh on the Dart Valley Railway where a train waits to leave for Totnes. (Photograph by David Andress.)

Surviving branch lines now employ diesel or electric multiple units for passenger services. This two-coach EMU was photographed recently on the Lymington Branch (Southern Region) between the Pier and Town stations.

country branch line services and this was later accelerated with the policies of rationalisation and economy.

Those branches which survived these cutbacks were streamlined for greater efficiency and economy. Sidings, passing loops and any other now unnecessary tracks have been lifted, and in some cases the line has been kept open only as far as one of the intermediate stations. On some branches traffic is now limited to passengers and the goods facilities have been closed. Other branches have been kept open for bulk freight of some type but the unprofitable passenger services have been abandoned. The lines which still carry passengers usually do so in diesel or electric multiple units (DMUs or EMUs) and there have been big reductions in staffing.

The great disadvantage of modern branch lines from the modelling point of view is the very limited operational scope, and ideally the lines are best modelled in the days of steam, preferably at a time when there was still a good deal of traffic, both passenger and goods, so that operation will be interesting. The most suitable choice for the beginner is the short, single track, feeder branch line, the classic country branch. However, if more space is available, the longer single track branch with its intermediate stations, longer trains, greater variety of locomotives and rolling stock and more interesting timetable, has much to offer. Another type of branch line, also interesting but less often modelled, is the cross country link between two main routes. These branches may be single or double track and while some have only light traffic, others are more similar to a main line in their operation. Suburban branches are rarely modelled; most are still in use but are now operated with DMUs or EMUs. Traffic can be intensive but such lines are more suited to the experienced modeller rather than the beginner. A further category of branch line is the industrial branch, built to serve one or a number of industries. Traffic on such lines may be almost entirely limited to one type of bulk load, coal, iron ore, clay, oil and so on, or may be mixed, with the line serving a variety of different industries or a dock area. Though the country branch is usually regarded as the best choice for the modeller, particularly the beginner, one of the smaller industrial branches can also be a good basis for an interesting layout.

There are many books covering various aspects of prototype branch lines. Most of these describe particular branches or areas and are invaluable if you are modelling the line concerned. However there are also some more general books which will give the reader a good idea of how the branch lines came into being, what they were like in their heyday, how they operated and how they changed over the years. Younger readers who did not have the opportunity to visit the lines in steam days will find that these books can give them some of the atmosphere and feel of the country branches. Older readers will enjoy the memories the books bring back! Three books I have found interesting and informative are *Branch Lines* by O.S. Nock, *British Branch Lines* by H.A. Vallance and *The Country Railway* by David St John Thomas. The first two are out of print, though I have seen them both on sale second hand recently so you may come across them. You should certainly be able to borrow them through your local library. Though such books may not provide any specific information that you will need for your own layout, reading them will give you a familiarity with the subject and will fill in the background in a way which will help you to create a realistic branch line layout.

Why model branch lines?

In the early days of railway modelling the emphasis was very much on the locomotives, rolling stock and track, with lineside features limited to a few structures such as station buildings and platforms, signal boxes and engine sheds. The 'scenery' was often no more than a railway poster or two behind the tracks. The rest was provided by the enthusiast's imagination which also allowed him to run main line trains of only three or four coaches to a 'Euston' with only two platforms quite happily! During the 1940s with the increasing popularity of 00 scale and under the influence of various modellers of whom John Ahern was outstanding, the idea of creating a realistic miniature landscape for the railway to run through and serve became widely accepted. This emphasis on realism also meant that the caricature of a main line terminus with platforms only long enough for three coach trains had to go!

Because we are modelling a whole system rather than just a few separate items which could be displayed on shelves or in a cabinet we must find space to accommodate our layout. The problem of finding adequate space is often emphasised but there are other factors which must also be taken into account. To complete a model railway there are many models to be constructed or purchased and time and money will be required. Thus when planning a layout we must consider not only the space available to accommodate it but also the amount of time and money we can afford and how long a period we are prepared to let the construction of the layout take. Obviously there is no point in planning a large and complex system if there is space for only a very small layout. What is often less evident to the beginner is the heavy commitment in hours of work and in cost involved in the building of a large model railway. It is essential not to be too ambitious in the choice of a first layout.

If we want to build a model railway that is as realistic as possible within these restrictions of space and of outlay in terms of time and money we must look for a suitable prototype. The country branch line, especially in the days of steam, has much to recommend it as a choice. The passenger trains often consisted of only two or three coaches pulled by a small tank engine, or were short push-pull trains, so that we can model trains of realistic length even on a small layout. Goods trains were also short but often had an interesting variety of rolling stock. Station layouts were usually fairly simple with only a limited number of points permitting economy both in space and in the cost of the trackwork. An attractive branch line type of layout can be developed easily from the train set and it can be an ideal first permanent scale layout with considerable scope for attractive scenery and structures.

During the 1950s the branch line model railway concept was developed considerably. At that time the idea was not so much to provide a suitable subject for beginners as to enable more experienced modellers to create a model railway which would look realistic and operate in an authentic manner within the confines of a small space. The short prototype trains allowed the modeller to run scale length trains despite the small size of his layout. Because the station track layouts are simple on branch lines they can be compressed to fit onto a model railway while still retaining their essential features so that the model can be operated according to prototype practice and following a proper timetable.

Because the aim was realistic operation, the point-to-point track arrangement, which represents the prototype railway running from one town to another, was generally preferred to the continuous run schemes typical of the train set. To provide the greatest interest in the least possible space, attention was concentrated on the branch line terminus and the now classic branch line terminus to fiddle yard design was developed. The fiddle yard consists of hidden sidings representing the rest of the railway system and on which trains can be rearranged by hand. Such a track plan can be fitted onto baseboards of various shapes but a popular arrangement is on two narrow baseboards

The atmosphere of a country branch line terminus, together with the village it serves, faithfully captured in miniature by the expert modelling of Allan Downes. The superbly realistic buildings were all scratch-built. The scale is 4 mm to the foot. (Photographs by Brian Monaghan.)

joined to form an L shape and often fitted into the corner of a room. This design has the advantage of giving the greatest running possibilities in a minimum area and often a layout of this shape can be accommodated in a room whereas a conventional rectangular baseboard would not be acceptable as it would block the centre of the room too much.

When the idea of modelling a branch line terminus was first put forward there was very little in the way of ready-to-run equipment and kits available. Thus the choice of a layout for which relatively little track and few points were required and which could be operated realistically with only one locomotive, two or three coaches and a few wagons meant that, even though most of the items needed had to be hand built, the layout could be completed within a reasonable length of time. In the years since then there has been a dramatic change in the availability of ready-to-run models and kits and in the standards of accuracy and detail of these models. Nowadays the beginner can go into a model railway stockist and buy off the shelf the locomotives needed for a branch line layout without difficulty, especially in 00 scale. The models will be inexpensive but will run well, and the accuracy to scale and degree of detailing will be better than any but an expert scratchbuilder could achieve. The ready availability also of assembled points and flexible track of excellent quality and of easily made up structure kits means that even a beginner can fairly quickly bring a layout of this type to the stage where it is interesting to operate and view. The country setting allows the modeller to add simple but attractive scenery to complete the model.

Great Western branches are particularly popular and are very well catered for with commercial models but other prototypes can also be followed just as successfully though a little more work on the part of the modeller may be required. Because so many enthusiasts have constructed branch line model railway layouts, the majority being based on Great Western Railway prototypes, there have been suggestions from time to time that the subject has become hackneyed and that modellers should choose other prototypes or another form of railway to model. Fortunately as railway modelling is a hobby you are free to do just as you wish. For those who want to model something a little different there is plenty of choice. However, if you like the idea of a Great Western Railway branch line do not be put off by such comments. The great popularity of this particular subject can be seen as a measure of how successful a choice it has been for many modellers and as an indication that it is likely to be for you also. Because the GWR is the most popular it has the greatest variety of ready-to-run and kit models available, making it easier to have an interesting layout with a varied locomotive roster and selection of rolling stock.

However, conversely, do not be talked into modelling a branch line because of the ease and convenience, or because of limited space, if you do not like branch lines. To produce a good layout, one which will provide the most interest and enjoyment for you the builder and operator, you must choose a subject you like and for which you feel an affinity and interest. Never build something just because you feel you should as the modelling will become a chore. There are alternatives to a branch line model suitable for even the smallest spaces.

Advantages and disadvantages

I have already mentioned a number of advantages which a branch line layout can offer but it might now be convenient to sum these up. Also, inevitably with any compromise, such as is almost always necessary with a model railway, there are some disadvantages and we can consider these here as well.

The key feature of a branch line layout is that it offers realistic operation and appearance in a minimum space. Because the layout is small it can be completed within a limited budget, both in terms of money and of the time the modeller can devote to construction. It is simple so should not be beyond the skill and knowledge of the novice. As the amount of track is limited it is relatively easy to lay it all accurately and smoothly so that good running can be achieved and the small size of the layout will mean that maintenance can be easily and quickly carried out. For these reasons a branch line layout is particularly suitable for the beginner, especially the young modeller. Such a layout can be fitted conveniently into a bedroom without interfering with sleeping, studying and so on and, if necessary, it can be constructed so that it is portable, enabling it to be moved and stored without difficulty.

The usual design employed means that the layout can be extended easily by the addition of further sections or can be incorporated into a larger layout later. Alternatively, once it has been completed and has provided entertainment, both in construction and operation, it can be scrapped without the loss of too much outlay in time and money. It will have more than paid for itself in the enjoyment and experience it has given the modeller and, of course, many of the purchased items such as track, structures, locomotives and rolling stock can be reused on later layouts. It may even be possible to use the baseboards again.

The disadvantages of a branch line layout mainly relate to its limitations in scope, both in the amount of construction work which can be carried out and in the operational possibilities. The modeller may find that all too soon there is little more that can be built, though we will look later in this book at ways in which we can extend this even on a very small layout. The operational limitations are perhaps even more significant as only a simple timetable can be worked and once this has been repeated a number of times interest may well wane.

A failing of the classic branch line scheme of terminus to fiddle yard is that the latter, which may be almost half the layout, is hidden from view. Thus on an already small layout, the visible part, the section which is of most interest, is even further limited in size.

However, if extension of the layout is possible the disadvantages can be overcome. Building new sections for the model keeps up the construction interest and, of course, operation becomes more complicated and entertaining as the layout is made larger. A fine example of a branch line layout which began as a small and simple model but which has been developed over a period of some 25 years into a large and extensive model railway is the Reverend Peter Denny's 'Buckingham Branch'. If you would like to see the full potential of branch line modelling I recommend that you read the excellent account given by the Reverend Denny in his book *Buckingham Great Central* published by Peco.

Prototype or freelance

Because of the emphasis on realism in branch line modelling the beginner may have the initial impression that the object is to model a particular prototype branch line station exactly to scale. This is not, however, what is really intended. Though the layout at many of these stations was simple the area occupied was usually considerable and to reproduce the track arrangement accurately to scale would take quite a large space. This may well be more than we have available, and if we should have this amount of space it could be used more productively to model a more complex and interesting station. In fact it is very questionable whether it would be desirable to model to exact scale anyway. Though we are fairly meticulous about scale accuracy with respect to our loco-

Harold Bowcott's 00-scale layout measures 8 ft by 4 ft 9 ins and is hinged to one wall of the room for convenient storage when not in use. This picture shows the layout in the hinged up position. The shelves for storing locomotives and rolling stock are fixed to the wall and fit neatly into the central operating well of the layout. (Photograph by Brian Monaghan, courtesy *Railway Modeller.*)

motives, rolling stock and generally for the structures, we do not usually model the track layout to scale. Ironically, we may well find that the station would look wrong if we did! There are, I think, two main reasons for this, in effect, optical illusion. First of all we are not used to getting the sort of overall aerial view of the prototype that we have of the model, as we would need to be on a hill or up in a helicopter to do so. We normally look at parts of the prototype station from various ground level positions. Perhaps even more important is the fact that we have become accustomed to seeing some selective compression in model railway layouts and we now regard it as normal and realistic. There is certainly an advantage in this compression, in addition to the space saving, in that it enables us to leave out the relatively uninteresting parts while retaining and bringing more closely together the features we like and which give the prototype, and hence the model, its character and appeal. These departures from exact scale do not mean that the model will not be authentic, merely that we are portraying the atmosphere and workings of a branch line station as an artist would, rather than a surveyor. Another advantage for the single handed operator, and most small layouts should be designed to be conveniently worked by one person even if two or more will operate them from time to time, is that compressing the track plan in this way will bring all parts of the station within easy reach.

The key feature of branch line stations, therefore, is that the simple track arrangements they employ can be compressed significantly without losing their essential characteristics. Such compression is limited by the number of points, as these must be modelled roughly to scale whereas other tracks can be reduced in length much more easily. Thus the potential compression is much greater for a branch line station with few points than for a main line station with more complex trackwork.

There are several choices open to us in selecting a station to model. We can copy a prototype station as exactly as possible, with some compression of the track plan as necessary or we can base our model on a particular prototype station but adapt it to suit our requirements and interests. Taking this a little further is the idea of modelling an imaginary station based closely on the practice, style and architecture of a specific company or area perhaps, for example, taking typical Great Western Railway features. Some modellers have applied this idea very successfully to the creation of a station for a branch line which could have existed but which was never built. A fine example is the Reverend Peter Denny's

'Buckingham Branch' for which he created the station which could have been built if the Great Central Railway had reached the real town of Buckingham. Though his line is imaginary it is based accurately on Great Central Railway practice in the year of 1907 for locomotives, rolling stock, structures and details. The fidelity to prototype and period has created an authentic, even though imaginary, model railway.

At the opposite end of the spectrum to the exact model of a particular prototype station is the completely freelance railway, created in its entirety by the modeller and not based on any real railway company. Though this may sound an easy solution in which anything goes and there is no need to bother about research, it is in fact much more difficult to create a convincing model in this way. It has been successfully done but requires considerable knowledge of real railways and also a good deal of imagination and skill to achieve the right effect. The classic example is John Ahern's 'Madder Valley Railway' now on permanent display at Pendon Museum. This expert modeller created his own railway in a realistic but imaginary setting and managed to blend the many diverse prototypes he modelled into a harmonious and balanced whole. He even succeeded in mixing standard-gauge locomotive models in 4 mm scale with narrow-gauge prototypes modelled to a slightly larger scale, all running on the same tracks, without spoiling the effect of realism and authenticity! If you do wish to create a freelance model railway it is important to have a clear idea at the outset of what you are working towards, otherwise there is the danger that the model may become an unrealistic mixture. It is much easier to use a prototype as your guide.

Some modellers have modelled a specific prototype station accurately with successful results. An excellent example is the model of the Watlington Branch built in EM by members of the Mid Hants Model Railway Group, and described in more detail later in this book. This exhibition layout is based very closely on the track layout of the prototype and the structures

Below left *A goods train passes through a cutting realistically modelled from offcuts of softboard broken up and fixed together to give the appearance of rock strata.* (Photo by Brian Monaghan, courtesy *Railway Modeller.)*

Below right *Joypol village on Harold Bowcott's 00-scale layout. Because the maximum depth to permit the layout to fold up against the wall is 9 inches the height of the buildings in the village had to be kept to a minimum and it was not possible to add the chimney pots. The cut out in the top of the backscene at the top left of the photograph is to clear the picture rail and the buildings of the village have been arranged to be clear of the rail. The factory at the right of the scene conceals the controls.* (Photograph by Brian Monaghan, courtesy *Railway Modeller*.)

are all accurate replicas of the real railway buildings at this Oxfordshire terminus. Recreating in miniature a prototype which may have been closed and abandoned years before can be a very satisfying project and of considerable historical interest. If you model a local line you may well find that many people from your area are interested in the layout even though they are not model railway enthusiasts, because they remember the branch as it was in the days of steam. Modelling a specific station in this way may involve you in a good deal of research to find out exactly how it looked at the time your layout will be set. This in itself can be very interesting and can add to the enjoyment of the modelling.

There are, however, some disadvantages to this approach. Such a project does tend to be strictly limited in scope. Once you have completed the track layout as it was in the prototype and have constructed all the buildings and have bought or built suitable locomotives and rolling stock, there is not really any further possibility for development. The timetable operated by the prototype may also be so limited that the model is not very interesting to run.

Another problem is that it may be difficult or impossible to find a prototype which has all the features you would like to include in a model, or one which has sufficient interest to make a good model. Alternatively, if you do find such a prototype it may well be too large for the space you have available.

The ideal solution for the average modeller is either to adapt a particular prototype until it does meet his requirements or to build up a composite station from various desirable features from a number of different prototype stations. Obviously an effort should be made to choose design features, structures and so on which will combine well together. Try also to give a unity to the whole design by basing it on the practice of one company or region.

When it comes to actually designing or selecting a track plan and layout design there is much to be said for the beginner choosing a plan which has been published in a magazine or book. Even though branch line stations and layouts tend to be simple there are pitfalls for the beginner in designing his own. It is important that the layout should permit realistic and interesting operation and that the maximum benefits are obtained from the space which is available. The number of workable arrangements for small layouts is quite limited and all have already been used many times so there is little to be gained in trying to come up with a completely new and original scheme. The beginner is best advised to take advantage of the experience of the experts and to choose one of their track plans. Many have appeared in the model railway magazines over the years and selections of those which have appeared in *Railway Modeller* magazine have been gathered together by Cyril Freezer into booklets of track plans and have been published by Peco. Of these *60 Plans For Small Railways* in particular includes a number of branch line layouts suitable for the beginner. If you do base your layout on a published track plan there is no reason, of course, why you should not make minor changes to the arrangement of the tracks and other features to suit the space available and your requirements. However, do remember that most of these designs are already as compact as possible so do not try to squeeze them into smaller spaces than those suggested. There is no difficulty, if you have slightly more space than absolutely necessary, in expanding the track plan to fit and the layout will usually be improved by this. The scenic suggestions given on the published plans can be altered to suit your own ideas.

It can be difficult to visualise exactly how a layout will look when constructed from viewing the small scale track plan alone and you may find it helpful to draw the plan out full size before making a decision on whether to build it. The lining paper used beneath wall paper is convenient for this as it comes in rolls and is cheap and easy to obtain. You may also find it useful, particularly if you are redesigning the scenery, to build a small scale model (say 1 inch to 1 foot) of the model railway layout to see how it will appear in three dimensions.

Your choice of layout will be dictated to some extent by the space available. It is advisable, anyway, as I mentioned earlier, to choose something fairly small and simple for a first layout so you can get it to a reasonably complete stage within a relatively short time. Give some thought to the operational possibilities and to the sort of locomotives and rolling stock you would like to run on the layout before making your choice. The geographical setting can generally be wherever you wish. For the most part the track layouts for small stations are similar between different companies and by modelling appropriate scenery and selecting suitable structures and details you can locate your railway anywhere in the country. In the next two sections we can look at some of the designs used for branch line layouts, both the general arrangements for the layouts and the station designs.

Layout schemes

Though there are varied layout designs they tend to conform to a few set patterns. The basic essentials of the classic branch line terminus type of layout are the terminus itself and the fiddle yard to which it is linked. If necessary these can be positioned close together with a minimum of track length between. The yard is usually concealed, at least partly, and the track to it passes through a tunnel mouth, under an overbridge or through some other form of scenic break. The provision of a siding or sidings lying in front of the fiddle yard helps to make it less noticeable, gives extra shunting opportunities and makes some visible use of the part of the layout otherwise taken up by the fiddle yard. A typical small layout of this type was constructed in TT scale by Chris Ellis when he was living in a bedsitter. The track plan is shown here. A small quarry was modelled in front of the fiddle yard adding scenic interest as well as an industrial siding to be shunted.

In an effort to provide space for a more interesting terminus, yet still be able to fit the railway into a small or moderate sized room without preventing other uses of the room, a very significant development took place. The design was bent to an L shape to fit into a corner of the room with the arms extending along the two adjacent walls. This design permitted the maximum of operation and interest in a minimum of space and, in addition, encroached much less onto the room than other designs of the same area would have done. Again, a siding or line to a dock, mine or other feature can be positioned in front of the fiddle yard helping to conceal it and making additional use of the area available. If there is space for it, the terminus to fiddle yard type of layout can easily be extended by adding extra sections between the two ends of the layout. If necessary these additional units can be portable, as can indeed the whole layout, and can be stored away except when actually operating the layout.

If the rectangular format more usually

A *The basic branch line terminus to fiddle yard scheme.* **B** *The addition of a siding or sidings in front of the fiddle yard helps to conceal it and also adds to the interest of the layout.* **C** *Chris Ellis built this TT scale branch line layout in a space of only 5 feet by 1 foot when he was living in a bedsitter. The layout follows the basic arrangement shown in* **B** *with a quarry siding in front of the fiddle yard.*

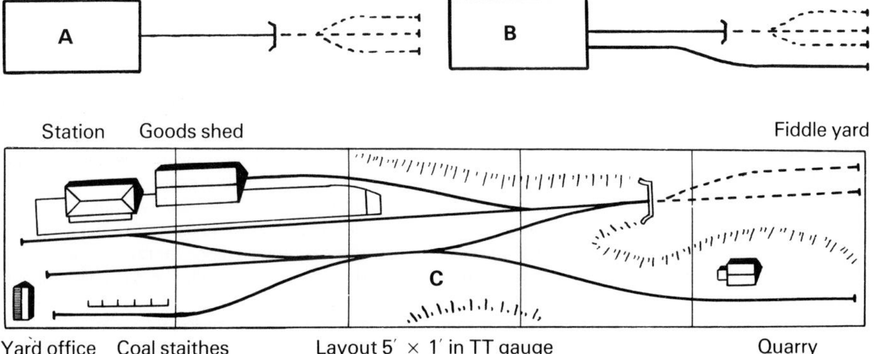

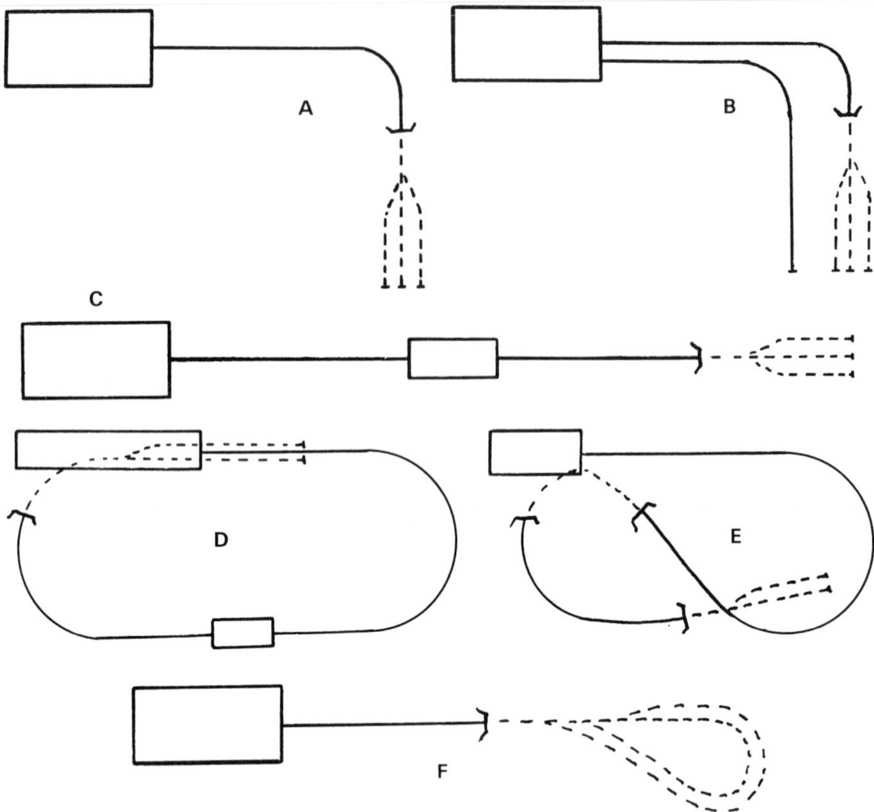

A *The terminus to fiddle yard design can be bent to an L shape to fit into the corner of a room, a very convenient arrangement.* **B** *Again a siding can be positioned in front of the fiddle yard.* **C** *The terminus to fiddle yard scheme lends itself to easy extension by adding extra sections between the terminus and the fiddle yard. The additional section or sections can include one or more intermediate stations and other features of operational or scenic interest.* **D** *If desired the terminus to fiddle yard design can be arranged to fit onto the conventional rectangular baseboard usually employed for the oval type of track plan. Here the fiddle yard is placed beneath the terminus.* **E** *Here a spiral design is employed.* **F** *In N gauge the small radius curves which can be employed enable a reversing loop with one or more holding sidings to be used in place of the usual fiddle yard.*

employed for the oval continuous track arrangement should be preferred, a terminus to fiddle yard design can be accommodated on it successfully by bending it into an oval or spiral shape.

The terminus to fiddle yard scheme was developed with 00 scale in mind but is also suitable for other scales including 0, TT and N. The small radius curves which can be employed in N scale, particularly on hidden sections where realism is not important, means that a different arrangement can be fitted onto the narrow baseboard if desired. Instead of the conventional fiddle yard a reverse loop together with one or more holding sidings can be utilised.

An interesting alternative to the usual design, first employed I believe by Maurice Deane, is to fit the branch line layout onto a rectangular baseboard with the fiddle yard behind the terminus but concealed from it by a low backscene. This arrangement has two advantages. The modeller can easily reach both the terminus station and the fiddle yard from his operating position in the central well. It also makes it simple to include a link to allow continuous running for locomotives to be run in, or for times when the modeller would like to just sit back and watch the trains in action without the need for any shunting. The link can be concealed so that the realism of the point-to-point scheme is not impaired. This type of layout can also be extended.

Another alternative is to model a through station on a continuous run design. This loses some of the advantages of the terminus design but does make a change from the more typical schemes. If a cross country branch is modelled there is more scope for variety in the choice of locomotives and rolling stock than on a small feeder branch. Part of the oval is concealed and hidden sidings are provided here for use as a fiddle yard.

Station design

The main feature of the typical branch line

G *The Maurice Deane terminus to fiddle yard design with a low backscene separating the two and with a concealed link to allow continuous running.* **H** *This arrangement can also be extended by adding a branch from the oval.* **I** *On a continuous run oval scheme part of the oval can be concealed and hidden sidings provided there for use as a fiddle yard.*

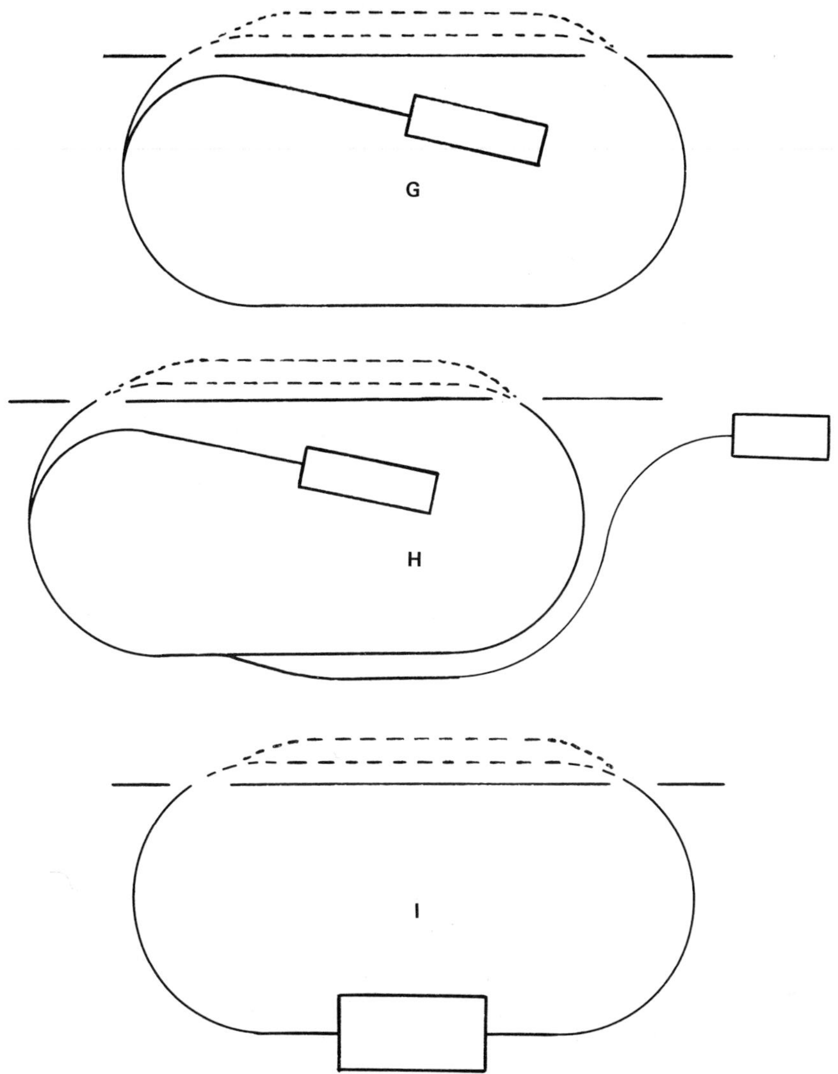

layout is the station, usually a terminus, less often a through station or junction. Obviously we should make the station as interesting as possible, both in appearance and in operating potential. The scope depends on the space available, and if this is small, the station may have to be very simple, but operation will then be very limited. The accompanying diagrams show a selection of typical station track plans ranging from small to moderate in size, and the layouts described later in the book provide further examples of stations of various types.

If only push-pull passenger trains, railcars or diesel or electric multiple units are employed, a branch line terminus, in its simplest form, need only have the single track with a platform beside it, and in many cases modern branch line termini have been reduced to this form. The train arrives, the driver and guard change positions, and the train departs in the opposite direction. However, such operation is not very interesting for the modeller and it is more usual to provide a run-around loop to enable the engine to reach the other end of the train for the journey back to the junction. The loop can either be placed alongside the platform or can be on the line beyond the platform. In either case it will usually be shared by goods trains also, these being scheduled to arrive and shunt between passenger trains. At larger stations a separate run-around loop may be provided for goods trains. The loop, or loops, must, of course, be long enough to hold the trains and there must also be sufficient room on the track beyond it for the locomotive. For 00 eight inches will usually be adequate for the small engines typically used on branch lines, though it would be worthwhile checking on the lengths of any locomotives which you plan to run on your layout.

The platform can be single with tracks on one or both sides. An attractive arrangement is to have a shorter bay at one side which can be used for a railcar, or for vans for milk, parcels and mail. An alternative is to have a platform each side of the two tracks with a release crossover forming a run-around formation. If desired, a shorter bay can be provided, in addition, at one side. At a junction station one line can curve away and a platform between it and the straight track can serve both. In general it is worth noting that a slightly curved platform is more attractive in model form than the more usually chosen straight type.

Goods facilities can be very simple, with trains sharing the run-around loop with

Typical branch line terminus station track plans. (Not to scale.) **A** *A very simple terminus with run-around loop and two sidings, one for a small goods shed, the other for engine coal and water.* **B** *Another small station with goods shed and coal staithes.* **C** *Passenger traffic is more important at this small terminus with two platforms for passengers with a bay platform for milk and parcels. There is a single goods siding with goods shed.* **D** *In this design the run-around loop is on the line before the station platform. Facilities include goods shed, coal staithes and an engine shed with coal and water.* **E** *This larger terminus has a siding serving a nearby factory. There is a two track engine shed while the goods shed and goods platform serves two sidings.* **F** *A larger terminus serving a small port. In addition to the run-around loop for the station itself there is a second run-around loop for the sidings for the wharf and the oil depot so that shunting can be carried on here without blocking the main line or the station.*

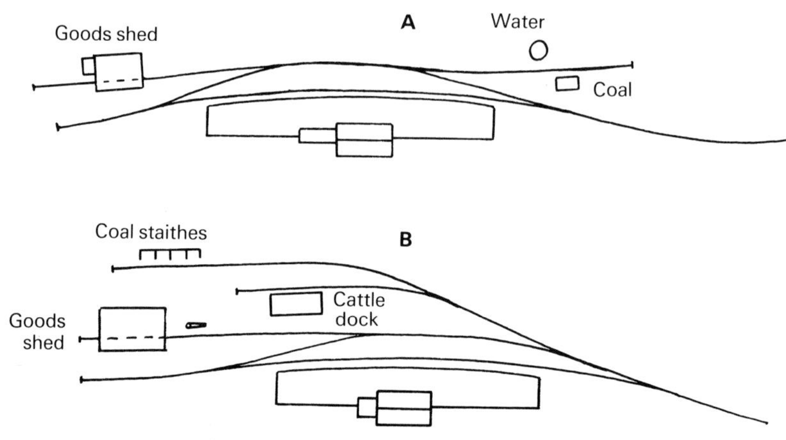

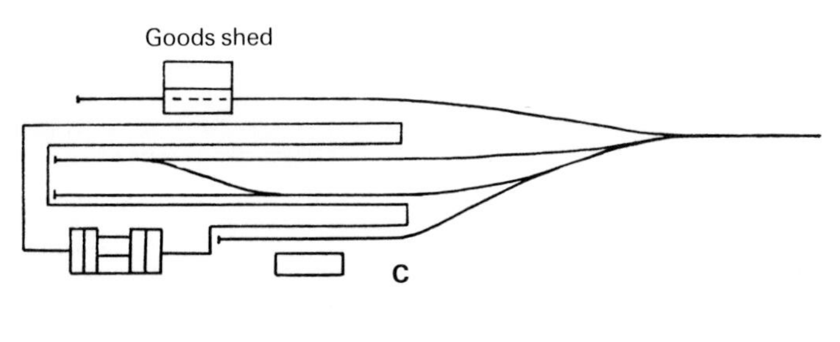

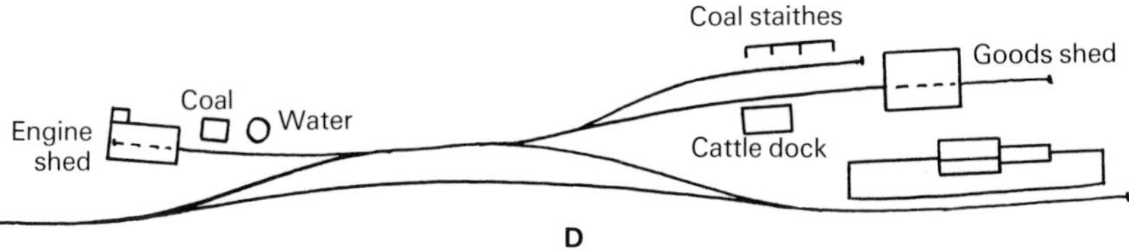

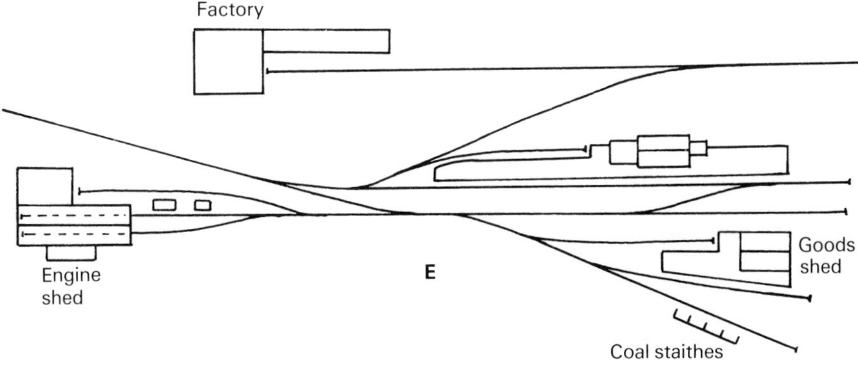

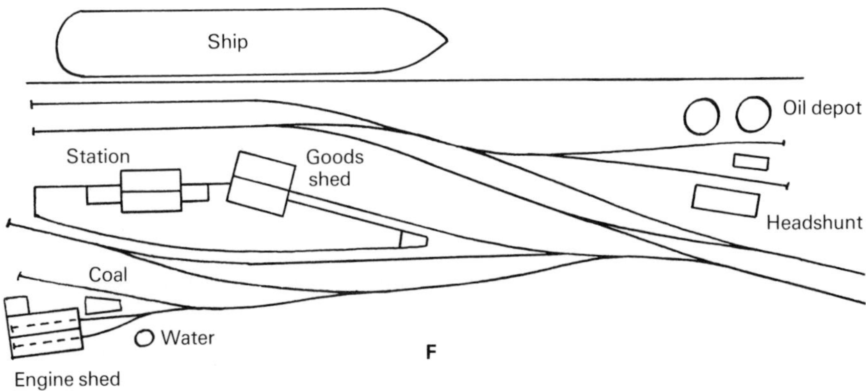

Layout schemes

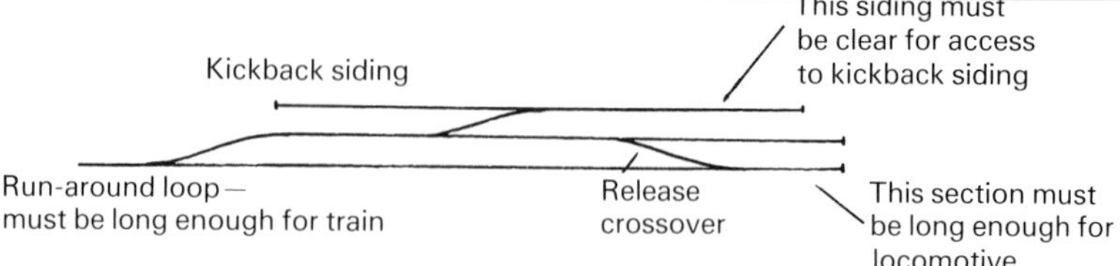

A run-around loop with a siding and a kick back siding.

passenger trains, and with only one or two sidings. If extra sidings can be included, operation will be more interesting as additional facilities can be provided. Typically, a small terminus may have a goods shed, coal staithes and a cattle dock. If a siding to a small factory, a dairy, a wharf, or some other source of extra traffic can also be fitted in, so much the better. At larger stations there may be more sidings and a headshunt may be included so that shunting can be carried out without interfering with the arrival and departure of passenger trains. A separate run-around loop for goods trains will also increase the operational flexibility of the station.

When planning sidings and loops try to avoid reverse or 'S' curves as these may cause problems in running, and even derailments. Kick-back sidings are sometimes included on a model railway layout. Access to one of these is only possible if the siding from which it leads is empty already or is cleared at the time. Because of this the modeller may find that he does not use the kick-back siding as he does not want to be bothered with carrying out the extra moves required. Conversely, however, we can take the view that anything which involves more shunting movements adds to the operating activity and makes the layout more interesting. It is a matter of personal choice whether you want to keep operation simple and easy or to make it as complex as you can. Modellers who particularly enjoy shunting may choose to include one or more kick-back sidings on their layouts because of the complications they introduce. Provided the modeller is prepared to shunt them, these sidings are convenient from the planning point of view as they often utilise space which cannot be otherwise used.

Engine servicing facilities will also be required. If the engine, or engines, are not shedded at the terminus all that is needed is a small coal stage from which coal is loaded by hand into the bunkers, a water tank and an ash pit. However, it is more interesting to provide a small engine shed as well. This will also give the opportunity to display a second engine on the shed track rather than having to hide it away in the fiddle yard. A turntable can be installed if tender locomotives are to be operated, but this facility may take up more space than you are able to spare.

To sum up, we should endeavour to make the station as interesting as possible with as many facilities as can be included to give the maximum traffic and operational potential. The more sidings we can provide the more of our rolling stock can be out on show instead of hidden away in the fiddle yard. If we can include an industry or two at the station this will increase the amount and type of goods traffic and also give us the opportunity to model interesting structures. Examples include small factories, a dairy, a timber yard, a wharf or a gas works.

Fiddle yards

As the fiddle yard is an integral component of the classic branch line model railway layout we should perhaps consider in more detail the various forms that this feature may take. The use of these hidden sidings, which represent the rest of the railway system to which our terminus is theoretically linked, enable us to operate our station realistically in a minimum of space. When the idea was first developed modellers provided these tracks with run-arounds and operated the yards very much as a normal station would be. Sometimes a turn-table or sector plate was included at the end of the tracks to allow the engines to be transferred from one line to another and, also with the former, to be turned as well.

However, as the sidings were hidden from view anyway modellers soon found it was easier, quicker and more convenient to ignore prototype practice and merely to provide a bank of storage sidings on which the locomotives and rolling stock could be re-arranged by hand. Hence the name 'fiddle yard'. An alternative to the original scheme of a set of sidings fed by points is the provision of a traverser table with a single track lead, an arrangement which results in a considerable saving in space. The table is moved back and forth to give access to its sidings. The traverser need not be elaborate, all that is needed is a

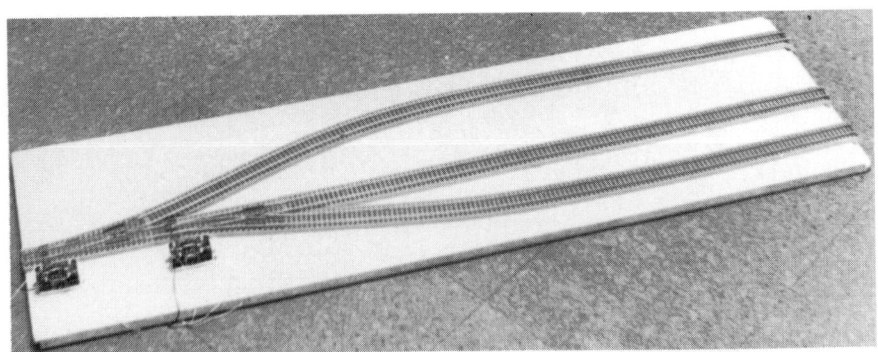

The very simple fiddle yard used with the 00-scale Stonepark Lane branch line terminus layout. In operation a board padded with foam rubber is fitted across the right-hand end to prevent trains running off the sidings.

simple sliding board moved by hand, with spring brass contacts completing the circuit for electrical supply to whichever track is lined up with the entry track. A variant on this device is to have a large sector plate carrying the sidings, as in the fiddle yard constructed by the Mid Hants Model Railway Group for their Watlington Branch layout and illustrated here. This plate pivots so that each of the sidings it carries can be alligned with the entry track. A neat arrangement made with an ordinary small bolt holds the plate in position and ensures that the selected siding is accurately lined up with the entry track.

The Reverend Peter Denny, well known for his superb 4 mm scale Buckingham Branch layout, has made some interesting further developments to fiddle yard design. Finding that the rearrangement of trains in the fiddle yard was proving a rather uninteresting chore for one operator on his model railway, he devised an ingenious detachable five track fiddle yard. The yard has raised sides at each end of which there are grooves into which small end pieces can be slid. When all the trains have entered the sidings, the end pieces are fitted into place preventing the trains from rolling off, and the whole yard is detached from the layout, turned end for end, and replaced. This reverses all the trains at once and, as soon as the end pieces are removed, operation can begin again. This is an excellent scheme provided that the trains are fairly short, as they will be on a branch line layout, so that the yard is not too large for easy

This neat sector plate type of fiddle yard constructed by the Mid Hants Model Railway Group for their EM scale Watlington Branch layout saves both on points and on space. This shows the simple but effective method of alignment and locking used.

Mike Sharman built this three-track train turntable for his broad gauge 4 mm scale period exhibition layout. The turntable reverses entire trains and takes the place of a fiddle yard.

handling while turning. A length of four feet should be adequate yet reasonable for handling. For a layout which must be stored away between sessions a convenient arrangement is to house the terminus on top of a chest of drawers, preferably with a cover which hinges up for operating, and to design the fiddle yard to fit as a drawer below. The original style Denny fiddle yard is ideal for this purpose.

I say 'original' because the Reverend Denny has since elaborated on his design to produce an even more ingenious arrangement, which allows reversal without the need for detaching and lifting the yard. With a mechanism based on Meccano parts, the yard is designed to move away a short distance to give clearance after which the whole fiddle yard can be rotated as a train turntable to reverse it. The yard is then moved in again to meet the layout. This fiddle yard is described in detail in an article by Peter Denny in the March 1954 issue of *Model Railway News.* Both the Denny fiddle yard designs combine the benefits of a fiddle yard and a reversing loop but occupy less space than the latter. Mike Sharman, another expert modeller, has recently constructed a train turntable, shown here, for his 4 mm scale broad gauge period exhibition layout, and this is used in a similar way.

When designing a fiddle yard for your layout there are certain points to be considered, no matter which type of yard is chosen. Particularly important, of course, are the number and length of the hidden sidings. While these may be limited by the space available they will also be influenced by the lengths of the trains you plan to operate and the number of trains you will have. These will depend to some extent on the amount of stock you own and on the number of locomotives you have. Train length will also be related to the track arrangements at the station, with the train lengths limited to that which can be accommodated on the run-around loop.

The amount of rearranging by hand which you plan to carry out also has a bearing on the design of a fiddle yard. If you will merely be reversing whole trains on a Denny style fiddle yard you can lay the tracks relatively close together, whereas if you intend to shuffle the stock around extensively in the yard you will need more space between the sidings for convenience and to avoid damage to the locomotives and stock by knocking them over. You may wish to conceal the fiddle yard from view with scenery or structures but you must, of course, take care that it is sufficiently easily accessible for convenient operation, for maintenance and in case of derailments.

Though fiddle yards and hidden sidings are particularly associated with point-to-point lines they can also be usefully employed to add operating potential to layouts based on other track patterns. For example, the rear of an oval can be concealed and sidings can be provided here for train holding or for use as a fiddle yard. Similarly, on an out-and-back scheme, hidden sidings can be led from the reversing loop. As I mentioned earlier, in N scale, where a 180 degree turn can be made in as little as 20 inches of baseboard width, a reversing loop is a feasible alternative to the more usual fiddle yard arrangement employed in 00 scale. If a little more space is available this loop can be combined with hidden sidings giving a more versatile scheme.

Locomotives and rolling stock

One of the advantages of building a branch line layout is that interesting and realistic operation can be carried out with a very limited selection of stock so that the initial financial outlay for locomotives and rolling stock can be very modest. A country branch will typically have one or more small tank engines, though small tender locomotives are also suitable if you prefer. If you use the latter, a turntable can be installed, and will add interest to the engine servicing facilities at the station, if sufficient space is available. However, a turntable is not essential as tender first running was acceptable prototype practice. An occasional through train can provide an excuse to run a larger locomotive if you wish.

The enthusiast is now well catered for in 00 scale; in N scale there is an adequate but more limited selection. For TT scale there are now no ready-to-run British prototype models available and the modeller must build from kits or scratch. In 00 ready-to-run locomotive models include the Airfix GWR 61XX Prairie and 14XX 0-4-2 Tank, the Lima GWR Class 45XX Prairie and Class 94XX 0-6-0 Pannier Tank, the Grafar Class 94XX Pannier 0-6-0 Tank, the Palitoy Mainline LNER and BR J72 0-6-0 Tank, the Wrenn SR Class R1 0-6-0 Tank and the Hornby GWR Class 57XX 0-6-0 Pannier Tank, among others. The GWR predominance is evident! The Hornby Class M7 0-4-4 Tank, useful for Southern branch line layouts, is unfortunately no longer in production, though may be obtainable second hand. There are also a number of excellent white metal kits from various manufacturers for locomotives suitable for branch lines.

For a GWR branch line of appropriate period, a model of one of the streamlined diesel railcars built in the 1930s and early 1940s would be an interesting addition. K's plan to reintroduce their 4 mm scale kit shortly and a Lima ready-to-run model of Railcar No 22 built at Swindon in 1941 to a newer, more angular, design will also be available soon. A kit for a fine model of a GWR Steam Railmotor is produced in 4 mm scale (and also in 7 mm scale) by Mallard Models.

For a modern branch line layout Modern Traction Kits (MTK) offer a range of Diesel Multiple Units. Various diesel locomotives have been used for passenger and freight services

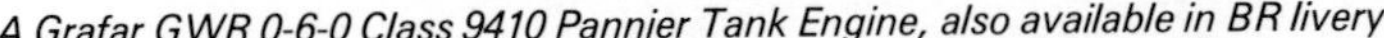

A Grafar GWR 0-6-0 Class 9410 Pannier Tank Engine, also available in BR livery.

Above *An Airfix 6110 Class GWR 2-6-2 Prairie Tank.* **Below** *A Lima Class 45XX Small Prairie Tank, seen here in GWR colours but also produced in BR lined black livery* **Bottom** *A Wrenn SR Class R1 0-6-0 Tank.* **Above right** *Langley Miniature Models produce a white metal kit for the Great Western Railway streamlined diesel railcar in N scale designed to fit onto a Lifelike diesel chassis. This picture shows the completed model* (Photograph by courtesy of Langley Miniature Models.) **Right** *A Wills Finecast 2-4-0 'Metro' Tank. This cast metal kit model can be built as the open cab version as shown here or with a closed cab.* (Photograph by courtesy of Wills.)

on branch lines. Modern Traction Kits and Q Kits both produce ranges of diesel locomotive kits in 4 mm scale. For goods services on some branches BR Class 08 shunters have been employed; in 00 a ready-to-run model is made by Wrenn and there is a kit manufactured by Modern Traction Kits.

In N scale the range is more limited but Grafar have ready-to-run models of the GWR and BR Class 94XX Pannier Tank, a Prairie Tank in GWR and BR livery, and 0-6-0 Tank Engines for other railway companies. There is a steadily increasing selection of cast metal kits designed to fit onto various commercially produced chassis. Langley Miniature Models, for example, have recently introduced a cast metal and etched brass kit for a GWR 14XX 0-4-2 Tank Locomotive and Autocoach. This firm also makes kits for the GWR streamlined diesel railcar and twin railcars designed to fit onto Lifelike GP 40 chassis. The carriages used on local passenger trains on branch lines were often older mainline stock passed down to the minor lines, though the GWR also used auto-coaches and 'B' sets. Through trains were usually made up of corridor coaches. A good range of ready-to-run and kit models are available, particularly in 00 scale.

Goods traffic was mainly carried in open wagons and in vans, with coal and foodstuffs forming the bulk of the traffic, though the transport of livestock, especially cattle, was also of some importance. Special stock will need some reason for its presence, for example, an appropriate industry on the line. There is an excellent range of wagons and vans both ready-to-run and kit models in 00 and a lesser but adequate selection in N.

Generally, the selection of locomotives, coaches and goods stock is good and is improving all the time so that the enthusiast should have no problem in providing adequate stock for a branch line layout, certainly in the two most popular scales.

Structures and scenery

More general information on structure modelling is provided in another book in this series, *PSL Model Railway Guide 3, Structure Modelling,* but there are a few relevant comments which I would like to make here. At branch line stations the structures are, or were, usually fairly small and simple and there were relatively few of them at a typical small terminus. All these features are advantageous for the beginner working in a small area.

The station buildings would include a booking office and a parcels office, a waiting room, toilets, a staff room and a lamp room as basic features at a small station. At larger terminii more facilities would be provided. If it was necessary for passengers to cross from one platform to another there might be a footbridge though often the passengers would use a barrow crossing. Other structures usually present include a goods shed, an engine shed and a signal box.

For the initial construction of the layout the modeller can utilise kits from the excellent ranges available. These include the accurate models of specific prototypes produced as full colour card kits by Prototype Models; many of these are replicas of branch line structures and are ideal for a layout of this type. The Superquick, Bilteezi and Builder Plus ranges also include a number of buildings suitable for branch line layouts. Plastic kit models are offered by Airfix, Malvern Models and Peco, while Hornby make a selection of colour printed, plastic, clip-together structure kits for 00 scale. Grafar have a range of ready made structure models in N scale.

Later the modeller may wish to replace some or all of the kit built models by scratch-built models to provide greater authenticity for a model of a specific branch, or to give more individuality, or to enable the modeller to include replicas of prototype buildings he particularly likes.

Information about buildings on specific branch lines may be available in books on these railways, and in some cases scale drawings are included. Two excellent books of this type are *Great Western Branch Line Termini,* Vols 1 & 2, by Paul Karau, and a fine model of Wallingford station inspired by Vol 1, built by Iain C. Robinson was described in the November 1979 issue of *Railway Modeller* magazine. This article gives a full description of the methods used by Mr Robinson to scratch-build these structures, methods which will be just as useful for other buildings, and I recommend it to would be scratch builders. Another useful book, also from the Oxford Publishing Company, is *Great Western Architecture,* a very comprehensive survey of GWR buildings.

Other books providing drawings of attractive structure models suitable for branch line layouts, both railway buildings and lineside structures, together with useful information on construction include John Ahern's *Miniature Building Construction* published by Argus, and *Downesplans Book 2 Railway Buildings,* by Allan Downes, published by Peco. Platform details and other accessories are available as plastic or white metal models from Mikes Models, Dart Castings, Airfix, John Piper (accessories) Ltd, Ratio and other manufacturers.

Above right *Prototype Models make a range of colour printed card structure kits in 2 mm, 4 mm and 7 mm scales. These attractive models are accurate replicas of actual railway buildings and many are ideal for branch line layouts. The selection of 4 mm scale models shown here includes from left to right: Chalford Goods Office, Standard GWR Signal Box, Wilmcote Station Shelter, Tetbury Engine Shed and Chalford Station, all from the Great Western.* (Photograph by courtesy of Prototype Models.)

Right *The station buildings at 'Stonepark Lane', an 00-scale branch line terminus, were constructed from a Superquick kit. Despite its impressive appearance the structure measures only 9 inches by 7½ inches.*

The structures on the Watlington Branch layout, including this beautifully detailed station building, were scratch-built by Barry Fisher. All are accurate replicas of the prototype railway buildings.

The modelling of scenery for model railway layouts is also covered in another book in this series, *PSL Model Railway Guide 4, Scenery.* The scenic work is important on a branch line layout because one of the essential features of this type of model is that it should be realistic. This can only be achieved if the setting is modelled with as much care and attention to detail as the railway itself. Initially, in an effort to get the layout complete enough for operation fairly quickly, the modeller may prefer to keep the scenic work basic and simple. Later more detail can be added and, as the layout will be relatively small, there is no reason why the scenery should not be brought to quite a high standard of detail and realism without too much work being required.

Operation

One of the advantages of branch line modelling is that the resulting layout can be operated in a realistic and authentic manner. Thus instead of merely running trains around at random we have a proper pattern of operation and this makes the layout much more interesting to use. If you model a particular prototype exactly you may wish to follow the working timetable for the branch concerned. Though these were originally issued only to employees, many have now been published. For example, the books *Great Western Branch Line Termini* Vols 1 & 2 contain the working timetables for the branches described. Alternatively, some research may be necessary to obtain details for the line you are modelling. If you adapt a prototype or have created your own station from various features from different prototypes you can either use a prototype timetable or can devise your own.

Prototype timetables are often rather limited and operation following one may not be of great interest so it may be preferable to make up your own to suit. When following a timetable there are two main schemes of operation. The first method is to run the trains according to time. Since a branch line timetable will have long pauses between trains when nothing is happening it is necessary to use a speeded up time system with an hour on the timetable represented by five or ten minutes of actual time. Often a clock in which the gearing has been altered to produce this speeding up is employed, or more simply movements of the minute hand are read off so that five minutes or ten minutes on the clock are taken to represent an hour. In fact this system is at its best on a larger layout where there is more than one operator and the time on the clock then provides a constant factor to which all the operators work. By reference to the clock, train movements are carried out in the correct order, trains meet and pass at the right times and places, and so on. Thus orderly operation can be achieved.

On a small layout, where there is often only one operator, much of this is irrelevant and unnecessary and the second method is more suitable. Here the operator works to the timetable sequence but ignores the actual time. Once a particular movement has been carried out he goes on to the next in the sequence. Thus train movements are carried out in the correct order and the pattern of running is maintained.

It is quite easy to develop a timetable for your own branch line terminus starting with a few trains, passenger and goods, and adding more as you buy or build more locomotives and rolling stock. At first just develop a single day's operation, arranging it so that after you have worked the timetable sequence through the trains will be back in their original positions ready for the next session. Later you can devise different timetables for other days such as Wednesday (market day) Saturday and Sunday. As you become more experienced you can add extra trains, unscheduled specials, maintenance of way trains, and so on. Additional interest can be supplied by an occasional breakdown or derailment which will cause delays and changes to the schedule. However it is best to let your timetable develop as you go along rather than trying to devise a complicated scheme from the very start.

Generally in planning the layout and its operation we want as many train movements as possible at the station to keep up the interest in operation. Thus it is usually better, for example, to run a passenger train of two or three coaches round which the engine must run to reverse the train, rather than an auto-train or railcar which merely runs back in reverse, though these can be included in the timetable to add variety. Similarly we need as many different facilities as possible at the station to increase the variety of rolling stock and the amount of shunting needed when goods trains arrive. The subject of operation is dealt with in detail in another book in this series, *PSL Model Railway Guide 5, Operating Your Layout.*

Further developments

Earlier I mentioned that while it is convenient for the beginner that a branch line layout could be brought to a fairly complete state reasonably quickly, this can also be a disadvantage as the modeller may then find he loses interest because the scope for any further construction appears very limited. In this section I want to explore some of the possibilities for extending the interest.

The enthusiast who enjoys scratch-building and super-detailing may like to gradually replace all the structures, perhaps originally simple kit models, by highly detailed hand-built models, perhaps based on actual prototype structures. If internal lighting and interior detailing are also provided the construction work can be extended even further. Similarly there are many opportunities for fine detailing with the addition of lamps, seats, barrows and other accessories of appropriate company style and period to the platforms and station areas. Human and animal figures are available commercially both as plastic and as cast metal models. The former may be painted or unpainted when purchased, the latter are only available unpainted. Careful painting, and in some cases additions or alterations to clothing, tools held in the hands, and so on, can improve and individualise the models.

Many trackside details can be added to give a more realistic and authentic appearance. Some of the accompanying photographs show such details on the Watlington Branch layout built by members of the Mid Hants Model Railway Group. The point rodding, made up from etched brass parts manufactured by Colin Waite, is particularly effective. Such detailing is fiddly to add but can keep the modeller amused for some time and the results are worth while as the finished appearance is most realistic. In the same way the scenery beyond the tracks can be systematically brought up to a very high standard of detail. Individual plants of recognisable varieties can be modelled as has been done on the magnificent dioramas in the Pendon Museum.

All this additional construction work can be carried on without interrupting operations on the layout. Further improvements can be the provision of realistic road vehicles, lorries, vans, cars, buses, motorcycles and bicycles of appropriate period, either made up from commercial kits or scratch-built. Further scope for construction lies in the replacement of the ready-to-run locomotives and rolling stock employed to get the layout into operation fairly quickly by kit or scratch-built models. Alternatively you may wish to retain your original

Very realistic track detailing on the EM gauge Watlington Branch layout built by the Mid Hants Model Railway Group. **Left** *Sleepers form this simple block across the rails preventing stock from running off the end of the track.* **Above right** *Though the points are operated electrically with point motors beneath the baseboard, dummy point levers have been added for authenticity.* **Above far right** *The beautifully modelled point rodding made up from Colin Waite parts gives a complete appearance to the track area.*

roster but add to it slowly by building extra models.

An interesting way of increasing the potential of a limited layout is to provide locomotives, rolling stock and accessories for two distinct and different periods, for example pre- and post-grouping. In many cases structures have survived relatively unchanged for many years so the basic track layout, structures and scenery can serve both periods. By changing the locomotives and rolling stock, and accessories such as motor vehicles and human figures (because of the changes in fashions of dress) we can represent different periods on the layout. Thus we can provide scope for additional locomotive and rolling stock construction as well as giving variety in appearance when operating the layout. For their Watlington Branch exhibition layout the Mid Hants Model Railway Group have locomotives and rolling stock for both pre-grouping and post-grouping periods and this has made the layout more interesting, both for them to operate and for the public to view.

All the above suggestions have been made on the assumption that no extension of the layout is possible. However, it may well be that additional sections can be constructed, even if they must be portable units to be stored away when not actually in use, to fit onto the original layout. The terminus to fiddle yard type of layout is particularly suitable for this as extra sections can be made, as convenient to the modeller, and when complete can be fitted between the original sections. These additional units may be purely scenic or can include a through station or a halt to add interest to the timetable operation. If more space becomes available you may even be able to model the junction station. Eventually the branch line may become merely part of a larger layout.

Another idea which can be considered is the modelling of a narrow-gauge feeder line as an addition to your branch line model. A prototype example is the Swanage Branch with exchange sidings at Furzebrook and at Eldon Sidings where clay was transferred from the narrow-gauge lines from the clay pits of Purbeck. Another alternative would be a narrow-gauge feeder from a stone quarry or a mine. Such a line could be fitted into a relatively small space but will add greatly to the operational possibilities as well as being very attractive scenically.

Other types of branches

Modern

Though the original concept of branch line modelling referred essentially to the steam worked lines in a period up to the 1950s, a number of branch lines have survived and are still in operation today. There have, however, been considerable changes with the introduction of diesel or electric motive power and with the various modifications designed to improve cost effectiveness by modernisation and automation. Track layouts have been simplified by removing tracks no longer necessary with the cessation of goods traffic and with no need for run-around facilities for the diesel or electric units employed for passenger traffic. Station buildings have been altered, though many original structures can still be seen. Some buildings have been demolished to save on repairs, painting and rates payments. Small stations are unmanned with tickets sold on the train or at the larger stations. Colour light signalling has in many cases replaced the semaphore signals previously present and barrier crossings or train operated unguarded level crossings have taken over from the old gated crossings. Though there have been so many changes there are still many features which will make these lines interesting in model form. There is also the great advantage of being able to directly observe the prototype which is being modelled thus ensuring accuracy and an authentic atmosphere. The biggest drawback is the very limited operational scope most of these branches now offer, often little more than a DMU shuttling back and forth, with no opportunities for shunting.

However, some branches do offer rather more interesting operation and a good case is made by J.G. Glover in the September 1979 issue of *Railway Modeller* magazine for Bourne End station as the basis of a modern branch line layout. The article and accompanying track plan are well worth consideration if you are interested in the idea of modelling a present day line. Suitable rolling stock is available in kit form in both 00 and N from Modern Traction Kits, who offer a good range of DMUs. The modeller who likes DMUs would find such a branch an ideal setting for an interesting selection of kit built models. Later, if desired, it could be incorporated into a larger layout, perhaps a main line scheme, as a branch from it.

Modern goods and industrial branches can still offer interesting and busy operation and later in this book I want to look at a goods branch serving a dock and industrial area in Poole which would make a good basis for a layout. The other modern period branch line we can consider modelling is the preserved line.

Preserved

For the modeller who likes, and has perhaps already collected, a wide variety of locomotives, a selection which would not normally be seen together because of their origins, period or type, a very attractive solution can be to model a preserved line. One can then even include some foreign engines if they take your fancy as there are several prototype precedents for this! For example, the Nene Valley Railway has locomotives from Denmark, Sweden and France, as well as continental rolling stock including Danish and Norwegian coaches, while the Kent & East Sussex Railway roster of locomotives includes an American Tank and a Norwegian State 2-6-0 Tender Engine.

You might like to base your layout on an actual preserved line. This has the advantage that you can visit the branch to see and photograph everything and there is often plenty of published data about the locomotives, rolling stock, stations and so on. The model could be a representation of the line as it is now, or as the preservation society hope to make it. Such a model could be very satisfying and could also have considerable publicity value for the railway. Providing locomotive and rolling stock models for most lines should not be a problem using the standard commercial products.

Another approach would be to model a branch line you like which has been closed, as though it had been preserved. This will give you more freedom in the design of the layout and in the choice of locomotives and rolling stock than if you were modelling an actual preserved line. A third alternative is to model an entirely imaginary preserved line of your own design.

There are many interesting details which can be added to a layout representing a preserved branch line. There may be locomotives and rolling stock awaiting or undergoing repairs, some scrapped items kept to provide spare parts for other equipment, many parts lying around, and perhaps numerous visitors, many with cameras taking pictures! Often equipment not normally seen on a branch line, such as a heavy breakdown crane, has been acquired by preserved lines and is to be seen at the station or in the workshop area. There may also be a small museum of other items such as traction engines, vintage cars or buses and so on. If you model a station on the preserved line as one combined with British Rail then you have the perfect excuse for including everything from vintage steam engines on the preserved line to the High Speed Train on the BR tracks! All on the one layout!

Foreign

Just as the branch line layout concept was essentially related to the steam period it was also really applied to British prototypes, especially the Great Western Railway branch lines. However, there does seem to be an increasing interest in modelling foreign railways, usually American or European. This, I think, is partly due to increasing familiarity with these prototypes through holidays abroad and the availability of information in both British and foreign railway and model railway books and magazines. The importation of models of foreign locomotives and rolling stock, and of kits for structures, mostly of excellent quality, also has a significant influence. Thus the popularity of modelling German railways must surely be related to the excellence both in variety and in quality of the range of models available in various scales, particularly HO and N.

There has at times been criticism in the British model railway press of foreign prototype layouts, especially German based lines, built by British modellers. In many cases the models appear unrealistic because the modeller is insufficiently familiar with the prototype, its setting and its methods of operation. Now if the enthusiast is happy with his layout and derives enjoyment and pleasure from it then its inaccuracies are unimportant. This is, after all, a hobby and it is up to the individual how he builds and operates his layout. However, most modellers will find that a realistic and authentic layout based accurately on the appearances and practices of the prototype will give the most satisfaction. To achieve this it is important to familiarise yourself with everything about the prototype

Useful details for modellers at Shackerstone Station, once a branch line junction station on the Midland Railway and now preserved, include a gas lamp, an MR boundary marker and the advertisements.

and its setting. Operating practice and track layout is often rather different from the British system and this should be taken into account when designing a layout.

For American modelling the range of ready-to-run models, kits and parts in HO and N scales is excellent and the enthusiast can obtain a great deal of information about modelling American branch and short line railroads from reading one or more of the fine model railroad magazines produced in the United States.

The range of European models in HO and N scales is also very good though the emphasis is almost entirely on ready-to-run equipment; this is generally of excellent quality. Some countries, particularly Germany, France and Switzerland, are very well catered for by the manufacturers but for others there is much less available. There is a good deal of prototype information available, in English, for the modeller, and several countries have model railway magazines, though here there may be language problems, of course. Ideally one should visit the country concerned and take as many photographs as possible to guide you in the modelling of the setting, the trackside details, and so on, in addition to the more obviously important locomotives, rolling stock and railway buildings.

For other countries of the world much converting or scratch building will be required to complete a layout and such a project is only really suitable for the more experienced modeller with a particular interest in, and knowledge of, the railway system concerned.

Research

I have already commented on the value of general background reading to the branch line modeller in giving some idea of the character and appearance of the prototype lines. If you are planning to base your layout on a particular station, or on several stations selecting the features you like from each and combining them, then more specific information will be required. The research involved in obtaining this will not only be invaluable in the construction of a realistic model but can also be very interesting and enjoyable in itself.

At the time when branch line modelling was first put forward as a good choice there were many branch lines still operating and they were still using steam locomotives. Thus if one of these lines was chosen as the prototype to be followed, simply visiting the railway would enable the modeller to obtain and record all the information needed. Now most of the branches have closed and those which have survived have often been considerably modified. If the enthusiast wishes to model a line which is still in use, as it is today, then there is, of course, no problem as a visit to the line with camera and notebook will give him all the data required. It is particularly convenient if the line is fairly local to the modeller's home so that return visits can be easily made as necessary to obtain further information or to check on details which have been previously overlooked. This is a point worth considering in the choice of prototype. You may want to model a branch which is still in operation as it was at an earlier period, perhaps in the later days of steam. Even though there will probably have been changes in the track layout, structures, and so on, much valuable information can still be obtained from visits. This data will be a useful basis to which you can add as you refer to books, photographs and maps describing and illustrating what the line was like before the recent modernisation.

Even on lines which have been closed, perhaps for many years, it is worth while visiting the site if you can. Though the tracks have been lifted you can often still see the line of the track and the type of scenic setting. Some structures may still be there and even though these may be in very poor condition the basic dimensions can still be accurately measured. Sometimes you will find that old station buildings have been converted into private houses and again, despite the alterations, it may be possible to obtain useful measurements. Remember that closed lines are now usually privately owned land and buildings and that you have no automatic right of access no matter how worth while you feel your research is. However, a polite request and explanation of why you want to view the site will usually meet with co-operation from the owner.

An alternative source of prototype information is from published work. Though the present day modeller is at a disadvantage compared to the enthusiast in the 1950s when it comes to viewing the prototype, he has a much greater range of published data available to him. A very great deal of information regarding branch lines has appeared in print, with more coming out all the time and, if the line you wish to model has been covered, much of your research may already have been done for you.

The model railway magazines have featured many prototype branch lines over the years, with descriptions, photographs, usually track plans and, often, suggestions on modelling. Because the articles are generally slanted towards the modeller they are particularly helpful in providing the information he requires. Back issues of model railway magazines are often to be found in second-hand book shops, and specialist booksellers, such as Lens of Sutton, hold extensive stocks of back numbers. The prototype railway magazines have also featured many useful and informative articles on branch lines and again back issues can be obtained from second-hand and specialist booksellers. Many model railway clubs have collections of magazines in their libraries which are available to members. Alternatively you may find that members have

The track has been lifted on this branch line in Northumberland but the signal cabin remains. Though there is minor damage the structure is essentially intact enabling the modeller to obtain accurate measurements.

personal collections of magazines which include the issues to which you want to refer.

Various categories of books are available on the subject of branch lines. I have already mentioned those offering a more general coverage, with three examples. A second type of book is the photographic album or pictorial book. These again usually give a fairly general coverage, though this time in pictures, often of branch lines in one area or region. These books are useful for background, atmosphere and, in some cases, from the scenic modelling aspect.

There is also a steadily increasing number of detailed books on particular branch lines or stations and these are invaluable if your chosen prototype is covered. The Oakwood Press have an extensive list of railway titles, a number of which are on branch lines. The Oxford Railway Publishing Company Ltd (OPC) have published a series of Branch Line Histories and there are further titles planned. Two excellent books from this publisher are *Great Western Branch Line Termini* (Vol 1) and (Vol 2) both by Paul Karau. The first covers Fairford, Lambourn, Tetbury, Wallingford, and Watlington, while the second features Abbotsbury, Ashburton, Hemyock, Moretonhampstead and Princetown. The surveys of the stations are very detailed with many photographs and drawings suitable for the modeller, and even working timetables. This firm also offers pictorial albums on Great Western, Scottish, LNER and Southern branch lines. Recently published by Wild Swan Publications (WSP) is *Branch Lines of the Southern Railway* by George Reeve & Chris Hawkins which provides excellent coverage of four Southern branches, including Swanage and Hayling. There are also useful books on specific aspects of railways which can be very helpful in modelling. For example *A Pictorial Record of Great Western Signalling* by A. Vaughan and *A Pictorial Record of Southern Signals* by G. Pryer, both published by OPC.

You may be able to obtain details of the track layout of the prototype in which you are interested from one of these books or from magazine article coverage. Alternatively many station plans are available through the BR/OPC Joint Venture (302 Holdenhurst Road, Bournemouth). An extensive range of GWR station track plans is already available with SR stations to follow shortly. Under this arrangement between British Rail and the Oxford Publishing Company many plans of structures, locomotives, rolling stock, etc and a wide range of photographs are also available to the modeller.

If the station or branch in which you are interested is not covered in this way Ordnance Survey maps will provide details in many cases. The large scale maps are needed for this purpose and may be available at libraries in the area concerned. Photographs of the station or branch can be invaluable in the creation of a realistic model and there are a number of firms specialising in railway photographs. I have already mentioned the BR/OPC Joint Venture. Lens of Sutton also have an excellent range, while Aerofilms of Boreham Wood have many photographs of stations, both period and modern, from the air which may be useful in planning your layout and in modelling the scenery.

Layouts

Having taken a fairly general look at the idea of branch line modelling I would now like to show you a few examples in various popular scales, though I would emphasise that 00 scale is really the ideal choice for the beginner. The layouts vary considerably in size and while two are closely based on particular prototype branches the others are not modelled on any specific lines though they do follow the general practices of the prototype.

Stonepark Lane

This L-shaped branch line terminus to fiddle yard 00-gauge layout is an example of what can be achieved using mainly commercially available items, in some cases modified to suit the situation. Much of the construction work was carried out by Paul Holmes who originally owned the layout but some modifications have been made by Ralph Fenwick, the present owner, who also plans to extend the layout when more space becomes available. The track layout is simple and only six points have been used, four at the terminus and two in the fiddle yard, which represents the junction with the main line at the other end of the branch.

The main section of the layout is L shaped and rests permanently on bookcases in the corner of the room. Two additional sections are temporarily fixed onto this for operating sessions. A simple fiddle yard with two points leading to three sidings fits on beyond the beach while a narrow strip of chipboard with a single track is positioned at the station end of the layout to make shunting of the goods siding more convenient. Later it is hoped to expand this to include some industrial sidings or a small harbour.

The baseboards are pieces of three-quarter inch thick chipboard and, as they are fitted onto the top of bookcases, bracing was not needed for further strengthening. Track and turnouts are Peco, mostly laid on foam underlay. Additional ballast and careful painting of the underlay and the sides of the rails has given a very realistic appearance and the foam makes the track very smooth and free running. The points near the level crossing are hand operated but the others at the terminus are moved by Peco point motors concealed by buildings or scenery. The points in the fiddle yard are operated by Hammant & Morgan point motors. The buffers are from Peco kits.

The station buildings were assembled from the Superquick Terminus station kit while the platforms were built up from thick card. The goods shed is a modified Superquick kit. The low relief structures at the rear give the impression of a road behind the station with houses and shops along it. Though they occupy very little space they complete the scene very effectively. The small hill, through which the line passes in a cutting and a short

Stonepark Lane is an 00-gauge branch line terminus constructed by Paul Holmes. Most of the buildings are based on commercially produced kits.

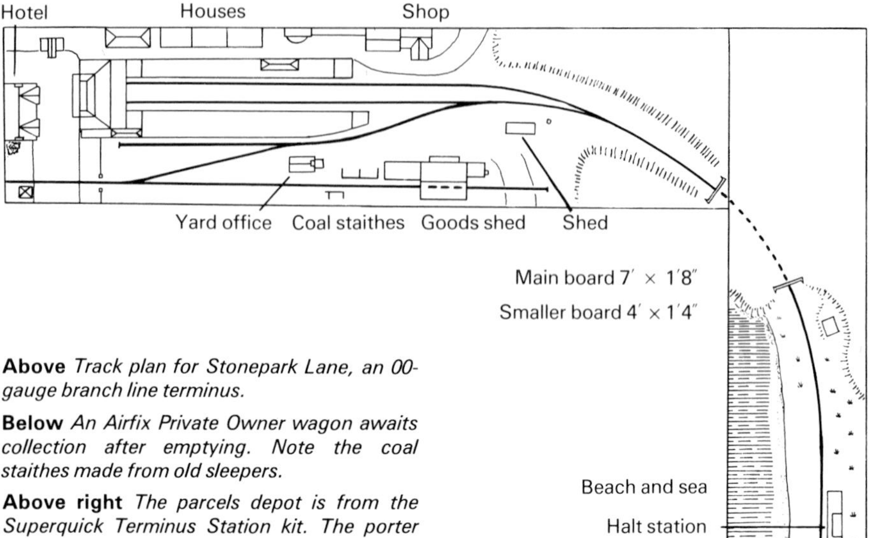

Above *Track plan for Stonepark Lane, an 00-gauge branch line terminus.*

Below *An Airfix Private Owner wagon awaits collection after emptying. Note the coal staithes made from old sleepers.*

Above right *The parcels depot is from the Superquick Terminus Station kit. The porter and milk churns are Merit products and the GWR Siphon F van was built from a K's kit.*

tunnel, has a basis of chunks of polystyrene foam supporting chicken wire netting. Over this is a covering of Mod-Roc and plaster, painted appropriately and with suitably coloured scenis dressings applied over it. The sea is ripple glass over painted hardboard.

The layout is operated as a Great Western branch using a simple timetable. The locomotives now include a Hornby 0-6-0 Pannier Tank, a Lima Small Prairie and Airfix 14XX Class 0-4-2 and Prairie Tanks. A Lima GWR diesel railcar will be added to the roster as soon as it is on the market. Coaches include four Triang clerestories, one of which is a brake end, an Airfix autocoach and a BSL kit built autocoach. Goods stock is from various ready-to-run ranges, together with a K's kit built GWR Siphon van. A Hornby light crane forms part of an engineers department train used for maintenance of way and for derailments.

The terminus is unusual in not having a run-around loop and a release cross-over could have been included on the two main platform roads, making operation more convenient. However, an isolated section has been provided at the end of each of these tracks so that another engine can be used to pull the train out and release the original engine. This is not necessary for the push-pull trains.

Stonepark Lane illustrates how an interesting and attractive branch line layout can be built in relatively little space and at low cost. Even though most items on the layout are readily available commercial products, the resulting model is realistic and individual.

The Sherrington branch

Sherrington is a typical branch line terminus model of the type so popular in 00 gauge but the choice of N gauge has meant that only a

Below and bottom *Two views of Sherrington Station, an N-scale branch line terminus. Most of the structures on this layout were scratch-built. The excellent scenic work has created a very realistic overall appearance.*

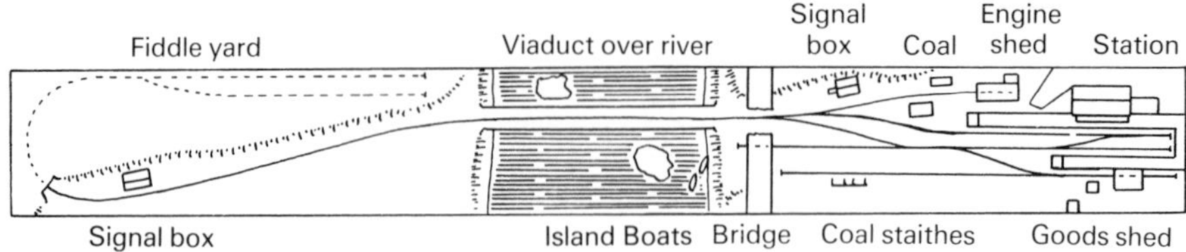

Track plan for the N-scale Sherrington Branch.

minimum of space has been necessary for an interesting layout. The terminus section measures only 4 feet by 15 inches and the fiddle yard section is identical in size. A linking section 28 inches by 15 inches completes the layout, the overall dimensions of which are thus 10 feet 4 inches by 15 inches. Because such small radius curves can be employed in N gauge a 180 degree turn has been possible on the 15-inch wide baseboard to reach the fiddle yard sidings. Thus this section of the layout provides a full length of visible line and scenery as well as accommodating the hidden sidings.

Sherrington was originally owned by J. Harvey Watkins who carried out most of the construction work on the station section. He later sold the layout to Eric Kay who developed it further adding the river section with its impressive viaduct. Baseboard construction follows conventional methods with a wood fibre insulation board top supported by wood framing. The three sections bolt together and the detachable wooden legs are also bolted into position. When not in use the layout is easily taken apart into small units which can be stored or transported without difficulty. The track and points are all Peco with all the points controlled by Peco point motors mounted

A Grafar GWR Prairie Tank on shed at Sherrington. The typical water tower and coaling stage were scratch-built from card and plastic.

beneath the baseboard top. The track was glued directly down onto the insulation board and ballasted with granite dust giving a very realistic appearance. Landscaping was carried out with plaster bandage material and Polyfilla while the rock faces are made from cork. After painting the scenery surface various scenic dressings were sprinkled on to give the appearance of grass, earth, and so on. The river was painted appropriately and then given a coat of gloss varnish to produce a wet look.

All of the structures at the terminus, with the exception of the station building—a modified Pola kit, were scratch-built. Construction was from plastic card, commercial brick and slate papers and stone embossed plastic sheet. The large viaduct over the river was modelled from polystyrene foam carved to give the effect of stonework. Many small details such as signs, signals and telegraph poles, scratch-built from odds and ends, add to the overall effect of the model. Locomotives and rolling stock are ready-to-run models from various ranges appropriate to a Great Western branch in the later days of steam. The layout is operated to timetable and when two operators are available a simple bell code can be employed between the station and fiddle yard. The layout has been shown at a number of exhibitions very successfully.

The Swanage branch

This 00-gauge model railway shows that a branch line layout need not be small and simple! The prototype Swanage line, opened in 1885, branched from the main Wareham-Dorchester route at Wogret Junction and then ran nearly ten miles to Swanage. The only intermediate station was at Corfe Castle, approximately half way along the branch. The line was an important one and in the busy holiday periods each summer there were many long distance trains arriving at Swanage, with through trains from as far afield as the Midlands and the North. Freight was also important, particularly the traffic in clay. The branch was operated by steam until 1967 when diesel units took over and carried on the local services. The line was closed in 1972 except for the short section from Wogret Junction to Furzebrook which has remained in operation for the bulk freight traffic in clay and oil. The Swanage Railway Society was formed in 1972 with the aim of reopening the branch and trains

Track plan for the EM-gauge Watlington Branch constructed by members of the Mid Hants Model Railway Group.

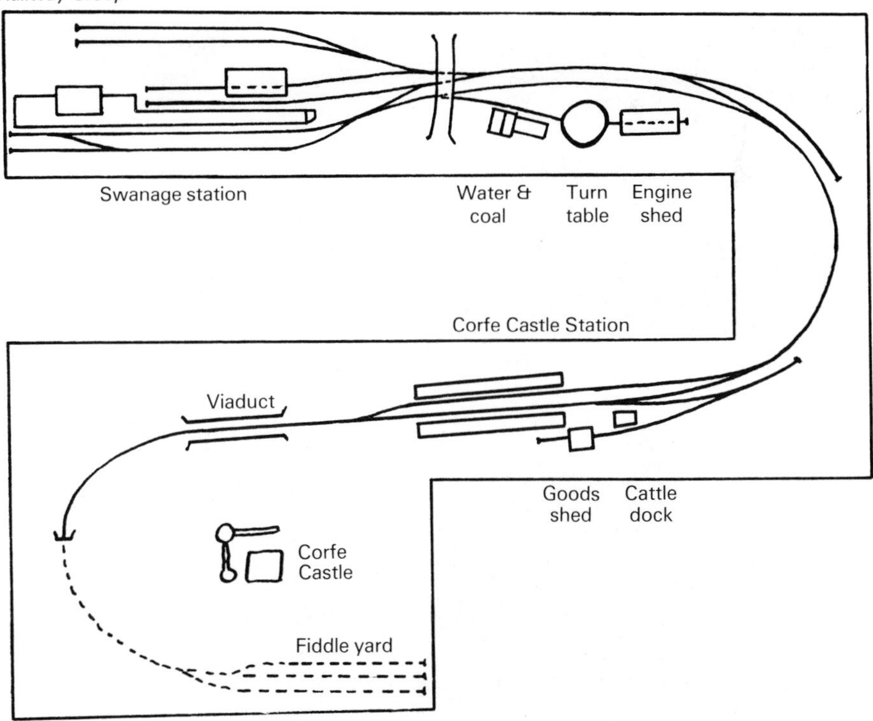

are run over a short length of track at Swanage at weekends.

The 00-gauge model was constructed some years ago by Terry Jenkins and other members of the Isle of Purbeck Model Railway Club as an exhibition and club layout. The aim was to reproduce the appearance and atmosphere of the real line as accurately as possible within the limitations imposed by space and finance. The layout of the stations at Swanage and Corfe Castle has been based quite closely on the prototype but naturally the line between has been markedly compressed. Even so the model requires a large room to accommodate it.

Baseboard construction was heavier than usual on home layouts to withstand the harder usage of exhibition halls and club room but otherwise followed the usual methods. Track and points were entirely hand built to reduce expense. The scenery was built up from plaster bandage material and plaster, painted and then covered with scenic dressings. Lichen was used extensively for bushes, hedges and trees, though some Britains trees were also included on the layout. An interesting method of construction was developed for the stone railway and other buildings on the model, including the accurate replica of the ruined Corfe Castle which is a major scenic feature of the layout. Over a basis of thick card a layer of Pyruma (Kos) fire cement was applied and scribed to represent the individual stones of the

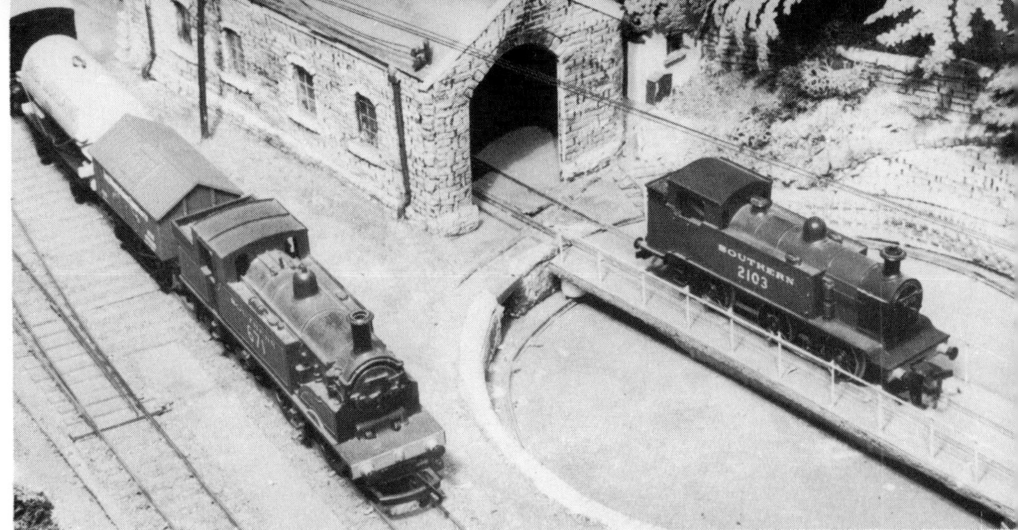

Left *Corfe Castle station on the 00-scale Swangage Branch layout built by Terry Jenkins and other members of the Isle of Purbeck Model Railway Club. The station buildings and goods shed were scratch-built with stonework modelled by scribing Pyruma fire cement.*

Below left *Swanage water tower and coaling stage scratch-built in 4 mm scale.*

Above *As a Triang 0-4-4 M7 Class Tank Locomotive arrives at Swanage with a goods train a Hornby 0-6-0 Tank is about to run off the turntable into the engine shed.*

Right *The ruins of Corfe Castle realistically modelled in 4 mm scale for the Swanage Branch layout.*

buildings. The cement was then allowed to harden and the resulting effect was very good.

Locomotives and rolling stock used on the line belonged to various club members. Most are ready-to-run models though many have been repainted or modified. The basis of the locomotive roster were Triang M7 0-4-4 Tanks and a variety of 0-6-0 Tank Engines, though larger locomotives were also run on through trains. Timetable operation following the original prototype working timetables could be carried out but at shows more intensive running was often provided to maintain interest for the spectators. A change in clubrooms necessitated the sale of the layout some time ago.

The Watlington Branch

The Watlington Branch has been one of my favourite lines ever since I first came across the descriptions of Watlington and Aston Rowant stations by John Ahern in *Model Railway News* back in August and September 1950, so I was delighted to see this model by the Mid Hants Model Railway Group at a recent exhibition. The layout, in EM gauge, is based very accurately on Watlington station and gives a realistic picture of how this terminus must have appeared.

The prototype branch from Princes Risborough to Watlington was opened in 1872 by the Watlington & Princes Risborough Railway Company but it was taken over in 1883 by the Great Western. The line was operated on the 'One Engine in Steam' principle, the locomotive being shedded at Watlington overnight. The working timetable consisted of Up and Down goods trains in the morning and evening, with passenger trains during the day.

The model features the end of the line from Lewknor Halt to Watlington and the layout is

A general view of the approach to Watlington Station on the EM gauge layout constructed by the Mid Hants Model Railway Group. The EM gauge track and the overall high standard of the modelling have created a very realistic appearance. Note the nail in hinge method of joining the baseboard sections, visible in the foreground on the right. The bell at the rear is used for communication between fiddle yard and terminus operators when timetable running is in progress.

18 feet 6 inches long, including the fiddle yard, which is of an interesting design with four sidings on a large sector plate. The Group plans to extend the distance between Watlington and Lewknor Halt stations and later it is hoped to incorporate the layout as a branch line terminus on another layout which is at present under construction.

The baseboards are of the solid top with supporting framing type and have detachable legs; the layout can be transported to exhibitions in two cars or in a small van. Track and points were hand-built using EM Gauge Society components, with SMP track employed on the sector table in the fiddle yard. All points are controlled by Hammant & Morgan motors fitted beneath the baseboard top, but dummy hand levers are also included on the model for realism. Locomotive control is by linked section using Scalespeed controllers.

The beautifully detailed structure models were made from plastic card and are accurate replicas of the real buildings on the branch. The scenery was shaped from polystyrene foam covered with plaster and given a realistic texture while trees were modelled with wire trunks and branches and foliage of scouring pads. Many small details including telegraph poles, fences and signs have been accurately modelled and there are numerous figures in appropriate period dress. Most of the figures are detachable for storage and are fixed in

A view of Lewknor Bridge Halt on the Watlington Branch. The structure was scratch-built. The gas lamps are from the Mike's Models range of cast metal accessories.

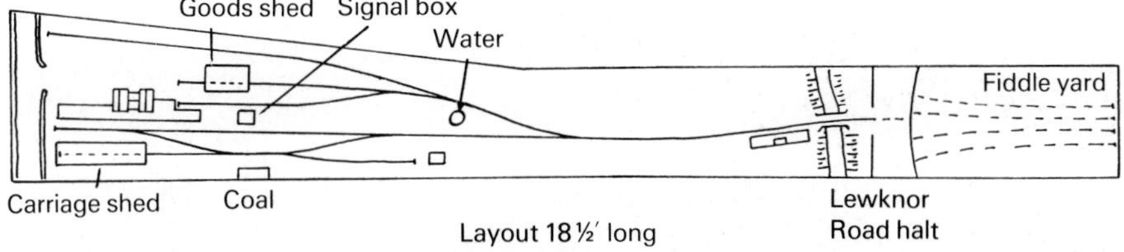

The Swanage Branch as modelled by the Isle of Purbeck MRC. (Not to scale.)

place on the layout by means of a wire attached beneath one foot which fits into a hole in the baseboard surface.

At exhibitions the layout can be operated using two sequence tables, one based on the Working Timetable of the 1920s/30s, the other an expanded version to show visitors a wider display of rolling stock and requiring more than one locomotive at Watlington. Most of the locomotives used on the layout were constructed from white metal and etched brass kits, with added details, and a few were scratch-built. Most of the locomotives are fitted with Mike Sharman wheels. Coaches are ready-to-run models suitably modified, mainly Triang clerestories, or from Ratio Coach parts cut and spliced together appropriately. The goods stock is from kits, mainly Slater's and Ratio, together with some scratch-built items. An interesting feature is the provision of locomotives and rolling stock for two distinct periods, pre- and post-grouping, adding to the variety and hence to the appeal of the layout. Regrettably, Barry Fisher who was the instigator of this layout and who built the structures, died suddenly in January 1979.

The Fort Ness Branch

This N-scale layout built by Alan Copas is an interesting example of a continuous oval track design with part of the oval concealed and provided with sidings to form a fiddle yard. The visible part of the layout features Fort Ness, a small through station between Inverness and Glasgow. When the branch to Fort William is constructed it will lead off from the front right-hand side of the layout and Fort Ness will become a junction station. In the meantime the arrangement of hidden tracks within the dotted line and the rear of the backscene forms a mock-up of the intended track plan for Fort William, enabling Alan to try out the design in advance.

The period of the layout is set at the time of the transition from steam to diesel to that both forms of motive power can be represented. Locomotives and rolling stock are mainly ready-to-run models from various manufacturers. Operation as a through station and junction allows Alan to justifiably run larger locomotives and longer trains than on a branch.

Track plan of the Fort Ness N-scale layout constructed by Alan Copas.

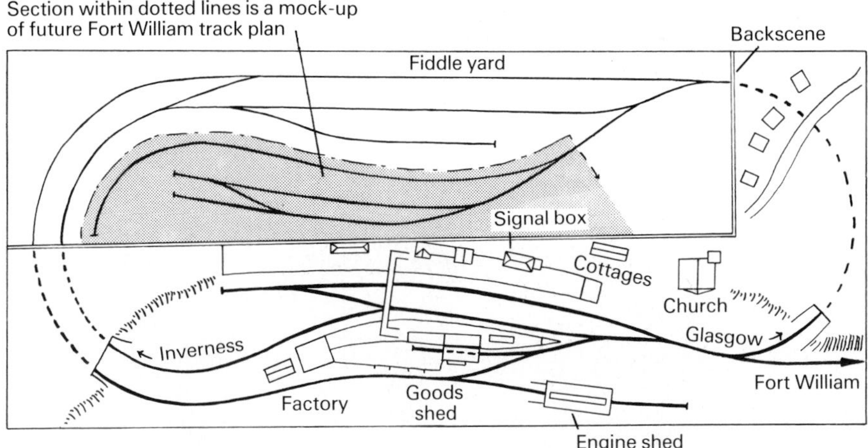

Above *A through passenger train made up of Minitrix coaches hauled by a Minitrix British Rail Type 2 diesel at Fort Ness on the N-scale layout constructed by Alan Copas. The main station building was made up from a Hambling's Bilteezi card kit. The attractive backscene has been assembled from pictures cut from calendars.*

Below *The goods shed at Fort Ness was built by Alan Copas from a Highfield card kit while the canopy behind it is from a Pola kit. The footbridge in the left background is an old Lone Star model.*

Bottom *This J89 0-6-0 is used on the Fort Ness branch for shunting duties. The cast metal body is mounted on a Minitrix chassis.*

Construction of the baseboard and scenery follows conventional methods. Extensive use of lichen has been made in the modelling of realistic vegetation. The track in the visible section of the layout is all Peco, whereas in the hidden sidings, various makes of points are fitted so that they can be tried out. The structures include both card and plastic kit models. The card kits are from the Hambling's Bilteezi and Highfield ranges, while there are plastic kits from Pola and Vaupe. The signal box, footbridge and some of the road vehicles are old Lone Star models which have been repainted. Other road vehicles are by Wiking and the human figures are Peco and Merten models.

A realistic feature of the layout is the very effective backdrop made up by combining suitable pictures from various calendars. Careful selection, positioning and matching of these pictures together with skilful blending of the modelled scenery with the flat background has given a very realistic impression of depth to the scene. The backdrop conceals the remainder of the oval and the fiddle yard.

Market Redwing

This Great Western layout in TT gauge depicts a small but busy terminus in an imaginary location somewhere between Plymouth and Exeter, but off the main line—access being by a single line. There are two branch lines from Market Redwing, one to Castle Deeping and the other to Cory Bay which is a small seaside town. This arrangement enables a branch line train to travel between Castle Deeping and Cory Bay with Market Redwing being the junction in the middle.

Traffic on the line is typical of that seen in a West Country market town with a Cattle Special from Exeter and a Milk Train from Cory Bay which works through to London. On the passenger side there is *The Coryman Express* which journeys to London daily. An overnight-sleeper-parcels train from Carlisle also works into Market Redwing and this is returned at the end of the day's operations. To complete the passenger service a stopping train from Plymouth also arrives which includes a parcels van for a through working to Cory Bay.

The period modelled is just after nationalisation in the 1948-50 period although Great Western motifs are evident on locomotives and rolling stock. The layout was built with exhibitions in mind and it has appeared at numerous shows. It was designed so that when not in use the layout sections can be stored on racks in a large cupboard. Baseboard construction is of the open frame type using 2 inch by 1 inch timber while pieces of floorboard form the base for the trackwork. The track is Wrenn, glued to a cork strip and, while the glue is still wet, granulated chippings are sprinkled over the complete area. Once dry the surplus is swept away giving a realistic effect. The point work is

Keith Gowen's TT-gauge Market Redwing layout. (Not to scale.)

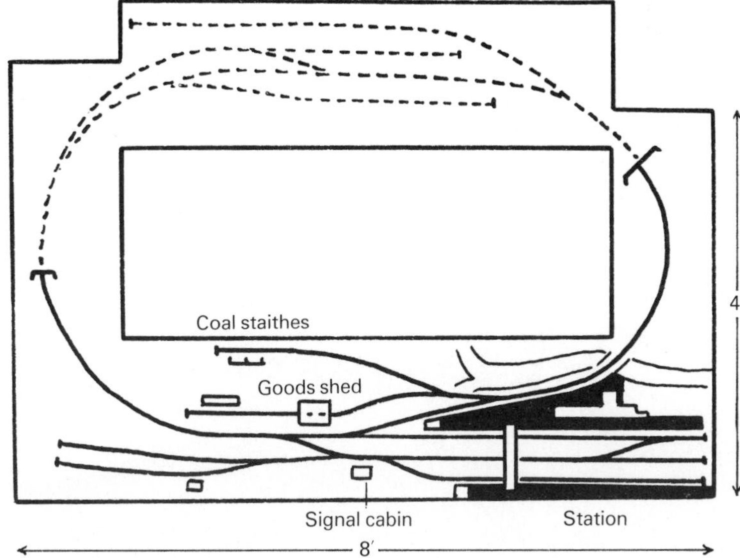

Left *A branch line goods train approaches Market Redwing station with the cattle dock to the left and the carriage sidings on the right.*

Below *The approach to Market Redwing station showing the Wrenn pointwork. The signal cabin and goods shed are made up from Hambling's Bilteezi sheets. Note the token exchange apparatus in the left foreground.*

Right *Market Redwing junction station on Keith Gowen's TT scale Great Western layout. The station buildings are from Bilteezi card kits and the footbridge is a modified Triang product.*

dealt with in a similar manner with a copper-clad sleeper replacing the original tie bar; this together with loop wiring gives trouble free operation. The scenery was mostly made from chicken wire covered with Mod-Roc and painted. Some areas have coloured flock sprinkled over glue to give a textured effect.

The working signals are a feature of the layout and were constructed from Bec kits with 3 mm Society signal arms. They are operated by piano wire passing through copper tubing. The level crossing also works and is made from a combination of wood and plastic pieces together with some parts from the Airfix 00-scale level crossing kit. These operating features are popular at exhibitions.

The buildings are mainly constructed from Hambling's Bilteezi printed card kits suitably modified for the situation. For example, the goods shed was made up from parts from several sheets of the 00 scale Warehouse/School/Narrow Gauge Locomotive Shed kit with Airfix Engine Shed windows. The station platforms are built from balsa wood covered with brickpaper while fine sandpaper was used for the top surfaces. The rolling stock is basically Triang although various Ian Kirk and 3 mm Society products are beginning to replace the Triang vehicles. The locomotives are of Triang origin with kit-built bodies and are all super detailed to give a more realistic effect.

When exhibited the layout operates on an hourly programme which gives a complete day's operations, and there is a card system which indicates to the public just what moves are taking place. Control is with a Hammant & Morgan Clipper controller and self isolating points. The programme cannot be smoothly

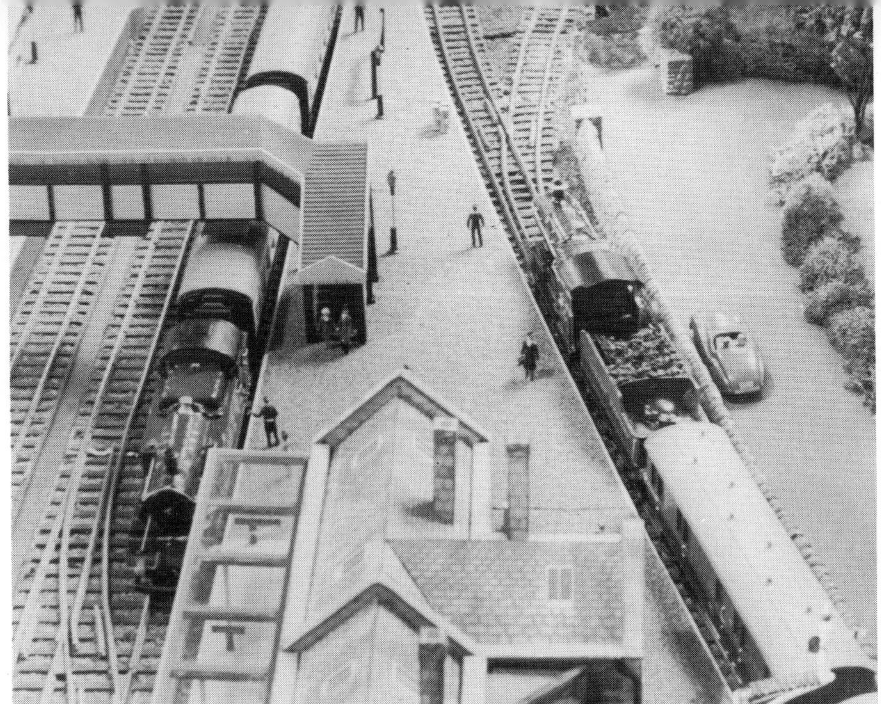

run unless the fiddle yard sidings ae operated efficiently and a comprehensive work list is drawn up for this purpose. Thus both the operator and the fiddle sidings assistant know exactly what is going to happen next ensuring straightforward operation. The programme has been designed so that all the trains appear to run for a reason and to be earning revenue, not just aimlessly going round and round a circuit.

Unterlenningen

Unterlenningen is a typical model German branch line terminus in N gauge and it again illustrates the advantages of this small scale in enabling an interesting station to be modelled in a minimum of space. Though the terminus has sufficient facilities to permit entertaining operation it only occupies a baseboard 60 inches by 20 inches. The branch line and terminus are designed to form part of a larger main line layout with a junction station at a later date, but can be operated in the meantime with a fiddle yard. The period has been set to allow the use of both steam and diesel power and facilities for refuelling both have been provided at the terminus together with a combined engine shed and workshop building.

Baseboard construction follows conventional methods with chipboard braced by timber framing; with the relatively narrow baseboard and the strong top surface of chipboard, 1 inch by 1 inch wood was considered sufficient for the framing rather than the more usual 2 inch by 1 inch material. On this surface there are two hidden tracks which will form part of the main line. Above them is supported a further sheet of chipboard on which Unterlenningen station is constructed. Track

Track plan for Unterlenningen, an N-scale German branch line terminus.

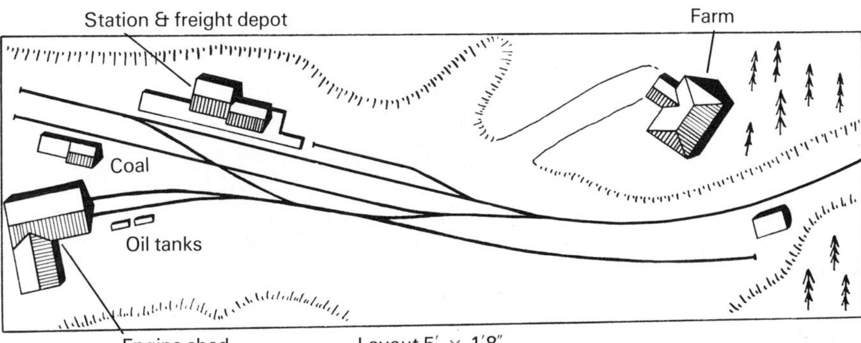

Left *A German prototype branch line terminus in N scale. The layout section illustrated here measures only 60 inches by 20 inches showing how little space is required for branch line modelling in this scale.*

Below left *Unterlenningen Station was built from a Kibri kit. The short passenger train is headed by a Fleischmann model of a German Federal Railways Class BR 91 0-6-0 Tank Engine. This small locomotive is ideal for branch line use.*

and points are from the Arnold range and are ballasted with cork granules. The structures are all made from plastic kits from Pola and Kibri. An excellent range of realistic structure model kits from German prototypes in N scale is available from these and other manufacturers and the kits are readily obtained in this country. The landscape was shaped with thin plywood formers supporting plaster bandage material. Over this there is a covering of Polyfilla which has been painted appropriately. Scenic dressings applied over this give the surface a realistic texture. Cork bark has been used for cliff faces and rocks and the bushes are of lichen. Numerous commercial tree models of the 'bottle brush' type give a realistic conifer forest effect. Even though the individual trees are simple models the massed appearance is very good. Road vehicles are from the excellent Wiking range. At present the layout is lacking in human figures but these will shortly be added using Preiser and Merten models.

The locomotives and rolling stock are all ready-to-run commercial models mainly from the Arnold and Fleischmann ranges, which include a good selection of smaller locomotives, steam and diesel prototype, suitable for branch line use. Operation follows conventional patterns but the area is assumed to be popular with tourists in the summer thus creating extra passenger traffic.

Layout ideas

To complete this book I would like to look briefly at three branch lines which are still very much operational today to see how we might use each as the basis for a layout. The lines are interesting in appearance and operation as they are now, but if one prefers there is nothing to stop us turning back the clock to steam days while still using information and ideas from these branches. All three are within fairly easy reach of my home showing that it can be worthwhile looking around the area in which you live when seeking a suitable prototype. Each has unusual and interesting features and only one was operated by the Great Western, the other two being Southern lines, showing that there are alternatives to the typical GWR branch line model!

The Weymouth Harbour Tramway

The Weymouth Harbour Tramway is a single track branch which winds its way along for a mile in the streets of Weymouth from the main Weymouth station to the quay. The line was opened for passengers in 1880 and was jointly owned by the London & South Western Railway and the Great Western Railway but was operated by the GWR. For many years the line was worked by a variety of small tank engines but now boat trains from Waterloo (Southern Region) are hauled through to the quay by main line diesel locomotives. Today it is a remarkable sight on a busy summer day with the streets teeming with holiday visitors and crowded with parked cars to see a boat train slowly rumbling along preceded by police and railwaymen checking that the track is not obstructed. On one side there is the harbour with many small boats, on the other side of the street there are buildings including shops, warehouses, pubs and so on, many of which would be very attractive in model form and which are very suitable for modelling in low relief. At one point a street is carried across the harbour on a bridge which also spans the road along which the track runs.

I have drawn up a plan based on the Weymouth Harbour Tramway for an along-the-wall layout measuring 10 feet by 1½ feet in 00 gauge. The track layout at the terminus is fairly typical of branch line station designs with a run-around loop at the passenger platform and with sidings serving, in this case, the quayside and warehouses at the rear. I have also included a small engine shed with coal and water. However, the choice of prototype does have advantages over the usual country branch line terminus both in the setting and in the operational possibilities. Instead of the usual simple scenic setting this layout has a crowded town scene around the line providing great scope for the modeller who enjoys making

Right *Weymouth Harbour Tramway with a boat train on its way from the quay towards Weymouth station. Note the rails inset into the roadway and the bell mounted on the front of the locomotive above the coupling.*

Below *Track plan for an 00-gauge branch line terminus layout inspired by the Weymouth Harbour Tramway.*

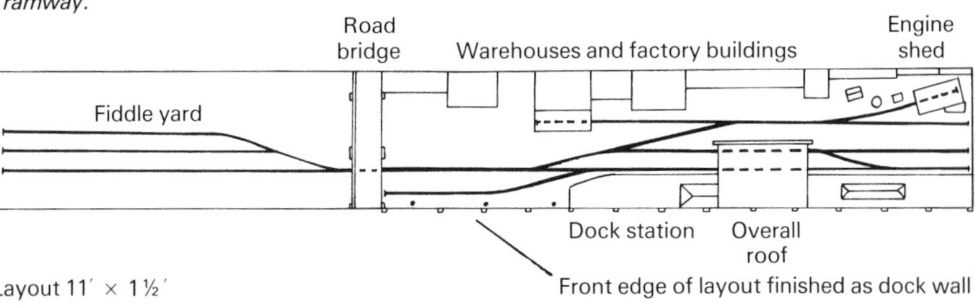

90

Above *The boat train at Ferry's Corner showing the congested surroundings.*

Left *This fish merchants store is typical of the buildings along the quay. The buildings could be very effectively modelled in low relief on a narrow layout.*

Right *A through train crosses the viaduct as it returns from Lymington Pier station to Lymington Town station.*

buildings and adding small details such as human figures, road vehicles, lamps, street signs and so on. For the best effect the low relief structures at the rear should be based on actual prototypes. The front of the layout can be modelled to represent the edge of the quay giving a very neat and finished appearance and I have used the road bridge as a scenic break to conceal the entrance to the fiddle yard at the left. The station platform is at the edge of the quay so that passengers can go directly up the gangways onto the ferries. I have sketched in an overall roof covering part of the platform and the two tracks.

The layout could be modelled for either steam or diesel operation, the coal and water facilities at the small engine shed being replaced by a diesel fuel oil tank for the latter. Operation can be interesting with passenger trains arriving to connect with ferry sailings and these trains can include main line coaches; if more space is available for the layout the platform and run-around loop could be lengthened with benefit, as at present only short trains can be run. A small steam or diesel shunting locomotive can be employed sorting wagons and vans and shunting them onto the appropriate sidings.

Lymington

This 4½-mile long branch leaves the main Southampton-Bournemouth line at Lymington Junction, 1 mile west of Brockenhurst and runs to Lymington Town and Lymington Pier. The branch to the Town station was opened in 1858 by the Lymington Railway Company and was taken over 20 years later by the London & South Western Railway. This company extended the branch another ½ mile from the Town station to reach the Pier. The regular ferry service from Lymington Pier to the Isle of Wight has provided a great deal of traffic for the branch and has ensured its survival despite the many closures which have taken place elsewhere. The branch was steam operated until 1967 when it was electrified and it is now worked by electric multiple units (EMUs). The run-around loops and sidings at both Lymington Town and Lymington Pier stations have been removed leaving only the single line and, although the branch is still interesting in appearance, operation is limited in scope even though there are hourly trains for much of the day. I have based my suggested layout on the early 1960s when the track layouts were more interesting, giving more operational possibilities. An excellent book on the line, *The*

Lymington Town station is an attractive structure and would make an interesting model. Unfortunately the impressive train shed which covered part of the platform and the platform track has been removed.

Above *Lymington Pier signal cabin is a small brick-built structure which faces out across the river. Note the 'W' (whistle) sign for trains approaching the viaduct. The cabin was built in the 1950s.*
Below *Lymington Pier station with its distinctive curved canopy.*

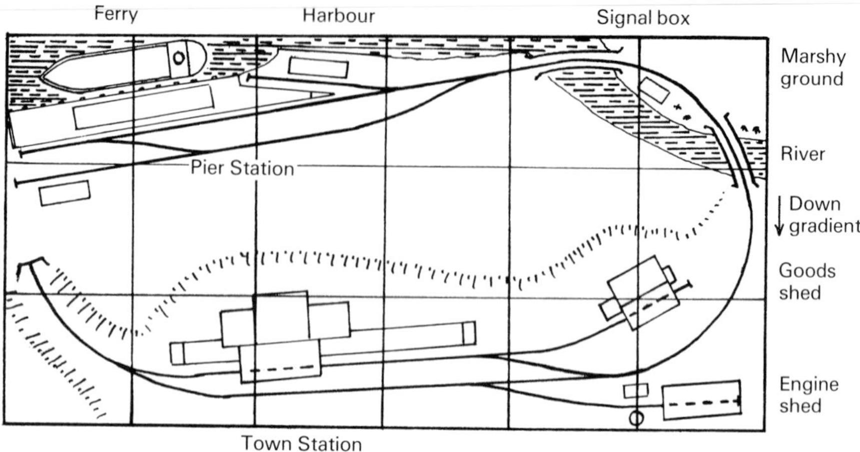

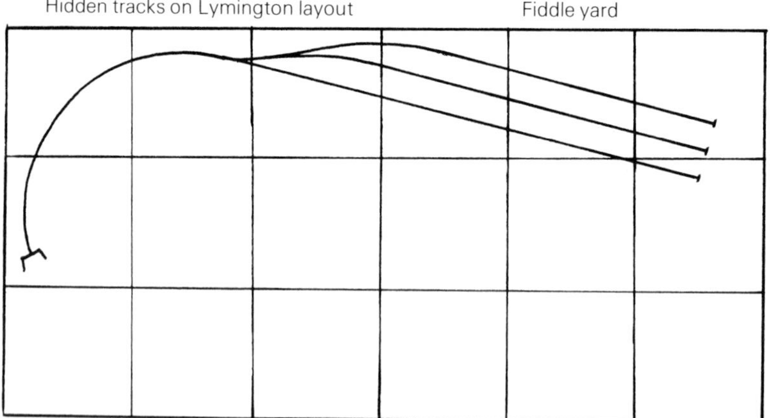

Track plan for a layout based on Lymington.

Lymington Branch by P. Paye (The Oakwood Press), has recently been published and the author includes sketches of the track plans at various periods together with a great deal of other information on the branch.

Although the layout could be of the usual along the wall or L shape in the corner of the room type I recalled a layout plan I had seen some years ago in *Model Railway News,* with a terminus and a through station on a rectangular baseboard with the track leading to a fiddle yard beneath the terminus. The design seemed an ideal basis for this layout and I have used this arrangement but have based the stations on the Lymington Town and Pier prototypes. It was necessary to alter the position of the goods shed at the former and to omit most of the sidings there but the Pier station is essentially similar to the real one.

The layout has attractive scenic possibilities with the river and harbour, complete with ferry. The Skinley range of blueprints includes a small car ferry which, though smaller than the ferries used on the Lymington to Isle of Wight run, would be an attractive addition to the scene. If you wish, a row of houses, together with the Railway Hotel, can be placed behind the Town station. Along the centre of the layout a ridge of hills or a double-sided backdrop would scenically separate the two sides of the layout and give a greater impression of distance between the two stations. Operational scope will be rather greater than for the usual terminus to fiddle yard design because of the additional through station at which extra train movements can take place. The layout is designed for 00 gauge in an area of 6 feet by 3 feet but could be built in N gauge in a correspondingly smaller space.

Hamworthy Goods Branch

This line has an interesting history. It branches from the old Southampton & Dorchester Railway at Hamworthy Junction and serves what was the original Poole station, on the west side of the harbour. This station was opened in 1847 and in about 1860 the single track of the branch was doubled. However trafic on the line became less as further lines were built and the present Poole station in the centre of the town was opened in 1872. The line was closed to passengers in 1896 and was singled again but is still open for freight. The station became Hamworthy Goods but the building is now derelict. However the line is still busy with the yard shunted daily, usually by a Class 33 locomotive and with a daily Freightliner train to Southampton. There are also Cartic trains carrying imported cars to the Midlands. The branch serves the Lower Hamworthy wharves and industrial area. Industries here include a coal yard, oil depots, ship repair slipway, yacht builder, sand and gravel hoppers, cement hoppers and an engineering works.

My plan inspired by the Hamworthy Branch is for an L-shaped layout with a fiddle yard concealed by low relief structures at the right-hand end. From these hidden sidings trains arrive at the run-around loop and the stock is then shunted onto the appropriate sidings serving various industries. There are sufficient of these to make for interesting operation particularly if one of the card order schemes for deciding on the destinations for the rolling stock is employed. The lap point at the right-hand end of the run-around loop is typical in industrial yards and the one at Lower Hamworthy is shown in one of the photographs. For 00-gauge points of this type are available commercially from Piko and Fleischmann; they are equivalent to a right-hand and a left-hand point combined and occupy less space than two separate points. Curves on the layout are of small radius but this is typical of industrial and dockside areas and they will cause no problems with the small locomotives

The coal wharf at Lower Hamworthy with the Ruston & Hornsby diesel shunting coal wagons.

Industries in Lower Hamworthy include **(above)** *a fuel oil depot;* **(below)** *a ship repair yard;* **(above right)** *a gravel hopper;* **(right and below right)** *the coal wharf and depot. All of these can be modelled effectively.*

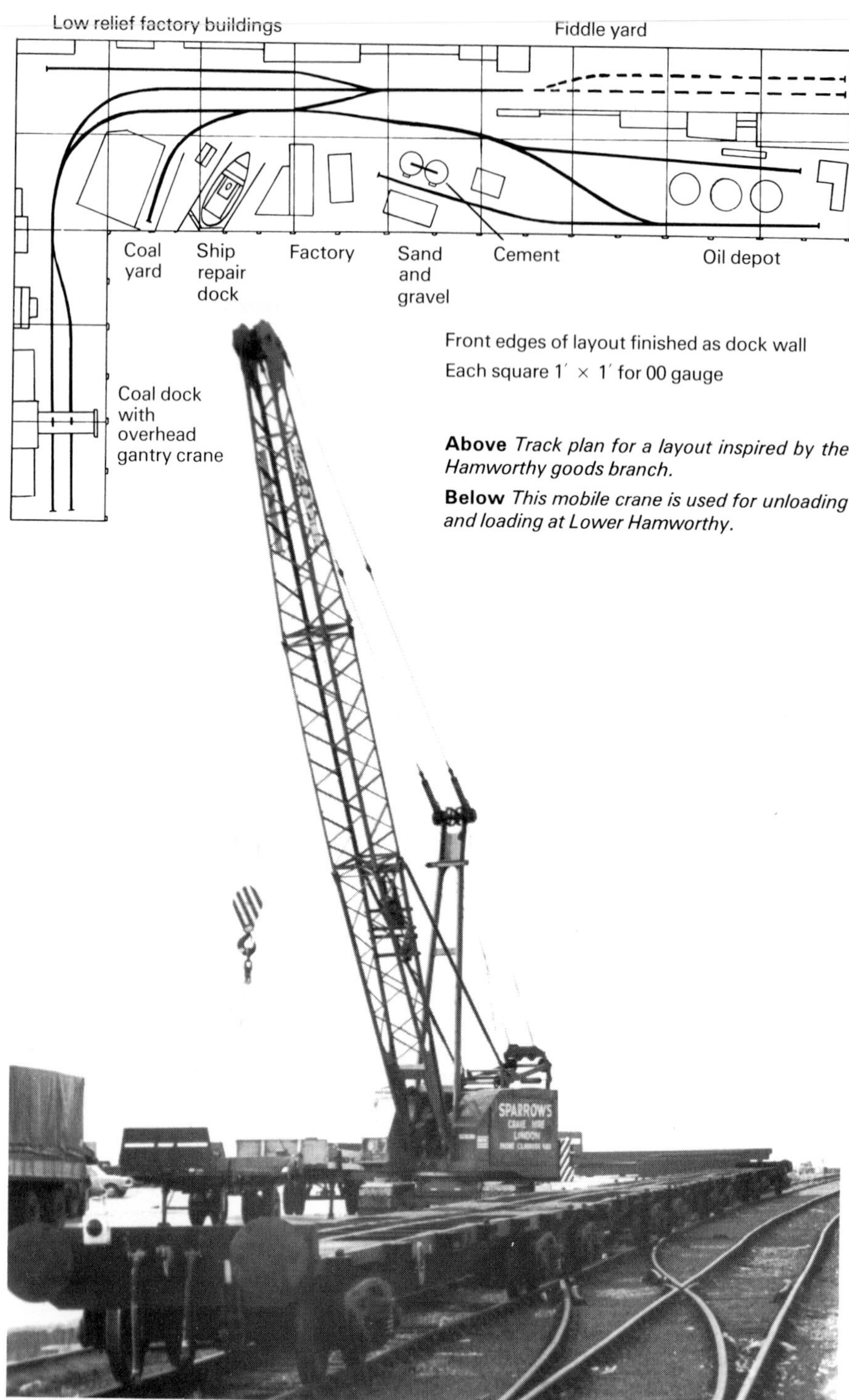

Above *Track plan for a layout inspired by the Hamworthy goods branch.*

Below *This mobile crane is used for unloading and loading at Lower Hamworthy.*

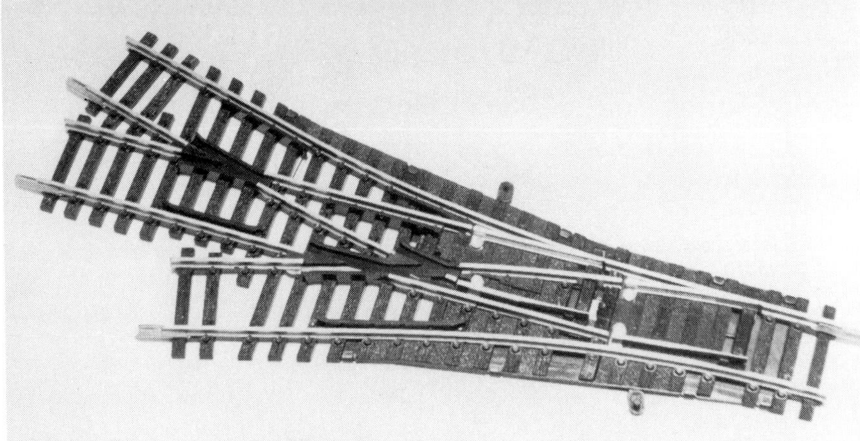

Top *Complex pointwork at Lower Hamworthy includes a lap point at the left of the picture. The tracks are not all still in use.*

Above *The Fleischmann range of H0-scale track includes this lap point useful for cramped situations, for example, in industrial areas.*

suitable for shunting on this layout. For enthusiasts who enjoy shunting, operation on the layout will offer considerable scope. Though the prototype carries only freight traffic, the modeller could run a few trains for the workmen giving the opportunity for some limited passenger traffic. The variety of industries served enables a wide range of rolling stock to be justifiably run on the layout, including some special types if desired. There is a good selection of ready-to-run and cast metal kit locomotives, both steam and diesel prototypes, which will be suitable for the line.

Scenically the scope of the layout is almost unlimited with numerous interesting industrial buildings to be constructed and with many small details which can be added to the area around the tracks. There are some excellent plastic kits for oil tanks, cement hoppers, cranes and other industrial structures made by Kibri, Faller, Vollmer and other manufacturers. Though strictly these are HO rather than 00 scale most of these models will look realistic on an 00-gauge layout. The ship repair slipway is an interesting feature and well worth including on a layout. The ship model can be scratch-built, perhaps following one of the Skinley blueprints, or you can adapt one of the plastic kit models on the market. The front edge of the layout can be finished to look like the wall of the dock giving a very realistic effect. At the rear of the layout low relief buildings give an impression of depth and completeness. Behind this only a sky blue backdrop will be needed.

Above *This 00 scale Johnson 0-4-0 was constructed from a K's kit. It would be ideal for a small industrial branch line.*

Below *Graham Bailey modelled this realistic dock scene in N scale. The ship model is the Novo* Shell Welder.

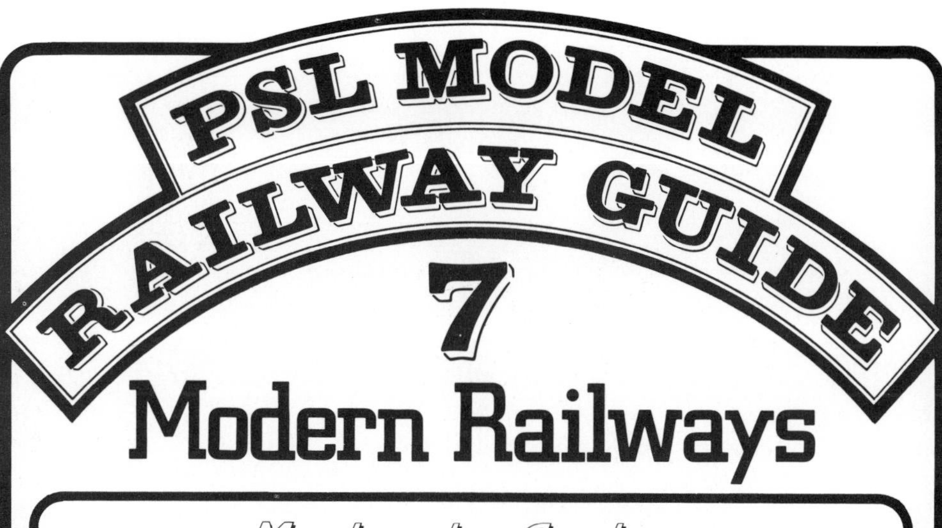

Modern Railways

Michael Andress

Contents

Introduction

Though many modellers still prefer to recreate the days of steam in miniature on their model railways there has been increasing interest recently, particularly among younger enthusiasts (many of whom do not remember steam on British Rail), in the modelling of modern railways. Such a choice has much to offer and a very interesting layout can be constructed based on the contemporary scene.

The aim in this book is to look at various aspects of the railways today from the modelling point of view and to indicate some of the differences from the railways as traditionally modelled. These changes are wide reaching and involve much more than the mere substitution of diesels or electrics for steam locomotives. Not only does the present day railway look different but there are also very significant changes in its operation.

The modeller's locomotive and rolling stock requirements are generally well catered for by the trade, at least in 00 scale, and new items appear regularly; in some cases the models are available even before the prototype goes into service! The intention here is to give some indication of what is available as ready-to-run models or in kit form and describe how these can be improved by alterations and detailing to make them more accurate and realistic. Taking this a little further we also find that it is often possible to convert models which are produced commercially to represent prototypes for which no models are available.

The scope of modern railway modelling is very wide and coverage cannot be complete in a book of this size. Rather the aim has been to provide some basic information and ideas to get you started. I hope that you may then be encouraged to learn more about the prototype and to develop your own ideas on how it can be realistically modelled.

I am most grateful to the four modern railway enthusiasts who have contributed sections to this book. John Glover is well known as a photographer of the contemporary railway scene and he is also interested in its representation in model form. He has designed three layouts of varying sizes, based on modern BR practice, for this book. Michael Alderton and John Payne are two expert and prolific diesel modellers. Their comprehensive survey of BR diesels and how they can be modelled is illustrated with many examples of their own model locomotives. Allan Dare is particularly interested in modern rail freight operation and he has provided a guide to this part of BR's activities, together with suggestions on how these services may be modelled.

I would like to thank all those modellers who have allowed me to use photographs of their models to illustrate this book. I am also grateful to those manufacturers who have assisted me with pictures of, and information on, their products.

The modern diesel multiple unit and colour-light signals, framed by a Victorian cast iron arch at York Station, typify the blend of old and new seen on British Rail today, a combination we can effectively represent in our modelling.

Above *The locomotive stabling and refuelling point on D. Bowe's modern image 00-scale layout. The railway has an impressive roster of diesel and electric locomotives* (Brian Monaghan, D. Bowe and *Railway Modeller*).

Below *The main yard on the modern image 00-scale layout built and operated by D. Bowe. Trains visible include a Freightliner, a company train of new cars from the factory, a diesel multiple unit and a block oil tanker train. Note the lamps in the yard and the modern signal cabin in the right foreground* (D. Bowe, Brian Monaghan and *Railway Modeller*).

Advantages and disadvantages

Railway modelling offers such a vast scope of different interests incorporated in one hobby that it is difficult to categorise the advantages and disadvantages of any particular aspect. One enthusiast, for example, with little skill or experience in construction may wish to build a layout which is large and complex enough for interesting and varied operation in a limited time. For him, availability of suitable commercial products will be essential. Another modeller, with little space for a layout and no great interest in operation, may prefer to spend much of his time researching and scratch-building only a few locomotives and items of rolling stock. Thus what may be an important advantage to one may be irrelevant or even a disadvantage to another. So in considering benefits and difficulties in choosing to model modern railways, I have looked at the situation from the average modeller's viewpoint.

A major advantage in modelling the contemporary scene is that we can so easily obtain accurate data on the prototype. Not only is there a great deal of information available in books and magazines but, best of all, one can go out and look at, measure and photograph the real thing. The benefits from this should not be underestimated. Much of the realism of a railway layout depends on the correct modelling of the many small details. Although each in itself is relatively insignificant, the cumulative effect is very important in achieving the right overall appearance and atmosphere. For a modern image layout it is easy to get these correct by direct reference to the prototype; on a period model railway it is much more difficult and some points may even be impossible to verify. The present approach to prototype photography, with the inclusion of more of the setting and surroundings, is also helpful to the modeller as a study of published pictures will often provide ideas and information on trackside details. Another recent trend is the publication of more colour photographs and these can be very useful for livery details, in showing the effects of weathering, and so on.

The modern image modeller benefits from the good selection of models now available commercially and the situation will be even better in the future as new releases appear. This means that the modeller who does not wish to construct his own locomotives and rolling stock can easily acquire an adequate roster of equipment—but there is still the opportunity to increase the scope and variety by conversion or scratch-building.

There is, for me, an even more important benefit in modelling the contemporary railway scene. I find that my interest in the prototype is enhanced so that I gain even more enjoyment from riding on and observing the full size railway. Similarly study of the real thing provides information and ideas which stimulate my modelling. Thus I gain increased pleasure from both prototype and model, and this is surely what the hobby is all about!

A number of objections have been voiced, largely, I suspect, by the 'dyed in the wool' steam enthusiasts, to the idea of modern railway modelling. While these may at first sight appear discouraging they are not always so valid when considered a little more closely. A favourite criticism is that diesels are just 'boxes on wheels' and that they 'all look alike'! A glance through any modern pictorial album will show the fallacy of these statements and, in fact, British Rail has had an appealing variety of diesel locomotives in operation in recent years. Not only are the various classes distinctly different but there are many minor variations within classes adding to the interest. In some cases the detail differences even permit identification of individual members of a class without reference to the numbers!

Another objection is that too much space is needed for a modern layout and the trains are too long to be realistically represented. However, these are problems faced by most railway modellers and are by no means limited to modern image layouts. In fact the simplification that has been carried out in many places on the real railways, with the removal of passing loops, run-around tracks and sidings,

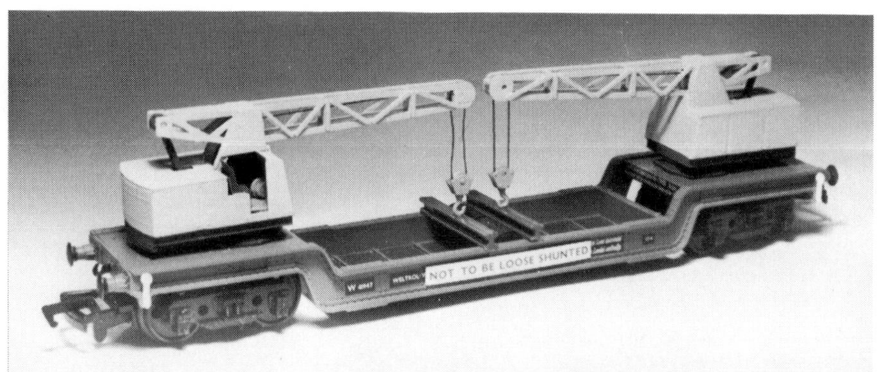

Above *Modern railways employ an interesting, but rarely modelled, selection of equipment for track layout and maintenance work. This track relaying unit was built in 00 scale by Ralph Fenwick using a Mainline well wagon with cranes from Airfix military vehicle kits. A full description of construction is given in* PSL's Practical Guide to Railway Modelling.

An example of the variations to be found within a locomotive class. **Below** *37 063, one of the first group of Class 37 Co-Co Diesel Electric locomotives to be delivered to British Rail, has gangway doors, split headcode boxes and horns situated behind small circular grilles on the front of the nose.* **Bottom** *37 250, one of the second group of Class 37s, has a revised nose layout with a four-character headcode box and horns mounted on the cab roof. Further variations on this locomotive are the oval instead of large round buffers and the small snow ploughs which have been fitted.*

Top *The Hornby model of the High Speed Train in 00 scale* (Hornby).

Above *Modern trains need not be long! On the Isle of Sheppey a Class 33 with a short train of steel rods approaches the Kingsferry bridge over the Medway. The train is fully fitted and therefore does not require a brake van* (John Glover).

closure of goods yards, singling of track, and so on, makes it easier to model the prototype realistically in the space available. Train lengths, for comparable trains, are often shorter today than in the days of steam and there are certainly many examples of very short trains, both passenger and freight, to be seen running on the modern railways.

It has also been claimed that the trains are drab and boring now. In reality there is still an interesting selection of rolling stock, including many colourful and distinctive privately-owned freight vehicles. On the passenger side the coaching stock, the diesel and electric multiple units, the HSTs and the APTs, provide considerable variety in design and colour schemes. Modern locomotive liveries are also more colourful and, because repainting a large roster of diesels is a gradual process, livery changes have resulted in a mixture of different colour schemes to be seen running on BR at any one time. Further interest can be added with one or more small diesel locomotive painted in private company colours for use on industrial tracks.

The modern modeller can even find valid reasons for running a few steam locomotives on the layout if he wishes, without loss of realism. An occasional steam-hauled enthusiasts' special can be operated over the main line or one or more small industrial engines can be employed on private sidings.

John Payne built this model of a diminutive Ruston Hornsby 48 HP diesel-mechanical shunter from scratch. Despite its small size the model can haul six wagons with ease (Michael Alderton and John Payne).

Another good scheme is to include a section of a preserved line on the layout. This could perhaps be a branch line, abandoned and now re-opened as a tourist attraction, running from a station on the modern main line. Such a feature will allow great scope for variety in the choice of locomotives and rolling stock and could be very interesting both scenically and operationally.

The structures on a modern layout can also give great variety because of the differing architectural styles and construction materials employed at various periods. Thus old buildings of stone, brick or wood, perhaps in poor condition or even derelict, provide an interesting contrast with modern glass and concrete or prefabricated structures.

The idea of modelling branch lines has become very popular, especially in the form of a small country terminus station linked to a fiddle yard. Such a choice enables a layout, realistic in both appearance and operation, to be built in a small space. Today many branch lines have been closed and those that do remain open have usually been simplified, by the removal of any unnecessary tracks and closure of many facilities. Often either the passenger services or the freight traffic has been discontinued. Because of these changes it has been claimed that branch lines are unsuitable for modern railway modelling. There is some validity in this statement in that the original concept of branch line modelling was firmly based on the station layouts and operating practices of the steam era. However, even though the character of these lines has undoubtedly changed, some of the branches still open today could form the basis for interesting layouts.

To close this section a word of caution would perhaps be appropriate. No matter what the apparent benefits are of choosing modern image, or for that matter any other aspect of railway modelling, do not be tempted unless you really are interested in the subject. Most model railways, unless very small, are long term projects and you will only be able to maintain the interest and enthusiasm essential for success if your choice of prototype and period has real appeal for you.

Above left *The black and yellow visibility stripes used on shunting locomotives add colour to the modern liveries. This Class 08 was photographed at York station. Note the heavy spillage on the hopper wagons at the front of the train which can easily be reproduced with white paint.*

Above right *Added interest is given to modern liveries by a number of special schemes. This panel appears on Class 86 electric locomotive No 86235 'Novelty' to commemorate the 150th anniversary of the Liverpool and Manchester Railway's opening.*

Below *A derelict station platform shelter. Modelling such a structure requires care to achieve the right effect.*

Layout suggestions

by John Glover

Why model the modern railway scene? Perhaps it is surprising that we need even ask, but since so many layouts recall the days of steam, which finally ceased commercial service in the 1960s, the question is worth posing. There can be little doubt that the steam locomotive itself is mainly responsible for that choice of period. For many it is a fabulous 'living creature' and its recreation in model form, even as a plastic body concealing an electric mechanism, which may even be in the tender, brings back fond memories. Yet distance of time tends to lend enchantment to this nostalgic view; in reality the steam locomotive was dirty and inefficient. While it was capable of impressive performances from time to time, steam could never provide the quality of service offered by British Rail today.

Recent years have seen a growth of interest in the modern scene, and the model railway trade is at last beginning to support the modern modeller to some effect, albeit with some startling gaps, particularly in the field of multiple units. The modeller of today analysing the contemporary scene, will find that there is greater variety than he perhaps suspected, with many worthwhile avenues to follow. Far more than just dieselisation or electrification is implied; new methods of working, simplification of the permanent way, resignalling and station modernisation are but some of the changes from the steam age which can be incorporated. At the same time, if there are any particular features of the traditional scene which appeal these can often be retained without loss of realism. Semaphore signalling, for instance, still exists in pockets on even quite important main lines, although most modellers will adopt colour-light signals with a sigh of relief. As in the real thing, multiple aspect signalling has no moving parts! Let us therefore consider briefly the main business of the modern railway.

Inter-City Nearly half of British Rail's passenger revenue is contributed by this group of services, which run between principal centres, usually on a regular hourly frequency throughout the day. On the electrified West Coast Main Line between Euston and Glasgow a typical formation is a locomotive of Class 87 or 86/2 with a rake of air-conditioned Mark II or Mark III coaches; at present these are supplemented by the prototype versions of the Class 370, better known as the Advanced Passenger Train or APT. On the East Coast Main Line, the services between Kings Cross, West Yorkshire and Edinburgh are in the hands of the diesel High Speed Trains or Inter-City 125s. Similar sets are in operation between Paddington and the West of England/South Wales and on the North East—South West route via Birmingham.

Slightly lower down the scale come the locomotive-hauled diesel services. The top rank locomotives for these duties are Classes 50, 47, 46 and 45, with a string of Mark II coaches (either air-conditioned or non air-conditioned varieties), or perhaps even elderly Mark I coaches of early 1950s design. Mark I stock can still be seen in large quantities; in particular the vast majority of catering vehicles are Mark I, as are all the gangwayed brake vehicles (BG).

On the secondary Inter-City network and excursions, less powerful locomotives such as the Classes 40, 37, 33 and 31 may be employed, almost invariably with Mark I stock. A detailed examination of illustrations appearing in the various railway publications will give some clues as to what trains and formations can be seen in different parts of the country, but even the shortest Inter-City service will not normally load to less than five vehicles.

London and South East This group covers all the suburban services operating in South East England within a line stretching roughly from Clacton through Northampton to Bournemouth. It is typified by electric traction with multiple unit trains operating at close headways, using either third rail electrification, as on the Southern Region, or overhead power supplies, as elsewhere. On principal routes the tracks are shared with Inter-City trains and the

PASSENGERS
CROSS RAILWAY
BRIDGE

Top left *A Class 86 electric locomotive arrives at Euston with a typical West Coast train formed of a Mk I BG (57 feet long) and Mk III coaches (75 feet long)* (John Glover).

Above left *Some of the North Warwickshire trains terminate at Shirley. A Metro-Cammell diesel multiple unit crosses to the up line for the return working. This unit is in the smart but short-lived 'refurbished' livery. Note the old and new notices warning about crossing the line by the bridge and the duplicated bridge number plates. Small details such as these will add to the realism of a layout* (John Glover).

Left *A Class 25 with a pick-up freight descends the bank at Cradley LMR towards Stourbridge. Few pick-up goods trains remain now. Note the long welded rail at the side of the running track awaiting future installation* (John Glover).

Top *A Class 47 locomotive about to leave a road-stone depot with a trainload of aggregate in privately-owned hopper wagons. Over half of British Rail's freight carryings are in company trains like this, many of them using special wagons purpose-built for customer's requirements. Company trains operate for one customer and run between specific terminals carrying bulkloads of commodities such as oil and petroleum products, roadstone and minerals, and new cars* (British Rail).

Above *Typical of the waiting accommodation provided for passengers on the platforms now is the 'bus shelter' type of structure. This can be modelled easily using plastic card and clear plastic sheet.*

general scale of operation is beyond what most would wish to recreate in model form. Nevertheless, there are gems to be found within this vast area, whose overall importance in revenue terms is only a fraction less than the Inter-City group. Astonishingly, there are no ready-to-run models of ordinary British electric multiple units available in any gauge.

Provincial services This category contains the remainder, ranging from the suburban services provided in cities such as Manchester and Liverpool to the diesel multiple unit (dmu) operated rural services which remain. The dmu is the principal means of traction. This sector is characterised by its diversity.

Parcels Whilst many parcels are carried by passenger train, parcels trains consisting of bogie or, occasionally, four-wheeled vans are run to convey newspapers and Post Office mails as well as rail parcels. These may use passenger stations or special parcels depots. The parcels themselves are often carried in the familiar BRUTE trolleys, which can be loaded complete into the vans.

Freight 85 per cent of freight traffic now moves in train loads between private sidings. The traditional mixed freight train and the local goods yard are now rare indeed. Haulage of coal and coke remains the principal rail freight traffic. Conveyed exclusively in British Rail owned wagons, the modern colliery to power station service consists of 30 or so 32-ton

Top *Older bridges and other structures on the railway often require repair or replacement. On the modern 00-scale layout, owned by Michael Alderton and John Payne, the scaffolding and workmen add interesting detail to this river bridge.*

Above *Abandoned siding and derelict cattle dock modelled on the 00-scale modern layout of Michael Alderton and John Payne is typical of the effects of changing freight traffic operations on the modern railway.*

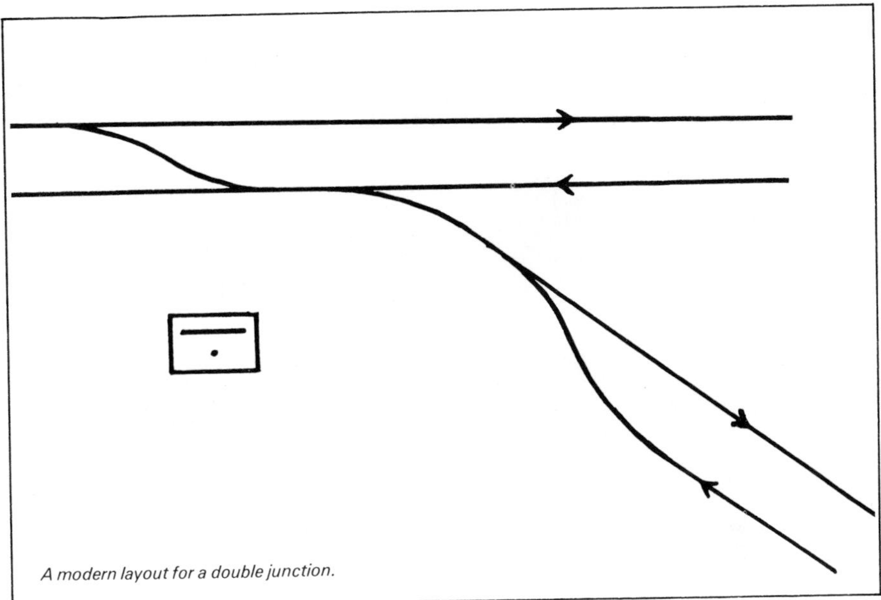

A modern layout for a double junction.

Merry-go-round Hopper wagons permanently attached to a locomotive of Class 47 or 56. Wagons of lesser capacity still abound, but those not equipped with a continuous brake operated from the locomotive are being withdrawn. Only trains including unbraked wagons would normally have a guard's brake at the rear.

Next in importance is iron and steel traffic, followed by earth and stones and then petroleum products. The latter groups are often conveyed in colourful privately-owned specialised vehicles which account for 20 per cent of the total wagon fleet. Merchandise traffic may be conveyed by Freightliner container services between principal points where special cranage to road vehicles is provided; for lesser quantities a modern wagon-load system, known as Speedlink, operates at speeds of up to 75 miles per hour, using the long wheelbase air-braked wagon fleet.

Modernisation of the railway system has resulted in many other physical changes which are of relevance to the modeller. A prime objective has been simplification. Thus the dmu or emu can be driven from either end and does not require run-around facilities at termini. This saves time and effort as well as pointwork. Occasional engineers' trains can be propelled to and from site or, alternatively, a locomotive can be attached at each end. On a grander scale, locomotives regularly push trains from Weymouth to Bournemouth (Class 33/1) and from Edinburgh to Glasgow Queen Street (Class 47/7) and pull them back again.

The track is also different, with traditional bullhead rail now relegated to secondary lines and sidings. The modern standard is a flat-bottomed rail clipped to concrete sleepers and welded into long lengths. Ballasting is deep and well built up at the sides of the track to prevent lateral movement. Point and crossing work remains timber mounted, but simplified, as complex track formations are costly to build and maintain. Consequently, ordinary turnouts are used in preference to items such as slip points and diamond crossings unless there are compelling reasons to do otherwise. As an example, a modern layout for a double junction is shown. Although the inability to make certain parallel movements simultaneously reduces the capacity of the junction, this can be offset through modern colour-light signalling. Through such means the headways between succeeding trains can be reduced and a greater flexibility in operation achieved. The use of bi-directional signalling in station areas, for instance, enables trains in either direction to use any platform instead of conforming to the 'keep left' principle applied historically in Britain.

Track reductions can also follow a resignalling project, quite apart from the changes which may stem from variations in the volume and nature of the traffic carried. Thus singling of previously double track is often found, and modern safety precautions

Some gated crossings operated from signal boxes are still to be found in use though many have been replaced by barrier crossings. This example is at Goring-by-Sea on the Southern Region.

eliminate the hand-over of a token for single line working between signalman and driver. Indeed the signalman may be many miles away in a remotely situated signalling centre. Often the remains of rationalisation schemes are visible, with abandoned track beds and disused platforms in station areas.

Although the Victorians built the railways to last, the life of structures is not indefinite. All structures are subject to the ageing process but the enforced renewal of station buildings and bridgework is perhaps the most noticeable result. The opportunity is invariably taken to rebuild according to more modern needs and station buildings are generally more compact and simpler than the legacies of the last century. In recent years a trend has been evident in the renovation of old buildings rather than demolition, but the 'bus shelter' type of accommodation, especially at unstaffed stations, is commonplace. Reconstructed overbridges will always allow for increased clearances for overhead electrification, and both over- and under-line bridges may need to take account of wider roads. Level crossings are an unmitigated nuisance to the railway operator and the traditional swing gates are being eliminated as quickly as funds allow. They are replaced by full lifting barriers (often controlled remotely by a signalman using closed circuit television to survey them), automatic half barriers, or the simple automatic open crossings which are protected solely by flashing lights and an audible warning.

Lastly, one must not forget the staff, their uniforms have been updated more than once in the last 20 years. Also, if their duties take them on or about the track, the wearing of an orange mini-vest is obligatory—and very easily modelled.

From this necessarily brief preamble it will be seen that the railway modeller has to make sizeable adjustments to convert from the steam age. Whether or not to go the whole hog and model the present day and future only, or to compromise by using some traditional features, is a personal decision, but the layout plans suggested below demonstrate some of the possibilities.

Plan 1 is not based on any particular real life location but sets out to enable prototypical main line operation in a moderate sized room. Exclusive use of the room is not required as this is strictly a wall-hugging layout and would be suitable for a boy's bedroom, for instance. Many modellers wish to indulge in main line running, and this layout makes provision for six-coach passenger trains. A local multiple unit service is superimposed and there is scope for parcels and block freight traffic. There is also a locomotive stabling area which could include a fuelling installation. There are no

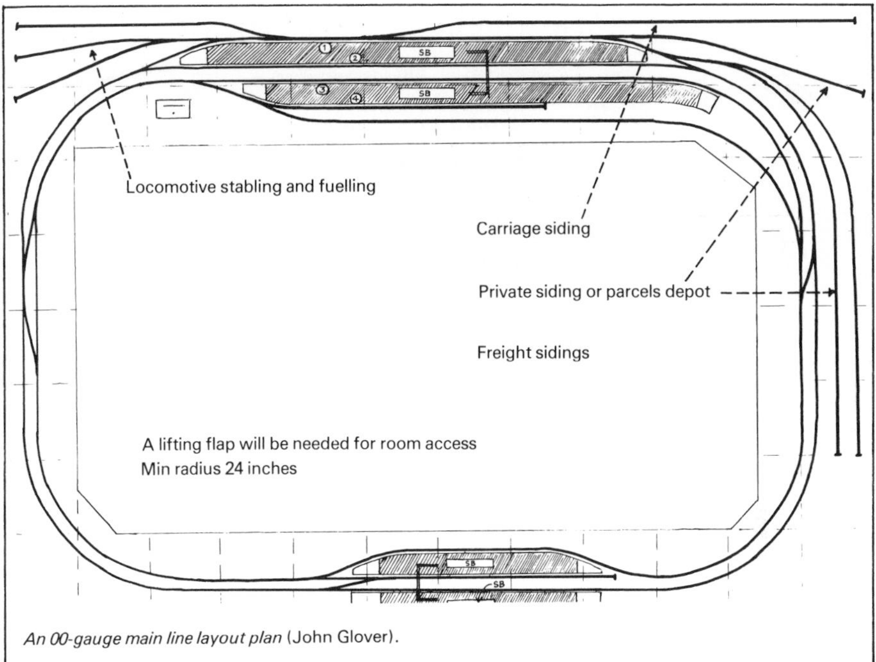

An 00-gauge main line layout plan (John Glover).

hidden sidings, and increased siding capacity to take spare trains would be advantageous if space permits. The layout is not set in any particular part of the country and the spread of British Rail (rather than regionally inspired) architecture, means that adaptation needs are minimal.

Operation is as follows. An Inter-City train is usually kept on each of the main circuits using Platforms 2 and 3 as appropriate. Termination from either direction can be achieved in Platform 1, where locomotives can be exchanged and the stock stabled in the carriage siding. A suitable formation would be Brake Second Open, Open Second, Open Second, Buffet Car, Open First, Brake First Open. Note that First and Second Class accommodation is usually separated by any catering facilities; the composite coach is now unusual as none have been built since 1964. There is usually a much higher element of Second Class than First Class, and this should be reflected in the model.

Parcels traffic would be dealt with in Platform 1 when it is not otherwise occupied. A parcels train consisting of a mixed vintage of rolling stock has been a common sight until very recent times, with pre-nationalisation designs still appearing in considerable numbers. The trade has now responded, offering a wide choice of model vehicles.

Freight traffic can depict the industries of the modeller's choice. Either a train of bogie tank wagons carrying oil (or of roadstone hoppers) would look most effective, although the latter suffer from the inherent defect that they must be permanently 'loaded' or 'empty'. A small Freightliner or Speedfreight terminal might also be a popular choice, and there are plenty of other possibilities from within the ranges offered. Using the facilities at the rear of the main station, trains can arrive and depart in either direction. The loop on the inner circuit is provided so that a freight may be held clear of a passenger service.

The shuttle train service is worked by a diesel multiple unit. For maximum effectiveness, platform lengths are sufficient for four cars; at less busy periods (assuming 2 x 2 car units), one unit might be detached and placed in one of the platforms. Electrification on either the third rail or the overhead system is a possibility and an electric multiple unit would make an unusual model. The whole layout could, of course, be equipped for (prototype!) electric traction and allow electrically-hauled trains throughout, with diesel power retained for shunting only.

A totally modern operation is assumed and blue liveried locomotives are essential. Recent years have seen more variation in locomotive liveries and these have percolated through to

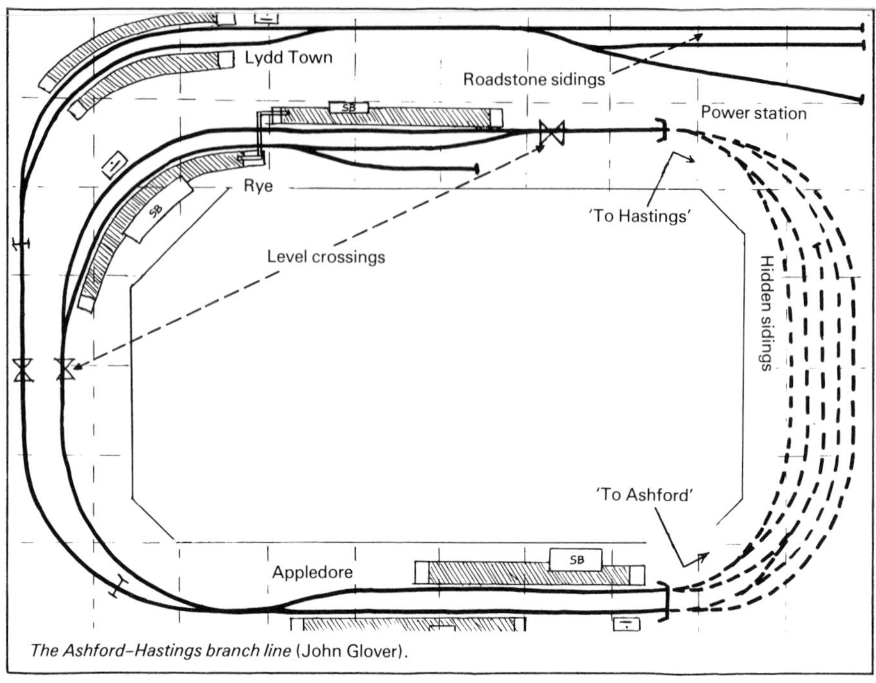

The Ashford–Hastings branch line (John Glover).

the models offered on the ready-to-run market. Diesel multiple units are especially varied and can reasonably appear in all blue, the 'refurbished' livery of grey with a blue stripe, or the standard blue and grey. In 1982 there was even a dmu running round in red livery for advertising purposes!

Before leaving the main line layout, it may be useful to mention the question of compatibility between different types of locomotives and rolling stock. The traditional method of braking trains in Britain was the automatic vacuum brake and heating was provided by steam piped from the locomotive. Today, all this has changed and the air brake is standard with electric train heating/air conditioning as required. During the modernisation period the traditional systems were retained initially and not all classes of vehicle are dual fitted. Details of which pieces of equipment are fitted with which system can be obtained from the pocket books published by Ian Allan Ltd and others, but it should be noted that mixed systems of heating or braking are not possible in any one train. Other points of importance are that air conditioned rolling stock are only normally seen behind locomotives of Classes 31/4, 45/1, 47/4, 47/7, 50, 55 and 81-87, and that goods brake vans are only needed if any portion of the train has no continuous brake operative.

A more relaxed attitude to operation will be evident in Plan 2. The branch line is a deservedly popular prototype, and this layout depicts a portion of the cross country Ashford-Hastings line. The real service has been the subject of closure proposals in the past, but the route is still retained and is operated by a variety of Southern Region diesel multiple units. Once being double track throughout its 26½ miles, it has been singled between Appledore and Ore, with a passing loop retained at Rye where the hourly trains in each direction cross. At peaks the service is augmented and the single line sections do impose some constraints. Thus the 07.10 from Hastings, having missed out three intermediate stations en route, leaves the single line at Appledore at 07.38 to allow the 07.28 from Ashford to proceed. It then stands for eight minutes so as to provide an 08.00 arrival in Ashford.

As befits a former South Eastern Railway line, the platforms are staggered at most stations, and the original architecture remains. In the flat country (on the edge of Romney Marsh), level crossings abound and all types of protection are found. Locomotive-hauled passenger trains are rare, but summer excursions to Rye with a Class 33 diesel and Mark I stock have been a feature of this line. There is one branch, formerly a passenger line

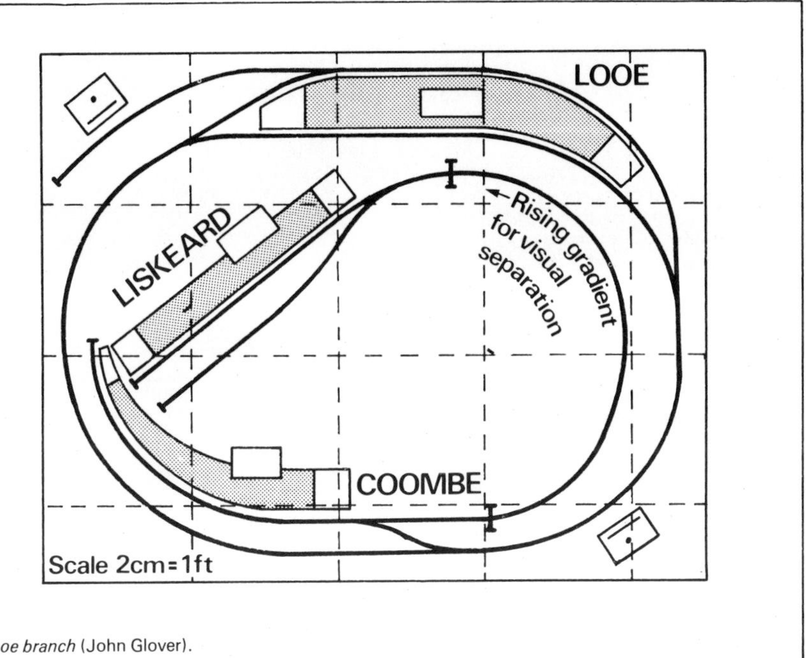

The Looe branch (John Glover).

to New Romney but now servicing only a siding for the nuclear power station at Dungeness and a roadstone siding at Lydd. Passenger trains were withdrawn in 1967; these ran to and from Ashford, leaving the 'main' line at Appledore.

The model is based on a continuous circuit with hidden sidings. Appledore and Rye have been selected for the plan, together with the branch. The basic service could be provided by a selection of models of dmu Classes 203/5/6/7 for which kits are available, although other unit types can be substituted. Freight would be handled by a Class 33, or perhaps a Class 47 or 73; the method of operation would be to run round trains in the remains of Lydd Town station and then propel the wagons to the sidings. The siding at Rye can be used for stabling defective vehicles, or holding engineers equipment. Embellishment of these basic operations is entirely feasible, and a reversing facility has been included in the hidden sidings so that an Ashford-Lydd passenger service could be operated.

It must be admitted that this plan still requires the availability of a fair sized room, so Plan 3 has been devised to suit the man who has started with a 6 ft and 4 ft baseboard and found it too big. The subject is the Liskeard-Looe branch in Cornwall, although much modeller's licence has been taken.

Below *Coombe station in 1979. Although the train has only just arrived from Looe, the signalman has already set the road for Liskeard. The short length of the platform and the simple nature of the station is evident in this view. The line on the right leads to the china clay works* (John Glover).

Nevertheless the prototype remains recognisable—just! This remarkable line has its platform at the junction station at Liskeard at right angles to the main line; the branch then descends under that line, throws off a freight spur at Coombe where the passenger trains reverse and at last assume their southerly course to the seaside town of Looe. Unsurprisingly, the passenger trains are diesel multiple units, but a Class 37 might appear on the China Clay freights.

The plan is drawn for a solid baseboard which is 4 ft 6 in by 3ft 6 in, although it might be possible to shave both these dimensions if essential. The Liskeard-Coombe-Looe service is provided by a Class 121 single unit dmu, with trailer if required; both can be simply converted from the Lima models. A representation of the freight service circulates around the continuous track at the lower level. If propelling movements are 'authorised' by the modeller, even with only the two sidings in the plan, a great deal of fun may be had. Train lengths must be kept short, and the absolute maximum of stock would be two dmu cars, one of the smaller diesel locomotives (a Class 25 or an 08 diesel shunter would look better than a Class 37), and a handful of wagons to choice.

The modern scene has much to offer and the possibilities are endless. This selection of ideas only scratches the surface of modern modelling which has the infinite advantage that research is possible through personal observation. Yet the railway is far from static and a continuous process of evolution is taking place. An accurate model of the railway of today will become a historical model in its own right in the future.

Readers may also like to refer to a number of other interesting layout ideas devised by John Glover, again based on various British Rail lines, which have appeared in issues of *Railway Modeller* magazine. These include: August 1979—'Worcester'; September 1979—'Bourne End'; November 1979—'Liskeard'; February 1980—'Eridge'; May 1980 (The Special Extra)—'Bromsgrove'; August 1980—'Silvertown' and September 1980—'Godley Junction'.

Top left *Class 207 no 1312 stands at Appledore with the 07.10 Hastings–Ashford. The goods shed is no longer in use for rail traffic* (John Glover).

Above left *Rye Station, Southern Region, is an example of a traditional station building still maintained in excellent condition today. The addition of the BR symbol and name are the only changes of note. The building would make a very attractive model* (John Glover).

Top *'Tadpole' unit of Class 206 No 1206 leaves Rye for Hastings past the well known windmill. A layout based on this line should include a model of the windmill to help set the scene. Note the abandoned track bed on the right* (John Glover).

Above *At Rye, Class 206 unit no 1206 crosses Class 205 unit no 1111. Note the lights and closed circuit TV cameras controlling the crossing in the background. On the right is the engineers siding. Note also the simple facilities on the platform* (John Glover).

Above *Liskeard, Western Region. The Looe branch platform with the single unit diesel awaiting departure* (John Glover).

Below *Coombe Junction signal box and level crossing in 1979. The signal box has now been closed and the track layout at the station further simplified* (John Glover).

Modelling diesel locomotives

by Michael Alderton and John Payne

Although diesel locomotives had been around for some time, it was not until 1958 that the first of the present main-line diesel locomotives, introduced initially under the diesel locomotive pilot scheme of 1955, began to make any significant impact on the grip of steam. Diesel introduction to British Railways at this time became so prolific, and made such rapid progress, that by 1963-64, steam had virtually disappeared from London and, by 1968, steam was gone.

Slowly events have turned full circle, gone are the conglomeration of small diesel shunters, gone are the Bo-Bos and Baby Deltics, gone are the Westerns and Warships, and surely the greatest loss of all must be that of the Deltics.

At first the model manufacturers were slow to exploit the new form of rail traction, but happily the situation has been corrected, and now one major company even manages to have its models running before the prototypes appear in service on British Rail, so that today all the current main-line diesel locomotives are available to the modern image modeller as ready-to-run items.

Let us quickly take stock of the various groups of locomotives which are running: Type 1—up to 1000HP and including all the diesel shunters; Type 2—1000-1475HP; Type 3—1500-1750HP; Type 4—2000-2750HP; and Type 5—3000HP and above. Locomotive numbers now begin with the class number, followed by a three-digit number which indicates any sub-division, and locomotive identification, ie, 47 420 is a Type 4 locomotive of the seventh type, built by Brush, 420 indicates it is a 47/4, ie, fitted with dual, or electric, train heating equipment and is the 20th such locomotive of this sub-division.

Diesel shunters can be split into two groups, locomotives under 350HP, and those up to 1000HP. Of the first group, the small shunters were allocated classes 01 to 07, and of this group only the 03 remains in service today.

03 & 04 0-6-0 DM Models of the 03, and the earlier 04, are available only in kit form. MTK produce whitemetal kits of both locomotives. Airfix used to produce a plastic kit of the 04, whch it was possible to motorise using a chassis kit produced by Eames, sadly neither are available now.

The MTK kits are complete except for motor, wheels and gears. All the castings are good, though a little thick, with a fair amount of flash to be removed. Assembly of the chassis is straightforward, but should be carried out on a piece of plate glass to ensure that the frames are square. One pitfall to avoid when assembling the chassis is to ensure that the throw of the cast jackshaft cranks matches the throw of the cranks of the wheels you intend to fit. When assembling the body parts ensure that the verticals are vertical when viewed from all sides, and follow the instructions carefully. The buffer beams are a little crude, plus the cab roof, and proportions of the cab windows do not appear to be quite right, however these minor problems should not cause too much trouble to the average modeller.

Most of the 03s have a runner permanently coupled to them to ensure that the track circuits are actuated, and if you are modelling one of the airbrake-fitted locomotives do not forget the extra reservoirs and associated pipework.

In the case of the 04 be careful about buffers, as some locomotives were fitted with oval ones, and others had round ones; likewise some locomotives were fitted with recessed front steps and a cut-out in the running plate, whereas others were fitted with a simpler design of step and no cut-outs. Also worth mentioning are the tramway versions which were legally required to have the wheels and motion enclosed behind skirts.

There are no models available of the 01, 02, 05, 06 and 07 shunters, but as these are all now withdrawn it would seem unlikely that a model from a major manufacturer will follow; however, models are available for two designs of small shunter that fell outside the present numbering system.

The first of these two designs are a small number of 165HP diesel electric 0-6-0 shunters operated by the Western Region Civil Engineers department. These locomotives are still in use today and are based on a standard industrial locomotive built by Ruston Hornsby of Lincoln. MTK have produced a kit of this locomotive, employing the same construction methods as the 03 and 04 kits described earlier. Many years ago Trix produced a model of this design of locomotive, the body casting was superb but the chassis was poor, and again these models have become very hard to find now.

A conversion based on the MTK kit of the Ruston 165HP 0-6-0 is the 0-4-0 diesel mechanical version of the locomotive—a pair of these locomotives were operated by the Eastern Region until the late 1960s. A new chassis is the major change but the cab front and the roof have to be rebuilt, and the radiator and front running plate shortened. Both vesions of this locomotive would be ideally suited to an industrial layout.

The second of the unclassed designs are the now withdrawn NBL 0-4-0 diesel hydraulics. Although a little bit early for the true modern image modeller, they provide a useful link with our steam friends. MTK produce a whitemetal kit for one of the very early versions of this locomotive, D2700-2702. Although not strictly accurate, it does provide a fair representation of the prototype. The kit follows normal MTK practice as described previously, the body being based on the industrial version of the locomotive, fitted with a large headlamp front and rear. These are easily removed and standard BR marker lights and lamp irons substituted.

The remaining members of the class—D2703-2707—were built to a revised design and cannot be constructed from the MTK kit, but many years ago Playcraft used this version for the basis of a 'starter' locomotive in their range of model railway equipment. Only the body of the locomotive is of any interest to the serious modeller and, even so, major surgery is required to make a presentable model. To complete the locomotive a scratch-built chassis is required as the original Playcraft version incorporated outside frames. Again, this model is very hard to find now.

Turning our attention to the large shunters, those that fall in the group 350-1000HP, Classes 08 to 14; only the 08 and 09 remain in service.

08 & 09 0-6-0 DE There are currently three versions of the 08/09 shunter available, produced by Hornby, Wrenn and Lima, though these are soon to be joined by a fourth version from Mainline. The model produced by Hornby is a poor representation and for modelling purposes can be dismissed. The two remaining versions produced by Wrenn and Lima represent the earlier version 08 and the later 08/09 respectively. It should be pointed out that the only difference between the 08 and 09 is that the latter has a higher top speed.

Both models can be very simply improved by just painting the cranks and coupling rods the correct colours. Progressing from this the removal of mould lines and, in the case of the Lima version, the replacement of the moulded hand-rails with wire ones, followed by a repaint, can work wonders. A word of caution though, due to the size and age of the class, a number of variations have crept in over the years. The most obvious visual differences are in the layout and variations of battery boxes/equipment cupboards on the bonnet sides, plus the cab doors are either panelled wooden ones or sheet metal. On the Lima model there is a large cubicle just ahead of the fuel tank, covering the lower set of air filter elements, which is used to house the air brake equipment, plus the cab doors are of the sheet metal variety, whereas the Wrenn model has a different battery box layout and the earlier design of cab door. The choice is yours, it depends on the period you model, but Southern fans don't forget the waist level air brake hoses on your 09s.

10, 11 & 12 0-6-0 DE Although a little early for the modern image period, these three classes all use the basic 08 body. The Class 10 is really only an 08 with a different engine, and the Class 11 is again a basic 08 body, but this time with slightly smaller wheels. Finally the Class 12 built at Ashford from components supplied by English Electric is also similar to the 08 but is fitted with the Bulleid-Firth-Brown wheels peculiar to the Southern.

13 0-6-0 + 0-6-0 DE Before leaving the English Electric shunters we must not overlook the Class 13 which is a conversion based on a pair of 08 shunters. The two locomotives are permanently coupled together, one of them having its cab cut down to waist height. To produce a model of this locomotive a pair of 08 shunters is required, preferably the Wrenn version. It sounds an easy conversion and it is, but don't forget to use a drawing and some photographs.

14 0-6-0 DH This is the final locomotive in our review of the large shunters, being a 650HP unit which employed a hydraulic transmission and a jackshaft drive positioned within the wheelbase. MTK have produced an etched brass kit of this locomotive designed to

Top *This Class 04 shunter was constructed with an Airfix kit body on a scratch-built chassis* (Michael Alderton and John Payne).

Above *A Class 03 shunter and runner; the locomotive was built from an MTK kit* (Michael Alderton and John Payne).

Below *This N scale 04 diesel shunter model was built from an ABS cast metal body kit mounted on a Minitrix chassis.*

Above *A Class 17 constructed from an MTK kit* (Michael Alderton and John Payne).

Below *Graham Farish produce a number of diesel locomotive models in N scale in ready-to-run form including this 08 seen here with a Peco tank wagon. This firm also offers the HST in N scale.*

Above *A Class 08 shunting at the quarry; the locomotive has a Kitmaster body mounted on a scratch-built chassis* (Michael Alderton and John Payne).

Below *A modified Wrenn Class 20 with extra details* (Michael Alderton and John Payne).

fit a Jouef chassis, incorporating the same jackshaft drive as the prototype. However, with Jouef having gone into liquidation, it may well be hard to obtain. In adapting the locomotive to fit the Jouef chassis, MTK have made the body far too short but the detail is of the high standard we have come to expect from etched brass kits.

Four other locomotive designs, Classes 15, 16, 17 and 20, conclude the Type 1 group, each of these locomotives are of the Bo-Bo diesel electric type, and were all designed as freight locomotives. Unfortunately there are no kits or ready-to-run models available of either the Class 15 or 16. However, MTK produce a kit of the Class 17, and Wrenn a model of the Class 20.

17 Bo-Bo DE The MTK kit of the Class 17 is a whitemetal body kit which includes a set of correct bogie sideframes, but no bogies, being originally designed to take a pair of K's four-wheel motor bogies. The castings are of a satisfactory standard, and build up into a very nice locomotive. However, the K's motor bogies are no longer available and there is no alternative but to scratch-build a new chassis employing a central motor, driving each bogie through a cardan shaft. Motorising this locomotive is one of the more challenging projects for the modern image modeller, though a little more space could be gained by modelling one of the locomotives fitted with Rolls-Royce engines and the raised engine hatches on each bonnet.

20 Bo-Bo DE Wrenn produce an excellent, if somewhat dated, model of the original batch of Class 20s. The only major fault of the model is that the cab sides are parallel, when they should taper inwards to the rear. It is not hard to modify the model to incorporate the taper, it just depends on the individual, if the time and energy involved are worthwhile.

The Class 20s were built in three batches, and there are significant visual differences between each group. The original batch—D8000-8034—were fitted with oval buffers, a ladder on the right-hand side of the bonnet just forward of the large radiator, a stiffening bar across the centre of the radiator and a sand box for each wheel. The second batch—D8035-8127—were fitted with large round buffers, no ladder, no radiator stiffener and sandboxes only for the outer wheels of the bogies. The locomotives in these two batches were all fitted with headcode discs, and locomotives D8070-8127 were fitted with tablet catcher recesses built into the cab sides and were intended for the Scottish region.

The final batch were fitted with headcode boxes instead of discs and had stress-relieving holes cut in the lower bogie members, otherwise they are identical to the second batch. A point worth noting is that locomotives of any group can be found with almost any, if not all, of the variations, indeed, some accident victims have headcode discs at one end and an indicator box at the other end.

Moving on to the next group—the Type 2s—the locomotives in this group can be likened to the Hall's, B1's, King Arthur's, Black five's, etc, suitable for all but the most demanding of duties.

21 Bo-Bo DE This was the original classification of the NBL Bo-Bo diesel electrics which were subsequently modified, becoming the Class 29, and will be covered under that heading.

22 Bo-Bo DH The only model available of this locomotive is the whitemetal kit produced by MTK. The castings are generally good, but it would appear that little or no allowance has been made for shrinkage during the casting process, so the resulting model is under length and a considerable amount of time and effort needs to be expended to achieve a satisfactory result from this kit.

The kit follows the same principles as the Class 17 kit described earlier, consisting of a set of body castings, and bogie sideframes, but lacking motor bogies. As is the case with most MTK kits, a suitable motor bogie kit is available, however we have found a tendency for them to be troublesome. Having tried a number of different motor bogies in this locomotive, the only effective solution seems to be the construction of a chassis incorporating a central motor, driving each bogie through a cardan shaft, as in the case of the Class 17.

Another course worth pursuing is a major conversion based on a Hornby Class 29, though it may be more practical to scratch-build. Visually these locomotives changed very little; apart from D6300-6305, which had a different radiator grille layout, the only major change was the fitting of headcode boxes.

23 Bo-Bo DE At present no ready-to-run model or kit is produced of this locomotive. However, if you are not faint-hearted, it is possible to make a satisfactory model of this locomotive using a Hornby Class 37 body as the basis of a heavy conversion. A suitable chassis can be made by stretching the Wrenn Class 20 chassis, which not only has bogies of the correct wheelbase, but the sideframes are almost identical in appearance to those on the Class 23. The only obvious changes to these locomotives were the early removal of the nose-mounted ladders and the fitting of four-character headcode boxes when the class

Above *Three modified Hornby models at Deanport. Hauling the freight train is a Class 25/3 while two Class 24s double head a passenger train* (Michael Alderton and John Payne).

Below *A Class 22 constructed from the kit made by MTK (Modern Traction Kits)* (Michael Alderton and John Payne).

received modified engines.

24 Bo-Bo DE A whitemetal kit of this locomotive is available from MTK. This kit follows the same principles as the MTK kits described earlier; again a separate motor bogie kit is available. Early versions of this kit were supplied with the cabs cast as one piece, but later versions have a revised arrangement where the cab sides, front and roof are separate castings. The kit is supplied with sufficient parts to produce either the early headcode disc-fitted version, or the later variant with roof-mounted headcode boxes. D5000-5049 (24 005, 24 001-049) are Class 24/0 and D5050-5150 (24 050-150) are Class 24/1 and differ only in fuel and water tank capacities. D5000-5113 were built with headcode discs, the remaining members of the class being fitted with roof-mounted indicator boxes.

In addition to the MTK kit, the Hornby model of the 25/1 can be converted to a Class 24 by adding bodyside valences, flush fitting cab doors, by repositioning the cabside window bar and modifying (or removing) the indicator boxes as required.

25/0 Bo-Bo DE These early Class 25s are almost identical to the later 24/1 and were numbered D5151-5175 (25 001-015). The only differences are the revised cabside window design and recessed cab doors. Both the MTK Class 24 kit and the Hornby Class 25/1 can easily be modified to fall into this division.

25/1 Bo-Bo DE This group of locomotives—D5176-5232 (25 026-082)—incorporate the standard Class 25 indicator box with the addition of the horns which were moved from the buffer beams, and the bodyside valences were omitted; otherwise they are identical to the Class 25/0. The Hornby model of the 25/1 is very accurate, with superb performance being powered by a ringfield motor. A whitemetal kit of this locomotive is also available from MTK.

25/2 Bo-Bo DE D5233-5299 (25 083-149) and D7500-7567 (25 150-217) constitute the 25/2 sub-division. These locomotives have a completely redesigned cab, with the centre windscreen extended downwards in line with the outer windscreens, and the bodyside grilles replaced with a line of seven and eight filter panels between the cantrail, and the engine roof hatches.

The Hornby model can be converted to represent this version, but care must be taken when choosing a number, as only D5233-5288 were fitted with steam heating equipment and, as such, are the only versions to have fuel and water tanks as fitted to the Hornby model. The MTK kit of the 25/3 can be easily modified to the Class 25/2. A final point to bear in mind when modelling this group of locomotives is that D7568-7597 (25 218-247) were built out of sequence and are of the earlier 25/1 style.

25/3 Bo-Bo DE The final version of these locomotives—D7598-7677 (25 248-327)—are not fitted with water tanks, making them identical to most of the 25/2 variants, the only difference being the cabside tablet catcher recesses fitted to D7605-7677 (25 248-327). MTK produce a whitemetal kit of this locomotive and the Hornby 25/1 can be converted to represent this version.

26 & 27 Bo-Bo DE The Class 26 and Class 27 locomotives can be dealt with under one heading as they utilise the same design of bodyshell. The Class 26 locomotives can be

A Baby Deltic passing Deanport scrapyard. The locomotive is a conversion with a Hornby Class 37 body mounted on a Wrenn Class 20 chassis (Michael Alderton and John Payne).

split into two groups, the first 20 locomotives—D5300-5319 (26 001-020)—were built for use in England and are distinguished by having drop-light cabside windows and oval buffers and form the Class 26/0 sub division. The remaining locomotives—D5321-5346 (26 021-046)—were built for use in Scotland and have sliding cabside windows, tablet catcher recesses and large round buffers and are classified 26/1. One locomotive in this group—D5320 (26 028)—has acquired oval buffers. Both groups of locomotives were built with headcode discs, however, several have been fitted with headlamps and the first seven 26/0 locomotives have now lost their train heating boilers and water tanks and received slow speed control equipment for use with merry-go-round trains. The only major visual change to these locomotives is the plating over of all the cab door windows and, in certain instances, the tablet catcher recesses have been plated over as well.

The Class 27 locomotives, like the Class 26, were built in two groups, the first 23 locomotives—D5347-5369 (27 001-023)—being destined for the Scottish region and the remaining locomotives—D5370-5415 (27 024-044, 27 101-118, 27 119-124)—were allocated to England. The Scottish locomotives were built with sliding cabside windows and tablet catcher recesses, whereas the English versions were fitted with drop-light cabside windows, all being fitted with roof-mounted headcode boxes instead of the more dated headcode discs fitted to the Class 26. Eight of the English locomotives—D5370-5378 (27 024-031)—were intended for freight work and are not fitted with train heating boilers or water tanks and are easily identified as such.

Locomotives 27 001-044 form the 27/0 class and locomotives 27 101-112 form the 27/1 class and differ only in being air braked, and push-pull fitted. The first of these locomotives—D5374 (27 101)—was one of the English freight locomotives, being specially modified to form the first member of this class. Locomotives 27 201-212 form the 27/2 class, being push-pull fitted, and equipped with electric train heating equipment. The only visual differences are the eth cables and a small grille adjacent to one of the cab doors. As with the Class 26, the tablet catcher recesses are now being plated over.

It should be noted that the numbers do not necessarily following a logical sequence and great care is required when selecting a number for a model of one of these locomotives. MTK produce whitemetal kits of both the 26 and 27 that will make up into any of the variants described; it is also possible to convert the Lima model of the Class 33 into any of the Class 26 or Class 27 variants.

28 Co-Bo DE Apart from the Deltics, this unusual class of 20 locomotives—D5700-5719—were the only locomotives to be fitted with two-stroke diesel engines. Currently no model is available of this locomotive, although some years ago a model was produced by Hornby Dublo, but this has now become very collectable. The model was superb, incorporating a one piece die-cast body, powered by the now famous Hornby Dublo ringfield motor.

29 Bo-Bo DE Fifty-eight locomotives were built for the Eastern and Scottish regions, 38 for the Eastern and the remaining 20 for Scotland. These locomotives proved to be very unreliable and the Eastern region locomotives were transferred to the Scottish region so that the whole class were near the NBL Co who built them. In an attempt to improve reliability, one locomotive D6123 was fitted with a Paxman engine which proved to be a success, leading to a further 19 locomotives being modified in the same manner. The modified locomotives were allocated Class 29, and the unmodified versions were allocated Class 21. However, both groups of locomotives were withdrawn before receiving their new numbers.

As built the Class 21 locomotives were fitted with headcode discs. However, a small number of them had the discs removed and replaced with four-character headcode boxes. The locomotives selected for conversion to Class 29 were not chosen in numerical order but were taken in a random manner from the first 38 members of the original class of locomotive. When converted to Class 29 a number of external changes took place, a revised windscreen wiper arrangement was fitted to each cab and a pair of small grilles were fitted to each bodyside, one in place of a window, with the other one directly below.

Hornby produce a model described as a Class 29 that should be described as a Class 21 as it is based on one of the few unmodified locomotives that received four-character headcode boxes in place of the headcode discs, which in turn limits the number of locomotives the model can represent. With care the Hornby model can be modified to produce both versions of these locomotives and, by enlarging the windscreens and lowering the body on the bogie pivots, it is possible to capture the true character of these locomotives.

31 A1A-A1A DE When introduced, the Brush Type 2 locomotives were fitted with Mirrlees engines and were intended to be designated Class 30 but were redesignated

Above left *End detailing on the Airfix 00-scale model of the Class 31. Compare with the model converted into a Class 31/0 by Michael Alderton and John Payne.*

Above right *Class 31/0 locomotive modified from the Airfix Class 31 model* (Michael Alderton and John Payne).

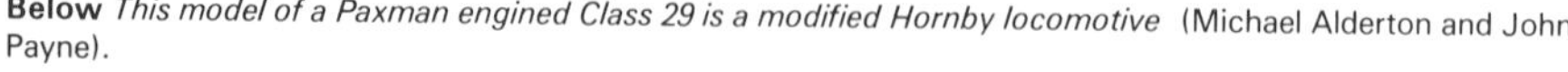

Below *This model of a Paxman engined Class 29 is a modified Hornby locomotive* (Michael Alderton and John Payne).

Class 31 when the replacement English Electric engines were fitted. Of the 263 locomotives that form this class, the first 20 locomotives were built with headcode discs and electromagnetic control equipment which makes them incompatible with the rest of the class. When new these locomotives were numbered D5500-5519 and, with the exception of D5518, were renumbered 31 001-019, becoming Class 31/0. The remaining members of the class—D5520-5862—with the addition of a modified D5518, were renumbered as Class 31/1 (31 101-327) or, if rebuilt with electric train heating equipment, as Class 31/4 (31 401-418).

With the exception of the Class 31/0 locomotives, the remaining machines were built with the more normal electro-pneumatic control equipment and, as supplies permitted, the locomotives were built with a revised design of cab roof incorporating a four-character headcode box in place of the earlier air vent, so avoiding the need for headcode discs which gave these locomotives a more modern appearance. This change was spread over a group of 30 locomotives—D5531-5560 (31 113-142)—and care should be taken to select the correct number when modelling a locomotive from this group.

The eth fitted locomotives, Class 31/4, were selected at random from the main group of locomotives and, again, care should be taken when choosing a number for a model of one of these locomotives due to the way they were selected. Two excellent models of the Class 31 have been produced by Hornby and Airfix. The Airfix model has a slight edge over the Hornby version by virtue of a better mechanism and crisper bogie detail. However, both body mouldings are first class.

The easiest version of these locomotives to model is the Class 31/4 by simply adding eth jumper cables and renumbering; even the 31/0 variant, involving a little more work in the shape of roof ventilators, and headcode discs, is not beyond the capabilities of the junior modeller. However, be very careful to check before choosing a locomotive to model as there have been many livery changes and detail changes over the years; some locomotives used in East Anglia even acquired tablet catcher recesses!

33 Bo-Bo BE This class of locomotive is the big brother of the Class 26 and 27, using the same basic bodyshell, with minor modifications, but having a larger engine. This was possible due to the locomotives being built with eth equipment and the space that would have been occupied by steam heating equipment was vacant, so allowing room for the larger engine.

As built there were two main groups of locomotives, the largest group being built to the normal loading gauge, but the last 12 built to a reduced width for use on the Hastings line with its restricted loading gauge. With the coming of the Bournemouth electrification scheme, 19 of the normal locomotives were selected at random and fitted for push-pull working.

Under the current numbering system the largest group of locomotives—33 001-065—form the 33/0 class, consisting of standard design locomotives. The locomotives selected for conversion to push-pull working form the 33/1 class, being numbered 33 101-119, and differ from the normal locomotives by the addition of buckeye couplings, waist level brake hoses and control cables, and a revised cab handrail layout. The 12 Hastings loading gauge locomotives are classified 33/2, being numbered 33 201-212, and remain in original condition, apart from the addition of slow speed control equipment for their coal train duties in Kent.

Both MTK and Lima produce models of this class of locomotive. The MTK kit, following their normal principles described earlier, contains sufficient parts to allow either 33/0 or 33/1 versions to be built. The Lima model is based on one of the 33/0 locomotives, first appearing as an H0 scale model, but now happily revised and available in 00 scale. This is an excellent model which can be very easily converted to one of the 33/1 variants. It is currently available in all of the livery versions carried by the prototypes. It would be extremely difficult, but not impossible, to convert one of these models to one of the 33/2 variants, however, it would be a matter of personal choice whether the final result would justify the time and effort needed to produce one of these locomotives.

35 Hymek Bo-Bo DH The Hymeks were the only locomotives with hydraulic transmissions to come under the Type 3 power classification. No changes were made to the locomotives during their short lives and, although allocated Class 35, no members of the class ever carried a new number. The only model of this locomotive is produced by Hornby, the early versions suffered from having bogies of the incorrect wheelbase. However, the latest version incorporating the ringfield motor is free of this fault; otherwise both versions are excellent, although they tend to sit slightly too high on their bogies.

37 Co-Co DE This class of locomotive can be divided into two groups, the first group—D6600-6608 and D6700-6819 (37 300-308 and 37 001-119)—was delivered new with gangway doors, split headcode boxes and the horns located behind small circular grilles on the front of the noses. The second group of locomotives—D6820-6999 (37 120-299)—was built with a revised nose layout, incorporating a four-character headcode box, revised layout and roof-mounted horns. Some of the locomotives have received oval buffers in place of the original large round type and, more recently, certain locomotives have appeared with the valences around the buffers stocks cut away. It is worth noting that the locomotives fitted with roof-mounted horns are banned from the Liverpool Street Station area due to the clearance problems between the catenary and the horns.

Again only one model of this locomotive is available and this is produced by Hornby and based on a member of the second group of locomotives. The body moulding is superb but the model as a whole is let down by its chassis. Early versions of this model were fitted with the Class 31 bogie, which is not correct for the Class 37. Later versions are fitted with the ringfield bogie from the Class 47, which again is not correct for the Class 37, and, to make matters worse, the wheelbase of both bogies is incorrect for this class of locomotive. There are two solutions to this problem. The first would be to use the Lima Class 50/Deltic chassis suitably shortened (the Class 37, Class 50, and Deltics all share a common design of bogie), or the second method would be to use the Airfix Class 31 chassis with either Ks, or perhaps the old Kitmaster Deltic bogie sideframes glued on as overlays.

40 1Co-Co1 DE This class of locomotive has not received any major changes during its life which affect the external appearance. However, as built, they did fall into three distinct groups. The first group—D200-324 (40 001-124)—were the first large group of production design Type 4 locomotives to be delivered to British Railways. They were being fitted with headcode discs and gangway doors and, in the case of some of the very first locomotives, a small ladder positioned on the driver's side of the noses beside the gangway doors; however, these ladders were soon removed. The second group of locomotives—D325-344 (40 125-144)—were identical to the first group, apart from being built with split headcode boxes in place of the headcode discs. The final group of locomotives—D345-399 (40 145-199)—were again identical to the first group of locomotives, apart from receiving four-character headcode boxes and not having gangway doors.

It must be stressed that having listed the three main design changes, variations do occur—for example, D260-266 (40 060-066) of the first group, allocated to Scotland, were all fitted with four-character headcode boxes at some time during their lives, so check thoroughly before starting any modelling.

At present there are three models of this class of locomotive available, two are kits and the third is a ready-to-run model produced by Jouef. Taking the kits first, one is produced by MTK and follows their normal construction methods as described earlier. The second kit is made by Q Kits and is available in any one of three options, either as a body and bogie sideframe kit with no wheels or motor, or with the addition of a set of parts for one motor bogie and one unpowered bogie, or with the addition of a set of parts for two motor bogies. The motor bogies are supplied with the Mashima can type motor as standard and the performance of the completed model is excellent. The body of the Q Kits model is a one-piece fibreglass resin moulding and, as supplied, requires the windows cutting out, a time-consuming, though not difficult, job.

At the time of writing, the ready-to-run model of the Class 40 is still available, however, the manufacturers, Jouef, have recently gone into liquidation and the models could soon disappear from the shops. This is an excellent model, based on one of the members of the first group of locomotives to be built, however, the body is a little too wide, but with careful super detailing it is possible to overcome this minor fault.

41 Warship A1A-A1A DH The five members of this class—D600-604—never survived in service long enough to receive their new classification officially. As the first large diesel hydraulics to be delivered to the Western Region they retained a semi-prototype status and as such were relegated to secondary and freight duties as soon as sufficient production Warships became available to cover their mainline duties. The only model available of these locomotives is a whitemetal kit produced by MTK which again follows their normal construction methods, incorporating sufficient parts to build the locomotives in their original form with headcode discs, or in their later modified form with split headcode boxes.

42 & 43 Warship Bo-Bo DH The main difference between these two classes of locomotive lay only in their internal equipment, the engines and transmissions coming from different manufacturers. The locomotives were built in two groups, one group at Swindon, and the other group by NBL of Glasgow. When first introduced, D800-812 were fitted with the old GWR three-digit train describers and

A modified Joueff Class 40 at Deanport (Michael Alderton and John Payne).

headcode discs, whilst the remainder of the class—D813-870—had standard four-character headcode panels from new, D800-812 being modified to conform at a later date.

This locomotive is very popular with the model trade, there being no fewer than four versions produced over the years. The first version to appear was produced by Trix and was based on one of the first locomotives in their original form. This was not an outstanding model and is now very rare. The second version to appear was a superb model produced by Fleischmann, disappointingly made to H0 scale. This leaves the two latest versions, produced almost simultaneously by Lima and Mainline. Taking the Lima model first, the body moulding is a little bit thick, though the detail is sharp and the motor is the standard Lima ringfield unit driving wheels of the correct diameter. The bogies are neatly moulded but the brakes do not line up with the wheel treads. The Mainline model has a very finely detailed body, including a number of separate wire handrails. The bogies are superbly detailed with the brake blocks just about in line with the wheels.

Both of these models are dimensionally accurate and therefore look very much alike. However, the Mainline version is dearer, but has much more detail, whereas the Lima model tends to be the better performer of the two. When it comes to purchasing one of these models it is very much a case of the old saying, 'You pays your money and takes your choice'.

44 1Co-Co1 DE The class 44 locomotives were the forerunners of the Class 45 and 46, only differing from these later locomotives by having a lower powered engine, headcode discs and gangway doors. When new these locomotives were numbered D1-10, later becoming 44 001-010, the only variation within the class being D9 and D10 (44 009 and 44 010) which were built with a different bodyside grille layout. No models of this class of locomotive are available from the trade, however, it is relatively easy to modify one of the Class 45/46 models which are available.

45 & 46 1Co-Co1 DE Externally there are no major differences between the Class 45 and 46; however, they were built in two distinct groups. The locomotives numbered D11-D31 and D68-107 were built with the earlier split headcode boxes but without gangway doors. Locomotives D32-67 and D108-165 were built with a pair of two-character headcode boxes fitted centrally in each nose. The final group of locomotives—D166-193—were built with standard four-character headcode boxes.

In the early 1970s 50 Class 45 locomotives were stripped of their steam heating equipment and fitted with eth equipment, so becoming Class 45/1, the only outward change being the new eth jumper cables. At the same time a number of locomotives from both classes began to receive new nose ends fitted with a pair of marker lights and, in certain cases, locomotives also began to receive modified roof panels. These modifications were carried out during heavy overhauls and depended very much on the condition of the original components.

There are three models available of these

Above *Larry Goddard modified a Palitoy Mainline Class 45 model to produce this 00-scale Class 44. Note the longer side grille and vertical off-centre bar* (Larry Goddard).

Below *A modified Palitoy Mainline Peak at Westend* (Michael Alderton and John Payne).

locomotives, comprising two kits and one ready-to-run, all based on the Class 45 variants. The two kits are produced by MTK and Q Kits, both following the manufacturers' normal construction methods outlined earlier. The ready-to-run locomotive is produced by Mainline and is an excellent model of one of the interim versions of the Class 45, fitted with a pair of two-character headcode boxes; however, it is marred by one error. For some reason, the buffer beams have been moulded as part of the body, rather than in the correct position as part of the bogies, but this fault can be easily rectified. All three models can be very simply modified to represent the Class 46 locomotives or, with a little more work, can be modified to represent a Class 44.

47 Co-Co DE The Class 47 has undergone very few changes in its life, the only major change is the fitting of thermostatically controlled radiator shutters in place of plain grilles. As a rule these shutters were fitted when the locomotives received air brake equipment, but this should not be taken for granted, as some early locomotives received air brakes and no shutters. All locomotives were delivered with standard four-character headcode boxes, though many have since been replaced with marker lights. Over the years these locomotives have been divided into the following sub-classes as a result of equipment changes:

47/0—the standard Class 47 with steam heating equipment, numbered 47 001-298.

47/3—the standard Class 47 without steam heating equipment, numbered 47 301-381.

47/4—the standard Class 47 fitted with eth equipment, numbered 47 401-585.

Diesel hydraulics at Deanport. From left to right, super-detailed Lima Western, Hornby Hymek and Lima Warship (Michael Alderton and John Payne).

47/7—the push-pull fitted Class 47, employed on the Edinburgh-Glasgow Inter-city services, numbered 47 701-712.

47/9—the modified Class 47 used as a test bed for the prototype diesel engines subsequently fitted to the Class 56 and 58 locomotives. This locomotive is numbered 47 901.

Hornby and MTK both produce models of this class of locomotive, the MTK kit following their normal principles. The Hornby model, although accurate, is spoilt by having a number of heavy mould lines and sitting too high on its bogies, however, its performance is very good, being powered by a ringfield motor.

50 Co-Co DE These locomotives, originally numbered D400-449 (50 001-050), have received virtually no changes which affect their appearance since they were introduced in 1968. The first two locomotives appeared with waist level jumper cables for multiple operation from new, the remainder of the class receiving these cables at Crewe works some time after delivery. The only changes to the class have been the fitting of marker lights in place of the headcode panels, and a single high intensity headlamp in the centre of the cab fronts.

Three models of these locomotives are available at present, with another promised from Lima. The three current models are all kits, produced by MTK, Q Kits and Jidenco. Having already looked at MTK and Q Kits, and as the previous comments are still valid, it is worth concentrating on the Jidenco model. Diesel locomotives are difficult to produce as etched kits due to the compound nature of the bodyside/roof curves which need special bending tools to form the shape of the main body component. For this reason Jidenco are now concentrating on steam locomotives and rolling stock, though this model may well appear under the MTK label. But whether it is MTK or Jidenco it does not matter, this kit has overcome these problems exceptionally well. The main body and roof component is a pre-formed brass etching with the cab front/roof assemblies cast in whitemetal. This kit incorporates a wealth of detail to a very high standard, resulting in an excellent model which is designed to fit the Lima Deltic chassis. Even though the bogies are slightly under length it does not detract from the kit's appearance. Overall this kit offers an accurate and well detailed model with a chassis which provides more than adequate performance.

At the time of writing, the Lima Class 50 has yet to appear, however, if it is like their Warship and Western, it will be excellent value for money.

52 Western Co-Co DH Once again this class of locomotive, numbered D1000-1073, received only minor modifications with almost no effect on their external appearance. Arguably the most handsome of diesel locomotives they were synonymous with the Western Region, all carrying names prefixed by the word 'Western'.

The model trade has again excelled itself with no fewer than four models available, two of which are kits, one from MTK and the other from Q Kits, both following their normal construction methods. The other two models are ready-to-run versions from Hornby and Lima, both are dimensionally accurate and have body mouldings of a high standard, with the Hornby model possibly having the edge with slightly crisper detail. However, the windscreen pillars are printed on the glazing material, and the leading portions of the body skirt are mounted on the bogies to allow the locomotive to negotiate sharp curves, whereas the Lima model has a moulded windscreen unit, and correct body skirts without the gap found on the Hornby model.

Both models are powered by ringfield motors, the Hornby model being more mechanically refined but fitted with slightly undersize nickel plated wheels, whilst the Lima version has chemically blackened wheels of the correct diameter. The performance of both models is superb, and overall there is little to choose between the two, the Lima model representing excellent value for money, with the Hornby model being just that much dearer so, once again, it is a matter of personal preference.

55 Deltic Co-Co DE During their outstanding lifetime the Deltics remained relatively free from major external changes, all receiving names during the first few years of service, being numbered D9000-9021 (55 001-022). Early in their lives they all received a pair of additional small ventilators above each nameplate position and various locations were tried for the horns on several locomotives before the position (just in front of the windscreens) was settled. During 1968 the class were fitted with eth equipment, and the standard sockets and jumper cables appeared and, finally, the headcode boxes were either fitted with black overlays, incorporating a pair of opaque discs, or were blanked off completely, apart from a pair of circular cut-outs.

Both Q Kits and Lima produce models of this class of locomotive. The Q Kits model is good value for money and, like their previous products, well repays the time and effort spent on construction. The Lima model follows the general comments about their other products though, as mentioned under the Class 50 heading, the bogies are a little under scale length. This model has recently been updated and now represents excellent value for money.

56 Co-Co DE This is the latest class of locomotive to appear on British Rail and was built in two separate batches. The first group—56 001-030—were built in Rumania and have detail differences such as a radiused cab front handrail, and rubber surrounds to the small triangular cabside windows. The second group—56 032-120—were built by BREL and incorporate a straight cab front handrail, and no rubber surround to the small triangular cabside windows. Locomotives built from around 56 050 have a redesigned cab front and buffer beam. The buffers have also been changed from large round ones to oval ones and the horn housing and marker lights are slightly different.

Two kits are available of these locomotives, one from MTK and the other from Q Kits, there being little to choose between them, both following their established construction methods. Another solution involves modifying a Hornby Class 47 bodyshell which is dimensionally correct, however, a scratch-built motor bogie and chassis would be needed as the wheelbase within each bogie is unequal.

58 Co-Co DE Currently this is the only new locomotive design due to appear on British Rail, being designed with a view to potential export orders. At least one model is proposed—Hornby intends to release their version at the same time as the prototype enters service.

Pre-production prototypes

No survey such as this would be complete

without a brief look at the fore-runners of the present day diesel locomotive fleet. In 1947-48 the LMS-designed Co-Co diesel electric locomotive 10000 entered service, followed shortly after by its companion 10001. Three years later, in 1951, the Southern Railway-designed Co-Co diesel electrics 10201 & 10202 appeared, to be joined in 1954 by the third member of the group, 10203, which became one of the major influences in the design of the Class 40. All five of these pioneer mainline diesels were powered by progressively improved versions of the same English Electric diesel engine, which was further developed to see service in the Class 40, 50 and 56.

In 1955 the prototype Deltic appeared, followed in 1961 by Falcon. In 1962 two prototypes appeared—the very successful DP2 (which formed the basis of the Class 50 design) and the ill-fated Lion. Finally, in 1968, the 4000HP locomotive, Kestrel, appeared, subsequently being sold to Russia. With the exception of the prototype Deltic, models of all these locomotives are available from Q Kits. A model of the prototype Deltic was produced by Kitmaster in the early 1960s and is now very rare. It would not be an impossible task to produce a model of the prototype Deltic, or for that matter DP2, from one of the Lima Deltics.

Below *This interesting model of the 4000HP locomotive,* Kestrel, *which was sold to Russia after trials in Britain, was built from a kit manufactured by Q Kits* (Q Kits).

Bottom *A Class 56 rumbles slowly over a river bridge at the head of a train of coal hoppers. The locomotive has a converted Hornby Class 47 body mounted on a scratch-built chassis* (Michael Alderton and John Payne).

Other prototype locomotives such as the LMS/NBL 827HP Bo-Bo DE 10800, which probably formed the basis of the Class 16 design, the SR/Paxman 500HP 0-6-0 DM 11001, and the unorthodox Fell 2000HP 4-8-4 DM, all played their brief part in the development of the diesel locomotive fleet. However, due to their short lives and limited appeal, no manufacturer has yet contemplated producing kits of these locomotives, so they remain strictly within the scratch-built field.

Even though this survey is intended for the modern image modeller, it raises the question, is there really such an animal? We are all really historical modellers, for many of the classes described here are just memories, with classics such as the Westerns and the Deltics now departed, and many of those classes that remain are slowly being reduced or withdrawn for a number of reasons. So, before it is too late, let us see how we can preserve our own favourite pieces of history in miniature.

To begin with in modelling any of the locomotives described in this survey, it is imperative that you consult as many drawings and photographs of the prototype as possible. We have only mentioned the major changes which occurred, but many minor alterations also took place such as the repositioning of lamp brackets, especially on the Western Region, changes to windscreen wipers and handrails, and the control cables and hoses mounted on the buffer beams. If you are able to photograph the particular locomotive you wish to model, then do so, the time spent on this type of research will be well repaid, especially when you come to painting. There are now so many modified liveries and associated variations applied to diesel locomotives that it would take a book just to describe this one aspect. However, it is now our intention to outline briefly the principles for super-detailing any of the ready-to-run models covered by this survey, and it should be remembered that these principles are basically the same for any of the kit-built locomotives we have mentioned.

Having purchased the model of your choice, very carefully dismantle it and place all the parts in a box for safe keeping. Strip the body right down to the basic shell, removing the glazing, buffers and, where required, handrails. It is almost certain that a repaint will be needed after any detailing work, so it is wise to remove the manufacturer's paint work. There are many ways this can be done, two of the most reliable methods are: 1) immersing the body in car hydraulic brake fluid, and when the paint is soft removing it with an old toothbrush, repeating the process until all the paint is off, followed by a wash in warm soapy water. However, this fluid can damage some plastics so it is essential to try brushing just a little on to a part of the body which is hidden to check for any softening before immersing the whole body. 2) using a proprietary model paint stripper such as Modelstrip. It is worth noting that certain paints can only be removed by one or other of these methods, so if the first method you try for removing paint fails, try again with the other, and make a note for future reference.

Having spent a large sum of money on your model you will not want to ruin it, so take great care with the next stage. Remove any flash or moulding lines; some manufacturers also use moulded lines as a guide for painting and these should be removed as well. Any blemishes found at this stage can be dressed out with light filing and emery paper. If the mark is deep use a little body filler. If the handrails are moulded as part of the bodyshell, drill either end of the handrail with a No 76 drill held in a pin chuck; this provides an accurate location for the new wire ones, and the old plastic ones can then be removed with a sharp knife. It is bad enough to have to replace a body shell due to over enthusiastic work with your craft knife, but fingers cannot be replaced as easily, so take great care! At the same time the engine and train heating boiler exhaust ports can be opened out, and the holes for any control cables and hoses on the buffer beams can now be drilled. When these operations are complete, thoroughly wash the body in warm soapy water and leave to dry. When you are certain that all the work is complete the body can be painted with a suitable undercoat. This serves two purposes: 1) it will show up any faults and missed blemishes, etc, 2) it provides a good key for the finishing coats of paint.

Having decided on your final livery, paint the locomotive body accordingly, and leave to dry for a good 24 hours between coats (British Rail colours are available in the Precision Paints range). Having done this paint the edges of the window frames matt black; this will help to disguise the thickness of the body moulding and the deception is completed by fitting flush glazing. This is a simple but tedious job, but the results are well worth the effort, completely hiding the thickness of the body. The same comments apply to indicator boxes. It is also wise to put some pieces of black plastic sheet behind the bodyside windows as this prevents light passing through an empty model, thus making it more convincing. Assemble any interior detail such as control desks, bulkheads and crew, after they have been painted, and finally fit the new wire handrails.

The bogies may be exceptionally well

detailed and require little or no extra work but do not forget the speedometer cables, mileage recorders and slow speed control equipment. Some bogies have solid portions and would benefit from fretting out, however, check before cutting as some designs of bogie will be weakened by this treatment. Finally we come to pick-ups. Most models have very good motors, but are let down by the number of pick-ups fitted; therefore fit extra pick-ups to as many wheels as possible and you will be pleasantly surprised by the improvement.

Many models sit roughly 2-3 mm too high so that the couplings do not foul the body. This can usually be overcome by modifying the bogie pivots when the chassis is reassembled. The distance from the top of the rail to the centre of the buffers should be 14 mm for 4 mm scale models. Having rebuilt the chassis, check that it runs smoothly and negotiates your trackwork, then fit any extra weight you want, re-unite the body and chassis and again check that all runs sweetly.

Now come the final touches such as windscreen wipers, brake, heating and control cables and lettering. Various types of wire including 15 amp fuse wire and guitar 'G' strings are useful for the cables, wires and pipes. For lettering, the range of transfers is considerable, ranging from dry print through waterline transfers to the more advanced Methfix and Pressfix types. Each modeller will have his own preferences and techniques; however, waterslide transfers are one of the simplest and cheapest forms, especially when used with one of the proprietary solvent systems such as the American Solvaset or Micro-sol.

The door handles and kicking plates should be touched in with steel paint, followed by any other touching up that may be required. This should produce a locomotive in ex-works condition and it can then be weathered down to any state you wish from a well kept, slightly worn locomotive to one that is in the poorest condition possible.

Readers intending to add extra details to their ready-to-run diesel locomotive models may like to avail themselves of the convenience of the Adpaks series of parts, rather than having to make the additional details themselves. The range includes kits of parts for detailing the Lima Western, Warship and Deltic, the Jouef Class 40, the Airfix Class 31, the Mainline Peak and the Hornby Hymek. The packs contain cast metal and wire parts and other items, together with full instructions for fitting. Chris Leigh has recently introduced a kit of cast metal and etched parts for detailing the Lima dmu or for converting it into the Class 121 single unit railcar.

Diesel locomotive bodies can be scratch-built using any of the usual materials and techniques. Probably the most popular construction material is plastic card. This is produced in a range of thicknesses, is easy to cut and shape, and has a smooth grainless surface finish. Assembly is convenient, using one of the solvent cements. The flat surfaces are easily modelled with the sheet plastic, building them up in layers if desired to make the glazing of windows and the modelling of ventilation grilles more convenient. To model the curved areas the plastic card can be laminated to build up sufficient thickness, allowing ample time for the plastic to harden completely again after cementing, then shaped with files and sandpaper. (An alternative method for forming simple curves is to soften the plastic card with heat and then mould it to the required shape using a wooden former.) The material is easily scribed to represent flush doors and panels while overlays of thin plastic can be fixed in place to model other panels and access hatches. The surface takes paint well, producing a good representation of a metal surface, and detailing is easily carried out as for the ready-to-run models.

Diesel locomotives carry an array of pipes on the buffer beams but these are largely omitted from commercial models; their addition will considerably improve the appearance of these models. This photograph shows a Class 25/3 at Tyne Yard (David Andress).

Electric locomotives and catenary

The extension of the overhead electrified system is a major feature of British Rail's development plans although financial constraints mean that Britain is lagging behind many other European countries in the proportion of electrified to non-electrified trackage. Despite its importance in the modern railway scene, relatively few modellers have chosen to include electrified lines on their layouts. Undoubtedly one of the reasons is that for a realistic effect the modeller must install a catenary system. For a layout of any size this can be expensive to build up from commercial parts or very time-consuming to construct from scratch. However, the modeller who is prepared to go to the trouble and expense of installing overhead electrification will find that it adds greatly to the interest of his or her layout and enhances the modern image appearance. The recent introduction of three excellent ready-to-run models, the Lima Class 87, the Hornby Class 86 and Advanced Passenger Train, together with the choice of commercially produced catenary systems now available may encourage more modellers to go electric. Several other prototypes have been marketed as ready-to-run models in the past, including the EM1 (later the BR Class 76) from Trix, the EM2 (later the BR Class 77) from Triang, and the Class 81 with versions from Liliput, Hornby Dublo and Triang, but none of these is currently available.

Catenary systems are made by Sommerfeldt (imported by M & R Model Railways Ltd), by Vollmer (imported by Liliput Model Railways (UK) Ltd), by JV (imported by Hadley Hobbies Ltd) and by Lima. All are for continental prototypes but include equipment similar to the type used on British Rail; all provide instructions for installation. As always, study of the prototype will help you to achieve accuracy and realism in your modelling.

The extensive Southern Region third rail electrified system has also been largely neglected by modellers and little has been produced commercially. However, the unusual and interesting Class 73 and Class 74 (withdrawn in 1977) electro-diesels are both available as MTK kits. There are no ready-to-run electric multiple units on the market but MTK do offer some examples as kits.

A train on the Tyne & Wear Metro. The addition of a short length of a modern transit system such as this to a railway layout would be of considerable interest but scratch-building or conversion would be necessary as no commercial models for this line are available.

Above *A section of realistic catenary modelled in HO scale using Sommerfeldt parts. The scene is on a Fleischmann exhibition layout. The range of catenary parts includes types suitable for use on British prototype layouts.*

Below *A busy scene on D. Bowe's modern image layout. Note the variety of modern structures mainly built from kits. The catenary system is Triang, no longer available* (D. Bowe, Brian Monaghan and *Railway Modeller*).

Passenger stock

None of British Rail's pre-nationalisation coaches now remain in passenger service though many are still in use on engineers' trains. The first of the standard coaches of BR design were built in 1951 and production of this Mark I stock continued until 1962. Construction was of the conventional type with a separate underframe and body. These coaches are still widely used, particularly on secondary main line services. Except for the High Speed Train catering cars, all buffet and restaurant coaches are Mark I stock and sleeping cars are also of Mark I type. Ready-to-run models are available from Hornby, Lima and Mainline and kits for various coaches from MTK.

Experiments by BR led to the development of a coach of integral body and underframe construction and these Mark II coaches were built in groups designated Mark II a-f in the period 1963-1973. Though there are differences between each group, a major distinction is that Mark II, Mark IIa, Mark IIb and Mark IIc do not have air conditioning while Mark IId, Mark IIe and Mark IIf do. The air conditioned stock makes up most of the main line locomotive-hauled trains; ready-to-run models are made by Airfix. The non-air conditioned Mark II coaches are run when necessary on the main routes but are essentially employed on the secondary main lines; ready-to-run-models are available from Hornby (Mark II) and Lima (Mark IIb). MTK offer a range of Mark II types in kit form.

The latest BR coaches are the 75 ft long Mark III cars designed by BREL and built at Derby; these coaches are of sophisticated design for maximum comfort and high speed running. They are the standard HST coaches but are also employed on some locomotive-hauled services, particularly the West Coast Main Line route. Ready-to-run models are available from Hornby, including a buffet car, and Jouef. The Jouef models are full scale length but the Hornby coaches are a little under scale length, with one window omitted, to allow them to be accommodated more easily on a layout.

There have been changes, not only in the design and construction of the passenger rolling stock, but also in the operation of the services. The very successful Inter-City concept of fast, regular-interval services, with maximum productivity from both locomotives and coaches, requires standardisation of train formats permitting rapid turn-arounds and ease of servicing. Thus the older system of running through-coaches to be dropped off at various branch junction stations along the main line can no longer be operated. Instead, passengers must change to local services at these points.

The push-pull train, the basis of passenger services on so many branch lines in the steam era, has not disappeared entirely and examples are still to be found, though in modern form. Sections of the Inter-City trains from London-Waterloo to Bournemouth continue on the non-electrified line to Weymouth as push-pull trains in the charge of Class 33/1 locomotives. A push-pull service is also operated between Edinburgh and Glasgow; in 1980 new trains, each made up of a Class 47/7 'auto-fitted' push-pull locomotive, five Mark III coaches and a driving brake open second coach, replaced trains of Mark II stock with a Class 27/1 locomotive at each end fitted with through train control. Any of these would be interesting in model form.

Another modern service which is very effective in model form is the Motorail train. Appropriate sleeping cars, day coaches, car flats and Cartic wagons are available as ready-to-run items, making it easy to start a service on your layout. Facilities at the terminals are usually simple, with little more than an easily modelled loading ramp required.

Many branch lines and minor routes have been closed by BR in recent years for economic reasons. Those branches which remain open for passenger services, and many other routes, are now operated by diesel multiple units or, in electrified areas, by electric multiple units. The dmus have been built by a number of different manufacturers and show a

Top *The Mainline 00-scale Mk I Buffet Restaurant coach.*

Above *A Class 33/1 fitted for push-pull operation on the Bournemouth–Weymouth route at the rear of its train as it accelerates away from Parkstone towards Bournemouth.*

Right *The driving cab of a converted Mk II Brake 2nd Open for use on the Edinburgh–Glasgow push-pull services with Class 47/7 power and Mk III intermediate coaches* (John Glover).

Below *The front of the Lima 00-scale Diesel Multiple Unit showing the highly detailed underframe.*

Above *A rail bus with an Airfix body mounted on a Piko chassis passes a track maintenance crew at work* (Michael Alderton and John Payne).

Below *The Motorail Terminal at Brockenhurst. The facilities are simple, essentially a siding for the Motorail flats and a ramp at one end to allow the cars to be driven on to the flats, therefore modelling should be easy.*

considerable variety in design as well as in livery and this, together with their short length, often only three, two, or even one unit, makes them ideal for modelling.

Lima have recently introduced a ready-to-run model of the Class 117/2 built by the Pressed Steel Company and this can also be converted into other types, for example, the single unit Class 121. Expected shortly from Hornby is a ready-to-run model of a three unit (motor brake composite/motor composite/trailer second) Class 110 set built by the Birmingham Railway Carriage & Wagon Co in 1961 and operating in the Yorkshire area and to Blackpool. Earlier ready-to-run models no longer available include a Metro-Cammell from Triang Hornby and a Trans-Pennine unit (slightly underscale for 4 mm) from Trix. Kits for a wide selection of dmus are produced by MTK. Because the areas in which particular classes of dmu operate are often rather restricted, be careful to choose an appropriate type for the location in which your layout is set. Parcels stock is available ready-to-run from Lima and as kits from MTK.

John Glover has also, in his section, given some indication of the types of services operated on British Rail today; study of photographs and of the real thing will provide much additional information on these services and on the make up of passenger trains in various areas.

Freight services
by Allan Dare

A cold winter's morning, at Wolverton on the West Coast Main Line. All is quiet for, although the snow has ceased, the nearby road is still impassable. Away in the distance, across the River Ouse, the Northamptonshire hills shine white against a threatening sky. Suddenly, a mile away to the north, the green lights of the signals flicker as the pantograph of a southbound train passes before them. Shortly after this, the yellow front of the electric locomotive can be seen, and then the long cavalcade of the train snaking across the viaduct. Then it is upon us. Leaning to the curve the train roars past, a cloud of white spindrift streaming behind it. The rumble of fast moving wagons shatters the silence—red and grey opens with paper from Fort William, blue Transfesa fruit vans on their way back to Spain, green tankers with powdered chemicals from Whitehaven, brown and silver ferry vans with whisky for Italy. The tail lamp vanishes under the bridge as the 'Speedlink' train heads south at a mile a minute. Then the flicker of the signals tells of another southbound train . . . .

Yes, there is drama and colour aplenty in British Rail's modern freight operations—and good modelling material as well. So how do we set about modelling the freight trains of today? Perhaps the first thing to realise about today's railfreight business is that it is very different from that of only a few years ago, let alone that of the age of steam which is favoured by so many enthusiasts. There is a great deal more involved than just taking a typical old fashioned goods train and putting a diesel on the head end instead of a steam engine! Modern freight trains use different wagons, different terminals and different operating methods from their predecessors, so it is useful to know how things are done. The commercial set-up has also changed, with service levels and rates negotiated directly with the customer rather than from scales controlled by Parliament. This commercial freedom is arguably the most important of all—but certainly impossible to model!

Modern freight trains have several distinguishing features. Of course, for a start they are hauled by diesel or electric locomotives—and even some classes of these had disappeared before things really began to change. Wagons are mostly high capacity jobs and often privately owned. Trains are faster, with 60 mph being common and 75 mph not unusual—a far cry from the days when wooden-bodied coal wagons ran 'hot' at anything over 20 mph! Brake vans are notable by their absence. Goods yards are now rare and most BR freight customers now have their own private sidings. Above all freight operations are now carefully planned and monitored by the 'TOPS' computer system to give the best possible service.

Types of trains

A number of different types of freight train are to be seen on British Rail today:

Freightliners are special fast container trains, conveying International Standard (ISO) 'boxes' on 'skeletal' flat wagons. The containers are owned either by Freightliners themselves, who are a BR subsidary, or by private owners such as the shipping companies, making the trains very colourful affairs. Freightliner trains run to fast schedules between special terminals situated in most large cities and ports. At these terminals large gantry cranes transfer the containers to either ships or lorries, giving a door-to-door service.

Company trains are just that, trains run exclusively for one customer. They run direct between private sidings without re-marshalling, hence the other names of 'block', or 'trainload', trains. Wagons on such trains are normally all of one type and are often privately owned. All kinds of traffic are conveyed by company trains but the commonest are bulk commodities such as oil, chemicals, cement, aggregates and cars.

Merry-go-round trains are a special type of block train, linking coal mines to power stations and other large coal users. The special railway-owned hopper wagons are designed so that both loading and unloading can be carried

A Freightliner container train heads down the West Coast Main Line (British Rail).

out while the train is on the move. The trains thus travel in a continuous circle between pit and power station, hence the name.

Speedlink trains are the express wagonload freights of today, having come into prominence in the late 1970s. Connecting up the main freight centres in both industrial and rural areas, their tightly timetabled runs convey all kinds of traffic—steel, soup, paper, Guinness, china clay—anything that needs to be moved in less than trainload quantities. As a result, all kinds of modern air-braked wagons are to be seen, both BR and privately owned. Continental wagons are also very common, for the fast growing Speedlink network has helped to attract the equally rapid growth in traffic with Europe via the train ferries from Dover and Harwich. As well as serving the major marshalling yards, Speedlink trains also serve the private sidings of individual customers where traffic so warrants—thus a Speedlink service would be appropriate on many layouts. (For a picture, see top of p 50.)

Finally come the **Trippers**. These are the local freight trains, feeding traffic to and from local sidings and the Speedlink services, and also to the remaining, but fast disappearing, 'conventional' trains (that is, those with the old, small, slow-speed wagons). Trip trains convey all kinds of traffic and wagons, according to the needs of local industry.

Lastly, it should be mentioned that modern freight trains vary considerably in length. The idea that they are all long and run only on main lines is a fallacy. A Speedlink train at the end of its run may have only three or four wagons; while traffic such as stone or fertiliser is as much at home on a country branch as on a main line.

Locomotives

Needless to say, modern trains need modern locomotives. Steam, of course, is out, but so strictly are the early diesels. Such classes as the 29, 35 (Hymek), 42 (Warship), and even 52 (Western) had all been withdrawn before really modern freight services got under way. And, of course, blue locomotives are required; the old green colour scheme had disappeared long before the era in question. Incidentally, don't worry whether a locomotive is in the so called 'railfreight' livery with the large symbol on the side or not—in reality such locomotives are used on all kinds of services. One thing that is important, however, is the type of brake system a locomotive has. Most modern freight trains employ air brakes but some engines still only have the old vacuum system. However, some locomotives in every class are equipped for air, so unless you wish to match the exact number of the locomotive to the characteristics of the train it is hauling, no problems should occur. The exceptions are the newer 56, 87 and 58 classes which are only equipped for air and thus cannot be used on trains with the older vacuum-braked wagons.

Top *The Hornby 00-scale Freightliner wagon.*

Above *A block train of 100T bogie oil tankers on the West Coast Main Line. Note the lack of a brake van on this fully fitted train* (British Rail).

The model trade now provides a good range of modern locomotives. The 50 and 55 Classes, as made by Lima, are mostly used on passenger trains, but most others are essentially mixed traffic machines. Classes 56 and 58 are, however, solely freight engines; the forthcoming model of the latter from Hornby should thus be a most attractive piece of motive power for the modeller interested in freight services. One problem is the provision of shunting locomotives. Whilst there are several models of the standard BR Class 08, there are no accurate models of the many privately-owned diesels to be seen on industrial sidings all over Britain. However, many private firms have purchased second-hand BR locomotives, such as 08s, which now operate in their own colour schemes and these can easily be duplicated by repainting. Otherwise one can convert continental models; many European diesel shunters are similar to British industrial locomotives and a little work on such a model will produce a very suitable engine.

Wagons

The most striking aspect of the modern freight railway is undoubtedly the wagon fleet. Fast disappearing is the short wheelbase, unbraked 'bugbox on wheels' of British tradition, with its poor payload and slow speeds. In its place

Speedlink trains provide reliable transits, usually overnight, for traffic in wagonload quantities. Speedlink services, using high capacity wagons, run to a strict timetable at speeds of up to 75 mph. Unlike previous wagonload services the wagons are not shunted at intermediate marshalling yards but, instead, the trains call at key junctions to attach groups of wagons brought from customers' private sidings or the nearest freight terminal. A national network links main centres of industry in Britain and also has Continental connections through the train ferry ports of Harwich and Dover. Speedlink is complementary to Railfreight's main business of bulk freight traffic in trainloads and the Freightliner system of door to door movements for containers. In this picture a Class 47 locomotive is hauling a Speedlink train rather unusually consisting entirely of VDA 45T vans. Normally the make-up of these trains is much more varied (British Rail).

have come high capacity jobs; up to 51 tonnes on four wheels or 102 tonnes on bogies. Air brakes, longer wheelbase and sophisticated suspension enable the modern wagon to run at high speeds, whilst features such as full length doors, fold-away roofs, corrugated floors or pressurised discharge systems make for easy cargo handling. Bright colours are the order of the day, with BR wagons in red and grey (although many still remain in maroon or brown), and the many private owner wagons in all colours. In addition, there are the many wagons which come over from Europe. These also can be either railway or privately owned and of every shape, size and colour. In general, railway-owned wagons are used to haul such traffic as coal, steel and general merchandise, whilst more specialised traffic, such as cement, cars, oil, grain, stone and fertiliser, moves in private vehicles. These are to be seen anywhere there is a regular flow of traffic and are often hired out by leasing firms such as Procor or BRT.

In addition to the new air-braked wagons, which have mostly been introduced in the past ten years, a number of older wagons have their part to play in modern freight operations. These are short wheelbase vacuum brake types such as Presflos (for cement) or Tipfits (for stone). These still have a few years of useful life left in them and are often to be seen formed into block trains. And, of course, many of the older wagons from the 1950s are still to be seen on 'conventional' trains, though pre-nationalisation types are now very rare indeed.

As has been indicated earlier, the question of brake type is very important. Whilst the vacuum brake is now officially obsolete and will eventually disappear, its existence in the meantime can cause problems. Vacuum and air brakes are incompatible and this affects not only the type of engine used, as mentioned above, but also how the wagons are marshalled. Thus if the front part of a train is air braked and the rear vacuum braked, the rear part will be effectively unbraked, hence the description of such a train as 'partially fitted'. In such cases a brake van is needed on the end of the train. Brake vans are now only required for partially fitted trains or when certain toxic chemicals are being conveyed. To a certain extent one can tell a wagon's brake type from its colour—grey for unfitted, brown for vacuum, maroon or red for air. Unfortunately this does not help with private owner wagons nor for those BR air braked wagons which were first painted brown. Otherwise, the design of the wagon gives a clue, virtually all modern looking wagons are air braked, but the most reliable guide is a wagon's TOPS code. This is a three-letter code painted above the wagon number, used as part of BR's computer control system. The last letter describes the brake type—A for air, V for vacuum, X for dual braked.

It is only very recently that the model trade

A typical modern wagon. Note the airbrakes, sophisticated suspension and 'TOPS' code. The livery is very colourful with a white tank, grey stripe, dark green lettering and red symbol (British Rail).

has started to produce models of modern freight wagons. Even now, only ready-to-run wagons are available with no kits. However, a useful variety is now made in both 00 and N scales, and this can be enhanced with simple conversions. In describing what is available the three letter TOPS codes are used as these are the most convenient form of reference.

In 00 Hornby produce a 45T van (VDA), 45T open (OAA), 45T steel carrier (SAA) and merry-go-round hopper (HAA). They also make a ferry van (VIX) and 50T tanker (TTA), with a Freightliner flat (FGA) and 100T tanker (TEA) soon to appear. These all come in a variety of liveries, reflecting both private owners and the changes in BR colours of late. The other main manufacturer in 00 is Lima with the 50T stone hopper (PGA) in a number of authentic liveries. Due soon are a bogie fertiliser van (PWA), 100T tanker (TEA) and grain hopper (PAV). The Lima car carrier is a model of a continental wagon, but similar to the Procor wagon in Britain and thus could be of use. In addition a number of older wagons are suitable for modern operations. These include the Prestwin and Tippler from Hornby, and the kits for the Presflo and 35T tanker from Airfix.

The range of wagons cited above can easily be extended with some judicious rebuilding. Adding higher ends to a Hornby OAA produces an OBA, whilst the SAA can be rebuilt into a plate wagon (SPA) or steel sided open (OCA), or just given a flat floor for carrying tractors and the like. The Freightliner flat can be given a wooden floor with sloping ends, to make it into a 'Lowliner', as used for carrying lorries. The chassis from the Airfix tanker can be used to make the simple MTV stone carrying wagon, while the bogies form the new Lima wagons can be used to update conventional bogie bolster wagons—just as BR has done. As modern wagons are essentially of welded steel construction and use many standard parts (for instance, most airbraked BR 4 wheelers use a standard chassis) conversions such as these are easily undertaken, using plastic card and spare kit parts. The main problem is getting drawings and information but with the steady increase in interest in the modelling of modern railways such data is beginning to appear in the railway press, both prototype and model.

The biggest gap in what is available concerns continental wagons. As remarked earlier, wagons from many European railways are now seen on British Rail tracks but no suitable models are available. Of course, continental model manufacturers produce many fine wagons but as these are to the smaller HO scale they are out of proportion on a British 00 scale layout—even if the smaller British loading gauge is taken into account. Thus such excellent models as the Roco VTG 'Ferrywagon' bogie van are of little use to us, which is a great shame.

A small range of modern wagons is also available in N scale. Lima make a Freightliner flat, whilst Peco produce some vans, opens and plate wagons (admittedly 1960s vehicles in modern colours) and some very nice tankers and grain hoppers. As with 00 there is a lack of continental wagons and there is a similar problem of scale difference.

Traffic

Which wagons you run on your layout will, of course, be affected by what part of the country it is supposed to be located in. For example, merry-go-round coal trains are not to be seen in the West Country whilst, conversely, one sees numerous china clay trains there. However, although most things are produced only in certain areas they are consumed everywhere. Thus grain from the flatlands of East Anglia is railed to whisky distilleries in the Scottish Highlands, and stone from the green hills of Somerset comes by the trainload to London's construction industry. So the wagons you run on your layout will be very much decided by the kind of freight terminals modelled and the types of traffic they are supposed to be handling. Of course, if you have the space for a continuous run you can operate all kinds of wagons as they can run in through trains 'on the way to somewhere else'. Certainly a long Freightliner behind double-headed electric locomotives, or a varied Speedlink formation behind a Class 47 would look extremely impressive. Furthermore, whether you have a continuous run or just a small terminus, don't fall into the trap of thinking that modern freight operations only concern the big cities. Rural areas give rise to much of BR's freight traffic—where else would stone be quarried or fertiliser used? And many market town stations act as distribution centres for the surrounding areas.

Terminals

Freight terminals, that is any place where wagons are loaded or unloaded, can form the most interesting and important part of a layout. Thus a little thinking here will pay dividends. This is because freight handling facilities have changed enormously in recent years and are now very different from those portrayed on more traditional model railways. The old fashioned goods yard, with its hand crane, goods shed and coal merchants' staithes, has largely disappeared, to be replaced by more specialist facilities. Nowadays the few remaining goods yards, 'full loads depots' as they are now called, each serve a wide area and then only where there is profitable regular traffic. This is why the small suburban coal yards, familiar to most modellers, are now rarely seen. Surviving full loads depots now often deal with a few customers only, served by a variety of Speedlink and block train services. Wagons will vary with the traffic, but ferry vans are increasingly common. Often such depots act as distribution centres, housing perhaps a stone terminal or cement depot, as well as dealing with general merchandise. Modelling such depots is relatively easy. The main requirement is plenty of hard standing next to the tracks, so that road vehicles can draw up alongside the wagons. Otherwise it is a case of providing cranes and/or fork lift trucks; as these are often 'hired in' as appropriate, they can vary greatly in design. If specialised facilities are required, these can be made in the same way as those at private sidings, described below.

Two special types of goods yard that are now common in the larger towns and cities are the International Freight Terminal and the Freightliner Terminal. The former deal specifically with traffic to and from the continent, with full customs, warehousing and forwarding agents' facilities making them literally 'inland ports'. If modelling one, provide plenty of hard standing and some modern looking warehouses—for example, colourfully painted, single storey, steel-clad structures. Freightliner Terminals are designed for the rapid transfer of containers between rail and road, and are the main means of dealing with traffic for customers without their own sidings. They are typified by large yellow painted gantry cranes and plenty of space for lorries and spare containers. Continental manufacturers such as Faller make some nice kits which, despite being HO scale, would be suitable for a Freightliner Terminal on a British layout.

Private sidings

Over 90 per cent of BR freight traffic now moves through private sidings. One or more of these will thus add much interest to a modern layout. There is a great variety of types and sizes of private sidings and if you are to model one successfully it helps to have a good knowledge of the industry concerned. This way you will be able to plan the correct buildings and facilities and the right types and proportions of traffic. Such information can be gained from magazines (not just those on British railways, incidentally, as many American model railroad magazines contain useful ideas and information), from books in your public library or by observing real industry. Apart from the value to your modelling, you will find such research a lot of fun in itself!

Big industrial plants such as steelworks, oil refineries and cement works, have extensive internal railway systems, linked to British Rail. These receive raw materials in, and ship out the finished product, often in complete trainloads. Unless you wish to base your entire layout on such a plant, they are perhaps too large to model convincingly. However, a large installation can easily be represented by just

Typical of many of the latest wagons in train ferry service is this bogie van from Germany which is in brown, silver and yellow (British Rail).

modelling the exchange sidings, where wagons or trains are handed over from BR locomotives to industrial shunters and vice-versa. Such a set of sidings, with the industrial line disappearing 'off stage' under a bridge to a fiddle yard, could allow the running of a wide variety of trains and wagons. Having such an industry 'off stage' is especially useful for mines, quarries and other plants where open wagons run loaded in one direction and empty in the other, as it allows the loads to be changed in the fiddle yard. Even better, two sets of wagons, one loaded, one empty, can be worked in perpetual circuits, giving the impression of a uni-directional flow for each.

Most private sidings are, however, nothing like as large. Instead they are likely to be a simple siding or two, serving a factory to which the occasional wagons are delivered by Speedlink or trip trains. The types of wagons will depend on the sort of factory; continental fruit vans at a cannery, grain hoppers at a brewery, sheeted opens at a papermill and so on. The possible variety is endless, for most industries use rail freight at some stage in their processes and, as the advantage of using the modern railway becomes more widely known, so the number of industries using its services increases.

Even more common is the 'railhead' style of siding. These are located at the local distribution centres for particular products. Thus we have simple sidings for cement silos, fertiliser warehouses, steel stockholders, oil tank farms and so on. Even in suburban areas coal concentration depots are found, where complete trains of coal hopper wagons are discharged, and the various grades of fuel distributed by road to local factories and coal merchants. Most railheads are like this, dealing with inwards traffic such as raw materials, fuel and finished products, and are operated by private firms rather than the railway. They are often located in local market centres, where the railway is convenient either to the final users or to a good road. In many cases, the land used was once the goods yard of a small town station. Occasionally, however, such sidings are used for outwards traffic. A good example is grain, which is collected by road from local farms, dried and stored at the railhead, and then sent on by train to flour mills, breweries and distilleries. In more industrialised areas a similar process is to be seen with scrap metal.

A recent development of the railhead concept, and owing much to the success of Speedlink, is the distribution depot. Typically these are owned and operated by road hauliers or freight forwarders, and are, in effect, modern, privately-owned goods yards. The haulier provides local road transport and warehouses, but uses Speedlink services in preference to road trunking for the long haul.

Modelling all these small sidings, be they industries, railheads or whatever, is simple. Track layouts are mostly basic, often no more than a simple siding off the main line, or a loop and a locomotive release neck. Structures and buildings will vary according to the traffic being handled. There are many good kits for factories and industrial plants available. Bilteezi and Builder Plus card kits make a useful start and the wide range of plastic kits from the European manufacturers have many uses. Don't be put off by the latter being to the slightly smaller continental scales; industrial structures in real life vary considerably in size. Kitbashing, and the imaginative use of plastic sheet, structural shapes and spare plastic kit

A typical Freightliner terminal showing the layout of tracks, access roads and container stacking areas (British Rail).

parts, can help reproduce most types of industrial plant. Remember to include appropriate loading and unloading facilities. If these seem too complicated to model in full, for example, the mass of pipework used for filling tankers, you can always partly conceal it by putting it under cover, using plastic girders and corrugated sheet painted to represent steel and cladding.

Similar factors apply when building a model railhead, though here you may have to be more explicit if the purpose of your depot is to be obvious. Thus a steel stockholders will need a gantry crane and a storage area, a cement terminal will need storage silos and an oil depot—tanks and pipe racks. Stone and coal depots can be reproduced by having the track run out on to a trestle, with space between the rails for the material to drop from the hopper wagons into storage bins. If you do not have room for this, model a dummy unloading house, with an inclined conveyor belt rising from its base and running to the storage dumps. Many railheads merely require a large warehouse, for example, for fertiliser, and a haulier's distribution centre, with the tracks running either into the building or alongside the loading doors. The Builder Plus factory is ideal for this. All that is needed are the building, railway tracks and space for lorries, a few large signs announcing the name and nature of the business, and you are away.

Lineside details

No railway works in isolation from the world at large. Your modelling of the modern rail freight scene will be greatly helped by the inclusion of appropriate lineside details. So, leave out such traditional features as milk churns, cattle docks, hand cranes and wooden barrels, and substitute more modern equipment instead. Chief of these is the pallet, the square wooden framework on which all kinds of goods are transferred between train, lorry and warehouse. These can easily be made from scrap plastic; they are around 4 ft square by 6 in deep. If you can, include such mechanical handling equipment as forklift trucks, gantry cranes and even air compressors (for unloading cement and other powders).

Take care with road vehicles; nothing looks worse than a World War 2 gun tractor masquerading as a modern juggernaut! Admittedly, little is available from the trade, but the Davric Foden tipper is a good kit of a most useful prototype, and it is easy to make semi-trailers which can stand around a yard waiting for a load. There are some well-detailed plastic modern lorry models available from continental manufacturers but these are under scale for British layouts. One interesting detail, if you are modelling a marshalling yard or other busy freight centre, would be a white Portakabin, representing a TOPS office, and demonstrating the increasing sophistication of modern freight operation.

Information

As I hope I have indicated above, modern rail freight operations are a large and fascinating subject, and one which cannot be separated from industry in general. To model them successfully you will need information, not only on such obvious matters as wagons and operating methods, but also on the traffic patterns of whichever aspects of industry and distribution your layout portrays. As mentioned earlier, details on relevant industries can be gained from a number of sources; it is with the railway matters that our problems begin. This may seem surprising but as most enthusiasts have hitherto concerned themselves mostly with the steam age and the traditional methods of freight handling on the railway, little has been published on more modern aspects. However, the situation is improving and the model railway press is beginning to cover the present day scene in some detail with useful articles of late in *Railway Modeller, Model Trains* and *Scale Trains.* The magazine, *Modern Railways*, is invaluable for keeping up with prototype developments. There are many useful books, including the photographic albums covering the various diesel and electric locomotive classes published by Oxford Publishing Co, Ian Allan Ltd and other publishers, and the excellent paperback *BR Diesel Freight in the Era of Specialisation*, by Michael Oakley (published by D. Bradford Barton Ltd). As to what kind of freight is handled where, the OPC *Rail Atlas of Britain* and the Geographia map sheets of British Rail are good for showing the location of private sidings and freight terminals.

The best way of gaining information, however, is to look at the prototype. So, when you see a freight train passing, take a close look and try to work out what it is, where it is going, what the traffic is and why it is marshalled as it is. Similarly, if there is a British Rail freight terminal or a private siding near you, have a look to see what traffic is being handled and how. But stay on the right side of the fence and do not trespass!

Finally, when you are planning any aspect of a modern model railway—pause and think! Ask yourself such questions as, 'What is the logical way to handle this traffic?' or 'How would the prototype lay out these sidings?'. After all British Rail and its customers are just as keen to save money and space while providing easily used facilities as you are! So, remember the Golden Rule: for a convincing layout, model reality, don't just copy someone else's model railway. This applies to all layouts but nowhere more so than on modern ones, where prototype practice diverges so greatly from that of traditional modellers.

Structures and scenery

The contemporary railway scene presents an interesting blend of old and new structures. Some of the older buildings are abandoned and derelict, even partly demolished, while others have been modified for changes in use, or have new extensions or additions. The new buildings are modern in style and may be of a prefabricated construction. For the modeller a variety of older structures are available as kits. These require careful finishing to produce an old, grimy and weathered appearance. Do not be misled into thinking that the choice of an old and crumbling prototype building can be an excuse for slipshod modelling covered up by heavy weathering. On the contrary, just as much care in construction and rather more attention to the prototype, particularly regarding the texture and colouring, are needed for a realistic result.

Relatively little is available commercially for modern structure models. Hornby make a snap together pre-coloured kit for an 00-scale diesel locomotive shed which would be a good basis for a modern motive power depot. Because the servicing and refuelling facilities for diesel locomotives are simpler than for steam engines, and no turntables are needed, a diesel depot or stabling point can be modelled more easily and in a smaller space; another advantage of a modern image layout. A modern signal box is available as a kit from Merit. Some of the plastic kits made by the continental manufacturers are for modern structures, both railway and non-railway buildings, and a number of these are suitable in style for use on a British prototype layout. However, they are underscale for British 00 and N scales so care must be taken that this is not too obvious, by suitable selection and positioning. Included in these ranges are oil refuelling and storage tanks, useful for a diesel depot; an engine and carriage washing unit is also available.

Kits, kit conversion and scratch-building of structure models are covered in some detail in *PSL Model Railway Guide 3: Structure Modelling* to which the reader is referred for further information. Scratchbuilding techniques for modern buildings are generally similar to those for older structures, though glass and concrete structures with large areas of windows may be most conveniently modelled using perspex sheet as the basic walls, with overlays of thin plastic card with the window openings cut out.

The scenic modelling is, of course, essentially the same as for a period layout and the materials and methods which can be employed are described in full in *PSL Model Railway Guide 4: Scenery.* As always, observation of the real thing is desirable for realistic results. There are a number of small scenic details for which styles have changed over the years and care must be taken with these to choose appropriate items for the contemporary scene. An obvious example is in clothing; styles change frequently and distinctively. Thus it is important to select model figures with suitable clothing from the wide range of figures on the market. If necessary, modifications can sometimes be made by cutting or filing, or by building up with filler, or by the addition of extra clothing from paper. The orange safety vests now worn by railway workers, and others, can easily be represented by painting the appropriate areas.

Road vehicles are also important in setting the period of a layout. Though one sees a few 'old bangers' and the occasional restored veteran, most cars and lorries on the road today are less than 10 years old, and this should be reflected on your model. Road signs, road markings, crossings, parking meters, advertisements and posters should also be in the appropriate modern style.

A scenic background will complete the picture and the simplest method is to use commercially-produced items. The Peco range includes city and dock sheets with buildings suitable for a modern scene. If in doubt about the correct style for any of the scenic details you can go out and look for yourself—one of the advantages of modelling the present day railways.

Above *Typical of diesel refuelling facilities is this scene of the Tyne Yard. Modelling would be straightforward, employing the usual materials and methods.*

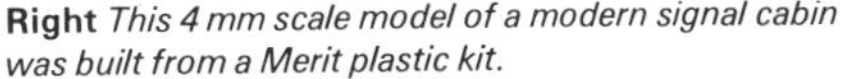

Right *This 4 mm scale model of a modern signal cabin was built from a Merit plastic kit.*

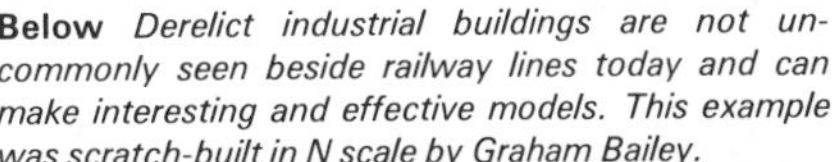

Below *Derelict industrial buildings are not uncommonly seen beside railway lines today and can make interesting and effective models. This example was scratch-built in N scale by Graham Bailey.*

Top *This modern hotel and restaurant building model was built from a Kibri HO-scale kit. Though based on a Continental structure the model would be equally suitable for use on a British prototype layout. It is seen on a Fleischmann exhibition layout.*

Above *This modern diesel or electric locomotive shed was constructed from a Kibri kit. The model shown is in N scale but an HO-scale version is also available.*

Left *A small oil refuelling tank suitable for an industrial diesel modelled using an Airfix tank wagon body mounted on a supporting frame built up from Plastruct girders.*

Above *A modern office block and service station in 00-scale constructed from Linka castings and typical of many buildings seen today* (Linka).

Right *This gravel hopper is typical of a number of modern industrial installations available as plastic kit models from Continental firms and suitable for use on British layouts. The model, in HO scale, is from the Kibri range.*

Below *This fine model of a modern cosmetics factory was scratch-built by Ken Ball for the Macclesfield Model Railway Group's 'Longacre' layout* (Ken Ball and Brian Monaghan).

Top *The Peco series of full colour scenic backgrounds in 00 and N scales includes this modern city scene* (Peco).

Above *Two 15 mph speed restriction signs at Liverpool Street station. Model signs are easily assembled from kits available commercially and are an essential lineside detail for a modern layout.*

Left *Michael Alderton and John Payne have fitted operating colour-light signals throughout their modern 00-scale layout. The relay box is a Merit product while the railwayman using the telephone is the man from the Merit telephone box kit with an orange safety vest painted on.*

Track and lineside details

Much can be done to enhance the realism and interest of the track and lineside areas by the addition of small details such as point motors, automatic warning system track magnets, relay boxes, ballast bins, lineside huts and so on. These can all be simply modelled using plastic, card, wood and odds and ends from the scrap box. Accurate models of speed restriction signs are available as easily made up etched brass parts from Smiths and R. Alderman. Mileposts and gradient signs are also on the market as ready-made and kit items. Parts left over from track laying or maintenance, or ready for use in future repair work, are often to be seen lying beside the track; these include sleepers, rail lengths, point parts and so on. Sometimes simple racks made up from old sleepers and rail are used to hold the spare rail lengths. All these details are easy to model and will realistically dress up the trackside area. Today one often sees places where track and sidings have been lifted; sometimes only the rails have been removed and the sleepers are still in place but overgrown with grass and weeds. An effective little scene on a layout would be a track lifting gang at work on a disused siding with the track partly removed. The Preiser range of figures includes several with picks, shovels and other tools which could be utilised.

Several firms make working colour-light signals of realistic appearance and these are very effective on a modern image layout. An interesting contrast can be introduced by also including some semaphore signals as one still sees a mixture in use. Where the latter are being replaced you may see both types together with crosses fitted over the colour lights to show that they are not yet in operation; modelling this would be a neat detail touch for a modern layout. Barrier crossings, of the half barrier type, are made by Peco, while some of the continental manufacturers make operating barrier crossings of European type which can be converted for British use.

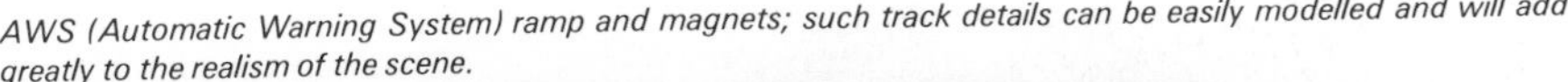

AWS (Automatic Warning System) ramp and magnets; such track details can be easily modelled and will add greatly to the realism of the scene.

Above *This realistic electrical equipment housing is from a Pola HO-scale kit. Positioning was not finally decided when the picture was taken; when permanently installed the base will be blended into the ground for better appearance.*

Below *This scene on the modern layout operated by Michael Alderton and John Payne shows some of the many lineside details which can be included with an old coach converted into an office and store, complete with outside toilet, a lineside hut, lengths of rail, sections of pipe, and so on.*

Above *Where semaphore signals are being replaced by colour-light signals, both types may be found together, as in this photograph taken in Southampton. Note the cross on the colour-light signal showing that it is not yet in use.*

Below *A modern lifting barrier type level crossing at Egham, remotely controlled from Feltham signal box. Note the closed circuit TV cameras scanning the crossing. 4VEP unit, 7830, heads the 08.34 Guildford–Waterloo via Ascot over the crossing* (John Glover).

Weathering

The concept of weathering models has become popular in recent years and the technique has added greatly to the realism of model railways. The treatment represents the effects of rain, dust, grime, rust, spillage and wear and tear, as well as the general toning down of colours at a distance due to atmospheric haze. It also enhances the texture and detailing of the surfaces. While such weathering adds to the realism of any model railway, I consider it to be particularly important for a modern layout. A period model railway can represent a somewhat idealised version of the prototype. The modeller may well wish the locomotives and rolling stock to be in an ex-works condition, with the livery colours bright and clean. Nostalgia will permit us to see this as an accurate representation of the period.

However, if we model the present day railway we can view and study the prototype so easily and frequently that we cannot ignore the wear and tear, grim and rust which are clearly visible, and must apply judicious weathering to our models if we are to achieve a realistic representation. There are many methods of weathering favoured by different modellers but basic to them all is close observation of the real thing. If possible it is very helpful to take colour photographs to which you can refer when actually carrying out the work on your models.

A popular method is to apply a thin wash of black, grey or grey-brown to locomotives and rolling stock, brushing vertically to give the effect of streaking due to rain washing the dirt and grime downwards. Additional colour can be painted on along the lower edges of the sides and ends where grime collects and where dust and dirt are thrown up from the track. Bogies and underframes should be painted a brown-grey rather than black. After the initial overall wash of colour has dried, additional touches can be applied using a trace of colour on an almost dry brush drawn lightly over the surface. This dry brushing technique is very effective in highlighting, and hence emphasising, the details. Rust spots, patches and streaks can be added as appropriate using one of the commercially-produced rust colour paints. A little gloss black will simulate oil spillage.

If you have an airbrush you will find it very useful for weathering, particularly for applying a light overspray of grey or grey-brown to tone down the original colours. You can vary the degree of weathering to give the appearance of almost new stock right through to very grimy and neglected locomotives, coaches or wagons, giving extra variety and interest to your trains. However, do take care not to overdo the effect but keep it subtle and unobtrusive; again reference to the real thing is all important. Structures should also be weathered and it is important not to overlook the track. An airbrush is very useful for applying overall weathering to the track, followed by painting the sides of the rails with rust colour. Finally clean the tops of the rails to leave them shiny.

Weathering is very much a personal thing and you should experiment for yourself to see which method you prefer—or even if you want to do it at all. You can also learn much by looking at the methods used by other modellers and the results they achieve, and I do not mean just railway modellers. Military modelling enthusiasts have put a great deal of thought and experiment into developing realistic weathering techniques and we can gain much useful information from them on methods which we can use, or can adapt for use, on railway layouts.

Narrow-Gauge Railways

Michael Andress

Contents

14
PAMELA

Introduction

One of the major recent developments in the hobby of railway modelling has been the great growth of interest in narrow gauge. At one time this was a subject suitable only for the experienced worker who could scratch-build everything required or who, at the very least, was capable of carrying out major alterations to the available standard-gauge models and parts. However, the introduction of many commercial models, kits and parts over the last few years has brought narrow-gauge railway modelling within the reach of all, even the complete beginner.

There seem to have been several factors combining to initiate the now considerable popularity of this type of modelling. The success of the prototype preservation work, particularly for the 'Great Little Trains of Wales' has led to a much greater public awareness of and interest in narrow-gauge railways. On the modelling scene the appeal of P.D. Hancock's superb 4 mm scale 9 mm gauge 'Craig & Mertonford Railway', a pioneer layout in this field, and its imaginative presentation in the model railway press must surely have created many potential narrow-gauge modellers. Finally, the appearance of the Eggerbahn ready-to-run models in 3.5 mm scale 9 mm gauge made it possible for anyone to build a layout without having to make their own locomotives, rolling stock or track.

Another commercial development of less obvious relevance but actually just as significant was the introduction of N gauge with many commercially produced items of excellent quality which could be adapted easily for use on narrow-gauge layouts using 9 mm gauge track. Although the commercial products have made this type of modelling much easier now, it still has much to offer for the modeller who would like to exercise his or her imagination and ingenuity, with a vast range of interesting and sometimes eccentric prototypes waiting to be modelled. With narrow-gauge it is perfectly possible to create a unique layout which is very different from the type of model railway usually seen.

My aim in this book is to look at the various features of narrow-gauge railways and the advantages they offer, to consider the choice of scale and gauge, and to give the reader some idea of what is currently available commercially in the form of ready-to-run models, kits and parts, and of how these may be modified and adapted. As far as possible I have tried to illustrate my points and to show the great scope of this type of modelling with photographs of models and layouts in various scales. The pictures show the work of many modellers and will, I hope, give the reader ideas and inspiration for his or her own layout. In both text and pictures I have concentrated on the most popular scales and gauges but most of the ideas and information presented here will also be useful for other models.

I would like to thank all those modellers who have allowed me to use photographs of their models and layouts to illustrate this book. In particular I am indebted to Brian Harrap for providing information and pictures on the construction of dual-gauge trackwork. I am also grateful to those manufacturers who have helped me with information and/or photographs of their products.

Above left *A scene from P.D. Hancock's famous Craig & Mertonford Railway layout. This was one of the first layouts to be built to 4 mm scale 9 mm gauge and it created considerable interest in narrow-gauge railway modelling* (P.D. Hancock).
Left *This interesting 009 model is based on a German Schwartskopf chain drive locomotive. John Bruce utilised an N-scale diesel bogie chassis together with a scratch-built body for this attractive engine.*

The prototype

It is perhaps logical before we discuss narrow-gauge modelling to consider the prototype briefly, to clarify what we mean by narrow-gauge and to identify the features which will be advantageous to us in our modelling. There is some variance in the definition of narrow-gauge. Track gauge is the distance between the inner surfaces of the running rails and strictly speaking we can consider 4 ft 8½ in gauge to be standard and anything less than this as narrow gauge. However, in some countries, for example, New Zealand, the track gauge throughout the national system is 3 ft 6 in and in these countries it is not unreasonable to regard this gauge as 'standard', particularly as these railways are run as main line systems.

An alternative definition that can be used is that a line is narrow gauge if it is narrower than other railway tracks in the same area. Another classification which I have seen suggested is that the term narrow gauge should be applied to any track between 3 ft 6 in and 1 ft 6 in in width. Lines with a gauge less than 4 ft 8½ in but greater than 3 ft 6 in are known as sub-standard and those less than 1 ft 6 in are regarded as miniature railways. However, although the above definitions are of interest, from our point of view as modellers it is really the purpose, the type of construction and the method of operation which are the key concepts in giving the characteristics of narrow gauge as it is usually modelled.

Generally all narrow-gauge railways were built because they were cheaper to construct than a standard-gauge line would have been. The saving was of the order of between one and two thirds of the cost of a standard-gauge railway, the greatest economies being where the terrain was most difficult. With the 3 ft 6 in lines, for example, the New Zealand Railways, there were significant savings, although the network was built up as a mainline system. Thus, though New Zealanders may strictly be narrow-gauge modelling (often using S scale on 00-gauge track) when representing their national railways, the result is essentially similar to standard-gauge modelling, with no great saving in space, and with operation more typical of standard- than narrow-gauge practice.

It is with the narrower gauges, less than 3 ft 6 in, that we find a very different character. These smaller gauges permit sharper curves and steeper gradients, avoiding in the prototype much of the expense of cuts, fills and tunnels, by enabling the line to follow the contours of the terrain. Locomotives are small and interesting, often all the engines on the line are different and frequently they are elderly or even ancient! The rolling stock is also likely to be varied. The stations are small with simple track arrangements and the whole operation is much more casual and leisurely, being more akin to light railway operating practice. These are the typical prototypes for narrow-gauge modelling.

Though today passenger traffic (particularly tourists) is so important to many of the surviving narrow-gauge railways, most lines were originally built to serve industries. The Welsh narrow-gauge railways were mainly constructed for the transport of slate from the many quarries; passenger traffic in the early days was largely limited to workmen travelling to and from the quarries. However, there were exceptions and, though the Vale of Rheidol line was built to serve several large lead mines, it was also intended to take advantage of the developing tourist trade in the area. The Welshpool & Llanfair, (built in a more rural border area) carried passengers and general goods, especially agricultural.

Elsewhere in the world narrow-gauge railways have been built to meet the transport requirements of a very wide range of industries, including mines, quarries, cement works, brickworks, sandpits, steelworks, gas works and power stations. On the agricultural side the timber, sugar beet and cane, and peat industries have been major users. The book, *Industrial Narrow Gauge Railways in Britain* by Peter Nicholson (D. Bradford Barton Ltd) gives some idea of the diversity of industries served by these lines in this country. If we include the

Above *This 3 ft 6 in gauge New Zealand Railways electric locomotive is strictly narrow gauge but the locomotives and rolling stock and the system of operation are more typical of standard gauge practice than of narrow gauge as it is usually modelled.*

Below *Typical of narrow-gauge prototypes chosen for modelling is this train on the 2 ft gauge Leighton Buzzard Light Railway. The locomotive,* Pixie, *is an 0-4-0 Kerr Stuart saddle tank built in 1922.*

Above *A view of the impressive limeworks on a 4 mm scale layout built by members of the Romsey & District Railway Modellers Society. The limeworks were largely scratch-built but some structure kit parts were included. Note the 6 mm gauge trains, representing 1 ft 6 in prototype gauge, in the foreground. The locomotives were scratch-built.*

other industrial lines and the many more general railways carrying passengers and freight throughout Britain, Europe and the rest of the world the choice of prototype and the scope of narrow-gauge railway modelling becomes immense.

If you would like to model your layout on one of the Welsh lines there is a great deal of information, including photographs and plans, easily to hand and you can also visit the railway to get the atmosphere of both line and setting. Kits and parts on the market will help you to build up a roster of suitable locomotives and rolling stock without difficulty. Similarly you can choose a continental line, for example, one of the Austrian, German or Swiss railways still operating and again adequate information (some in English and a good deal in German) and models are available. A visit to such a railway may be possible and your layout may thus provide a good excuse for a most enjoyable holiday!

Alternatively you might like to choose something very different from the usual and have a unique model. A layout based on one of the railways on the islands off the north west German coast, such as Sylt, or on an East African line, or on the Fijian sugar cane railway are all possibilities for an intriguing model and there are many other prototypes which would be just as unusual and interesting. Enough information for a realistic model is usually available if you are prepared to search for it and this background work is all part of the fun. An authentic model of one of these lesser known prototypes could be a very satisfying project.

Obviously I haven't the space here to discuss the prototype in any detail. There are many books now available on prototype narrow-gauge railways in Britain and abroad; indeed we have never been so well served with published information as we are today. Though this does not compensate for the disappearance of so many lines it does help greatly with our modelling. I suggest that you read all you can about the prototype railways; the more you know about the real thing the more accurate and realistic your modelling is likely to be.

Above *Terry Onslow's attractive 4 mm scale narrow-gauge Port Newydd & Llwyd Railway layout was inspired by the Welsh slate mining industry and railways. This view shows the station at Port Newydd* (Terry Onslow).

Right *This rail auto on P.D. Hancock's Craig & Mertonford Railway layout was built from an American Kemtron kit long discontinued. The vehicle is typical of many converted from road to rail use by railroads in the United States and elsewhere* (P.D. Hancock).

Below *Howard Coulson's 009 Eitomo layout is based on East African narrow-gauge lines and the resulting model is both attractive and unusual. Locomotive No 16 has an N-scale Minitrix 0-6-0 chassis; the body uses a number of parts from Airfix plastic locomotive kits, particularly the Pug, the remainder being built up from plastic. The coal wagon is a converted N-scale American gondola car.*

Advantages of narrow gauge

Many of the features which make the prototype narrow-gauge railways so appealing—the individuality of the locomotives, the small size of the engines and rolling stock, the tiny but interesting stations and other structures, and the shortness of the lines—are the very ones which make them so suitable for modelling. The choice of prototype is always very important in building an effective and pleasing model and almost all narrow-gauge prototypes reproduce well. The factors which lead to such a significant cost saving over standard-gauge lines on the real railways also give a great space advantage in the model. Sharp curves, short trains and small stations with simple track layouts are all too often unavoidable on model railway layouts but are not unrealistic when working in narrow gauge. Not only is it possible to fit a layout into a smaller space but it will look better. The short trains do not occupy as much of the scene and therefore make the layout appear relatively larger. Similarly the trains travel more slowly, giving the impression that they are running a greater distance. Even the fact that the rails are closer together gives the illusion of a longer track and larger layout. Because the locomotives and rolling stock are smaller and the trains shorter, the passing loops and the sidings can be shorter than on a standard-gauge line so that there is a greater proportion of track between stations, again giving the impression of a longer run. Gradients can be steeper and this, together with the sharp curves, enables a more interesting layout to be accommodated in the area available.

A narrow-gauge layout can always be built in a smaller area than a comparable standard-gauge layout in the same scale. Conversely, with the same space at our disposal we can either have a more complex narrow-gauge layout or can model to a larger scale. It is even possible with some narrow-gauge prototypes to build a model representing the whole length of the line in only a moderate space. At the very least, however, narrow-gauge modelling in a small scale such as 009 means that a fully working layout can be fitted into a 3 ft by 2 ft area. So even if you haven't the space for a full size 00-gauge layout you will surely have room for a narrow-gauge line.

If you already have a standard-gauge layout the addition of a narrow-gauge 'feeder' will increase the scenic and operational interest considerably without requiring much, if any, more space. Similarly on a narrow-gauge layout there is much to be said for including at least one or two standard-gauge sidings where transfer of goods can take place, or even a little dual-gauge track.

Below *Two attractive railcars built by Graham Lindley for his 009 Lydd Valley layout. Both are models of County Donegal prototypes, and have bodies scratch-built in card and balsa. In each case an Atlas N-scale 0-6-0 chassis with the centre wheels removed is used as a power bogie.*

Scale and gauge

Some of the basic terms in railway modelling are often used rather loosely and this can be confusing for the beginner. Because scale and gauge are fundamental in our terminology when discussing narrow-gauge modelling I would like to begin by explaining their use. Gauge, as I have mentioned earlier, is the track width, measured between the inner surfaces of the running rails. The British prototype standard gauge is 4 ft 8½ in and there is a wide range of gauges narrower than this which have been employed in Britain and elsewhere. Scale refers to the proportion between the prototype and the model. For example, for 00 the scale is 4 mm to the foot; that is each foot on the prototype is represented by 4 mm on the model. Originally 00 was used to refer to the gauge only, that is 16.5 mm, but more recently there has been a tendency to refer to 00 scale, meaning 4 mm scale models, and though the purists may not approve, this is a convenient and easily understandable usage. If the term 00 scale is used and the gauge is not specified then it implies 00 gauge, that is 16.5 mm representing prototype standard gauge.

When we speak of narrow-gauge models we need to be more specific about the actual track gauge as well as the scale used. A widely recognised symbol system to indicate this has been devised. Capital letters give the scale employed for the models, followed by a small 'n' or 'm' showing it to be narrow gauge in either the foot 'n' or metric 'm' system of measurement. A final number indicates the prototype gauge in either feet or centimetres. Thus 00n2¼ refers to 00 scale, 4 mm to the foot, models of narrow-gauge prototypes running on 2 ft 3 in gauge track (9 mm gauge). Some of the foot and metric gauges are the same; for example, H0n2½ is the same as H0m75.

Now if we choose to model a particular prototype narrow gauge there are many possible scale and gauge combinations but these fall into two main alternatives. We can choose a specific scale and calculate the model track width which will be correct for the prototype gauge. For example, if we wish to model a 2 ft 6 in gauge prototype in 4 mm scale then the gauge would be 10 mm. Alternatively we can select the gauge for our models and work back to find the scale we will need to employ. If we use 9 mm gauge track and intend to model a 2 ft gauge prototype the scale would be 4.5 mm to the foot. If either the scale or the gauge will be one which is not commercially produced it is usually easier to use a gauge which is available, with a non-standard scale rather than vice versa. This means that mechanisms, chassis, axles and wheelsets can be employed without adaptation, making modelling much simpler.

In fact, narrow-gauge modelling is made much easier because there are a number of what have been called 'coincidence combinations' where the track and wheels from standard gauge in one scale can be used (particularly if we are prepared to compromise a little) for a narrower prototype gauge in another commercially available scale. Thus, for example, locomotive chassis designed for standard-gauge N-scale models can be used for models of 2 ft 3 in gauge prototypes modelled in 00 scale. The convenience of these 'coincidence combinations' is so great that they are employed for almost all narrow-gauge modelling.

The great popularity of 00 (in Britain) and H0 (in Europe and the United States) scales and the extensive developments in N scale in recent years have meant that the majority of narrow-gauge modelling is in either 00 or H0 scale on 9 mm (N) gauge or with 00/H0 gauge utilised for 0 scale. In the remainder of this book I intend to concentrate on these scale/gauge combinations as they are not only the most popular but are also the ones best suited to the beginner. As many modellers may already have a standard 00-gauge layout to which they may like to add a narrow-gauge line, the choice for them is limited to 00 scale and 9 mm gauge is then the most convenient. Larger scale narrow-gauge modelling has also had a considerable boom in the last few years and I

Above *There are three different gauges on the 4 mm scale Wiltshire Limeworks layout built by the Romsey & District Railway Modellers Society. In the foreground a train on the 6 mm gauge line crosses a standard (16.5 mm) gauge track while the elevated tracks at the rear are 9 mm gauge. Note also the abandoned tracks at the right of the scene.*

will devote a separate chapter later in the book to this subject.

However, to show the scope of choice in scale and gauge which exists and so that you will be familiar with these combinations which are in use when you see them mentioned in model railway magazines and books, the following listing is included. I do certainly recommend though that the beginner should choose the 00 scale/N gauge or 0 scale/00 gauge combination rather than one of the less commonly used ones.

Nn3 (N scale on Z gauge (6.5 mm) representing 3 ft gauge prototype.) This combination can also be used to model metre gauge, Nm, or 3 ft 6 in gauge, Nn3½. A few modellers in Britain and the United States have built narrow-gauge layouts in N scale using locomotives and rolling stock converted from Märklin Z scale models with either Märklin ready-made track or hand-built track. Unfortunately, the relatively high cost of the Z-scale models is likely to deter many enthusiasts but the combination has considerable potential for the modeller who would like an extensive narrow-gauge system in a very limited space or who wishes to add a narrow-gauge 'feeder' to an N-scale layout. Peco plan to introduce kits for this scale.

00n1½ (00 scale on Z gauge track representing 1 ft 6 in gauge.) Interest in this scale/gauge combination should be stimulated by the 'Waril' Class Hunslet 0-4-0 locomotive of the Sand Hutton Light Railway planned for early release as a brass kit by Merlin Locomotive Works, particularly if this is followed by other items.

00n2 & H0n2½ (These are respectively 4 mm scale (usually known as 009) and 3.5 mm scale (usually known as H09 or H0e) on 9 mm gauge track.) Strictly speaking the former is equivalent to 2 ft 3 in gauge prototype and the latter approximately 2 ft 6 in but both are used to model prototypes of from 2 ft (60 cm) to 2 ft 6 in (75 cm) gauge. The range of models, kits and parts available is considerable and is discussed elsewhere in this book.

H0n3 (This is 3.5 mm scale on 10.5 mm gauge track for 3 ft gauge prototypes.) It is popular in the United States where brass ready-to-run locomotives and rolling stock, numerous parts and a variety of rolling stock kits are on sale. Ready-made track, including some dual-gauge H0/H0n3 items, is also produced. Some of these products are available in Britain from specialist model railway shops, such as Victors.

00n3 (4 mm scale on 12 mm (TT) gauge track representing 3 ft gauge prototype.) Gem have produced a number of cast metal kits for Isle of Man Railway prototypes and Anbrico have recently introduced a cast metal kit for an Isle of Man (ex-County Donegal) railcar. TT3 mechanisms and other parts can be employed

Above *Two views of Colin Woolridge's 2 mm scale 5 mm gauge layout. The locomotives have bodies scratch-built from nickel silver sheet mounted on modified Marklin Z-gauge chassis. The wagons are adapted Marklin models while the three coaches were made from one Grafar coach cut into three and mounted on modified Marklin wagon chassis. The excellent scenery and scratch-built structures add to the realistic effect.*

Below *Colin Woolridge used two Marklin Z-gauge locomotive chassis regauged from 6.5 mm to 5 mm as the basis for this impressive Fairlie for his 2 mm scale 5 mm gauge (representing 2 ft 6 in gauge prototype) model railway.*

Above *Peter Bailey models in Sn2, $\frac{3}{16}$ inch to the foot scale on 9 mm gauge, representing 2 ft gauge prototype.* Tommy, *a 4-6-0 tank locomotive based on a Hunslet prototype, is based on a modified Fleischmann 2-6-0 chassis. The body was built up entirely of plastic except for the chimney and dome which are standard-gauge castings filed down to size. The coach was also constructed from plastic card.*

Left *This tram locomotive model, based on a Glyn Valley prototype, was constructed from a Peco cast metal body kit mounted on an Arnold N-scale chassis. The model is 4 mm scale on 9 mm gauge, that is 009* (Peco).

Above right *This small diesel hydraulic locomotive is one of the LGB range of locomotive models in 1:22.5 scale on 45 mm gauge* (Lehmann).

Right *An attractive Hunslet quarry engine in 016.5, 7 mm scale on 16.5 mm (00) gauge, constructed from a Peco body kit mounted on a Hornby chassis* (Peco).

for modelling in this scale/gauge combination.

H0m (3.5 mm scale on 12 mm gauge track for metre gauge prototypes.) This scale/gauge combination was formerly catered for by Zeuke of East Germany but ready-to-run locomotives and rolling stock, together with sectional and flexible track and points are now produced by Bemo. This scale and gauge has also been used by a few enthusiasts to model 3 ft 6 in gauge prototypes in H0 scale, H0n3½.

Sn2 (This is S scale, 3/16 inch to the foot, 1/64, on 9 mm (N) gauge track representing 2 ft gauge prototypes.)

Sn2½ (This is 3/16 inch to the foot, 1/64 (S) scale on 12 mm (TT) gauge track representing 2 ft 6 in gauge prototypes.)

Sn3½ (3/16 inch to the foot, 1/64, scale on 00 gauge, 16.5 mm track for 3 ft 6 in prototypes.) This scale/gauge combination is quite popular in New Zealand, Australia and South Africa and some kits are available for local prototypes in these countries.

5½ mm scale on 12 mm gauge track representing approximately 2 ft gauge. At one time Gem made a number of cast metal kits of Talyllyn and Festiniog Railway prototypes to this scale. It had the advantage of greater size than 4 mm scale with correspondingly more space for motors in the locomotives though this is less important now. Though track and TT gauge mechanisms and other parts are available, few other items are suitable and this is a considerable disadvantage.

On1¼ 7 mm scale on 9 mm (N) gauge track provides a fairly good approximation to 15 in prototype gauge.

On2¼ (7 mm scale on 16.5 mm gauge, also known as 016.5 in line with 009, equivalent to approximately 2 ft 4 in gauge prototype but also used for 2 ft, 2 ft 3 in and 2 ft 6 in gauges.) This is an attractive combination as the models are large enough to allow considerable detailing but a layout can be built in the same space as a comparable one in 00-scale standard gauge. The vast range of mechanisms, wheels, underframes and track parts intended for 00

and H0 can be used for convenience and economy and there is a good selection of accessories such as figures and road vehicles for 7 mm scale. Flexible track for 016.5 with typical narrow-gauge sleeper spacing and appearance is now available from Peco and there is an increasing range of locomotive and rolling stock kits, more details of which are given elsewhere in this book.

0n2½ (This is the US 0 scale, ¼ inch to the foot, on 16.5 mm gauge track.) The American equivalent of 0n2¼, it has similar advantages.

0m75 (0 scale models on H0, 16.5 mm, gauge track representing 75 cm gauge prototypes.) These models were introduced by Märklin as 0H0 in 1970 and ran on Märklin H0-gauge stud contact track. The range was limited but included a steam and a diesel outline locomotive with passenger and freight stock.

0n3 (American 0 scale, ¼ inch to the foot, 1/48 scale, on 19 mm gauge representing 3 ft gauge.) This is a popular scale/gauge combination in the United States with many fine brass locomotives and kits available. Some of these are imported into Britain by specialist model shops.

10 mm, 14 mm and 16 mm scales on 32 mm (0) gauge track (Representing respectively 3 ft, 2 ft 3 in and 2 ft gauge prototypes.) The large size of these models means that they can be very well detailed. Some modellers have used inexpensive 0-gauge locomotive and rolling stock models as a basis for narrow-gauge equipment in these larger scales, others have built from scratch. This type of modelling has become popular recently and it is discussed in more detail later.

G gauge (This is 13.5 mm scale, 1/22.5, on 45 mm (1) gauge track representing metre gauge prototypes.) Modelling in this scale/gauge combination is based on the LGB range of ready-to-run locomotives and rolling stock, together with track and many other items. It is further discussed in the section on large scale modelling.

Locomotives

Quite a number of ready-to-run narrow-gauge locomotive models have been produced for 9 mm (N) gauge track, though many of these have since been discontinued. The original Eggerbahn range included steam, diesel and electric locomotive prototypes, together with an attractive steam railcar. Although this range was later taken over by Jouef, none are now available except on the second-hand market. Jouef also produced a Decauville 0-4-0 Tank Engine for a time. Most of the ready-to-run models have been of continental locomotives though Minitrains made two realistic American models, a Baldwin steam 0-4-0 Saddle Tank and a Plymouth 4-wheel diesel, while Roco, in addition to a typical Austrian steam 0-6-0 Saddle Tank, produced a neat 6-wheel diesel.

The Liliput range is still in production and features an Austrian 0-6-2 Tank Engine, available with detail variations and with different colour schemes representing locomotives operated by a number of Austrian narrow-gauge lines, including the Zillertalbahn, and the Swiss Waldenburgerbahn engine *Eurovapor*. Also from this manufacturer is a realistic model of the Waldenburgerbahn 0-6-0 tank engine *G. Thommen*. Liliput also make a superb model of the Austrian Federal Railways Bo-Bo Class 2095.11 diesel locomotives in red or red and cream livery.

The West German firm-Bemo-has a steadily increasing range of H0e and H0m models accurately based on German and Swiss prototypes. The locomotives include a DB V51/V52 Bo-Bo diesel, an 0-6-0 tank engine, a DB Class 99 0-10-0 tank locomotive, and a Swiss Rhaetian Railway Ge4/4 Bo-Bo electric locomotive. For future release is the Rhaetian Railway Ge6/6 Co-Co electric 'Crocodile' which should be a most impressive model.

The ready-to-run models mentioned above are all to 3.5 mm scale but modellers have also used them on 4 mm scale layouts. The plastic bodies lend themselves to easy modification, ranging from minor detail changes to extensive rebuilding, or the bodies can be removed completely and replaced by new ones built up from card or plastic card. However, even more useful for rebuilding purposes is the wide range of N-scale models now available, particularly as some of them are relatively inexpensive. In some cases the bodies can be modified to make the models suitable for 00 or H0 narrow gauge. N-scale diesels, for example, can often be adapted quite simply by removing the cabin and replacing it by a larger one; a few extra details can also be added with advantage. Some steam locomotives can be similarly altered. The wide range of chassis made for N-scale is very useful for the modeller working in 00 or H0 scale on N gauge. These chassis are easily obtained, are usually very reliable in operation, and the wide variety means that most prototypes can be modelled, though some compromise with accuracy may be necessary. Suitable bodies can be fabricated from wood, card or plastic card and mounted on the chassis. The use of these commercial products makes it possible for modellers with experience only of working with plastic or card to build up a locomotive roster without difficulty.

The availability of commercially-made chassis has had a further benefit as a number of small manufacturers have been able to produce cast metal body kits designed to fit on to these ready-made chassis. This is a particularly pleasing development as there is now a good selection of British prototypes available in this form with more planned. The Chivers Finelines range includes the Welsh Highland Railway, *Russell*, the North Wales Narrow Gauge Railway, *Beddgelert* and *Gowrie*, the Lynton & Barnstaple, *Lew*, and a Campbeltown & Machrihanish 0-6-2T, all designed to fit on to the Minitrix N205 2-6-2T chassis. Also from this manufacturer are a Tralee & Dingle 2-6-0T to fit the Farish Hall chassis and the Dinorwic Quarry Hunslet, *Dolbadarn* to be mounted on the Arnold 0-4-0 chassis. Dundas Models produce a kit for the Welshpool & Llanfair Hunslet 2-6-2T No14 which can be modelled either in its original Sierra Leone Railway form or as it is now on

Above *This impressive 009 Garratt articulated locomotive was constructed by John Bruce. The engine has two Jouef 0-4-0 chassis with the bodywork scratch-built from plastic, together with parts from plastic kits and odds and ends from the scrap box.*

Right *Peter Bailey built this model of a Hunslet quarry locomotive in Sn2. The chassis is adapted from a Minitrain's Baldwin while the body was scratch-built entirely from plastic except for the hand rails.*

Below *This 4 mm scale 9 mm gauge model of the Welsh Highland Railway locomotive,* Russell, *was built from a Chiver Finelines cast metal body kit mounted on a Minitrix chassis by manufacturer, Roger Chivers. The model was painted by Larry Goddard* (Graham Boyes).

Above *A Minitrix N-scale 2-6-2 chassis.*

Below *The completed Lynton & Barnstaple 2-6-2 model in 009 built from the Stenning kit with Minitrix chassis* (R. Stenning).

Bottom *An 009 model of a Darjeeling Tank Locomotive built from the Langley Miniature Models cast metal body kit mounted on an Arnold N-scale chassis.*

the W & L, while the Lynton & Barnstaple 2-6-2T kit, formerly marketed by Weald Models, is now available from R. Stenning. Both these kits are arranged to fit on to the Minitrix N205 chassis. Another impressive model, a Leek & Manifold 2-6-4T, originally made by Centre Models, will soon be re-issued by ABS Models; this kit will fit on to the Minitrix 2-6-2 chassis.

For Talyllyn enthusiasts Gem have kits for the 0-4-0T engines *Douglas* (to fit the Arnold 0-4-0 chassis) and *Dolgoch* (to be mounted on the Arnold 0-6-0 chassis with the centre wheels removed). The Festiniog Railway Co have produced kits for a Baldwin 4-6-0, for *Mountaineer*, an Alco 2-6-2T, and for the 0-4-0 *Prince*. The Peco kits include a tram engine based on a Glyn Valley Tramway prototype and three freelance engines, a saddle tank, a side tank, and a Vari-kit which can be assembled in various ways to give different appearances. Each of the three freelance kits can be built as an 0-4-0 or an 0-6-0 as desired. Two interesting diesel body kits have been produced by Meridian Models, a Simplex and a Kerr Stuart. The latter is designed to fit a Minitrix 0-6-0 chassis but other chassis can also be employed. Members of the Wessex 009 Group have described the prototype Kerr Stuart narrow-gauge diesels and models based on the Meridian kit, using various chassis, in an article in the November 1977 issue of *Model Railway Constructor* magazine and this is a useful reference.

There are two other cast metal kits which are of interest though not of British prototypes. Langley Miniature Models make a body kit for a Darjeeling 0-4-0T to fit an Arnold Chassis and MS Models produce a kit for the body of a railbus loosely based on the German Wismar 4-wheel double-bonnet type. The kit can be assembled in various ways.

Recently imported from Japan are the models in the Joe Works H0e range of kits. These highly detailed brass and cast metal kits make up easily into very attractive models, mainly of Japanese, but also of American and German, prototypes. The locomotives include steam, diesel and electric outline models and range from tiny 0-4-0s to a Lima 2-truck Shay and an articulated 3-car electric railcar set.

Joe Works have now produced a British prototype to the special order of Victors, one of the firms selling this range of kits in this country. The model is a 4 mm scale 9 mm gauge Peckett 0-4-0 Saddle Tank *Gamecock* of the Cranmore Class. The brass kit includes the standard Joe Works 0-4-0 chassis and motor. Merlin Locomotive Works make a white metal body kit for *Midget*, a Bagnall style 0-4-0 saddle tank to fit the Joe Works chassis. Also from Merlin is a brass locomotive kit by Brian Clarke for a Port Class Dinorwic Quarry Hunslet.

Though the use of commercially available chassis for locomotives with cast metal bodies is very convenient it does mean a compromise with strict accuracy in many cases. As an example the Minitrix N205 chassis is employed for a number of different models, including some of prototypes which have outside frames and for which it is, of course, incorrect as it has inside frames. There are hopes that a more accurate chassis may be produced by one of the specialist manufacturers. Failing this modellers will either have to make more accurate chassis themselves or have them made specially, or be prepared to accept the compromise of using the commercially available ones.

For 016.5 the only ready-to-run models of which I am aware are the Märklin OHO series which were made to operate on stud contact track. The locomotives were an 0-6-0 steam engine and a 6-wheel diesel, both of continental type. There are a number of kits for models of British prototypes. DJH Kits offer a choice of four small locomotives for 016.5, the Festiniog Railway 0-4-0, *Prince*, and three freelance 0-4-0s of rather similar design. The kits are complete with chassis and motors and the modeller has only to supply paint, transfers, adhesive and couplings. Peco have cast metal body kits for two locomotives, a tram engine based on a Glyn Valley Tramway prototype to fit a Hornby 0-6-0 chassis and a Hunslet quarry locomotive to be mounted on a Hornby 0-4-0 chassis. For early release is a body kit for 0-4-2T, *Talyllyn*; a suitable chassis will be available from Wrightlines.

Vulcan Model Engineering have an etched brass and cast white metal kit for the Welshpool & Llanfair No14, designed to fit on to the Lima diesel shunter chassis. The kit includes outside frames and all details so that a very realistic model can be constructed. Another highly detailed and accurate kit is the Baldwin 4-6-0 originally produced by Chivers 'Finelines' and now to be re-issued in improved form by Wrightlines.

The very large selection of commercially-produced chassis available for 00 and H0 makes it easy for the modeller to find a suitable ready-made chassis on which to mount a scratch-built body for the prototype of his choice, though some compromise with strict accuracy may be necessary. As with the N-scale models used for 009, some of the 00- and H0-scale models can be modified for 016.5 use by removing the original cab and replacing it with a larger one and extra details can be added.

Rolling stock

In many respects the situation is rather similar to that with the locomotives. For 3.5 mm scale 9 mm gauge Eggerbahn, Jouef and Minitrains passenger and freight stock was largely freelance but based on continental prototypes; it is no longer available though you may find items second-hand from time to time. The Liliput and Bemo ready-to-run rolling stock models are still on the market; the Bemo models are also made in H0m as well as H0e. The models in both the Liliput and the Bemo ranges are highly detailed replicas of actual prototype vehicles, all of continental origin. There are 4-wheel and bogie passenger coaches from both manufacturers together with 4-wheel goods wagons and vans. The Liliput series also features some bogie freight vehicles while 6-wheel vans and a wagon are included in the Bemo range.

For British layouts in 4 mm scale 9 mm gauge, kits for passenger and goods stock are available in plastic, cast metal and etched brass. Dundas Models produce a range of wagon, van and coach kits which are freelance but are designed to be typical of rolling stock built around the turn of the century. The kits have moulded plastic bodies and cast metal chassis; Peco wheels are included. The Colin Ashby kits are also freelance; they are moulded plastic with Peco wheels, and the range includes eight different wagons. Mikes Models offer Talyllyn coaches and a slate wagon; the kits are cast metal with, for the coaches, plastic sides. The Micro Rail kits by Bill Brown have etched brass body and chassis parts with cast metal details; the range includes Festiniog, Glyn Valley and North Wales Narrow Gauge Railway coaches with other coach and wagon kits

Below *A Lynton & Barnstaple Special 3rd Class coach model in 009 built from a Langley Miniature Models kit. The model has a photo-etched body, cast metal parts and plastic bogies* (Langley Miniature Models).

Above *A scene on Graham Lindley's Lydd Valley 4 mm scale 9 mm gauge layout with the engine depot at the rear. The fine model of the Lynton & Barnstaple crane set was scratch-built by John Bruce; the vans are from the now discontinued Eggerbahn range. The locomotive is a model of the Festiniog Railway 'Mountaineer' built from the Festiniog Railway Co cast metal kit mounted on an Arnold chassis.* **Below** *Howard Coulson used Airfix tank wagon kits to model these two bogie tankers for his 009 Eitomo layout based on East African lines. Everything below the solebars was trimmed off and the models were then mounted on Jouef/Playcraft bogies. Other 009 or N-scale bogies could also be used.*

Above *These 7 mm scale 16.5 mm gauge wagons based on Talyllyn Railway prototypes were constructed from cast metal kits in the Wrightlines range.*

planned to follow. Langley Miniature Models make Lynton & Barnstaple coach kits with etched brass bodies, cast metal parts and plastic bogies and couplings, while Chris Leigh also has two Lynton & Barnstaple coaches in his range of kits. The Festiniog Railway Co produces a series of kits for Festiniog and Lynton & Barnstaple goods vehicles.

For 3.5 mm scale 9 mm gauge the Joe Works range of kits includes a selection of passenger and goods stock, together with a small crane wagon and two snow ploughs, one a wedge type and the other a rotary machine. The models are mainly of Japanese prototypes but some are essentially international in style.

The ready-to-run models and kits can be modified to introduce greater variety or to reproduce prototypes which are not otherwise available, but it is often more convenient to scratch-build new bodies and mount them on commercially available chassis. Dundas Models chassis are marketed separately and can be utilised or N scale chassis can be employed. In this way the scope is almost limitless and there is no reason why you should not be able to run any prototype stock you would like to have on your layout.

For 016.5 the only ready-to-run models were the coaches and goods stock in the Märklin 0H0 range. These were of continental type and, as far as I know, are no longer on the market. Wrightlines make a range of cast metal kits for Talyllyn wagons, together with wheels and other parts for scratch-building. Peco have coach, van and wagon kits with moulded plastic parts and the original range of 4-wheel stock is being extended with the addition of bogie vehicles utilising many of the same parts. DJH Kits offer a locomotive tender, two wagons and a guard's van in kit form.

Though the present range of models available as kits is rather limited the use of 00-scale chassis or parts with scratch-built bodies will give great scope for rolling stock construction, following whatever prototype the modeller wishes.

Track

Many modellers, particularly beginners, will find it convenient to use ready-made commercial track rather than build their own. The Peco 'Crazy' track originally introduced for 9 mm gauge is now also made for 16.5 mm gauge. The track is flexible, allowing it to be curved as required, and right- and left-hand and Y-points are produced for the 9 mm gauge; the original 9 in radius turnouts have been replaced now by 12 in radius points, providing a better appearance and smoother running. The plastic sleepers have a realistic wood grain surface and are slightly irregular in length and spacing, giving a good representation of typical narrow-gauge trackwork. For 016.5 Peco produce sets of sleepers to be fitted to their ordinary 00-gauge points to give a narrow-gauge effect, and this firm is to introduce a Y point for 016.5 shortly. Bemo make track, both sectional and flexible, for both H0e and H0m, and right- and left-hand turnouts are included in both gauges.

As we often use wheels and chassis intended for N scale as a basis for 00- and H0-scale narrow-gauge models it might seem logical to employ standard N-gauge track; similarly we could use standard 00-gauge track for 0-scale narrow gauge. The disadvantage with this is that the sleepers are too small, too close together and rather too regular. However, if the sleepers are largely concealed by modelling them almost completely buried in the ground with the effect of a rather overgrown track, then the appearance can be perfectly acceptable. This does give the advantage of being able to use the far greater variety of points and crossings which are produced for standard gauge; these include such items as 3-way points and slip points, both of which can be very useful but are difficult to make.

The track should be weathered to give a realistic appearance. A dull brown wash of paint can be applied to the sleepers to tone down the plastic finish, giving a weathered wood effect, while the rails are painted with rust colour, the running surfaces being wiped clean immediately afterwards. A little scenic dressing sprinkled on to the ballast will simulate weeds growing on the track.

Buffer stops on narrow-gauge railways show many variations in style but are usually of simple construction. Peco make a small sleeper-built buffer stop for 009, or suitable models can be made quickly and easily from wood or plastic. A useful detailing item in the Peco 009 range is a point lever moulded in plastic which will add a finishing touch to the lineside scene. Small wagon turntables are very common on narrow-gauge railways, especially in mines and quarries. The Peco 009 range includes a typical example but the modeller can also scratch-build small turntables of this type without difficulty. For locomotives a larger turntable is required, though smaller than would be needed for standard-gauge engines. Joe Works makes a kit for an H0e locomotive turntable with a span of 61 mm; the kit is complete and is easy to assemble and install. It is supplied to operate by hand but there is no reason why a motor drive should not be fitted if desired.

It adds greatly to the interest of a narrow-gauge layout if some standard-gauge tracks are included. The difference in width between these and the narrow-gauge tracks and the contrast in size between the standard- and narrow-gauge locomotives and rolling stock provides a comparison which emphasise the character of narrow-gauge railways. In the simplest form the narrow- and standard-gauge tracks are separate, perhaps running either side of a passenger platform or a goods transhipment shed, or side by side beneath a hoist used to transfer freight between standard- and narrow-gauge wagons. A useful item in the Liliput track range is a crossing with narrow- and standard-gauge track, enabling one to be brought across the other.

Even more interesting is the inclusion of dual (or even triple!) gauge trackwork on your layout. This was not very common on prototyie narrow-gauge railways in Britain but was frequently employed in some countries. In its

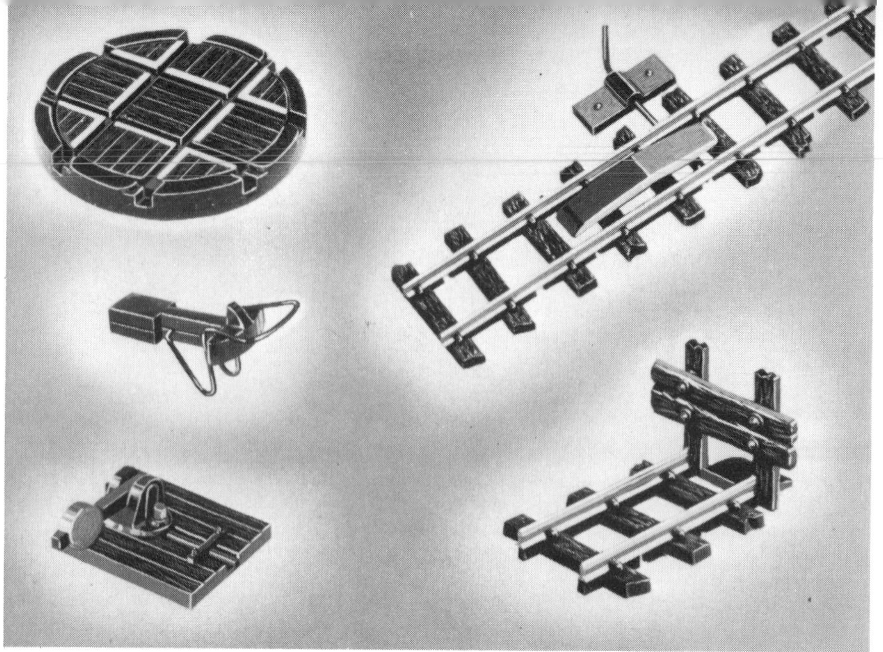

Above *Useful items in the Peco 009 range include a wagon turntable, an uncoupler, a buffer stop, a point lever and couplings* (Peco).

Below *A small locomotive turntable on the 60 cm gauge Swedish Ohs Bruk Railway. A rather similar model turntable for 009 is made in kit form by Joe Works.*

Bottom *A standard- and narrow-gauge crossing in Sweden.*

Top *Triple gauge (left) and dual gauge (right) at a Swedish factory and* **(above)** *simple merging of standard- and narrow-gauge track into dual-gauge (nearer the camera).*

simplest form a length of dual-gauge track has two outer rails used by standard-gauge equipment, while the narrow-gauge stock runs on one of the outer rails and on another rail laid between these at the appropriate distance. Pointwork takes various forms depending on whether it relates to one or both of the gauges and some examples are shown in the accompanying photographs. Brian Harrap is an expert in modelling dual- and triple-gauge track and I am most grateful to him for the following description of construction methods illustrated with examples of his work.

One of the most interesting facets of modelling narrow-gauge railways is their interface with standard-gauge lines. Many narrow-gauge systems do not have a connection at all with any standard-gauge railway but those that do must deal with the differing gauge problem as best they can. Often, and typically, the narrow-gauge line will feed a standard-gauge railway and may just share the same station buildings or platform. However, where there are industries along the narrow-gauge line at some distance from the interchange, to which it would be useful to take standard-gauge wagons, then special measures are needed. The required movement of standard-gauge wagons is sometimes achieved by carrying them piggy-back fashion on special narrow-gauge vehicles, especially in Europe, or dual-gauge trackwork may be laid.

Which system is used in any particular location rather depends on the circumstances. If there are relatively few standard-gauge wagons to be moved around a works or factory that is laid with narrow-gauge track or if the standard-gauge wagons are to be moved over some tramway type trackage through the town streets then the method of carrying these wagons on transporters is most likely to be used. There are several types of transporter but generally they are of one of two basic designs, a low slung narrow-gauge vehicle with standard-gauge rails along its length on to which the standard-gauge wagon can be shunted via a simple ramp, or special small narrow-gauge two-axle carrying trucks which are positioned so that there is one under each axle of a standard-gauge wagon. These small carrying trucks or rollbocks, as they are called, require rather more elaborate arrangements for getting the standard-gauge wagons on to them and they are really only suited to moving 2-axled standard-gauge wagons, those with 3 or 4 axles being much more easily moved on the rail-equipped transporters. These latter are the type more commonly in use today and they are certainly the easiest to copy in model form.

However, any form of transporter is a hindrance to railway operation and laying dual-gauge track is a better solution where this is practical and if traffic is sufficient to warrant it. When circumstances demand it, dual-gauge trackage of the most complex designs can be laid but anyone considering including a little dual-gauge trackwork on their narrow-gauge layout should not be put off by the fact that it looks complicated. Basically, dual-gauge trackage is as straightforward as ordinary track, there are just a few more rails involved, as can be seen by looking at the first diagram. This shows an ordinary narrow-gauge point with an extra rail laid on the outside to allow standard-gauge vehicles to travel over it on the diverging route. It is easy to see that to make this point dual gauge in both directions only one more rail need be laid as in the second diagram. Although it may appear rather involved, all that is required is one more point blade, one more frog and an obtuse angle crossing of the same type as is found on a diamond crossing. So what may have looked daunting at first is really just a logical assembly of standard parts that most railway modellers will already be familiar with. Thus anyone who has had experience of normal, either standard- or narrow-gauge, point construction should have little difficulty with dual gauge.

Whilst the principles of dual-gauge point construction are similar in any scale, most of my work has been done in H0-H09 using copper-clad sleepers and nickel silver rail and I would suggest this method for a first attempt. Any dual gauge track should be considered as standard (or broadest) gauge first with narrow gauge added, rather than the other way around, and is usually laid with standard-gauge size rail for both standard- and narrow-gauge lines. Therefore any proposed point construction would commence by laying sleepers as for standard gauge and I do this

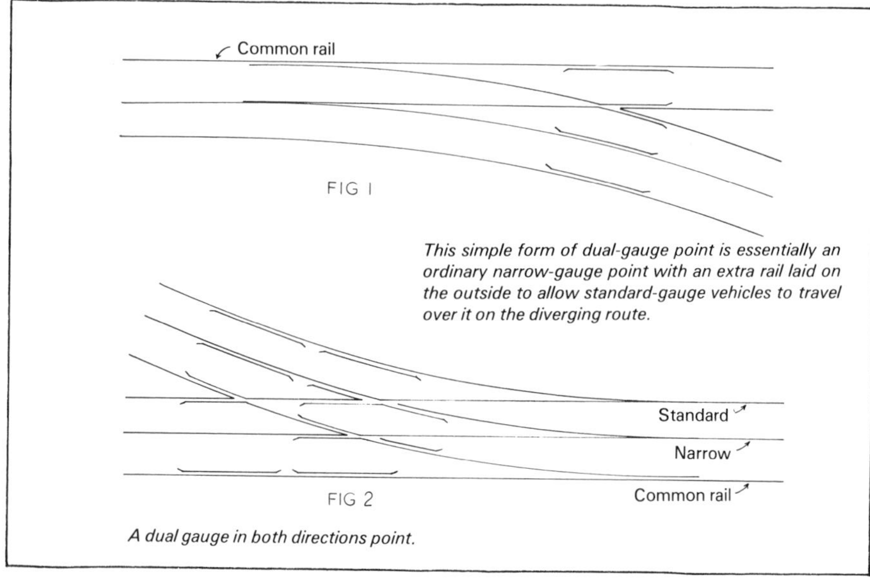

This simple form of dual-gauge point is essentially an ordinary narrow-gauge point with an extra rail laid on the outside to allow standard-gauge vehicles to travel over it on the diverging route.

A dual gauge in both directions point.

Above *HO-scale narrow-gauge transporter truck with continuous running surface for standard-gauge wagon wheels. Long wheelbase or bogie standard-gauge vehicles may be carried easily on this type, sometimes with a standard-gauge wagon spanning two transporters* (Brain Harrap).

Right *Dual-gauge track with narrow-gauge only point and* **(Below right)** *two turnouts for both standard and narrow gauge.*

directly on to my prepared drawing using double-sided transparent tape. To make a point of the fairly simple type shown in the first diagram I would lay the straight common stock rail first and then the standard-gauge diverging stock rail, followed by assembly of the frog nose as normal except, of course, that it will be gauged differently on each route; otherwise there is nothing special about it.

Next the check rails should be added and test wheels offered up to the frog nose to ensure that neither narrow- nor standard-gauge wheels pick at their respective side of the frog. Then the diverging stock rail can be laid; this rail is naturally parallel to the standard-gauge diverging stock rail but gauged to the common rail at the blade end and to the frog at the other. The other narrow-gauge check rail can then be installed to prevent picking of the frog. The wing rails can now be fitted as normal, making sure that they do not infringe the back to back gauge of either the standard- or the narrow-gauge wheelsets that you are using. Once the blades are in position, which in this case is the same as on a normal narrow-gauge point, and all the insulating gaps are cut, you are in the dual-gauge business.

Other simple types of dual-gauge points are shown and I would recommend practice on one or two of these before tackling the dual both routes type of point which is a little more

Above *Rollbocks at Möckmühl in West Germany where the 75 cm gauge Jagsttalbahn meets the standard gauge. Note also the simple hoist straddling narrow- and standard-gauge tracks in the background.*

Below *Standard-gauge HO-scale wagon on narrow-gauge rollbock transporters. The two rollbocks are not connected together; long coupling bars are used to link to other vehicles in a train* (Brian Harrap).

Above left *Dual-gauge track on Brian Harrap's HO-scale layout. Note that it is basically standard gauge with narrow gauge added. These dual gauge both routes points are all left hand but right hand are little different* (Brian Harrap).

Above right *It looks complicated but a careful study will show that all the frogs and crossings are the same as usual, they are just in close proximity. Pointwork like this is fascinating to shunt over* (Brian Harrap).

Below *Triple gauge is something to try after having mastered dual gauge. Construction principles are similar except that due to reduced working clearances it is often necessary to lay the narrowest gauge first. Triple once existed at Växjö in Sweden and still does at Gladstone in Australia* (Brian Harrap).

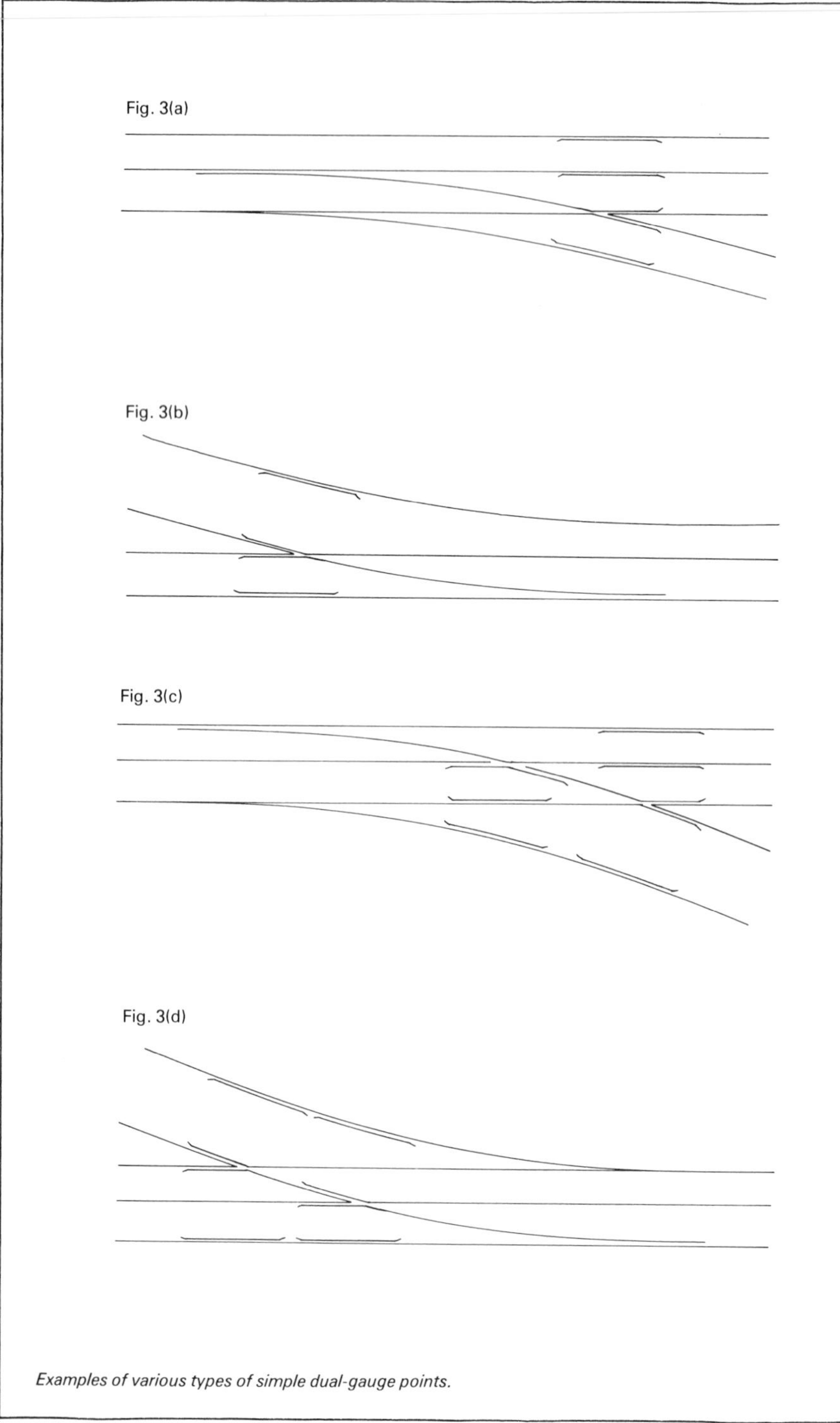

Examples of various types of simple dual-gauge points.

involved. Construction of the dual both routes point follows normal methods by laying out for standard gauge and assembling sleepers ready for laying rail. If you can arrange to get a sleeper under each of the frog noses and under the obtuse crossing, so much the better. Lay the straight stock rail as before, then the curved standard-gauge stock rail and the main frog nose and check rails all as for a standard-gauge point. Next lay in the narrow-gauge frog nose being careful to gauge correctly from the common rail on the straight side and from the outer rail on the diverging side (Narrow gauge one side, standard gauge the other). Accurate work here is important as it is all too easy to get the frog nose too far back and therefore of too wide gauge on one route or the other, leading to trouble later with narrow-gauge wheels dropping excessively at the frog. Note that the short leg of this narrow-gauge frog can be led straight into the wing rail for the standard-gauge frog and is easier to do than it may look.

Fit the remaining check rails associated with these two frogs as in the diagram. Incidentally, with any pointwork, try to arrange for the wing rails to end opposite the ends of the check rails as the finished work then looks so much better. Now lay in the common closure and wing rails. It is important to do this at this stage so as to have a rail to gauge the obtuse angle crossing to later. I usually make the obtuse crossing integral with its associated point blade. Take a length of rail and make a bend in the approximate place that the crossing will be, leaving enough material for the blade. Offer up and mark the length for the blade and cut off about one inch longer. File the blade and refit. Using gauges very carefully, position the rail and curve the diverging length and, at this stage, continually check the track gauge at the nose of the obtuse crossing. This must be exactly right or there will be worse wheel dropping than on a sloppy frog. When you are satisfied, mark off and trim the final length of the blade and then solder the rail in position, checking the gauge again as you go. Note that the straight leg of this crossing is gauged to the common rail at standard gauge and the curved leg is gauged to the common closure rail, previously laid, to narrow gauge.

The fitting of the remaining pieces of rail is fairly straightforward; file the ends of the rails to match the obtuse crossing and gauge to the appropriate common rails. Extra check rails are needed to stop wheels sliding the wrong side of the crossing and these can be positioned by trial and error. Whether you fit the K shaped check rail is up to you. It serves little purpose in the model but is usually, though not always, part of the prototype, so you may wish to add it.

Almost any piece of dual-gauge trackwork can be built up using these guidelines. The main thing is to be very accurate with gauge at crossings and frogs. I have not considered here how the blades are to be moved or the frogs switched as any of the methods currently used for standard gauge can be employed with dual gauge. I usually use a copper-clad throw bar and flex the blades but pivoted blades may just as easily be used. Note that both frogs are always of the same polarity and that the obtuse crossing needs no special switching.

Why don't you install some dual-gauge trackwork on your layout soon? Watching both standard- and narrow-gauge trains threading their way through a section of 'complicated' trackage is hard to beat!

The scenic setting

Obviously the same general principles and techniques apply to scenic work for narrow-gauge layouts as for standard-gauge model railways, both in planning and in construction. As I have already mentioned, a hilly or mountainous terrain is often chosen as the setting. Various methods can be employed for modelling this type of scenery. The basic framework is often built up from wood or hardboard formers covered with strips of card or with wire netting—though an alternative which has become popular recently is the use of expanded polystyrene. This latter material is very easy to cut and shape and can often be obtained without cost as it is widely used as a packing material; it is very light and thus especially popular for portable layouts. Over the basic shape of wood and card, or netting, or of expanded polystyrene, a covering of plaster bandage material will give a surface to which texturing and colouring can conveniently be applied to complete the modelling of the ground surface.

Because narrow-gauge layouts are often small the modeller is able to bring the model to a very high standard of detail throughout, with the addition of all the small touches that are so important in creating interest and realism.

The subject of scenery modelling is covered in detail in *PSL Model Railway Guide 4: Scenery,* but the accompanying scenes on a number of narrow-gauge layouts show how various modellers have tackled this aspect of layout construction. Though most narrow-gauge model railway layouts feature rural, hilly or mountainous scenery, do not overlook the possibilities of an urban, factory or dockside setting. Many prototype narrow-gauge lines were built to serve industrial concerns, some of them in heavily built up areas, and the factory buildings and other structures can make a very interesting backdrop to your railway. The scope for super-detailing is considerable so that even a small layout of this type can provide enough construction work to keep you enjoyably occupied for some time.

Below *Attractive scenic work on Graham Mighell's Graell Junction 009 layout includes this realistically modelled derelict mine. Note the many small details which have been included.*

Above *The 0-4-4-0 Bagnall* Monarch, *hauls a passenger train along the river bank on Graham Lindley's Lydd Valley layout. Grass scenic matting has been used for the realistic grassy banks. Note the swans and the punt.*

Below *A realistic dock scene at Port Newydd on Terry Onslow's 009 layout. The ship is a much modified Airfix kit constructed by John Sondermann and Terry Onslow. The slate wagons were built from Mike's Models kits* (Terry Onslow).

Above *A scene on the 016.5 layout representing the middle section of the Talyllyn Railway built by the Wessex Group of the Talyllyn Railway Preservation Society. The tent is an appropriate touch in view of the popularity of the prototype line with holidaymakers.*

Below *This working incline at the slate quarry is a very impressive feature on Terry Onslow's Port Newydd & Llwyd Railway layout. The rock face has a foundation of wire netting covered with Mod Roc; Cove Adhesive was used for the final surface treatment. The buildings were constructed from balsa wood covered with Pyruma fire cement scribed to represent individual blocks* (Terry Onslow).

Structures

The structures of narrow-gauge lines tend to be small and relatively simple in design, though by no means lacking in interest. In fact they are often very attractive with considerable character and charm. There are very few structure models specifically for narrow gauge available but this is not a significant disadvantage as many of the kits for buildings based on prototypes used on standard-gauge railways can easily be adapted. Also many modellers like to scratch-build their own structures; this permits greater individuality and also enables specific prototypes of choice to be modelled.

Among the plastic kits Heljan offer an H0 scale model of Mariefred station building on the Swedish 60 cm gauge Östra Södermanlands Railway (ÖSlJ). Some of the Swiss, German and Austrian stations in other manufacturers' ranges may be based on narrow-gauge prototypes; if not they would certainly be suitable for such use. Pola make a small narrow-gauge engine shed kit in H0 scale, and similarly some of the smaller standard-gauge kits can also be employed if you are modelling a Swiss, German or Austrian line.

If, on the other hand, you choose to model United States prototypes there are a number of narrow-gauge structures featured in the ranges of craftsman type wood kits available from various American manufacturers. These build up into superb models with exquisite detailing provided by numerous cast metal items. Most are H0 scale but there are a few in 0 scale.

For modellers of British prototypes it is a question of converting or scratch-building. The Airfix plastic structure kits, particularly the station, stone church (not at present available), engine shed, signal box, coal office and platelayers hut, are useful as a starting point and some very attractive narrow-gauge models have been created by converting these kits.

In many ways, however, scratch-building is the most satisfying of all. You can choose any prototype you like and which is appropriate to your line and your models will be different from those on any other layout. If you are working in 016.5 you will have to scratch-build as there are no suitable kits available for British structures. Construction follows the usual methods utilising card, wood, plastic card or other materials as preferred. *PSL Model Railway Guide 3: Structures Modelling* covers these techniques in detail so I will not repeat them here. The photographs accompanying this section show conversions and scratch-built models using various materials and will give you some idea of the possibilities.

Whatever method you use, do choose your prototypes carefully to ensure that they are suitable for the character and location of your line. Select them so that they will be in keeping with the surroundings and also so they will look right together. Railway buildings in a particular area are often all made from similar materials, whether they are brick, stone or wood, and frequently also in the same architectural style. Attention to such points in modelling will help to create a unified appearance in the scene. Conversely, too much mixing of different and inappropriate styles of building can spoil the realism entirely.

There are also several smaller items which can conveniently be considered here. Water towers show quite a variety of styles and different construction materials in the prototype. R. Stenning includes a cast metal kit for a small water tower in his range of models. The kit is closely based on a tower with a slate base and timber-clad tank at Dolgoch on the Talyllyn Railway. Other types can be built up using the usual materials and methods employed for larger structure models. Coaling stages on narrow-gauge railways are usually simple affairs made from wood or stone and are easily modelled. If you run diesel locomotives on your layout you will need one or more refuelling tanks; these can be modelled very satisfactorily with tanks from some of the Airfix military vehicle kits or from the Airfix tank wagon kit. The range of cast metal kits from Mikes Models includes several small cranes and hoists in 4 mm scale and these are ideal as goods yard cranes, coal hoists and so on for narrow-gauge layouts.

Above *Lyddford Station on Graham Lindley's 009 layout. The station building is an Airfix kit covered with random stone paper. Locomotive No 14 at the platform is based on a North British Locomotive Co metre gauge 2-8-0 and utilises an Atlas 0-8-0 chassis. The Kerr Stuart diesel shunting the siding at the rear of the station was built from a Meridian Models kit.*

On the prototype, facilities were often provided for the transfer of freight between the narrow and standard gauge. These could take the form of a goods shed or simply a platform, perhaps with a cover or canopy, with the standard-gauge line at one side and the narrow-gauge track on the other. To allow for the smaller size of the narrow-gauge rolling stock the narrow-gauge track will need to be at a slightly higher level than the standard gauge so that the platform height is uniform. Here the wagons and vans are loaded and unloaded by hand or possibly with a small crane. For heavier transfers a light gantry or hoist is sometimes provided, straddling a standard- and a narrow-gauge track. When transfers involve bulk materials such as ore, gravel or coal the narrow-gauge track can be elevated so that the material can be tipped down a chute into standard-gauge wagons on a track beneath.

To avoid the expense of transferring freight between standard and narrow gauge some narrow-gauge lines, particularly on the continent, use transporter wagons or rollbocks. As Brian Harrap has mentioned earlier, with this system the standard-gauge vans, wagons or tankers are carried over the narrow-gauge line to their final destination either on low transporter wagons or on special narrow-gauge bogies. Transporter wagons were rare in Britain but were employed on the Leek & Manifold Railway and a 4 mm scale model is available as a cast metal kit from ABS Models. On the 4ft gauge Padarn Railway in North Wales the situation was reversed with the 1 ft 10 in gauge quarry wagons from the Dinorwic slate quarries carried over the wider gauge tracks on special transporter wagons, each carrying four of the tiny quarry trucks down to the port. On the continent both transporter wagons and rollbocks have been used quite extensively and both are available in very realistic model form in both H0e and H0m from Bemo.

Bridges of various types will add interest to a

Above *The engine depot on Graham Lindley's 009 layout. The workshop and crew room at the rear are part of a Pola kit; the corrugated iron roofed shelter in front is scratch-built as are the water tower and the diesel fuel tank. The water crane is a Mike's Models kit.*

layout. They also provide scenic breaks in the train journeys, making the length of run appear greater and thus giving the impression of a larger layout. As I have already mentioned, narrow-gauge railways were often built in hilly or mountainous country where the advantages over the standard gauge are greatest. The narrower tracks, sharper curves and steeper gradients which are possible give the maximum economies in such difficult terrain. Similarly modellers often choose this type of setting to provide the greatest interest and scope in a limited space. Thus both the prototype and the model are likely to need bridges. These can be lighter in construction than is necessary for standard gauge and may be built of wood, stone, iron, steel or brick, or of some combination of these materials. The size varies with the location, small where the line crosses a tiny stream to large where a wide valley is to be traversed. Very large bridges are best avoided on your layout unless you have a lot of space as they tend to dwarf the rest of the railway. However, one of the advantages of narrow-gauge modelling is that a bridge of only moderate size can look quite large and impressive in relation to the small engines and rolling stock which cross it.

Some of the small H0-scale plastic kit bridges from the various continental manufacturers are very suitable for 00 or H0 scale narrow-gauge lines. Light bridges, ideal for narrow gauge, can also be constructed by using parts from N-scale kits for 00 or H0 narrow gauge, or from 00- or H0-scale kits for 0 narrow gauge. Another useful source of girders and other parts are footbridge and signal gantry kits. The girders from the Airfix Signal Gantry kit, for example, are suitable for a girder bridge for an 009 line. Alternatively, bridges of this type can be scratch-built using the extensive range of plastic girders and other parts from Plastruct. Other bridges can be scratch-built utilising the usual structure modelling materials and techniques. Wooden bridges can be built up from stripwood, either

Above *This narrow-gauge station building was largely scratch-built from plastic card with facings of stone course embossed plastic card but the lean-to, roof, lamps and downpipes are from an Airfix Engine Shed kit modified as necessary to fit.*

Below *This water tower for 4 mm scale is based on the tower at Dolgoch on the Talyllyn Railway; it was assembled from a cast metal kit manufactured by R. Stenning.*

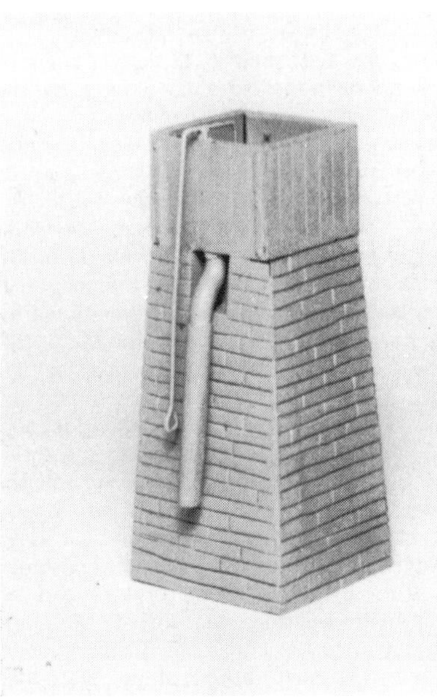

balsa or hard wood. Stonework can be represented by embossed stone course or random stone plastic card or by applying individual 'stones' of thin plastic card to a basic structure built up from wood or thick plastic card. Alternatively stonework can be scribed in a layer of Polyfilla or Peco Texture Modelling Compound applied over a base of wood. Another very realistic method is to cast the stonework in plaster, either using Linka moulds or making your own.

It is important to choose a type of bridge which is appropriate to the location and also to the geographical locality. You should also plan your scenery so that any bridges appear necessary and do not look as if they have only been added because you wanted some bridges on your layout. It is usually more interesting and realistic to have two or more smaller bridges of differing styles rather than one large structure. Whatever type of bridge you build it is very important that it is set into the scenery so that is really looks as though the bridge was actually constructed at the site and the track then laid over it. If the bridge has the appearance of being built on the workbench from a plastic kit and then just planted down on top of the scenery, we cannot hope for a realistic effect.

The accompanying photographs show a variety of model bridges on narrow-gauge layouts and give some idea of the possibilities. If you plan a kit conversion or intend to scratch-build a bridge model, the best results are likely to be achieved if you base your model on an actual bridge; you will then be certain

Top and above *Two bridges on the 009 layout built by the Middlesbrough Model Railway & Tramway Club. The top one is a trestle bridge which was scratch-built from stripwood.*

that the design is correct from the engineering and architectural aspects.

Tunnels are very useful on model railway layouts. By concealing part of the track, particularly on an oval design track plan, they give a more realistic appearance and can also make the length of run seem longer. They can also be used to lead to hidden storage sidings, a fiddle yard or other concealed tracks. However, we must use them with discretion. On prototype railways tunnels are very expensive to build and are therefore avoided if at all possible. Indeed one of the advantages of narrow-gauge lines is that the sharp curves and steep gradients which can be used often reduce or eliminate the need for tunnels, the tracks being able to follow the contours of the terrain. Thus if we are to preserve the realism of our model we must make sure that the scenery is planned and constructed so that any

Above left *Terry Onslow built this fuel tank for his 009 layout from a shortened Airfix Tank Wagon kit tank; the boiler is a Mike's Models kit. The locomotive is a model of the Talyllyn Railway 0-4-0,* Douglas, *built from a Gem cast metal kit* (Terry Onslow).

Left *The water tower base is card coated with Peco Texture Modelling Compound while the tank and filler pipe are copper tube and wire. The coal hoist is a Mike's Models kit.*

Above *A realistically modelled road overbridge on the Talyllyn Railway layout built in 016.5 by members of the Wessex Group of the TRPS.*

tunnels we build appear to have been unavoidable.

Particular care is needed on the so-called 'rabbit' or 'rabbit warren' layouts where full advantage has been taken of the sharp curves and steep gradients possible in 009 to pack as much length of run into a small area as we can, and on which the trains pop in and out of tunnels like rabbits in burrows! The length of run is achieved by using overlapping loops of track and a winding run and, to preserve any realism and credibility, it is essential to conceal parts of the track with tunnels. To justify these the scenery must be appropriately chosen—usually very rugged and rocky mountainous terrain. With proper planning and execution the results can be very effective. On some prototype narrow-gauge railways in mountainous areas the line gains height by a series of loops; the Darjeeling is a classic example but the same device is also employed on lines in Switzerland, so that, provided the scenery is suitably arranged, the overlapping loops on a layout need not be unrealistic.

On standard-gauge model railways the height and width of the rolling stock is fairly uniform and is within the regular loading gauge. Thus it is usually simple to ensure that any tunnel mouths and tunnels will have adequate clearance for any stock likely to be used on the layout now or in the future. Because of the variable size of narrow-gauge locomotives and rolling stock, particularly as modellers often have stock based on prototypes from several different railways, perhaps with different gauges and often with varying loading gauges, it is advisable to allow rather generous clearances in tunnels. Remember that you may want to add some larger stock at a later date and that you will be unable to do so unless you have provided sufficient clearance. This also applies to clearances on curves, either between adjacent tracks or for scenery and structures beside the line. You may later wish to run longer coaches

Above *A disused tunnel mouth modelled in Polyfilla with balsa stripwood planking.*

so allow enough space for the greater overhang which will result on the curves. Howard Coulson has made a careful study of standards and clearances for 009 and he presented his findings in detail in an article in the February 1980 issue of *Model Railway Constructor* magazine; I would recommend obtaining a copy for reference if you are working in 009.

It is also essential to provide adequate access to the inside of any tunnels on your layout so that you can retrieve, without risk of damage, any trains which stall or derail within the tunnels. It is usually possible to arrange this access from the side or rear of the layout beneath the hill or mountain but occasionally it is necessary to construct the scenery so that a section over the tunnel can be lifted out as required to give access.

The tunnel portals on narrow-gauge lines are usually of simple style and construction; they may be of rock, stone, brick or wood. Rock portals can be carved in plaster while timber portals can be built up from balsa or hard wood stained and weathered. Brick tunnel mouths may be represented with brickpaper on card or wood, or can be modelled with Linka brickwork castings. For stone portals we can use plastic card, scribed, with individual 'stones' of thin plastic card applied, or with a facing of embossed stone course plastic card. Alternatively the stonework can be carved in a layer of plastic, Polyfilla or Peco Texture Modelling Compound applied to a basic wooden form. Another method is to cast the stonework in plaster or Linka Casting Compound using Linka moulds or ones made by the modeller. Whatever form of construction is employed the portals should be set into the scenery properly with any gaps or cracks between them and the hillside filled in with plaster.

Details

There are many details we can add to make a layout more attractive and interesting to view and operate. In fact, the scope is almost limitless and this detailing can provide enjoyable modelling for the enthusiast long after the layout is otherwise complete. Study of the work of experienced scenic modellers either at exhibitions or as featured in photographs in the model railway magazines will often give you ideas for additional details you can include on your layout. Look also at how they use these details to enhance the overall effect.

Human and animal figures form an important part of the scene on a model railway layout, suggesting life and activity. Here there is considerable advantage in the use of a well-established commercial scale, particularly 00 or H0, as there are many figures of excellent quality available as painted or unpainted plastic or as cast metal models. (A range of unpainted cast metal figures in 0 scale is produced by ABS Models.) Greater variety can be introduced by modifying the available models to produce different poses. Many other small items for detailing station and goods yard areas are commercially produced. These include seats, gas lamps, luggage, barrows, trolleys, tools, barrels, drums, boxes, crates, sacks, and so on from various manufacturers.

Road vehicles also add interest to the scheme, either in the station or goods yard or on roads in town or country. Many plastic models are produced in H0 scale by firms such as Wiking and Kibri, while cast metal kits for 00- and 0-scale model road vehicles are available from British manufacturers. The Airfix military vehicle kits lend themselves to easy adaptation and modification for civilian use, or the parts from these well detailed but inexpensive kits can be used for scratch-building suitable models.

For rural or period layouts horse-drawn vehicles are attractive and appropriate. The Preiser range of H0-scale models includes several different types; 00-scale horse-drawn vehicles can be built from Airfix or Slater parts. There is also a cast metal horse and cart kit

Below *Milborne Station on Bob Goodwin's 009 layout. The station building was constructed from thick card with stonework represented by Peco Texture Modelling Compound scribed and painted. The gas lamps on the platform are from the Mike's Models range.*

Above *Effective modelling by Graham Mighell on his 009 Graell Junction layout. Note the repair work being carried out on the hotel building and the many other small details which add interest to the scene.*

produced by Dart Castings. This latter firm has a range of other useful detailing items for country scenes such as sign posts of various types, post boxes, a horse trough, and so on. Langley Miniature Models make a motor cycle and sidecar (complete with rider), a delivery boy and his bicycle, and other cast metal models. The range also includes the parts to construct a lock scene, complete with canal narrow boats. Merit make a wide selection of accessories in plastic including a telephone box, bicycles and stand, barrels, drums, carboys, milk churns, dustbins, and so on, all very useful for scenic detailing. The John Piper range also has many useful items including luggage and tools, and other manufacturers also produce items for scenic modelling. In addition there is, of course, great scope for scratch-building small details to complete the scene using scraps of plastic, card, wood, wire, thread, and odds and ends.

I have already commented that, because a narrow-gauge layout can be built in a small area, it is perfectly feasible for the whole layout to be brought up to a very high standard of finish and detail. It can be very satisfying to be able to model to such a degree of super-detailing—something which would be difficult or impossible to achieve on a larger layout. Working to a high standard in this way also means that you can spend more time modelling on even a small layout.

Another method of extending the interest is to use your model to represent two different periods. In many cases there has been little change in the setting or structures of a railway over many years. Often in photographs it is only the changes in details such as the dress of the passengers and railway employees, the road vehicles in the background, and perhaps the locomotives and rolling stock in use that give a clue to the date. Thus by modelling two sets of figures and road vehicles, and perhaps some additional locomotives and rolling stock, we can use the same layout to depict the line at two very different periods. For example, we can model it in the early days when it was a railway transporting slate from the quarries and today as a preserved line carrying tourists and enthusiasts. The construction of the extra items will prolong the modelling interest while the choice of the two periods will give variety in both appearance and operation.

Layout suggestions

Planning for narrow gauge is essentially similar to that for standard gauge and the basic track arrangements apply to both. However, the design details are somewhat different and, to take full advantage of the sharper curves, steeper gradients, shorter trains, and other special features of narrow-gauge railways, the layout should be planned with these in mind. It is not, therefore, usually desirable to take a standard-gauge plan, merely reduce it to a smaller area and build it in narrow gauge.

In 009 very small layouts have been built and operated, some of them incorporating a continuous run in areas as small as 2 ft by 1 ft or less. However, these minute layouts tend to be gimmicky and toy-like and if a very small space is all that is presently available it is probably better to build a scene, or module, featuring a station, locomotive depot or industry which can later be fitted into, or extended to form, a larger layout. In fact, even if there is adequate space initially this is a good way for the beginner to try out narrow-gauge modelling as, in an area of only, say, 2 ft by 1 ft, he or she can lay some track, build scenery and structures, and test locomotives and rolling stock. By working in such a small area the whole scene can be completed quickly and easily without much expense. The scene should be as complete in itself as possible but designed to be incorporated into a larger layout later. If your ideas have altered by then or if your standard of modelling has noticeably improved, the original scene can be scrapped without too much loss in time or money. These points are worth bearing in mind as attemping to build too large a layout at the beginning can be very discouraging because progress seems so slow and any changes you want to make as work advances, and you gain experience, are likely to be expensive and time-consuming.

You may wish to use one of the plans which have appeared in the model railway magazines, perhaps altering it a little to suit your own requirements, or you may prefer to design your own layout from scratch. Either way it is useful to draw the track plan out to a large scale or even, if your layout is fairly small, full size. You can use cheap lining paper from a decorating shop for this purpose. Drawing it out like this will make visualisation of the finished layout much easier and will help you to find out if you will want to make changes before you start actual construction.

When planning your layout remember that it will enhance the realism both scenically and operationally if your railway has a clear purpose. It may be to transport slate or ore from the quarries or mines in the hills down to the standard-gauge line or the dock for transhipment, it may be to move materials around a large factory complex or shipyard, or it may be to provide rides for tourists. For a modeller with an interest in military matters also, a line set in France during World War I would be an interesting and unusual subject for a layout. Interchange with the standard-gauge and perhaps dual-gauge trackwork add interest and are discussed earlier.

To complete this section I have selected four narrow-gauge railways which would make good models. All four are still in operation, three of them as preserved lines, but they are very different in setting, character and original purpose. At least two have already been successfully modelled.

The Talyllyn Railway

It is perhaps appropriate to consider this line first for it was with the Talyllyn Railway that railway preservation as we know it today really began. This 2 ft 3 in gauge line was opened in 1866 to carry slate from the quarries at Bryn Eglwys, near Abergynolwyn, down to Tywyn; the railway was also planned to provide a passenger service from the start. The slate traffic continued for many years, though showing a steady decline, until the quarries closed in 1947. The owner of the railway, Sir Henry Haydn Jones, then kept the line open, depending entirely on passengers, until his death in 1950, when closure and scrapping seemed inevitable. However, a group of enthusiasts met and formed a society to take

Top *A view of the trackwork at Tywyn Wharf Station on the Talyllyn Railway.*

Above *The engine shed and workshop at Tywyn Pendre on the Talyllyn Railway.*

over the operation of the railway with a volunteer workforce, at that time a completely new idea. The success of the venture is now well known and has been followed by many other preservation schemes elsewhere in Britain and later throughout the world.

The original passenger route runs 6½ miles from Tywyn Wharf Station, where slate was transferred to standard-gauge wagons, to Abergynolwyn, climbing 200 feet through the Fathew Valley in attractive scenery. A further extension to Nant Gwernol was opened in 1976 after much hard work by the members of the TRPS. The Talyllyn Railway works and locomotive and carriage sheds are at Tywyn Pendre.

The original locomotives, the 0-4-0T *Dolgoch* and the 0-4-2ST *Talyllyn*, both built by Fletcher Jennings & Co of Whitehaven, have been rebuilt, and additional motive power which has

Above *A scene on the 7 mm scale 16.5 mm gauge model of a section of the Talyllyn Railway built by the Wessex Group of the Talyllyn Railway Preservation Society. The locomotive is a model of the 0-4-2 tank* Talyllyn.

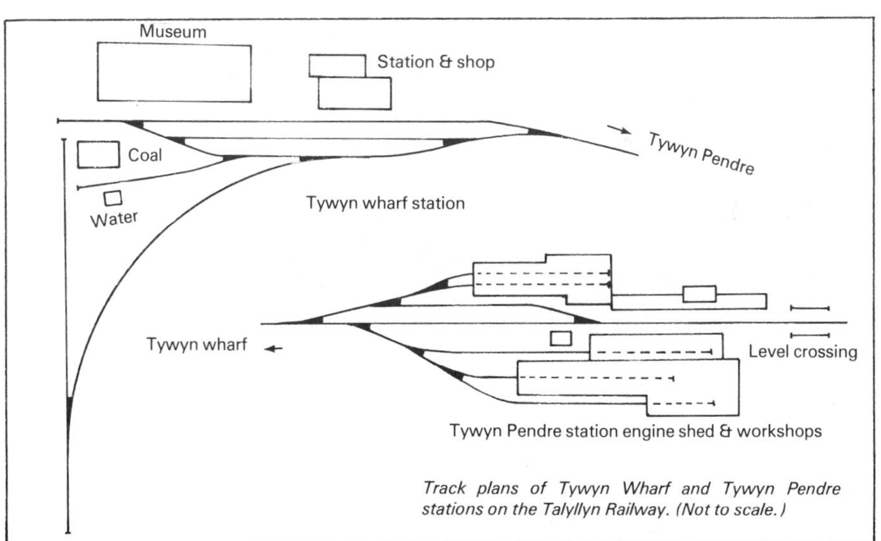

Track plans of Tywyn Wharf and Tywyn Pendre stations on the Talyllyn Railway. (Not to scale.)

been acquired includes two ex-Corris Railway 0-4-2Ts renamed *Sir Haydn* and *Edward Thomas*, and an Andrew Barclay 0-4-0T, *Douglas*, which had previously been used by the RAF. There are also several diesel locomotives used on works trains. The locomotive livery is dark Brunswick green with yellow lining. The rolling stock includes four 4-wheel coaches and a 4-wheel brake van with a side ticket window which have survived from the original stock and have been restored. There are also coaches from other lines which have also been restored or rebuilt, together with a number of 4-wheel and bogie coaches newly built for the railway at Tywyn. Most of the passenger stock is painted red with green lining. Some 40 or 50 goods wagons are used on work trains.

For the modeller, information on the line is readily available in books and magazine articles; an excellent general account is given in J.I.C. Boyd's book, *Narrow Gauge Railways in Mid-Wales*, (Oakwood Press) and includes scale drawings of the locomotives *Talyllyn*, *Dolgoch* and *Douglas*, and of the original coaches and wagons. A visit to the railway is the ideal way to obtain further information and photographs. The Greenwich and District Narrow Gauge Railway Society have built an accurate model in 009 of Tywyn Wharf Station as it was in the period 1969-71; to ensure strict accuracy members of the society carried out a detailed survey of the site. Alternatively you may be more interested in building a model based less exactly on the prototype but still having much of its character.

For 009 Gem make body kits for *Dolgoch* and *Douglas* and kits for coaches and wagons are available from Mike's Models. Models of stock from other lines can also be used just as the prototype railway has acquired coaches and wagons from other companies. The remaining locomotives and rolling stock can be built up using scratch-built bodies mounted on commercial chassis. The structures will also have to be scratch-built but R. Stenning offers a neat cast metal kit model of the water tower at Dolgoch.

In 016.5 the locomotive *Talyllyn* will soon be available in kit form from Peco (body) and Wrightlines (chassis) while wagons are already on the market as cast metal kits from Wrightlines. Other locomotives and rolling stock can be built up from scratch as shown by the models on the 7 mm scale layout constructed by members of the Wessex Group of the Talyllyn Railway Preservation Society depicting the middle section of the railway from just below Rhydyronen to a little beyond BryngIas. The Talyllyn Railway has much to offer the modeller and several successful models of the line or sections of it have been built. Many freelance narrow-gauge layouts have been based on or inspired by this railway.

The Sittingbourne & Kemsley Light Railway

This line shows a considerable contrast to the Talyllyn Railway but is no less interesting for the modeller. The 2 ft 6 in gauge railway was opened in 1906 to serve a paper mill and, as the mill and the associated dock facilities developed and expanded over the years, the railway also became more extensive. In 1948 the mills were taken over by the Bowater Group; the railway continued in use, was well maintained and the locomotive roster was increased. One of the new locomotives was *Monarch*, a Bagnall 0-4-4-0 articulated tank

Below *Monarch is a 2 ft 6 in gauge Bagnall 0-4-4-0 articulated tank engine built in 1953 for the Bowater Railway and later transferred to the Welshpool & Llanfair where this photograph was taken.*

engine built in 1953. However, in the 1960s, a work study showed that the line was uneconomic and it was eventually closed in 1969. On closure the firm passed the section of the railway between Sittingbourne and Kemsley Down over to the Locomotive Club of Great Britain for preservation. Six locomotives were also handed over, three Bagnall 0-6-2 Tanks *Alpha*, *Superb* and *Triumph*, and three Kerr Stuart 0-4-2 Saddle Tanks, *Leader*, *Melior* and *Premier*, together with a selection of rolling stock.

The setting for the railway is very different from the Welsh hills of the Talyllyn. Here the area is flat and marshy with industry very much in evidence. The line is carried on a low viaduct for a quarter of a mile after leaving Sittingbourne and this is an important feature which should be included on a model. Another characteristic part of the scene is the large steam pipes alongside the track and, at various points, bridging the line.

Scratch-building would be necessary for the locomotives and rolling stock as none are available commercially, although N-gauge chassis can be utilised with bodies constructed from plastic for convenience. The rolling stock is unusual, especially the workmen's coaches, the bogie pulp and paper wagons and the 4-wheel hoppers, and should be modelled accurately to give a good representation of the trains. David Hammersley has built some realistic models of the locomotives and rolling stock in 009 for his layout based on Sittingbourne and some of these are shown in the accompanying pictures.

An excellent booklet, *Bowater's Sittingbourne Railway* by Arthur G. Wells, has been published by the Locomotive Club of Great Britain. It gives a full account of the railway and its locomotives and rolling stock, together with scale drawings of two of the locomotives, a 14-ton bogie pulp wagon and a 5-ton hopper wagon. Track plans of the various sections of the railway and a good selection of photographs are also provided. The booklet will be an invaluable guide if you wish to model the line and, of course, there is no substitute for a personal visit armed with camera and notebook.

Bottom Triumph, *one of the Bagnall 0-6-2 Tank Engines on the line.*

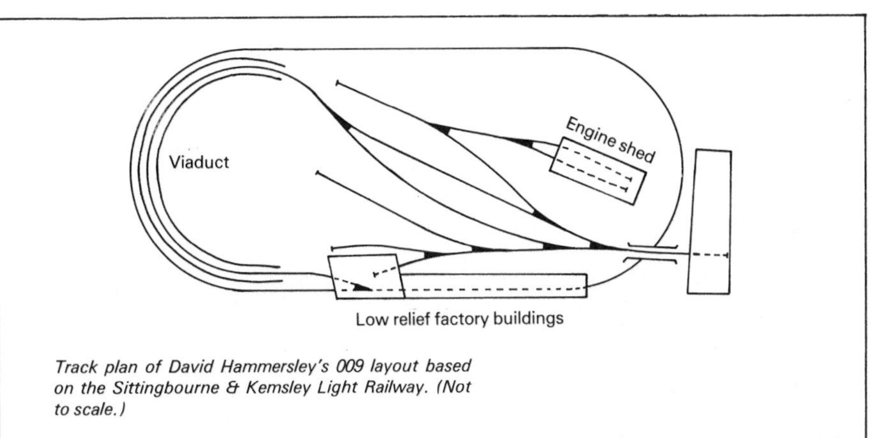

Track plan of David Hammersley's 009 layout based on the Sittingbourne & Kemsley Light Railway. (Not to scale.)

Above *The viaduct on the Sittingbourne & Kemsley Light Railway. The piping carried along the route of the line and the industrial nature of the area can be clearly seen.*

Above *The coaches on the line are unusual and very distinctive.*

Above right *One of the china clay hopper wagons on the line.*

Right *David Hammersley's realistic scratch-built model of a hopper wagon.*

Left and below *Note the selection of realistically modelled locomotives and rolling stock in these views of David Hammersley's layout.*

Above *Graham Lindley has modelled* Monarch *in 009. His model was scratch-built on a Bachmann N-scale GP40 Bo-Bo chassis converted to outside cranks and frames. The locomotive is an interesting addition to his Lydd Valley layout.* **Below** *An overall view of David Hammersley's 009 layout based on the Sittingbourne & Kemsley Light Railway.*

Above left Premier *of the Sittingbourne & Kemsley Light Railway is a Kerr Stuart 0-4-2 saddle tank.*
Above right *David Hammersley's model of the similar* Alpha *captures the appearance of the prototype very well. This model is scratch-built on a Liliput 0-6-2 chassis.*

The Waldenburgerbahn

The Waldenburgerbahn with its 750 mm (2 ft 5½ in) track gauge is the narrowest railway in Switzerland and it was also the last narrow-gauge railway in that country to be run exclusively by steam. The line, which shares the standard-gauge main line station at Liestal, a few miles south-east of Basel, runs eight miles up the valley to the terminus at Waldenburg.

The railway was opened in November 1880 in an effort to increase traffic, trade and industry in the valley. One of the leaders in planning the line was Gedeon Thommen of Waldenburg, after whom locomotive No 5, now preserved at Liestal Station, was named. Originally the railway was planned to continue beyond Waldenburg to Balsthal, but financial difficulties prevented this. When the line was built a gauge of 750 mm was chosen because for much of the route the tracks were to be laid beside the road and there would not have been space for a wider gauge.

As long ago as 1910, the first study for the electrification of the railway was carried out and in 1912 and again in 1925 estimates were given by a firm in Basel for electrification of the line and at the same time re-laying the track to metre gauge. Later, an expert report recommended electrification but not the change of gauge, on the grounds of cost. However, central government approval for the scheme was not at that time forthcoming and it was not until 1953 that electrification was carried out.

Because of the many delays in the change to electric propulsion, the steam service lasted for 73 years and the railway was the last narrow-gauge line in Switzerland to be exclusively steam powered. Of the eight locomotives which have served the line during its years of steam No 5, *G. Thommen*, is on display at Liestal Station and No 6, *Waldenburg*, is exhibited in the Swiss Museum of Transport in Lucerne. Both these locomotives were made by the Swiss Locomotive & Machine Co, Winterthur, and, together with WB No 4 they were the smallest locomotives in Switzerland. A steam service is still run occasionally for tourists and enthusiasts with an 0-6-2 tank locomotive, *Eurovapor*, built at Linz in 1900. The routine services today are provided by three motor coaches of the BDe 4/4 type smartly turned out in an orange and yellow livery. The line is not only still operating on a commercial basis but regularly shows a profit!

The railway would be a good choice for modelling. The wooded valley and the small Swiss towns make an attractive setting and there are enough suitable models commercially available to give the modeller a good start in H0e. Liliput make models of WB No 5, *G. Thommen*, and of the old style 4-wheel coaches for its train, together with a model of 0-6-2 tank, *Eurovapor*. Other rolling stock from the Liliput and Bemo ranges would also be suitable for use on the line. Models of the motor coaches could be constructed with scratch-built bodies of plastic card mounted on

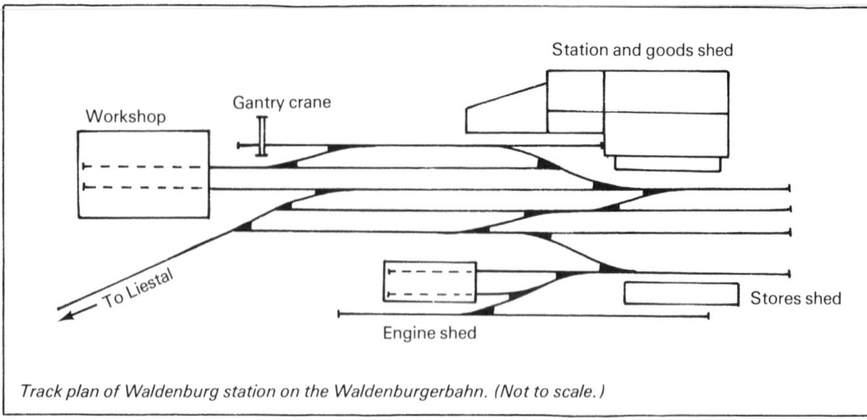

Track plan of Waldenburg station on the Waldenburgerbahn. (Not to scale.)

Below *Waldenburg station and goods shed are combined in a single building, here seen from the track side. The motor coach and trailer on the siding near the station building are waiting to return to Liestal.*
Bottom *The Liliput HO9 model of the Waldenburgerbahn 0-6-0,* G. Thommen.

Top *WB 0-6-2 298.14,* Eurovapor, *is used for steam specials on the line. This locomotive is also available as an HO9 model from Liliput.*

Above *Liliput also make models of the old tramway type coaches of the railway in HO9.*

N-gauge diesel chassis and the bogie passenger stock now in use could be similarly made to fit on to N-gauge coach chassis.

Pantographs and catenary parts for a working overhead electrification sytem are made by Sommerfeldt and are available in Britain from shops handing continental products. Many suitable kits for station buildings, goods sheds, workshops, houses, hotels, shops and so on are available from European manufacturers such as Pola, Kibri, Faller and Vollmer. Information on the railway is not very readily available in Britain but there is a German language pictorial book, *Die Waldenburgerbahn*, by Claude Jeanmaire-dit-Quartier (published by Verlag Eisenbahn) which may be stocked by book and model shops specialising in European railways.

The Östra Södermanlands Järnväg

The ÖSlJ was the first preservation project in Sweden and was formed in 1959 as a group within the Swedish Railway Club to collect, restore and operate locomotives and rolling stock from Sweden's seven 60 cm gauge passenger lines. At first, operation was limited to weekends on a short brickworks line but, in 1964, when the 2½ mile long standard gauge Läggesta-Mariefred branch was closed, the SJ (Swedish State Railway) handed it over to the ÖSlJ. After relaying to 60 cm gauge the line was opened to traffic in July 1966. In June 1970 it was extended ¼ mile from Mariefred Station to Mariefred Pier making a direct link with the Steamer, *Mariefred*, which sails on Lake Mälaren to and from Stockholm.

The site is ideal. Mariefred, a small old town with the impressive 16th century Gripsholm Castle in a beautiful lakeside setting, is a tourist attraction itself and is within easy reach of Stockholm by train, road or lake steamer. The railway has proved very popular with the visitors and has been successful in building up an impressive selection of locomotives and rolling stock. Among the nine steam locomotives operational are No 5, *Hamra*, an 0-4-4-0T built by Orenstein & Koppel in 1902 and No 7, *Helgenäs*, a delightful little 0-4-2ST built by Hudswell Clarke in 1889, the oldest engine on the railway. In addition there are three diesel locomotives, a petrol engined locomotive and a battery electric. There is also a 4-wheel petrol-engined railbus originally constructed from a 1930 Volvo car; this vehicle came from the 802 mm gauge HFJ and was rebuilt to 60 cm gauge by the ÖSlJ. The railway has an attractive selection of passenger coaches, mainly bogie vehicles, from seven different Swedish lines. Goods and service stock includes vans, open wagons, flat trucks, tippers and, rather unusual on narrow gauge, a bogie tanker from the Munkedals Railway, together with a small crane and a snow plough.

The ÖSlJ is a very attractive line and would make a good model. The locomotives and rolling stock are not available as commercially produced models so scratch-building and the use of N-gauge chassis would be necessary for an accurate model. The lovely wooden station building at Mariefred is produced in H0 scale as a plastic kit by Heljan; the other structures could be constructed from scratch without undue difficulty. The engine shed and workshops at Mariefred are fairly simple in style. The delightful little eight-sided structure at the Pier Station will require care in modelling but should be very effective when completed. The layout will be enhanced scenically if the modeller can include at least part of Gripsholm Castle and the edge of the lake.

There is an excellent Swedish language book, *Östra Södermanlands Järnväg 1966-1976*, published by Frank Stenvalls Förlag, Malmö, which gives a detailed account of the railway and its locomotives and rolling stock. Information in English is less readily available but a good article on the ÖSlJ by C.E.A. Buckle did appear in *Narrow Gauge Times* No 9, Winter 1977-8.

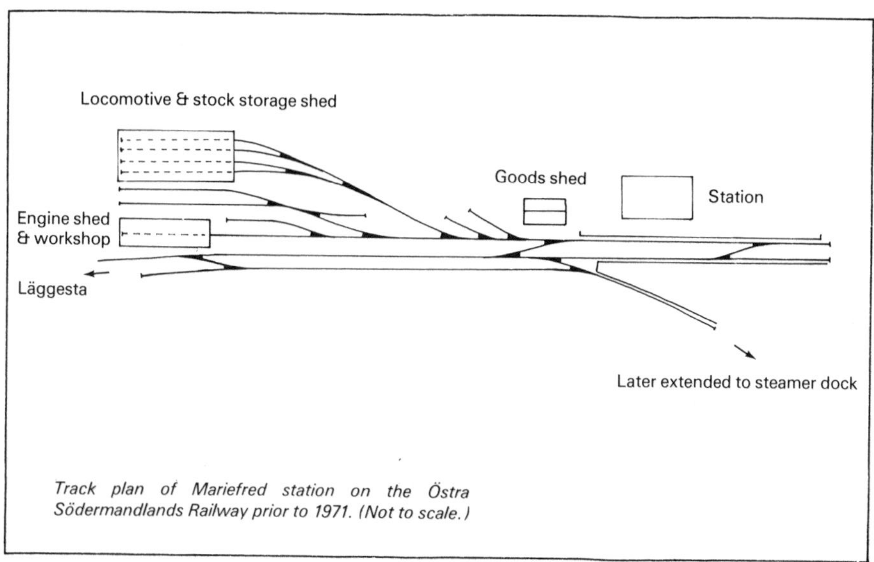

Track plan of Mariefred station on the Östra Södermandlands Railway prior to 1971. (Not to scale.)

Above *ÖSlJ No 6 hauls a train away from Mariefred towards Läggesta through typical lineside scenery.*

Below *The battery electric locomotive,* Garpen, *built in 1916 by ASEA. Mariefred Station building is at the rear with the goods shed on the left.*

Above left *The picturesque wooden shelter at the Mariefred steamer berth served by the extension of the line from Mariefred Station.*

Above *Mariefred Station building on the Ostra Södermanlands Railway. An HO-scale model of this attractive structure is available in plastic kit form from Heljan.*

Left *ÖSlJ No 5,* Hamra, *an Orenstein & Koppel 0-4-4-0 tank built in 1902.*

Below left *Engine shed and workshop at Mariefred. The structure, though attractive, would be fairly simple to model.*

Below *This double slip point was installed in 1971 together with two others during improvements and developments to the track layout at Mariefred. The track on the right rear of the picture leads to the steamer station.*

Large scale modelling

There has been a considerable interest recently in modelling narrow-gauge prototypes to much larger scales than most railway modellers usually employ. The resulting models have a very appealing bulk and weight and the large scale permits a much greater degree of detailing. There are two main groups depending on the gauge of track used, 0 gauge, 32 mm, and gauge 1, 45 mm, and I would like to consider these separately.

G gauge

In 1968 the German firm, Lehmann, introduced its LGB system at the International Toy Fair. This is a range of ready-to-run models built to 1/22.5 scale (approximately 13.5 mm to the foot) running on 45 mm gauge, the equivalent of metre gauge in the prototype. The system began essentially as a large scale train set with clip-together track which could be laid down indoors or, due to its very robust construction, out of doors. However, the models are beautifully detailed and are, for the most part, accurate replicas of actual prototypes, so that the system is also of great interest to the serious narrow-gauge enthusiast. The development of the range has been steady since its introduction and there is now a remarkable selection of locomotives, of steam, diesel and electric prototype, and rolling stock. Most are of continental prototypes, mainly German, Swiss and Austrian, but there are some American items.

Below *This 0-4-0 tender locomotive is one of the LGB range of models to 1:22.5 scale on 45 mm gauge. The model is powered by two motors, one in the engine and one in the tender. The prototype operated on the KPEV* (Lehmann).

Bottom *The LGB range of 4 wheel and bogie coaches includes this Rhaetian Railway 1st/2nd Class Corridor Coach. The interior is fully detailed* (Lehmann).

Above *The LGB model of the DB V 51/V 52 Series Bo-Bo diesel locomotives is an accurate model of the prototype. Two motors give excellent traction* (Lehmann).

Left *The LGB track system includes a double slip point* (Lehmann).

Above right *This LGB beer wagon is finished in white with blue lettering* (Lehmann).

Right *This beautiful 16 mm scale model of a 4-4-0 locomotive used on the Fiji Free Train was built by Don Boreham, President of the Merioneth Railway Society.*

The track system has straight and curved, of various radii, pieces, left- and right-hand points with a choice of two radii, crossings, a 3-way turnout and even a double-slip point. Flexible track is also available allowing greater freedom in layout design. Electrification is by the normal 2-rail method and power is supplied through a transformer/controller (though batteries can be used) and the system includes a full range of electrical equipment, together with electronic controllers. Parts are produced for a catenary system from which models of overhead electric prototypes can be controlled.

Some of the larger locomotives such as the South German Railway Co 0-6-6-0 Mallet, the DB V51/V52 Bo Bo diesel and the Rhaetian Railway Ge 6/6 Co electric 'Crocodile' have two motors providing even greater power. Though these locomotives are superb in quality and detail, pride of place must go to the hand-built locomotives which are available in very limited numbers, ordered in advance. These have included Argentinian, Indian and Chinese prototypes and they really are collectors items!

The system is remarkably complete and includes many accessories. A few structure kits and other items suitable for use with LGB layouts are available from other manufacturers. From Lehmann there is also a track planning book and stencil, and a German language magazine, *LGB Depesche*, published twice yearly.

Though the system is essentially based on continental prototypes there is still scope for modelling British narrow gauge in this scale, either by modifying or converting the locomotives and rolling stock or by scratch-building bodies and using the LGB replacement parts and components which can be purchased separately.

10 mm, 14 mm and 16 mm scales on 32 mm gauge

The idea of modelling large scale narrow gauge on 32 mm (0) gauge track seems to have become popular through the work of a number of imaginative and ingenious narrow-gauge enthusiasts who formed a group, the Merioneth Railway Society. These modellers realised that the Triang Big Big Train models produced as toy train sets for youngsters provided inexpensive chassis on which scratch-built bodies could be mounted to make model narrow-gauge locomotives and rolling stock of an appealing size. The modelling was to 10, 14 or 16 mm scale depending on the gauge of the prototype. For example, a 2 ft

gauge locomotive modelled to 16 mm scale would be exactly correct to gauge on 32 mm gauge track. The Triang models were discontinued after a time, were later re-introduced by Novo, but have again vanished from the market. However, this has not reduced the interest in this type of modelling and an appreciable number of enthusiasts are now working in 32 mm gauge, mainly using 16 mm scale. Various commercial products such as the Lima 0-scale models and the Faller E Train, which is approximately 12 mm scale on 32 mm gauge track, can be converted.

There was also a train set from Timpo very similar to the Triang models but for an American prototype which was also useful for conversion purposes. There are also several specialist manufacturers now offering kits, parts and accessories for 16 mm scale 32 mm gauge. Tenmille produce kits for Talyllyn coaches, while Kidner Kits have a Festiniog slate wagon and a Cliffe Hill Granite Co side-tipping wagon in kit form, together with a selection of parts for scratch-building. Merlin Locomotive Works have a selection of unpainted cast resin figures to 1/20 scale for use with 16 mm scale or LGB. Colin Binnie & Son (Miniature Engineering) offer a range of parts including wheels, axle boxes, and couplings which will be very useful to the scratch-builder in this scale. Peco are planning to produce flexible 32 mm gauge track of narrow-gauge type.

In this large scale the emphasis tends to be on the locomotives and rolling stock rather than on scenery and structures and there has also been a move towards live steam locomotives operating outdoors. A number of very attractive garden layouts have been built and give a great deal of pleasure. A good selection of live steam locomotives is now available from various manufacturers; two of the leading firms are Archangel Models and Merlin Locomotive Works. However, this aspect of the hobby, though very enjoyable, is really beyond the scope of the present book.

There have been suggestions for naming 16 mm scale narrow gauge on 32 mm gauge track as Mn2 or SM32 but at the time of writing agreement does not appear to have been reached by the various groups concerned. Some idea of the interest in this large scale modelling can be seen from the fact that there are now two active clubs, The Merioneth Railway Society and The Association of 16 mm Narrow Gauge Modellers, both of whom issue regular magazines or newsheets.

Clubs, magazines, books and manufacturers

Clubs and societies

Membership of a club or society can be of great benefit to the railway modeller, whether a beginner or a more experienced enthusiast, and this is especially so with specialised interests such as narrow gauge. It is an excellent way of meeting people with similar interests and you will soon make friends among the other members. Some modellers like to work in groups to construct layouts and you may well find that you can participate in such a project. This can be very useful experience for a beginner and an opportunity to learn a great deal about how to build a layout while working under the guidance of more knowledgeable modellers. Even if you prefer to work as an individual rather than as part of a team you will find that fellow members can help you with advice and information on all aspects of narrow-gauge modelling, from construction techniques and locating drawings and photographs to where to obtain kits and parts.

Though the specialist clubs and societies tend to be nationwide in their membership, unlike the local model railway clubs, you will probably find from their membership lists that there are some enthusiasts in your area with whom you can meet regularly. In some cases, for example, the 009 Society, there are local or regional groups within the society. Some of the clubs put on exhibitions of their own and others participate in shows put on by other model railway clubs; these will give you the opportunity to meet other enthusiasts as well as seeing layouts that members have built. The societies often publish magazines or newsheets for members and these will also give you ideas and information to help you in your modelling, details of new items available, and lists of items which other members wish to sell or exchange. (The details about the following societies were correct at the time of going to press.)

The 009 Society Membership Secretary: 3 Bottrill Street, Nuneaton, Warwickshire CV11 5JA.

The 7 mm Narrow Gauge Association Hon Membership Secretary: Bill Corser, 3 Arnhem Way, Woodhall Spa, Lincolnshire LN10 6TJ.

The Greenwich and District Narrow Gauge (Railway) Society Hon Secretary: Dave Brewer, 124 Blackheath Hill, Greenwich, London SE10 8AY.

The Merioneth Railway Society Hon Treasurer: Dave Ashley, 14 Whitelands Avenue, Chorleywood, Hertfordshire.

The Association of 16 mm Narrow Gauge Modellers A.F. Webb, 82 Leigh Road, Eastleigh, Hampshire SO5 4DT.

Readers might also like to consider membership of a society concerned with all aspects of prototype narrow-gauge railways:

The Narrow Gauge Railway Society Membership Secretary: P.A. Slater, The Hole in the Wall, Bradley, Ashbourne, Derbyshire.

Magazines

There are several magazines and newsheets for narrow-gauge modellers; some of these are available only to club or society members.

HOeSG PO Box 787, Station 'A' Fredericton, New Brunswick, Canada E3B 5B4. A recently introduced international newsletter for development and standardisation of HOm/HOe/HOz model railroading.

009 News—The Newsletter of the 009 Society, issued monthly to members. Membership Secretary, 3 Bottrill Street, Nuneaton, Warwickshire CV11 5JA.

Narrow Lines—The Official Journal of the 7 mm Narrow Gauge Association. Issued six times a year to members. Editor, Don Mason, 'Tan-y-Bwlch', Astral Drive, Hucknall, Nottinghamshire NG15 6FP.

Merioneth Mercury—The Journal of the Merioneth Railway Society. Issued three times a year to members. Editor, Stuart Baker, 58 Sandringham Crescent, South Harrow, Middlesex HA2 9BT.

16 mm Today—The Newsheet of The Association of 16 mm Narrow Gauge Modellers. Issued to members together with 16

Mil Exchange. Editor, J. Wenlock, 19 Fford Meirionnydd, Rhosddu, Wrexham, Clwyd, LL11 2LA.

Merlins Messenger Editor, David John, Station Villa, Nant Garedig, Carmarthen, Dyfed. Covers large scale narrow-gauge railway modelling.

Narrow Gauge and Short Line Gazette Editor, Robert W. Brown. Published bimonthly by Gazette Publications, One First Street, Suite C, PO Box 26, Los Altos, CA 94022, USA. Covers American narrow-gauge railroad modelling.

LGB Depesche German language magazine published twice yearly. Covers modelling with LGB system of large scale narrow-gauge models. May be available from LGB stockists.

Articles on narrow-gauge modelling also appear from time to time in the model railway magazines, *Railway Modeller, Scale Trains, Model Railway Constructor* and *Model Railways.*

Magazines featuring prototype narrow-gauge railways include:

The Narrow Gauge Issued quarterly to members of The Narrow Gauge Railway Society. Editor, M. Swift, 47 Birchington Avenue, Birchencliffe, Huddersfield, HD3 3RD.

Narrow Gauge Times has now been incorporated into *Railway Times*, published by Railway Times Publications, Blaenau Ffestiniog, Gwynedd. Editor, Pete Nicholson, Railway Times, Southwood Lane, Cheltenham, Gloucestershire GL50 2QH.

Books

Narrow Gauge Railway Modelling by D.A. Boreham (Model and Allied Publications.)

Narrow Gauge Adventure—The Story of the Craig & Mertonford Railway by P.D. Hancock (Peco.)

Klein- & Nebenbahnen im Modell by Hans-Joachim Spieth and Gernot Balcke (Alba Buchverlag, Düsseldorf.)

There are numerous books on prototype narrow-gauge railways including general surveys, detailed descriptions of individual railways, pictorial albums, and so on. Lack of space precludes listing them here but a book or model railway shop which specialises in railway books should be able to show you a good selection. Books on American and European narrow-gauge railways are also becoming increasingly available in this country through specialist firms.

Manufacturers

The following listing of manufacturers, together with some stockists, is probably not complete but I hope that it may be of assistance to modellers who wish to obtain models, kits and parts. I believe the addresses to be accurate at the time of compilation but, of course, these may change from time to time and readers are advised to check, where possible, from advertisements appearing in current issues of magazines before writing to manufacturers. Please remember that some of the specialist manufacturers are enthusiasts who run part time businesses for mail order only and that attempting to visit them without prior arrangement may be inconvenient both for them and for you.

ABS Models, 39 Napier Road, Poole, Dorset BH15 4LX. Cast Metal kits for 009. Mail order through Wrightlines.

Archangel Models, 43 Cock Lane, High Wycombe, Buckinghamshire HP13 7DY. Live steam locomotives.

Colin Ashby, 16 Newlaithes Road, Horsforth, Leeds, Yorkshire LS18 4LG. Plastic wagon kits for 009.

Bemo H0m and H0e ready-to-run locomotives and rolling stock, track, etc. Available in Britain from Liliput Model Railways (UK), ECOS, Victors, etc.

Colin Binnie & Son (Miniature Engineering), 12 Elm Close, Wells, Somerset. Live steam locomotive, wheels and other parts for large scale.

Bob's Models Ltd, 520 Coventry Road, Birmingham 10. Specialist stockist of narrow-gauge models.

Bill Brown, 9 Mendip Drive, Nuneaton, Warwickshire CV10 8PT. Micro Rail etched brass coach kits for 009.

Chivers Finelines, 49 St Christines Avenue, Leyland, Preston, Lancashire PR5 2YS. Cast metal locomotive kits for 009.

Coopercraft, 25 Swain Street, Watchet, Somerset TA23 0AD. Wagon kits for 16 mm scale.

Charles Covey, 572 Kingston Road, Raynes Park, London SW20. 7 mm scale parts.

DJH Models, Leadgate Industrial Estate, Lope Hill Road, Consett, County Durham DH8 7RS. 016.5 locomotive and wagon kits.

Dundas Models, 9 Dundas Street, Bo'ness, Scotland EH51 0DF. 009 locomotive, coach and wagon kits.

ECOS, 22 Britannia Road, Parkstone, Poole, Dorset BH14 8BB. Stockists of LGB, Liliput and Bemo models.

Festiniog Railway Co, Harbour Station, Porthmadog, Gwynedd LL49 9NF. Cast metal locomotive and rolling stock kits in 009.

GEM Model Railways, 31a Rhos Road, Rhos-on-Sea, Clwyd, North Wales L28 4RR. 009 cast metal locomotive kits.

Joe Works H0e brass locomotive and rolling stock kits. Available from Victors, Merlin Locomotive Works and M.G. Sharp.

Kidner Kits, 185 Leamington Road, Styrechale, Coventry, CV3 6JZ. 16 mm scale wagon kits.

LGB Complete G gauge system. Available in Britain from ECOS, etc.

Langley Miniature Models, 166 Three Bridges Road, Crawley, Sussex RH10 1LE. 009 locomotive and coach kits.

Chris Leigh, 46 Meadow Way, Old Windsor, Berkshire SL4 2NY. 009 coach kits.

Liliput Model Railways (UK) Ltd, No 4 Factory Unit, Station Yard, Industrial Estate, Bala, Gwynedd, North Wales. Importers of Liliput and Bemo models.

MS Models, PO Box 23 Stroud, Gloucestershire. 009 railbus body kit, 4 mm scale cast metal detailing items.

Meridian Models, 124 Blackheath Hill, Greenwich, London SE10 8AY. Cast metal locomotive kits for 009 and 16 mm scale parts.

Merlin Locomotive Works, 3 Banwy Estate, Llanfair Caereinion, Welshpool, Powys. Narrow-gauge locomotives and rolling stock in 009, 016.5 and 16 mm scales and live steam locomotives.

Micro Mold (See Tenmille Products.)

Micro Rail (See Bill Brown.)

Mike's Models, Holt House, Caswell Bay, Swansea. 009 coach and wagon kits and 4 mm scale cast metal accessories.

Peco, Pritchard Patent Product Co Ltd, Beer, Seaton, Devon EX12 3NA. Locomotive, coach and wagon kits for 009 and 016.5, track for 009, 016.5 and 32 mm gauge, etc.

Pro-Scale 016.5 etched brass coach kits. Available from Victors.

Renoster Scale Models Ltd, 71 London Road, Sevenoaks, Kent. South African Railways locomotive and rolling stock kits in Sn 3½.

M.G. Sharp Models, 712 Attercliffe Road, Sheffield S9 3RP. Stockists of Joe Works models and European and US models.

R. Stenning, 29 Treyford Close, Ifield, Crawley, Sussex RH11 0JN. Cast metal 009 locomotive, rolling stock and water tower kits.

Tenmille Products, Station Road, East Preston, Littlehampton, West Sussex. 16 mm scale 32 mm gauge coach kits.

Triassic Model Works, D. Bradwell, 15 Clifton Court, Marlow Road, High Wycombe, Buckinghamshire HP11 1TE. 16 mm scale wheels and other parts.

Victors, 116 Pentonville Road, Islington, London N1 9JL. Stockists of Joe Works models and European and US models.

Vulcan Model Engineering, 36 Northampton Street, Birmingham B18 6DX. 016.5 locomotive kit.

Jack Wheldon, 16 East Sands, Burbage, Marlboro', Wilts. Live steam locomotives and parts.

Wrightlines, 141 Portland Road, Bournemouth BH9 1NG. 016.5 locomotive chassis and rolling stock kits. Mail order for ABS Models.